CW01281408

MINORITY RIGHTS IN EUROPE
—
EUROPEAN MINORITIES AND LANGUAGES

MINORITY RIGHTS IN EUROPE

EUROPEAN MINORITIES AND LANGUAGES

Editor-in-Chief:

Snežana Trifunovska

Guest Editor:

Fernand de Varennes

T·M·C·Asser Press
The Hague

Published by T·M·C·ASSER PRESS
P.O.Box 16163, 2500 BD The Hague, The Netherlands

Sold and distributed in North, Central and South America
by Kluwer Academic Publishers
101 Philip Drive, Norwell, MA 02061, USA

In all other countries, sold and distributed
by Kluwer Law International, Distribution Centre,
P.O.Box 322, 3300 AH Dordrecht, The Netherlands

ISBN 90-6704-127-0

All rights reserved.
© 2001, T·M·C·ASSER PRESS, The Hague, The Netherlands

No part of the material protected by this copyright notice may be reproduced or utilized in any form or by any means, electronic or mechanical, including photocopying, recording, or by any information storage and retrievel system, without written permission from the copyright owner.

FOREWORD

According to some sources there are around 5,000 national minority groups living in the contemporary world, and about 3,000 linguistic groups. However, this is probably a discretionary assessment as it seems that there are no exact figures with respect to the number and size of minority groups. The existing estimates are usually based on different and sometimes not very clear criteria and mostly take into account those groups and numbers which are the result of the individual choice of a person and are not based exclusively on the objective differences. Notwithstanding this, a brief calculation would indicate that in Western Europe 14.7% of the total population belongs to minority groups, and the same percentage exists in the Central and Eastern European region – 14.7%, whereas in the countries belonging to the Commonwealth of Independent States this percentage is slightly higher – at 18.9%.

Throughout the history of the European continent minorities have had a significant impact on political stability and security. Currently, most of the situations of internal tension as well as conflicts, whether internal or international, involve inter-ethnic relations. Thus the international community at large and – for the European minorities more importantly – the European institutions have placed minority issues high on their agenda. Apart from the United Nations bodies which are dealing with the issues of minorities in all countries all over the world, the OSCE institutions and the Council of Europe are two of the most important European institutions involved in the protection of (European) minorities. However, mention also deserves to be made of other regional institutions like the Council of the Baltic Sea States and/or the Central European Initiative which within the framework of their mandate also deal with the issues surrounding minorities.

This publication was supposed to be published as the first volume of the *European Yearbook on Minorities*. However, because of its thematic approach, it was decided to publish it under the broad title *Minority Rights in Europe*. It is aimed to primarily fill the lack of a publication dealing with an issue of minorities in the OSCE area in a systematic way. Its purpose is to provide a more detailed insight into some of the aspects concerning minorities. Its final purpose is to provide information which should facilitate discussion in the scientific, governmental and non-governmental circles dealing with both human rights protection and security issues, and to assist in finding solutions to particular minority situations. This is all in accordance with the ideal of building a united Europe with guaranteed certain (minimum) levels of human rights and minority protection.

This volume consists of three main parts dealing with the theme of minority languages: (a) academic discussion; (b) activities and documents of international organisations and bodies; and (c) national activities and documents, which provides information on the available legislation and developments taking place at the national level. With the last part our purpose is to provide an insight into the compliance of national governments with the commitments undertaken at the international level and to facilitate a (comparative) analysis of European countries with respect to the documents and activities at the national level.

It had been expected that this volume would appear during the course of 1999 or at the beginning of 2000. However, as so often happens, various reasons and unexpected obstacles during its preparation contributed to delays for which we hope the readers shall accept our apologies. Certain efforts have been done up to the last moment of its publication to provide for an up-dated information, however, the work on most of the articles contributed by various experts was closed in autumn 1999-early spring 2000.

It should be pointed out that probably more than in certain other cases, publications on minorities, especially those containing statistical information, are bound to sometimes contain imprecise and even contradictory information. This is due to various reasons, but mostly to the great dynamism of changes which take place in demographic, legal and political fields involving minorities. In this case such a risk exists for Part Three of this publication in particular, since, despite the efforts of the Editor, the sources used for its preparation have not always been consistent.

For the preparation of this volume our gratitude should be extended to various persons and institutions which have participated and assisted in various ways:

- to the authors who have taken part by means of their contributions
- to the Office of the OSCE High Commissioner on National Minorities, the Council of Europe Human Rights Department, the UN Office of the High Commissioner for Human Rights, the Office of the Council of the Baltic Sea States and the Secretariat of the Central European Initiative
- to the Ministries for Foreign Affairs of Croatia, the Czech Republic, Denmark, Finland, France, Georgia, Hungary, Iceland, Ireland, Kazakhstan, Latvia, Liechtenstein, Lithuania, Malta, Portugal, Romania, the Slovak Republic, Spain and Switzerland, as well as to Germany's Ministry of the Interior, and
- to the conscientious student assistants Gülşen Karaer and René Wesel.

Special gratitude is extended to Alan Stephens, Publishing Director of Kluwer Law International, who throughout the period of preparing this publication has unreservedly supported and assisted the project.

Finally, sincere thanks should be extended to Prof. Willem van Genugten, Chairman of the Editorial Board, to Mr. John Packer, member of the Editorial Board, as well as to other members of the Editorial Board, who provided valuable advice and suggestions throughout the preparation of this volume.

In setting up this publication the Centre for Migration Law of Nijmegen University's Law Faculty played a crucial role. Having great appreciation for the significance of minority issues for, in and beyond European countries, its understanding and cooperation proved to be indispensable. In this sense it should be pointed out that by its supportive role and friendly assistance the Centre for Migration Law has made the actual work on this volume possible.

Finally, we hope that the planned continuation of this publication on other minority aspects will succeed in bringing together all those who are considered experts in the field throughout the European continent, as well as those who are involved in various ways and are interested in minority issues. By publishing this book, the T.M.C. Asser Institute hopes to promote an on-going discussion on minorities and thereby to contribute to their satisfactory protection.

Dr. Snežana Trifunovska

Editor-in-Chief
Nijmegen, September 2000

EDITORIAL BOARD

Chairman:

- Prof. Dr. W. van Genugten, Professor at Tilburg and Nijmegen Universities, The Netherlands

Members:

- Dr. Arie Bloed, Director of COLPI, Budapest, Hungary
- Prof. Dr. Asbjørn Eide, Norwegian Institute of Human Rights, Oslo, Norway
- Prof. Dr. Budislav Vukas, Professor of the Law Faculty, University of Zagreb, Croatia
- Prof. Dr. Cees Flinterman, Director of the Netherlands Institute of Human Rights (SIM), Utrecht, The Netherlands
- Prof. Dr. Gudmunder Alfredsson, Professor of Law and Director of Raoul Wallenberg Institute of Human Rights and Humanitarian Law, University of Lund, Sweden
- Mr. John Packer, Director of the Office the OSCE High Commissioner on National Minorities, The Hague, The Netherlands
- Prof. Dr. Dr. Rainer Hofmann, Professor of Walther Schücking Institut für Internationales Recht, Christiian-Albrecht-Universität, Kiel, Germany
- Prof. Dr. Vojin Dimitrijević, Center for Human Rights, Belgrade, Yugoslavia

Editor-in-Chief

- Dr. Snežana Trifunovska, Senior University Lecturer, University of Nijmegen, The Netherlands

TABLE OF CONTENTS

Foreword	V
Editorial Board	VIII
Abbreviations	XIII

Part One – Academic Discussion

Fernand de Varennes
The Linguistic Rights of Minorities in Europe 3

Dónall Ó Riagáin
All Languages – Great and Small: A Look at the Linguistic Future of Europe with Particular Reference to Lesser Used Languages 31

Marcia Rooker
Non-Territorial Languages: Romany as an Example 43

Francesco Palermo
A Never-Ending Story? The Italian Draft Bill on the Protection of Linguistic Minorities 55

Floris van Laanen
The Frisian Language in the Netherlands 67

Giovanni Poggeschi
Linguistic Rights in Spain 85

Sia Spiliopoulou Åkermark
Steps Towards a Minority Policy in Sweden 103

Part Two – International Activities and Documents

United Nations

Cecilia Thompson
The Protection of Minorities within the United Nations 115

Documents
- International Covenant on Civil and Political Rights, 1966 139
- Declaration on the Rights of Persons Belonging to National or Ethnic, Religious and Linguistic Minorities, 1992 140

Council of Europe

Snežana Trifunovska
Protection of Linguistic Rights within the Council of Europe — 145

Documents
– European Charter for Regional or Minority Languages, 1992 — 159
   Chart of Signatures and Ratifications by the European Charter
   for Regional or Minority Languages — 172
   Reservations and (Territorial) Declarations — 172
– Framework Convention for the Protection of National
   Minorities, 1995 — 190
   Chart of Signatures and Ratifications by the Framework
   Convention for the Protection of National Minorities — 197
   Reservations and (Territorial) Declarations — 198
– Parliamentary Assembly Recommendation 1383 (1998) on
   Linguistic Diversification — 202

The European Union

Gabriel von Toggenburg
A Rough Orientation through a Delicate Relationship: The EU's
Endeavours for its Minorities — 205

Documents
– Judgement of the European Court, *Bickel/Franz* v. *Italy* case, 1998 — 235

Organization for Security and Cooperation in Europe

Edwin Bakker
Linguistic Rights and the Organization for Security and
Cooperation in Europe — 241

John Packer
The Protection of Minority Language Rights through the Work of
OSCE Institutions — 255

TABLE OF CONTENTS XI

Documents
- Document of the Copenhagen Meeting of the Conference on the Human Dimension of the CSCE, 1990   275
- The Oslo Recommendations Regarding the Linguistic Rights of National Minorities and Explanatory Note, 1998   278
- Correspondence of the OSCE High Commissioner on National Minorities with some OSCE Countries   299

Council of the Baltic Sea States

Ole Espersen and Hanne Fugl
Protection of Rights of Persons belonging to Minorities in the Baltic Sea States   319

Central European Initiative

Snežana Trifunovska
Activities of the Central European Initiative in the Field of Minorities   329

Documents
- CEI Instrument for the Protection of Minority Rights   333

Part Three – National Activities and Documents

Introductory Remarks   341

The OSCE High Commissioner on National Minorities, Max van der Stoel
Report on the Linguistic Rights of Persons Belonging to National Minorities in the OSCE Area, March 1999   347

Survey of National Activities and Documents   389

- Albania   389
- Andorra   391
- Armenia   392
- Austria   396
- Azerbaijan   398
- Belarus   404
- Belgium   407
- Bosnia and Herzegovina   410
- Bulgaria   413

- Croatia 415
- Cyprus 423
- Czech Republic 427
- Denmark 433
- Estonia 438
- Finland 450
- France 468
- Georgia 469
- Germany 473
- Greece 478
- Hungary 479
- Iceland 495
- Ireland 496
- Italy 499
- Kazakstan 501
- Kyrgyzstan 503
- Latvia 506
- Liechtenstein 521
- Lithuania 523
- Luxembourg 530
- Macedonia (The Former Yugoslav Republic of) 531
- Malta 535
- Moldova 537
- Monaco 547
- The Netherlands 547
- Norway 549
- Poland 551
- Portugal 554
- Romania 556
- Russian Federation 559
- San Marino 563
- Slovak Republic 564
- Slovenia 570
- Spain 573
- Sweden 575
- Switzerland 577
- Tajikistan 580
- Turkey 582
- Turkmenistan 585
- Ukraine 587
- United Kingdom 592
- Uzbekistan 594
- Yugoslavia (Federal Republic of) 597

ABBREVIATIONS

AA	*Ars Aequi* (magazine)
AB	*Administratiefrechtelijke Beslissingen* (magazine)
ARRvS	*Afdeling Rechtspraak van de Raad van State* [Legal Division of the Council of State]
AWCP conditions	Autonomy, Welfare and Culture Protection conditions
B.F.S.P.	British and Foreign State Papers
Bijlagen I / II	*Bijlagen bij de Handelingen van de Eerste/Tweede Kamer der Staten-Generaal* [Annex to Hansard of the First/Second Chamber of the States-General]
CEI	Central European Initiative
CoE	Council of Europe
CoR	Committee of the Regions and Local Authorities
CTS	Consolidated Treaty Series
E.H.R.R	European Human Rights Reports
ECHR	European Convention for the Protection of Human Rights and Fundamental Freedoms
ECJ	European Court of Justice
EMBNET	Ethnic Minority Business Network
ENAR	European Network Against Racism
ETS	European Treaty Series
Handelingen I/II	*Handelingen van de Eerste/Tweede Kamer der Staten-Generaal* [Hansard of the First/Second Chamber of the States-General]
HR	*Hoge Raad*, Supreme Court
ICCPR	International Covenant on Civil and Political Rights
ILO	International Labour Organization
MELIN	Minority European Languages Information Network
MvT	*Memorie van Toelichting*, explanatory notes
NJ	*Nederlandse Jurisprudentie* (magazine)
NV	*Nota naar aanleiding van het Verslag*, Memorial in pursuance of parliamentary report
OJ	Official Journal of the European Community
PBF	*Provinciaal Blad van Friesland*, official journal of the province of Frisia
PCIJ	Permanent Court of International Justice
S.C.R.	Supreme Court Reports
SAAs	Stabilisation and Association Agreements
SOU	Statens offentliga utredningar
Stb.	*Staatsblad*, official journal The Netherlands
Stcrt.	*Staatscourant*, official gazette The Netherlands
Trb.	*Tractatenblad*, treaty series The Netherlands

UNHRC	United Nations Human Rights Committee
UNTS	United Nations Treaty Series

Part One

Academic Discussion

THE LINGUISTIC RIGHTS OF MINORITIES IN EUROPE

Fernand de Varennes[*]

1. INTRODUCTION

'The importance of language rights is grounded in the essential role that language plays in human existence, development and dignity. It is through language that we are able to form concepts, to structure and order the world around us. Language bridges the gap between isolation and community, allowing humans to delineate the rights and duties they hold in respect to one another, and thus live in society.'[1]

There is a steadily growing movement to clarify the extent and content of what are commonly referred to as 'minority rights' at the Council of Europe. But this trend can also be seen at the European Union, which has gone as far as to make respect for minority rights one of the 'political criteria' for admissions of new States to the Union.

Yet in a sense our understanding of the rights of minorities has not progressed as rapidly as in the case of other segments of society which have received specific measures of protection as part of the implementation of general human rights provisions. The rights of women and children have been the subject of a number of treaties and other documents for a few decades now, while in the case of the rights of minorities, which will be subjected here and also involve measures for the implementation of general human rights provisions, the same process has only really occurred in contemporary Europe in the last few years with the entry into force of both the European Charter for Regional or Minority Languages (further on: European Charter) and the Framework Convention for the Protection of National Minorities (further on: Framework Convention). At the United Nations, the process has in fact hardly progressed at all, with the rights of minorities only clarified in a non-binding – and quite timid – declaration.

This comparatively slow pace of development in relation to the rights of minorities can be attributed to a number of factors, including the long-standing

---

[*] Director, Asia-Pacific Centre for Human Rights and the Prevention of Ethnic Conflict, Murdoch University, Australia

[1] Re *Manitoba Language Rights*, (1985) 1 S.C.R. 721, at p. 744 (Canada).

S. Trifunovska (Ed.), *Minority Rights in Europe: European Minorities and Languages*
© 2000, T.M.C. Asser Press, The Hague, The Netherlands

debate on what exactly is a minority or a national minority, and whether 'minority rights' are collective rights, largely the application of existing individual rights or even some new emerging standards. Furthermore, there is, no doubt, a degree of unease from States who feel any recognition of minority rights might be a threat to their unity or the equality of all citizens.

This article will not attempt to address all of those matters. Its scope is much more modest and will mainly focus on clarifying the rights of persons belonging to minorities in the area of language. It will also be shown how the 'linguistic rights' of minorities actually refer to the application of universal human rights and freedoms in specific situations. Thus the linguistic rights of minorities in Europe will be addressed and conceptualised not as isolated elements, but as part of an evolving, comprehensive framework based on respect for human worth and dignity, and the effects of the promotion and protection of human rights. In order to do this, it may be helpful to first step back in time and look at some of the precursors of the various recent European treaties and instruments with an impact on the linguistic rights of minorities.

2. EMERGENCE OF 'LINGUISTIC RIGHTS'

2.1 The antiquity of the rights of persons belonging to linguistic minorities

It is a common mistake to assume that the rights of linguistic minorities in Europe have only emerged with the adoption of recent Council of Europe treaties such as the European Charter and the Framework Convention. The reality is much more complex: for hundreds of years there have existed treaties in Europe with provisions relating to the use of language or aimed at individuals of a particular language group.

The 1516 Treaty of Perpetual Union between the King of France and the Helvetic State contained a provision identifying those who were to receive certain benefits as the 'Swiss who speak no language other than German'.[2] The Final Act of the Congress of Vienna of 1815[3] also had measures aimed at protecting the Poles' nationality. Indirectly, this resulted in the possibility for the Polish minority in some parts of the empire to use Polish for official business.[4]

It is also often forgotten that treaties with provisions protecting religious or ethnic minorities sometimes had linguistic ramifications. For example, in the

---

[2] François Dessemontet, *Le droit des langues en Suisse*, Éditeur officiel du Québec, Québec, (1984) p. 29.

[3] B.F.S.P. 1814-1815, Vol. II (1839), at pp. 7-55.

[4] Art. 1 of the Final Act of the Congress of Vienna: 'Les Polonais, sujets respectifs des hautes parties contractantes, obtiendront la conservation de leur nationalité, d'après les formes d'existence politique que chacun des gouvernements, auxquels ils appartiennent, jugera convenable de leur accorder.'

nineteenth century when the Muslim minority in Greece had largely adopted the Turkish language, an 1881 treaty guaranteeing the free exercise of the Islamic faith, the maintenance of Islamic courts and other community structures also implicitly provided for the continued use of the Turkish minority language as part of the Muslim religious and community activities.[5] Other treaties were even more explicit in providing that cultural institutions, including minority language schools, were to be protected.[6]

The recognition and protection of the rights of linguistic minorities at the European level became more visible at the end of the First World War under the so-called minorities treaties overseen by the League of Nations. Although not limited to Europe strictly speaking, nor being a universally applicable regime for the protection of minority rights in all of Europe, most of the minorities treaties applied to European States.

The minorities treaties fell into three categories. The first category included treaties imposed upon the States of Austria, Hungary, Bulgaria, and Turkey. The second dealt with new States born of the remains of the Ottoman Empire and States whose boundaries were altered under the self-determination principle (Czechoslovakia, Greece, Poland, Romania, and Yugoslavia). The third category included a number of special provisions relating to minorities in Åland, Danzig, the Memel Territory, and Upper Silesia, as well as a series of five unilateral declarations made by Albania, Lithuania, Latvia, Estonia, and Iraq upon their admission to the League of Nations.[7]

The first two categories of treaties described above incorporated the right to equality of treatment and non-discrimination, the right to citizenship, the right of minorities to establish and control their own institutions, a State obligation to provide equitable financial support to schools in which instruction at the primary level would be in the minority language where warranted by sufficient numbers,

---

[5] Convention for the Settlement of the Frontier between Greece and Turkey, 24 May 1881, Vol. 158 CTS 367, Art. 7. See other similar provisions involving Muslim minorities in the Treaty of Peace between Serbia and Turkey, Art. 7, signed 14 March 1914 in Constantinople, (1913-1914) Vol. 219 CTS 320, at p. 322, and the apparent protection of private schools of numerous linguistic and religious minorities in Art. 29 of the Treaty of Peace between Austria-Hungary, Bulgaria, Germany and Turkey, and Romania, signed 7 May 1918 in Bucharest, (1917-1918) Vol. 223 CTS 241, at p. 264.

[6] See for example the case of the Vlach minority, who speak a distinctive form of Romanian, whose schools were protected under the Treaty of Peace between Bulgaria, Greece, Montenegro, Romania and Serbia, signed 10 August 1913, (1913) Vol. 218 CTS 322, at pp. 335-337; see also the provisions regarding German language schools in Arts. 38 to 41, Treaty between Germany and Romania supplementary to the Treaty of Peace, 7 May 1918, signed in Bucharest, (1917-1918) Vol. 223 CTS 304, at pp. 311-312, and the provisions regarding Turkish language private schools for members of the Muslim minority living in Serbia, Article 9 of the Treaty between Serbia and Turkey, signed at Constantinople on 14 March 1914, Vol. 219 CTS (1913-1914) 320, at p. 324.

[7] See 'Study on the Rights of Persons belonging to Ethnic, Religious and Linguistic Minorities' (1976), UN Special Rapporteur Francesco Capotorti, UN Doc. E/CN.4/Sub.2/384/Add.1-7.

and the recognition of the supremacy over other statutes of laws protecting minority rights. In addition, a certain degree of territorial autonomy was provided for minority groups in some cases.

Specifically on the issue of language, it has been pointed out that:

> 'As regards the use of the minority language, States which have signed the Treaties have undertaken to place no restriction in the way of the free use by any national of the country of any language, in private intercourse, in commerce, in religion, in the press or in publications of any kind, or at public meetings. Those States have also agreed to grant adequate facilities to enable their nationals whose mother tongue is not the official language, either orally or in writing, before the courts. They have further agreed, in towns and districts where a considerable proportion of nationals of the country whose mother tongue is not the official language of the country is resident, to make provision for adequate facilities for ensuring that, in the primary schools [...] instruction shall be given to the children of such nationals through the medium of their own language, it being understood that this provision does not prevent the teaching of the official language being made obligatory in those schools.'[8]

The treaties included essentially two principle types of provisions: firstly, individuals belonging to linguistic minorities, amongst others, would be placed on a footing of equality with the other nationals of the State; secondly, the means to preserve the characteristics of minorities, including language, would be ensured.

The Permanent Court of International Justice explained in one of its key opinions how the two type of measures interact:

> 'These two requirements are indeed closely interlocked, for there would be no true equality between a majority and a minority if the latter were deprived of its own institutions and were consequently compelled to renounce that which constitutes the very essence of its being a minority.'[9]

As a result, nationals belonging to linguistic minorities were to enjoy the same treatment in law and in fact as other nationals. In particular, they had an equal right to establish schools and institutions at their own expense. Such schools were distinct from State schools where the minority language was the language of instruction. Finally, in those towns and districts where the minorities constituted a considerable proportion of the population, they would be assured of an equitable share in the enjoyment and application of sums provided out of public funds under State, municipal, or other budgets for educational, religious or charitable purposes.

---

[8] Idem., at pp. 18-19.
[9] Advisory Opinion on *Minority Schools in Albania*, (1935) PCIJ, Series A/B, No. 64, 3, at p. 4, also known as the *Minority Schools in Albania* case.

2.2 The Evolution of the Rights of Persons Belonging to Linguistic Minorities in International Law and Europe

Since 1945 there has been an emphasis on the universal protection of individual rights and freedoms:

> 'Throughout the discussions on human rights at the United Nations Conference on International Organisation, the minorities treaties were not referred to, but a considerable amount of influence was brought to bear in favour of a 'new covenant' and a fresh approach.'[10]

International instruments incorporating provisions related to language came into being at an increasingly frequent pace. On 10 December 1948, the UN General Assembly proclaimed the Universal Declaration of Human Rights.[11] Article 2(1) provides that 'everyone is entitled to all rights and freedoms set forth in this Declaration, without distinction of any kind, such as [...] language'. Pursuant to the ILO Convention No. 107 of 1957 concerning Indigenous and Tribal Populations,[12] protected indigenous populations have the right to be taught in their mother tongue or, where this is not practicable, in the language most commonly used by the group to which they belong.

One of the most often-quoted international treaty provisions dealing with minority rights is of course Article 27 of the International Covenant on Civil and Political Rights (ICCPR), which provides that:

> '[i]n those States in which [...] linguistic minorities exist, persons belonging to such minorities shall not be denied the right, in community with the other members of their group, [...] to use their own language.'

In the area of education, the Convention Against Discrimination in Education of 1960[13] prohibits, under Article 1, 'any distinction, exclusion or preference' based upon language or other grounds, which 'has the purpose or effect of nullifying or impairing equality of treatment in education'. The Convention makes it clear, in Article 2(b), that it does not constitute discrimination to establish or maintain, for linguistic reasons, separate educational systems or institutions.

The Convention also provides in Article 5(1)(c), that it is essential to

> 'recognise the right of members of national minorities to carry on their own educational activities, including the maintenance of schools and, depending on the educational policy of each State, the use or the teaching of their own language,'

---

[10] Warwick McKean, *Equality and Discrimination under International Law*, Clarendon Press, Oxford, United Kingdom (1983) p. 53.
[11] General Assembly Resolution 217 A (III), UN GAOR, 3rd Session, Resolutions, Part 1, at p. 71 (1948).
[12] Vol. 328 UNTS p. 249.
[13] Vol. 428 UNTS p. 93.

provided that

> 'this right is not exercised in a manner which prevents the members of these minorities from understanding the culture and language of the community as a whole and from participating in its activities, or which prejudices national sovereignty.'

A number of peace treaties concluded in Europe following the Second World War included provisions in which language also figured more or less prominently. The treaties signed with the Allied and Associated Powers in 1947 provided that each State concerned should take all measures necessary to secure to all persons within their jurisdiction, without distinction as to language, the enjoyment of human rights and freedoms, including freedom of expression, of press and public opinion, and of public meeting.[14]

In addition, many countries in Europe have more recently concluded bilateral agreements dealing with some of their linguistic minorities, at times providing for the protection of language and cultures, and for the maintenance of minority schools.[15]

Finally, in the last few years, international and regional treaties, declarations and other instruments containing language rights have proliferated. Amongst the more prominent are the UN Declaration on the Rights of Persons Belonging to National or Ethnic, Religious and Linguistic Minorities (further on: UN Declaration), the draft UN Declaration on the Rights of Indigenous Peoples, the Vienna Declaration on Human Rights, the ILO Convention No. 169 concerning Indigenous and Tribal Peoples in Independent Countries, the CEI Instrument for the Protection of Minority Rights, the Oslo Recommendations Regarding the Linguistic Rights of National Minorities and the The Hague Recommendations Regarding the Education Rights of National Minorities.

3. LINGUISTIC RIGHTS OF MINORITIES AND PRIVATE ACTIVITIES

The rights of minorities in Europe in the area of language from a legal point of view emanate from either existing legislation or treaty obligations. The vast majority of European countries with sizeable minorities have a wide range of administrative measures or legislative provisions dealing with some recognised

---

[14] Treaty with Italy, Vol. 49 UNTS at p. 3; Treaty with Romania, Vol. 42 UNTS at p. 3; Treaty with Bulgaria, Vol. 41 UNTS at p. 21; Treaty with Hungary, Vol. 41 UNTS at p. 135; Treaty with Finland, Vol. 49 UNTS at p. 203; Austrian State Treaty, Vol. 217 UNTS at p. 223.

[15] Including, among many others, the Agreement on the Cooperation between the Ministry of National Education of the Republic of Poland and the Ministry of Education of the Republic of Belarus, the Agreement on the Cooperation between the Ministry of National Education of the Republic of Poland and the Ministry of Education of Ukraine, and the Agreement between the Ministry of National Education of the Republic of Poland and the Ministry of Culture and Education of the Republic of Lithuania Regarding the Educational System and University Education.

use of minority languages, even if they do not necessarily grant minority languages an official status. While it is not possible to summarise here the various State practices in terms of the linguistic rights of minorities in Europe, there are a number of sources where this information can be found.[16]

If one moves away from the mistaken assumption that minority rights such as those involving language are 'group rights' and examines more closely the content of various European and international treaties and decisions, it is possible to tentatively identify a core of linguistic rights upon which there seems to be fairly widespread agreement in Europe and at the international level. While there may still be no consensus on some issues, including the vexing matter as to what exactly is meant by the term 'national' minority as opposed to a minority *simpliciter*, it is possible to outline a number of rights which are based on widely accepted fundamental human rights principles.

These rights can also be divided into two broad categories for purposes of analysis, based upon whether they involve public authorities attempting to impose their own linguistic preferences on the private activities of individuals, or conversely whether a situation deals with an individual seeking to have public authorities provide a service or respond to the individuals' linguistic preferences in activities involving State authorities.

Essentially, State measures which have the effect of preventing the use of a minority language in private activities can be in breach of a number of well-established rights in international law and Europe, as well as increasingly recognised in a variety of bilateral and multilateral treaties, and other documents. Generally speaking, government attempts to regulate the language used in the private sphere, such as in commercial activities, in private publications, in the family or community, etc., may run foul of the right to private and family life, freedom of expression, non-discrimination or the right of persons belonging to a linguistic minority to use their language with other members of their group.

Therefore, although commentators and most experts usually refer to the rights contained in treaties such as the Framework Convention and the European Charter, as well as in other influential documents such as the UN Declaration, as being 'minority rights', it is clear that in the private sphere what are involved are in fact the application of basic individual human rights which impact in the area of language.

What follows is an attempt to break down exactly how these various rights apply in private activities to better illustrate the scope and content of the linguistic rights of minorities.

---

[16] See 'Report on the Linguistic Rights of Persons Belonging to National Minorities in the OSCE Area', Organization for Security and Co-operation in Europe, The Hague, 1999. There is also valuable information on national policies and legislation on linguistic rights in Europe available through the Internet at sites such as the UNESCO MOST project at http://www.unesco.org/most/ln1.htm and MERCATOR Legislation at http://www.troc.ec/mrcator/-index.htm which was set up by the European Commission.

3.1 Right to correspond and communicate

In Europe as elsewhere, a State cannot stop individuals from using a minority language in private correspondence or communications (including in private business or commercial correspondence, by telephone, electronic means, etc.). Such an attempt would clearly be a breach of a variety of rights, including the freedom of expression, the right to private life, non-discrimination, and would probably be a denial of a person's right to use their own language with other members of their group in the case of a minority in provisions such as Article 27 of the ICCPR. There are of course possible limitations permitted depending on the nature of the right or freedom involved. For example, some restrictions are permitted to the freedom of expression where necessary for purposes of public health. However, in a general sense none of the permissible limitations under international law or European treaties would allow for a blanket prohibition on the private use of a minority language for correspondence or communication.

Specifically in Europe, in addition to the guarantee of freedom of expression which is enshrined in the Convention for the Protection of Human Rights and Fundamental Freedoms (ECHR) and under which would be protected the right to use a minority language in private correspondence and communications, there is also a treaty provision which directly refers to such a right:

> 'The Parties undertake to recognise that every person belonging to a national minority has the right to use freely and without interference his or her minority language, in private and in public, orally and in writing.'[17]

3.2 Cultural and Musical Expression

Although there have not been many attempts in recent times in Europe to make it illegal to play a song, present a theatre presentation, opera, etc., either in private or in public, in a minority language, such prohibitions have occurred. They would, were they to be attempted today, clearly be in violation of rights such as the freedom of expression, non-discrimination, and also Article 27 of the ICCPR. It is implied in a large number of instruments which recognise the right of members of a minority to use their own language in private and in public, such as Article 10 of the Framework Convention. It is also more clearly set out in Article 12 of the European Charter. This provision essentially establishes not only that States must not prohibit such activities, but that they must even in some situations actually promote them:

> 1. With regard to cultural activities and facilities – especially libraries, video libraries, cultural centres, museums, archives, academies, theatres and cinemas, as well as literary work and film production, vernacular forms of cultural expression, festivals and the culture industries, including *inter alia* the use of new technologies – the Parties

---

[17] Art. 10 of the Framework Convention.

THE LINGUISTIC RIGHTS OF MINORITIES IN EUROPE 11

undertake, within the territory in which such languages are used and to the extent that the public authorities are competent, to have power or play a role in this field:
a. to encourage types of expression and initiative specific to regional or minority languages and foster the different means of access to works produced in these languages;
d. to ensure that the bodies responsible for organising or supporting cultural activities of various kinds make appropriate allowance for incorporating the knowledge and use of regional or minority languages and cultures in the undertakings which they initiate or for which they provide backing; etc. [...].'

3.3 The name or surname of individuals

This 'minority right' has been found to be part of the right to private and family life, both in Europe and in the UN human rights systems.[18] It is furthermore part of the rights of ethnic and linguistic minorities under Article 27 of the ICCPR. It is also contained in an increasing number of international and regional treaties and other documents dealing either with minorities,[19] including Article 11(1) of the Framework Convention:

'The Parties undertake to recognise that every person belonging to a national minority has the right to use his or her surname (patronym) and first names in the minority language and the right to official recognition of them, according to modalities provided for in their legal system.'

A State cannot prevent an individual from having a name or surname which is not in an official language or prescribed list. Once again, this right of linguistic minorities is in fact protected under existing human rights regimes under the right to private and family life, but has also been reiterated in minority rights treaties.

3.4 Designations of localities and topography

The private use of topographical names in a minority language cannot be prohibited by a State. This would constitute a violation of freedom of expression, and possibly Article 27 of the ICCPR. A number of treaties and other international or regional documents directly mention such a right.[20]

While a government cannot ban the private use of topographical or place-names in a minority language, it does not mean that the State itself must

---

[18] *Coeriel and Aurik* v. *Netherlands*, UN Human Rights Committee, Communication No. 453/1991, UN Doc. CCPR/C/52/D/453/1991 (1994); *Burghartz* v. *Switzerland*, European Court of Human Rights, Judgement of 22 February 1994, 18 E.H.R.R. 101.

[19] See for example Art. 11 of the Central European Initiative for the Protection of Minority Rights and Recommendation 1 of the Oslo Recommendations Regarding the Linguistic Rights of National Minorities.

[20] Art. 14 of the CEI Instrument for the Protection of Minority Rights, and Art. 11 of the Framework Convention.

officially recognise or use these names or designations. The issue of official toponomy arises in relation to the use of a minority language by public authorities, discussed later in this article.

3.5 Public displays on private posters, commercial signs, etc.

Treaties such as the Framework Convention indicate in Article 11 that 'every person belonging to a national minority has the right to display in his or her minority language signs, inscriptions and other information of a private nature visible to the public'.

But this is not just a minority right. Decisions at the international level have made it clear that freedom of expression includes the right to linguistic expression in private activities.[21] Members of minorities in Europe and elsewhere therefore have the right to use their language of choice in private 'expression' activities under this freedom. This would therefore apply to the language used in the private display of signs, posters, etc. of a commercial, cultural or even political nature.

Another point to keep in mind in this respect is that a particular script is a component of a language. Since the private use of a minority language is protected under the freedom of expression, it follows that the private use of a particular script, including the script of a minority script (Cyrillic, Greek, Latin, etc.) would also be protected under this fundamental human right.[22]

It should however be pointed out that the right to use a minority language in these circumstances does not prevent the State from requiring some use of an official language in conjunction to the minority language if it does not prevent the actual exercise of the freedom of expression.[23]

3.6 Private media and publications

Members of a minority cannot be prevented from publishing privately in their own language since such activities fall squarely within the realm of freedom of expression. It is also likely to be protected under Article 27 of the ICCPR and similar provisions. In the European context, there is in addition to fundamental human rights guarantees specific recognition of this right, both in Article 9 of the Framework Convention and Article 11(2) of the European Charter. Article 9, for example, states the following:

> '3. The Parties shall not hinder the creation and the use of printed media by persons belonging to national minorities. In the legal framework of sound radio and television

---

[21] *Ballantyne, Davidson and McIntyre* v. *Canada*, UN Human Rights Committee Communications Nos. 359/1989 and 385/1989, 31 March 1993.

[22] See specifically on this point Fernand de Varennes, *Language, Minorities and Human Rights*, Martinus Nijhoff, The Hague (1996) p. 105.

[23] *Ballantyne, Davidson and McIntyre* v. *Canada*, op. cit. n. 21.

broadcasting, they shall ensure, as far as possible, and taking into account the provisions of paragraph 1, that persons belonging to national minorities are granted the possibility of creating and using their own media.'

Neither freedom of expression nor more specific provisions dealing with this issue impose on States the obligation to provide financial assistance or resources to make publishing in a minority language possible. There would appear to be nevertheless an obligation to act in a non-discriminatory way if States already provide financial or material assistance to private publication activities. For example, Recommendation 7 of the Oslo Recommendations Regarding the Linguistic Rights of National Minorities would seem to apply to funding for private minority language publications and media:

'If the State actively supports activities in, among others, the social, cultural and sports spheres, an equitable share of the total resources made available by the State shall go to support those similar activities undertaken by persons belonging to national minorities. State financial support for activities which take place in the language(s) of persons belonging to national minorities in such spheres shall be granted on a non-discriminatory basis.'

3.7 Private broadcasting

A State which attempts to prevent the use of a particular language in private radio or television broadcasting would clearly be in breach of a right recognised in an important number and cross-section of international legal and political documents.[24] To give but one example, Article 9(3) of the Framework Convention:

'The Parties shall not hinder the creation and the use of printed media by persons belonging to national minorities. In the legal framework of sound radio and television broadcasting, they shall ensure, as far as possible, and taking into account the provisions of paragraph 1, that persons belonging to national minorities are granted the possibility of creating and using their own media.'

Prohibiting private minority language broadcasting would also be breaching freedom of expression, would in all likelihood constitute a form of discrimination, and may very well be inconsistent with Article 27 of the ICCPR and similar provisions.

3.8 Right to create and operate private educational facilities

Members belonging to a minority have had in Europe a historically long recognised right to create and operate their own educational facilities under the

---

[24] Art. 18 of the CEI Instrument for the Protection of Minority Rights, Art. 9 of the Framework Convention, and Art. 11(3) of the European Charter.

League of Nations in a series of legally-binding treaties, thus pre-dating even the creation of the United Nations.[25] In terms of international law, it is often assumed such a right is inherent to Article 27 of the ICCPR.[26]

Linguistic minorities in Europe therefore have the right to use their language as a medium of instruction under existing human rights treaties at the international level, but it should be pointed out that that does not involve schools operated by public authorities, since this particular situation only deals with private schools or classes.

Even though this right deals with private activities, one should also keep in mind that it is possible for public authorities to impose some requirements on these private activities. For example, States may require that all minority students in private schools or classes must learn the official language up to a reasonable level of fluency. States may also impose 'non-linguistic' standards as to the quality of instruction.

The vagueness of the human rights treaties in this regard has to a large degree been rectified in Europe by clearer, more precise provisions in treaties and other instruments. To give but one example, the wording used in Article 13 of the Framework Convention indicates that:

> '1. Within the framework of their education systems, the Parties shall recognise that persons belonging to a national minority have the right to set up and to manage their own private educational and training establishments.
> 2. The exercise of this right shall not entail any financial obligation for the Parties.'

European documents also tend to clarify that while States have the obligation to officially recognise the validity of the education received in these private facilities (diploma, university admission, etc.) as long as educational quality standards are met, there is no general obligation to provide financial or other support for these facilities. However, non-discrimination also applies (at least according to international law and most other treaties with the notable exception of the ECHR) in all areas of State involvement. If States already provide financial or material assistance to private schools, minority educational facilities would correspondingly be entitled to similar support in a non-discriminatory manner. There appears to be widespread recognition of this right in legal and political documents.[27]

---

[25] See for example Advisory Opinion on *Minority Schools in Albania*, (1935) PCIJ, Series A/B, No. 64, 3, at p. 17.

[26] See de Varennes, op. cit. n. 22, at pp. 157-158.

[27] Including Art. 16 of the CEI Instrument for the Protection of Minority Rights; paragraph 32.2 of the Document of the Copenhagen Meeting of the Conference on the Human Dimension, Recommendation 10 of the The Hague Recommendations Regarding the Education Rights of National Minorities, and Art. 14 of the Framework Convention.

3.9 Worship, religious practices or observance

Minorities in Europe and elsewhere are free to use their own language during religious worship or other religious practices in the sense that a State prohibition in this area would be a violation of the freedom of expression, as well as be inconsistent with specific provisions contained in a number of European documents.[28] For example, it would seem to run foul of the obligation described in Article 5(1) of the Framework Convention:

> 'The Parties undertake to promote the conditions necessary for persons belonging to national minorities to maintain and develop their culture, and to preserve the essential elements of their identity, namely their religion, language, traditions and cultural heritage.'

Such an attempt to abolish or restrict the use of a minority language by the State against the wishes of the members of a religious or linguistic community could furthermore constitute a form of discrimination inconsistent with the guarantees contained in human rights treaties in international law, as well as a violation of Article 27 of the ICCPR and similar provisions.

3.10 Marriage or other civil rites

When a particular religious ceremony also involves an official act as can be the case in marriage rites, a State cannot prevent the use of a minority language during the private part of the ceremony. To do so would constitute a breach of freedom of expression, and possibly a breach of private and family life. It would in all likelihood also involve a denial of the rights of individuals to use their own language with other members of their minority group.

Although the issue has never been considered at the international level, the State may require that the 'official' part of the 'private' marriage rites – if it involves a minister, priest, official or rabbi exercising State authority – be in an official language, in addition to but not excluding the minority language.

3.11 Language restrictions in private economic activities

As in other private activities, a State cannot prevent an individual or corporate entity from using their preferred language in the economic field. This means that private persons and institutions cannot be stopped from using a minority language in private business relationships.[29] This is reflected in 'European standards' such as Article 13 of the European Charter (which speaks of the need

---

[28] See Art. 12 of the CEI Instrument for the Protection of Minority Rights and paragraph 32.3 of the Document of the Copenhagen Meeting of the Conference on the Human Dimension.

[29] Art. 13 of the European Charter.

for governments not to prohibit, exclude or restrict 'the use of regional or minority languages' in economic activities) and especially Recommendation 12 of the Oslo Recommendations Regarding the Linguistic Rights of National Minorities which states that:

> 'All persons, including persons belonging to national minorities, have the right to operate private enterprises in the language or languages of their choice. The State may require the additional use of the official language or languages of the State only where a legitimate public interest can be demonstrated, such as interests relating to the protection of workers or consumers, or in dealings between the enterprise and governmental authorities.'

This 'minority right' is also a basic right contained in all international human rights treaties, since the restriction or prohibition of the use of a minority language between an employer and his or her employees, between a small business owner and a client, or on the advertisements or posters in relation to private commercial activities, would be a violation of freedom of expression, as mentioned earlier.[30]

A State may nevertheless validly require that another language in addition to a minority language be used in private commercial activities in some cases. If a State adopted measures requiring the use of an official language, but not excluding the use of a minority language, then both languages could be used and there would generally not be a breach of freedom of expression, or discrimination in these business activities if, as contained in Recommendation 12 of the Oslo Recommendations, the forced joint use of the official and minority languages is for a 'legitimate public interest'.[31]

There are however situations where a government's requirement to use an official language in conjunction with the preferred language of a minority in private economic activities could be a violation of international human rights law and European standards involving minority rights. For example, a requirement that all the employees of a private business be able to speak the official language would in all likelihood be an unreasonable demand and therefore discriminatory. Furthermore, in the case of smaller businesses, a bilingualism requirement could more likely be seen as a discriminatory measure than for large businesses, since such a requirement imposes a particularly heavy burden on small business owners who may have to hire additional or new employees in order to comply with the requirement, translate documents at their own expense in both languages, etc. In the case of small business owners such a burden may be quite unreasonable and therefore discriminatory. Additionally, this type of requirement could be seen as in fact preventing certain individuals from engaging in private activities, and thus seem particularly objectionable.

---

[30] Raimo Pekkanen and Hans Danelius, Special Rapporteurs, 'Human Rights in the Republic of Estonia', in *Human Rights Law Journal*, Vol. 13 (1991), No 5-6, pp. 236-256, at p. 241, and *Ballantyne, Davidson and McIntyre* v. *Canada*, op. cit. n. 21.

[31] *Ballantyne, Davidson and McIntyre* v. *Canada*, op. cit. n. 21.

With larger commercial activities, a bilingualism requirement in the workplace may not automatically be a heavy or cumbersome burden, depending on the exact nature of what exactly is being required.

3.12 Use within private groups or organizations

Any attempt to prevent the use of a minority language in the activities of private groups or organisations, such as cultural societies, minority associations, etc., would constitute a breach of freedom of expression, possibly be discriminatory, and most certainly be in violation of minority rights contained in provisions such as Article 27 of the ICCPR.

A State could nevertheless require that a private group or organisation keep its financial records and other types of official documentation in an official language, as long as it does not prevent the group or organisation from also keeping these same documents in their own language.

This right of minorities is also spelt out in Europe in Recommendation 6 of the Oslo Recommendations:

> 'All persons, including persons belonging to national minorities, have the right to establish and manage their own non-governmental organisations, associations and institutions. These entities may use the language(s) of their choosing. The State may not discriminate against these entities on the basis of language nor shall it unduly restrict the right of these entities to seek sources of funding from the State budget, international sources or the private sector.'

Council of Europe treaties also guarantee the same right, although in more general terms under the right to use freely and without interference his or her minority language (Article 10 of the Framework Convention and Article 13 of the European Charter).

3.13 Use by political associations or parties

Political parties or associations are not part of the administrative structure of the State and therefore cannot be prevented from using a minority language, even during elections. Their activities are therefore part of the private domain, even if in many countries these are heavily regulated by the State. A prohibition on the use of a minority language would be in violation of the freedom of expression, Article 27 of the ICCPR, as well as probably being discriminatory, as well as probably Article 10 of the Framework Convention and Article 13 of the European Charter.

Any use of a minority language that involves the public authorities (such as registration of a political party or association, broadcasting of political messages on State-controlled media, etc.) falls outside the private domain. It therefore involves mainly whether or not a particular restriction or requirement is discriminatory, rather than problems of freedom of expression, or of Article 10 of the Framework Convention or Article 13 of the European Charter as will be shown in the next section dealing with the use of minority languages and public authorities.

4. THE USE OF MINORITY LANGUAGES BY STATE AUTHORITIES

'Public authorities, particularly in a modernizing situation, are inevitably and increasingly drawn into language questions through the spread of citizen participation in politics, the provision of more administrative services, and perhaps most of all through the development of State-supported education. This means that one of the most successful methods for pacifying religious differences at an earlier date, namely, the withdrawal of the State from the arena of conflict, or de-politicization, is not available for most linguistic conflicts, and other methods of conflict resolution must be found. One can have separation of church and State, but in advanced societies separation of language and State is simply not possible. A major consequence of this central role of language in the communication network is that it is closely linked with most of the professional and bureaucratic employment opportunities, with the result that conflicts over language frequently involve high personal stakes in terms of career prospects for the groups concerned, and most of all for their most articulate and well-educated elites. Language conflicts therefore concern not simply languages as such, but tangible economic benefits as well.'[32]

The 'minority rights' referred to until now involve language choices and preferences in private activities. Yet for linguistic minorities it is often the use of – or rather refusal to use – their language by State authorities which gives rise to much controversy and difficulties.

To put it simply, it is on the one hand fairly unanimous in Europe and at the international level that individuals are generally free to use their language of choice in private matters. What is less clear on the other hand is whether – and especially under what conditions and to what extent – State authorities may also have a legal obligation to use minority languages themselves.

The issue should not be confused with whether a State should 'officially' recognise a language. State authorities in all countries of the world often use non-official languages in 'minority languages' for various purposes, such as government publications in foreign languages to promote tourism or business ventures, or during a trial when a defendant, accused or witness does not understand the language of court proceedings. What is more controversial is the extent to which State authorities are obliged to provide services and respond in non-official languages.

Despite a degree of hesitancy in some milieus, there does appear to be a growing legal acceptance in Europe that States have a positive obligation to

---

[32] Kenneth D. McRae, *Conflict and Compromise in Multilingual Societies: Belgium*, Wilfrid Laurier University Press, Waterloo, Canada (1986) pp. 3-4.

provide public services and respond in the non-official or minority language preferred by individuals in 'appropriate' circumstances, such as where the numbers and geographic concentration of the speakers of a minority language and the State's resources make it a viable option. The Framework Convention, the European Charter, and the Oslo Recommendations Regarding the Linguistic Rights of National Minorities, to name but a few, all reflect this emerging consensus, as will now be shown in specific areas of State involvement.

4.1 Minority language use by public authorities in general

Recent treaties and instruments in Europe and elsewhere often embody the concept of a 'sliding-scale' approach as a proper response to the use of the language of minorities by public authorities. None of these documents suggest that there is a collective, unqualified right to have minority languages used by public authorities. On the contrary, all of them identify the conditions where such a minority right exists, usually connected to the need for public authorities to respond to the linguistic preferences of individuals. In other words, there is no automatic 'right to language' in the contacts and exchanges between individuals and the State machinery. What exists instead is a right 'where appropriate'. In some cases, as when an individual faces a particularly serious disadvantage in court proceedings held in a language s/he does not understand, a State will be obliged to use the minority language even if there are hardly any speakers of that specific language in the country. In such a case, public authorities only have to use a minority language for a limited purpose (the State need only provide for an interpreter), and this right exists regardless of the number of individuals affected or their territorial concentration. But in most cases of use of a minority language, these two last factors are central to determine the extent of a minority's language rights.

The CEI Instrument for the Protection of Minority Rights (Article 13: 'whenever in an area the number of persons [...] reaches [...] a significant level'), the Framework Convention (Article 10: 'In areas inhabited by persons belonging to national minorities traditionally or in substantial numbers, if those persons so request and where such a request corresponds to a real need, the Parties shall endeavour to ensure, as far as possible [...]'), the European Charter (Article 10: 'within the administrative districts [...] in which the number of residents [...] justifies the measures specified below and according to the situation of each language'), and the Oslo Recommendations Regarding the Linguistic Rights of National Minorities (Recommendation 13: 'In regions and localities where persons belonging to a national minority are present in significant numbers and where the desire for it has been expressed [...]'), all recognise that there is a gradation that must be respected as to the degree public authorities must use a minority language.

Essentially, this 'sliding-scale approach' requires that where public authorities at the national, regional or local levels face a sufficiently large number of individuals who use a minority language, these authorities must provide an appropriate level of service in this language.

For example, in the case of local districts and their administration where minorities are concentrated, local authorities should generally provide for an increasing level of services in their language as the number of speakers of a particular language increases. Beginning at the lower end of what will be called a 'sliding-scale model', and moving to a progressively higher end, this would imply:

1. making available widely used official documents and forms for the population in the non-official or minority language or in bilingual versions;
2. the acceptance by authorities of oral or written applications in the non-official or minority language;
3. the acceptance by authorities of oral or written applications in the non-official or minority language, and response thereto in that language;
4. having a sufficient number of officers, who are in contact with the public, in place to respond to the use of the non-official or minority language;
5. being able to use the non-official or minority language as an internal and daily language of work within public authorities.

Not to provide an appropriate, i.e. 'sliding-scale', response could also be a form of discrimination as to language under human rights treaties such as Article 26 of the ICCPR (although not under the more limited Article 14 of the Council of Europe's ECHR). Individuals whose fluency in a State's official language is generally lower than that of a native user of the language would experience a disadvantage. This does not mean that such State linguistic preferences are automatically discriminatory, since Article 26 of the ICCPR does not prohibit all distinctions, even if they are disadvantageous to some. However, in some situations, especially where it would be relatively simple for public authorities to accommodate to some degree the language of a large minority, such as where a minority may represent 25 percent or more of the population, not to use their language as is 'appropriate' in the circumstances could be deemed to be unreasonable or arbitrary in light of the disadvantages caused, and therefore discriminatory.[33]

4.2 Public instruction and minority languages

There is historically a long-standing recognition that a State not only **should** provide for public schooling in a minority language, but also that it **must** do so under certain conditions. During the League of Nations era, the minorities treaties contained provisions specifically involving the use of a minority

---

[33] See on this point the analysis in de Varennes, op. cit. n. 22, at pp. 56-105.

language as a medium of instruction in the State school system when appropriate:

> 'Provisions will be made in the public educational system in towns and districts in which are resident a considerable proportion of Albanian nationals whose mother-tongue is not the official language, for adequate facilities for ensuring that in the primary schools instruction shall be given to the children of such nationals, through the medium of their own language, it being understood that this provision does not prevent teaching of the official language being made obligatory in the said schools.'[34]

One Permanent Court of International Justice decision stated that Article 9 of the Polish Minorities Treaty which called for adequate public facilities for ensuring to the children of Polish nationals of other than Polish speech primary instruction through the medium of their own language, represented the right of 'minorities the members of which are citizens of the State to enjoy [...] amongst other rights, equality of rights [...] in matters relating to primary instruction'.[35]

Such a right is not, however, necessarily limited to minorities, since it can be linked to the general prohibition of discrimination. Where a substantial number of students of a minority are concentrated territorially, it would be unreasonable – and therefore a breach of non-discrimination – for a State not to use their language as a medium of instruction in public schools as appropriate. In other words, equality and non-discrimination in public education may require the use of a minority language as a medium of instruction to some degree because of the disadvantage suffered by members of a national minority who are less fluent in the official language of the State.

Even if this view were to be contested, treaties and other instruments in Europe and in international law make it unanimously clear that this is a recognised minority right.[36] For example, Article 14 of the Framework Convention states:

> '2. In areas inhabited by persons belonging to national minorities traditionally or in substantial numbers, if there is sufficient demand, the Parties shall endeavour to ensure, as far as possible and within the framework of their education systems, that persons belonging to those minorities have adequate opportunities for being taught the minority language or for receiving instruction in this language.'

All of these instruments recognise at the same time that public education in a minority language must not exclude instruction of the official language.

---

[34] Advisory Opinion on *Minority Schools in Albania*, (1935) PCIJ, Series A/B, No. 64, 3, at p. 21, also known as the *Minority Schools in Albania* case.

[35] *Treatment of Polish Nationals in Danzig* (1932), PCIJ, Series A/B, No. 44, 1, at p. 9.

[36] For example, the The Hague Recommendations Regarding the Education Rights of National Minorities, Art. 4 of the UN Declaration on the Rights of Persons Belonging to National or Ethnic, Religious and Linguistic Minorities, Art. 17 of the CEI Instrument for the Protection of Minority Rights, Art. 14 of the Framework Convention, and Art. 8 of the European Charter.

Members of a minority (and others) must be able to learn the official language to a reasonable degree of fluency. Once again, Article 14 of the Framework Convention provides an illustration of the nature of this right which has attained widespread acceptance:

> '3. Paragraph 2 of this article shall be implemented without prejudice to the learning of the official language or the teaching in this language.'

Not to provide opportunities to learn the official or majority language could possibly lead to the creation of 'linguistic ghettos' or exclude minorities from employment or educational opportunities – which would in turn constitute a discriminatory policy.

4.3 The use of minority languages by judicial authorities

As with other situations involving the use of a minority language by public officials, treaties and other instruments provide for a 'sliding-scale' approach within the judicial system. One of the more detailed treaty provisions that applies such a model is Article 9 of the European Charter, which describes the need to increase the use of a minority language in criminal, civil and administrative tribunal proceedings where 'the number of residents [...] justifies the measures'. The same approach is embodied in other documents, such as Recommendations 18 and 19 of the Oslo Recommendations Regarding the Linguistic Rights of National Minorities:

> '18. In regions and localities where persons belonging to a national minority are pres??ent in significant numbers and where the desire for it has been expressed, persons belonging to this minority should have the right to express themselves in their own language in judicial proceedings, if necessary with the free assistance of an interpreter and/or translator.
> 19. In those regions and localities in which persons belonging to a national minority live in significant numbers and where the desire for it has been expressed, States should give due consideration to the feasibility of conducting all judicial proceedings affecting such persons in the language of the minority.'

The situation involving judicial authorities, as with any type of State preferences, is also one which raises a potential issue of discrimination. The language used during court proceedings is a form of State endorsed 'disadvantage' which can negatively impact individuals who are not as fluent as native speakers of the official language. In some situations, because of the seriousness and scale of this disadvantage, it may be discriminatory not to provide for some appropriate degree of use of the minority language by judges and other court officials. What this implies is the application of a sliding-scale model which takes into account these disadvantages and a State's resources and ability to respond in a reasonable way. It is this non-discriminatory approach, and European standard, which one can find in documents such as the European

Charter and Oslo Recommendations Regarding the Linguistic Rights of National Minorities.

Confirmation of the pertinence of non-discrimination can be found in a recent decision of the European Court of Justice.[37] Although the European Union does not have competence in the area of language policy, the Treaty establishing the European Community does contain provisions dealing with non-discrimination and freedom of movement which can in some situations offer a degree of protection in the area of 'linguistic rights', as surprising as this may initially sound.

An Austrian citizen, Mr. Bickel, and a German national, Mr. Franz, visiting the Trentino-Alto Adige region (South Tyrol) of Italy were charged with minor criminal offences in separate incidents. Criminal proceedings in this region, and more specifically the Province of Bolzano, can be conducted in either German or Italian, but this linguistic right under Presidential Decree No. 670 of 30 August 1972 is limited to German-speaking citizens of the Province. A further decree (Presidential Decree No. 574 of 15 July 1988) adds that judicial authorities must use the language of German- or Ladin-speaking citizens in their dealings and documents with these citizens.

Bickel and Franz both requested that judicial proceedings be held in German, even though they were not citizens of Italy and thus not entitled to this linguistic right under existing Italian legislation. The matter eventually found its way to the European Court of Justice, the plaintiffs claiming that to deny them the right to a trial in German was discrimination on the basis of nationality in relation to the freedom to provide services and freedom of movement since they could not enjoy a benefit enjoyed by some Italian nationals.

The European Court of Justice agreed, with the result that a consequence of the European Union may be an extension of linguistic rights to unexpected categories, although one should not read too much into the decision. The case does emphasise that in the context of a Community based on the principles of freedom of movement and of establishment, the protection of the linguistic rights of individuals is of particular importance. It also confirmed that non-discrimination on grounds of nationality under Community law applies to all nationals of Member States, and that consequently:

> '16. [...] the exercise of the right to move and reside freely in another Member State is enhanced if the citizens of the Union are able to use a given language to communicate with the administrative and judicial authorities of a State on the same footing as its nationals. Consequently, persons such as Mr Bickel and Mr. Franz, in exercising that right in another Member State, are in principle entitled, pursuant to Article 6 of the Treaty, to treatment no less favourable than that accorded to nationals of the host State so far as concerns the use of languages which are spoken there. [...]
> 26. [...] rules [...] which make the right, in a defined area, to have criminal proceedings conducted in the language of the person concerned conditional on that person being

---

[37] *Bickel and Franz v. Italy*, Case C-274/96, ECJ Judgement of 24 November 1998.

resident in that area, favour nationals of the host State by comparison with nationals of other Member States, exercising their right to freedom of movement and therefore run counter to the principle of non-discrimination [...] '

What should be remarked upon, and which appears to have been overlooked by most commentators in Europe, is the Italian Government attempt to sway the Court by arguing that the right to a trial in German was in fact a specific measure for the protection of the German-speaking (Tyrolean) national minority of Alto Adige, which it undoubtedly is, and thus should not be extended to individuals who were not members of that national minority.

The European Court of Justice concluded that the aim of protecting a national minority would in no way be undermined if citizens of Member States of the Community who were German-speaking, but not members of the Tyrolean national minority, were to be extended to right to a trial in their language. An important lesson from this decision is the potential of using non-discrimination so that non-citizens and individuals who are not members of a national minority may still be able to enjoy existing linguistic rights through the application of non-discrimination.[38]

As mentioned earlier, the right to proceedings in a minority language is not the only linguistic right which individuals may be entitled to in judicial affairs. Any accused, including persons belonging to linguistic minorities, has the right to an interpreter in criminal cases for translation of proceedings, including court documents, if he or she does not understand the language used in criminal proceedings. A number of international decisions confirm this right and give some indication of its scope and limitations.[39] The right does not depend on considerations such as the number of speakers of a minority language or their territorial concentration in a State. It is an absolute right once it has been shown that an accused does not understand the language of proceedings. Once again, the right is found in a large number of international human rights treaties[40] as well as more specific minority rights instruments.[41]

---

[38] The European Court of Justice had made similar comments in an earlier decision, *Ministère Public* v. *Mutsch*, Case 137-84, (1985) European Court Reports 2681, where it indicated that non-discrimination applied to EU migrants not only in relation to their work, but also in respect to 'social advantages' even if they area unrelated to employment. One of these advantages, according to the Court, was the possibility for a migrant to use his own language in court proceedings, and that this would facilitate the free movement of persons within the Community by contributing to the integration of the migrant in his host country.

[39] *Isop* v. *Austria*, Application 808/60, 5 Yearbook of the European Convention on Human Rights 108; *Dominique Guesdon* v. *France*, Communication No. 219/1986; *Kamasinski* v. *Austria*, Judgement of 19 December 1989, European Court of Human Rights.

[40] Art. 14(3)(f) of the ICCPR, and Art. 6(3)(e) of the Council of Europe's ECHR.

[41] Recommendation 17 of the Oslo Recommendations Regarding the Linguistic Rights of National Minorities, and Art. 10(3) of the Framework Convention.

Similarly, individuals, including members of minorities, have the linguistic right to be informed promptly of the nature and cause of a criminal accusation.[42] Under this 'linguistic right', public authorities must use a minority language where an individual does not understand the language used by State officials in criminal charges. This is a right universally referred to in international human rights treaties and most minority instruments.[43]

4.4 Use of names by public authorities

As mentioned earlier, a State which prohibits the private use of a person's first name or surname in a minority language (and other languages) breaches the right to private and family life. But the right to private and family life may not necessarily oblige public authorities to use or officially recognise an individual's name or surname in a minority language. Such a refusal could nevertheless be seen as a discriminatory practice if it is deemed to be unreasonable. Since some individuals are denied a benefit or privilege enjoyed by others (the benefit or privilege of having their name recognised and used by public authorities in their own language), there is a distinction as to language that could be argued as unreasonable and therefore discriminatory. In fact, there are few arguments to support a policy where public authorities refuse to recognise or use an individual's name or surname because it is in a minority or unofficial language. Additionally, treaties and other instruments emanating from Europe make it clear that public authorities must recognise and use such a name for official purposes. This is for example spelt out, among others,[44] in Article 11(1) of the Framework Convention:

> 'The Parties undertake to recognise that every person belonging to a national minority has the right to use his or her surname (patronym) and first names in the minority language and the right to official recognition of them, according to modalities provided for in their legal system.'

4.5 Topographical names and descriptions

Both legal and political documents now seem to recognise that it is 'reasonable' for States to accommodate the language of minorities where they are territorially concentrated in sufficient numbers. Minorities in Europe would thus appear to have the 'linguistic right' for local and regional public authorities to use the

---

[42] *Brozicek* v. *Italy* (1989) European Convention on Human Rights, Series A, No. 167.

[43] Art. 14(3)(a) of the ICCPR, and Art. 6(3)(a) of the Council of Europe's ECHR, Recommendation 17 of the Oslo Recommendations Regarding the Linguistic Rights of National Minorities, and Art. 10(3) of the Framework Convention.

[44] These are, among others, Art. 11 of the CEI Instrument for the Protection of Minority Rights and Recommendation 1 of the Oslo Recommendations Regarding the Linguistic Rights of National Minorities.

name of towns, geographical places, even street or road names in a minority language, if necessary in conjunction with the official language, where this is appropriate.[45] To illustrate when this arises, one could look at the wording of Article 11(3) of the Framework Convention:

> 'In areas traditionally inhabited by substantial numbers of persons belonging to a national minority, the Parties shall endeavour, in the framework of their legal system, including, where appropriate, agreements with other States, and taking into account their specific conditions, to display traditional local names, street names and other topographical indications intended for the public also in the minority language when there is a sufficient demand for such indications.'

Once again, this right can be seen as the adoption of a non-discriminatory practice in terms of language.

4.6 Public media and minority languages

Like any other type of State service, benefit or activity, the involvement of the State in public media must conform to the requirements of non-discrimination. Public authorities must therefore adopt a sliding-scale model: if the State controls, operates or finances any media, they should do so in a non-discriminatory fashion.

This view of non-discrimination, as well as the provisions of some human rights treaties and political commitments in a number of documents, suggest that an appropriate and reasonable policy by public authorities must be based on the numerical importance of the speakers of a minority language, their location and geographic concentration, etc.

This 'minority right' is confirmed in Europe by a number of provisions in various documents, such as Article 11 of the European Charter, and Recommendation 9 of the Oslo Recommendations Regarding the Linguistic Rights of National Minorities.

The explanatory note which accompanies the Oslo Recommendations also sets out why such a linguistic minority right exists, linking it to existing basic human rights such as freedom of expression and non-discrimination in international and European law:

> 'The issue of access to publicly funded media is closely linked with the concept of freedom of expression. Article 9(1) of the Framework Convention [for the Protection of National Minorities] stipulates that the freedom of expression of persons belonging to national minorities includes the freedom to impart information and ideas in the minority language, without interference by public authorities, and goes on to say that 'members of minorities shall not be discriminated against in their access to the media.' Article 9(4) of the Framework Convention stipulates that 'Parties shall adopt adequate measures in order

---

[45] Including Art. 14 of the CEI Instrument for the Protection of Minority Rights, Art. 11 of the Framework Convention, and Art. 10(2)(g) of the European Charter.

to facilitate access to the media for persons belonging to national minorities.' This implies that a national minority consisting of a substantial number of members should be given access to its fair share of broadcast time, on public radio and/or television, with the numerical size of the minority in question having a bearing on its share of broadcast time.

Numerical strength and concentration, however, cannot be seen as the only criteria when judging the amount of broadcast time to be allocated to any given national minority. In the case of smaller communities, consideration must be given to the viable minimum of time and resources without which a smaller minority would not meaningfully be able to avail itself of the media.

Moreover, the quality of the time allotted to minority programming is an issue that needs to be approached in a reasonable, non-discriminatory manner. The time-slots allotted to minority language programming should be such as to ensure that persons belonging to a national minority can enjoy programming in their language in a meaningful way. Hence, public authorities should ensure that this programming is transmitted at reasonable times of the day.'

Broadcasting frequencies are not part of the private realm, which means that public authorities are not legally obliged to grant a private broadcasting frequency every time it is demanded by a minority.

However, the European Court of Human Rights in *Informationverein Lentia and Others* v. *Austria*[46] pointed out that public authorities when exercising their regulatory powers by allocating airwave frequencies had to observe their obligations under international legal instruments. Thus, this means that a State must consider a minority's right to communicate with its members in its language, *via* the airwaves.

In a State where public authorities favour exclusively the majority or official language, the linguistic and cultural needs of speakers of a minority language are qualitatively and quantitatively disregarded. Such a policy could be discriminatory, and probably a violation of Article 27 of the ICCPR, if minorities found themselves unreasonably excluded or disadvantaged in terms of operating private stations using their language.

If the State is actively involved in newspaper publication, it should likewise devote a fair proportion of resources and/or space for the use of minority languages when parts of its population involve sufficiently large linguistic minorities.[47]

4.7 Minority language, public office and the electoral process

Excluding individuals from being candidates or from holding an elected public position because they do not speak the official language could constitute an unreasonable, and therefore discriminatory, restriction. In light of the importance of a free and democratic process open to all citizens, such an exclusion because

---

[46] Case 36/1992/381/455-459.
[47] See also Art. 11(1)(a) of the European Charter.

of the linguistic preferences of public authorities is an extremely serious measure which would likely be prohibited in most situations as discrimination as to language.[48]

As pointed out in a number of European decisions, neither freedom of expression, nor the limited non-discrimination provision of the Council of Europe's ECHR, guarantee a right to use a minority language in official State activities connected to the electoral process. In the case of the registration of a political party, the European Court of Human Rights has indicated there is no unqualified obligation for public authorities to accept such a document.[49]

However, under a general non-discrimination provision such as that contained in Article 26 of the ICCPR, this type of function is an example of an administrative activity by public authorities. When dealing with a numerically important or territorially concentrated minority, it could be described as unreasonable for public authorities not to use a minority language to some degree. This means that under the sliding-scale model of what is 'reasonable' or 'appropriate', public authorities would have to use the national minority language in terms of proceeding with the registration of documents and in other aspects of the electoral process as may be required in consideration of what is non-discriminatory. Although not many European or other instruments deal directly with this right, there is some direct support for such an approach. Recommendation 15 of the Oslo Recommendations Regarding the Linguistic Rights of National Minorities refers to the following:

'In regions and localities where persons belonging to a national minority are present in significant numbers, the State shall take measures to ensure that elected members of regional and local governmental bodies can use also the language of the national minority during activities relating to these bodies.'

This implies not only that individuals who speak a non-official language may be elected to public office, but additionally that governmental bodies must also, where appropriate, permit the use of minority languages where there is a sufficiently large demand.

What should also be made clear is that this does not signify that every minority language must be accommodated in every situation by elected bodies.[50]

---

[48] Previous attempts by minorities to obtain the right to use of their language in the electoral process, such as in *Fryske Nasjonale Partij* v. *Netherlands* (1986) 45 Decisions and Reports 240, at p. 243, by claiming a State is obliged to respect their freedom of expression have failed at the international or European levels because the electoral process is part of the 'public' sphere and not a private activity.

[49] Idem.

[50] In the situation where elected politicians were prevented from taking up their office for refusing to take a parliamentary oath in Dutch in Mathieu-Mohin and Clerfayt, (1987) *European Convention on Human Rights*, Series A, No. 113, at p. 25, the European Court of Human Rights essentially concluded that such a linguistic requirement affecting the principles embodied in Art. 3

The costs and difficulty of providing, for example, translation must be taken into account in determining whether not using a minority language is discriminatory in a particular context.

In view of the fundamental role and prominence of political activities in a democratic setting, it would seem that elected public institutions must be flexible in taking measures to permit the use of a minority language in order to ensure the effective participation of minorities in public affairs.[51]

5. CONCLUSION

'Does not the sun shine equally for the whole world? Do we not all equally breathe the air? Do you not feel shame at authorizing only three languages and condemning other people to blindness and deafness? Tell me, do you think that God is helpless and cannot bestow equality, or that he is envious and will not give it?'
Saint Constantine (Cyril)[52]

The rights of linguistic minorities include a panoply of guarantees which have mainly emerged in the second half of this century from the credo announced in the Universal Declaration of Human Rights of a 'faith in fundamental human rights, in the dignity and worth of the human person, in the equal rights of men and women and of nations large and small'.

These rights are based on the acknowledgement and acceptance of the human person in all of his or her diversity. Just as one's colour of skin should not diminish one's worth or dignity, so the State should not be prejudiced in its conduct towards or relationship with linguistic minorities.

It is therefore an often repeated error to assume that the protection of the rights of minorities is somehow inconsistent with or different from 'individual' human rights. On the contrary, by being founded on the recognition of the intrinsic value of the human person's dignity and worth, human rights have gone beyond mere tolerance of human differences: respect of the individual includes valuing human diversity. To deny minority individuals access to certain benefits, or to disadvantage them because of language is - under certain conditions – no longer permissible. Their human differences must be respected and accommodated to some degree whenever possible.

Despite differences in emphasis and terminology in documents emanating from the Council of Europe and other sources, there is by and large in Europe acceptance that States must provide for some degree of use of minority

---

of the First Protocol of the ECHR could not be deemed to be unreasonable, and therefore discriminatory.

[51] See Art. 10(2)(e) & (f) of the European Charter, and paragraph 35 of the Copenhagen Document of the Conference on the Human Dimension of the CSCE (now OSCE).

[52] Quoted in Joshua A. Fishman (Ed.), *Readings in the Sociology of Language*, Mouton and Co. N.V. Publishers, The Hague (1968) p. 589.

languages where reasonable and feasible to do so, as well as generally permit individuals to freely use minority languages in private activities.

Although there may still be some debate and disagreements on their exact extent and content, minority rights in the area of language are not 'special' or 'collective' rights, but the actual implementation of widely recognised individual human rights as this article has tried to show. Even if not everyone agrees on this proposition, it remains that in the European context, the linguistic rights of minorities have been widely approved in a wide-ranging number of treaties, resolutions, and political documents, as well as in the practices of many States.

In other words, there appears to be a European consensus visible through instruments such as the European Charter, the Framework Convention, and the Oslo Recommendations Regarding the Linguistic Rights of National Minorities, that human dignity and respect for human differences can and must be accommodated whenever possible as part and parcel of human rights within a democratic framework, and that includes respecting what may be described as the linguistic rights of minorities.

ALL LANGUAGES – GREAT AND SMALL
A Look at the Linguistic Future of Europe with Particular Reference to Lesser Used Languages

Dónall Ó Riagáin*

1. INTRODUCTION

The 1982 World Conference on Cultural Policies, organised by UNESCO in Mexico, in its final declaration,[1] defined culture as being, in its widest sense, *'the whole complex of distinctive spiritual, material, intellectual and emotional features that characterise a society or social group. It includes not only the arts and letters, but also modes of life, the fundamental rights of the human being, value systems, traditions and beliefs.'* Language is, in the first instance, a means of communication. But it is a lot more than that. It is a communal tool, developed and refined by its users, to express their ideas, their beliefs, their feelings. It reflects a people's development, their shared historical experience and their sense of community. It is a receptacle where a people's most intimate and finest thoughts can be recorded, stored and transmitted, not only to other contemporary members of the community, but even from one generation to another, from one era to another. It is the mainspring of culture. Small wonder then that language has played such a pivotal role in relationships between peoples, be these relationships problematic or amicable.

Some people would argue that the concept of the modern nation-State, as a sovereign entity, entitled to the allegiance of all its citizens, can be traced to the Peace of Westphalia in the 17th century. Personally, I would favour the school of thought that claims that the true prototype of the modern nation-State was, in fact, the first French Republic. At the time of the Revolution France was not yet a nation of citizens: rather she was a federation of provinces.[2] It is estimated that only 30% of the French population spoke standard Île-de-France French at the end of the 18th century. The majority spoke a variety of what are now called regional languages – Occitan, Corsican (close to the language of Tuscany), Breton, Basque, a variation of Dutch, Catalan, varieties of German in Alsace and

---

[*] Former Secretary General of the European Bureau for Lesser Used Languages, currently Special Adviser of the Bureau in its Dublin Office.
[1] Adopted by the World Conference on Cultural Policies, Mexico, 6 August 1982.
[2] E.N. Williams, *The Ancien Régime in Europe*, Penguin Books, London (1970).

S. Trifunovska (Ed.), *Minority Rights in Europe: European Minorities and Languages*
© 2000, T.M.C. Asser Press, The Hague, The Netherlands

Lorraine, not to mention the *langues d'Oïl* such as Gallo and Picard. This situation presented no great problem for the *ancien régime*. If the populace paid their taxes, participated in the occasional war and protested loyalty to the monarchy, then the King had no problem with his subjects speaking whatever language they chose. The Revolution ended all of that. The people were now citizens, entitled to certain rights but above all owing fealty to the State.

The modern nation-State was of its nature bureaucratic and also centralist. It attached great importance to having its influence extend into hitherto largely untouched domains of life – education, public administration and commerce. While the French revolutionaries started with a very liberal agenda they quickly switched to an authoritarian and centralist one, inspired by people like Abbé Gregoire. State and nation, citizenship and nationality, were perceived as being synonymous. One State, one nation and [...] of course, one language. Unity meant uniformity. With the establishment of unified nation-States in Germany, Italy, the United Kingdom [to mention but some cases] during the 19th century one can trace the beginning of the decline for most of Europe's small linguistic communities. The only two political entities which were notable exceptions were the Austro-Hungarian and Ottoman Empires where the sheer scale of linguistic diversity rendered the imposition of a monolingual policy impossible.

The solutions imposed by the victors of the First World War left more problems unsolved than solved. Borders were changed in a purely arbitrary manner, very often without the slightest regard to the wishes of the people concerned. A British statesman, involved in negotiating the Treaty of Versailles, is reputed to have turned to one of his officials and said, 'Remind me, old chap, was it Upper Silesia or Lower Silesia we gave away this morning?'

A decade later, Hitler was to exploit some of these anomalies with a ruthless efficiency. For example, the existence of a German-speaking minority in the Südatenland provided a ready-made excuse for invading Czechoslovakia. Rather than learning from their earlier mistakes, the victorious powers, at the end of the Second World War seemed to be as blinkered as ever and even more suspicious of minorities than before. They felt that the best way of ensuring stability in Europe was to keep minorities in firm check and to accord priority to the absolute integrity of nation-States. It must be said that people like Stalin, Franco, Tito and Salazar did produce a certain form of 'stability' within their own States but at a frightening cost in terms of human liberty and dignity.

Finding ways of accommodating diversity is a real challenge and not one which can be put to one side indefinitely. Our continent is a linguistic and cultural mosaic. In the European Union alone almost forty autochthonous languages are spoken. Should we care to take the greater Europe as our measure we would have to multiply this figure many times. In the Russian Federation, there are no fewer than 175 minorities officially recognised, each with their own language.

In a word, linguistic diversity is the norm in Europe – not the exception. The European Union has eleven official and working languages. Of course, some languages are more widely used than others either as mother-tongue or as languages of wider communication. A Eurobarometer survey,[3] published in July 1994, but not including Austria, Sweden or Finland, which had just acceded to the Union, showed that German was the most widely used language as a mother-tongue by the citizens of the EU – at 24%. Italian and English tied for second place at 17% each. French came a close third at 16%. A further question on foreign languages spoken showed quite a different picture with English being known by 25%, French by 13% and German by only 8%. It is worth noting that all of these languages are minority languages in a European context.

But leaving aside the relative strengths of these major languages, we discover that 40-50,000,000 EU citizens speak a language other than the main official language of the country of which they are citizens. In the member States of the European Union alone there are almost fifty communities speaking over thirty autochthonous European languages, other than the dominant, majority languages of the States in which they live. These do not include the African and Asian languages introduced in recent decades by immigrants and guest workers. If one discounts micro-States like San Marino and Monaco, Iceland is the only European State without a linguistic minority. For instance, in France we find Breton, Dutch, Lëtzebuergesch, Occitan, a variety of German, Basque and Corsican. In Italy there are no fewer than thirteen minority language communities. In the UK we find Welsh, Scottish Gaelic, Irish, Cornish and Scots, including the variety of that language spoken in Northern Ireland. I have not included the Gaelic of the Isle of Man nor the varieties of Norman-French spoken on the Channel Islands as neither Man nor the Channel Islands are strictly part of the UK.

These small linguistic communities can be categorised in many different ways. For political and pragmatic reasons, rather than for socio-linguistic ones, the following model can be useful:

1. The national languages of two small EU member States, which by any international criteria are lesser used, i.e. Irish and Lëtzebuergesch. Should Malta accede to EU membership sometime in the future, Maltese, one of the few Semitic languages spoken in Europe, can be added to this short list;
2. The languages of minority communities which live in one, but only one, EU member State, e.g. Friulan in Italy, Sorbian in Germany or West Frisian in the Netherlands;
3. The languages of minority communities who live in two or more EU member States, e.g. Basque, which is spoken in both Spain and France, Occitan and Catalan which are spoken in France, Spain and Italy, and the Sami language which can be heard in Norway, Sweden, Finland and ever part of the Russian Federation;

---

[3] Eurobarometer No. 41.

4. Languages which are majority languages in some States but which are spoken by minorities in others, e.g. German in Belgium, Italy and Denmark, Danish in Germany, Finnish in Sweden and Greek in parts of southern Italy;
5. Autochthonous languages, which have been spoken in Europe for centuries but which are non-territorial, i.e. the Jewish languages (Yiddish and Judeo-Spanish) and the languages of the Sinti and Roma.

Some of these language communities are large and some tiny. An estimated seven million people speak Catalan – more that speak either Finnish of Danish, although the latter two are official and working languages of the EU. There are probably only 2-3,000 speakers of Saterfrisian in Germany and of Croatian in Molise in Italy. Some enjoy high levels of official recognition (e.g. Basque in the Basque Autonomous Community in Spain or German in the South Tirol in northern Italy) while the very existence of some language communities is not acknowledged by the authorities in other instances (e.g. Slav-Macedonian, Aroumain and Arvanite in Greece).

2. TOWARDS LEGAL RECOGNITION

In 1998 we celebrated the golden jubilee of the Universal Declaration of Human Rights.[4] The Universal Declaration has but one important reference to language – in Article 2:

> 'Everyone is entitled to all the rights and freedoms set forth in this Declaration, without distinction of any kind, such as race, colour, sex, **language**, religion, political or other opinion,, national or social origin, property, birth or other status' (emphasis added).

The importance of this article, however modest it might seem on first reading, should not be underestimated. The concept has been enunciated that certain rights should not be denied to any person on the grounds of language. Of course, this concept needed to be elaborated.

Twelve years later the UN adopted its Convention Against Discrimination in Education.[5] This Convention defined *'discrimination'* as being *'distinction, exclusion, limitation or preference which, being based on [...] language, [...] has the purpose or effect of nullifying or impairing equality of treatment in education [...]*. It went on to recognise the right of national minorities to use or teach their own languages.

The UN in the International Convention on the Elimination of all Forms of Racial Discrimination,[6] the International Covenant on Economic, Social and

---

[4] Adopted by the UN General Assembly on 10 December 1948.
[5] Adopted on 14 December 1960.
[6] Adopted on 21 December 1965.

Cultural Rights,[7] the International Covenant on Civil and Political Rights[8] and the Convention on the Rights of the Child[9] restated and further developed the principle first enunciated by it in the Universal Declaration. Undoubtedly, the most important UN document on this topic is the Declaration on the Rights of Persons belonging to National or Ethnic, Religious and Linguistic Minorities.[10] The Declaration recognises the rights of persons belonging to minorities to *enjoy their own culture and to use their own language, in private and in public, freely and without interference or any form of discrimination.*

The International Labour Organisation echoed similar sentiments in its Convention concerning Discrimination in respect of Employment and Occupation[11] and its two conventions on indigenous and tribal peoples.[12] UNESCO followed the same route with its Convention against Discrimination in Education[13] and its Recommendation on Participation by the People at large in Cultural Life and their Contribution to it.[14]

But it was in the Council of Europe that the most important development from a legal viewpoint was to take place. In 1984 the Standing Conference of Local and Regional Authorities held a public hearing in the Palais de l'Europe to consider the position of Europe's regional and minority languages. This was the launching pad for the preparation of the European Charter for Regional or Minority Languages,[15] which after a gestation period of eight years, was accorded the legal form of a convention by the Committee of Ministers of the Council of Europe in 1992. The Charter was and remains a unique document. It does not pertain to minorities, less still to ethnic groups. It does not even speak of linguistic communities – just languages and users of languages. This Jesuitical approach sidesteps the psychological block some States have about minorities, national or otherwise, and focuses on the languages themselves. But of course every living language has to have a community which uses it, otherwise it would not be living. And by according rights to languages the Charter *inter alia* confers rights on those who use them.

The Charter is cleverly designed also in as much as ratifying parties have to choose a minimum of 35 paragraphs or sub-paragraphs from Part III of the Charter which deals with Measures to Promote Regional or Minority Languages

---

[7] Adopted on 16 December 1966.

[8] Adopted by the UN General Assembly on 16 December 1966, entering into force on 23 March 1976.

[9] Adopted on 20 November 1989.

[10] Adopted on 18 December 1992.

[11] Adopted by the ILO General Conference on 25 June 1958.

[12] ILO Convention No. 107 concerning the Protection and Integration of Indigenous and other Tribal and Semi-Tribal Populations in Independent Countries, adopted on 26 June 1957, and the ILO Convention No. 169 concerning Indigenous and Tribal Peoples in Independent Countries, adopted on 27 June 1989.

[13] Adopted on 14 December 1960.

[14] Adopted on 26 November 1976.

[15] Adopted on 23 June 1992.

in Public Life. This part is set out in a domain by domain basis so every contracting party has to make a real and tangible commitment to implement concrete measures.

At the end of 1998 no fewer than 18 European States had signed the Charter and eight of these – Norway, Finland, Hungary, the Netherlands, Liechtenstein, Switzerland, Croatia and Germany – had ratified it. It seems as if France, the great bastion of centralist language policies, will sign the Charter in 1999. The UK has already publicly pledged to sign and ratify. Signatures are also anticipated from Italy and Sweden this year.

In 1996 the Foundation on Inter-Ethnic Relations published The Hague Recommendations Regarding the Education Rights of National Minorities. These had been compiled by a small expert working group at the request of the OSCE High Commissioner on National Minorities, Max van der Stoel. In October of the same year the High Commissioner asked the Foundation to consult another small group of internationally recognised experts with a view to receiving their recommendations on an appropriate and coherent application of the linguistic rights of persons belonging to national minorities in the OSCE region. This resulted in the publication in February 1998 of the Oslo Recommendations Regarding the Linguistic Rights of National Minorities. These two documents are interesting in that all of the recommendations contained therein are based on existing international legal instruments. In short, they give a fascinating overview of what legal provisions are in place and what are their implications for language policy.

3. THE EUROPEAN UNION AND LANGUAGE

In Europe the European Communities, now known to us as the European Union, were steadily evolving as the dominant socio-economic bloc in the post-Second World War period. The European Coal and Steel Community was formed as far back as 1951 and the European Economic Community and EURATOM came into existence with the adoption of the Treaty of Rome in 1956. What was fascinating about these developments was that there was no reference to language, culture or education in the treaties establishing the Communities except a listing of languages in which official versions of the Treaties were being made available. The official and working languages were defined by a Council decision. Schuman and Monet foresaw the interdependence of the French and German coal and steel industries as the cornerstone of the new European order, not culture nor language.

Indeed it was originally intended that the European Coal and Steel Community would have only one official and working language – French. Paradoxically, opposition to this idea came, not from the Germans, but from the Flemings who could not accept a monolingual French-speaking institution choosing a Flemish city, Brussels, as its capital while refusing to extend parity to the Dutch language. The new Community quickly found itself with four official and working languages – French, Dutch, German and Italian. Interestingly, the only authentic (as distinct from official) version of the Treaty establishing the European Coal and Steel Community is the French one.

With the accession of Denmark, Ireland and the UK these four languages became six, then nine as Spain, Portugal and Greece joined the club and finally eleven with the arrival of Sweden, Finland and Austria. Irish, while not an official or working language is a 'treaty language' – that is to say that versions of the Treaties and other important documents are available in Irish and enjoy equal official status with those in the eleven official and working languages of the EU. Irish may also be used in the European Parliament and in the European Court of Justice subject to certain conditions. This high number of official languages compares strikingly with the UN which has only six, and the Council of Europe and NATO, which have only two – French and English.

Although all eleven official and working languages enjoy legal equality, their actual use displays anything but equality. Indeed one can conclude that *de facto* there are only two major working languages – French and English. A study carried out by the Gerhard-Mercator-Universität, Duisburg a few years ago clearly demonstrates this.[16]

Use of languages by EU institutions:

	EU institutions		EU Member States	
	Oral	Written	Oral	Written
French	69	75	54	56
English	30	25	42	41
German	1	<0.5	3	2
Others	<0.5	<0.5	1	1

The European Communities, as the Union was then called, had from its inception a number of official and working languages – now eleven – but no policy in relation to other lesser used languages. The first step towards a new and more inclusive approach began in 1979 when John Hume, a Northern Ireland MEP and now Nobel Peace Prize laureate, supported by a number of deputies from other member States tabled a motion for resolution calling for a report to be made on the lesser used languages of the Communities. This was passed to a parliamentary committee which appointed an Italian deputy, Gaetano Arfé, to prepare a report and motion for resolution on these languages. This

---

[16] Gerhard-Mercator-Universität, Duisburg, *New Language Planning Newsletter* (Central Institute of Indian Languages), 9 (June 1995) No. 4.

resolution,[17] which was adopted in 1981, called for recognition to be given to these languages in the critical domains of education, public administration, mass media and social life. The following year, 1982 the EU budget contained for the first time a modest budgetary provision for promoting these languages. A further resolution[18] on his topic, again from Arfé, was adopted in 1983. The same year the European Parliament established a small Intergroup to monitor the position of these languages. The Intergroup is still active and meets almost every month during the plenary sessions of parliament in Strasbourg. Further reports and resolutions, one in 1987 from a Flemish deputy, Willy Kuijpers[19] and another in 1994 from a member from Ireland, Mark Killilea[20] were adopted without difficulty. A total of 321 deputies voted for the Killilea Resolution, six abstained and only one voted against.

The development of a more positive and holistic approach to European integration was reflected in the Maastricht Treaty of 1992. For the first time ever, articles on Education and Culture now appeared in the EU Treaty. In many respects the new articles are cautious to the point of being conservative. Nevertheless, they reflect a positive development in thinking, the importance of which should not be underestimated. Article 126 (Education) speaks of *the responsibility of the Member States for the content of teaching and the organisation of education systems and their cultural and linguistic diversity.* Article 128 (Culture) declares that the *Community shall contribute to the flowering of the cultures of the Member States, while respecting their national and regional diversity* [...]. So now we have in the Treaty a commitment to *cultural and linguistic diversity* and also to *national and regional diversity.*

The European Commission (DG XXII) is now about to propose that a Legal Act be adopted by the main institutions of the EU to establish a multi-annual action programme to support regional and minority languages. It is to be known as ARCHIPEL. A draft of the proposed Act will be considered by the Commission in early March 1999. If accepted by the Commission it will then have to go before the European Parliament and the Council of Ministers, the Committee of the Regions having first given an opinion. Because of the impending European elections it is unlikely that this procedure will be completed before early 2000. Nevertheless, when adopted it will signal another major breakthrough in that the work in favour of lesser used languages, promoted by the Parliament for the past seventeen years, will at last be put on a formal legal basis.

---

[17] Resolution on a Community charter of regional languages and cultures and on a charter of rights of ethnic minorities, adopted by the European Parliament on 16 October 1981.

[18] Resolution on measures in favour of minority languages and cultures, adopted by the European Parliament on 11 February 1983.

[19] Resolution on the languages and cultures of regional and ethnic minorities in the European Community, adopted by the European Parliament on 30 October 1987.

[20] Resolution on linguistic and cultural minorities in the European Community, adopted by the European Parliament on 9 February 1994.

4. THE EUROPEAN BUREAU FOR LESSER USED LANGUAGES

The first Arfé Resolution was a metaphorical ice-breaker in that one of the main EC institutions had now taken a positive stance on the issue of regional and minority languages. However, how were the proposals contained in the Resolution to be implemented? The Socialist Group in the European Parliament – (Arfé was a member of that group at the time) – convened a colloquy in Brussels in May 1982 to examine the proposals contained in the Resolution and to see how best they might be implemented. As well as interested deputies, Commission officials and key-note speakers, representatives of most of the linguistic communities in question were also invited. These representatives expressed the view that they needed an organisation which could speak and act on their behalf at European level. The European Bureau for Lesser Used Languages was thus established, albeit in an embryonic form. Its aim was to conserve and promote the lesser used, autochthonous languages of the European Communities, together with their attendant cultures.

The author was elected its first President and he and the other five persons set about making the Bureau a reality. The Irish Government offered a grant-in-aid and the following year a subvention was obtained from the newly established EC budget line for regional languages and cultures. Seventeen years later the Bureau now has committees in thirteen of the fifteen EU member States, an office in Dublin and an information centre in Brussels. It enjoys NGO status with the UN (ECOSOC), UNESCO, and the Council of Europe. It receives 90% of its funding from the EU, the remaining 10% comes from subventions from the Irish, Luxembourg and Frisian Provincial Governments and from the Germanophone Community in Belgium. Free office accommodation is made available by the Communauté française in Belgium.

The Bureau engages in a number of different forms of activity. Advocacy is probably its most important activity or, in less diplomatic parlance, lobbying. This work entails seeking support for initiatives in the European Parliament, the Committee of the Ministers and the Council of Europe. Members of the Bureau were particularly active in promoting the European Charter for Regional or Minority Languages at all stages of procedure. They were also active in advancing some of the key resolutions in the European Parliament, particularly the Kuijpers and Killilea Resolutions. This work is also carried out at national and regional level – in persuading governments to sign and ratify the European Charter and in seeking support for education through the medium of lesser used languages, for instance.

Facilitating an exchange of information and experiences among those working for lesser used languages is another aspect of the organisation's work. The Bureau publishes a newsletter, Contact-Bulletin, three times per year in bilingual, French/English format. It also produces booklets, reports, posters and videos. It organises a Study Visit Programme which enables around eighty language activists per year to visit another region and to see at first hand what is being done to promote the lesser used languages there. It was instrumental in establishing the Mercator, a series of information/documentation centres which provide information in the key domains of education, media and legislation. It organises workshops, seminars and conferences often in association with other bodies.

The establishment of a news agency, to provide information on lesser used languages, is one of the organisation's major projects at the present time. Another is the development of a form of Associate Membership which will be open to local, provincial and regional authorities, as well as official language planning boards.

5. WHAT DOES THE FUTURE HOLD?

Europe has been undergoing many changes over the past forty years. The establishment and growth of the European Union has entailed the ceding of part of their sovereignty by the member States and their sharing of a common sovereignty in certain areas. Parallel to this we have seen the development of a strong regional policy with funds flowing from the centre of the EU to peripheral regions which were underdeveloped. In short, the old nation-State concept of the 19th century seems to be in rapid and probably terminal decline. These two trends (Euro-centralisation and regionalisation) are likely to continue. The introduction of the common currency will unleash growing pressures for more central control, particularly in the domain of fiscal policy. On the other hand, enlargement will increase pressure for the transfer of more and more credits to underdeveloped regions.

The empowerment of regions has brought with it greater respect for regional languages and cultures. Indeed to support lesser used languages is now the politically correct position even if there is a gap between theory and practice in expressing this support in practical terms. The proponents of these languages can indeed be pleased with what they have achieved over the past two decades.

But public opinion can be fickle. New pressures are beginning to be felt – pressures which can only increase with increased centralisation on the one hand and enlargement on the other. And one of these pressures is to limit the number of working languages and even possibly reduce the number of existing working languages. Most commentators would agree that it is becoming increasingly evident that a new language cannot be added each time a new State joins the Union. Interpretation and translation services are already under strain with eleven working languages. The principle of geometric progression comes into play with the addition of each new language. If Hungarian, Polish or Estonian were added, interpreters would have to be found to interpret and translate from the new language into and from each one of the existing languages. It has been suggested that maybe three working languages would suffice – English, French and German. But can anyone seriously expect the Dutch, the Danes or the

Swedes, not to mention the Spaniards and the Italians to easily accept a *de facto* downgrading of their national languages? Realistically, the most that is likely to be agreed is an embargo on any additional languages, with the possible exception of one Slavic language, probably Polish, and the gradual legitimisation of the *de facto* situation which already exists, i.e. the dominance of two working languages.

In such a scenario a case might be made for a distinction to be made between languages of internal communication and languages of service to the citizen. If the concept of European citizenship is to mean anything then surely it must mean that all citizens of the EU are entitled to receive services and information about them in their own language. Such a policy could be implemented at modest cost in cooperation with the relevant national and regional governments. Again, such a strategy would be in keeping with the principle of subsidiarity.

Diversity of language and culture have never been a cause for conflict. It has been a refusal to accept and respect such diversity that has given rise to discrimination, institutional violence, resentment, alienation and ultimately conflict. This is not to contend that implementing a language policy which is respectful of diversity is always free of problems. Very often the relationship of one language community to another can be coloured by political or other factors and their perception of each other tainted with memories of past injustices. Besides this, a bilingual or multilingual language policy bears a price tag which may seem prohibitive to some. But very often this price is a lot lower than that accompanying conflict! It is all too easy to know the price of everything and the value of nothing. Nevertheless, available resources are inevitably limited and the creation and implementation of a language policy needs to be approached in a sympathetic, yet realistic, manner by all concerned. A case could be made for international organisations, such as the Council of Europe or the OSCE, to set up panels of experts whose expertise and impartial advice could be made available to governments and linguistic minorities when difficult situations arise.

Another factor which needs to be taken into consideration is the deeply felt human desire to belong. In an era of ever increasing homogenisation and urbanisation people have a deeply felt need for a sense of roots – of belonging to some distinct community, to some place, to some distinct culture. The maintenance of linguistic diversity can contribute a lot to meeting this need. Our ability to have each and every European citizen feel comfortable with his/her shared European identity may depend a lot on how the Union treats the citizen's national or regional identity and respects the linguistic and cultural mosaic which is Europe.

Having all European citizens being able to speak European languages other than their own is a stated objective of the European Union. The era of monolingualism is rapidly passing and our polyglot future will inevitably see changes in patterns of language usage. Diaglossic language use is now the norm for many of us. One language is used for one purpose, another language in another situation. Code switching in meetings at European level is everyday practice. Sometimes a language may not be dominant in any particular domain but may be used extensively among networks of speakers in a number of domains. The time when language communities could be delineated neatly with lines on a map may be ending. Increased levels of bilingual and multi-lingual ability, the greater mobility of persons and the ongoing urbanisation of society are already posing challenges to a purely territorial conceptualisation of language space. These challenges may also be windows of opportunity for lesser used languages as are certain technological developments, e.g. digital television, desk-top publishing or the web. The person whose mother-tongue is lesser used may be able without undue effort to use this language extensively and at the same time draw on languages of wider communication as is necessary. One thing is clear. These are challenges worth facing in a spirit of determination and optimism.

NON-TERRITORIAL LANGUAGES: ROMANY AS AN EXAMPLE

Marcia Rooker[*]

1. INTRODUCTION

Non-territorial languages have a long and interesting, but rather unknown history on the European continent. These languages survived and developed despite the fact that their speakers lived dispersed over the continent and often had to cope with an environment which was hostile to them and their language. The ultimate example is of course Yiddish, probably the best known non-territorial language, but used in everyday life only in some remote parts of Europe, due to the fact that most of its speakers fell victim to Nazi persecution. Nowadays, for the first time in history a more positive attitude towards these languages can be observed, but much is left to be desired.

The term non-territorial language is rather new. The first, and up to now only, international instrument to mention non-territorial languages is the 1992 European Charter on Regional or Minority Languages. The definition of non-territorial languages in Article 1(c) of the Charter is as follows:

'languages used by nationals of the State which differ from the languages used by the rest of the State's population but which, although traditionally used within the territory of the state, cannot be identified with a particular area thereof.'

The explanatory memorandum gives two examples of languages that qualify as non-territorial: Romany and Yiddish, languages connected with the Roma and Jewish communities respectively. Some States ratifying the Charter have identified more languages as non-territorial.[1] This article will mainly focus on Romany, the first language of millions of Europeans and the most problematic one when it comes to guaranteeing its place among other minority and non-minority languages.

---

[*] Researcher, Faculty of Law, Nijmegen, the Netherlands.
[1] Germany has identified Low German as another non-territorial language; the Netherlands has declared that it will treat the Lower-Saxon and Limburger languages as non-territorial, although these two languages are connected to certain regions.

S. Trifunovska (Ed.), Minority Rights in Europe: European Minorities and Languages
© 2000, T.M.C. Asser Press, The Hague, The Netherlands

2. ROMA AND ROMANY

The number of Roma and related groups[2] is estimated at seven to eight and a half million in Europe,[3] with the majority living in Central and Eastern Europe, and a substantive number on the Iberian peninsula. Certainly not all Roma speak Romany. Taking into account the fact that the persecution of Roma started almost the moment they arrived in Europe it is surprising that Romany still exists.[4] The exclusion of its speakers from mainstream society may at the same time be an explanation for the survival of Romany.[5] But the attempts to ban the language, to force another language on its speakers for 'their own good' or for less commendable reasons, did take its toll.

Some groups of Roma do not speak Romany, as for example the majority of Roma in Hungary.[6] Other groups have not entirely adopted another language but speak a language that linguists classify as 'para-Romany', which is a language with a grammar taken from another language and to a greater or lesser extent a Romany vocabulary. The Kaló spoken on the Iberian peninsula and the Anglo-Romany of Great Britain are examples of para-Romany.[7]

Many Romany dialects have maintained an Indian grammatical structure and a Romany vocabulary influenced by other languages. The Indian roots of the language are unchallenged among linguists.[8] This does not automatically mean that the ancestors of the people that speak Romany today came from India. Physical anthropology should help to give the answer to that question. But this science discipline is emotionally charged and has not yet come up with the definite answer on the origin of the Roma.[9] Loan words are a key to the journeying of Romany from India to Europe and even across the Ocean to the Americas. Loan words from other languages can be found in every variety of Romany, and other languages have taken loan words from Romany. Today Romany-speakers from different parts of Europe may have problems understanding each other. According to some there is reason to speak of a group of

---

[2] The term 'Roma' will be used as the general term for the people related to the Romany language, as the majority of Romany speakers are Roma. When appropriate the terms Sinti or Kale will be applied, meaning people closely related to Roma, who live in North-West Europe and the Iberian peninsula respectively, and who also speak a Romany dialect.

[3] Jean-Pierre Liégois and Nicolai Gheorghe, *Roma/Gypsies, a European Minority*, London (1995) p. 7.

[4] Donald Kenrick and Grattan Puxon, *The Destiny of Europe's Gypsies*, Sussex (1972).

[5] Milena Hübshmanova, 'Bilingualism among Slovak Roma', *International Journal of the Sociology of Language*, 19 (1979) p. 37.

[6] David Crowe, *A History of Gypsies in Eastern Europe and Russia*, London (1996) pp.69-107 for the history of Roma in Hungary.

[7] Jean Pierre Liégois, *Roma, Gypsies, Travellers*, Strasbourg (1994) p. 47.

[8] Ian Hancock, 'The Development of Romani Linguistics', in Mohamed Ali Jazayery and Werner Einter (Eds.), *Languages and Cultures*, Berlin (1988) p.183.

[9] Angus Fraser, *De Zigeuners*, Amsterdam (1994) p. 33.

related languages rather than of one Romany language.[10] In this sense, one linguist states that his research revealed a network of sixty forms of Romany.[11]

A common feature (of all forms) of Romany is that it is traditionally unwritten, and thus passed down orally. This may have hampered the development of Romany, as writing is a means by which to stabilise and cultivate a language. Songs, tales, proverbs and anecdotes fulfil the role literature has in other languages.[12] Nowadays serious attempts are being made by Roma and linguists to agree on a unified way of spelling Romany.

During its World Conference held in 1971 the International Romani Union, a Roma organisation, established a Language Commission with the task of dealing with the issues of the Romany language by taking convergence into consideration but at the same time respecting the variety of Romany dialects as the starting point for its work. In 1990 at a conference in Poland an alphabet and a protocol for the meaning of this alphabet in different dialects was decided upon. Once this step is taken the next will be to intensify the standardisation and work on comprehension between the different dialects.[13] The work of the Romani Union and other Roma spokesmen have contributed to putting the Romany language on the European agenda.

An exception to this development are the Sinti in Germany and the Netherlands as they are, indeed, very protective of their language: it should remain unwritten, outsiders are not supposed to learn it.

3. PRACTICAL OBSTACLES WITH RESPECT TO THE DEVELOPMENT OF ROMANY

For the first time in history the view is gaining ground that Romany is a real language and its speakers are a real minority and not a bunch of vagrants speaking a kind of argot.[14] The principle that Romany as a European language is entitled to exist, to be used, and to develop like any other European language, may become increasingly accepted now, but there is no tradition whatsoever to facilitate the use of this language in any respect. Policies to develop and encourage, or at least not hamper, the use of this language have hardly hatched out of the egg. Romany differs from other European languages in many ways; policies for other minority languages cannot merely be applied to Romany. It will take more before Romany is on an equal footing with other European

---

[10] Aangus Fraser, Idem., p. 298.
[11] Terrence Kaufman, 'Review of Weer Rajendra Rishi's Multilingual Romany Dictionary', *International Journal of the Sociology of Language* 19 (1979) p. 134.
[12] Milena Hübschmanova, op. cit. n. 5, p. 37; she gives, in fact, a much more detailed description of the cultural and linguistic structure of Romany than is reproduced here.
[13] Jean Pierre Liégois, op. cit. n. 7, p. 57.
[14] Idem., p. 44.

languages. Those governments who take a positive attitude towards Romany have to surmount a number of difficulties.

First, there is hardly any theoretical framework for Romany. No ages, not even decades of scientific work have unveiled the details of grammar, vocabulary or changes in the language. There is no tradition of stabilising and cultivating the language in this way. As stated above, traditionally Romany is an unwritten language which takes many forms so that Romany speakers from different parts of Europe do not understand each other.

Furthermore, the native speakers of Romany belong to the lowest strata in Europe. Only very few have an education that enables them to contribute to the development of a theory of the language. Most theoretical knowledge of Romany comes from scientists who do not speak it as a first language.

The most obvious way to keep a language alive is by teaching it. It will not come as a surprise that there is hardly any experience with teaching Romany to children at school or outside school and that there are hardly any people qualified to teach the language. Teaching material is not available as a matter of course. And, Romany being a non-territorial language, the speakers do not conveniently live together, thus it may prove difficult to gather enough Roma children to make up a class. The decisive factor is whether governments are able and willing to fund a policy to strengthen the position of Romany.

4. STATES' ATTITUDES TOWARDS TEACHING ROMANY

Two perspectives can be distinguished when talking about mother tongue education: the survival of the language, and what is best for the education of children. Education in the mother tongue is beneficial both for the development of the language[15] and for the development of the children.[16] Neither perspective seems to be very popular when it comes to Romany.

A large number of States prefer to ignore the fact that it has Romany speakers among its citizens. Telling in this respect is the information on Romany in a document published by the Council of Europe on the situation of regional or minority languages.[17] Only six out of the twenty-three countries that contributed to this report submitted information on the Romany language. Two countries, Ireland and Malta, do not have Romany speakers among its citizens. That leaves fifteen States that do count speakers of Romany or para-Romani, but have reason to ignore this fact.[18] It should be noted, however, that some countries with large Roma minorities did not contribute to this document at all: Romania, Bulgaria

---

[15] Fernand de Varennes, 'To speak or not to speak', UN Doc. E/CN.4/Sub.2/AC.5/1997 WP.6, para. 14.

[16] De Varennes, *Language, Minorities and Human Rights*, The Hague (1996) p. 192 ff.

[17] Council of Europe Doc. DELA (94) 1 Rev. Strasbourg, 1995.

[18] Austria, Belgium, Cyprus, Denmark, Germany, Italy, Luxembourg, the Netherlands, Norway, Portugal, Spain, Sweden, Switzerland, the United Kingdom and Turkey.

and the Czech Republic. The six countries that do mention Romany are Finland, Greece, Hungary, the Slovak Republic, Slovenia and Poland. These last two States only mention the existence of Romany speakers. If there is any state policy it remains unreveiled here. Some information on Poland is available from other sources. Fourteen schools experiment with Romany teaching, Poland reported to the UN Human Rights Committee in 1997.[19]

The information submitted by the four other States is not very extensive either. Greece admits that there are no educational facilities for teaching Romany to the 7,000 Roma living in Thrace, as Romany is not written. And Roma do speak Turkish or Greek alongside their mother tongue, the Report adds so as to explain why there is no real need to change the situation. No information is submitted on Roma living in Greece outside Thrace.

In the Slovak Republic Romany is not part of the national school curriculum, but some elementary schools in Kosice experiment with bilingual teaching in 'zero-classes': classes to prepare the Roma children for the regular Slovak school.

The developments in Finland and Hungary seem to be a little more encouraging. Finland reported that the majority of its 7,000 Roma can speak Romany to some extent, but that Finnish is – generally speaking – their first language. Since 1990 Roma pupils in the region of Helsinki can take evening classes in Romany. The instructors are Roma who graduated from an elementary course in the Romany language in 1990. Hungary reveals that approximately 70% of the estimated 500,000-700,000 Roma living in Hungary speak Hungarian as a first language, whereas the other 30% speak different kinds of Romany. Despite the high number of Hungarian-speaking Roma the report devotes an entire section to 'the situation of Gipsy languages': Roma languages are not used for official purposes, they are not taught at schools as 'there are virtually no qualified teachers who speak those languages'. But the Government does think it necessary to promote the gypsy languages. Several newspapers and books (including the bible and language courses) have been published with government money. And radio and TV programmes in Romany are regularly broadcasted. It is remarkable that in the two States that have done the most to promote the Romany language, Romany is in fact not the first language of the majority of Roma.

The developments in the States with large Roma minorities that did not contribute to this document, Romania, Bulgaria and the Czech Republic, are mixed. From other sources it becomes apparent that since 1989 Bulgaria has had a rather positive attitude towards teaching Romany. A Romany textbook has been published, but finding and training people to teach the language seems to be problematic.[20] Still, Bulgaria reports that 499 pupils receive education in their mother tongue from ten teachers.[21] Romania informed the UN Human Rights

---

[19] UN Doc. CCPR/C/95/Add. 8, 1997.
[20] UN Doc. CERD/C/299/Add.7, p. 26, § 103, 1996.
[21] CERD/C/299/Add.7 p. 23, 1996.

Committee that it has special classes for training teachers in Romany.[22] Whether any Roma children are already being educated in their mother tongue remains unclear.

The Czech Republic appears to have an entirely different approach to Roma pupils:

> 'The Roma minority has never requested education in its own language; on the contrary, they do not seem inclined to sponsor separate schools providing instruction in the Roma language. Special schemes targeting Roma pupils are not based on the 'education in minority language' principle - on the contrary, the imperative task is to eliminate the linguistic, social and cultural handicaps which prevent Roma children from completing elementary education and entering secondary schools.'[23]

For the time being the imperative task to eliminate the linguistic, social and cultural handicaps is being carried out by sending the majority of Roma children to remedial schools, forever blocking their access to secondary education and thus consolidating their marginal position. A lack of knowledge of the Czech language is one of the main reasons why many Roma children qualify for remedial teaching.[24] On 15 June 1999 a group of parents, with the help of a local lawyer and the European Roma Rights Centre, filed a complaint with the Czech Constitutional Court and the Ostrava School Bureau charging the Ministry of Education and local school authorities with segregation by sending Roma children to remedial special schools because of their ethnic identity. In case domestic remedies are not effective an application with the European Court of Human Rights in Strasbourg should be expected to follow.[25]

Thus, on one side of the spectre there is Finland, for many years trying to preserve the Roma language and now able to offer evening classes by skilled teachers for the Roma in and around Helsinki; and at the other end is the Czech Republic convinced that speaking Romany is a linguistic handicap. In between are the States that do not have a policy with regard to the Romany language or are experimenting and developing mother tongue education for the Roma.

From the point of view that Romany is a language worthy of existence and a tool to improve the deplorable situation of the majority of Roma in Europe, the situation is pathetic. A gleam of hope may come from international law.

---

[22] CCPR/C/95/Add.7, p.58, § 249-250, 1997.

[23] UN Doc. CERD/C/289/Add.1, § 133, 1997.

[24] *A Special Remedy, Roma and Schools for the Mentally Handicapped in the Czech Republic*, ERRC Country Report, 1999.

[25] James Goldston, 'Lawsuit filed by Roma challenge Racial Segregation in Czech Schools', *Roma Rights* 2(1999), pp. 52-54.

5. THE EUROPEAN CHARTER ON REGIONAL OR MINORITY LANGUAGES

The importance of the European Charter on Regional or Minority Languages with respect to non-territorial languages is in the first place in its recognition of the existence of these languages. The protection which it guarantees is that the general principles for all minority languages apply *mutatatis mutandis* to non-territorial languages (Article 7(5)). The general principles can be found in Part II of the Charter and include the recognition of the language as an expression of cultural wealth; resolute action to promote the language in order to safeguard it; the provision of forms and means to teach and study the language; promotion of transnational exchanges when the same language is used in another state. Apart from these affirmative measures the States have to eliminate any act of discrimination related to the use of the minority language. And of course the needs and wishes of the speakers of the minority language have to be taken into consideration, even more so with respect to speakers of a non-territorial language.

For the time being nowhere have the objectives and principles of the Charter been fully implemented with respect to Romany. To move on from the negative stereotype of Roma as vagrants and thieves to the recognition of their language as an expression of cultural wealth that needs promotion, is certainly quite a big step which will take time.

Furthermore, according to Article 7(5) of the Charter 'the nature and scope of the measures to be taken to give effect to this Charter shall be determined in a flexible manner, bearing in mind the needs and wishes, and respecting the traditions and characteristics, of the groups which use the languages concerned'. This can easily be used as an escape clause. Traditionally Romany has not been a language of instruction, neither has it been even looked upon as a real language.

A more positive explanation of this phrase is that the measures to be taken to give effect to the Charter are not only found in the policy developed to meet the objectives and principles of Article 7, but also in Part II of the Charter. Part III provides a catalogue of minority language rights, like education in the mother tongue and the use of the minority language in the media. States can select for specified minority languages to be bound by a minimum of thirty-five provisions from Part III (Article 2(2)). 'Flexible' in this respect means that less than thirty-five provisions can be selected for a non-territorial language or the condition that certain provisions have to be selected (Article 2(2)) can be applied less strictly. Up to now only Germany has interpreted the Charter in this way.

At the time of ratification of the Charter more States made declarations or reservations concerning Romany or non-territorial languages in general. By the beginning of 1999 eight countries had ratified the Charter and declared which provisions listed in Part III applies to what minority or regional language,

Liechtenstein being an exception as it declared that no regional or minority languages are spoken on its territory.

As stated above, the general principles of Part II apply *mutatis mutandis* to non-territorial languages. States therefore do not need to mention Romany explicitly in this respect. And indeed, Hungary, Norway and Switzerland do not mention Romany in their declarations, though there were countries, like Finland and the Netherlands, which did declare that the provisions of Part II will apply to Romany. On the other hand, Croatia has made a reservation with respect to the provisions of Article 7(5). That means that the general principles contained in Part II of the Charter will not be applied to non-territorial minority languages. It is worth mentioning, however, that according to Croat official statistics, about 5,000 Roma reside in Croatia, making up 0.1% the approximate 4,784,265 population,[26] most of whom arrived in Croatia relatively recently. During the Second World War about 28,000 Roma were killed by the Ustaša, together with the German and Italian occupiers.[27]

Germany not only protects the non-territorial Romany language by applying the general principles of Part II but also indicates which provisions of Part III will apply to Romany in which *Land* or in the entire territory. Germany made a selection of the Charter provisions aimed at ensuring the teaching of Romany history and culture; facilitating the use of Romany in civil and administrative procedures; allowing the use of family names in Romany; encouraging and/or facilitating the use of Romany in the media and in printing; ensuring no limitations in law on Romany in economic and social life; and finally co-operating with neighbouring countries on several subjects with respect to Romany or not hampering contacts with Romany speakers from other countries. Besides, some *Länder* have declared that additional provisions will apply to Romany. For example, with respect to education and with respect to cultural activities. The German selection of provisions may reflect for the most part the rights which Roma and Sinti already enjoy, but still, Germany has to be commended for recognising these rights in this way and setting the tone as to how the Charter can be applied.

As the Charter is a not self-executing document, there is a reporting system and a Committee of experts to inform the Committee of Ministers of the progress made with the implementation of the Charter. The Charter gives ample room to NGOs to inform the Committee of their views concerning the implementation of the Charter. Thus, the Charter gives minorities an opportunity to voice their grievances, although its main aim is the protection of the regional or minority languages and not the speakers of these languages.

---

[26] UN Doc. HRI/CORE/1/Add.32, para. 9, p.4, 1994.
[27] Grattan Puxon, 'Romanes and Language Policy in Yugoslavia', *International Journal of the Sociology of Language*, 19 (1979) p. 84 with reference to Kenrick and Puxon (1972) p. 115.

6. THE FRAMEWORK CONVENTION ON THE PROTECTION OF NATIONAL MINORITIES

The other recent Council of Europe minority treaty is the Framework Convention on the Protection of National Minorities. This Convention contains articles on the use of minority languages (Articles 10, 11 and 14), providing for the right to use the minority language in private and public, to use names in the minority language and the right to learn one's minority language. But the basic precondition for the protection of the Romany language is the recognition of Roma as a national minority. This is especially important in the light of the fact that the States parties to the Convention could not agree on a definition of 'national minority'. Consequently, some States have, at the time of ratification of the Convention, made declarations and listed minorities to which the Convention would apply. By June 1999 there had been 26 ratifications (25 by member States and 1 by a non-member State) with 12 reservations and declarations concerning the application and implementation of the Framework Convention. Malta and Liechtenstein declared that no minorities live on their territories; five States came up with a definition of 'national minority': Estonia, Luxembourg, Russia, Switzerland and Austria. Austria limited protection to those minorities that fall within the scope of its 1976 Law on Ethnic Groups. Roma with Austrian nationality are one of the minorities recognised under this Law. Denmark only recognises the Germans in South Jutland as a minority. And finally Germany, Slovenia and the Former Yugoslav Republic of Macedonia (FYROM) mention Roma specifically in their respective declarations.

Like the Charter, the Convention is not a self-executing document and therefore much depends on the reporting system. The Committee of Ministers monitors the implementation, assisted by an advisory committee. This seems paradoxical as this Convention is open for signature for States that are not members of the Council of Europe and therefore do not participate in the work of the Council of Ministers, while at the same time member States that have not ratified the Convention are involved in that they have a say in its implementation. Pursuant to Article 25(1) the first State reports due to be submitted within a year of the entry into force of the Convention in respect of a Contracting Party,[28] have already been submitted but not yet discussed. Anyhow, it would be interesting to discuss briefly the report submitted by Croatia. If taken into consideration that Croatia did make a reservation with respect to non-territorial languages when ratifying the European Charter for Regional and Minority Languages (deposited on 5 November 1997), its position could not be different with respect to Roma language rights under the Framework Convention. In fact, the Croat attitude towards Roma and Romany is rather clear: the problem lies in the fact that some children do not attend classes and

---

[28] The Framework Convention entered into force in 1 February 1998, on the first day of the month following the expiration of a period of three months after the date on which twelve member States expressed their consent to be bound (Article 28(1)).

there are those who do so and 'are incorporated in the regular schooling system in the Croatian language[...][having the possibility to] successfully become part of the social environment in which they live.'[29] Roma children will only succeed in Croatia when they adapt, which as a position is, of course, contrary to the spirit of the Framework Convention.

7. ARTICLE 27 OF THE UNITED NATIONS COVENANT ON CIVIL AND POLITICAL RIGHTS

On the international level Article 27 of the UN Covenant on Civil and Political Rights gives protection to members of minorities, with the possibility of an individual complaint if the state concerned has ratified the 1966 First Optional Protocol to the Covenant. In its General Comment No. 23 the Human Rights Committee has elaborated its interpretation of Article 27.[30] It is a liberal interpretation which states that, for example, the protection under Article 27 extends to non-citizens. With respect to the use of a minority language, members of minorities are entitled to use their language in private and in public. It should be distinguished from the right to freedom of expression and the right of accused persons to interpretation during criminal proceedings. States are obliged to take positive measures to protect members of minorities and to report to the Human Rights Committee on the measures taken in the reporting period. The Committee recognises that Article 27 is an individual right but this individual right depends 'in turn on the ability of the minority group to maintain its culture, language or religion. Accordingly, positive measures by States may also be necessary to protect the identity of a minority and the rights of its members to enjoy and develop their culture and language and to practice their religion, in community with the other members of the group.'

Thus States should not only refrain from banning the language and similar destructive measures but should also enable minorities to speak and develop their language, and to ensure that they have the possibility and means to do so. On the UN level the question that arose with respect to the Council of Europe's Framework Convention, i.e. whether it applies to Roma, does not occur, as the Human Rights Committee gives this liberal interpretation of the term 'minority'.

8. CONCLUSION

There are very few examples of good practice with respect to the linguistic rights of the Roma. In this respect one should mention the evening classes organized for Roma living in the Helsinki region in Finland or education provided in the

---

[29] CoE Doc. ACFC/SR (99) 5 p. 151.
[30] UN Doc. A.49/40 pp. 107-110.

mother tongue for 499 Roma pupils in Bulgaria. In addition to this, in Hungary and Romania the good intentions of the respective governments to improve the situation of Roma are notable. However, it should be pointed out that there are only a few hundred, not even a thousand out of the millions of the European Roma population, whose linguistic rights are respected to a certain extent. During the last decade there have been changes for the better, but there is still a long way to go. Compared to other languages, Romany, as a non-territorial language has no sound basis for maintenance and development: there is no theoretical framework, no experience with teaching the language, its speakers belong to the lowest strata in society and therefore have little power to push forward their demands, and most importantly, a mainstream society still has to get used to the idea that Roma have the same human rights as others and are entitled to enjoy them.

The existing international protection of the Romany language leaves much to be desired. The Charter on Regional or Minority Languages treats it in a stepmotherly fashion, while it more desperately needs protection than many other regional or minority languages. The European Framework Convention's main shortcoming is the absence of a definition of 'national minority' giving States the opportunity to exclude Roma from the protection guaranteed by the Convention. The UN Covenant on Civil and Political Rights protection is very general, but does demand that States take positive measures to ensure members of minorities, among other things, the use of their language. A serious, if not the most serious, obstacle is the lack of financial means needed to develop the theoretical framework and to provide teaching materials, training of teachers, organisation of classes, and/or even separate schools for Romany speakers. With the majority of the Roma living in the poorest parts of Europe and facing much more and often acute problems, there is little hope that the situation will improve in the near future.

A NEVER-ENDING STORY? THE ITALIAN DRAFT BILL ON THE PROTECTION OF LINGUISTIC MINORITIES

Francesco Palermo*

1. THE ITALIAN CONSTITUTIONAL MINORITY PROTECTION SYSTEM. GENERAL REMARKS

Within the Italian territory approximately 2.5 million people (4.5% of the population) belong to (at least) 12 minority groups. This fact makes Italy the EU country in which most minorities live.[1] It is important to stress that the Italian Constitution takes only the language as a distinctive feature to identify minorities, because of the basic assumption that all Italian citizens are members of the Italian nation, which is, in fact, a nation of nations. This fact does not mean that minority features other than linguistic are not recognized, but only that the protectional mechanisms are different. For the 'other' minorities (racial, sexual, religious, and so on) the general provision of the equality clause in Article 3 has been enacted, while linguistic minorities are protected on the basis of the special measures announced in Article 6.

In addition, not all the linguistic minorities are officially recognized, so that, under the Italian constitutional law's point of view, it is correct to speak about 'protected' linguistic minorities. The third preliminary element for the comprehension of the Italian 'minority Constitution'[2] is the difference in the minority safeguard system not only between protected and unprotected minorities, but also between the different protected minorities. It is also (not only possible, but also necessary) to distinguish the diverse protection systems within the constitutional law.

The criterion for the identification of protected minorities basically relates to territory. The affirmative minority rights are connected primarily to a territory rather than to its inhabitants, so that in the Italian constitutional system,

---

* Dr. Jur. Francesco Palermo, Researcher at the European Academy of Bolzano/Bozen (South Tyrol, Italy).

[1] Further information in: Ministero dell'Interno, 'Ufficio centrale per i problemi delle zone di confine e delle minoranze etniche. Primo rapporto sullo stato delle minoranze in Italia', Roma (1994).

[2] This expression has been developed by *Roberto Toniatti*, 'La rappresentanza politica delle minoranze linguistiche: i ladini fra rappresentanza 'assicurata' e 'garantita'', *Le Regioni* (1995) p. 1271.

S. Trifunovska (Ed.), *Minority Rights in Europe: European Minorities and Languages*
© 2000, T.M.C. Asser Press, The Hague, The Netherlands

personally-related minority rights are rarely recognized; this means, for instance, that a French-speaking inhabitant of the Aosta Valley can only make use of his/her linguistic rights within his/her Region. Furthermore, belonging to a linguistic minority is generally only based on the free will of each individual, with a degree of partial exception in the Province of Bolzano.

1.1 The asymmetrical element

Article 6 of the Constitution, the general provision for minority protection, does not specify if this defence should be granted by a general provision (framework law) or by different measures for every (protected) minority. For reasons factual (the difficulty in drafting a general provision which satisfies the requests of the different minorities) and legal (the international anchoring of a certain minority, such as the South Tyrolean one), a general law was never passed by the national Parliament, and every (recognized) minority now enjoys different treatment. This could probably be seen as a violation of the equality principle which imposes equal treatment for the social groups sharing the same legal nature.[3] This is the usual result in almost all the constitutional systems (and now also recognized by the Framework Convention on the Protection of National Minorities of the Council of Europe), because of the impact of extra-legal elements (such as the number of the minority group members, their political cohesion, the influence of foreign national States). In Italy, however, the different legal condition of the minorities is particularly evident.

For this reason, Italy is at the same time one of the most advanced countries with respect to minority protection and a State in which many small minority groups are in danger of being definitively assimilated in the near future. There are many possible explanations for this situation, not least the economic feature (some affirmative rights, like for example the linguistic ones, are very expensive for the State budget), but the result is that this situation even works against the survival of the smaller groups. In any case, the relevance in a legal perspective is that the Constitutional Court not only invited Parliament to establish at least a minimum standard for all the groups, but in fact also recognised (i.e., accepted) the different protection of minority groups as an unavoidable element of the Italian 'minority Constitution' (Pronunciation Nos. 28/1982, 62/1992 and 15/1996).

1.2 The legislation

The briefly described constitutional principles should be concretised through ordinary laws. Under the laws recognising the concrete minority rights of certain groups the following should be mentioned: the articles of the civil and criminal procedure code with respect to the right to use one's own language in legal

---

[3] For this interpretation see Sergio Bartole, 'Minoranze nazionali', *Novissimo Digesto Italiano*, Appendice, V (1982), p. 45.

proceedings (usually with the aid of an interpreter, with the exception of the Province of Bolzano, where it is possible to conduct proceedings in the German language), the laws which guarantee political representation for some minority groups (for instance in the European elections for South Tyrol and Aosta Valley, Article 12(9), Law of 24 January 1979, No. 18), the possibility to constitute schools in the language of the minorities (in South Tyrol, Friuli-Venezia Giulia and Aosta Valley, Articles 4 and 9, Law of 30 July 1973, No. 477), special provisions for the media (for the German, the French and the Slovene minority), and many others.[4] Nevertheless, all these measures only recognize the diversity in the legal status of the various minorities, providing legal recognition to a pre-existing factual situation.

The best example to demonstrate how Italy only creates an asymmetrical minority protection system, is the case of the framework law on minority issues. The small minorities always request a framework law on this matter, which ensures a minimum standard of protection, as a consequence of the disposal of Article 6 of the Constitution, and even the Constitutional Court on some occasions stressed the utility of such a law (Pronunciation No. 312/1983). In spite of many attempts to pass a framework law, which indicates the recognized minorities and provides a minimum standard of protection (the most important and concrete was Proposal No. 612/1991), this law has never been enacted.

1.3 The regional minority protection system

The most important criterion adopted by the Italian Constitution for minority protection is the territorial autonomy of the regions where such groups live. Obviously, the more developed the self-government, the easier the recognition and the protection of the minority groups at a local level, because small groups at a national level can become, in a local governance perspective, numerically more significant, or even the majority in its territory, such as in South Tyrol and in the Aosta Valley. This criterion is in fact very efficient in the cases of larger and territorially compact minorities, whereas for smaller and more scattered groups it is an inadequate protection instrument. As a consequence, the most safeguarded (protected) minorities in Italy are the larger linguistic groups, living in border areas adjacent to the respective national States: German speakers along the Austrian border, French speakers along the French border, Slovene speakers near Slovenia.

Since 1970, when Regions with ordinary autonomy were set up, some smaller minorities have also slowly become more safeguarded. Nowadays, many Regions have laws on the protection of minorities living in their territory: Piemonte has passed a law in favour of the French-provençal and the Walser speaking group, Veneto for German and Ladin speakers, Molise for Albanians and Croats, Basilicata for the Albanians, Calabria for the Provençal speaking

---

[4] For example, the Law on the Protection of the Slovene Minority, which is under approval by the Parliament (AC 229) (http://www.camera.it/dat/leg13/lavori/sk0500/fronresp/02290a.htm).

minority. In most of these cases, these laws have shown their ineffectiveness, containing too general and even utopian provisions which the Region could never be able to apply for economic and political reasons.

Obviously, not every Italian Region where linguistic minorities are living has passed laws for their protection, so that many groups do not have any legal instrument to safeguard them: French-provençal speakers in Liguria, Albanians in Abruzzo, Campania and Puglia, Greeks and Provençal speakers in Puglia. As a last point of general information it is important to stress that almost all municipal basic statutes (merely administrative rules) where non-Italian speaking groups live, mention as a municipal duty safeguarding and improving the situation of these groups.

After these brief but necessary general remarks on the Italian constitutional minority protection system, it should be easier to understand the legal and historical background to the Draft Bill on the protection of minorities.

2. HISTORICAL BACKGROUND AND APPLICABILITY OF THE DRAFT BILL

On June 17th 1998 the Chamber of Deputies (the Lower Chamber of Parliament) approved a general law on the 'protection of historical linguistic minorities'.[5] At this point in time (August 1999) the text is still waiting to be approved by the Senate. Actually, it is not possible to foresee if and when the Senate will definitively enact the law, because it is not on top of the political agenda and if the draft is amended by the Senate, there must be another vote in the Chamber.

In order to understand the importance of the general law on minority protection, its historical background as well as its fields of application must be briefly described.

2.1 Historical background

The different legal treatment of each minority is at the same time the main reason for the aim of the small and unprotected minorities to obtain a general law, granting a basic standard for the protection of every minority living in Italy.

Since many decades proposals for a general law on minority protection have been presented to Parliament, but for different reasons it has not been possible to pass a bill. During the VIIth legislative period (1979-1983) a first complete draft was presented, but it was never discussed. The same happened during the Xth (1987-1992) and the XIIth period (1994-1996): due to the political crisis in Italy, the Parliament never had the time to deal with the issue of minority protection. The most serious attempt was made during the XIth period (1992-1994). In 1991 the Chamber approved the draft general law on the protection of 'historical'

---

[5] Draft Bill, Chamber of Deputies, XIIIth legislative period, No. 169, AC 169, AS 336. Text: http://www.camera.it/_dati/leg13/lavori/stampati/sk0500/frontesp/0169.htm

linguistic minorities presented by a Member of Parliament, Labriola,[6] but also in that case the Senate did not have the time to enact the law because of the anticipated elections in 1992.

The present law is based mainly on the draft of 1991, as far as the list of the protected minorities as well as the minority rights provided by the law are concerned. Nevertheless it must be said that the draft bill on which this paper focuses will not solve the problem of the different legal treatment of the minorities: the social and political differences between the minorities still produce legal differences in their status.

2.2 Protected minorities

Article 2 of the draft Bill deals with the range of the law's application. It states that 'according to Article 6 of the Constitution and in accordance with the general principles laid down by European and international institutions,[7] Italy protects the language and culture of the Albanian, the Catalan, the German,[8] the Greek, the Slovene and the Croat populations, as well as those speaking French, Provenzial, Friulan, Ladin, Occitan and Sardish. The law protects all the 'small' minorities historically living on Italian territory,[9] whereas it does not apply to the so-called 'new minorities', i.e. immigrants. Their legal protection still remains an open problem.[10]

As far as territorial application is concerned, the law grants to the provincial assemblies the competence to identify the geographical areas in which the minority rights can be applied. The initiative can also be taken by citizens and municipal representatives of the concerned minorities (Article 3).[11] It has to be pointed out that the competence concerning this matter should have been transferred to the regional assemblies rather than to the provincial ones (as

---

[6] Draft Bill, Chamber of Deputies, XIIIth legislative period, AC 612.

[7] Especially the Framework Convention of the Council of Europe, adopted on November 10th, 1994 and opened for signature on February 1, 1995. Italy ratified it on November 3, 1997. The Convention entered into force on February 1, 1998. See Sergio Bartole, 'La Convenzione-quadro del Consiglio d'Europa per la protezione delle minoranze nazionali', *Rivista italiana di diritto e procedura penale* 2 (1997) p. 567.

[8] The German-speaking population of South Tyrol is not affected by the Law. 'German populations' are therefore only Cymbres and Mocheni (settled in the Province of Trento), the Walser (Piemonte and Aosta Valley), the Carnic people in the Province of Belluno and the small German-speaking groups in the provinces of Vicenza and Udine. A constitutional law for the protection of German populations in the Province of Trento, granting them more advantageous cultural and political rights will be finally approved by Parliament within 1999.

[9] The list mirrors the census of minorities prepared by the Ministry of Internal Affairs. See *Ministero dell'Interno, Ufficio centrale per i problemi delle zone di confine e delle minoranze etniche*, Primo rapporto sullo stato delle minoranze in Italia, Roma 1994.

[10] The Law of 22 July 1998 (provisions for immigrants) does not provide minority rights to immigrants. At present, no draft bill has been presented in this regard, whereas there are more than 40 drafts concerning the protection of different autochthonous minorities.

[11] The initiative can be taken by 15% of the residents in the affected municipalities or by one-third of the municipal deputies (Art. 3 para. 1).

provided by the original proposal): although the provinces are smaller and closer to the citizens (the above mentioned minorities mainly live in small villages), only the regions are defined as political bodies and the protection of minorities is certainly a political and not a merely administrative issue. On the contrary, the possibility of democratic participation on the part of the concerned citizens is a positive fact. It reflects the principle of belonging freely and voluntarily to minorities: every citizen who feels that he/she belongs to a minority or who simply wishes to promote the minority culture in his/her municipality can take the initiative on this matter.

The law will not apply to the special regions, i.e. to the five Italian regions which have a higher degree of autonomy. That means that it does not concern the stronger and already protected minorities, like in particular the German-speakers in South Tyrol, the French-speakers in Aosta and the Slovenian-speakers in the area of Trieste. Every autonomous region can decide to enact some provision of the law as far as it contains innovative principles. This is due to the intention to protect only the 'small' (i.e., the unprotected) minorities, but some problems could arise, in particular as far as the 'small' minorities living in the special regions are concerned. The problem does not affect the Ladins living in Trentino[12] and South Tyrol (because they are already more protected by the autonomy statute than under the proposed law), but it can be an issue for the Friulans in Friuli-Venezia Giulia, the Catalans and the Sards in Sardinia. They will therefore not be directly protected by the law, and a regional bill will be necessary in this matter. Politically, this might not be easy, especially for the Friulans.

3. THE CONTENTS OF THE DRAFT BILL

Because of the length of this article it is impossible to describe in detail all the cultural and linguistic rights provided by the draft. Nevertheless, it will be sufficient to underline the most important of them (language use in schools and in the public sector, place-names, family names, media) to understand that the law, when enters into force, will be a fundamental step towards effective minority protection also for the less important minorities. The rights provided by the draft bill will guarantee the survival of the threatened small minority groups traditionally living within the Italian territory.

Articles 4 to 7 of the draft deal with one of the most sensitive issues in the field of minority protection: the teaching of a minority language and culture in schools. The bill allows minority languages to be taught at school. In particular, in nursery schools the minority languages will be permitted in educational

---

[12] Also for the Ladins residing in Trentino a constitutional law is awaiting approval of Parliament. It grants them political representation in the provincial council of Trento. In August 1999 some additional provisions on the protection of the Ladin minority in Trentino entered into force.

activities, whereas in elementary and secondary schools the language, the culture and the traditions of the local communities can be taught as a subject. Teaching of the minority language shall be required by the parents (Article 4(5)), whereas each school can decide to teach minority culture and traditions, which will be a compulsory subject for every pupil. The Ministry of Public Education will co-finance the teaching programmes and can provide further regulation on this matter (Article 5). Finally, universities may promote research activities in these fields (Article 6).

As for the public use of minority languages, it will be possible to use minority languages in the municipal and provincial councils and governments; in this case, translation into Italian must be provided for those who do not understand the minority language (Article 7). The local authorities may also publish their official acts (and also acts of the State and of the Regions) in the minority language, but at their own expense. In addition, the minority language will be allowed in written and oral relations with the public administration located in the area, except from the relations with the army and the police (Article 9(1)). Italian remains in any case the only official language (Article 8). The minority languages can be used in the judiciary too, but only in proceedings conducted by a justice of peace (the lower range of the judicial system, Article 9(3)); in any case, the codes of civil and criminal procedure grant the right for everyone to speak his/her own language in court proceedings and to be assisted by an interpreter (Article 109 Code of Criminal Procedure and Article 122 Code of Civil Procedure).

With regard to official place-names (toponyms), the law states that the municipalities may add to the Italian city and road names also the 'traditional names' (Article 10). Furthermore, the persons whose family names have been italianized in the past, have the right to use the original form of their names (Article 11). This extends to all the people belonging to minorities the right to personal identity, happened in South Tyrol after the Second World War, when German names were re-introduced after the fascist regime.

In the fields of the mass-media, the Ministry for Communications and public broadcasting shall jointly establish (generic) 'conditions in order to grant minority protection' (Article 12(1)). More concretely, also the Regions will be able to sign conventions with the public and private broadcasting authorities in order to ensure the transmission of news, cultural and educational programmes in the minority languages (Article 12(2)). Regions, Provinces and municipalities may also grant financial aid to the media in order to implement the use of minority languages (Article 14).

It is important to point out that all the mentioned linguistic and cultural rights will not unduly burden the State's budget. A 'national fund for the protection of linguistic minorities' (around 5 million EUROs per year) will be established, as well as a special fund provided by the Ministry of Education (1 million EUROs per year). In addition to these costs, the State cannot spend more than 4 millions EUROs per year. Finally, the total costs for the State may not be more than 10 million EUROs per year. The reminder of the costs will be sustained by Regions, provinces and municipalities, in accordance with the 'federalist wind' which has been blowing through Italy in the last decade.

4. CONCLUDING REMARKS

Once it enters into force, the new law will provide a reasonable solution to the issue of 'small minorities'. The small minority groups will be protected by a general legal measure, implementing the principle of Article 6 of the Italian Constitution. This law represents, on the one hand, a unique historical occasion to grant to each linguistic minority living in Italy a minimum standard of protection. Unfortunately, on the other hand, the Italian policy is often quite difficult to foresee, and the approval by the Chamber does not automatically mean that the Senate will definitively enact the law. It is therefore necessary not only to underline the positive and negative aspects of the draft bill, but also to briefly describe what might happen if the law will not be approved.

4.1 The lacking aspects of the draft

The Italian 'minority Constitution' is based on three basic principles:[13]

1. The linguistic criterion, i.e. minorities are only linguistic minorities. According to the Italian constitutional tradition, based on the French-derived 'citizenship approach' and avoiding the concept of 'ethnicity', the Italian 'nation' is built up of many linguistic groups. The concept of 'nation' is to be understood as *demos* and not as *ethnos*.[14] Legally speaking, in Italy there are no 'ethnic', but only 'linguistic' minorities;
2. The legal condition for the protection of minorities is their legal recognition. Only officially recognized minorities can be protected with special instruments. Otherwise, only the equality principle and the principle of non-discrimination can be applied;
3. The minority rights are coupled with the territory and not with the persons. Persons belonging to a (recognized) minority can use their minority rights only within a certain territory (the territorial principle instead of the personal

---

[13] See Francesco Palermo, 'Self-Government (and Other?) Instruments for the Prevention of Ethnic Conflicts in South Tyrol', in Mitja Zagar, Boris Jesih, Romana Bešter (Eds.), *The Constitutional and Political Regulation of Ethnic Relations and Conflicts*, Institute for Ethnic Studies, Ljubljana (1999) p. 299.

[14] See Alessandro Pizzorusso, 'Commento all'art. 6', in G. Branca (a cura di), *Commentario alla Co-stituzione*, Bologna-Roma (1975) p. 296. For the concepts of nation as *demos* and as *ethnos* see Carlo Casonato, *Minoranze etniche e rappresentanza politica: i modelli statunitense e canadese*, Trento (1998) p. 22.

principle).[15] A German-speaker who is an inhabitant of South Tyrol, for example, may use his mother tongue in legal proceedings only in South Tyrol and not in Rome. As a consequence, the minorities are protected mainly through regional autonomy.

As far as recognition is concerned, the present draft is an important step, because it provides the necessary legal condition for positive actions in favour of all the 'small' minorities. Nevertheless, different to the draft of 1991, the present law does not provide legal recognition for 'historical' minorities such as Roma and Sinti. Politically speaking, this is due to the right-wing parties, which voted in favour of the law in Parliament only if the Roma and Sinti were not included in the list.[16] Nevertheless, from a historical point of view, the exclusion of the Roma and Sinti from the list of the 'historical' minorities living in Italy is not correct, because they have been settled in Italy at least since the XIVth century.[17] The exclusion of these populations will probably be criticized by the 'European and international organizations', according to whose principles this law shall operate (Article 2).[18]

Finally, also the linguistic criterion seems to have been neglected by the draft. In fact, Article 2 seems to distinguish between 'ethnicity' and 'language', stating that Italy 'protects the language and culture of the Albanian, the Catalan, the German, the Greek, the Slovene and the Croat *populations*, as well of the ones *speaking* French, Provenzial, Friulan, Ladin, Occitan and Sardish'. It is true that the second group of minorities has been living in Italy for many centuries, but this is also true for Albanians, Catalans, Greeks, Slovenes and Croats.[19] What is the difference between the two groups? Do French, Provenzial, Friulan, Ladin, Occitan and Sardish speakers perhaps have Italian 'blood', and do the others belong to different 'nations'? Are not all the groups a constitutive part of the (multicultural) Italian 'nation'? More attention by the Senate seems to be necessary on this aspect.

---

[15] In this sense see the recent judgement of the Italian Constitutional Court No. 213/1998 (on the right to use a minority language in military trials).

[16] The draft of 1991 and also the present draft in its original formulation did include the Roma and Sinti in the list. The issue was extensively discussed in Parliament: the leftist parties wanted to include the Roma and Sinti in the law, according to the recommendations of the Council of Europe, whereas the conservative parties wanted to exclude them completely.

[17] According to some sources, those populations have been settled in Italy since the Xth or the XIth century. See Ministero dell'Interno, Primo rapporto..., op. cit. n. 1, p. 364.

[18] See note No. 6.

[19] Albanians and Croats came to Italy in the XIVth century. Catalans were settled in Sardinia since the city of Alghero was taken by the Crown of Aragon in 1354. Greek populations have lived in Italy since the age of the Byzantium Empire.

4.2 The positive aspects of the draft

The cultural and linguistic rights provided to minorities by the draft are of a great symbolic but also concrete importance. At the same time, they do not imply an undue burden for the State budget: in the actual political and economic situation, this means that there will be a chance for the law to be enacted.

The low economic costs of the law has a double positive effect. On the one hand, it grants the until now unprotected minorities basic cultural rights at a low cost for the State. On the other hand, the concrete implementation of the minority rights will be carried out basically by the Regions, the provinces and the municipalities. As a political consequence, the minorities will clearly identify the level of government which is responsible for their issues, and they will be able to determine minority policy at the local level.

The budgetary provisions of the draft are an example of the promotion of local autonomies, a principle which has been increasingly applied in Italian legislation in the recent years, building a federal system step by step and not by means of constitutional reform. The promotion of autonomy as a means to attain more effective governance also affects the field of minority protection. Some years ago the Constitutional Court stated that only the State, by granting the unity of the Italian Republic and the principle of equality between the citizens, could intervene in the field of minority protection.[20]

Another important provision concerns the official status of the Italian language (Article 1(1)). The multi-cultural composition of the Italian 'nation' is emphasized by recognizing the minority languages. This provision does not have practical consequences, because the official status of the Italian language and the promotion (or in some cases even the co-officiality) of minority languages is provided by other laws (like for example Article 99 of the Autonomy Statute of Trentino-South Tyrol), but its symbolic importance should be underlined: the principle of Italy's cultural pluralism will now be extended to the whole national territory. For this reason, the mentioned principle should rather be anchored in the Constitution, in Article 6.

Furthermore, two additional provisions have to be mentioned. Firstly, Italy will also be allowed to promote the cultures present in Italy in foreign countries (Article 1 and Article 19(2)), that is of course mainly the Italian culture, but also its minority cultures, which are a constitutive part of the Italian one. Secondly, Italy will promote inter-regional and cross-border co-operation, especially in order to safeguard and implement minority languages and cultures (Article 19(2)).

As for its structure and its basic principles, the present draft is similar to that presented in 1991. Like all the old drafts, it contains a list of the minority languages and cultures which shall be protected under the law; except for the Roma and Sinti, the list indicates the same minorities as in 1991. What has deeply changed since 1991 is the legal and political framework concerning

---

[20] In particular Judgement No. 32/1960.

autonomy and minority protection in Italy. Even if the mega-constitutional change failed in 1998,[21] the so-called administrative federalism has taken place in Italy step by step during the last decade.[22] The brighter regional and local (municipal) autonomy is a new important instrument for minority protection.

For this reason, unlike 10 years ago, the actual legal framework in Italy is probably in itself sufficient in order to grant genuine protection to all the minorities living in Italy. This fact will be taken into consideration, especially if political difficulties will lead to another failure in the approval of the law. Indeed, the ripe autonomy attained in Italian regionalism nowadays allows the Regions and the local authorities to protect the minorities even in the absence of a general State law.

As a consequence, at the present moment the bill is less important than it was ten years ago, as has been shown by a recent judgement of the administrative Court of the Region Friuli-Venezia Giulia. A municipality stated in its basic law the obligation to protect and promote the Friulan language, but the provision was rejected by the State, arguing that minority protection cannot be considered a goal of local authorities, especially in the absence of a national legal framework. The Court decided that Regions and municipalities are able to adopt legal and administrative provisions also in the field of minority protection, i.e. in the field of State competence.[23]

Therefore, the approval of the draft will represent an important step towards the implementation of minority protection in Italy, but the same goal can be pursued by the local authorities too, by means of their autonomous powers.

---

[21] See Francesco Palermo, Giovanni Poggeschi, 'Devolution and Federalism. The case of Italy and Great Britain', in Sergio Ortino, Mitja Zagar (Eds.), *Changing Faces of Federalism. Political Reconfiguration in Europe*, to be published in 1999.

[22] Many very important laws reforming public administration and the system of self-government have been approved in the last decade. The largest set of reforms began with the law on reorganising ministerial bureaucracy (Act No. 400 of 1988), that was followed by the reform of local self-government (Act No. 142 of 1990), containing a number of ground-breaking provisions to improve the efficiency of municipalities and provinces. Closely connected with that law was the new set of rules on administrative procedure (Act No. 41 of 1990), simplifying and rationalising the functioning of State, regional, provincial and municipal administrations. Act No. 81 of 1993 was a politically very significant step towards raising awareness of local self-government, with the introduction of direct elections for mayors and provincial presidents. Act No. 46 of 1995 then introduced a technically complicated and overall totally impractical arrangement, nonetheless also introducing *de facto* a direct popular vote for regional presidents. This process of carrying out a far-reaching reform of the system of self-government was crowned in 1997 by two extremely important legislative acts (Act No. 59 of 1997 and Act No. 127 of 1997), commonly known as the 'Bassanini Acts', named after Minister Bassanini. In particular, the first (Act No. 59) provided for a delegation to the Government for issuing decrees to transfer to the regions all powers including those still reserved for the State. The practical translation of that law, by means of a series of decrees issued between the summer of 1997 and the spring of 1999, will reverse the criterion of residual power in Italy, since the State will only remain in possession of those functions that had not been transferred to the regions.

[23] Tribunale Regionale di Giustizia Amministrativa – Regione Friuli-Venezia Giulia, Judgement No. 783/1996.

Finally, it must be pointed out that minority protection does not only mean the protection of 'historical' minority groups, but it also safeguards the 'new' immigrant cultures. Minority protection means the protection of those who cannot integrate in society for economic, linguistic and cultural reasons. Not only is protection of languages and cultures important, but also protection of the individuals who keep those languages and cultures alive. Hopefully after the approval of the bill on 'historical' minorities a law for the protection (and not only for the repression) of immigrants will also be passed.

Post scriptum: On November 25, 1999, the Italian Parliament finally approved the bill on the protection of minorities in its original wording.

THE FRISIAN LANGUAGE IN THE NETHERLANDS

Floris van Laanen[*]

1. INTRODUCTION

It is said that in the beginning all people on earth spoke the same language. Apparently, it is only thanks to Noah's descendants that nowadays we are blessed with a huge variety of languages.[1] It seems that our ancestors wanted to build a tower which was to reach up to heaven. By doing so, they displeased the Lord. He then interrupted building activities by causing a confusion of languages among the people. Subsequently, He scattered the people all over the earth.

Probably we will never know what language these first of mankind spoke. Once, a lady at the eighteenth century Court of Versailles said: 'What a dreadful pity that the bother at the tower of Babel should have got language all mixed up; but for that, everyone would always have spoken French'.[2] I presume that that was merely one of the noble lady's desires.

1.1 Central question and limitations

In this contribution I will deal with some aspects of one of the post-Babel languages,[3] the Frisian language ('Frysk' in Frisian, 'Fries' in Dutch). The central question being the position of the Frisian language in Dutch law, the analysis which follows will be limited in three ways:

The most obvious limitation is, of course, the discussion only with respect to the situation of one language, i.e. Frisian. It is one of the languages spoken in the Kingdom of The Netherlands. The Kingdom is a State with a kind of a federal system, which is governed by the Charter for the Kingdom of The Netherlands.[4] According to its preamble, the Kingdom consists of The Netherlands (which

---

[*] Fourth year student of International and European Law, Law Faculty, University of Nijmegen, The Netherlands.
[1] Genesis 10:32 and Genesis 11:1-9.
[2] According to a letter by Voltaire to Empress Catherine the Great, 26 May 1767. Quoted in: B.J. Palmer, *The Oxford library of words and phrases; Volume I; The concise Oxford dictionary of quotations*, 2nd ed., Oxford (1988), p. 265.
[3] And perhaps even the pre-Babel language, who knows?!
[4] *Statuut voor het Koninkrijk der Nederlanden* (Act of 28 October 1954, Stb. 1954.503; most recently amended by the Statute Act [Rijkswet] of 7 September 1998, Stb. 1998.579).

S. Trifunovska (Ed.), Minority Rights in Europe: European Minorities and Languages
© 2000, T.M.C. Asser Press, The Hague, The Netherlands

used to be called 'the Realm in Europe'[5]), The Netherlands Antilles and Aruba. In former times the Kingdom's territory was much larger, including for example Belgium (until 1839), The Dutch East Indies (the present Indonesia, until 1949) and Surinam (until 1975). In reigning over this whole territory, linguistic policies have always been of particular concern to the Dutch Government.[6] Nowadays the Kingdom is confronted with many languages. Partly, these languages have been imported by modern immigrants (Turkish, Arabic etc.). Some other languages, such as Papiamento (in the Caribbean part of the Kingdom), Low Saxon and Frisian, have been spoken in the Kingdom for many centuries.

Secondly, there is a geographic limitation. Frisian is spoken both in The Netherlands and in Germany. In my article I will only deal with the Dutch situation, thus excluding the position of the Frisian language under the German law and in cross-border situations.

Thirdly, there is a legal limitation with the focus being primarily on Dutch national law. With the exception of Chapter II and some remarks in the Conclusion, attention will be only paid to international law if it is relevant for a better understanding of national law.

1.2 Some remarks on the Frisian language

Frisian is a Germanic language spoken in the German Länder of Schleswig-Holstein and Niedersachsen as well as in the Dutch province of Friesland ('Fryslân' in Frisian, 'Friesland' in Dutch).[7] Frisian is most closely related to the English language, and documents in Frisian go as far back as the 13th century.[8] In those days Frisian was an official language, a position which it lost in the 15th century because of political reasons.[9] A standard spelling has been agreed upon by provincial States in a bye-law, there is an authoritative dictionary in 20 volumes, and grammar is embodied in several handbooks, the most authoritative being the 1985 'Frisian reference grammar'.[10] Furthermore, it should be noted that the Government states that Dutch and Frisian are The Netherlands' indigenous languages.[11]

---

[5] Articles 1 and 2 of the 1887 Constitution (Act of 10 August 1887, Stb. 1887.144). The present Constitution originates from and/or is based on the 1983 Constitution (Acts/Statute Acts of 19 February 1983, Stb. 1983.17 to 51; most recently amended by the Statute Act of 6 October 1999, Stb. 1999.454).

[6] See for example K. Groeneboer (Ed.), *Koloniale taalpolitiek in Oost en West; Nederlands-Indië, Suriname, Nederlandse Antillen en Aruba*, Amsterdam (1997).

[7] F.J. de Varennes, *Language, Minorities and Human Rights*, diss., Maastricht (1996), p. 41.

[8] Microsoft, Encarta '95; *The Complete Interactive Multimedia Encyclopedia*, (1994).

[9] Handelingen I, 1994/1995, p. 1160 (Postma MP).

[10] Bijlagen II, 1994/1995, 24092, 5, p. 4 (MvT).

[11] Bijlagen II, 1993/1994, 23543, 3, p. 2 (MvT).

Friesland has a population of some 610,000 people.[12] 54.8% of the population states that Frisian is their mother tongue; 94,3% of Friesland's inhabitants have a passive knowledge of Frisian; 74.0% actually know how to speak Frisian; 64.5% are able to read Frisian; and finally, 17.0% are also used to writing in Frisian.[13] Regarding civil servants of the province of Friesland, 30% know how to write in Frisian and 83% are able to read texts in Frisian.[14]

2. SOME REMARKS ON RELEVANT INTERNATIONAL LAW

It is obvious that the role of international law in the field of language can hardly be overestimated. Apart from provisions of international law dealing with expression, private life and non-discrimination in general, such as provisions of the ICCPR[15] and ECHR[16], there are provisions dealing with indigenous peoples, national minorities and their languages in particular. Mention deserves to be made of Article 27 of the ICCPR, the Framework Convention for Protection of National Minorities, the European Charter for Regional or Minority Languages, the European Parliament's Resolution on Cultural and Linguistic Minorities and the Draft Declaration on the Rights of Indigenous Peoples.

Article 27 of the ICCPR prohibits the denial of the right of ethnic, religious or linguistic minorities to enjoy their own culture, to profess and practice their own religion, or to use their own language, all this in community with other members of their group. It is the Government's opinion that the Frisian-speaking population forms such a linguistic minority.[17] This opinion is supported by the Council of State.[18] After all, it was agreed that Article 27 should cover only 'separate or distinct groups, well-defined and long-established on the territory of a State'.[19] It should be mentioned that the fact that Frisian is considered to be one of The Netherlands' indigenous languages, and thus the fact that the Frisians may be an indigenous people, is not an obstacle for bringing the Frisians under the scope of Article 27.[20] What then are the obligations of the States parties? According to the 'travaux préparatoires', the original proposal, which implied

---

[12] Wolters-Noordhoff, *De Grote Bosatlas Basisstatistiek 96/97*, Groningen (1996), p. 3.

[13] D. Gorter/R.J. Jonkman, *Taal yn Fryslân op 'e nij besjoen*, Leeuwarden 1995 (results: http://www.ned.univie.ac.at/publicaties/taalgeschiedenis/nl/fries.htm.). In 1984 the figures were 90%, 70%, 65% and 10% (D. Gorter et al., *Taal yn Fryslân*, Leeuwarden (1984), results: Bijlagen II, op. cit. n. 11, 3, p. 7 [MvT]).

[14] D. Gorter/R.J. Jonkman, *Taal op it wurk fan provinsjale amtners*, Leeuwarden (1993), (results: Bijlagen II, op. cit. n. 11, 5, p. 7 [NV]).

[15] Trb. 1969.100.

[16] Trb. 1951.54.

[17] Bijlagen II, op. cit. n. 11, 3, p. 8 (MvT).

[18] Bijlagen II, op. cit. n. 11, B, p. 6 (Council of State's advice).

[19] M.J. Bossuyt, *Guide to the 'travaux préparatoires' of the International Covenant on Civil and Political Rights*, Dordrecht/Boston/Lancaster (1987), p. 494.

[20] De Varennes, op. cit. n. 7, pp. 134 and 135, referring to UNHRC case law (*Lovelace* v. *Canada*, *Kitok* v. *Sweden*, *Ominayak* v. *Canada*).

that a State had to ensure to national minorities certain linguistic and cultural rights, was rejected. The text which was adopted seems to imply that the obligations of the States would be limited to permitting the free exercise of the rights of minorities.[21] This is also the view of the Dutch Government.[22]

In the 1995 Council of Europe's Framework Convention for the Protection of National Minorities there are some provisions on minority languages as well.[23] For example, a person belonging to a national minority has the right to use freely and without interference his or her minority language, in private and in public, orally and in writing (Article 10). Furthermore, there are specific articles on the use of first names, surnames and geographic names in the minority language (Article 11), on research (Article 12) and on learning the minority language (Article 14). However, although The Netherlands has signed the Framework Convention, it has not yet ratified it.

The Netherlands is party to the 1992 European Charter for Regional or Minority Languages.[24] In conformity with Dutch constitutional law, the Charter was approved by the Act of Parliament in 1996.[25] Instead of conferring individual or collective rights on persons using a regional or minority language, the Charter imposes on States parties an obligation to take measures in order to ensure and improve the position of those languages.[26] It is the Dutch Government's opinion that Frisian is a regional or minority language as defined in Article 1, sub. (a) of the Charter: a language that is traditionally used within a given territory of a State by nationals of that State who form a group numerically smaller than the rest of the State's population and different from the official language(s) of that State.[27] A concrete result of signing the Charter was the establishment of a consultative organ on the Frisian language in 1998.[28] According to the Government, one of the reasons for signing the Charter was that it provides the position of the Frisian language in the province of Friesland with a solid legal basis, which is in conformity with the Government's policy.[29]

The use of the words 'provides a solid legal basis' is remarkable: it might be concluded that in the Government's opinion such a solid legal basis had not existed before the signing of the European Charter. In my view a substantial part of such a basis had already been created by several acts of parliament, such as the Act of 4 May 1995[30] and the Act of 11 May 1956[31]. Furthermore, the non-

---

[21] Bossuyt, op. cit. n. 19, p. 496.
[22] Bijlagen II, op. cit. n. 11, 3, p. 8 (MvT).
[23] Text available on: http://www.conventions.coe.int/treaty/en/Treaties/Html/157.htm
[24] Trb. 1993.1 and 199.
[25] Act of 26 January 1996, Stb. 1996.136.
[26] Bijlagen II, op. cit. n. 10, 3, p. 1 (MvT).
[27] Bijlagen II, op. cit. n. 10, 3, p. 2 (MvT); Bijlagen II, op. cit. n. 11, 3, p. 9 (MvT); Bijlagen I, 1994-1995, 23543, 23d, p. 1 and 2 (NV).
[28] See: *Instellingsregeling consultatief orgaan Friese Taal* (Ministerial regulation of 15 January 1998, Stcrt. 1988.33).
[29] Bijlagen II, op. cit. n. 10, 3, p. 3 (MvT).
[30] Stb. 1995.302 on the use of Frisian in relations with administrative authorities.

existence of the European Charter does not preclude the legislator from initiating legislation which could improve the status of the Frisian language. My view is supported by the fact that the Government originally intended to pass the Charter's Approval Act in advance of the Acts of 4 May 1995 and 14 September 1995. This could not be achieved because of political reasons and capacity problems at the Ministry for Foreign Affairs.[32] Moreover, the Government acknowledges that the text of the Charter is much broader than this national legislation; it even states that national legislation and the Charter will be mutually reinforcing.[33]

The Resolution of the European Parliament on Cultural and Linguistic Minorities[34] was adopted in 1994. In it, the European Parliament expresses its opinion that a suitable legal status should be created for minority cultures and languages. This includes the use and promotion of these languages and cultures in the fields of education, judicial affairs, public administration, the media, toponymy and other parts of public and cultural life. It should be noted that the legal force of such resolutions is rather weak.

Finally, some attention should be paid to the Draft Declaration on the Rights of Indigenous Peoples.[35] As mentioned before, Frisian is considered to be one of The Netherlands' indigenous languages. For that reason, it could be concluded that the Frisians are an indigenous people. As with the concept of national minority, international law does not give an answer to the question of how an indigenous people should be defined. It is claimed that the crucial element is that they are the original inhabitants of the land on which they have lived from time immemorial.[36] The Draft Declaration contains some rights regarding the indigenous people's language. For example, an indigenous people has the right to revitalise, use, develop and transmit to future generations its language, writing system and literature, and it has the right to designate and retain its own names for communities, places and persons (Article 14). There are also provisions on the use of an indigenous language in the fields of education and the media. It should be noted that the Declaration has not yet been adopted. Once it will be adopted, being merely a declaration it will not have legally binding force.

---

[31] Stb. 1956.242; as amended by the Act of 14 September 1995, Stb. 1995.440 on the use of Frisian in relations with judicial authorities.
[32] Bijlagen II, op. cit. n. 10, 3, p. 1 (MvT).
[33] Bijlagen II, op. cit. n. 11, 3, p. 9 (MvT) and Bijlagen II, op. cit. n. 10, 5, p. 1 (NV).
[34] Resolution of 9 February 1994, OJ C 61/110.
[35] UN Doc. E/CN.4/Sub.2/1994/56.
[36] De Varennes, op. cit. n. 7, p. 238.

3. THE DUTCH CONSTITUTION

3.1 Language and the Dutch constitution

Together with Denmark, The Netherlands is the only European Union member State having a written constitution which has no section therein on the country's (official) language.[37] Regarding the Kingdom of the Netherlands such a section cannot be found in the Charter for the Kingdom either. In the 1970s the Institute for Linguistic Integration (*Instituut voor Taal-integratie*) suggested that the Constitution should be amended, so as to add a fundamental right to use one's mother tongue. A Member of the Dutch Parliament, H.J.G. Waltmans, while speaking in Parliament, pointed out that it concerned a matter which determined the further development of the Frisian language and culture.[38] In response, the Government though supporting this development, did not support the proposed amendment.[39] In 1995 the issue arose again in a proposal for an amendment submitted by two Members of Parliament, A.K. Koekkoek and E. van Middelkoop.[40] They wanted to insert an article in the Constitution implying that the promotion of the use of the Dutch language is a matter of concern to the Government.[41] In the explanatory notes the initiators wrote that it was not their objective to weaken the position of minority languages in general and of Frisian in particular.[42] This, they stated, would be contrary to the European Charter for Regional or Minority Languages and recent Dutch legislation concerning the public use of the Frisian language.[43] Nevertheless, a large number of representatives were worried about the position of the Frisian language, which was one of the reasons why the Second Chamber rejected the proposal. In my opinion the promotion of the Dutch language, as proposed in the bill, does not (necessarily) exclude the promotion of Frisian. Therefore I do not see any objection, resulting from the position of the Frisian language, to amending the Constitution as proposed. With regard to the use of the Dutch language in an ever growing European Union, it may even be considered to be useful to insert such an article, despite the fact that it is not strongly formulated.

---

[37] Bijlagen II, 1995/1996, 24431, A, p. 4 (Reaction to the Council of State's advice).
[38] Handelingen II, 1976/1977, p. 1981 (Waltmans MP).
[39] Bijlagen II, op. cit. n. 11, 3, p. 8 (MvT).
[40] Bijlagen II, op. cit. n. 37, 2 (Bill).
[41] 'Artikel 22a. De bevordering van het gebruik van de Nederlandse taal is voorwerp van zorg van de overheid.'
[42] Bijlagen II, op. cit. n. 37, 3, p. 2 (MvT).
[43] See the more detailed discussion on this aspect further on in the text.

3.2 Fundamental rights in the Dutch Constitution

Chapter 1 of the Dutch Constitution contains 23 sections granting basic classical and social rights,[44] while in other chapters of the Constitution other rights like, *inter alia*, the prohibition of the death penalty, can also be found. Some of these rights are of course very much connected with expression in general and language in particular. Before turning to the relationship between the position of the Frisian language and some of these constitutional fundamental rights, some general remarks should be made on the fundamental rights as established by the Dutch Constitution.

Firstly, it should be noted that according to Dutch law fundamental rights primarily concern the relationship between the State authorities and its subjects (vertical operation).[45] However, it is the Government's opinion that fundamental rights could also operate in relationships between citizens themselves (horizontal operation). Unfortunately, the Government's statements on this matter are very vague. The case law of the Supreme Court shows that a court should balance the interests of both parties to a dispute when dealing with this kind of question.[46]

Secondly, the constitutionality of acts of parliament and treaties may not be reviewed by the courts. Such a review, both on material and on formal grounds,[47] is prohibited by Article 120 of the Constitution. The Supreme Court extended the scope of the prohibition by ruling that testing an act of parliament against fundamental principles of law and the Charter for the Kingdom is also prohibited by Article 120.[48] However, the importance of this prohibition must be slightly reduced, because Article 120 does not prohibit testing acts of parliament against provisions of treaties or of resolutions adopted by international institutions that are binding on all persons.[49] There is, indeed, an impression that Article 120 leaves too much competence to the legislative power. More importantly, it places the Dutch courts in a somewhat peculiar position by entitling them to test acts of Parliament against provisions of international law, but not against similar provisions contained in the Constitution, which can be used as an argument to suggest that Article 120 should be repealed, or at least amended.

Thirdly, it is important to realize that there is a system of limitations to fundamental rights. Such a limitation is lawful if it conforms to a constitutional

---

[44] For a brief description of these fundamental rights in English see: C.A.J.M. Kortmann/P.P.T. Bovend'Eert, *The Kingdom of the Netherlands; an introduction to Dutch constitutional law*, Deventer (1993), p. 129-142. For an analysis in Dutch: C.A.J.M. Kortmann, *Constitutioneel recht*, 3rd ed., Deventer (1997), p. 341-431.

[45] Bijlagen II, 1975/1976, 13872, 3, p. 15 (MvT) and HR 26 April 1996, AB 1996.372, *Gemeente Rijssen* v. *Universal Star Production GmbH*.

[46] See for example HR 22 January 1988, NJ 1988.891, *JBO* v. *Brucker*.

[47] For the latter: HR 27 January 1961, NJ 1963.248, *Van den Bergh* v. *Staat der Nederlanden*.

[48] HR 14 April 1989, NJ 1989.469, *Staat der Nederlanden* v. *LSVB and Kruisbrink*.

[49] See also Article 94 of the Constitution.

limitation clause or, sometimes, criteria developed in case law.[50] Regarding the former, sometimes the legislator (that is the Government (the monarch and ministers) and Parliament) is exclusively competent to do so, and sometimes the legislator may delegate the power to other offices. This should be determined by the text of the limitation clause.[51]

4 THE RELATIONSHIP BETWEEN FUNDAMENTAL RIGHTS IN THE DUTCH CONSTITUTION AND THE FRISIAN LANGUAGE

In principle individuals are allowed to use the Frisian language in private correspondence, communications, cultural and musical expression, private use of topographical names, private parts of (religious) ceremonies, private media and publications, private broadcasting, private economic activities and private (political) groups and organizations. If the Dutch Government would try and prevent individuals from doing so, it would be in breach of the freedom of expression, the right to private life and/or the right to non-discrimination as guaranteed by the Dutch Constitution.

Freedom of expression is guaranteed by Article 7 of the Constitution. Paragraph 1 focuses on the press: no one shall require prior permission to reveal thoughts or opinions through the press, without prejudice to everyone's responsibility established by act of parliament. Paragraph 2 focuses on television and radio: rules concerning radio and television shall be laid down by act of parliament; there shall be no prior supervision of the content of a radio or television broadcast. Paragraph 3 focuses on the remaining category of means: no one shall be required to submit thoughts or opinions for prior approval in order to reveal them by means other than those mentioned in the preceding paragraphs of Article 7, without prejudice to everyone's responsibility established by act of parliament. In Article 10 of the Constitution it is stated that everyone shall have the right to respect for his privacy, without prejudice to restrictions laid down by or pursuant to an act of parliament. Finally, there is a general non-discrimination article, Article 1: discrimination on any ground (some of the grounds are listed) is not permitted. This includes, of course, discrimination on the (non-listed) ground of language.[52] It should be mentioned that any differentiation on the basis of knowledge of the Frisian language is prohibited as well, if there is no reasonable and objective justification.[53]

---

[50] Kortmann/Bovend'Eert, op. cit. n. 44, p. 133; Kortmann, op. cit. n. 44, p. 360-361.
[51] Kortmann/Bovend'Eert, op. cit. n. 44, p. 108; Kortmann, op. cit. n. 44, p. 318-320.
[52] This was also the opinion of Koekkoek and Van Middelkoop (Bijlagen II, op. cit. n. 37, A, p. 4 [Reaction to the Council of State's advice]) and of the Government (Bijlagen II, op. cit. n. 11, 3, p. 8 [MvT]).
[53] Bijlagen II, op. cit. n. 11, 3, p. 8 (MvT).

With respect to the media, I note that pursuant to Article 170 of the 1987 Media Act[54] there is a fund which promotes Dutch cultural broadcasting productions (*Stichting Stimuleringsfonds Nederlandse Culturele Omroepproducties*). It subsidizes the development and production of cultural radio and television broadcasts, one of the requirements being that for the most part the Dutch or Frisian languages are spoken.[55] Furthermore, there is a Frisian regional broadcaster (*Omrop Fryslân*), which broadcasts television and radio programmes both within the territory of the province of Friesland and on a national level.[56]

Regarding private correspondence and private communications an additional remark should be made. Very often a letter, a telephone or a telegraph will be used for correspondence and/or communication. Article 13, paragraph 1 of the Constitution guarantees the privacy of correspondence, except in the cases laid down in an act of parliament, by order of court. Paragraph 2 protects the privacy of telephone and telegraph communication, except in the cases laid down in an act of parliament, by or with the authorization of those designated for the purpose by the act of parliament. Therefore, enforcement of any prohibition on using the Frisian language in private correspondence or communication would lead in most cases to an infringement of the privacy of correspondence or telephone and telegraph communication.

The general principle is clear: there is the freedom of expression, the right to private life, the right to privacy of correspondence and communication and the right to non-discrimination. However, apart from the right to non-discrimination, limitations on these rights and freedoms are allowed. Therefore, according to national law it would be possible for the legislator (in the case of the freedom of expression and privacy of correspondence and communication) or for the legislator and, if designated, an office with delegated authority (in the case of the right to private life) to limit the use of the Frisian language in the fields which are mentioned above. It should be noted that such a limitation, which at the moment does not exist, would violate certain international obligations (such as Articles 8 and 10 ECHR and Articles 17, 19 and 27 ICCPR) if they are not in conformity with the limitation criteria mentioned there. A limitation would also violate Article 1 of the Constitution if it is of a discriminatory nature.

With regard to the latter, one can express concern about the increasing number of job advertisements, in which local or provincial authorities require prospective civil servant to have knowledge of the Frisian language. This matter was specifically addressed by the Council of State and the Government: the Government complied with the Council's recommendation to change certain formulations in the explanatory notes to the Act of 4 May 1995 in order to prevent the possible misunderstanding that learning the Frisian language would

---

[54] *Mediawet* (Act of 21 April 1987, Stb. 1987.249; most recently amended by the Act of 22 December 1999, Stb. 1999.573).
[55] http://www.stimuleringsfonds rtv.nl/hand/inleiding/html
[56] See also: http://www.dds.nl/~cvdm/perb/12-06-98.htm

be a requirement for being appointed as a provincial civil servant.[57] Of course, there may be a reasonable and objective justification for such a requirement: it is not difficult to imagine why it is required for a provincial advisor in the field of communication to be able to speak Frisian.[58] However, in this context it is difficult to understand why it is considered necessary for a municipal head of the department of facility affairs to speak Frisian,[59] if it is not considered to be necessary for a civil servant who grants environmental permits in the same municipality.[60]

5. USE OF FRISIAN LANGUAGE BY AND IN RELATIONS WITH STATE AUTHORITIES

5.1 Rules on the use of the Frisian language in relations with administrative authorities[61]

A very important aspect of the position of a language in a State is, of course, the possibility for individuals and State authorities to use a particular language in mutual relationships. From the very beginning of the Kingdom of The Netherlands, the legislator has been aware of this, as can be seen by referring to an 1830 Royal Decree on the use of languages in The Netherlands.[62] Article 7 of this Decree provided that Dutch shall be used in administrative, financial and judicial affairs in all Dutch provinces except Limburg.[63] Various courts confirmed the view that Dutch is the official administrative language,[64] though, for reasons which are unclear, they did not base their judgements on the Decree.

Article 107, paragraph 2 of the Constitution urges the legislator to lay down general rules of administrative law. This was done in the General Administrative Law Act 1992.[65] In 1995 seven sections, Articles 2:6 up to and including 2:12, on the use of language in relations with administrative authorities were inserted.[66] Two reasons underlie the adoption of this amendment.[67]

---

[57] Bijlagen II, op. cit. n. 11, B, p. 7 ([Reaction to] Council of the State's advice).
[58] *Binnenlands Bestuur*, 5 May 2000, p. 34.
[59] *Binnenlands Bestuur*, Idem, p. 42.
[60] *Binnenlands Bestuur*, 21 April 2000, p. 66.
[61] See also: T.C. Borman, 'De taal in het rechts- en bestuurlijk verkeer', *Ars Aequi* (1996), p. 28-34.
[62] Royal Decree of 4 June 1830, Stb. 1830.19.
[63] Limburg's exclusion was due to the political situation at the time. The Decree intended to regulate the relationship between Dutch and French as administrative languages, and in those days French was a much-spoken language in Limburg.
[64] Case law – amongst others by the Legal Division of the Council of State – listed in Bijlagen II, op. cit. n. 11, 3, p. 3 (MvT).
[65] *Algemene wet bestuursrecht* (Act of 4 June 1992, Stb. 1992.315; most recently amended by the Act of 28 January 1999, Stb. 1999.30).
[66] Act of 4 May 1995, Stb. 1995.302.

Firstly, the States General, presuming that the general rule that Dutch should be used in relations with State authorities had always remained uncodified, had requested for codification.[68] This presumption seems to be doubtful, since the above-mentioned 1830 Royal Decree had never been formally repealed.[69] In addition, it should be mentioned that the Government laid down its opinion on the use of the Frisian language both in administrative relations and in judicial relations, in a 1953 parliamentary document (the Cabinet's Position) and in a 1993 agreement.[70] The Cabinet's Position was a reaction to riots which took place on 16 November 1951 (the so-called *knuppelvrijdag* or 'truncheon Friday') between the police and adherents of the *Fryske Beweging* (Frisian Movement), caused by a judge who did not allow the use of the Frisian language in court.[71] It was necessary to codify the rules in an act of parliament because of uncertainty surrounding the question whether or not these documents were binding upon third parties.[72]

Secondly, the 1830 Royal Decree was still in force and the Legal Division of the Council of State had ruled that an act of parliament was required in order to allow exceptions to the general rule that Dutch is the language in relations with administrative and judicial authorities.[73]

Thus, the general rule that administrative bodies and their staff use the Dutch language is laid down in Article 2:6, first part of paragraph 1 of the General Administrative Law Act. However, there are two exceptions to this general rule:[74] (1) a statutory provision may create an exception (Article 2:6, second part of paragraph 1); and (2) another language may be used if this is more efficient and if the interests of third parties are not harmed in a disproportionate manner (Article 2:6, paragraph 2). The position of the Frisian language, elaborated in Articles 2:7 up to and including 2:12 of the General Administrative Law Act, is an example of a statutory exception to the general rule.[75]

These articles lead to four types/possibilities of use of the Frisian language: oral and written use by an individual and oral and written use by the administrative authority. Article 2:7, paragraph 1 provides that all individuals may use the Frisian language in relations with administrative authorities which are established in the province of Friesland. However, paragraph 1 is not

---

[67] Bijlagen II, op. cit. n. 11, 3, p. 1 (MvT) and preamble of the Act of 4 May 1995, Stb. 1995.302.

[68] See for example: Bijlagen I, 1990/1991, 21800 VII, 135d (Motion by Postma MP).

[69] Bijlagen II, op. cit. n. 11, 3, p. 3 and 20 (MvT) and article II of the Act of 4 May 1995, Stb. 1995.302.

[70] Bijlagen II, 1953/1954, 3321, 1 (Cabinet's Position of 9 December 1953) and *Bestuursafspraak Friese taal en letterkunde* (Agreement of 8 November 1993, Stcrt. 1993.237).

[71] Handelingen II, 1993/1994, p. 6103 (Kalsbeek-Jasperse MP).

[72] Bijlagen II, op. cit. n. 11, 3, p. 7 (MvT).

[73] ARRvS 17 January 1985, AB 1986.73, *Spithorst* v. *Gedeputeerde Staten van Friesland*.

[74] Bijlagen II, op. cit. n. 11, 3, p. 4 (MvT).

[75] Bijlagen II, op. cit. n. 11, 3, p. 17 (MvT). Other exceptions are listed in Bijlagen II, op. cit. n. 11, 5, p. 11 (NV), also referring to Fryske Akademy/Berie foar it Frysk, *Lykbe-rjochtiging en it Frysk. Momintopname fan in ûnfolsleine rjochtsstaat*, Leeuwarden 1987.

applicable if the administrative authority requests that the Dutch language be used, on the ground that using the Frisian language would lead to a disproportionate burden (paragraph 2). The counterparts of Article 2:7 are Articles 2:8 and 2:9. Administrative authorities may use Frisian orally within the province of Friesland (Article 2:8, paragraph 1). Again, paragraph 2 provides an exception: paragraph 1 is not applicable if the opposite party requests that the Dutch language be used, on the ground that using Frisian leads to an unsatisfactory state of affairs. Decentralized administrative authorities which are established in Friesland may lay down rules on the use of Frisian in written proceedings (Article 2:9). With regard to administrative authorities of the province of Friesland, this was done by provincial states in 1999.[76] Documents will be bilingual if they have to be used outside the province of Friesland as well or if they contain or prepare general binding rules (*algemeen verbindende voorschriften*) or policy rules (*beleidsregels*) (Article 2:10). Anyone may request a translation of documents which are written in Frisian upon payment of (a part of) the costs. An interested party can obtain a translation for free if the document contains a relevant decision or minute of a meeting (Article 2:11). In meetings of representative bodies Frisian may be used; that which is said in Frisian will be entered in the minutes in Frisian (Article 2:12).

5.2 Rules on the use of the Frisian language in relations with judicial authorities

Rules on the use of Frisian in relations with judicial authorities have been laid down in the 1956 Act on the Use of the Frisian Language in Judicial Matters.[77]

Article 1 provides that oaths and affirmations that are required by law may be made in the Frisian language, unless the words of the oath or affirmation are (partly) laid down in the Constitution. Article 1 is an exception as provided for in Article 2 of the 1911 Act on the Wording of the Oath.[78] For that reason, oaths or affirmations which have to be made in court, such as oaths or affirmations made by witnesses, experts and interpreters, may be made in Frisian. This is not limited to courts in the province of Friesland.[79] Former Article XI of the Constitution contained the words of the oaths or affirmations to be made by the King and the regent. Since this article was repealed in 1999,[80] the present Constitution no longer prescribes any words for oaths or affirmations. The words of 'constitutional' oaths or affirmations are now laid down in the 1992 Act on

---

[76] *Oardering oangeande it skriftlik brûken fan de Fryske en de Nederlândske taal troch bestjoerorganen fan de provinsje Fryslân*, http://www.fryslan.nl/html-ned/home.html

[77] *Wet gebruik Friese taal in het rechtsverkeer* (Act of 11 May 1956, Stb. 1956.242; most recently amended by the Act of 28 January 1999, Stb. 1999.30).

[78] *Wet vorm van de eed* (Act of 17 July 1911, Stb. 1911.215).

[79] Bijlagen II, 1953/1954, 3553, 3, p. 4 (MvT).

[80] Statute Act of 6 October 1999, Stb. 1999.454.

Swearing and Inauguration of the King,[81] the 1994 Swearing of the Regent Act[82] and the 1994 Swearing of Ministers and Members of the States General Act.[83] These oaths or affirmations may be made in Frisian as well, and in practice this has been done by some Frisian Members of Parliament.[84]

Persons speaking in a court established in the province of Friesland may use the Frisian language (Article 2). A suspect or witness who wishes to use Frisian in criminal proceedings in a court outside the province of Friesland, may use Frisian if the suspect or witness demonstrates an insufficient knowledge of Dutch (Article 12). In criminal proceedings the president of the court may order that an interpreter shall be present (Article 3). The same applies to civil and administrative proceedings, provided that there will be no needless delay of the proceedings (Articles 4 and 5). In principle, what is said in Frisian will be entered in the minutes in Frisian; the president of the court may order a translation into Dutch (Article 6). Documents, except for summonses and charges, may be written in Frisian, if necessary with a translation (Article 7).

Article 8 deals with documents and statements which have to be registered in a public register, for example deeds of conveyance of real estate (Article 3:89 of the Civil Code). These documents may be written in the Frisian language. However, instead of the original Frisian documents, official translations in Dutch will be registered; the Frisian documents will be attached (paragraphs 1 and 2). Specific rules on notarial deeds in Frisian can be found in Article 42 of the 1999 Office of Notary Act;[85] rules on registration of Frisian documents in the land register were laid down in Article 41 of the 1991 Land Register Act.[86] Article 8, paragraph 3 of the Act of 11 May 1956, as amended, provides that birth, marriage and death certificates are made both in Frisian and in Dutch, which is an exception to the general rule that they are only made in Dutch.[87] With respect to birth certificates it should be noted that the registrar may only refuse first names proposed by the person registering the birth, if the name is inappropriate or if it corresponds with an existing surname which is not also a usual first name (Article 1:4, paragraph 2 of the Civil Code). This leads to the conclusion that the registrar may not refuse a Frisian name merely because it is a Frisian name: the grounds for refusing a first name have been listed exhaustively.

---

[81] *Wet beëdiging en inhuldiging van de koning* (Statute Act of 27 February 1992, Stb. 1992.121).

[82] *Wet beëdiging van de regent* (Statute Act of 25 March 1994, Stb. 1994.250).

[83] *Wet beëdiging ministers en leden Staten-Generaal* (Act of 27 February 1992, Stb. 1992.120).

[84] For example Atsma MP, on 19 May 1998: http://www.telegraaf.nl

[85] *Wet op het notarisambt* (Act of 3 April 1999, Stb. 1999.190).

[86] *Kadasterwet* (Act of 6 June 1991, Stb. 1991.376; most recently amended by the Act of 3 April 1999, Stb. 1999.190).

[87] Art. 17, paragraph 1 of *Besluit burgerlijke stand 1994* (Royal Decree of 25 February 1994, Stb. 1994.160; most recently amended by the Royal Decree of 27 March 1998, Stb. 1998.176).

5.3 Geographic names

Throughout the centuries the name of the 'province' of Friesland has sometimes changed. As early as 1579 we find the name 'Vriesche Ommelanden' in the Constitution.[88] From 1801 onwards, however, the Dutch name of 'Friesland' has been used.[89] Article 1 of the former 1962 Provinces Act[90] listed the 12 Dutch provinces, one of them being 'Friesland'. However, this situation changed with the entry into force of the new 1992 Provinces Act[91]: the list of provinces disappeared. For this paragraph, Article 156 of the present Provinces Act is relevant. According to paragraph 1 of Article 156, provincial states can change the name of the province. The decision has to be notified to the Minister of the Interior. It will enter into force at least one year after its date. Provincial states of Friesland have used their power to change the province's name: in 1995 they changed the name from the Dutch 'Friesland' into the Frisian 'Fryslân'.[92] The decision entered into force on 1 January 1997. A similar power has been granted to the municipal council with regard to the names of the municipalities (Article 158 of the 1992 Local Authorities Act[93]). Some of the Frisian municipal councils actually used this power,[94] the others did not.

It is the Government's opinion that the power to establish and change the names of villages, streets etc. is a part of the autonomous legislative power of the municipal council.[95] This power is granted by Article 124 of the Constitution.[96] As early as 1953 the Government stated that, in principle, it would not use its power to nullify municipal bye-laws on this matter.[97] That the power to change the names of villages may lead to some practical problems, is demonstrated by the question of traffic signs in the municipality of Tytsjerksteradiel.[98] The local council changed the names of the municipality's villages in the 1980s. In its decision, the council ordered new traffic signs indicating built-up areas. In The Netherlands, these signs contain the name of the village and, in a smaller letter,

---

[88] Van Hasselt, *Nederlandse staatsregelingen en grondwetten*, 17th ed., Alphen aan den Rijn (1987), p. 5.
[89] Art. 21 of the 1801 Constitution: Van Hasselt, Idem., p. 107.
[90] *Provinciewet* (Act of 25 January 1962, Stb. 1962.17).
[91] *Provinciewet* (Act of 10 September 1992, Stb. 1992.550; most recently amended by the Act of 28 January 1999, Stb. 1999.30).
[92] *Beslut fan Provinsjale Steaten fan Friesland* (Decision of 13 December 1995, PBF 1996.7).
[93] *Gemeentewet* (Act of 14 February 1992, Stb. 96; most recently amended by the Act of 11 November 1999, Stb. 1999.505).
[94] Boarnsterhim, Ferwerderadiel, Gaasterlân-Sleat, Littenseradiel, Skarsterlân, Tytsjerksteradiel, Wûnsteradiel, Wymbritseradiel. Source: internet, op. cit. n. 76.
[95] Bijlagen II, op. cit. n. 11, 3, p. 9 (MvT).
[96] On autonomous legislative power see: H.Ph.J.A.M. Hennekens/H.J.A.M. van Geest/R. Fernhout, *Decentralisatie*, 4th ed., Nijmegen (1998), p. 14-18, 59-86.
[97] Bijlagen II, op. cit. n. 70, 1, p. 2 (Cabinet's Position of 9 December 1953).
[98] B. Olmer, 'Rimram in Tietjerk om plaatsnamen', *De Telegraaf*, 4 May 2000. Further information was provided by the municipal spokesman.

the name of the municipality. The council determined the layout of these signs: the official Frisian name, in a normal letter; the Dutch translation, in a somewhat smaller letter; and the municipality's name in the smallest letter. After a few years, some of the traffic signs had to be replaced and the council ordered new ones. The layout of these new signs differed significantly from the old one, this being caused by a ministerial rule, issued pursuant to an Order in Council, on the layout of Frisian traffic signs. As a result, some members of Tytsjerksteradiel's council complained about the non-implementation of the council's decision. This resulted in an exceptional position, granted by the Ministry of Transport and Public Works: Tytsjerksteradiel's traffic signs were saved…

5.4 Public instruction[99]

Education is essential for preserving and promoting language and culture. It is the Government's opinion that the bilingual situation in Friesland requires special attention at all levels of education. The instruction in Friesland has to offer possibilities for students to educate themselves in their native language, as well as to prepare students for life in a bilingual society. For that reason the Minster for Education has to promote, initiate and adopt legislation on the position of the Frisian language in the field of education.

Regarding primary education the position of the Frisian language is primarily dealt with in Article 9 of the 1981 Primary Education Act.[100] In principle, the official school language is Dutch, but Frisian may also be used in areas where Frisian is a much-spoken language (paragraph 8). This is in conformity with the general idea that instruction in the mother tongue is, at least at the initial levels of education, the most effective way to instruct children.[101] Paragraph 4 provides that, apart from the subjects mentioned in paragraphs 1, 2 and 3, there will be instruction in the subject of Frisian language at primary schools in the province of Friesland, unless the provincial executive (*Gedeputeerde Staten*) has granted an exemption from this requirement. Pursuant to paragraph 5, some main targets have been laid down in a 1998 Royal Decree.[102] These targets concern, for example, sufficient speaking, reading and writing skills. The State refunds expenses entitled in instruction in the Frisian language to the province of Friesland, which has to ensure a student-based distribution to the schools (Article 134, paragraph 2). Furthermore, the State provides for educational guidance on the subject of Frisian and it encourages that final tests, which have an advisory function in admitting a child to a certain type of secondary education, will be prepared.

---

[99] See also: Chapter 4 of the *Bestuursafspraak*, op. cit. n. 70.

[100] *Wet op het primair onderwijs* (Act of 2 July 1981, Stb. 1981.468; most recently amended by the Act of 2 December 1999, Stb. 1999.527).

[101] De Varennes, op. cit. n. 7, p. 184.

[102] *Besluit kerndoelen primair onderwijs 1998* (Royal Decree of 2 June 1998, Stb. 1998.354; most recently amended by the Royal Decree of 27 July 1998, Stb. 1998.487).

With respect to secondary education, rules can be found in the 1963 Secondary Education Act.[103] During the first three years of secondary education Frisian is a compulsory subject for students in the province of Friesland, unless the inspector of education has granted an exemption from this requirement (Article 11a, paragraph 2, sub. b). Again, main targets have been laid down in a Royal Decree.[104] Regarding special secondary education, Frisian may be taught in schools in the province of Friesland, though this is not compulsory (Article 135, paragraph 3). Finally, the State provides for educational guidance, a co-ordinator and final examinations in the subject of the Frisian language.

6. CONCLUSION

Once an official language of The Netherlands, the Frisian language is nowadays primarily spoken in the Dutch province of Friesland. This Germanic language is considered to be a minority language as defined in several international documents, which was one of the reasons for the Dutch Government to initiate legislation on the position of the Frisian language in The Netherlands. The Dutch legislation provides the Frisians and their language with a stronger position than required is by Article 27 of the ICCPR. The right of a linguistic minority to use its own language in community with other members of its group is sufficiently guaranteed by several constitutional fundamental rights. Since no special measures granting specific rights to a minority are required, the specific legislation on, for example, the use of Frisian in relations with administrative authorities must therefore be regarded as being 'excessive' in this context. However, this kind of legislation is not excessive in the context of the European Charter for Regional or Minority Languages and the Draft Declaration on the Rights of Indigenous Peoples. On the contrary, The Netherlands has committed itself to applying some 50 provisions of the Charter concerning education (Article 8), judicial authorities (Article 9), administrative authorities and public services (Article 10), the media (Article 11), culture (Article 12), the economy and social life (Article 13) and cross-border exchanges (Article 14). In the field of language, literature, education in an indigenous language and the media, the Draft Declaration also provides rights to indigenous peoples. Special legislation was also required in order to fulfil the European Parliament's wishes, as laid down in its Resolution on Cultural and Linguistic Minorities. It will also be required in order to comply with the Framework Convention for the Protection of National Minorities, once it will enter into force for The Netherlands.

In the Constitution itself there is no provision on language as efforts to insert such an article have never reached the point of acceptance. However, the

---

[103] *Wet op het voortgezet onderwijs* (Act of 14 February 1963, Stb. 1963.40; most recently amended by the Act of 28 October 1999, Stb. 1999.474).

[104] *Besluit kerndoelen en adviesurentabel basisvorming 1998-2003* (Royal Decree of 15 October 1997, Stb. 1997.484).

Constitution contains several fundamental rights which are related to expression and the use of language. In principle, individuals enjoy freedom of expression, a right to private life, a right to non-discrimination and a right to privacy of correspondence and communication. It should be noted that these rights can be limited (in most cases by an act of parliament) and that they operate primarily in a vertical direction, as discussed in Chapter 3 of this article.

In addition, as analysed in Chapter 4, detailed rules on the use of the Frisian language in relations with administrative authorities were laid down in the 1992 General Administrative Law Act, whereas the use of Frisian in judicial matters is regulated by the 1956 Act on the Use of the Frisian Language in Judicial Matters, as amended. The 1992 Provinces Act and the 1992 Local Authorities Act, as well as Article 124 of the Constitution, are of certain relevance too, as they provide a legal basis for changing toponymical names from Dutch into Frisian. Several acts in the field of education provide rules for the use and teaching of Frisian in schools.

As mentioned above, the enjoyment of certain fundamental rights can be limited by an act of parliament. Furthermore, the existing acts of parliament can be repealed or amended. Thus, it still remains possible to severely limit the position of the Frisian language. However, this seems to be a highly improbable scenario for various reasons. Firstly, such limitation would be contrary to international law guaranteeing fundamental rights and protecting minority languages. Secondly, such measures would be contrary to Article 1 of the Constitution which cannot be limited in any way. And finally, it would be contrary to continuous Government policy on the position of the Frisian language, which originates from the 1950s.

LINGUISTIC RIGHTS IN SPAIN

Giovanni Poggeschi*

This article deals with the most important legal events and discusses legal norms and judicial decisions relating to linguistic rights in Spain that have occurred during the period 1997-1998 and partly covering 1999. In order to make the reading somewhat easier it is necessary to explain that the terms 'region' and 'regional' are translations of the Spanish *Comunidad Autónoma* and *autonómico/a*. The author thanks all the civil servants, librarians and activists in the defence of minority languages in Spain for their assistance.

1. OVERALL CONSIDERATIONS AND CONSTITUTIONAL ARRANGEMENTS

Linguistic rights in Spain and the development of the regional State go along together, in the same way that the restoration of democracy with the Constitution of 1978 coincides with the decentralisation of the territorial structure of the State.

To begin with the legal data, it is necessary to analyse the two basic articles of the Spanish Constitution aiming to regulate the regional framework and linguistic rights. Article 2 states that the

> 'Constitution is based on the indissoluble unity of the Spanish nation, the common and indivisible homeland of all Spaniards, and recognises and guarantees the right to autonomy of the nationalities and regions which make it up and the solidarity among all of them.'

The text of Article 3 is as follows:

> '1. Castilian is the official Spanish language of the State. All Spaniards have the duty to know it and the right to use it.
> 2. The other languages of Spain will also be official in the respective autonomous communities, in accordance with their Statutes.
> The richness of the linguistic modalities of Spain is a cultural patrimony which will be the object of special respect and protection.'

---

* Researcher at the European Academy of Bolzano/Boze, Italy.

S. Trifunovska (Ed.), Minority Rights in Europe: European Minorities and Languages
© 2000, T.M.C. Asser Press, The Hague, The Netherlands

Article 2 derives from the combination of two apparently conflicting principles: the idea of the coexistence of different peripheral nationalities and the existence of an unique Spanish nation. This theoretical construction could at first glance seem artificial and ambiguous, while in reality it is bold and clever. It is bold because it sets the presence of differentiated societies as the basis of the *Estado autonómico*, and clever because it adapts local needs to the central State guarantee of indissolubility. The term 'nation' may in this way correspond with the term 'nationality' (the Spanish term 'nationalities' corresponds to the term 'national minorities' used in Central and Eastern Europe).

The Spanish Constitution does not use the term 'minority' as many other Constitutions do, like for instance the Italian. The reason for this lies in the number of persons speaking Catalan, Basque and Galician, who are in total several millions, so that the utilisation of the word minority would indicate a depreciation of those important regional languages and cultures.

Spain has been during the last five centuries, with few exceptions, a very centralised State. At the beginning of the eighteenth century, the strengthening of the absolutist State led to the abolition of the few institutions that had been formerly left to the regions, especially to Catalonia. The few attempts to implement democracy in Spain were made through federal, or almost-federal projects, like in the draft of the Constitution of 1873 and by the experience of the Republican Constitution of 1931, which shaped the *Estado integral*, a composed State with a broad autonomy for Catalonia and the Basque Countries.[1]

Twenty years after the adoption of the Constitution, the consolidation of linguistic rights is one of the peculiar features which shapes the open model of Spanish regionalism.

2. THE CENTRAL STATE

The territorial model of regional Spain creates a sort of concentration of linguistic rights relating to the local languages only in the areas where they are spoken. Spain is not in its entirety a plurilingual State, because the central institutions do not have to adhere to the duty of double officiality (like for instance in Canada or Belgium), apart from those which are in the territories where a regional language is indeed official.

On 6 April 1999 the *Tribunal Constitucional* delivered a judgement concerning linguistic rights. The decision is of no use from the practical point of view, because the norm which has been declared unconstitutional had been previously abolished. This has been done through the reform, which took place on 13 January 1999, of Law 30/1992 of 26 November 1992 on the legal regime

---

[1] José Antonio González Casanova, *Federalismo y autonomía. Cataluña y el Estado español (1868-1938)*, Barcelona (1979); Sebastián Martín-Retortillo Baquer & Enric Argullol Murgadas, *Aproximación histórica al tema de la descentralización (1812-1931)*, Madrid (1973); Manuel Gerpe Landín, *L'estatut d'Autonomia de Catalunya i l'Estat integral*, Barcelona (1977).

and procedure of the public administration.² Article 36 of this law was entirely dedicated to the use of language in the administrative procedure.

Article 36 of the above mentioned Law stated that it is compulsory to translate into Castilian all the documents issued in a co-official language, different from Castilian, by a public administration located inside an Autonomous Community with linguistic double officiality, when those documents are bound to take effect outside the territory of the region where they have been issued. To give an example, a document issued in Catalan in the town of Barcelona, and directed to Palma de Mallorca, in the Balearic Islands, where the Catalan language is also official, has to be translated into Castilian by the public administration which has initiated the procedure.[3] This regulation does not take in consideration the *trans-regional* diffusion of the 'the other languages of Spain', and it could be considered to be also contrary to Article 149(2) of the Spanish Constitution, which prescribes that

> '[...] without prejudice to the competences which the Autonomous Communities may assume, the State shall consider the service of culture a duty and essential attribute and shall facilitate cultural communication among the Autonomous Communities in agreement with them [...]',

at least when communications concern cultural matters.

The legitimacy of Article 36 of *Ley 30/1992* was raised by the Catalan Government. The *Tribunal Constitucional* declared that this provision is not in conformity with the Constitution in the part referring to compulsory translation in Castilian when the documents take effect in the territory of an Autonomous Community with the same official regional language. The Judgement recognises that in some cases the official status of the local language (*lengua propia*) of an Autonomous Community is not only bound to the territory of the Autonomous Community. Thus 'to compel to translate into Castilian all the documents, the dossiers and parts of those which are going to take effect outside the Autonomous Community, also when they do so in a territory where it is also official, from the language in which the document was originally drawn, means to refuse to acknowledge the official status of this language [...]'. The need of a translation into Castilian is a breach of the principle stated by Article 3(2) of the Spanish Constitution and by the corresponding regulations of the Autonomy Statutes which prescribe the principle of double officiality.

The described Judgement is not among the most important of those of the *Tribunal Constitucional* concerning linguistic rights,[4] but nevertheless it will be

---

[2] Ley 30/1992, de 26 novembre, *Legislación general de Régimen Jurídico de las Administraciones Públicas y del Procedimiento Administrativo Común*.

[3] Antoni Milian i Massana, 'Planificación en las Administraciones de las CC.AA. con doble oficialidad lingüística', *Revista Vasca de Administración Pública*, No. 44 (1996) p. 108.

[4] The 'historical' decisions of the Tribunal Constitucional on linguistic rights are 82 and 84 (of 1986), 46 (of 1991), 337 (of 1994) and 147 (of 1997): Giovanni Poggeschi, 'The linguistic struggle in the Almost Federal Spanish System', in *The Constitutional and Political Regulation of*

remembered because it adds one point to the score of the Autonomous Communities versus the Central State in the linguistic conflict. The division of competences between the Central State and the Autonomous Communities is not very clearly defined in the Spanish Constitutional system, that is why an important role has to be played by the Supreme or the Constitutional Court. The Autonomous Communities have surely gained a great deal of power also through some decisions of the *Tribunal Constitucional* but the role of the regional parties, which are fundamental to creating governmental coalitions, both in the Central Government and in the regional executives, is even more important.[5]

3. CATALONIA

Catalonia and the Basque Countries are the two Autonomous Communities with the highest number of provisions concerning the local language. The big difference between the two regions lies in the number of persons speaking the

---

Ethnic Relations and Conflicts, Ljubljana (1999) pp. 313-324. Here follows a brief analysis of four mentioned Judgements (337 of 1994 will be analysed in the chapter dedicated to Catalonia): Judgement 82 of 1986 sets some fundamental points on the status of officiality of the languages in Spain. It confirms the validity of the double linguistic officiality set up in the whole territory of the four Autonomous Communities (Catalonia, Basque Country, Galicia and Balearic Islands) and in some of the territory of Valencia (most of it) and Navarra (a small part). The Judgement is a reminder that official bilingualism policies involve the State Administration offices located inside the Autonomous Community. Both the State and the Autonomous Communities have the power to regulate linguistic matters in their respective areas of jurisdiction. There is of course the risk of some overlapping between the State and the Autonomous Communities in issues involving language policies, so Judgement 82 states that the Autonomous Communities do not have the right to establish provisions on the organisation and the functioning of State Administration offices, but they can impose some degree of official bilingualism based on the Constitution and the Statutes of the Autonomous Communities. Judgement 84 of the same year (and the same day too) concerning the linguistic law of Galicia declares that the second paragraph of Article 1 of this Law, which states that all the inhabitants of Galicia have the duty to know the local language and the right to use it, is contrary to the Constitution, because there is only the duty to know the Castilian language. Judgement 46 of 1991 refers to the use of languages in public administration. It puts an end to the behaviour of the Courts which had condemned the provisions of some CA or of some municipalities prescribing the duty to know the local language in order to become a civil servant. Judgement 46 of 1991 states that the obligation to know the co-official language in order to hold a certain post in public administration is not contrary to the principle of equality in Spain. Equality does not mean uniformity, otherwise the principle of the officiality of the regional languages would become meaningless. Judgement 147 of 1996 deals with the labelling of goods, an issue that is gaining ground in the protection of local languages all around Europe. It states that both the State and the bilingual Autonomous Communities share the competence. This double nature seems to inspire the very last State provision about labelling, which is Royal Decree 1268, enacted on 24 July 1997. This norm 'translates' the last EU directive on the labelling of alimentary goods containing sweeteners (n. 96/21). The Decree maintains the obligation to use 'the State official Spanish language, excepting (the labelling of) traditional products which are elaborated and distributed only within the framework of an Autonomous Community having its own language'.

[5] Gumersindo Trujillo, 'Reformas y neuvo horizontes del Estado autonómico en los años noventa', in Javier Corcuera Atienza (Ed.), *Los nacionalismos: glabalización y crisis del Estado-nación*, Madrid, Consejo Genral del Poder Judicial (1999), pp. 271-300.

regional tongue. Basque is an increasingly strong minority language, but it is always minoritarian, being spoken in its own *Comunidad Autónoma* by approximately 25% of the population. Much stronger is the percentage of Catalan speakers: more than a half of the population use it as a first language, but the most impressive and important data is that around 90% of the residents of Catalonia are able to speak it, and an even higher percentage of the people are able to understand it.

According to the Statute of Autonomy of 1982 – which is the basic law for the Autonomous Communities – Catalan is the official language, together with Castilian of course. The legislative pillar that had been the cornerstone and has put into practice the general linguistic provisions is the *Ley de normalización del catalán*, No. 7 of 18 April 1983. The term 'normalisation' is used in many linguistic laws of Spain, and it means that the minority language has to recover the ground that it has lost, for social, political and historical reasons, that has contributed to making it slip into 'abnormal' use. The 'language-normalisation' process has to take place in all the most important fields, like education, public administration and justice. But the constant changing of contemporary life persuaded the Catalan executive and Parliament of the necessity to reform the 1983 Linguistic Law. The new Law, called *Le Ley de política lingüística*, was enacted by the Catalan Parliament on 30 December 1997, under the jurisdiction of the Autonomous Community in accordance with Article 148(17) of the Spanish Constitution, which concerns the teaching of the local language and the encouragement of culture and research.

The spirit of the *Ley de política lingüística* (No. 1 of 7 January 1998), reflects some of the historical features of Catalanism, a movement that from the end of the last century has shown many nationalist aspects, but has rarely chosen a clear demand for independence from Spain. Nevertheless, all Catalan nationalists, even the most moderate and prudent, have a precise feeling that Catalonia is a different nation inside Spain.

The new Catalan Language Law was preceded by an intense parliamentary and social discussion which lasted about eight months. The key word of this discussion has been 'consensus'. The aim of the members of most parties inside the Catalan Assembly was to achieve a general agreement between all the political forces represented in the *Parlament* concerning the Law. The Law has been actually voted for by all parties (the moderate Catalan nationalists *Convergència i Unió*, led by the President of the Catalan Government, the *Generalitat*, Jordi Pujol, the socialists, the ex-communists and one of the two independentist parties) except the *Partido Popular*, the right-wing party led by José Maria Aznar, the President of the Central Government, and the traditional national party claiming the sovereignty of Catalonia, *Esquerra Republicana*. The first said that the Law was going too far and did not provide guarantees for the Spanish-speaking population, while the second considered it too weak as far as the promotion of the local language was concerned.

The new Language Law marks a further step in the 'normalisation' of Catalan. The new Catalan linguistic law does not include this term because it is thought, and declared in the Preamble, that the basic results of the first language normalisation process have already been achieved. But the provisions on such an important and sensitive issue must be renewed, because the world has changed over the last fifteen years, and a new law is necessary to adapt the needs of the Catalan people to the technological changes that may, if used in a certain way, weaken the minority language. As an example, computer programs, sold in Catalonia, are provided with instructions in English or in Spanish, but rarely in Catalan.

The Law is quite long and detailed.[6] It insists on the concepts of *llengua pròpia*, the traditional local language peculiar to the region, the Catalan, and official languages, both Catalan and Spanish. The status of officiality means that everybody has the right to use and to receive a proper response in any of the two languages, while the concept of *llengua pròpia* means that Catalan should be the normal means of communication in the fields of public administration and education. The consequence of the interpretation of the idea of *llengua pròpia* (in Catalan) is that Catalan has, or should receive, priority in many areas of social life, saving the right of using and learning Spanish. The concept of officiality includes the right not only to use but also to get a response in the official language used by the citizen. This right to receive an answer in the same official language used by the citizen cannot be implemented over a short period of time, but rather in a gradual and progressive manner. The right to be answered in the same language has to be reasonable: this means that it has to exist in public administration, but not at any cost with private enterprises or individual workers. To give an example, a taxi driver from Andalusia would not be punished if he provides an answer in Spanish to somebody who has spoken to him in Catalan.

A fundamental area touched upon by the new Catalan Linguistic Law is education. Supported by the Judgement 337/1994, of 23 December, of the *Tribunal Constitucional*, the Law declares the validity of the so-called 'immersion' model in non-university education,[7] and sets a number of provisions with the aim of enlarging the use of Catalan at the University level.

---

[6] Giovanni Poggeschi, 'La nuova legge linguistica catalana nel quadro dell'evoluzione dello Stato regionale spagnolo', *Le Regioni* 5 (1998) pp. 1107-1141.

[7] The peculiarity of the Catalan educational system stems from the single educational net. According to Art. 14(5) of the Catalan *Ley de Normalización* 'the Administration has to adopt the necessary means not to separate the children in different centres because of their language'. The schooling system is the same regardless of the mother tongue of the pupils. Subjects are mainly taught in Catalan but some subjects, for instance Spanish literature, have Spanish as the language of instruction. The struggle began when a group of parents of Spanish speaking pupils brought an action against some provisions of a decree implementing the Linguistic Law, requesting, *inter alia*, the possibility for their children to be totally educated in Castilian. The *Tribunal Constitucional* declared that the educational system of Catalonia almost totally conforms with the Constitution, saying that there is no freedom to choose the language of instruction. In order not to damage social cohesion, it is accepted that the Catalan system has only one educational net. The

But the very new part of the *Ley de política lingüística* concerns the use of Catalan by the media and in the sphere of economic activity. It includes some provisions establishing shares appointed to the Catalan language for television and radio broadcasts and the press. More precisely, all radio and TV channels under the control of the *Generalitat* – the numerous cable and private channels licensed outside Catalonia are excluded from the application of this Law – have to broadcast at least 50% of the time in Catalan, and radio music must include at least 25% of songs in Catalan. Similar provisions are made regarding the press, with reference to the subsidies that can be obtained by the publishers. The aim of Articles 28 and 29 is to stimulate the presence of the Catalan language in many fields of cultural industry, including information science.

The Law on the Linguistic Policy of Catalonia is typically 'interventionist'. The Catalan language is alive and widely spoken, but nevertheless within the Spanish State it is a minority language. The absence of a Catalan State is disadvantageous in the promotion of the language, if compared with the situation of other languages which benefit from the sovereignty of the country in which they are spoken, though the double identity, which most Catalans have, makes easier to be bilingual and this is a great personal benefit.

Some may point to the lack of strict regulations needed in the language sphere, so closely related to personal freedom(s). But it is impossible not to set some basic rules on the use of languages: maybe the citizens of some regions do not want a fully-developed system of linguistic rights, being satisfied with some cultural provisions. But more probably the citizens of Catalonia and the Basque Country wish to see their culture and language better protected and developed, and the parties which promote the regional languages take this desire into account. A very important feature of Catalan nationalism has always been the desire to integrate people coming from other parts of Spain, which will now have to include also many residents coming particularly from Northern Africa.

Maybe these kinds of measures, which regulate linguistic reality, somehow seem forced and against the principle of the linguistic free market, but lesser used languages need support and affirmative action, of course with the proviso that the population support such measures and by means which have to be proportional to each concrete situation. The risk of breaching the principles of European law has recently been underlined, and this point has to be taken into serious consideration.[8] The argument lies in Article 87 of Treaty of the European Community (formerly Article 92), and confirmed by the European Court of Justice: 'any aid granted by a Member State or through State resources in any form whatsoever which distorts or threatens to distort competition by favouring

---

only linguistic right of the pupil, states Judgement 337 of 23 December 1994 is to receive the instruction in a language that he/she can understand: Eliseo Aja et al., *La lengua de enseñanza en la legislación de Cataluña*, Barcelona, Institut d'Estudis Autonòmics (1994); Antoni Milián i Massana, *Derechos lingüísticos y derecho fundamental a la educación. Un estudio comparado: Italia, Belgica, Suiza, Canada y España*, Madrid, Civitas (1994).

[8] Tomás Ramón Fernández, 'Dictamen...', *Teoría y realidad Constitucional. Monográfico sobre Lenguas y Constitución*, 2 (1998) pp. 13-35.

certain undertakings or the production of certain goods shall, insofar as it affects trade between Member States, be incompatible with the common market'. On the other hand, the same author uses a very old-fashioned justification, at least in composed States, which considers the duty to know a regional language, a duty not prescribed by the Constitution, which only foresees this duty for the Castilian language, to be contrary to the principle of free movement and equality of persons inside the State.[9] The *Tribunal Constitucional* has confirmed in its jurisprudence that this theory, which confuses equality with uniformity, is a mistaken one (see for instance Judgement No. 37 of 28 July 1981).

The Catalan Linguistic Law has been the object of many complaints lodged with the Spanish Ombudsman,[10] the *Defensor del pueblo*, but so far he has not found any grounds to call for the intervention of the *Tribunal Constitucional*. Anyway, in certain proceedings, he has issued some advice and recommendations to the *Generalitat*,[11] demanding a careful application of the Constitucional principles in the implementation of the law through regulations and decrees, whose importance in the process of language normalisation is evident, maybe too much so if it is true that decisions which are so important should be taken directly within a legislative assembly which, better than the executive body, represents the interests of the citizens.[12]

4. THE BASQUE COUNTRIES (EUSKADI) AND NAVARRA

The uniqueness of the Basque language, the *Euskera*, and the strong feeling of autonomy, or often independence, spreading all over Euskadi, explain the great efforts which the Basque Government has been undertaking in strengthening the status of the local language. Differently from Catalan, the Basque language is a minority language being spoken regularly by only 20% of the population of Euskadi and by an even smaller minority in Navarra. For this and other reasons, and also the terrorist activities of E.T.A. should not be forgotten, the linguistic policies in Euskadi and in Navarra have to operate in a more difficult context than in Catalonia. The analysis will begin with Euskadi, and then the case of Navarra will be considered.

The Regional Government in Euskadi has been making great efforts in the 'euskaldunización', which means the 'basquenization' of public administration. Due to the regional legislation which requires knowledge of the Basque

---

[9] Juan José Solozabal Echevarria, 'El régimen constitucional del bilingüísmo. La Cooficialidad lingüística como garantia institucional', *Revista Española de Derecho Constitucional*, 55 (1998) pp. 28-31.

[10] 'Álvarez de Miranda destaca que no se respete el bilingüísmo oficial', *El País* (Cataluña), 23 June 1999, pp. 1-4.

[11] Fernando Álvarez de Miranda, 'Sugerencias y recomendaciones que formula el defensor del pueblo', *Teoría ...*, op. cit. n. 8, pp. 255-270.

[12] Tomás Ramón Fernández, 'La normalización del catalán como problema constitucional', *Documentación Administrativa* (1996), pp. 525-535.

language for civil servants, or at least it considers this knowledge to be a merit, the percentage of the Basque speakers within regional public administration, but less so within the public administration of municipalities (except the ones where the *Euskera* is widely spoken), is much higher than in the society as a whole.

In 1998 some decrees concerning the 'normalisation' of the Basque language in some fields of public administration were enacted. One of the most relevant is Decree 30/1998, of 24 February 1998, which regulates the process of normalisation of *euskera* in the *Ertzaintza*, the regional police which was created in accordance with the implementation of the 1981 Autonomy Statute.

The nature of the *Ertzaintza*, which have gained increasing importance in the last years also in the fight against terrorism, and which unfortunately have suffered some fatalities, requires at least the capability for the single agent to be able to speak in Basque, and of course in Castilian, while doing his work. Thus, within the framework of Law 6/1989, of 6 July 1989, of the *Función Pública Vasca*, and of the *Ley básica de normalización del euskera*, No. 10, of 24 November 1982, the present Decree regulates the process of mastering the Basque language by the police (*Ertzainas*). Two levels of knowledge are foreseen: the first demands only a capability to speak Basque, required for all agents of the *Ertzaintza*, while the second level also implies a good knowledge of the written language and is required for those in charge of preparing and issuing documents. There is a possibility to attend some free classes in the Basque language in order to be able to fulfil the linguistic requirements specified by the present Decree. Article 7 of the Decree foresees a 10-year period of linguistic planning.

By reading the Decree on the *Ertzaintza* one can realise how much importance is given to the broadening of the use of the local language, even if there is a kind of refrain that states that Catalan nationalism is more language-oriented than the Basque. Decree 30/1998, and all the regulations relating to implementation of the *euskera*, questions this common belief.

Another interesting document that we may quote is the *Convenio*, the Convention on Collaboration between the *Consejo General del Poder Judicial* (which is the highest organ of self-government of the judicial authorities in Spain) and the Basque Government, on the normalisation of the use of the *Euskera* in some fields of the judicial administration of the Basque Country.

The organisation of the judicial authorities is a typical State competence, though there are provisions to be found in some Autonomous Communities relating to certain aspects of judicial power: Catalonia has, in particular, a civil law which is peculiar to the region which is, at the same time respecting the basic State law, implemented by the *Generalitat*; and Euskadi and Navarra still retain their customs and an individual financial system. So there is some opportunity for the Autonomous Communities not to leave all the regulation of justice to the State, and the principle of double officiality is also valid in the bilingual Autonomous Communities, but, for many reasons, within the judicial system the knowledge of the regional languages is much less developed than in other fields, like public administration and education.

The knowledge of Catalan, Basque or Galician is not compulsory in order to become a judge, and even the knowledge of these languages adds little merit in drawing up the judiciary lists, which is the same for the whole Spain.[13] Nevertheless, some Autonomous Communities, especially Catalonia and Euskadi, are trying to promote the principle of double officiality within the judicial system of their regions. We can place the above mentioned Convention on collaboration between the *Consejo General del Poder Judicial* and the Department of Justice of the Basque Government, signed in April 1998, within this context. The Central Government has appealed to the *Tribunal Constitucional* because it considers that the Government of Euskadi has gone beyond its competence in proposing rules on the use of the Basque language inside the Courts located in Euskadi.

Another legal tool issued in the Autonomous Community of Euskadi during 1998 that may be interesting to mention is the Agreement of the Executive Council of the Basque Government which approves the plan for the normalisation of the use of the *euskera* in the public administration of the Autonomous Community of Euskadi for the period 1998-2002.

These most relevant and recent provisions from the Basque Country underline the importance given to the public administration in building up the Spanish Autonomous Communities. There is nevertheless a danger that the protection of regional languages will probably fade, if seen in the context of the trend towards privatisation which public administrations are facing all over the Western world.[14] The protection of *Euskera* would be less consistent and less in demand if merely the rules of competition in the market of languages would enter into play. It is true that the Basque public administration will always exist, but if some of the tasks would increasingly fall into private hands, then a civil (private) servant would probably not have the same linguistic obligations that an actual civil (public) servant has. Consequently, it would be possible that the knowledge of the *Euskera* would not be demanded of all employees.

The situation of Navarra is to a certain extent comparable to the one of Valencia, being a territory not completely officially bilingual. But the situation in Navarra is much more complicated, because the Linguistic Law (*Ley Foral* 18/1986), of 15 December 1986, provides a list of three different linguistic areas: the Basque zone, the mixed one and the non-Basque zone.

Among the legal documents aiming to promote of the *Euskera*,[15] the *Orden Foral* 39/1998[16] should be mentioned. It regulates collaboration on the

---

[13] Giovanni Poggeschi, 'La giustizia nei paesi plurilingui', *Informator* 3 (1997), p. 114 et seq.

[14] Antoni Milián i Massana, 'Allò 'públic' en l'extensió i en els límits de l'oficialitat lingüística. Reflexions a propòsit d'una eventual reforma de la llei de normalització lingüística a Catalunya', *Autonomies*, No. 21 (1996).

[15] A distinguished Basque author reminds us, however, that the aim of the regulations concerning the language in Navarra is not inspired by the principle of 'promotion', but rather, less

normalisation of the use of the *Euskera* within the framework of local administration between the Government of Navarra and the local bodies which had signed an Agreement on this matter in March 1994. The *Comunidad Foral* finances programmes aimed at strengthening the language in the Basque and mixed areas, and it is a good example of collaboration between different levels of government, a factor which has to improve in Spain.[17]

5. GALICIA

Not much has occurred in Galicia from a linguistic point of view in recent years. The linguistic normalisation seems to be on-going, but Castilian remains very important, especially in the larger towns. Diglossy, which means an alternative use of the two languages without a clear awareness of it, is a widespread habit in Galicia, due to the similarity of the two official languages, but also due to the historical *status* of inferiority of the local language in comparison with Castilian.

A symbolic and important change was introduced by State Law 2/1998 of 3 March 1998, which establishes that the Galician provinces of 'La Coruña' and 'Orense' will be officially called by their Galician names 'A Coruña' and 'Ourense'.

Among the numerous provisions that have been approved by the competent bodies – especially the *Xunta*, the Galician Government – during recent years,[18] it is interesting to mention the regulation (*Orden* in Spanish, *Orde* in Galician) of 27 February, which announces the setting up of classes in the Galician language for the *galegos* who reside abroad. Galicia, which is historically a land of massive immigration,[19] has a law (No. 4/1983, *de recoñecemento da galeguidade*) which is meant in particular for Galician people living outside Galicia, which, not surprisingly, follows the most important norm for of protecting the local Galician language (No. 3/1983).

---

ambitiously, to the idea of 'conservation': Edoardo Cobreros Mendazona, *El régimen juridico de la oficialidad del euskera*, Onati (1989), p. 145.

[16] Literally, Navarra is not an Autonomus Community, but a *Comunidad Foral*. The *fueros* are the ancient customs that are still in force in the Basque Countries (Euskadi) and in Navarra, recognised by the Spanish Constitution of 1978, which states in its first additional provision that '1. The Constitution protects and respects the historic rights of the territories with 'fueros'; 2. The general updating of the 'fuero' system shall be carried out, when appropriate, within the framework of the Constitution and of the Statutes of Autonomy'. The best work on the subject, which is a proposal for a new model of the Spanish Constitution, is the book written by Miguel Herrero De Miñón, *Derechos históricos y Constitución*, Madrid (1998).

[17] Eliseo Aja Fernández, 'Igualdad competencial y hecho diferencial', in Miguel Herreo de Miñon et al., *Uniformidad o diversidad de las Comunidades Autónomas*, Barcelona (1995) pp. 81-85.

[18] See the section dedicated to Galicia of the *Revista de llengua i dret*, nn. 28-29 and 30, written by Xosé González Martínez. This review contains very detailed sections on linguistic rights in the Autonomous Communities and in the Central State.

[19] In Argentina, the term *gallego* simply means Spanish, because most of the immigrants from Spain came from Galicia.

6. THE VALENCIAN COMMUNITY

The position of the Valencian language is very interesting to analyse, because it shows that different history may shape a different social and political attitude also in the presence of a similar, or even identical language.

In fact the *lengua propia* of the Valencian Community is considered by all the most prominent linguists to be a variation of Catalan, or at least belonging to the same linguistic group, no different from the peculiar variety of Catalan spoken in the Balearic Islands.[20] But the history of Valencia differently from the history of the *Principat* of Catalonia, contributed to the creation of a different identity which, with a few exceptions, does not recognise the leading role of Catalonia inside the *Països Catalans*. As a consequence, all the legal documents on the regulation of the language refer to the Valencian and not Catalan as the local language.

Therefore, the Judgement of the *Tribunal Constitucional* delivered on 21 April 1997 cannot be understood without these extra-judical elements. The origin of the Judgement lies in an Agreement signed at the University of Valencia on 20 July 1986 which allows the 'academic' utilisation of the term 'Catalan' to indicate the local language, without thus excluding the term 'Valencian' which can be found in the Autonomy Statute and in Law 4/1983, of 23 November 1983, on the *Uso y enseñanza del valenciano*, which is the local law of linguistic normalisation.

The use of the term 'Catalan' was declared to be not in conformity with the mentioned laws (the Statute and the Linguistic Law) by a Judgement of 18 May 1989 of an ordinary court, and the decision was confirmed by the *Tribunal Supremo* on 20 November 1992 on appeal. The University of Valencia submitted its claim to the *Tribunal Constitucional* through the *recurso de amparo* (which is a direct claim to the *Tribunal Constitucional*, unknown in many European countries like Italy or France, while it does exist in Germany under the title of *Verfassungsbeschwerde*), arguing that it had broken the principle of the autonomy of the universities.

The *Tribunal Constitucional* expressed the view that the possibility of using the term 'Catalan' to indicate the local co-official language did not amount to a breach of the Autonomy Statute of Valencia, thus opening the door to using the term 'Catalan' in all kinds of documents, in addition to the term 'Valencian', which also continues to be valid.

Just after the Judgement, on 20 May 1997 was pronounced, the Legislative Commission on Culture and Education of the Chamber of Deputies adopted a resolution (*Proposición no de ley*) declaring the unity of the Catalan language, without diminishing the respect for the legal denomination in the Valencian language inside the respective *Comunidad Autónoma*. Notwithstanding this,

---

[20] Carlo Tagliavini, *Le origini delle lingue neolatine*, Bologna (1982) p. 434; Hans Ingo Radatz, '"Katalanisch" oder "Valancianisch"? Zum sprachlichen Sezessionismus im Land Valencia', *Zeitschrift für Katalanistik*, 6 (1993) pp. 97-120.

from the spring of 1997 onwards, by the force of the *Proposición no de ley* and the above-described Judgement of the *Tribunal Constitucional*, Valencian has no longer been considered as the only language allowed.

7. THE BALEARIC ISLANDS

Also the Balearic Islands are part of the *Països Catalans*, or the 'philological Catalonia', to use the undervaluing expression of the historian Salvador de Madariaga.[21] Though a 'fear' of the Catalan political influence is less strong than in Valencia, it is also present in this archipelago and is accompanied by significant efforts for an effective restoration of the Catalan language.[22]

On 17 July 1997 the *Tribunal Constitucional* delivered its Judgement (No. 134) concerning the division of competence between the Central State and the Autonomous Community of the Balearic Islands. The question raised was who has the competence to establish criteria for exemption from learning the Catalan language in the non-university educational system of the Balearic Islands: the State or the Autonomous Community? In this particular case the problem concerned the sons of members of the armed forces who are stationed for only few years in the territory of the *Islas Baleares*. The concrete matter was regulated by the 1988 Agreement between the Ministry of Education and Science and the Ministry of Defence, that is to say, two State institutions.[23]

As military and defence matters are typical issues of State competence, the State claimed its authority to regulate the issue of exemptions from educational programmes as far as the children of the military were concerned. However, at the same time education belongs to regional competence, at least this has been the case in the Balearic Islands since 1994, the fact being that the Islands were the last Spanish bilingual Autonomous Community to which matters of education were transferred from Central Government.

So the *Tribunal Constitucional* had to decide upon a typical legal conflict. The Tribunal confirmed the competence of the *Comunidad Autónoma*, at the same time recognising that the issues of defence belong to State competence. However, in the concrete case the Tribunal established that there was no direct relationship with the 'organisation and operation' (*organización y*

---

[21] Salvador de Madariaga, *Storia della Spagna*, Bologna (1957).

[22] It is a necessary reminder that the process of the normalisation of Catalan in the Balearic Islands faces an additional problem: the increasing presence of foreigners from Northern European countries permanently residing in the region who are, with few exceptions, not interested in learning Catalan. The possibility, foreseen in some provisions of the Maastricht Treaty, that European citizens may vote for the administrative bodies of the place in which they have chosen their residence, outside the State of which they are citizens, has created a massive presence of new residents in the Balearic Islands whose linguistic integration seems even more difficult than the integration of newcomers from less-developed countries, because the 'rich' new residents tend to create their 'ghettos' without the feeling of a necessity to integrate which the 'poor' new residents tend to have.

[23] The Agreement was approved by Royal Decree 295/1988, of 25 March 1988.

funcionamiento) of the armed forces, while there was a stronger implication on the part of education, which belongs to the Autonomous Community. There was no need for the *Tribunal Constitucional* to stress the principle of linguistic officiality, which horizontally covers many matters, it was not sufficient to refer to competence in the field of education, which in the Spanish *Estado autonómico* belongs to the Autonomous Communities.[24]

It may be an interesting reminder that after 18 years of Government by the *Partido Popular* the *Comunidad Autónoma* of the Balearic Islands has a new Government, appointed after the elections of 13 June 1999, which is the result of a coalition between the Socialist Party and other smaller leftist Parties, included *Unió Mallorquina*, the strongest regional Party in the Islands. The new President, Francesch Antich, has declared that a great effort will be made to strengthen the status of the Catalan language in the region, mainly in the educational field.[25]

8. ASTURIAS

This is the only Autonomous Community, together with Catalonia, which has a general linguistic law enacted during the last two years. In fact the *Ley de uso y promoción del bable/asturiano*, approved by the Asturian Parliament on 23 March 1998, is meant to generally regulate the local language.

The year of enactment and the overall approach are the only two common aspects of the Catalan and Asturian Laws. In fact the Catalan Law is very much more ambitious, or better said, it is aimed at regulating a totally different society, in which the *lengua propia* is the most important communication tool for the majority of the citizens living in Catalonia, and is used in all fields of everyday life, from family banter to doctoral thesis.

While Catalan is recognised as a language both in official documents since the Middle Ages and by linguists, the majority of specialists do not consider *bable* to be a separate language. Its close similarity with Castilian allows one to conclude that *bable* is merely a dialect of Castilian, and this fact is also reflected in the perception of most people in Asturias. It is difficult to say how many people speak it, because many Asturians use a kind of regional Castilian which is influenced by *bable*. Few people speak the 'pure' Asturian.

Thus the protection of the Asturian language has to be subsumed under the third paragraph of Article 3 of the Spanish Constitution, being a 'mere linguistic modality'. There is no doubt, on the other hand, that Catalan has to be referred to the provision of the second paragraph of Article 2, which speaks of 'other

---

[24] It might be interesting to note that, according to Balearic legislation, the exemption from studying the Catalan language can only be relied upon for a maximum of three years.

[25] 'El nou Govern balear convertirà el català en idioma vehicular a l'escola', *Avui*, 19 July 1999.

languages'.[26] The 1981 Autonomy Statute of the principality of Asturias has two articles on the protection of the *bable*, whose learning, notwithstanding this, has not been made compulsory.[27]

The Asturian Linguistic Law is a 'soft law', especially the part relating to education in *bable*. In fact Article 10 states that:

> 'within the exercise of its competences, the principality of Asturias will guarantee the teaching of *bable/asturiano* at all levels and grades, in any case respecting the voluntary nature of the learning'.

Article 4 concerning the use of Asturian in administration looks much more ambitious, providing for the validity of any oral or written act submitted by citizens to the Asturian administration in the local language. The first paragraph of Article 4 states that:

> 'every citizen is entitled to use *bable/asturiano* and to express themselves in it, in the written as well as in the oral form.'

These provisions concern only the civil servants of the Autonomous Community of Asturias; Article 8 foresees for the municipalities only the possibility of providing validity to the acts in which Asturian is used.

It seems correct at this stage to speak of semi-officiality of Asturian. Of course this Law, even if it may present a decisive step for implementing the local language in many fields of social life, has to be followed by a series of implementary steps, such as regional decrees or even regulations by municipalities which aim to give some official recognition to the local language. And at the end of the day it will be the will of the people living in Asturias which will determine the possibility of broadening the use of this mere *modalidad lingüística*.

9. ARAGÓN

The socio-linguistic situation of Aragón is similar to the Asturian one. In fact, the Castilian language is used by an almost absolute majority of around 95% of its population. The remaining 5% use both Aragonese, once the most important

---

[26] It needs to be emphasised that the expression 'linguistic modality' covers all the idioms spoken in Spain, from Castilian, the unique official language throughout the whole Spanish territory, to the dialects like Asturian, Aragonese and Aranese (a dialect of Occitan), through the regional languages, which are Catalan, Basque and Galician. In this sense the term 'mere linguistic modality' indicates the idioms which are not languages, and consequently whose status is not official (with the only exceptions being the Basque in Navarra and Catalan in the franja of Aragón, which have the low-level protection of the 'mere linguistic modalities' even if they are in fact languages).

[27] Xosé Luís Garcia Arias, 'La lengua asturiana en la Administracion', *Revista de llengua i dret*, 2 (1983) pp. 137-139.

language all over the region,[28] and Catalan. The speakers of Aragonese only can be found in some areas in the foothills of the Pyrenees, while Catalan is spoken in the *franja*, an area along the border with the Autonomous Community of Catalonia.

The Autonomy Statute of Aragón contains an article on the protection of the languages of Aragón, which foresees that a future law of the Aragonese Parliament will regulate the details of this protection. So far, Parliament has not fulfilled the duty of the mandate of the above-mentioned provision, but some recent events have revealed that this lack of interest toward protecting the minority languages inside the Autonomous Community might be changing.

In fact, during 1999 the regional Parliament approved two laws which include brief references to the languages used in Aragón, showing a certain sensitivity for the issue. As Law No. 1/1999 deals with the Aragonese cultural heritage and Law No. 3/1999 with the succession in the case of death, the need for a general linguistic law remains. This has been underlined in an advice given by the *Comisión Especial de Política Lingüística* of the Aragonese Parliament on 6 November 1997, which urged the regional Government to elaborate a language law before the end of 1997. As it has already been pointed out, this law has not yet been enacted, but there is a draft which has been prepared by a joint Committee of some members of the regional Government and some organizations united in the *Plataforma para la Defensa de las Lenguas Minoritarias de Aragón*.[29]

This draft looks very ambitious, maybe too much so taking into consideration the socio-linguistic reality of Aragón. In fact, the draft is very long, detailed (53 articles, compared to the 18 of the Asturian law), and ambitious, because its aim is to give Aragonese and Catalan official status in the 'territories where they are prevailing, together with Castilian'. The sections on education, public administration and judicial authorityconfirm this ambitious attitude. One peculiar feauture of this draft is the list of municipalities where Aragonese and Catalan are predominant.

The new Parliament elected on 13 June 1999 will have to decide on whether this initiative will be given an opportunity or whether it will be set aside.[30]

---

[28] An historical analysis of the administrative use of Aragonese has been made by Francho Nagore Laín, 'Notas sobre el uso administrativo del aragonés', *Revista de llengua i dret*, 2 (1983) pp. 97-110.

[29] Among those institutions should be mentioned the Colla Unibersitaria por l'aragonés, which also publishes an interesting and complete electronic magazine, *'O lupo'*.

[30] The new President of the regional Government, the *Chunta*, Marcelino Iglesias, emanates from the *franja*, and this factor raises hopes to the supporters of minority languages in Aragón. The new Aragón President is socialist and is supported by a coalition of his party and the regionalists of the *PAR*, the *Partido aragonés*, who formerly supported the Government led by the *Partido Popular*: 'El PAR pone fin a doce años de pacto con el PP y dará la presidencia de Aragón al PSOE', *La Vanguardia*, 22 July 1999.

10. TRENDS IN SPAIN: TOWARDS A FEDERAL SPAIN? THE ROLE OF THE REGIONAL LANGUAGES IN THIS PROCESS

In this article much importance has been given to the cases of the 'minor' languages of Spain, especially to the Asturian, because this revival of the 'mere linguistic modalities' is a sign of success of the regionalization of democratic Spain. Of course the success of the development of the *Estado autonómico* does not only consist of the promotion of regional languages and cultures, but the linguistic factor is one of the most important aspects which form the *hecho diferencial*, the distinctiveness of certain regions inside the Spanish institutional framework.

In particular, Catalan nationalism greatly stresses the linguistic question, so that some critics speak of 'linguistic nationalism'.[31] In fact the Catalan language is the most evident and beloved feature of the distinctiveness of Catalan society. The detailed legislation on the language, which practically covers all fields of life, is a clear sign of that.

Thus, the search for linguistic roots that many Autonomous Communities are conducting should not amaze one: in this way they are looking for their own *hecho diferencial*, and this may seem a bit artificial and forced but it is also a sign of the need for a local identity which accompanies, and is not contradictory to, globalization. A recent important symbolic event has been the adoption of a Catalan law which allows for the creation of national teams in various sports. Nearly half million people had signed the draft to promote the initiative to *Parlament*.[32]

If the Autonomous Communities in Spain will gain more competences, always within the framework of the unity of the State and carefully not to unbalance the European framework, then surely the regulation of the other languages of Spain will be considered an increasing fundamental feature.

---

[31] Here could be quoted a publication which is a sharp critic of all Catalan nationalism, not only the linguistic form: Arcadi Espada, *Contra Catalunya*, Barcelona (1996).
[32] 'Aprobada la ley para que Cataluña tenga selecciones deportivas propias', *El País*, 29 July 1999.

STEPS TOWARDS A MINORITY POLICY IN SWEDEN

Sia Spiliopoulou Åkermark*

1. INTRODUCTION: THE SWEDISH CONSTITUTION AND OTHER EXISTING LEGISLATION

The Swedish Constitution[1] provides that the Government shall promote opportunities for ethnic, linguistic and religious minorities to *preserve and develop* their own cultural and community life (Chapter 1, Article 2(4)). This provision was introduced in 1976 but is only of a declaratory nature, not considered to have legal force and can therefore not be invoked by individuals or groups before the courts.[2] The Constitution does not give any definition of what is considered to be a minority in Sweden. Nor has there existed any legal and official declaration of specific groups as being Sweden's minorities. In another provision of the Constitution, however, specific reference is made to the Sami's right to reindeer breeding in conjunction with the right to property (Chapter 2, Article 20(2), introduced in 1994).

In spite of those provisions Sweden has not developed a co-ordinated policy on minority issues. Sweden's policy towards its traditional minorities, on the one hand, and towards immigrant and refugee groups, on the other, has been described as 'paradoxical'.[3] Until recently Sweden pursued a positive policy towards immigrants and refugees but has been reluctant to recognise a distinct minority status to well-established minorities. This has been recognised even officially. The recent inquiries concerning a possible ratification of the two Council of Europe minority treaties (the European Charter for Regional or Minority Languages and the Framework Convention for the Protection of

---

* Senior lecturer at the Faculty of Law, Uppsala University, Sweden.

[1] The Swedish Constitution consists of four documents: The Instrument of Government (1974), the Act of Succession (1810), the Freedom of the Press Act (1949) and the Freedom of Expression Act (1994). The provisions concerning minorities and the protection of human rights are included in Chapters 1 and 2 of the Instrument of Government and when referring to the Swedish Constitution in this article it is the Instrument of Government which is envisaged.

[2] C. Jonsson, L. Lerwall, and S. Spiliopoulou Åkermark, 'Race Equality in Sweden' forthcoming in the *European Review of Public Law*.

[3] Lauri Hannikainen, 'The Status of Minorities, Indigenous Peoples and Immigrant and Refugee Groups in Four Nordic States', *Nordic Journal of International Law*, 65 (1996), pp. 1-71, at p. 29.

S. Trifunovska (Ed.), Minority Rights in Europe: European Minorities and Languages
© 2000, T.M.C. Asser Press, The Hague, The Netherlands

National Minorities) are entitled 'Steps towards a Minority Policy'[4] and it is here explicitly stated that 'for Sweden to be able to ratify the Framework Convention, it should lay the foundation for a coherent and comprehensive minority policy. Such a policy must be explicitly designed to protect the national minority groups in Sweden and [...] to take measures which promote their opportunities for preserving and developing their culture and identity'.[5]

The fact that Sweden has been lacking a coherent minority policy does not mean that there have not existed any rules concerning the protection of minority cultures and languages. The two pillars of this legislation have been:

1. the right to receive training in the so-called home language;[6] and
2. the establishment of a Sami Parliament in 1992.[7]

School children belonging to a minority or to an immigrant group have a right to receive training in their home language.[8] The basic requirements are: one or both parents have a language other than Swedish as their mother tongue and this language is used by the child in everyday life; the child has some elementary knowledge of this language; the child wishes to learn this language. This right is stronger for the children of Sami, Tornedal Finns and Roma (on the minorities of Sweden see below), since they can receive such training even if they do not use their traditional language in their everyday life and at home. Indirectly, this legislation has been a recognition of the Sami, Tornedal Finns and Roma as minorities whose culture should be protected. About 80 different languages are taught in Swedish schools. On average for all groups entitled to home language training, it is estimated that 54.9% of the entitled pupils participate in home language training. Kurdish pupils' participation has been considerably higher (79%) while Norwegian has been followed by only 7% of the pupils entitled to such language training.[9] During the late 1980s and in the 1990s there have been severe cuts in the school budget and the teaching of home languages has been curtailed. Since responsibility for compulsory education lies with communities it is, however, quite difficult to have a complete and accurate picture of trends in the whole country.

---

[4] Reports SOU 1997:192 and SOU 1997:193 (SOU is the abbreviation of 'Statens offentliga utredningar', i.e. the State's official inquiries which are part of parliamentary *travaux préparatoires*). The reports include summaries in English as well as summaries in minority languages (Sami, Finnish, Romani, and Yiddish).

[5] SOU 1997:193, p. 17.

[6] Education Act 1985:1100 and Compulsory School Ordinance No. 1194 of 1994.

[7] Sami Parliament Act 1992:1433.

[8] There is terminological discussion as to whether the term 'home language' (hemspråk) or 'mother tongue' (modersmål) are most appropriate. See the discussion in Leena Huss, 'En ny syn på 'hemspråk' och 'modersmål' i den svenska skolan?' *Multiethnica*, 23 (1998), pp. 1-4.

[9] Erling Wande, 'Tornedalen', in Frank Horn (Ed.), *Svenska språkets ställning i Finland och Finska språkets ställning i Sverige*, The Northern Institute for Environmental and Minority Law, *Juridica Laponica* 14 (1996) pp. 116-137, at p. 126.

According to the Education Act (1985:1100) Sami children have the possibility to go to public Sami schools during their first six years of basic education. Sami is then included in the teaching plan for each year. Such schools exist in a few cities of Northern Sweden. The Sami Parliament (see below) is the supervisor of those schools.

The Sami Parliament (*Sametinget*) consists of 31 representatives elected by the Sami, but at the same time it is also a public administrative authority. The Sami Parliament has merely an advisory status and its main responsibility is to promote the Sami culture. It allocates governmental subsidies and directs work related to the Sami language. Its weak position has been criticised and then especially whether its status as an elected body representing an indigenous group is compatible with its public administrative tasks.[10]

The present article discusses mainly the considerations and proposals of the two inquiries concerning a possible ratification of the European Charter for Regional or Minority Languages[11] and the Framework Convention for the Protection of National Minorities.[12] The inquiries have dominated the discourse in Sweden during 1998 and are expected to lead to a draft bill and ratification of the Council of Europe treaties in 1999. For the first time, Sweden has had a real discussion concerning its minorities. Already one can see that this discussion has considerably raised the awareness of the general public and the media is more inclined to produce and present articles, radio and TV programmes on the situation and concerns of minority groups.

2. RECENT PARLIAMENTARY INQUIRIES CONCERNING A POSSIBLE RATIFICATION OF THE EUROPEAN CHARTER FOR REGIONAL OR MINORITY LANGUAGES AND THE FRAMEWORK CONVENTION FOR THE PROTECTION OF NATIONAL MINORITIES

Starting off with a Nordic comparison one finds that Finland ratified the European Charter for Regional or Minority Languages in 1994 with respect to the Sami, Swedish, Romani and 'other territorial languages', while it ratified the Framework Convention in 1997 without specifying in a declaration the groups covered.[13] Norway ratified the Charter in 1993 with respect only to the Sami language, and it ratified the Framework Convention very recently making no declaration as to the covered minority groups (March 1999).[14] So Sweden has been the last among the three to take a stand. This has been of particular

---

[10] Hugh Beach, 'The New Swedish Sami Policy – A Dismal Failure', in Eyassu Gayim and Kristian Myntti, (Eds.), *Indigenous and Tribal Peoples' Rights – 1993 and After*, The Northern Institute for Environmental and Minority Law, *Juridica Laponica*, 11 (1995) (reprint 1997) pp. 109-129.

[11] ETS No. 148 (adopted in 1992, entered into force in 1998).

[12] ETS No. 157 (adopted in 1994, entered into force in 1998).

importance for the Sami who live in all three countries and who find themselves being in a weaker legal position in Sweden in comparison with its neighbours. This is of course not something new; as an example one may mention that the Sami Parliaments in Finland and Norway have a stronger position than the one in Sweden;[15] Finland and Norway have ratified the ILO Convention No. 169 concerning Indigenous and Tribal Peoples while Sweden has not yet done so.[16]

In 1995 a committee under the name 'Minority Language Committee' (hereinafter referred to as 'the Committee') was appointed by the Swedish Government and was given the task to examine the possible ratification by Sweden of the European Charter for Regional or Minority Languages. The Committee was composed of representatives of the political parties in Parliament as well as representatives of the main minority groups in question, i.e. the Sami, the Finns, the Tornedalers, and the Roma.[17] The Jews were, however, not allowed to have a representative with a voting right in the Committee; later on they were granted the possibility to attach an expert to the Committee. In 1996 the task of the Committee was expanded by the Government to cover also the Framework Convention for the Protection of National Minorities of the Council of Europe. One of the most important tasks of the Committee was also to estimate the cost of proposed measures and to provide suggestions concerning the financing of these measures, under the basic understanding, however, that the public sector budget should be left intact.[18] From the very beginning this has been an important limitation in the workings of the Committee, since it meant that the Committee could propose only a reallocation of existing resources.

The results of the work of the Committee, presented in two separate reports, were made public in December 1997. During 1998 the reports were widely

---

[13] Council of Europe, Chart of Signatures and Ratifications as of 24 June 1999 (see the site http://www.coe.fr/tablconv/). The travaux préparatoires of the recent reform of the Finnish Constitution indicate that with 'other languages' are meant primarily the Jews and the Tatars. See Spiliopoulou, Athanasia, 'De nordiska ländernas behandling av den europeiska språkstadgan', in *Minoritesspråk i Norden*, Mariehamn, Finland (1995) pp. 28-40, at p. 34.

[14] Council of Europe, Chart of Signatures and Ratifications, op. cit. n. 13.

[15] This is also the conclusion of a recent doctoral thesis by Kristian Myntti on the political representation of minorities and indigenous peoples in the Nordic countries. (Kristian Myntti, 'Minoriteters och urfolks politiska rättigheter', The Northern Institute for Environmental and Minority Law, *Juridica Laponica*, 18 (1998).

[16] For an excellent comparison of Nordic policies see the already mentioned article by Lauri Hannikainen, 'The Status of Minorities, Indigenous Peoples and Immigrant and Refugee Groups in Four Nordic States', *Nordic Journal of International Law*, 65 (1996) pp. 1-71. A recent development of relevance is the appointment by the Swedish government in December 1997 of a one-man inquiry (Kommittédirektiv, Terms of Reference, Dir. 103 of 1997) concerning a possible ratification by Sweden of ILO Convention No. 169 on Indigenous and Tribal Peoples in Independent Countries. The main issue of consideration is expected to be that of ownership and possession of the lands traditionally used by the Sami for reindeer herding, hunting and fishing. There are now several cases before Swedish courts concerning disputes between the Sami and landowners in Northern Sweden. This report is also expected in 1999.

[17] On Sweden's minority groups see below.

[18] Kommittédirektiv (Terms of Reference) Dir. 84 of 1995.

discussed and the Ministry of Agriculture[19] requested and received comments from a number of public and other actors, including the concerned minorities themselves, non-governmental organisations, judicial authorities, academic institutions and the Discrimination Ombudsman (DO). The Government will now take into account all those comments and present its final proposal concerning the ratification of the treaties some time during the course of 1999.

2.1 Minorities in Sweden

First of all, one should recall that the Council of Europe has used the term 'national' minorities usually as meaning that members of minorities have to be citizens of the State concerned. This is explicitly stated as a requirement in the European Charter for Regional or Minority Languages.[20] Immigrants and so-called new minorities have been excluded from the protection offered by Council of Europe instruments.[21]

The Swedish reports have followed a different view as regards the granting of citizenship. It is noted that international law developments concerning minorities do not support a view limiting minority protection only to nationals and that Sweden's membership in the European Union also entails a greater mobility over national borders.[22] For those reasons the reports have not included a citizenship criterion when examining which groups should be regarded as national minorities and which languages should be afforded the protection of the Language Charter. This has the advantage of avoiding making artificial distinctions for instance between old and new Finns, old and recently arrived Jews, or Roma which have lived in Sweden for centuries and those who have arrived recently, e.g. from the former Yugoslavia.

In view of the fact that the Framework Convention does not include any definition or criteria for what is a 'national minority' the Committee used the following criteria for examining which groups should be regarded as national minorities in Sweden:

– the group should be distinguished by a marked degree of cohesion and not have a dominant position in relation to the rest of the population;

---

[19] The Ministry of Agriculture has traditionally been responsible for Sami issues and has therefore been seen as the appropriate ministry to handle minority issues at large.

[20] Art. 1(a) of the Charter defines a regional or minority language as a language 'traditionally used within a given territory of a State by nationals of that State who form a group numerically smaller than the rest of the State's population' and which is 'different from the official language(s) of that State'. The definition explicitly excludes 'dialects of the official language(s)' as well as 'the languages of migrants'.

[21] Athanasia Spiliopoulou Åkermark, *Justifications of Minority Protection in International Law*, Iustus Publishing Company and Kluwer Law International, Uppsala/Dordrecht (1997), pp. 92-96, 229-238.

[22] SOU 1997:193, pp. 43-44.

- it should have a distinctive character in terms of religion, language, traditions and/or culture;
- it should have historical or long-standing ties with Sweden;
- self-identification: both the individual members and the group as a whole must be prepared to preserve its identity.[23]

On the basis of these criteria the Committee concluded that the Sami, Tornedalers, Swedish Finns, Roma and Jews are the national minorities of Sweden and should be covered by the protection of the Framework Convention when Sweden ratifies it.

According to the data collected by the Committee there are about 15,000-20,000 Sami living in the northernmost part of Sweden. Tornedalen is a northern region on the border between Sweden and Finland. The Tornedalers (or Tornedalen Finns) are those speaking a special variety[24] of Finnish (Tornedal Finnish, called by the Tornedalers themselves *meänkieli* which means 'our language'). The exact number of the members of this group is difficult to assess. Their own association (*Svenska Tornedalingars Riksförbund*) estimates that there are today 50,000-60,000 persons speaking *meänkieli* in Sweden.[25] The biggest group of non-Swedes in Sweden is formed by the Finns. According to statistical data from 1994 there are approximately 440,000 persons of Finnish origin living in Sweden. Most of them have lived in Sweden less than 40 years and are thus a relatively new group. About 250,000 of them are estimated to use Finnish as their main language.[26] There are 15,000-20,000 Roma in Sweden today and they speak several different varieties of the Romani language.[27] It is evident in the study that there are lacking data and substantive studies concerning the various Romani varieties and their speakers. As a result, the reports have chosen not to point out a few groups or a few varieties of Romani as being dominant among the Roma in Sweden. The protection of the treaties should thereby cover all those varieties.[28] Finally, there are in Sweden approximately 20,000-25,000 persons who consider themselves to be Jews.[29]

The Committee found that worthy of protection under the European Language Charter are the following languages: Sami (including all its varieties such as South Sami, Lule Sami and North Sami), Finnish (including standard Finnish and *meänkieli*) and Romani (including all its varieties).[30]

---

[23] Idem., pp. 16, 47-53.
[24] The Committee has avoided using the term 'dialect' and speaks instead of 'varieties' of the Finnish, Sami and Romani languages.
[25] SOU 1997:192, pp. 127 and 371.
[26] Idem., p. 128.
[27] Idem., p. 141, SOU 1997:193, p. 52 and the study *Romer i Sverige – tillsammans i förändring* (Roma in Sweden – Together towards change) Ds No. 49 of 1997, p. 18.
[28] SOU 1997:1992, p. 143.
[29] This estimation is supported by the Jewish Central Council. SOU 1997:193, p. 53.
[30] SOU 1997:1992, p. 15.

A surprising and worrying result of the two reports has been that in spite of the recognition of the Jews as a national minority,[31] there was a rejection by the Committee of the recognition of Yiddish as a minority language.[32] The Committee found that Yiddish had not been used in Sweden during 'a sufficiently long time' and to 'a sufficiently large extent'. The Committee noted that Yiddish is spoken in Sweden today by a relatively small group of people, most of whom are elderly.[33] There is indeed a contradiction in the views expressed in the two reports! The Jewish expert attached to the Committee, Ms Susanne Sznajderman-Rytz, criticised this contradiction in a separate opinion.[34] The exclusion of Yiddish as a minority language has also been criticised by many of those who have supplied the Government with comments. The Swedish Discrimination Ombudsman, for instance, pointed out that the explanatory report to the Charter does not require a minimum number of speakers in order for the language to be covered by the protection of the Charter, even though the number of speakers is important for defining the appropriate scope of the various protective and promotional measures to be adopted for each language. The Ombudsman therefore recommended that Yiddish be recognised as a non-territorial language in accordance with Article 1(c) of the Charter.[35]

2.2 Proposals for measures to be taken in order for Sweden to satisfy the requirements of the Charter and the Framework Convention

(a) The Language Charter

The Committee examined which of the provisions of the Charter have already been fulfilled by existing legislation and practice. The Committee found that Sweden satisfies several of the requirements of Part II (Objectives and Principles) with respect to Sami, Finnish and Romani while 33 paragraphs or sub-paragraphs of Part III (Measures to promote the use of minority languages in public life) are satisfied with respect to Sami and 29 with respect to Finnish. The Committee observed, however, that the existing Swedish provisions are selective. The requirements of the Charter can only be fulfilled, said the Committee, in the context of a general minority language policy under which measures are coordinated and directed under the common objective of providing protection and support for regional and minority languages; and there is no such policy in Sweden today.[36]

The Committee examined the various provisions only from the perspective of the main minority languages while their various varieties were very marginally

---

[31] SOU 1997:193, p. 53.
[32] SOU 1997:192, pp. 143-149.
[33] SOU 1997:192, p. 148.
[34] SOU 1997:192, pp. 295-301.
[35] DO, Ombudsmannen mot etnisk diskriminering, Remissvar 1998-07-15, Dnr 157-98.
[36] SOU 1997:192, p. 16.

studied. This is the case not only for varieties of Romani which may be difficult to examine due to the absence of a territorial link, but also with respect to Sami (with its varieties South Sami, Lule Sami and North Sami) and Finnish (including, as mentioned earlier, standard Finnish and *meänkieli*). There is a risk therefore that any measures taken will benefit mainly the most dominant of the varieties (namely North Sami and standard Finnish). Both representatives of the minority groups and others have reacted against such a solution and observed that all the varieties accepted by the Committee should be particularly mentioned in legislation. As an example, protective measures should also be taken for regions where South Sami is used.[37]

The Committee has recommended that Sweden ratifies the Language Charter. As regards concrete measures, the Committee proposes:

a. the official recognition of Sami, Finnish and Romani as historical minority languages. Such recognition should preferably be provided in the Swedish Constitution;
b. that the languages, culture and history of the minorities be made required knowledge in the curricula of all compulsory and secondary education;
c. that at least one folk high school for each of the languages concerned should receive government assistance on a long-term basis so as to be able to function as linguistic and cultural centres;
d. that one public authority be given the task of monitoring education in minority languages. Such regular supervision is lacking today. The Committee proposed that the National Agency for Education (*Skolverket*) be entrusted with this task;
e. that also the Finnish and Romani speakers be given the possibility to have their voice heard in decision making concerning their language. As mentioned above, the Sami Parliament, has this opportunity with regard to the Sami language. The Committee, however, has not made any concrete proposals as to how this will be done. It has only noted the need;
f. the promotion of Nordic co-operation with a view to promoting the regional or minority languages spoken also in other Nordic countries;
g. for certain specifically identified municipalities in Northern Sweden, the Committee proposes, with regard to Sami and Finnish, that individuals be granted the right to use their own language vis-à-vis administrative authorities and courts. The authorities and courts would then be obliged to use Sami or Finnish for oral (but not written) communication with the individuals who have chosen to communicate in one of these languages; and
e. the Committee recommends also to examine the need and feasibility of using Sami and Finnish in pre-schools and care services for the elderly.

---

[37] See the separate opinion of Johansson Henning (representative of the Tornedalers in the Committee), comments by the Discrimination Ombudsman (loc. cit.) and comments by an expert group appointed by Uppsala University (1998-06-02, Dnr 1263/98).

(b) The Framework Convention

The Committee has proposed that Sweden ratifies the Framework Convention and that the concrete proposals coincide in general with those made with regard to the Language Charter. The Committee thus proposes the formal recognition of the national minorities (Sami, Finns, Tornedalers, Roma and Jews). The proposals made under the Framework Convention are of particular importance for the Roma who are considered to fall only under Part II of the Language Charter, and even more so for the Jewish minority which has not been covered by the proposals under the Language Charter. The Committee proposes the establishment of arrangements allowing the national minorities a say prior to the taking, implementation and evaluation of decisions that concern them. The Romani language and culture should be given a privileged position in public TV and radio programmes in the same way as Sami, Finnish and *meänkieli*. The proposals concerning the introduction of knowledge about the minorities in the school curricula and about the importance of folk high schools are extended to cover also the Jewish minority.

3. CONCLUSION

The recent proposals made in the field of minorities set the basis for a comprehensive minority policy in Sweden. This is already a big step. Unfortunately, the proposals say very little about the monitoring of the rights proposed. Apart from the suggestion concerning the responsibility of the National Agency for Education as the monitoring authority in educational matters, nothing is said concerning the enforcement of the rights before courts or other authorities.

The position of the Discrimination Ombudsman is unique in matters concerning racial discrimination in working life. One possibility would be to entrust the Discrimination Ombudsman with the supervision of the Language Charter and Framework Convention. It is remarkable that the inquiries on minorities did not take into account the work done at the very same time concerning proposed amendments of the Act against Ethnic Discrimination.

Neither do the reports of the Committee address the issue of the international supervision of the Language Charter and Framework Convention. The treaties provide for the creation of expert committees which will monitor the implementation of the instruments.[38] Sweden should work actively for an efficient and active supervision.

There is, in other words, still a lot left to do as regards the establishment of a comprehensive Swedish minority policy. At the same time it is important to remind oneself that such a policy should not be developed at the expense of more recent migrant groups.

---

[38] See Art. 17 of the Language Charter and Art. 26 of the Framework Convention.

Part Two

International Activities and Documents

UNITED NATIONS

THE PROTECTION OF MINORITIES WITHIN THE UNITED NATIONS

Cecilia Thompson*

> '[...]. The promotion and protection of the rights of persons belonging to national or ethnic, religious and linguistic minorities contribute to the political and social stability of States in which they live'
>
> (Preamble of the United Nations Declaration on the Rights of Persons Belonging to National or Ethnic, Religious and Linguistic Minorities[1])

Almost all European States have one or more minority groups within their national territories, characterized by their own ethnic, linguistic or religious identity which differs from that of the majority population. Harmonious relations among minorities, and between minorities and majorities and respect for each group's identity is a great asset to the multi-ethnic and multi-cultural diversity of European society. Meeting the aspirations of national, ethnic, religious and linguistic groups and ensuring the rights of persons belonging to minorities allows for dignity and equality for all individuals, furthers participatory development, and thus contributes to the reduction of tensions among groups and individuals – key elements in guaranteeing stability and peace both within and outside Europe.

During the twentieth century, major developments regarding the protection of minorities have taken place at the international level. The provisions guaranteeing minority protection under the auspices of the League of Nations were both innovative and of great historical significance. They were largely a result of the territorial changes which had taken place in Europe after the First World War. In order to guarantee peace and stability, the 1919 Peace Conference decided to set up and place under the guarantee of the League of Nations, a system of protection of minorities in the form of five Minorities Treaties concluded between the Allied and Associated Powers on the one hand, and the newly established or enlarged States such as Poland, Czechoslovakia,

---

* Human Rights Officer, Office of the High Commissioner for Human Rights, or Secretary of the Working Group on Minorities.
1 Adopted by the General Assembly on 18 December 1992 (GA Resolution 47/135).

S. Trifunovska (Ed.), Minority Rights in Europe: European Minorities and Languages
© 2000, T.M.C. Asser Press, The Hague, The Netherlands

Romania and Greece, on the other. Concurrently and with a view to ensuring a certain degree of reciprocity, similar obligations were imposed by the peace treaties on four of the vanquished States, namely, Austria, Bulgaria, Hungary and Turkey. Furthermore, this system of protection of minorities was reflected in the Treaties of Versailles (1919), Saint-Germain-en-Laye (1919), Neuilly (1919) and Trianon (1920). The provisions of these treaties focussed on ensuring that individuals belonging to minorities be placed on an equal footing with the other nationals of the State and that the characteristics of the minorities and their traditions be preserved. This regime for the international protection of minorities established after the First World War represented not only a significant development in the area of minority protection but more importantly, the establishment of the League of Nations represented the essential condition of the development of an international supervisory machinery.

After the Second World War, there seemed to have been general agreement that the system for minority protection established under the auspices of the League of Nations had too many gaps and that the political basis no longer existed. Whereas the functioning of the League of Nations had been linked to the need for a balance in Europe and to the resolution of the territorial problems arising from the Peace Treaties, the United Nations was in no way involved in the settlement of European territorial questions.

Until recently, the United Nations did not devote a high level of attention to the protection of minorities, as other rights have appeared more pressing. In recent years, however, there has been a sharpening of interest in issues affecting minorities as ethnic, racial and religious tensions have escalated, threatening the economic, social and political fabric of States, as well as their territorial integrity.

In 1947, the system for the protection of minorities, as groups, established under the League of Nations, which was considered by the United Nations to have outlived its political expediency was replaced by the Charter of the United Nations and the Universal Declaration of Human Rights. Although no specific reference is made to the protection of minorities, these instruments were based on the protection of individual human rights and freedoms and the principles of non-discrimination and equality. The view was that if the non-discrimination provisions were effectively implemented, special provisions for the rights of minorities would not be necessary. It was very soon evident, however, that further measures were needed in order to better protect persons belonging to minorities from discrimination, and to promote their identity. To this end, special rights for minorities were elaborated and measures adopted to supplement the non-discrimination provisions in international human rights instruments.

This chapter provides an overview of the non-discrimination clauses and the special rights contained in international human rights instruments and describes the mechanisms that have been established to monitor compliance with minority rights standards. It provides an analysis of the complaints procedures available in cases when violations have occurred, the early warning mechanisms which have been established to prevent conflict, and the role of non-governmental organizations in protecting and promoting the rights of persons belonging to minorities. Finally, it points to some of the minority issues which may prove particularly pertinent in the years to come.

1. PROVISIONS FOR THE PROMOTION AND PROTECTION OF THE RIGHTS OF PERSONS BELONGING TO MINORITIES

1.1 Prohibition of discrimination

Discrimination which affects minorities in a negative manner – politically, socially, culturally or economically – persists and is a major source of tension in many parts of the world.

Discrimination has been prohibited in a number of international instruments that deal with most, if not all, situations in which minority groups and their individual members may be denied equality of treatment. Discrimination is prohibited on the grounds of, *inter alia*, race, language, religion, national or social origin, and birth or other status. Important safeguards from which individual members of minorities stand to benefit include recognition as a person before the law, equality before the courts, equality before the law, and equal protection of the law, in addition to the important rights of freedom of religion, expression and association.

Non-discrimination provisions are contained in the UN Charter of 1945 (Articles 1 and 55), the Universal Declaration of Human Rights of 1948 (Article 2) and the 1966 International Covenant on Civil and Political Rights (Article 26) and on Economic, Social and Cultural Rights (Article 2). Such provisions also feature in a number of specialized international instruments, including: ILO Convention concerning Discrimination in Respect of Employment and Occupation No. 111 of 1958 (Article 1); International Convention on the Elimination of All Forms of Racial Discrimination of 1965 (Article 1); UNESCO Convention against Discrimination in Education of 1960 (Article 1); UNESCO Declaration on Race and Racial Prejudice of 1978 (Articles 1, 2 and 3); Declaration on the Elimination of All Forms of Intolerance and of Discrimination based on Religion or Belief of 1981 (Article 2); and the Convention on the Rights of the Child of 1989 (Article 2).

Non-discrimination clauses are also included in all of the basic regional human rights documents, such as the European Convention for the Protection of Human Rights and Fundamental Freedoms, the European Social Charter, and the Framework Convention on National Minorities (Council of Europe), the Document of the Copenhagen Meeting of the Conference on the Human Dimension of the CSCE (Conference (now Organization) for Security and Cooperation in Europe); the American Convention on Human Rights (Organization of

American States); and the African Charter on Human and Peoples' Rights (Organization of African Unity).

In order to better ensure the implementation of the non-discrimination provisions, and to give meaning to their content and scope, their interpretation has been elaborated by what is known as general comments or recommendations. General comments are adopted by the various committees established under the terms of the instruments themselves and entrusted to oversee their implementation. The purpose of these comments is, *inter alia*, to clarify the terminology used and to provide a clearer understanding of the content and scope of these rights. The two bodies which have most actively contributed to interpreting human rights are the Committee on Human Rights (responsible for overseeing the Covenant on Civil and Political Rights) as well as the Committee on the Elimination of Racial Discrimination (responsible for overseeing the Convention on the Elimination of All Forms of Racial Discrimination).

Discrimination has been interpreted to:

> 'imply any distinction, exclusion, restriction or preference which is based on any ground such as race, colour, [...] language, religion, [...] national or social origin, [...] birth or other status, and which has the purpose or effect of nullifying or impairing the recognition, enjoyment or exercise by all persons, on an equal footing, of all rights and freedoms'.[2]

The prevention of discrimination has been defined as the

> 'prevention of any action which denies to individuals or groups of people equality of treatment which they may wish'.[3]

Non-discrimination is understood to afford equal opportunities for a disadvantaged group as compared with the rights enjoyed by the majority population and non-discrimination applies to all individuals living within the jurisdiction of the State. It prohibits discrimination in any field, including in law or in fact, in the civil, cultural, economic, political and social sectors, which is subject to regulation and protection by State authorities.

In its General Comment on Article 18 of the Covenant on Civil and Political Rights on freedom of thought, conscience and religion, the Human Rights Committee mentioned that discrimination in the context of freedom of religion includes

> 'any tendency to discriminate against any religion or belief for any reasons, including the fact that they are newly established or represent religious minorities that may be the subject of hostilities by a predominant religious community'.

---

[2] General Comment 18 of the Human Rights Committee on non-discrimination under the Covenant on Civil and Political Rights, UN Doc. HRI/GEN/1/Rev.2 of 29 March 1996.

[3] UN Doc. E/CN.4/52, Section V.

Although at paragraph 3 of Article 18, limitations are permitted on the right to freedom to exercise one's religion or belief if such limitations are 'prescribed by law and are necessary to protect public safety, order, health or morals or the fundamental rights and freedoms of others', the comment emphasizes that this provision should be interpreted strictly. Protection under Article 18 is afforded to believers as well as non-believers and the parents or legal guardians have the freedom to choose the religious and moral education of their children in conformity with their own convictions. Stress is laid on the prohibition of discrimination against religious minorities, including non-believers, whether in the form of economic, or political privileges for followers of the majority religion, and the imposition of restrictions on the practice of non-dominant faiths.

Furthermore, the International Committee on the Elimination of Racial Discrimination has, in its General Recommendation No. XI on non-citizens as referred to at Article 1, paragraph 2 of the International Convention on the Elimination of All Forms of Racial Discrimination, stated that a State is not allowed to discriminate against a particular nationality of non-citizens living with in the State and under no circumstances to deny non-citizens the rights and freedoms provided for in other international human rights instruments.

1.2 Special rights for minorities

Special rights are not privileges but they are granted to make it possible for minorities to preserve their identity, characteristics and traditions. Special rights are just as important in achieving equality of treatment as non-discrimination. Only when minorities are able to use their own languages, benefit from services they have themselves organized, as well as take part in the political and economic life of States can they begin to achieve the status which majorities take for granted. Differences in the treatment of such groups, or individuals belonging to them, is justified if it is exercised to promote effective equality and the welfare of the community as a whole.[4] This form of affirmative action may have to be sustained over a prolonged period in order to enable minority groups to benefit from society on an equal footing with the majority.

Several international human rights instruments refer to national, ethnic, racial or religious groups, and some include special rights for persons belonging to minorities. These include: the Convention on the Prevention and Punishment of the Crime of Genocide (Article II), the Convention on the Elimination of All Forms of Racial Discrimination (Articles 2 and 4), the International Covenant on Economic, Social and Cultural Rights (Article 13), the International Covenant on Civil and Political Rights (Article 27), the Convention on the Rights of the Child (Article 30), the UNESCO Convention against Discrimination in Education (Article 5), the UN Declaration on the Rights of Persons Belonging to

---

[4] UN Doc. E/CN.4/52, Section V.

National or Ethnic, Religious and Linguistic Minorities, and the UNESCO Declaration on Race and Racial Prejudice (Article 5).

Regional instruments which contain special rights for minorities include the Framework Convention for the Protection of National Minorities (Council of Europe), the European Charter for Regional or Minority Languages (Council of Europe), and the Document of the Copenhagen Meeting of the Conference on the Human Dimension of the OSCE (Organization for Security and Cooperation in Europe).

a.   Article 27 of the International Covenant on Civil and Political Rights

The most widely-accepted legally-binding provision on minorities is Article 27 of the International Covenant on Civil and Political Rights which states:

> 'In those States in which ethnic, religious or linguistic minorities exist, persons belonging to such minorities shall not be denied the right, in community with the other members of their group, to enjoy their own culture, to profess and practise their own religion, or to use their own language.'

Article 27 of the Covenant grants persons belonging to minorities the right to national, ethnic, religious or linguistic identity, or a combination thereof, and to preserve the characteristics which they wish to maintain and develop. Persons belonging to minorities are to enjoy the rights 'in community with other members of the group', thereby affording the protection of their identity, including their culture, language and religion. In accordance with its General Comment under Article 27 (No. 23), the Committee stated that protection is afforded to all persons belonging to ethnic, religious and linguistic minorities within the jurisdiction of the State and cannot be limited only to citizens. Although Article 27 refers to the rights of minorities in those States in which they exist, its applicability is not subject to official recognition of a minority by a State, the recognition thereof is thus to be established on the basis of objective criteria. Article 27 does not call for special measures to be adopted by States, but States that have ratified the Covenant are obliged to ensure that all individuals under their jurisdiction enjoy their rights. This may require specific action to correct inequalities to which minorities are subjected.[5]

b.   Declaration on the Rights of Persons Belonging to National or Ethnic, Religious and Linguistic Minorities

The only United Nations instrument which addresses the special rights of minorities in a separate United Nations document is the Declaration on the Rights of Persons Belonging to National or Ethnic, Religious and Linguistic

---

[5]   General Comment of the Human Rights Committee 18 (37). For the full text see UN Doc. HRI/GEN/1 of 4 September 1992.

Minorities.[6] The text of the Declaration, while ensuring a balance between the rights of persons belonging to minorities to maintain and develop their own identity and characteristics, and the corresponding obligations of States, ultimately safeguards the territorial integrity and political independence of the Nation as a whole. The principles contained in the Declaration apply to persons belonging to minorities in addition to the universally recognized human rights guaranteed in other international instruments.[7]

The Declaration grants to persons belonging to minorities:

- protection, by States, of their existence and their national or ethnic, cultural, religious and linguistic identity (Article 1);
- the right to enjoy their own culture, to profess and practise their own religion and to use their own language in private and in public (Article 2 paragraph 1);
- the right to participate in cultural, religious, social, economic and public life (Article 2 paragraph 2);
- the right to participate in decisions which affect them on the national and regional levels (Article 2 paragraph 3);
- the right to establish and maintain their own associations (Article 2 paragraph 4);
- the right to establish and maintain peaceful contacts with other members of their group and with persons belonging to other minorities, both within their own country and across state borders (Article 2 paragraph 5); and
- the freedom to exercise their rights, individually as well as in community with other members of their group, without discrimination (Article 3).

States are to protect and promote the rights of persons belonging to minorities by taking measures:

- to create favourable conditions to enable them to express their characteristics and to develop their culture, language, religion, traditions and customs (Article 4 paragraph 2);
- to allow them adequate opportunities to learn their mother tongue or to have instruction in their mother tongue (Article 4 paragraph 3);
- to encourage knowledge of the history, traditions, language and culture of minorities existing within their territory and ensure that members of such minorities have adequate opportunities to gain knowledge of the society as a whole (Article 4 paragraph 4);
- to allow their participation in economic progress and development (Article 4 paragraph 5);
- to consider legitimate interests of minorities in developing national policies and programmes, as well as in planning and implementing programmes of cooperation and assistance (Article 5);

---

[6] Adopted by the General Assembly on 18 December 1992 (GA Res. 47/135).
[7] See Art. 8 of the Declaration.

- to cooperate with other States on questions relating to minorities, including the exchange of information and experiences, in order to promote mutual understanding and confidence (Article 6);
- to promote respect for the rights set forth in the Declaration (Article 7);
- to fulfil the obligations and commitments States have assumed under international treaties and agreements to which they are parties (Article 8 paragraph 1); and
- finally, the specialized agencies and other organizations of the United Nations system are encouraged to contribute to the realization of the rights set forth in the Declaration (Article 9).[8]

The General Assembly, on the occasion of the adoption of the Declaration, called on the international community to direct its attention to making the standards effective through international and domestic mechanisms. This included, in particular, the dissemination of information on the Declaration and the promotion of understanding thereof, appropriate mechanisms for its effective promotion and the consideration of the Declaration within the mandates of the relevant organs and bodies of the United Nations.[9]

2. THE IMPLEMENTATION OF SPECIAL RIGHTS AND THE PROMOTION OF FURTHER MEASURES FOR THE PROTECTION OF MINORITIES

2.1 Reporting procedure

In order to implement the rights of persons belonging to minorities which are contained in the International Conventions, committees have been established to monitor the progress made by States parties, in fulfilling their obligations, in particular in bringing national laws as well as administrative and legal practice into line with their provisions. The Committees which are of particular relevance to the implementation of minority rights are the Committee on Human Rights (which oversees implementation of the International Covenant on Civil and Political Rights); the Committee on Economic, Social and Cultural Rights (International Covenant on Economic, Social and Cultural Rights); the Committee on the Elimination of Racial Discrimination (Convention on the Elimination of All

---

[8] For an interpretation of the Declaration, see in particular: Patrick Thornberry, in *The UN Minority Rights Declaration*, edited by Alan Phillips and Allan Rosas, Abo Academe University Institute, 1993, pp. 11-71; Joseph Yacoub, in *Les Minorités, quelle protection?*, Paris, 1995, pp. 335-368; and Isse Omanga Bokatola 'La Déclaration des Nations Unies sur les droits des personnes appartenant à des minorités nationales ou ethniques, religieuses et linguistiques', *Revue Générale de Droit International Public* (1993) pp. 745-766.

[9] See GA Resolution 47/135 paras. 2-6.

Forms of Racial Discrimination); and the Committee on the Rights of the Child (Convention on the Rights of the Child).

States parties undertake to submit periodic reports to the respective Committees which outline the legislative, judicial, policy and other measures which they have taken to ensure the enjoyment of, *inter alia*, the minority-specific rights contained in the relevant instruments. When a State report comes before the respective Committee for examination, a representative of the country concerned may introduce it, answer questions from the expert members of the Committee, and comment on the observations they make.

The Committees provide States with a detailed set of reporting guidelines specifying the type of information required for the Committees to monitor a State's compliance with its obligations.[10] For reporting under Article 27 of the International Covenant on Civil and Political Rights for example, information contained in the report must be provided about minorities in a State, their respective numbers as compared to the majority, and the concrete measures adopted by the reporting State to preserve minorities' ethnic, religious, cultural and linguistic identity, as well as other measures to provide minorities with equal economic and political opportunities. Particular reference should be made to their representation in central and local government bodies.[11]

On the basis of the information they receive, the Committees can insist on a genuine dialogue with the reporting State. Once consideration of a State report has been concluded, the Committees issue 'concluding observations' which may state that violations of the rights of minorities have taken place, urge States parties to desist from any further infringements of the rights in question, or call on the respective Governments to adopt measures to improve the situation.

With reference to European countries, the respective committee have over the past year welcomed the constitutional and legal protection of minorities, the existence of boards or councils to advance the interests of minorities, the increasing participation of minorities in political, administrative and cultural institutions, as well as the conclusion of bilateral treaties between kin States providing for the protection of their respective minority groups. With regard to the respect of specific rights, the various committees welcomed measures adopted by European States such as the provision of State subsidies for the construction of places of worship, guarantees of national cultural autonomy, the promotion of multi-cultural and inter-cultural education, proportional participation of minorities in the army and the police, the provision of a fixed number of seats in Parliament, and the introduction of bills aimed at eliminating discrimination based on ethnic origin. The relevant Committees also expressed their concern with regard to continuing discrimination against certain minority groups such as the Roma, the lack of trained teachers of minority languages in

---

[10] For further details see 'Manual on Human Rights Reporting', United Nations Centre for Human Rights and United Nations Institute for Training and Research, United Nations, New York 1991.

[11] Ibid, p. 119.

public establishments, the under-representation of ethnic minorities in education, and the difficulties faced by minorities to acquire citizenship.

All the Committees make specific recommendations to States in their concluding observations on how they can better implement the rights contained in the international instruments they have subscribed to. The advice given by the Committees usually pertain to the necessary measures to be adopted by States to redress discrimination and to ensure the respect of the rights of persons belonging to minorities. Although these are not legally binding, States more or less respect the advice of the Committees, as they can in this way gain credibility with the international community by demonstrating good will in recognizing problems involving minorities and in redressing situations which have been brought to the attention of the Committees.

2.2 High Commissioner for Human Rights

The High Commissioner for Human Rights, the post of whom was established in 1993 by the General Assembly, has been entrusted with the task, among others, to promote and protect the rights of persons belonging to minorities.[12] In particular, the High Commissioner has been entrusted, by the General Assembly, to promote the implementation of the principles contained in the Declaration on the rights of persons belonging to minorities and to continue to engage in a dialogue with Governments concerned for that purpose.[13] To this end, a comprehensive three-pronged programme, has been elaborated to: promote and implement the principles contained in the Declaration on the rights of persons belonging to minorities; cooperate with other organs and bodies of the United Nations, including the international human rights community, and programmes of technical assistance and advisory services; and engage in dialogue with Governments and other parties concerned with minority issues. These three activities are interrelated and have preventive functions as their common element.

During visits to countries and in ongoing dialogue with Governments, the High Commissioner encourages the implementation of the principles contained in the Declaration and discusses problems and possible solutions concerning situations involving minorities. The High Commissioner further contributes to strengthening minority protection by providing guidance in respect of, and support to, the activities of the other bodies and organs of the United Nations. This includes, among others, the follow-up of minority-related resolutions of legislative bodies and the recommendations of the treaty bodies, of the Working Group on Minorities, and of the Special Rapporteurs.

---

[12] See General Assembly Resolution 48/141.
[13] See General Assembly Resolution 49/192.

2.3 Working Group on Minorities

In 1995, a five member Working Group on Minorities of the Sub-Commission for the Prevention of Discrimination and the Protection of Minorities was established, initially for a three-year period, in order to promote the rights as set out in the Declaration on persons belonging to minorities, and in particular to:

- review the promotion and practical realization of the Declaration;
- examine possible solutions to problems involving minorities, including the promotion of mutual understanding between and among minorities and Governments; and
- recommend further measures, as appropriate, for the promotion and protection of the rights of persons belonging to national or ethnic, religious and linguistic minorities.[14]

At the last session of the Economic and Social Council in 1998, a decision was taken to grant the Working Group a perennial mandate to hold one session of five working days annually.[15]

The Working Group is a forum for dialogue which serves two interdependent purposes:

Firstly, the Working Group acts as a process by which Governments, minorities and scholars come together to discuss issues of concern and seek solutions to problems identified. This leads to greater awareness about the differing perspectives on minority issues and consequently also increased understanding and mutual tolerance among minorities and between minorities and Governments. Secondly, it acts as a mechanism for arriving at peaceful and constructive solutions to problems involving minorities, and for the elucidation and elaboration of the principles contained in the Declaration.

During its sessions, the Working Group has focussed on the content, scope and application of the principles contained in the Declaration; the different measures which have been adopted to enable persons belonging to minorities to enjoy their own culture, profess and practise their own religion and use their own language; the role of multicultural and intercultural education in fostering tolerance and understanding between various groups in society; the effective participation of minorities in public life and decision-making processes; the contribution of regional and other mechanisms, as well as national institutions and non-governmental organizations to minority protection; conciliation and

---

[14] See Commission on Human Rights Resolution 1995/24.
[15] Decision 1998/2 ECOSOC 46 of 30 July 1998.

early-warning mechanisms to prevent the escalation of tensions and conflicts; and the definition of a minority.[16]

The Working Group is rapidly becoming the major focal point for the activities of the United Nations in the field of minority protection. It has recommended, *inter alia*, that: a database be established on good practices adopted in protecting the rights of minorities; information on national, regional and international recourse mechanisms be collected; the treaty bodies and Special Rapporteurs give due regard to minority issues in carrying out their mandates; the High Commissioner for Human Rights develop and implement procedures for conflict prevention; inter-agency cooperation on minorities be further promoted; and, regular seminars on subjects of particular concern to minorities. Three such seminars have been held to date before the sessions of the Working Group, the subjects of which have centred on intercultural and multicultural education, the role of the media in protecting minorities and the effective participation of minorities in public life and in decisions affecting them.

Although the Working Group has essentially focussed on thematic issues within the framework of the UN Declaration on the Rights of Persons belonging to National or Ethnic, Religious and Linguistic Minorities, information on specific situations and recommendations as to how minority problems can be addressed, is welcomed. This allows the members of the Working Group to arrive at possible solutions to minority issues and propose further measures for their protection at national, regional and international levels. Two major innovative decisions were taken by the Working Group at its 1998 session – the first refers to the possibility of the Working Group to undertake country visits in order to collect additional information on the status of minorities and the protection of their rights, and the second pertains to the transmission of information submitted by minority groups during the session, to respective Governments for their comments.

Participation in the sessions of the Working Group is open to Government representatives, inter-governmental organizations, non-governmental organizations involved in minority protection irrespective of whether they have consultative status with the Economic and Social Council (ECOSOC), and scholars versed in the subject.

3. INVESTIGATIONS, TECHNICAL ASSISTANCE AND ADVISORY SERVICES

The independent experts appointed by the United Nations to investigate and report on the human rights situation in specific countries, as well as thematic

---

[16] See the reports of the Working Group at its First, Second, Third and Fourth Sessions contained in: Docs. E/CN.4/Sub.2/1996/2; E/CN.4/Sub.2/1996/28; E/CN.4/Sub.2/1997/18; and E/CN.4/Sub.2/1998/18.

issues, often address concerns pertaining to the rights of persons belonging to minorities or are confronted with violations of minority rights. The conclusions and recommendations of these special rapporteurs are published and debated, bringing the issues they address to international attention and serving either as guidance for the Governments concerned or as a means of pressure to ease or eliminate the problems they have discovered. Of particular relevance are the reports on countries where minority rights are not respected, which often results in ethnic and religious tensions and inter-communal violence, and on thematic issues such as religious intolerance and racial discrimination.[17]

Over the past year, the Special Rapporteur on religious intolerance for example has reported on a visit to Germany undertaken in February 1997.[18] In his report, special attention was devoted to the study of legislation relating to tolerance and non-discrimination in the field of religion or belief, its implementation and the policy in force. The Special Rapporteur made specific reference to the situation of the Jewish and Muslim minorities in Germany. The Special Rapporteur on extrajudicial, summary or arbitrary executions paid special attention to violations of the right to life of, *inter alia*, persons belonging to ethnic minorities, and to this end, sent urgent appeals on behalf of persons belonging to minorities to their respective Governments. In his concluding remarks, the Special Rapporteur noted that one of the most prevalent targets of extrajudicial, summary or arbitrary executions has continued to be persons preventing and combating racial, ethnic or religious discrimination, and persons belonging to minorities.[19]

The Special Rapporteur on the situation of human rights in Bosnia and Herzegovina, the Republic of Croatia and the Federal Republic of Yugoslavia has continued to draw the attention of the international community to the situation of minorities in these countries. In Croatia, the Special Rapporteur noted that the failure to resolve the question of property rights has been a major obstacle to the return of Serb refugees who continue to face serious difficulties regarding access to properties given over to displaced and immigrant Croats. With reference to the situation in the Federal Republic of Yugoslavia, special attention has been paid to the situation of human rights in Kosovo, especially in regard to the demand of students of Albanian origin to return to school and university premises. With regard to the situation in Sandzak, the Special Rapporteur continued to receive information indicating discrimination against the Muslim community, especially in employment and education and that laws were selectively applied depending on a person's ethnicity.[20]

---

[17] Such reports are submitted to the General Assembly, the Commission on Human Rights and the Sub-Commission on the Prevention of Discrimination and the Protection of Minorities. They are available from the Document Section of the United Nations.
[18] UN Doc. E/CN.4/1998/6/Add.2.
[19] UN Doc. E/CN.4/1998/68.
[20] UN Doc. E/CN.4/1998/63.

The advisory services and technical assistance offered by the Office of the High Commissioner is a comprehensive programme for building national and regional human rights infrastructures funded through the Voluntary Fund for Advisory Services and Technical Assistance in the Field of Human Rights. Assistance is provided only in agreement with the Governments concerned, on the basis of requests received from them. In the area of minority protection, Governments may request qualified expertise on minority issues, including the prevention of disputes, to assist in existing or potential situations involving minorities. Assistance has been provided in drafting laws to protect and promote the identity and characteristics of minorities, the organization of training seminars on minority rights and workshops on peaceful conflict resolution techniques, the strengthening of confidence-building measures for different groups in society, and the provision of fellowships and scholarships. Further assistance is being provided in the field of constitutional and electoral assistance, human rights education and curriculum development, police training, the establishment and strengthening of national institutions, the administration of justice, the training of the military, and support to non-governmental organizations.[21]

States still remain reluctant to request technical assistance and qualified expertise in the area of minority protection. Some technical cooperation projects have however addressed minority-related issues. A number of relevant projects have been undertaken over the past year. One example was the organization of a major training course on human rights monitoring and law enforcement for International Police Task Force members of the United Nations Mission in Bosnia and Herzegovina and for civilian police monitors of the United Nations Transitional Authority in Eastern Slavonia. Another is a two-year project, in cooperation with UNESCO, to implement the Plan of Action for the United Nations Decade for Human Rights Education 1995-2004, and a further example pertains to the preparation of a human rights handbook on constitutions, parliament and conflict resolution with a view to enhancing training efforts carried out under the technical cooperation programme.

4. INTER-AGENCY COOPERATION

Inter-agency cooperation on minorities has been initiated and developed in order to better coordinate the responses of the agencies to issues involving minorities. Three consultations have been held to date, bringing together representatives of approximately ten agencies and inter-governmental organizations which address in one way or another the promotion and protection of the rights of persons belonging to minorities. Agencies which have been most extensively involved in these consultations include the World Health Organization (WHO), the United

---

[21] For further details see Fact Sheet No. 3 (Rev.1) on advisory services and technical cooperation in the field of human rights.

Nations Educational, Scientific and Cultural Organization (UNESCO), the International Labour Organization (ILO), the United Nations High Commissioner for Refugees (UNHCR), Habitat, and United Nations Development Programme (UNDP).

The consultations provide an opportunity for agencies to present their activities in various areas such as non-discrimination in education, the promotion and protection of the cultural rights of minorities, training programmes of in-house staff and minorities at the local level, the issue of citizenship and nationality and the use of minority-related databases. The discussions have focussed on possible cooperation on: joint input to the Commission on Human Rights, the Sub-Commission and its Working Group on Minorities, the provision of relevant information to be included on a web-site page, joint minority-related technical cooperation projects, submission of information on system-wide complaints procedures, input into the treaty bodies, the dissemination of the recommendations and resolutions of supervisory bodies, and the provision of training on minority-related human rights instruments at regional and national levels and generally the exchange of information.

This inter-agency cooperation has now been integrated into the regular sessions of the Working Group on Minorities, with part of the session devoted to a presentation by the agencies of the activities they have undertaken in the past year, followed by a discussion between members and participants of the working group and the agencies on issues of interest and of concern.

5. STUDIES

The protection of minorities has been the subject of a number of studies commissioned by the United Nations since the 1960's which have been undertaken principally by the Sub-Commission on the Prevention of Discrimination and Protection of Minorities. These studies have concerned: the legal validity of undertakings relating to the protection of minorities placed under the guarantee of the League of Nations,[22] the definition and classification of minorities,[23] the problem of the juridical treatment of minorities,[24] ways and means to facilitate the resolution of situations involving racial, national, religious and linguistic minorities.[25]

---

[22] UN Doc. E/CN.4/367 of 7 April 1950.
[23] Lake Success, New York, 1950, by the Secretary-General; 'Proposals concerning a definition of the term minority', by Mr. Jules Deschênes E/CN.4/Sub.2/1985/31 of 14 May 1985; 'Definition of minorities' by Mr. Stanislav Chernichenko, E/CN.4/Sub.2/AC.5/1996/WP.1 and E/CN.4/Sub.2/AC.5/1997/WP.1; 'Classification of minorities and differentiation in minority rights', by Mr. Asbjørn Eide E/CN.4/Sub.2/AC.5/1996/WP.2.
[24] 'Rights of persons belonging to ethnic, religious and linguistic minorities', by Francesco Capotorti, (United Nations Study Series No. 5).
[25] 'Possible ways and means to facilitate the peaceful and constructive solution of problems involving racial minorities', by Mr. Asbjørn Eide (E/CN.4/Sub.2/1993/34 and Add 1-4).

Since the adoption of the Declaration on the rights of persons belonging to minorities, the Secretary-General has prepared a number of reports for the General Assembly and the Commission on Human Rights, describing the measures undertaken by States, international organizations, organs and bodies of the United Nations, specialized agencies, and non-governmental organizations to give effect to the principles contained in the Declaration, and, more generally, in protecting and promoting the rights of persons belonging to minorities.

Defining a minority

What is a minority? Who defines a minority? Who are the beneficiaries of minority rights? These questions and the possible responses thereto have been the subject of a number of studies by experts of the Sub-Commission[26] and lengthy debates in many forums at which minority protection has been considered. No definite answers have been found and no satisfactory universal definition of the term 'minority' has proved acceptable. The absence of a definition has, however, neither precluded standard-setting or promotional activities nor hindered the establishment and work of the Working Group on Minorities.

The difficulty in arriving at an acceptable definition lies in the variety of situations in which minorities exist. Some live together in well defined areas, separated from the dominant part of the population while others are scattered throughout the national community. Some minorities base a strong sense of collective identity on a well remembered or recorded history, others retain only a fragmented notion of their common heritage. In certain cases, minorities enjoy – or have known – a considerable degree of autonomy. In others, there is no past history of autonomy or self-government. Some minority groups may require greater protection than others, because they have resided for a longer period of time in a country, or they have a stronger will to maintain and develop their own characteristics.

Despite the difficulty at arriving at a universally acceptable definition, various characteristics of minorities have been identified, which, taken together, cover most minority situations. The most commonly used description of a minority in a given State can be summed up as a non-dominant group of individuals who share certain national, ethnic, religious or linguistic characteristics which are different from those of the majority population. In addition, it has been argued that the use of self-definition which has been identified as 'a will on the part of the members of the groups in question to preserve their own characteristics' and to be accepted as part of that group by the other members, combined with certain specific objective requirements could provide a viable option.[27]

---

[26] See the studies of Mr. Jules Deschênes, Mr. Asbjørn Eide and Mr. Stanislav Chernichenko, all Members of the Sub-Commission at the time the studies were drafted.

[27] See the Study by Francesco Capotorti, op. cit. n. 24, at p. 96.

Some groups of individuals may find themselves in situations similar to those of minorities. These groups include migrant workers, refugees, stateless persons and other non-nationals, who do not necessarily share certain ethnic, religious or linguistic characteristics common to persons belonging to minorities. These particular groups are however protected against discrimination by the general provisions of international law, and have additional rights guaranteed in, for example, the International Convention on the Protection of the Rights of All Migrant Workers and Members of their Families;[28] the Convention relating to the Status of Stateless Persons; the Convention relating to the Status of Refugees; and the Declaration on the Human Rights of Individuals Who are not Nationals of the Country in which They Live.

6. COMPLAINTS PROCEDURES

Complaints about the violation of human rights, including minority-specific rights, can be brought to the attention of the United Nations. They may be submitted by an individual, a group or a State under a number of procedures, namely:[29]

- The confidential '1503 Procedure', which allows a working group of the Sub-Commission on the Prevention of Discrimination and Protection of Minorities, and ultimately the Economic and Social Council, to receive communications about situations that constitute a 'consistent pattern of gross violations' of human rights, including those of particular importance to minorities. Individuals or groups who claim to be victims of violations, or a person or group of people who has direct, reliable knowledge of such violations (including NGOs) may submit communications.
- The International Covenant on Civil and Political Rights which provides for State to State complaints under Article 41, if the State party has recognized the competence of the Committee on Human Rights to receive and consider such complaints. In this case, the Committee may consider communications to the effect that a State party claims that another State party is not respecting the rights in the Covenant, including Article 27.
- The Optional Protocol to the International Covenant on Civil and Political Rights which provides for individual communications alleging violations of the Covenant to be submitted to the Human Rights Committee on violations perpetrated by a State Party of any of the articles contained therein, including Article 27.

---

[28] As of August 2000, this Convention has not entered into force due to the lack of ratifications.

[29] For further information about how to submit communications, see Fact Sheet No. 7 entitled 'Communication Procedures', pages 4 to 8.

– The Convention on the Elimination of Racial Discrimination also permits communications from individuals or groups who claim to be victims of a violation of their rights as set out in the Convention, and for State to State complaints under Article 11 of the Convention.[30]

Further relevant complaints procedures are available under the Convention against Torture, and those established by the specialized agencies, in particular by the ILO and UNESCO.

7. EARLY WARNING MECHANISMS

Early warning mechanisms have been set up in order to prevent, *inter alia*, racial, ethnic or religious tensions from escalating into conflicts. Two types of provisions for early warning mechanisms established by the United Nations deserve to be mentioned in the context of minority protection.[31]

The High Commissioner for Human Rights has been entrusted with the specific task to prevent the continuation of human rights violations throughout the world. To this end, the High Commissioner plays a mediating role in situations which may escalate into conflicts by acting at the diplomatic level to obtain substantive results with individual Governments and by encouraging dialogue among the parties concerned.

The Committee on the Elimination of Racial Discrimination has established an early warning mechanism drawing the attention of the members of the Committee to situations which have reached alarming levels of racial discrimination. The Committee has adopted both early-warning measures and urgent procedures to prevent as well as to respond more effectively to violations of the Convention. Criteria for early warning measures could for example include the following situations: the lack of an adequate legislative basis for defining and prohibiting all forms of racial discrimination; inadequate implementation of enforcement mechanisms; the presence of a pattern of escalating racial hatred and violence or appeals to racial intolerance by persons, groups or organizations; and significant flows of refugees or displaced persons resulting from a pattern of racial discrimination or encroachment on the lands of minority communities.

---

[30] So far no State party has taken advantage of the procedure, which provides – unless the matter has been settled in another way – for the appointment of a conciliation commission.

[31] At regional level, the OSCE High Commissioner on National Minorities has been entrusted with the specific mandate to provide for early warning of potential conflict.

8. ROLE OF NON-GOVERNMENTAL ORGANIZATIONS

International non-governmental organizations (NGOs) play an important role in promoting and protecting the rights of persons belonging to minorities. They are – either directly or through their national affiliates – close to situations of tension and possible sources of conflict. They are frequently involved in mediation, and they are able to sensitize international as well as national public opinion when the rights of minorities are neglected or violated.

Through research, the publishing of reports, and by serving as channels and platforms for minority groups on the one hand, and by providing timely and factual information to governmental and inter-governmental bodies on situations involving minorities on the other, NGOs can have a significant impact in the field of minority protection.

How can NGOs contribute to the work of the United Nations?

NGOs can attend most meetings at the United Nations, including the sessions of the treaty bodies, the working groups, the Commission on Human Rights and the Sub-Commission on Prevention of Discrimination and Protection of Minorities. Attendance at, and participation in, the meetings are generally subject to having been awarded consultative status with the Economic and Social Council (ECOSOC). However, the Working Group on Minorities for example is open to the participation of all NGOs involved in minority protection, irrespective of whether they have consultative status.

The way in which NGOs can contribute are manifold:

- NGOs can encourage the adoption of measures at national level to effectively implement the provisions of the relevant international instruments, in particular the special rights for minorities and the principles contained in the United Nations Declaration on the Rights of Persons Belonging to National or Ethnic, Religious and Linguistic Minorities;
- NGOs can provide information about infringements of the rights of persons belonging to minorities by bringing these to the attention of the various United Nations human rights mechanisms, in particular the Commission on Human Rights and the Sub-Commission on Prevention of Discrimination and Protection of Minorities;
- NGOs can contribute to the implementation, at local, national and regional levels, of the minority-specific resolutions adopted by the various organs and bodies of the United Nations, in particular the Commission on Human Rights and the Sub-Commission, and the implementation of the relevant recommendations of the treaty bodies, the Special Rapporteurs and the Working Group on Minorities;
- NGOs can support the United Nations working group on minorities by: actively participating in its deliberations; providing accurate, objective and constructive information about situations involving minorities, conciliation

mechanisms, and ways in which minority protection can be strengthened; and contributing to the dialogue between minorities and Governments;
- NGOs can contribute to the reports of the State parties to the relevant international instruments by providing accurate and objective information for inclusion in the reports. Furthermore, NGOs can play an important role during the examination of state party reports by bringing to light information about serious situations warranting the attention of the relevant treaty bodies, and they can contribute to the implementation of the decisions and recommendations of the Committees.

9. THE PROTECTION AND PROMOTION OF THE RIGHTS OF LINGUISTIC MINORITIES

For hundreds of years, provisions relating to the use of language have been included in international treaties such as the 1516 Treaty of Perpetual Union between the King of France and the Helvetic Confederation and the 1815 Congress of Vienna.[32] At the international level, the recognition and protection of the rights of linguistic minorities was reflected in the minorities treaties concluded under the auspices of the League of Nations. These treaties provided for persons belonging to linguistic minorities to be treated on a basis of equality with other nationals of the State and guaranteed the means to preserve their language.

Since 1945, the preservation of language and the protection of linguistic rights has been considered an important element of individual human rights, warranting specific protection. The Universal Declaration of Human Rights in Article 2 paragraph 1 provides that

> 'everyone is entitled to all rights and freedoms [...] without distinction of any kind, such as [...] language'.

Article 27 of the International Covenant on Civil and Political Rights provides that

> 'in those States in which [...] linguistic minorities exist, persons belonging to such minorities shall not be denied the right, in community with the other members of their group, [...] to use their own language'.

The Convention against Discrimination in Education prohibits under Article 1

> 'any distinction, exclusion or preference based upon language [...]',

---

[32] Fernand de Varennes, 'To Speak or not to Speak – the rights of persons belonging to linguistic minorities', Document of the Working Group on Minorities E/CN.4/ Sub. 2/AC.5/1997/ WP.6, p. 2.

and the Convention on the Rights of the Child at Article 29 provides for

'the Development of respect for the child's [...] language [...]'

and at Article 30, that

'[...] a child belonging to a minority (in those States in which it exists) [...] shall not be denied the right, in community with other members of his or her group, [...] to use his or her own language'.

The UN Declaration on the rights of persons belonging to minorities at Article 1 suggests that States have an obligation to take legislative and other measures to protect the identity of minorities, including their right to speak their own language. Article 4 paragraph 2 provides that

'States shall take measures to create favourable conditions to enable persons belonging to minorities to express [...] their language'

and at Article 4 paragraph.3 to ensure that adequate opportunities are provided to minorities to learn, or to have instruction, in their mother tongue.

During the sessions of the Working Group on Minorities, a number of Government observers have raised the issue of the protection of linguistic rights. Examples include the positive measures adopted by: Austria regarding the Minority Schools Acts for the provinces of Carinthia and Burgenland governing schooling of the Slovene, Croat and Hungarian ethnic groups; Cyprus on the provision of financial assistance to minorities to enable them to maintain their own schools; the Russian Federation concerning instruction in minority languages; Norway on the use of the Sami language before the authorities in the Sami homeland; Romania regarding the Education Law to provide for the education in their mother tongue, and, Switzerland concerning the constitutional protection of the Latin linguistic minority.

A number of minority representatives expressed concern at the restrictions of the use of their own language in private and public, and with regard to the use of, and instruction in, tongue. Examples provided include: the Basque minorities in France and Spain; the Hungarian minority in Slovakia, the Former Republic of Yugoslavia and the Ukraine; the Assyrian, Circassian and Kurdish minority in Turkey; the Roma minority in central and Eastern Europe; and the Turkish minority in Greece.

The content, scope and interpretation of the language provisions contained in the United Nations Declaration and the extent of measures to be adopted by States in this regard was discussed during the sessions. One of the scholars provided an interpretation of State obligations under Articles 1 and 4 paras.2 and 3 on the existence and the linguistic identity of minorities as well as the use of, and instruction in, their own mother tongue.[33] In a commentary to the

---

[33] Document of the Working Group E/CN.4/Sub.2/1997/WP.6.

Declaration,[34] the Chairman of the Working Group stressed that language and educational policies of the state are crucial to protect the identity and characteristics of minorities. Denying minorities the possibility to learn their own language, or excluding them from instruction in their own language would be a violation of the obligation to protect their identity. As a minimum, members of minorities should be given the possibility to learn their mother tongue and have the right to establish their private institutions where the minority language is the main language of instruction. A representative of the Foundation on Inter-Ethnic Relations, in a working paper on the Hague Recommendations,[35] drew attention to issues relating to the language education policy as applied in States of Central and Eastern Europe.

In commemoration of the 50th anniversary of the Universal Declaration of Human Rights and the 90th anniversary of the Universal Esperanto Association, a seminar was organized at the United Nations in April 1998 on language and human rights and the role of States, the United Nations and Non-governmental organizations. The aim of the seminar was to discuss the provisions of linguistic rights in international human rights instruments and to consider ways in which to improve the implementation of linguistic rights. The participants agreed to strengthen networks of organizations working on this issue, draw the attention of the High Commissioner to concerns raised and exchange information and experiences with the Working Group on Minorities.

10. CONCLUSION

The body of international law which can be applied to minorities in Europe has shown a welcome development in the past two decades. The field of non-discrimination is well covered in international instruments and special rights have received greater attention in recent years with the adoption of the Declaration and the establishment of the Working Group on Minorities. Further evidence of the importance of minority rights is provided in reports by governments to international organizations, the studies of thematic or country rapporteurs, the work of NGOs, and academic research.

There is also evidence that much remains to be done. Many minorities are subject to serious and persistent violations of their basic rights. Long experience has shown that neither oppression – applied in defiance of international law – nor neglect of minority problems provides a sound basis for relations between groups. Enforced or involuntary assimilation has sometimes been attempted, but it has often failed. Although minority problems may change over time, there is no reason to believe that they, or the claims of minorities, will disappear, unless positive action is taken.

---

[34] Document of the Working Group E/CN.4/Sub.2/AC.5/1998/WP.1.
[35] Document of the Working Group E/CN.4/Sub.2/AC.5/1997/WP.3.

Unresolved situations and conflicts involving minorities indicate that further measures to address minority issues need to be adopted and new avenues of conflict resolution need to be sought. The effective implementation of the non-discrimination provisions and special rights, as well as of the resolutions and recommendations of the various organs and bodies of the United Nations can contribute to meeting the aspirations of minorities, and to the peaceful accommodation of different groups within a State. Tolerance, mutual understanding and pluralism should be nurtured and fostered through human rights education, confidence-building measures, and dialogue. Persons belonging to minorities, rather than being considered adversaries, should be allowed to contribute to the multi-cultural richness of our societies and be involved as partners in development. This is an essential condition for greater stability and peace within and across State borders.

DOCUMENTS

INTERNATIONAL COVENANT ON CIVIL AND POLITICAL RIGHTS

Of 16 December 1966, adopted by the General Assembly Resolution 2200A (XXI), entered into force on 23 March 1976 (999 UNTS 171)

[Extracts]

PART I

Article 1

1. All peoples have the right of self-determination. By virtue of that right they freely determine their political status and freely pursue their economic, social and cultural development.
2. All peoples may, for their own ends, freely dispose of their natural wealth and resources without prejudice to any obligations arising out of international economic co-operation, based upon the principle of mutual benefit, and international law. In no case may a people be deprived of its own means of subsistence.
3. The States Parties to the present Covenant, including those having responsibility for the administration of Non-Self-Governing and Trust Territories, shall promote the realization of the right of self-determination, and shall respect that right, in conformity with the provisions of the Charter of the United Nations.

PART II

Article 2

1. Each State Party to the present Covenant undertakes to respect and to ensure to all individuals within its territory and subject to its jurisdiction the rights recognized in the present Covenant, without distinction of any kind, such as race, colour, sex, language, religion, political or other opinion, national or social origin, property, birth or other status.
2. Where not already provided for by existing legislative or other measures, each State Party to the present Covenant undertakes to take the necessary steps, in accordance with its constitutional processes and with the provisions of the present Covenant, to adopt such other measures as may be necessary to give effect to the rights recognized in the present Covenant.
3. Each State Party to the present Covenant undertakes:
   a) To ensure that any person whose rights or freedoms as herein recognized are violated shall have an effective remedy, notwithstanding that the violation has been committed by persons acting in an official capacity;
   b) To ensure that any person claiming such a remedy shall have his right thereto determined by competent judicial, administrative or legislative authorities, or by any other competent authority provided for by the legal system of the State, and to develop the possibilities of judicial remedy;
   c) To ensure that the competent authorities shall enforce such remedies when granted.

Article 3
The States Parties to the present Covenant undertake to ensure the equal right of men and women to the enjoyment of all the civil and political rights set forth in the present covenant.

PART III

Article 26
All persons are equal before the law and are entitled without any discrimination to the equal protection of the law. In this respect, the law shall prohibit any discrimination and guarantee to all persons equal and effective protection against discrimination on any ground such as race, colour, sex, language, religion, political or other opinion, national or social origin, property, birth or other status.

Article 27
In those States in which ethnic, religious or linguistic minorities exist, persons belonging to such minorities shall not be denied the right, in community with the other members of their group, to enjoy their own culture, to profess and practise their own religion, or to use their own language.

DECLARATION ON THE RIGHTS OF PERSONS BELONGING TO NATIONAL OR ETHNIC, RELIGIOUS AND LINGUISTIC MINORITIES
GA/RES/47/135 92nd plenary meeting 18 December 1992

The General Assembly,

Reaffirming that one of the main purposes of the United Nations, as proclaimed in the Charter of the United Nations, is to achieve international cooperation in promoting and encouraging respect for human rights and for fundamental freedoms for all without distinction as to race, sex, language or religion,

Noting the importance of the even more effective implementation of international human rights instruments with regard to the rights of persons belonging to national or ethnic, religious and linguistic minorities,

Welcoming the increased attention given by human rights treaty bodies to the non-discrimination and protection of minorities,

Aware of the provisions of article 27 of the International Covenant on Civil and Political Rights concerning the rights of persons belonging to ethnic, religious or linguistic minorities,

Considering that the United Nations has an increasingly important role to play regarding the protection of minorities,

Bearing in mind the work done so far within the United Nations system, in particular through the relevant mechanisms of the Commission on Human Rights and the Sub-commission on Prevention of Discrimination and Protection of Minorities, in promoting and protecting the rights of persons belonging to national or ethnic, religious and linguistic minorities,

Recognizing the important achievements in this regard in regional, subregional and bilateral frameworks, which can provide a useful source of inspiration for future United Nations activities,

Stressing the need to ensure for all, without discrimination of any kind, full enjoyment and exercise of human rights and fundamental freedoms, and emphasizing the importance of the draft Declaration on the Rights of Persons Belonging to National or Ethnic, Religious and Linguistic Minorities in that regard,

Recalling its resolution 46/115 of 17 December 1991 and taking note of Commission on Human Rights resolution 1992/16 of 21 February 1992, by which the Commission approved the text of the draft declaration on the rights of persons belonging to national or ethnic, religious and linguistic minorities, and Economic and Social Council resolution 1992/4 of 20 July 1992, in which the Council recommended it to the General Assembly for adoption and further action,

Having considered the note by the Secretary-General,

1. Adopts the Declaration on the Rights of Persons Belonging to National or Ethnic, Religious and Linguistic Minorities, the text of which is annexed to the present resolution;
2. Requests the Secretary-General to ensure the distribution of the Declaration as widely as possible and to include the text of the Declaration in the next edition of Human Rights: A Compilation of International Instruments;
3. Invites United Nations agencies and organizations and intergovernmental and non-governmental organizations to intensify their efforts with a view to disseminating information on the Declaration and to promoting understanding thereof;
4. Invites the relevant organs and bodies of the United Nations, including treaty bodies, as well as representatives of the Commission on Human Rights and the Sub-commission on Prevention of Discrimination and Protection of Minorities, to give due regard to the Declaration within their mandates;
5. Requests the Secretary-General to consider appropriate ways for the effective promotion of the Declaration and to make proposals thereon;
6. Also requests the Secretary-General to report to the General Assembly at its forty-eighth session on the implementation of the present resolution under the item entitled "Human rights questions".

ANNEX
Declaration on the Rights of Persons Belonging to National or Ethnic, Religious and Linguistic Minorities

The General Assembly,

Reaffirming that one of the basic aims of the United Nations, as proclaimed in the Charter, is to promote and encourage respect for human rights and for fundamental freedoms for all, without distinction as to race, sex, language or religion,

Reaffirming faith in fundamental human rights, in the dignity and worth of the human person, in the equal rights of men and women and of nations large and small,

Desiring to promote the realization of the principles contained in the Charter, the Universal Declaration of Human Rights, the Convention on the Prevention and Punishment of the Crime of Genocide, the International Convention on the Elimination of All Forms of Racial Discrimination, the International Covenant on Civil and Political Rights, the International Covenant on Economic, Social and Cultural Rights, the Declaration on the Elimination of All Forms of Intolerance and of Discrimination Based on Religion or Belief, and the Convention on the Rights of the Child, as well as other relevant international instruments that have been adopted at the universal or regional level and those concluded between individual States Members of the United Nations,

Inspired by the provisions of Article 27 of the International Covenant on Civil and Political Rights concerning the rights of persons belonging to ethnic, religious or linguistic minorities,

Considering that the promotion and protection of the rights of persons belonging to national or ethnic, religious and linguistic minorities contribute to the political and social stability of States in which they live,

Emphasizing that the constant promotion and realization of the rights of persons belonging to national or ethnic, religious and linguistic minorities, as an integral part of the development of society as a whole and within a democratic framework based on the rule of law, would contribute to the strengthening of friendship and cooperation among peoples and States,

Considering that the United Nations has an important role to play regarding the protection of minorities,

Bearing in mind the work done so far within the United Nations system, in particular by the Commission on Human Rights, the Sub-commission on Prevention of Discrimination and Protection of Minorities and the bodies established pursuant to the International Covenants on Human Rights and other relevant international human rights instruments in promoting and protecting the rights of persons belonging to national or ethnic, religious and linguistic minorities,

Taking into account the important work which is done by intergovernmental and non-governmental organizations in protecting minorities and in promoting and protecting the rights of persons belonging to national or ethnic, religious and linguistic minorities,

Recognizing the need to ensure even more effective implementation of international human rights instruments with regard to the rights of persons belonging to national or ethnic, religious and linguistic minorities,

Proclaims this Declaration on the Rights of Persons Belonging to National or Ethnic, Religious and Linguistic Minorities:

Article 1
1. States shall protect the existence and the national or ethnic, cultural, religious and linguistic identity of minorities within their respective territories and shall encourage conditions for the promotion of that identity.

States shall adopt appropriate legislative and other measures to achieve those ends.

Article 2
1. Persons belonging to national or ethnic, religious and linguistic minorities (hereinafter referred to as persons belonging to minorities) have the right to enjoy their own culture, to profess and practise their own religion, and to use their own language, in private and in public, freely and without interference or any form of discrimination.
2. Persons belonging to minorities have the right to participate effectively in cultural, religious, social, economic and public life.
3. Persons belonging to minorities have the right to participate effectively in decisions on the national and, where appropriate, regional level concerning the minority to which they belong or the regions in which they live, in a manner not incompatible with national legislation.
4. Persons belonging to minorities have the right to establish and maintain their own associations.
5. Persons belonging to minorities have the right to establish and maintain, without any discrimination, free and peaceful contacts with other members of their group and with persons belonging to other minorities, as well as contacts across frontiers with citizens of other States to whom they are related by national or ethnic, religious or linguistic ties.

Article 3
1. Persons belonging to minorities may exercise their rights, including those set forth in the present Declaration, individually as well as in community with other members of their group, without any discrimination.
2. No disadvantage shall result for any person belonging to a minority as the consequence of the exercise or non-exercise of the rights set forth in the present Declaration.

Article 4
1. States shall take measures where required to ensure that persons belonging to minorities may exercise fully and effectively all their human rights and fundamental freedoms without any discrimination and in full equality before the law.
2. States shall take measures to create favourable conditions to enable persons belonging to minorities to express their characteristics and to develop their culture, language, religion, traditions and customs, except where specific practices are in violation of national law and contrary to international standards.
3. States should take appropriate measures so that, wherever possible, persons belonging to minorities may have adequate opportunities to learn their mother tongue or to have instruction in their mother tongue.
4. States should, where appropriate, take measures in the field of education, in order to encourage knowledge of the history, traditions, language and culture of the minorities existing within their territory. Persons belonging to minorities should have adequate opportunities to gain knowledge of the society as a whole.

5. States should consider appropriate measures so that persons belonging to minorities may participate fully in the economic progress and development in their country.

Article 5
1. National policies and programmes shall be planned and implemented with due regard for the legitimate interests of persons belonging to minorities.
2. Programmes of cooperation and assistance among States should be planned and implemented with due regard for the legitimate interests of persons belonging to minorities.

Article 6
States should cooperate on questions relating to persons belonging to minorities, *inter alia*, exchanging information and experiences, in order to promote mutual understanding and confidence.

Article 7
States should cooperate in order to promote respect for the rights set forth in the present Declaration.

Article 8
1. Nothing in the present Declaration shall prevent the fulfilment of international obligations of States in relation to persons belonging to minorities. In particular, States shall fulfil in good faith the obligations and commitments they have assumed under international treaties and agreements to which they are parties.
2. The exercise of the rights set forth in the present Declaration shall not prejudice the enjoyment by all persons of universally recognized human rights and fundamental freedoms.
3. Measures taken by States to ensure the effective enjoyment of the rights set forth in the present Declaration shall not prima facie be considered contrary to the principle of equality contained in the Universal Declaration of Human Rights.
4. Nothing in the present Declaration may be construed as permitting any activity contrary to the purposes and principles of the United Nations, including sovereign equality, territorial integrity and political independence of States.

Article 9
The specialized agencies and other organizations of the United Nations system shall contribute to the full realization of the rights and principles set forth in the present Declaration, within their respective fields of competence.

COUNCIL OF EUROPE

PROTECTION OF LINGUISTIC RIGHTS WITHIN THE COUNCIL OF EUROPE

Snežana Trifunovska[*]

1. INTRODUCTION

Prominent in the protection of human rights, the Council of Europe has, especially during the course of the last decade, undertaken a range of activities for the protection of national minorities. As in other international organizations, developments in Central and Eastern Europe after the fall of the Berlin Wall and the collapse of Soviet communism were a major catalyst in this respect. Over the last decade most Central and Eastern European countries have joined the Council of Europe as full members.[1] The activities of the Council of Europe under the aegis of the Committee of Ministers can be generally described as the following: the development of legal standards and the monitoring thereof, discussed in more detail together below under sub 3 and various programmes and projects, both bilateral and multilateral in the framework of activities with member States, discussed below under 4. Some other, related, activities are touched upon under 5. First, attention will focus on the work of the other main statutory body, the Parliamentary Assembly.

2. PARLIAMENTARY ASSEMBLY

In the post-Cold War period, or – more precisely – in the period 1990-1999, the Parliamentary Assembly frequently discussed human rights and minority protection issues. In this period it addressed a number of Recommendations to the Committee of Ministers relevant for the issues of minorities and human rights. In its Recommendation 1134 (1990)[2] the Parliamentary Assembly pointed out that

---

[*] Senior University Lecturer of the Law Faculty of Nijmegen, The Netherlands. With thanks to Mr. Frank Steketee, Programme Counsellor in the Secretariat of the Framework Convention for the Protection of National Minorities.

[1] At this moment in time the Council of Europe has 41 members, up from 23 in 1990.

[2] Adopted at the Assembly debate on 1 October 1990 (14th Sitting).

S. Trifunovska (Ed.), Minority Rights in Europe: European Minorities and Languages
© 2000, T.M.C. Asser Press, The Hague, The Netherlands

as the maintenance and further realisation of human rights and fundamental freedoms is one of the main assignments given to the Council of Europe, the Organisation 'must have the interests of minorities at heart'. The potential impact of minorities on peace and stability in Europe was also emphasized in a number of the Parliamentary Assembly documents.[3]

According to the Assembly national minorities are understood to be separate or distinct groups, well defined and established on the territory of a State, the members of which are nationals of the State and have certain religious, linguistic, cultural or other characteristics which distinguish them from the majority of the population. In its view persons belonging to minorities should have the following rights:

- to be recognized in the States in which they live;
- to maintain and develop their culture;
- to maintain their own educational, religious and cultural institutions; and
- to participate fully in decision-making on the matters of their concern i.e. which affect the preservation and development of their identity.[4]

Furthermore, linguistic minorities should have access to adequate types and levels of public education in their mother tongue and the right to obtain, provide, possess, reproduce, distribute and exchange information in their mother tongue regardless of frontiers.

In more general terms, States should take legislative, administrative, judicial and other measures guaranteeing the implementation of the rights of minorities. The measures provided should also contribute to the elimination of prejudices and fostering mutual knowledge and understanding as well as a climate of tolerance and mutual respect.

Finally, it was said that belonging to a minority also includes a duty to comply with the obligations arising from citizenship of or residence in a European State.

Apart from its interest in the protection of national minorities in general, the Parliamentary Assembly has in the past emphasised the significance of protection of minority cultures and languages, as well as in specific situations in various recommendations and resolutions. For example, Recommendation 1203 (1993) on Gypsies in Europe, Recommendation 1291(1996) on Yiddish culture and 1333(1997) on the Aromanian language and culture contain paragraphs dealing with the use of respective languages. One of the more recent documents is Resolution 1171(1998) on endangered Uralic minority cultures[5] in which the

---

[3] Of certain relevance are the following Recommendations to the Committee of Ministers: 1134(1990), 1177(1992), 1201(1993), 1255(1995), 1285(1996), 1300(1996) and 1345(1997).

[4] Parliamentary Assembly Recommendation 1134(1990) on the rights of minorities (Assembly debate on 1 October 1990, 14th Sitting).

[5] Parliamentary Assembly debate on 25 September 1998 (32nd Sitting).

Assembly expressed its concern about the endangered status of Uralic languages and cultures in the Russian Federation.

Of more general significance is Recommendation 1353(1998) on the access of minorities to higher education[6] in which the Parliament recommended to the Committee of Ministers that it should ask the governments of the States signatories to the European Cultural Convention to take account of the principle that all citizens should have the possibility to study their own language and culture in general, and on all levels, including the university level. One of the appropriate modalities of the implementation of this right would be the possibility for the students from minority groups to sit entrance examinations to higher education in their mother tongue. A system of bonuses given in the entrance examination on the basis of language could be envisaged as a means of encouraging persons belonging to linguistic minorities (paragraphs 6(vi) and (vii)). There should also be special courses in minority languages and cultures included in the curricula of teacher-training institutions (paragraph 6(ix)).

Finally, the Parliamentary Assembly Recommendation 1383(1998) on linguistic diversification[7] pointed to the significance of teaching in a variety of modern languages in the member States of the Council of Europe which would include, in case of sufficient demand, the teaching of languages of local minorities at school. The Committee of Ministers is recommended to invite member States to ensure the supply of teachers of minority languages and, in establishing networks of schools and colleges, to ensure diversity in the range of languages offered, including minority and less commonly taught languages.

3. LEGAL STANDARDS IN THE FIELD OF MINORITY PROTECTION ADOPTED BY THE COUNCIL OF EUROPE AND THEIR MONITORING MECHANISMS

The most important European document for the protection of human rights, the European Convention for the Protection of Human Rights and Fundamental Freedoms (ECHR) of 1950, does not contain any specific provision for the protection of minorities. The only article referring to national minorities is Article 14 which is, in fact, a non-discrimination provision providing that '[t]he enjoyment of the rights and freedoms set forth in the Convention shall be secured without discrimination on any ground such as [...] colour, language, religion [...] national or social origin, association with a national minority [...]'. Nonetheless, it must be borne in mind that individual human rights guaranteed under the ECHR such as the protection of private life, freedom of religion, freedom of expression, association and assembly can be of particular importance to persons belonging to national minorities.

---

[6] Parliamentary Assembly debate on 27 January 1998 (3rd Sitting).
[7] Parliamentary Assembly debate on 23 September 1998 (29th Sitting).

However, as from the beginning of the 1990s special emphasis was laid on work in the normative field concerning not human rights in general but minorities in specific. Accordingly, in February 1992 the Parliamentary Assembly requested the Committee of Ministers:

- to conclude as soon as possible the work (which was at that time under way) for the elaboration of a charter for regional or minority languages and to do its utmost to ensure the rapid implementation of the charter;
- to draw up an additional protocol on the rights of minorities to the European Convention on Human Rights; and
- to provide the Council of Europe with a suitable mediation instrument.

The first major legally binding document relevant for protection of minorities, the European Charter for Regional or Minority Languages, was adopted by the Committee of Ministers on 22 June 1992. Already in February 1993, the Parliamentary Assembly presented the Committee of Ministers with Recommendation 1201(1993) containing a proposal for an additional protocol. The proposal included a number of general principles like, *inter alia*, the prohibition of discrimination, the maintenance of religious, ethnic, linguistic and/or cultural identity, equality in law, as well as the prohibition of deliberate changes to the demographic composition of the region in which a national minority is settled to the detriment of that minority.[8] The proposed text contained also a definition of 'national minority' for the purposes of the European Convention on Human Rights.[9] In addition, the proposal included some more substantive rights of minorities on an individual basis and without any exception, such as the right to set up own organizations and political parties. In regions where minority presents a majority of the population, persons belonging to a minority should have at their disposal appropriate local or autonomous authorities or have a special status, matching the specific historical and territorial situation and in accordance with domestic legislation.

With respect to the use of minority languages the text provided for the right of persons belonging to minorities freely to use their mother tongue in private and in public, both orally and in writing. This right applies also to the use of the minority language in publications and in the audiovisual sector, as well as in the

---

[8] Parliamentary Assembly Recommendation 1201(1993) on an additional protocol on the rights of national minorities to the European Convention on Human Rights (Assembly debate on 1 February 1993, 22nd Sitting).

[9] According to Article 1 of the text a 'national minority' is considered to be a group of persons in a State who:
- reside on the territory of that State and are citizens thereof;
- maintain longstanding, firm and lasting ties with that State;
- display distinctive ethnic, cultural, religious or linguistic characteristics;
- are sufficiently representative, although smaller in number than the rest of the population of that state or of a region of that State;
- are motivated by a concern to preserve together that which constitutes their common identity, including their culture, their traditions, their religion or their language.

field of education, providing that every person belonging to a national minority has the right to learn and receive an education in his or her mother tongue at an appropriate number of schools and State educational and training establishments.

Further more significant steps in the field of minority protection were taken at the Vienna Summit of Heads of State and Government, held on 8-9 October 1993. At the Summit the following decisions were adopted:

a. to begin work on drafting a protocol complementing the European Convention on Human Rights in the cultural field by provisions guaranteeing individual human rights, in particular for persons belonging to national minorities, and
b. to draft a framework convention specifying the principles which States Parties commit themselves to respect in order to assure the protection of national minorities.

Thus, the Vienna Summit did not follow the recommendation of the Parliamentary Assembly to prepare an additional protocol containing rights for persons belonging to national minorities.

The issue of drafting instruments in the follow up to the Vienna Summit was entrusted to the Ad Hoc Committee of Experts on Minorities (CAHMIN). The Framework Convention for the Protection of National Minorities was adopted by the Committee of Ministers on 10 November 1994 and opened for signature on 1 February 1995. On the basis of the CAHMIN's Final Activity report concerning an additional protocol to the ECHR with individual rights in the cultural field, issued at the end of 1995, the Committee of Ministers decided in January 1996 to suspend this work. However, in March 1998, the Committee of Ministers requested the Steering Committee (CDDH) to draft an additional protocol or protocols to the European Convention on Human Rights which would broaden the application of Article 14 of the Convention and 'would contain a non-exhaustive list of discrimination grounds', and to elaborate it by 31 December 1999.

For the time being the Council of Europe's major contribution to the protection of minorities is the adoption of two legal documents: the European Charter for Regional or Minority Languages and the Framework Convention for the Protection of National Minorities. As part of the activities of the Council of Europe in the field of human rights protection, these documents present a landmark in the development of standard setting and supervisory mechanisms in the protection of minorities.

3.1 The European Charter for Regional or Minority Languages

The Charter was opened for signature in 1992, and entered into force (upon five ratifications) on 1 March 1998.[10] Its main objective is to provide for the protection of regional or minority languages and the promotion of the right to use them in private and public life. The Charter provides for a twofold system of protection. On the one hand, Part II of the Charter establishes that the Parties shall base their policies, legislation and practice on a number of objectives, *inter alia*: the recognition of the regional or minority languages as an expression of cultural wealth (paragraph 1(a)); the need for resolute action to promote regional or minority languages in order to safeguard them (paragraph 1(c)); and the provision of appropriate forms and means for teaching and study in regional or minority languages at all appropriate stages. The principles and objectives also include the elimination of unjustified discrimination, promotion of mutual understanding between all the linguistic groups of the country as well as consideration of the needs and wishes expressed by the groups which use minority languages. The principles are applied *mutatis mutandis* to non-territorial languages. On the other hand, Part III of the Charter transforms these principles into practical measures in specific fields. This flexible solution enables the Parties to customise their obligations to the very diverse situation of these languages. The ratifying State must therefore choose the provisions of the Charter it undertakes to apply to each of its regional or minority languages, provided that it accepts a minimum of 35 paragraphs or sub-paragraphs. In this sense, appropriate measures to promote the use of regional or minority languages in public life should be undertaken with regard to education, judicial authorities in civil, criminal and administrative proceedings, in administrative and public services, the media, cultural activities, economic and social life and transfrontier exchanges.

The Charter is a reflection of several considerations: (a) languages vary so greatly in their situations that they cannot be measured by the same yardstick; (b) the Charter reflects the Council of Europe's policy, which is centred on integration, not exclusion; (c) the Charter provides for a dynamic process, does not present an end result; and (d) the role played in this process by evaluation and monitoring will stimulate dialogue between States, and between States and the Council of Europe, and will make a wider public aware of the needs of regional and minority languages.[11]

---

[10] In October 2000 total number of ratifications and accessions was 11 (Croatia, Denmark Finland, Germany, Hungary, Liechtenstein, The Netherlands, Norway, Slovenia, Sweden and Switzerland), whereas there were 12 signatures not followed by ratifications (Austria, Cyprus, France, Iceland, Italy, Luxembourg, Malta, Romania, Spain, Macedonia (FYROM), Ukraine and the United Kingdom).

[11] Romedi Arquint, a member of the Parliament of the Canton Grisons, Switzerland, International Conference on the European Charter for Regional or Minority Languages, Regional or Minority Languages, No. 1, pp. 18-19.

To ensure that the implementation of each State's undertakings is effectively monitored, provision is made in the Charter for a monitoring mechanism. One year after the entry into force of the Charter for each State, the contracting parties are to present an initial periodical report, where they state the policies and measures that have been taken in order to fulfil their obligation in accordance with all the provisions in Part II and those chosen under Part III for each language. After the first report the State shall present three-yearly periodical reports on the evolution of the situation. These reports shall all be made public by the State.

There will then be an examination of these reports, as well as of any other information that has been submitted by interested bodies or associations, by an independent committee of experts. The committee has the possibility of organising 'on the spot missions' to a contracting party, during the examination of the report to gather further information from bodies and associations in the State, to visit institutions that use the various languages and to consult with the authorities. On the basis of all this information the Committee of Experts will submit its own report to the Committee of Ministers with appropriate proposals for recommendations, if considered necessary.

3.2 Framework Convention for the Protection of National Minorities

The Framework Convention for the Protection of National Minorities is the first legally binding multilateral document completely devoted to the protection of national minorities, i.e. persons belonging to national minorities. To date it is also the most comprehensive legal document in the area of protection of minorities.[12] Typical for the Convention is that it mostly contains principles and programme-type provisions, meaning that it articulates certain objectives and leaves it to the countries to pursue these objectives with a certain measure of discretion by taking their own circumstances and minority situations into consideration.

In the absence of a definition of the term national minority, 'as it was impossible to arrive at a definition capable of mustering general support of all Council of Europe member States',[13] the Parties must examine the personal scope of

---

[12] Pursuant to Art. 28 (1) the Convention entered into force on the first day of the month following the expiration of a period of three months after the date on which twelve member states of the Council of Europe expressed their consent to be bound by the Convention. Like the Charter on Regional or Minority Languages, the Framework Convention is opened to non-member States which can join it upon the invitation of the Committee of Ministers. By October 2000 the Framework Convention had been ratified by 32 countries members and non-members of the Council of Europe (Albania, Armenia, Austria, Azerbaijan, Bosnia and Herzegovina, Bulgaria, Croatia, Cyprus, the Czech Republic, Denmark, Estonia, Finland, Germany, Hungary, Ireland, Italy, Liechtenstein, Lithuania, Macedonia (FYROM), Malta, Moldova, Norway, Romania, the Russian Federation, San Marino, the Slovak Republic, Slovenia, Spain, Sweden, Switzerland, Ukraine and the United Kingdom) and signed by 8 countries (Georgia, Greece, Iceland, Latvia, Luxembourg, the Netherlands, Poland and Portugal).

[13] http://www.dhdirhr.coe.fr/minorities/eng/mine.htm

application of the Framework Convention, taking account of the specific circumstances prevailing in their countries. This has been subject of some concern as countries might seek to limit the applicability of the Convention only to certain groups while at the same time excluding other groups. The personal scope of application given to the Framework Convention is however subject to review under the monitoring mechanism.

Throughout five sections containing in total 32 articles, the Convention includes some basic and some more specific provisions dealing with, *inter alia*: non discrimination, equality, freedom of assembly, association, expression, linguistic freedoms including the use of minority languages in private and public, education, topographical names in the minority language(s), transfrontier contacts, participation in economic, cultural and social life, prohibition of forced assimilation, etc.

Though sometimes the provisions of the Convention are subject to criticism,[14] their implementation is, as indicated above, subject to review by the monitoring mechanism which will certainly increase their efficiency. The Framework Convention provides that monitoring is carried out by the Committee of Ministers, assisted by an advisory committee on the basis of periodical reports submitted by the States Parties. On 17 September 1997 the Committee of Ministers adopted the Rules on the Monitoring Arrangements under Articles 24 to 26 of the Framework Convention.[15] In accordance with Article 26 an Advisory Committee was created consisting of members with re-cognized expertise in the field of protection of minorities who serve in their individual capacity, and are independent and impartial in their work.[16] The first meeting of the Advisory Committee was held from 29 June-1 July 1998.

Each State Party is required to submit a report containing full information on the measures taken to give effect to the provisions of the Convention. The first reports must be submitted within a year of the entry into force of the Convention, whereas further reports are to be made on a periodical basis of five years and whenever the Committee of Ministers so requires.

In considering State reports the Advisory Committee may request additional information from States, and may receive and use information from other

---

[14] In its Recommendation 1255(1995) on the Protection of the Rights of National Minorities, adopted by the Assembly on 31 January 1995, the Parliamentary Assembly pointed out that the Convention is weakly worded and that it formulates a number of vaguely defined objectives and principles, the observation of which will be an obligation of the contracting States but not a right which individuals may invoke (paragraph 7).

[15] Resolution (97) 10: Rules adopted by the Committee of Ministers on the monitoring arrangements under Articles 24 to 26 of the Framework Convention for the Protection of National Minorities (17 September 1997).

[16] The Rules set up a procedure for the election and appointment of the members of the Advisory Committee: both ordinary and additional members (who will replace the ordinary members in case of their absence), are elected by the Committee of Ministers from the List of Experts Eligible to Serve on the Advisory Committee. Each Party to the Convention may submit to the Secretary General of the Council of Europe the names and the curricula vitae of at least two experts who have the required qualifications and capacity to serve on the Advisory Committee.

sources (for example, NGOs and individuals).[17] For this purpose, under certain conditions also bilateral meetings with the governments and other sources can be held. The Advisory Committee is to prepare opinions which are submitted to the Committee of Ministers. This body must adopt conclusions concerning the concrete measures of implementation of and compliance with the provisions of the Convention. It may further, where appropriate, adopt recommendations in respect of the country concerned. The Advisory Committee, if the Committee of Ministers has so decided, may also be involved in monitoring the actual implementation of the conclusions of the Committee of Ministers by the Parties. By the end of 1999 and throughout 2000 a number of State reports had been received, but no opinions had yet been adopted by the Advisory Committee.[18]

Besides the direct impact which the Framework Convention has already had on the development of national minority legislation, it also served as a basis for negotiating several bilateral treaties between the countries of Central and Eastern Europe relevant to minorities and minority protection.

4. INTERGOVERNMENTAL COOPERATION: PROGRAMMES AND PROJECTS

In addition to its work in the normative field, the Council of Europe has developed also other forms which contribute to the protection of minorities within the member States of the Council of Europe. In this sense briefly should be mentioned the intergovernmental cooperation which takes place through, *inter alia*, implementation of various programmes and projects. Actually, multilateral co-operation between Governments of the member States of the Council of Europe is traditionally a core activity of the Organization in the pursuit of its aim to achieve greater unity between member States based on common fundamental values. This work is set out in the Intergovernmental Programme of Activities that the Committee of Ministers adopts every year.

The Council of Europe has over the last decade developed the Activities for the Consolidation and Development of Democratic Stability in Europe (the ADACS programme), which aims at bilateral and other activities with individual member States. Two other parts of the Council of Europe relating to the protection of national minorities are also briefly discussed below, namely the Confidence Building Measures programme and the work of the European Commission against Racism and Intolerance. However, it has to be pointed out that many other areas of work of the Council of Europe are relevant to minority

---

[17] There are already a number of shadow reports which have been submitted by NGOs and individuals.
[18] Available up to date information at: http://www.human rights.coe.int/Minorities/index.htm

issues, but it is not possible to discuss them all in the context of this contribution.[19]

In the Intergovernmental Programme of Activities of the Council of Europe, the item 'Legal and Political Aspects of the Protection of National Minorities' covers the following:

- efforts to facilitate further signatures and ratifications through information meetings, conferences and seminars at national and local levels for government officials, parliamentarians, local authorities and NGOs aimed at increasing knowledge and awareness of the Framework Convention in member States;
- providing expert counselling on policy and legislation at the request of State authorities;
- organising training seminars for NGOs on using the Framework Convention;
- since 1998, the work of the Intergovernmental Committee of Experts on Issues relating to the Protection of National Minorities (DH-MIN),[20] which includes exchanges of views on policy areas, most notably so far on the participation of national minorities in decision-making processes,[21] exchanges of information on recent developments and the preparation of opinions for the Committee of Ministers on relevant topics.

The ADACS programme in the field of protection of national minorities includes information meetings and legislative and policy counselling identical and linked to those mentioned under the Intergovernmental Programme above, but in recent years the main thrust has been in the Joint Programmes with the European Commission. On 10 June 1996 an 18-month Joint Programme with the EU Commission's PHARE Programme on minorities in Central and Eastern Europe, was signed. It consisted of four separate projects: (a) regular meetings of the Governmental Offices for National Minorities to create a spirit of cooperation

---

[19] The Council of Europe aims to publish and overview of all its activities in this field during the course of 2000.

[20] Terms of reference:
- to act as a forum for the exchange of information, views and experience on policies and good practices for the protection of national minorities at the domestic level and in the context of international instruments;
- to identify and assess ways and means of further enhancing European co-operation on issues relating to the protection of national minorities and, where appropriate, to make proposals to this effect for consideration by the CDDH;
in so doing it shall, where appropriate,
- carry out or commission relevant policy research;
- involve in its work representatives of national minorities and non-governmental organisations with recognised competence in this field.

[21] Public documents (also available on web-site, see footnote 18):
- DH-MIN (99)1 – Replies to the questionnaire on Forms of Participation of Minorities in Decision-making processes.
- DH-MIN (99)2 – Synthesis of Replies to the questionnaire on Forms of Participation of Minorities in Decision-making processes.

and mutual understanding; (b) a scheme of study visits to promote an exchange of technical assistance between countries where Governmental Offices for National Minorities exist and those which are in the process of setting up similar structures; (c) a series of sub-regional workshops and seminars associating countries confronted by similar problems in order to define common solutions and to develop new cooperation schemes; and (d) pilot projects for professional training in areas relevant to the issue of national minorities (governmental officials, journalists, cultural administrators, teachers, etc.). Based on the success of this first programme, in 1998 a second Joint Programme with the European Commission, entitled 'National Minorities in Europe', was agreed upon, which would now be pan-European in its scope. The main aim of this Joint Programme is to make a significant contribution to the implementation and consolidation in practice of the protection of national minorities through: (a) strengthening bilateral and multilateral relations and cooperation between States, and (b) strengthening relations between governments and persons belonging to minorities. The programme has a thematic approach (specific themes will be dealt with in seminars, bilateral meetings, study visits, training sessions, etc.) and is carried out by applying flexible working methods. The programme includes involvement of Heads of Government Offices for national minorities of all member States of the Council of Europe (who should also take part in sub-regional events with neighbouring States) and applicant States, as well as the involvement of minority representatives.

The Joint Programme consists of a number of separate projects, notably: Periodic meetings of Heads of Government Offices for National Minorities; Minorities and Media; Minorities and Education; Participation of Minorities in Decision-making Processes; Integration and Tolerance; General Orientation Study Visits; Professional Training, and Publicity and Publications.

5. OTHER ACTIVITIES: CONFIDENCE-BUILDING MEASURES PROGRAMME

The Confidence-building Measures (CBM) Programme was established following the Summit of Heads of State and Government of the Member States of the Council of Europe which took place in Vienna in 1993. After the Summit, one of the key objectives of which was to achieve effective protection of national minorities, the Council of Europe drafted the Framework Convention for the Protection of National Minorities and developed a programme of confidence-building measures designed to improve tolerance and understanding between peoples.

The aim of the programme is to provide moral and financial support for projects developed by non-governmental partners, of which the main objective is to promote good relations between minorities and the majority.

The distinguishing feature of the Confidence-building Measures Programme is that, within an international organisation where the emphasis is on intergovernmental co-operation, it provides support for projects mainly submitted by non-governmental organisations. The upsurge of problems concerning majority-minority relations in specific countries has revealed the need to back up intergovernmental activities by implementing specific initiatives in particular fields in close co-operation with the majority and minority communities concerned.

The CBM Programme supports the implementation of projects designed to defuse possible tensions between different communities in order to break down the barriers that divide them. The aim is to enable those concerned to engage in dialogue, to learn and to work together so as to share experiences and to promote mutual knowledge and understanding. Confidence-building measures may cover various fields, in particular democracy, human rights, the media, education, culture, social cohesion, transfrontier co-operation and youth. The impact of projects in these fields is generally felt at the local level. They are therefore conceived as pilot projects or models for action that should stimulate the development of other, similar projects.

6. ECRI

Finally, for the Council of Europe's activities in the field of minorities, certain attentions deserves the work of the European Commission against Racism and Intolerance (ECRI). It is a mechanism which was established by the first Summit of Heads of State and Government of the member States of the Council of Europe (October 1993). ECRI's task is to combat racism, xenophobia, anti-semitism and intolerance at the level of greater Europe and in the perspective of the protection of human rights (the Council of Europe's mission). ECRI's members are nominated by their governments on the basis of their in-depth knowledge in the field of combating intolerance. They are nominated in their personal capacity and act as independent members. ECRI's programme of activities comprises three aspects:

- a country-by-country approach;
- work on general themes; and
- activities in relation to civil society.

Within the framework of the country-by-country approach, ECRI closely examines the situation in each of the member States of the Council of Europe and draws up, following this analysis, suggestions and proposals as to how the problems of racism and intolerance identified in each country might be dealt with. ECRI's reports are first transmitted in the form of draft texts to the member States concerned for a process of confidential dialogue with the national authorities of these countries. The content of the report is reviewed in the light of this dialogue. The report is then adopted in its final form and transmitted by ECRI to the government of the member State concerned, through the intermediary of the Committee of Ministers. The report is made public two months after this transmission, unless the government in question is expressly against making the report public. At the end of 1998, ECRI finished the first round of its country-by-country reports for all the member States. In January 1999, ECRI started on the second stage of its country-by-country work. This will take place over four years and will again cover all member States of the Council of Europe, with the aim of producing some ten individual country reports annually. In order to obtain as detailed and comprehensive a picture as possible as regards the situation of racism and intolerance in each country, a contact visit is organised for the relevant ECRI rapporteurs before the preparation of the new report on each country.

The second aspect of ECRI's programme includes work on policy recommendations and guidelines on those general themes which have a particular importance for combating racism and intolerance as well as operational activities on these subjects. The following work and activities can be cited as examples:

- preparation of general policy recommendations on combating racism and intolerance, on specialised bodies at the national level to combat racism and intolerance, on combating racism and intolerance against Roma/Gypsies as well as on national surveys on the experience and perceptions of discrimination and racism from the point of view of potential victims;
- collection and dissemination of collections 'on a variety of subjects chosen by ECRI'.

Relations with civil society are developed and maintained to make ECRI's activities against racism widely-known among the general public and among interested parties at the international, national and local levels, by means of information and raising awareness concerning the problems of racism and intolerance.[22]

7. CONCLUSION

During the last decade, the Council of Europe has taken a leading role in developing normative i.e. legally binding documents for protection of minorities within the member States. Whereas the Charter on Minority Languages has more indirect impact on minorities, as it by protecting minority languages contributes to the maintenance of minority identity, the proper implementation of the Framework Convention has rather direct effect on protection of individuals be-

---

[22] *Inter alia*: the regular production of an information bulletin and the website 'combating racism and intolerance': www.ecri.coe.int (a bilingual site with over 4,000 pages).

longing to minorities. Its contribution is already visible as the flow of information concerning minorities coming from the States parties to the Framework Convention, has already been established by the first reports arriving to the Council of Europe on the basis of Article 25 of the Convention. These reports serve as basis for further steps to be suggested by the Advisory Committee, and follow-up activities. In this sense it should be pointed out that one of the significant achievements of the Framework Convention up to now is the publicity given to the internal/national situation(s) involving minorities as not only governmental bodies but also non-governmental organizations and bodies concerned with human rights protection feel called upon to provide information on the basis of the above-mentioned Article 25.

It is without doubt that, taken into consideration the complexity of the issues involving minorities from the human rights and security perspective, strengthening and broadening of the work of the Council of Europe in the field of minority protection carries a potential of significantly contributing to the promotion of the rights of persons belonging to minorities in Europe. Some preconditions to that effect are already present. One should definitely mention that within the Council of Europe the most substantial normative framework for protection of minorities has been established, as well as a framework for a systematic follow-up; various forms of intergovernmental cooperation have been developed, projects set up and measures adopted for concrete issues and situations involving minorities; the Council of Europe is increasingly becoming a pan-European organization as by 41 member States it already now gathers large majority of the European States; and finally it has by now, achieved a great degree of transparency vis-à-vis other international organizations and forums as well as vis-à-vis its member States. These all preconditions provide certain guarantee that in the future it will continue to play a significant role in the field of minority protection.

DOCUMENTS

EUROPEAN CHARTER FOR REGIONAL OR MINORITY LANGUAGES
Strasbourg, 5 November 1992 (ETS No. 148)

Preamble
The member States of the Council of Europe signatory hereto,

Considering that the aim of the Council of Europe is to achieve a greater unity between its members, particularly for the purpose of safeguarding and realising the ideals and principles which are their common heritage;

Considering that the protection of the historical regional or minority languages of Europe, some of which are in danger of eventual extinction, contributes to the maintenance and development of Europe's cultural wealth and traditions;

Considering that the right to use a regional or minority language in private and public life is an inalienable right conforming to the principles embodied in the United Nations International Covenant on Civil and Political Rights, and according to the spirit of the Council of Europe Convention for the Protection of Human Rights and Fundamental Freedoms;

Having regard to the work carried out within the CSCE and in particular to the Helsinki Final Act of 1975 and the document of the Copenhagen Meeting of 1990;

Stressing the value of interculturalism and multilingualism and considering that the protection and encouragement of regional or minority languages should not be to the detriment of the official languages and the need to learn them;

Realising that the protection and promotion of regional or minority languages in the different countries and regions of Europe represent an important contribution to the building of a Europe based on the principles of democracy and cultural diversity within the framework of national sovereignty and territorial integrity;

Taking into consideration the specific conditions and historical traditions in the different regions of the European States,
Have agreed as follows:

Part I
General provisions

Article 1 – Definitions
For the purposes of this Charter:
 a. 'regional or minority languages' means languages that are:
  i. traditionally used within a given territory of a State by nationals of that State who form a group numerically smaller than the rest of the State's population; and
  ii. different from the official language(s) of that State; it does not include either dialects of the official language(s) of the State or the languages of migrants;
 b. 'territory in which the regional or minority language is used' means the geographical area in which the said language is the mode of expression of a

number of people justifying the adoption of the various protective and promotional measures provided for in this Charter;
   c. 'non-territorial languages' means languages used by nationals of the State which differ from the language or languages used by the rest of the State's population but which, although traditionally used within the territory of the State, cannot be identified with a particular area thereof.

Article 2 – Undertakings
1. Each Party undertakes to apply the provisions of Part II to all the regional or minority languages spoken within its territory and which comply with the definition in Article 1.
2. In respect of each language specified at the time of ratification, acceptance or approval, in accordance with Article 3, each Party undertakes to apply a minimum of thirty-five paragraphs or sub-paragraphs chosen from among the provisions of Part III of the Charter, including at least three chosen from each of the Articles 8 and 12 and one from each of the Articles 9, 10, 11 and 13.

Article 3 – Practical arrangements
1. Each Contracting State shall specify in its instrument of ratification, acceptance or approval, each regional or minority language, or official language which is less widely used on the whole or part of its territory, to which the paragraphs chosen in accordance with Article 2, paragraph 2, shall apply.
2. Any Party may, at any subsequent time, notify the Secretary General that it accepts the obligations arising out of the provisions of any other paragraph of the Charter not already specified in its instrument of ratification, acceptance or approval, or that it will apply paragraph 1 of the present article to other regional or minority languages, or to other official languages which are less widely used on the whole or part of its territory.
3. The undertakings referred to in the foregoing paragraph shall be deemed to form an integral part of the ratification, acceptance or approval and will have the same effect as from their date of notification.

Article 4 – Existing regimes of protection
1. Nothing in this Charter shall be construed as limiting or derogating from any of the rights guaranteed by the European Convention on Human Rights.
2. The provisions of this Charter shall not affect any more favourable provisions concerning the status of regional or minority languages, or the legal regime of persons belonging to minorities which may exist in a Party or are provided for by relevant bilateral or multilateral international agreements.

Article 5 – Existing obligations
Nothing in this Charter may be interpreted as implying any right to engage in any activity or perform any action in contravention of the purposes of the Charter of the United Nations or other obligations under international law, including the principle of the sovereignty and territorial integrity of States.

Article 6 – Information

The Parties undertake to see to it that the authorities, organisations and persons concerned are informed of the rights and duties established by this Charter.

Part II
Objectives and principles pursued in accordance with Article 2, paragraph 1

Article 7 – Objectives and principles

1. In respect of regional or minority languages, within the territories in which such languages are used and according to the situation of each language, the Parties shall base their policies, legislation and practice on the following objectives and principles:
    a. the recognition of the regional or minority languages as an expression of cultural wealth;
    b. the respect of the geographical area of each regional or minority language in order to ensure that existing or new administrative divisions do not constitute an obstacle to the promotion of the regional or minority language in question;
    c. the need for resolute action to promote regional or minority languages in order to safeguard them;
    d. the facilitation and/or encouragement of the use of regional or minority languages, in speech and writing, in public and private life;
    e. the maintenance and development of links, in the fields covered by this Charter, between groups using a regional or minority language and other groups in the State employing a language used in identical or similar form, as well as the establishment of cultural relations with other groups in the State using different languages;
    f. the provision of appropriate forms and means for the teaching and study of regional or minority languages at all appropriate stages;
    g. the provision of facilities enabling non-speakers of a regional or minority language living in the area where it is used to learn it if they so desire;
    h. the promotion of study and research on regional or minority languages at universities or equivalent institutions;
    i. the promotion of appropriate types of transnational exchanges, in the fields covered by this Charter, for regional or minority languages used in identical or similar form in two or more States.
2. The Parties undertake to eliminate, if they have not yet done so, any unjustified distinction, exclusion, restriction or preference relating to the use of a regional or minority language and intended to discourage or endanger the maintenance or development of it. The adoption of special measures in favour of regional or minority languages aimed at promoting equality between the users of these languages and the rest of the population or which take due account of their specific conditions is not considered to be an act of discrimination against the users of more widely-used languages.
3. The Parties undertake to promote, by appropriate measures, mutual understanding between all the linguistic groups of the country and in particular the inclusion of respect, understanding and tolerance in relation to regional or

minority languages among the objectives of education and training provided within their countries and encouragement of the mass media to pursue the same objective.
4. In determining their policy with regard to regional or minority languages, the Parties shall take into consideration the needs and wishes expressed by the groups which use such languages. They are encouraged to establish bodies, if necessary, for the purpose of advising the authorities on all matters pertaining to regional or minority languages.
5. The Parties undertake to apply, mutatis mutandis, the principles listed in paragraphs 1 to 4 above to non-territorial languages. However, as far as these languages are concerned, the nature and scope of the measures to be taken to give effect to this Charter shall be determined in a flexible manner, bearing in mind the needs and wishes, and respecting the traditions and characteristics, of the groups which use the languages concerned.

Part III
Measures to promote the use of regional or minority languages in public life in accordance with the undertakings entered into under Article 2, paragraph 2

Article 8 – Education
With regard to education, the Parties undertake, within the territory in which such languages are used, according to the situation of each of these languages, and without prejudice to the teaching of the official language(s) of the State:
- a. i. to make available pre-school education in the relevant regional or minority languages; or
  - ii. to make available a substantial part of pre-school education in the relevant regional or minority languages; or
  - iii. to apply one of the measures provided for under i and ii above at least to those pupils whose families so request and whose number is considered sufficient; or
  - iv. if the public authorities have no direct competence in the field of pre-school education, to favour and/or encourage the application of the measures referred to under i to iii above;
- b. i. to make available primary education in the relevant regional or minority languages; or
  - ii. to make available a substantial part of primary education in the relevant regional or minority languages; or
  - iii. to provide, within primary education, for the teaching of the relevant regional or minority languages as an integral part of the curriculum; or
  - iv. to apply one of the measures provided for under i to iii above at least to those pupils whose families so request and whose number is considered sufficient;
- c. i. to make available secondary education in the relevant regional or minority languages; or
  - ii. to make available a substantial part of secondary education in the relevant regional or minority languages; or

- iii. to provide, within secondary education, for the teaching of the relevant regional or minority languages as an integral part of the curriculum; or
- iv. to apply one of the measures provided for under i to iii above at least to those pupils who, or where appropriate whose families, so wish in a number considered sufficient;
- d. i. to make available technical and vocational education in the relevant regional or minority languages; or
  - ii. to make available a substantial part of technical and vocational education in the relevant regional or minority languages; or
  - iii. to provide, within technical and vocational education, for the teaching of the relevant regional or minority languages as an integral part of the curriculum; or
  - iv. to apply one of the measures provided for under i to iii above at least to those pupils who, or where appropriate whose families, so wish in a number considered sufficient;
- e i. to make available university and other higher education in regional or minority languages; or
  - ii. to provide facilities for the study of these languages as university and higher education subjects; or
  - iii. if, by reason of the role of the State in relation to higher education institutions, sub-paragraphs i and ii cannot be applied, to encourage and/or allow the provision of university or other forms of higher education in regional or minority languages or of facilities for the study of these languages as university or higher education subjects;
- f. i. to arrange for the provision of adult and continuing education courses which are taught mainly or wholly in the regional or minority languages; or
  - ii. to offer such languages as subjects of adult and continuing education; or
  - iii. if the public authorities have no direct competence in the field of adult education, to favour and/or encourage the offering of such languages as subjects of adult and continuing education;
- g. to make arrangements to ensure the teaching of the history and the culture which is reflected by the regional or minority language;
- h. to provide the basic and further training of the teachers required to implement those of paragraphs a to g accepted by the Party;
- i. to set up a supervisory body or bodies responsible for monitoring the measures taken and progress achieved in establishing or developing the teaching of regional or minority languages and for drawing up periodic reports of their findings, which will be made public.

2. With regard to education and in respect of territories other than those in which the regional or minority languages are traditionally used, the Parties undertake, if the number of users of a regional or minority language justifies it, to allow, encourage or provide teaching in or of the regional or minority language at all the appropriate stages of education.

Article 9 – Judicial authorities
1. The Parties undertake, in respect of those judicial districts in which the number of residents using the regional or minority languages justifies the measures specified below, according to the situation of each of these languages and on condition that the use of the facilities afforded by the present paragraph is not considered by the judge to hamper the proper administration of justice:
   a. in criminal proceedings:
      i. to provide that the courts, at the request of one of the parties, shall conduct the proceedings in the regional or minority languages; and/or
      ii. to guarantee the accused the right to use his/her regional or minority language; and/or
      iii. to provide that requests and evidence, whether written or oral, shall not be considered inadmissible solely because they are formulated in a regional or minority language; and/or
      iv. to produce, on request, documents connected with legal proceedings in the relevant regional or minority language, if necessary by the use of interpreters and translations involving no extra expense for the persons concerned;
   b. in civil proceedings:
      i. to provide that the courts, at the request of one of the parties, shall conduct the proceedings in the regional or minority languages; and/or
      ii. to allow, whenever a litigant has to appear in person before a court, that he or she may use his or her regional or minority language without thereby incurring additional expense; and/or
      iii. to allow documents and evidence to be produced in the regional or minority languages, if necessary by the use of interpreters and translations;
   c. in proceedings before courts concerning administrative matters:
      i. to provide that the courts, at the request of one of the parties, shall conduct the proceedings in the regional or minority languages; and/or
      ii. to allow, whenever a litigant has to appear in person before a court, that he or she may use his or her regional or minority language without thereby incurring additional expense; and/or
      iii. to allow documents and evidence to be produced in the regional or minority languages, if necessary by the use of interpreters and translations;
   d. to take steps to ensure that the application of sub-paragraphs i and iii of paragraphs b and c above and any necessary use of interpreters and translations does not involve extra expense for the persons concerned.
2. The Parties undertake:
   a. not to deny the validity of legal documents drawn up within the State solely because they are drafted in a regional or minority language; or
   b. not to deny the validity, as between the parties, of legal documents drawn up within the country solely because they are drafted in a regional or minority language, and to provide that they can be invoked against interested third parties who are not users of these languages on condition that the contents of the document are made known to them by the person(s) who invoke(s) it; or

c. not to deny the validity, as between the parties, of legal documents drawn up within the country solely because they are drafted in a regional or minority language.
3. The Parties undertake to make available in the regional or minority languages the most important national statutory texts and those relating particularly to users of these languages, unless they are otherwise provided.

Article 10 – Administrative authorities and public services
1. Within the administrative districts of the State in which the number of residents who are users of regional or minority languages justifies the measures specified below and according to the situation of each language, the Parties undertake, as far as this is reasonably possible:
   a. i. to ensure that the administrative authorities use the regional or minority languages; or
      ii. to ensure that such of their officers as are in contact with the public use the regional or minority languages in their relations with persons applying to them in these languages; or
      iii. to ensure that users of regional or minority languages may submit oral or written applications and receive a reply in these languages; or
      iv. to ensure that users of regional or minority languages may submit oral or written applications in these languages; or
      v. to ensure that users of regional or minority languages may validly submit a document in these languages;
   b. to make available widely used administrative texts and forms for the population in the regional or minority languages or in bilingual versions;
   c. to allow the administrative authorities to draft documents in a regional or minority language.
2. In respect of the local and regional authorities on whose territory the number of residents who are users of regional or minority languages is such as to justify the measures specified below, the Parties undertake to allow and/or encourage:
   a. the use of regional or minority languages within the framework of the regional or local authority;
   b. the possibility for users of regional or minority languages to submit oral or written applications in these languages;
   c. the publication by regional authorities of their official documents also in the relevant regional or minority languages;
   d. the publication by local authorities of their official documents also in the relevant regional or minority languages;
   e. the use by regional authorities of regional or minority languages in debates in their assemblies, without excluding, however, the use of the official language(s) of the State;
   f. the use by local authorities of regional or minority languages in debates in their assemblies, without excluding, however, the use of the official language(s) of the State;
   g. the use or adoption, if necessary in conjunction with the name in the official language(s), of traditional and correct forms of place-names in regional or minority languages.

3. With regard to public services provided by the administrative authorities or other persons acting on their behalf, the Parties undertake, within the territory in which regional or minority languages are used, in accordance with the situation of each language and as far as this is reasonably possible:
   a. to ensure that the regional or minority languages are used in the provision of the service; or
   b. to allow users of regional or minority languages to submit a request and receive a reply in these languages; or
   c. to allow users of regional or minority languages to submit a request in these languages.
4. With a view to putting into effect those provisions of paragraphs 1, 2 and 3 accepted by them, the Parties undertake to take one or more of the following measures:
   a. translation or interpretation as may be required;
   b. recruitment and, where necessary, training of the officials and other public service employees required;
   c. compliance as far as possible with requests from public service employees having a knowledge of a regional or minority language to be appointed in the territory in which that language is used.
5. The Parties undertake to allow the use or adoption of family names in the regional or minority languages, at the request of those concerned.

Article 11 – Media
1. The Parties undertake, for the users of the regional or minority languages within the territories in which those languages are spoken, according to the situation of each language, to the extent that the public authorities, directly or indirectly, are competent, have power or play a role in this field, and respecting the principle of the independence and autonomy of the media:
   a. to the extent that radio and television carry out a public service mission:
      i. to ensure the creation of at least one radio station and one television channel in the regional or minority languages; or
      ii. to encourage and/or facilitate the creation of at least one radio station and one television channel in the regional or minority languages; or
      iii. to make adequate provision so that broadcasters offer programmes in the regional or minority languages;
   b. i. to encourage and/or facilitate the creation of at least one radio station in the regional or minority languages; or
      ii. to encourage and/or facilitate the broadcasting of radio programmes in the regional or minority languages on a regular basis;
   c. i. to encourage and/or facilitate the creation of at least one television channel in the regional or minority languages; or
      ii. to encourage and/or facilitate the broadcasting of television programmes in the regional or minority languages on a regular basis;
   d. to encourage and/or facilitate the production and distribution of audio and audiovisual works in the regional or minority languages;
   e. i. to encourage and/or facilitate the creation and/or maintenance of at least one newspaper in the regional or minority languages; or

ii. to encourage and/or facilitate the publication of newspaper articles in the regional or minority languages on a regular basis;
f. i. to cover the additional costs of those media which use regional or minority languages, wherever the law provides for financial assistance in general for the media; or
ii. to apply existing measures for financial assistance also to audiovisual productions in the regional or minority languages;
g. to support the training of journalists and other staff for media using regional or minority languages.
2. The Parties undertake to guarantee freedom of direct reception of radio and television broadcasts from neighbouring countries in a language used in identical or similar form to a regional or minority language, and not to oppose the retransmission of radio and television broadcasts from neighbouring countries in such a language. They further undertake to ensure that no restrictions will be placed on the freedom of expression and free circulation of information in the written press in a language used in identical or similar form to a regional or minority language. The exercise of the above-mentioned freedoms, since it carries with it duties and responsibilities, may be subject to such formalities, conditions, restrictions or penalties as are prescribed by law and are necessary in a democratic society, in the interests of national security, territorial integrity or public safety, for the prevention of disorder or crime, for the protection of health or morals, for the protection of the reputation or rights of others, for preventing disclosure of information received in confidence, or for maintaining the authority and impartiality of the judiciary.
3. The Parties undertake to ensure that the interests of the users of regional or minority languages are represented or taken into account within such bodies as may be established in accordance with the law with responsibility for guaranteeing the freedom and pluralism of the media.

Article 12 – Cultural activities and facilities
1. With regard to cultural activities and facilities – especially libraries, video libraries, cultural centres, museums, archives, academies, theatres and cinemas, as well as literary work and film production, vernacular forms of cultural expression, festivals and the culture industries, including *inter alia* the use of new technologies – the Parties undertake, within the territory in which such languages are used and to the extent that the public authorities are competent, have power or play a role in this field:
   a. to encourage types of expression and initiative specific to regional or minority languages and foster the different means of access to works produced in these languages;
   b. to foster the different means of access in other languages to works produced in regional or minority languages by aiding and developing translation, dubbing, post-synchronisation and subtitling activities;
   c. to foster access in regional or minority languages to works produced in other languages by aiding and developing translation, dubbing, post-synchronisation and subtitling activities;

d. to ensure that the bodies responsible for organising or supporting cultural activities of various kinds make appropriate allowance for incorporating the knowledge and use of regional or minority languages and cultures in the undertakings which they initiate or for which they provide backing;
   e. to promote measures to ensure that the bodies responsible for organising or supporting cultural activities have at their disposal staff who have a full command of the regional or minority language concerned, as well as of the language(s) of the rest of the population;
   f. to encourage direct participation by representatives of the users of a given regional or minority language in providing facilities and planning cultural activities;
   g. to encourage and/or facilitate the creation of a body or bodies responsible for collecting, keeping a copy of and presenting or publishing works produced in the regional or minority languages;
   h. if necessary, to create and/or promote and finance translation and terminological research services, particularly with a view to maintaining and developing appropriate administrative, commercial, economic, social, technical or legal terminology in each regional or minority language.
2. In respect of territories other than those in which the regional or minority languages are traditionally used, the Parties undertake, if the number of users of a regional or minority language justifies it, to allow, encourage and/or provide appropriate cultural activities and facilities in accordance with the preceding paragraph.
3. The Parties undertake to make appropriate provision, in pursuing their cultural policy abroad, for regional or minority languages and the cultures they reflect.

Article 13 – Economic and social life
1. With regard to economic and social activities, the Parties undertake, within the whole country:
   a. to eliminate from their legislation any provision prohibiting or limiting without justifiable reasons the use of regional or minority languages in documents relating to economic or social life, particularly contracts of employment, and in technical documents such as instructions for the use of products or installations;
   b. to prohibit the insertion in internal regulations of companies and private documents of any clauses excluding or restricting the use of regional or minority languages, at least between users of the same language;
   c. to oppose practices designed to discourage the use of regional or minority languages in connection with economic or social activities;
   d. to facilitate and/or encourage the use of regional or minority languages by means other than those specified in the above sub-paragraphs.
2. With regard to economic and social activities, the Parties undertake, in so far as the public authorities are competent, within the territory in which the regional or minority languages are used, and as far as this is reasonably possible:
   a. to include in their financial and banking regulations provisions which allow, by means of procedures compatible with commercial practice, the use of regional or minority languages in drawing up payment orders (cheques,

drafts, etc.) or other financial documents, or, where appropriate, to ensure the implementation of such provisions;
b. in the economic and social sectors directly under their control (public sector), to organise activities to promote the use of regional or minority languages;
c. to ensure that social care facilities such as hospitals, retirement homes and hostels offer the possibility of receiving and treating in their own language persons using a regional or minority language who are in need of care on grounds of ill-health, old age or for other reasons;
d. to ensure by appropriate means that safety instructions are also drawn up in regional or minority languages;
e. to arrange for information provided by the competent public authorities concerning the rights of consumers to be made available in regional or minority languages.

Article 14 – Transfrontier exchanges
The Parties undertake:
a. to apply existing bilateral and multilateral agreements which bind them with the States in which the same language is used in identical or similar form, or if necessary to seek to conclude such agreements, in such a way as to foster contacts between the users of the same language in the States concerned in the fields of culture, education, information, vocational training and permanent education;
b. for the benefit of regional or minority languages, to facilitate and/ or promote co-operation across borders, in particular between regional or local authorities in whose territory the same language is used in identical or similar form.

Part IV
Application of the Charter

Article 15 – Periodical reports
1. The Parties shall present periodically to the Secretary General of the Council of Europe, in a form to be prescribed by the Committee of Ministers, a report on their policy pursued in accordance with Part II of this Charter and on the measures taken in application of those provisions of Part III which they have accepted. The first report shall be presented within the year following the entry into force of the Charter with respect to the Party concerned, the other reports at three-yearly intervals after the first report.
2. The Parties shall make their reports public.

Article 16 – Examination of the reports
1. The reports presented to the Secretary General of the Council of Europe under Article 15 shall be examined by a committee of experts constituted in accordance with Article 17.
2. Bodies or associations legally established in a Party may draw the attention of the committee of experts to matters relating to the undertakings entered into by that Party under Part III of this Charter. After consulting the Party concerned, the

committee of experts may take account of this information in the preparation of the report specified in paragraph 3 below. These bodies or associations can furthermore submit statements concerning the policy pursued by a Party in accordance with Part II.
3. On the basis of the reports specified in paragraph 1 and the information mentioned in paragraph 2, the committee of experts shall prepare a report for the Committee of Ministers. This report shall be accompanied by the comments which the Parties have been requested to make and may be made public by the Committee of Ministers.
4. The report specified in paragraph 3 shall contain in particular the proposals of the committee of experts to the Committee of Ministers for the preparation of such recommendations of the latter body to one or more of the Parties as may be required.
5. The Secretary General of the Council of Europe shall make a two-yearly detailed report to the Parliamentary Assembly on the application of the Charter.

Article 17 – Committee of experts
1. The committee of experts shall be composed of one member per Party, appointed by the Committee of Ministers from a list of individuals of the highest integrity and recognised competence in the matters dealt with in the Charter, who shall be nominated by the Party concerned.
2. Members of the committee shall be appointed for a period of six years and shall be eligible for reappointment. A member who is unable to complete a term of office shall be replaced in accordance with the procedure laid down in paragraph 1, and the replacing member shall complete his predecessor's term of office.
3. The committee of experts shall adopt rules of procedure. Its secretarial services shall be provided by the Secretary General of the Council of Europe.

Part V
Final provisions

Article 18
This Charter shall be open for signature by the member States of the Council of Europe. It is subject to ratification, acceptance or approval. Instruments of ratification, acceptance or approval shall be deposited with the Secretary General of the Council of Europe.

Article 19
1. This Charter shall enter into force on the first day of the month following the expiration of a period of three months after the date on which five member States of the Council of Europe have expressed their consent to be bound by the Charter in accordance with the provisions of Article 18.
2. In respect of any member State which subsequently expresses its consent to be bound by it, the Charter shall enter into force on the first day of the month following the expiration of a period of three months after the date of the deposit of the instrument of ratification, acceptance or approval.

Article 20
After the entry into force of this Charter, the Committee of Ministers of the Council of Europe may invite any State not a member of the Council of Europe to accede to this Charter.
In respect of any acceding State, the Charter shall enter into force on the first day of the month following the expiration of a period of three months after the date of deposit of the instrument of accession with the Secretary General of the Council of Europe.

Article 21
1. Any State may, at the time of signature or when depositing its instrument of ratification, acceptance, approval or accession, make one or more reservations to paragraphs 2 to 5 of Article 7 of this Charter. No other reservation may be made.
2. Any Contracting State which has made a reservation under the preceding paragraph may wholly or partly withdraw it by means of a notification addressed to the Secretary General of the Council of Europe. The withdrawal shall take effect on the date of receipt of such notification by the Secretary General.

Article 22
1. Any Party may at any time denounce this Charter by means of a notification addressed to the Secretary General of the Council of Europe.
2. Such denunciation shall become effective on the first day of the month following the expiration of a period of six months after the date of receipt of the notification by the Secretary General.

Article 23
The Secretary General of the Council of Europe shall notify the member States of the Council and any State which has acceded to this Charter of:
   a. any signature;
   b. the deposit of any instrument of ratification, acceptance, approval or accession;
   c. any date of entry into force of this Charter in accordance with Articles 19 and 20;
   d. any notification received in application of the provisions of Article 3, paragraph 2;
   e. any other act, notification or communication relating to this Charter.

In witness whereof the undersigned, being duly authorised thereto, have signed this Charter.
Done at Strasbourg, this 5th day of November 1992, in English and French, both texts being equally authentic, in a single copy which shall be deposited in the archives of the Council of Europe. The Secretary General of the Council of Europe shall transmit certified copies to each member State of the Council of Europe and to any State invited to accede to this Charter.

CHART OF SIGNATURES AND RATIFICATIONS BY THE EUROPEAN CHARTER FOR REGIONAL OR MINORITY LANGUAGES
(Situation as in October 2000)

States	Signature	Ratification	Entry into force
Austria	05/11/92		
Croatia		05/11/97	05/11/97	01/
Cyprus	12/11/92		
Denmark	05/11/92	08/09/00	01/01/01
Finland	05/11/92	09/11/94	01/03/98
France	07/05/99		
Germany	05/11/92	16/09/98	01/01/99
Hungary	05/11/92	26/04/95	01/03/98
Iceland	07/05/99		
Italy	27/06/00		
Liechtenstein	05/11/92	18/11/97	01/03/98
Luxembourg	05/11/92		
Malta	05/11/92		
Netherlands	05/11/92	02/05/96	01/03/98
Norway	05/11/92	10/11/93	01/03/98
Romania	17/07/95		
Slovenia	03/07/97	04/10/00	01/01/01
Spain	05/11/92		
Sweden	09/02/00	09/02/00	01/06/00
Switzerland	08/10/93	23/12/97	01/04/98
the former Yugoslav Republic of Macedonia	25/07/96		
Ukraine	02/05/96		
United Kingdom	02/03/00		

Treaty open for signature by the member States and for accession by non-member States.
Non member States: None.

RESERVATIONS AND (TERRITORIAL) DECLARATIONS
(Updated information available at http://conventions.coe.int/treaty)

CROATIA

Reservation and Declarations contained in the instrument of ratification, deposited on 5 November 1997

Reservation:
The Republic of Croatia declares, in pursuance of Article 21 of the European Charter for Regional of Minority Languages, that in respect of the Republic of Croatia the provisions of Article 7, paragraph 5, of the Charter shall not apply.

Declarations:
The Republic of Croatia hereby declares that, in accordance with Article 2, paragraph 2, and Article 3, paragraph 1, of the European Charter for Regional of Minority Languages, it shall apply to Italian, Serbian, Hungarian, Czech, Slovak, Ruthenian and Ukrainian languages the following paragraphs of the Charter:
Article 8:
  Paragraph 1, sub-paragraphs a (iii), b (iv), c (iv), d (iv), e (ii), f (ii), g, h;
Article 9:
  Paragraph 1, sub-paragraphs a (ii), a (iv), b (ii), b (iii), c (ii), c (iii), d; Paragraph 2, sub-paragraph a;
Article 10:
  Paragraph 1, sub-paragraph a (iii), a (iv) b, c; Paragraph 2, sub-paragraphs a, b, c, d, g; Paragraph 3, sub-paragraphs a, b, c; Paragraph 5;
Article 11:
  Paragraph 1, sub-paragraphs a (iii), d, e (ii); Paragraph 2; Paragraph 3;
Article 12:
  Paragraph 1, sub-paragraphs a, f, g;
Article 13:
  Paragraph 1, sub-parasgraphs a, b, c;
Article 14

The Republic of Croatia further declares, with regard to Article 1, paragraph b., of the Charter, that pursuant to Croatian legislature, the term 'territory in which the regional or minority languages is used' shall refer to those areas in which the official use of minority language is introduced by the by-laws passed by the local self-government units, pursuant to Article 12 of the Constitution of the Republic of Croatia and Articles 7 and 8 of the Constitutional Law on Human Rights and Freedoms and the Rights of National and Ethnic Communities or Minorities on the Republic of Croatia.

DENMARK

In accordance with Article 2, paragraph 2, and Article 3, paragraph 1, of the European Charter for Regional or Minority Languages, Denmark declares that it will apply the following provisions of Part III of the Charter to the German minority language in Southern Jutland:
Article 8
  Paragraph 1 a iii; b iv, c iii/iv, d iii; e ii, f ii, g; h; i; Paragraph 2;
Article 9
  Paragraph 1 b iii; c iii; Paragraph 2 a/b/c;
Article 10
  Paragraph 1 a v; Paragraph 4 c; Paragraph 5;
Article 11
  Paragraph 1 b i/ii, c i/ii; d, e i, f ii; g, Paragraph 2;
Article 12
  Paragraph 1 a; b; d; e; f; g; Paragraph 2; Paragraph 3

Article 13
 Paragraph 1 a; c; d; Paragraph 2 c;
Article 14, a; b.

The Danish Government considers that Article 9, paragraphs 1 b iii, and 1 c iii, does not preclude that national procedural law may contain rules which require that documents produced in a foreign language before courts as a general rule be accompanied by a translation.

Declaration contained in a Note Verbale from the Permanent Representation of Denmark handed at the time of deposit of the instrument of ratification on 8 September 2000

The Danish Realm comprises Denmark, the Faroe Islands and Greenland.
Section 11 of Act No. 137 of 23 March 1948 on Home Rule of the Faroe Islands states that 'Faroese is recognized as the principal language, but Danish is to be learnt well and carefully, and Danish may be used as well as Faroese in public affairs.' By virtue of the said Act the Faroese language enjoys a high degree of protection and the provisions of the Charter will therefore not be applicable to the Faroese language, cf. Article 4 (2) of the Charter. For this reason, the Danish Government does not intend to submit periodical reports according to Article 15 of the Charter as far as the Faroese language is concerned.
Denmark's ratification of the Charter does not in any way prejudice the outcome of the negotiations on the future constitutional status of the Faroe Islands.
Section 9 of Act No. 577 of 29 November 1978 on Greenland Home Rule states that:

'1. Greelandic shall be the principal language, Danish must be thoroughly taught.
2. Either language may be used for official purposes.'

By virtue of the said Act the Greenlandic language enjoys a high degree of protection and the provisions of the Charter will therefore not be applicable to the Greenlandic language, cf. Article 4(2) of the Charter. For this reason, the Danish Government does not intend to submit periodical reports according to Article 15 of the Charter as far as the Greenlandic language is concerned.

FINLAND

Declarations contained in the instrument of acceptance, deposited on 9 November 1994

Finland declares, according to Article 2, paragraph 2, and Article 3, paragraph 1, that it applies to the Saami language which is a regional or minority language in Finland, the following provisions of Part III of the Charter:
Article 8:
 Paragraph 1, sub-paragraphs a (i), b (i), c (i), d (ii), e (ii), f (ii), g, h, i; Paragraph 2

Article 9:
   Paragraph 1, sub-paragraphs a (ii), a (iii), a (iv), b (ii), b (iii), c (ii), c (iii), d; Paragraph 2, sub-paragraph a; Paragraph 3
Article 10:
   Paragraph 1, sub-paragraphs a (iii), b, c; Paragraph 2, sub-paragraphs a, b, c, d, e, f, g; Paragraph 3, sub-paragraph b; Paragraph 4, sub-paragraphs a, b; Paragraph 5
Article 11:
   Paragraph 1, sub-paragraphs a (iii), b (i), c (ii), d, e (i), f (ii); Paragraph 2; Paragraph 3
Article 12:
   Paragraph 1, sub-paragraphs a, b, c, d, e, f, g, h; Paragraph 2; Paragraph 3
Article 13:
   Paragraph 1, sub-paragraphs a, c, d; Paragraph 2, sub-paragraphs b, c
Article 14:
   Paragraph a; Paragraph b

Finland declares, according to Article 2, paragraph 2, and Article 3, paragraph 1, that it applies to the Swedish language which is the less widely used official language in Finland, the following provisions of Part III of the Charter:
Article 8:
   Paragraph 1, sub-paragraphs a (i), b (i), c (i), d (i), e (i), f (i), g, h, i; Paragraph 2
Article 9:
   Paragraph 1, sub-paragraphs a (i), a (ii), a (iii), a (iv), b (i), b (ii), b (iii), c (i), c (ii), c (iii), d; Paragraph 2, sub-paragraph a; Paragraph 3
Article 10:
   Paragraph 1, sub-paragraphs a (i), b, c; Paragraph 2, sub-paragraphs a, b, c, d, e, f, g; Paragraph 3, sub-paragraph a; Paragraph 4, sub-paragraphs a, b; Paragraph 5
Article 11:
   Paragraph 1, sub-paragraphs a (iii), b (i), c (ii), d, e (i), f (ii); Paragraph 2; Paragraph 3
Article 12:
   Paragraph 1, sub-paragraphs a, b, c, d, e, f, g, h; Paragraph 2; Paragraph 3
Article 13:
   Paragraph 1, sub-paragraphs a, c, d; Paragraph 2, sub-paragraphs a, b, c, d, e;
Article 14:
   Paragraph a; Paragraph b

Finland further declares, referring to Article 7, paragraph 5, that it undertakes to apply, *mutatis mutandis*, the principles listed in paragraphs 1 to 4 of the said Article to the Romanes language and to the other non-territorial languages in Finland.

FRANCE

Declarations contained in the full powers handed to the Secretary General at the time of signature of the instrument, on 7 May 1999

I. France intends to make the following declaration in its instrument of ratification of the European Charter for Regional or Minority Languages:
1. In so far as the aim of the Charter is not to recognise or protect minorities but to promote the European language heritage, and as the use of the term 'groups' of speakers does not grant collective rights to speakers of regional or minority languages, the French Government interprets this instrument in a manner compatible with the Preamble to the Constitution, which ensures the equality of all citizens before the law and recognises only the French people, composed of all citizens, without distinction as to origin, race or religion
2. The French Government interprets Article 7-1, paragraph d, and Articles 9 and 10 as posing a general principle which is not in conflict with Article 2 of the Constitution, pursuant to which the use of the French language is mandatory on all public-law corporations and private individuals in the exercise of a public service function, as well as on individuals in their relations with public administrations and services.
3. The French Government interprets Article 7-1, paragraph f, and Article 8 to mean that they preserve the optional nature of the teaching and study of regional or minority languages, as well as of the history and culture which is reflected by them, and that the purpose of this teaching is not to remove from pupils enrolled in schools on the national territory the rights and obligations applicable to all those attending establishments providing the public education service or associated therewith.
4. The French Government interprets Article 9-3 as not opposing the possible use only of the official French version, which is legally authoritative, of statutory texts made available in the regional or minority languages, by public-law corporations and private individuals in the exercise of a public service function, as well as by individuals in their relations with public administrations and services.

II. France will specify in its instrument of ratification of the European Charter for Regional or Minority Languages, pursuant to Article 3-1 thereof, the regional or minority languages to which the measures to be selected in accordance with Article 2-2 shall apply. In conformity with Article 2-2, France intends to undertake to apply some or all of the following paragraphs or sub-paragraphs of Part III of the Charter:
Article 8:
    sub-paragraphs 1.a.iii, 1.b.iv, 1.c.iv, 1.d.iv, 1.e.i, 1.e.ii, 1.f.ii, 1.g, 1.h, 1.i; Paragraph 2
Article 9:
    Paragraph 3
Article 10:
    sub-paragraphs 2.c, 2.d, 2.g
Article 11:
    sub-paragraphs 1.a.iii, 1.b.ii, 1.c.ii, 1.d, 1.e.ii, 1.f.ii, 1.g; Paragraph 2; Paragraph 3
Article 12:
    sub-paragraphs 1.a, 1.b, 1.c, 1.d, 1.e, 1.g; Paragraph 2; Paragraph 3

Article 13:
sub-paragraphs 1.b, 1.c, 1.d; sub-paragraphs 2.b, 2.e
Article 14:
Paragraph a; Paragraph b

GERMANY

Declarations contained in a letter from the Permanent Representation of Germany, dated 16 September 1998, handed to the Secretary General at the time of deposit of the instrument of ratification, on 16 September 1998.
Minority languages within the meaning of the European Charter for Regional or Minority Languages in the Federal Republic of Germany shall be the Danish, Upper Sorbian, Lower Sorbian, North Frisian and Sater Frisian languages and the Romany language of the German Sinti and Roma; a regional language within the meaning of the Charter in the Federal Republic shall be the Low German language.
Pursuant to Article 3, paragraph 1, of the Charter, the Federal Republic of Germany specifies the regional or minority languages to which the provisions selected pursuant to Article 2, paragraph 2, of the Charter shall apply upon the entry into force of the Charter in the Federal Republic of Germany:

Danish in the Danish language area in *Land* Schleswig-Holstein:
Article 8:
Paragraph 1 a iv; b iv; c iii/iv; d iii; e ii; f ii/iii; g; h; i; Paragraph 2
Article 9:
Paragraph 1 b iii; c iii; Paragraph 2 a
Article 10:
Paragraph 1 a v; Paragraph 4 c; Paragraph 5;
Article 11:
Paragraph 1 b ii; c ii; d; e ii; f ii; Paragraph 2
Article 12:
Paragraph 1 c; d; e; f; g; Paragraph 2; Paragraph 3
Article 13:
Paragraph 1 a; c; d; Paragraph 2 c
Article 14 a; b

Upper Sorbian in the Upper Sorbian language area in the Free State of Saxony:
Article 8:
Paragraph 1 a iii; b iv; c iv; d iv; e ii; f iii; g; h; i; Paragraph 2
Article 9:
Paragraph 1 a ii; a iii; b ii; b iii; c ii; c iii; d; Paragraph 2 a
Article 10:
Paragraph 1 a iv/v; Paragraph 2 a; b; g; Paragraph 3 b/c; Paragraph 4 c; Paragraph 5
Article 11:
Paragraph 1 b ii; c ii; d; e i; f ii; Paragraph 2
Article 12:
Paragraph 1 a; b; c; d; e; f; g; h; Paragraph 2; Paragraph 3

Article 13:
Paragraph 1 a; c; d; Paragraph 2 c

Lower Sorbian in the Lower Sorbian language area in *Land* Brandenburg:
Article 8:
Paragraph 1 a iv; b iv; c iv; e iii; f iii; g; h; i
Article 9:
Paragraph 1 a ii; a iii; b iii; c iii; Paragraph 2 a
Article 10:
Paragraph 1 a iv/v; Paragraph 2 b; g; Paragraph 3 b/c; Paragraph 4 a; c; Paragraph 5
Article 11:
Paragraph 1 b ii; c ii; d; e i; Paragraph 2
Article 12:
Paragraph 1 a; b; c; d; e; f; g; h; Paragraph 2; Paragraph 3
Article 13:
Paragraph 1 a; c; d

North Frisian in the North Frisian language area in *Land* Schleswig-Holstein:
Article 8:
Paragraph 1 a iii/iv; b iv; c iv; e ii; f iii; g; h; i; Paragraph 2
Article 9:
Paragraph 1 b iii; c iii; Paragraph 2 a
Article 10:
Paragraph 1 a v; Paragraph 4 c; Paragraph 5
Article 11:
Paragraph 1 b ii; c ii; d; e ii; f ii; Paragraph 2
Article 12:
Paragraph 1 a; b; c; d; e; f; g; h; Paragraph 2; Paragraph 3
Article 13:
Paragraph 1 a; c; d
Article 14 a

Sater Frisian in the Sater Frisian language area in *Land* Lower Saxony:
Article 8:
Paragraph 1 a iv; e ii; f iii; g; i
Article 9:
Paragraph 1 b iii; c iii; Paragraph 2 a
Article 10:
Paragraph 1 a v; c; Paragraph 2 a; b; c; d; e; f; Paragraph 4 a; c; Paragraph 5
Article 11:
Paragraph 1 b ii; c ii; d; e ii; f ii; Paragraph 2
Article 12:
Paragraph 1 a; b; c; d; e; f; g; Paragraph 2; Paragraph 3
Article 13:
Paragraph 1 a; c; d

Low German in the *Länder* Free Hanseatic City of Bremen, Free and Hanseatic City of Hamburg, Mecklenburg-Western Pomerania, Lower Saxony and Schleswig-Holstein:
Obligations regarding Low German in the territory of the *Länder* Free Hanseatic City of Bremen, Free and Hanseatic City of Hamburg, Mecklenburg-Western Pomerania, Lower Saxony and Schleswig-Holstein:
Article 8:
    Paragraph 1 a iv; e ii; g
Article 9:
    Paragraph 1 b iii; c iii; Paragraph 2 a
Article 10:
    Paragraph 1 a v; c; Paragraph 2 a; b; f
Article 11:
    Paragraph 1 b ii; c ii; d; e ii; f ii; Paragraph 2
Article 12:
    Paragraph 1 a; d; f; Paragraph 3
Article 13:
    Paragraph 1 a; c
and additionally:

– in the Free Hanseatic City of Bremen:
Article 8:
    Paragraph 1 b iii; c iii; f i; h
Article 10:
    Paragraph 2 c; d; e
Article 11:
    Paragraph 1 g
Article 12:
    Paragraph 1 b; c; e; g
Article 13:
    Paragraph 2 c

– in the Free and Hanseatic City of Hamburg:
Article 8:
    Paragraph 1 b iii; c iii; d iii; f ii; h; i
Article 10:
    Paragraph 2 e; Paragraph 4 c
Article 11:
    Paragraph 1 g
Article 12:
    Paragraph 1 g
Article 13:
    Paragraph 1 d; Paragraph 2 c

– in *Land* Mecklenburg-Western Pomerania:
Article 8:
　Paragraph 1 b iii; c iii; d iii; h; i
Article 10:
　Paragraph 4 c
Article 12:
　Paragraph 1 b; c; e; h
Article 13:
　Paragraph 1 d; Paragraph 2 c

– in *Land* Lower Saxony:
Article 8:
　Paragraph 1 f iii; i
Article 10:
　Paragraph 2 c; d; e; Paragraph 4 a; c
Article 12:
　Paragraph 1 b; c; e; g; Paragraph 2
Article 13:
　Paragraph 1 d
Article 14 a; b

– in *Land* Schleswig-Holstein:
Article 8:
　Paragraph 1 b iii; c iii; f iii; h; i; Paragraph 2
Article 10:
　Paragraph 4 c
Article 12:
　Paragraph 1 b; c; g
Article 13:
　Paragraph 1 d; Paragraph 2 c

The separate specification of these provisions for the territories of each individual *Land* is in keeping with the federal structure of the Federal Republic of Germany and takes into account the situation of each of these languages in the *Land* in question.

The Romany language of the German Sinti and Roma in the territory of the Federal Republic of Germany and Low German language in the territory of the *Länder* Brandenburg, North-Rhine/Westphalia and Saxony-Anhalt shall be protected pursuant to Part II of the Charter.
Part II of the European Charter for Regional or Minority Languages shall be applied to Romany, the minority language of the German Sinti and Roma in the territory of the Federal Republic of Germany, and to the regional language Low German in the territory of the *Länder* Brandenburg, North-Rhine/Westphalia and Saxony-Anhalt upon its entry into force in the Federal Republic of Germany in accordance with the declaration of the Federal Republic of Germany of 23 January 1998. The objectives and principles laid down in Article 7 of the Charter shall form the bases with regard

to these languages. At the same time, German law and Germany's administrative practice thus meet individual requirements laid down in Part III of the Charter:

With regard to Romany – for the territory of the Federal Republic of Germany:
Article 8:
　　Paragraph 1 f iii; g; h
Article 9:
　　Paragraph 1 b iii; c iii; Paragraph 2 a
Article 10:
　　Paragraph 5
Article 11:
　　Paragraph 1 d; e ii; f ii; g; Paragraph 2
Article 12:
　　Paragraph 1 g; Paragraph 3
Article 13:
　　Paragraph 1 a; c; d
Article 14 a:

and additionally:
– in *Land* Baden-Württemberg:
Article 8:
　　Paragraphs 1 a iv, 1 e iii
Article 10:
　　Paragraph 4 c
Article 12:
　　Paragraphs 1 a, 1 d; f; Paragraph 2

– in *Land* Berlin:
Article 8:
　　Paragraph 1 a i/ii; b i/ii/iii/iv; e i/ii/iii; i; Paragraph 2
Article 11:
　　Paragraph 1 b i/ii: c ii; e i/ii
Article 12:
　　Paragraph 1 a; d; f

– in the Free and Hanseatic City of Hamburg:
Article 8:
　　Paragraph 1 b iv; c iv
Article 11:
　　Paragraph 1 b ii; c ii
Article 12:
　　Paragraph 1 a; d; f

– in *Land* Hesse:
Article 8:
　　Paragraph 1 a iii/iv; b iv; c iv; d iv; e iii; i; Paragraph 2

Article 11:
   Paragraph 1 b ii; c ii; e i
Article 12:
   Paragraph 1 a; d; f; Paragraph 2

– in *Land* North-Rhine/Westphalia:
Article 8:
   Paragraph 1 e iii; Paragraph 2
Article 12:
   Paragraph 1 a; d; f; Paragraph 2

– in *Land* Lower Saxony:
Article 12:
   Paragraph 1 a; d; f

– in *Land* Rhineland-Palatinate:
Article 8:
   Paragraph 1 a iv; e iii
Article 11:
   Paragraph 1 c ii
Article 12:
   Paragraph 1 a; d; f

– in *Land* Schleswig-Holstein:
Article 10:
   Paragraph 1 a v; Paragraph 2 b; Paragraph 4 c
Article 11:
   Paragraph 1 b ii; c ii
Article 12:
   Paragraph 1 a; d; f; Paragraph 2

With regard to Low German:

– in *Land* Brandenburg:
Article 8:
   Paragraph 1 a iv; b iv; c iv; f iii; g
Article 9:
   Paragraph 2 a
Article 10:
   Paragraph 2 b; Paragraph 3 c
Article 11:
   Paragraph 1 b ii; c ii; d; e ii; f ii; Paragraph 2
Article 12:
   Paragraph 1 a; f; g

– in *Land* North-Rhine/Westphalia:
Article 8:
   Paragraph 1 e iii; g; h; Paragraph 2
Article 9:
   Paragraph 1 b iii; c iii; Paragraph 2 a
Article 11:
   Paragraph 1 d; Paragraph 2
Article 12:
   Paragraph 1 a; d; e; f; g; h; Paragraph 2
Article 13:
   Paragraph 1 a; c; d

– in *Land* Saxony-Anhalt:
Article 8:
   Paragraph 1 a iv; b iv; c iv; g; h
Article 9:
   Paragraph 2 a
Article 11:
   Paragraph 1 b ii; c ii; e ii; Paragraph 2
Article 12:
   paragraph 1 a; f; g; h

The separate specification of these provisions for the territory of each individual *Land* is in keeping with the federal structure of the Federal Republic of Germany and takes into account the situation of each of these languages in the *Land* in question.

In accordance with the national distribution of competencies, the way in which the above-mentioned provisions of Part III of the Charter are implemented through legal regulations and Germany's administrative practice with due regard to the objectives and principles specified in Article 7 of the Charter shall be the responsibility of either the Federation or the competent *Land*. Details will be provided in the procedure for implementing the federal act with which the legislature consents to the Charter as laid down in the Memorandum to the Charter.

HUNGARY

Declarations contained in the instrument of ratification, deposited on 26 April 1995 and completed by a Note Verbale[1] from the Ministry of Foreign Affairs of Hungary, dated 12 March 1999, registered at the Secretariat General on 16 March 1999.

---

[1] The Note verbale read as follows:
The Ministry of Foreign Affairs of the Republic of Hungary presents its compliments to the Secretariat General of the Council of Europe and has the honor to draw its attention to a technical error contained in the instrument of ratification deposited by the Republic of Hungary, namely that the languages enumerated in respect of which Hungary makes undertakings concerning Part III of the European Charter for Regional or Minority Languages, do not include the Serbian language.

Hungary declares, according to Article 2, paragraph 2, and Article 3, that it applies to the Croatian, German, Romanian, Serbian, Slovak and Slovene languages, the following provisions of Part III of the Charter:

Article 8:
   Paragraph 1, sub-paragraphs a (iv), b (iv), c (iv), d (iv), e (iii), f (iii), g, h, i; Paragraph 2
Article 9:
   Paragraph 1, sub-paragraphs a (ii), a (iii), a (iv), b (ii), b (iii), c (ii), c (iii); Paragraph 2, sub-paragraphs a, b, c
Article 10:
   Paragraph 1, sub-paragraphs a (v), c; Paragraph 2, sub-paragraphs b, e, f, g; Paragraph 3, sub-paragraph c; Paragraph 4, sub-paragraphs a, c; Paragraph 5
Article 11:
   Paragraph 1, sub-paragraphs a (iii), b (ii), c (ii), e (i), f (i), g; Paragraph 3
Article 12:
   Paragraph 1, sub-paragraphs a, b, c, f, g; Paragraph 2; Paragraph 3
Article 13:
   Paragraph 1, sub-paragraph a
Article 14:
   Paragraph a; Paragraph b

LIECHTENSTEIN

Declaration contained in the instrument of ratification deposited on 18 November 1997:

Indeed, the Republic of Hungary, by Decision No. 35/1995 (IV.7) of the Parliament, of which an official translation in French is appended, has ratified Part III of the Charter, accepting also the Serbian language and with the same options as those enumerated in the instrument of ratification of 19 April 1995. Hungary's obligations with regard to the Serbian language become therefore operative from the date of entry into force of the European Charter for Regional of Minority Languages in respect of Hungary.

Decision of the Parliament No. 35/1995 (IV.7)
On the ratification of the European Charter on Regional or Minority Languages and on the undertakings taken by the Republic of Hungary in conformity with its Article 2, litt. 2,

The Parliament, on a proposition from the Government:
Ratifies the European Charter on Regional or Minority Languages, elaborated on 5 November 1992, which text is reproduced in Appendix No. 1.
Agrees that the undertakings taken in conformity with Article 2, litt. 2, of the Charter reproduced in Appendix No. 2 extend to the Croatian, German, Romanian, Serbian, Slovakian, Slovenian languages.
Invites the President of the Republic to issue the instrument of ratification.
Invites the Minister of Foreign Affairs to deposit the instrument of ratification and the inventory of the undertakings taken.

The Principality of Liechtenstein declares in accordance with Article 2, paragraph 2, and in accordance with Article 3, Paragraph 1, of the European Charter for Regional or Minority Languages of 5 November 1992, that there are no regional or minority languages in the sense of the Charter in the territory of the Principality of Liechtenstein at the time of ratification.

NETHERLANDS

Declaration contained in the instrument of acceptance, deposited on 2 May 1996:

The Kingdom of the Netherlands accepts the said Charter for the Kingdom in Europe.
Declarations contained in a Note Verbale handed over by the Permanent Representative of the Netherlands at the time of deposit of the instrument of acceptance, on 2 May 1996.
The Kingdom of the Netherlands declares, in accordance with Article 2, paragraph 2, and Article 3, paragraph 1, of the European Charter for Regional or Minority Languages, that it will apply to the Frisian language in the province of Friesland the following provisions of Part III of the Charter:
Article 8:
Paragraph 1, sub-paragraphs a (ii), b (ii), c (iii), e (ii), f (i), g, h, i; Paragraph 2
Article 9:
Paragraph 1, sub-paragraphs a (ii), a (iii), b (iii), c (ii), c (iii); Paragraph 2, sub-paragraph b
Article 10:
Paragraph 1, sub-paragraphs a (v), c; Paragraph 2, sub-paragraphs a, b, c, d, e, f, g; Paragraph 4, sub-paragraphs a, c; Paragraph 5
Article 11:
Paragraph 1, sub-paragraphs a (iii), b (ii), c (ii), f (ii); Paragraph 2
Article 12:
Paragraph 1, sub-paragraphs a, b, d, e, f, g, h; Paragraph 2; Paragraph 3
Article 13:
Paragraph 1, sub-paragraphs a, c, d; Paragraph 2, sub-paragraphs b, c
Article 14:
Paragraph a; Paragraph b

The Kingdom of the Netherlands further declares that the principles enumerated in Part II of the Charter will be applied to the Lower-Saxon languages used in the Netherlands, and, in accordance with Article 7, paragraph 5, to Yiddish and the Romanes languages.
Declaration contained in a Note Verbale from the Permanent Representation of the Netherlands, dated 18 March 1997, registered at the Secretariat General on 19 March 1997
The Kingdom of the Netherlands declares, in accordance with Article 2, paragraph 1, of the European Charter for Regional or Minority Languages of 5 Nov-

ember 1992, that the principles enumerated in Part II of the Charter will be applied to the Limburger language used in the Netherlands.

NORWAY

Declarations contained in the instrument of ratification, deposited on 10 November 1993:

We undertake to carry out the provisions contained in Parts I, II, IV and V of the Charter and also in accordance with Article 2, paragraph 2, the provisions contained in the following articles, paragraphs and sub-paragraphs of Part III of the Charter:

Article 8:
    Paragraph 1, sub-paragraphs a (iii), b (iv), c (iv), d (iv), e (ii), f (ii), g, h, i; Paragraph 2
Article 9:
    Paragraph 1, sub-paragraphs a (i-iv), b (i-iii), d; Paragraph 2, sub-paragraph a; Paragraph 3
Article 10:
    Paragraph 1, sub-paragraphs a (iii), b, c; Paragraph 2, sub-paragraphs a, b, c, d, e, f, g; Paragraph 3, sub-paragraph b; Paragraph 4, sub-paragraph a; Paragraph 5
Article 11:
    Paragraph 1, sub-paragraphs, a (iii), b (i), c (ii), e (i), f (ii), g; Paragraph 2
Article 12:
    Paragraph 1, sub-paragraphs a, d, e, f, g, h; Paragraph 2; Paragraph 3
Article 13:
    Paragraph 2, sub-paragraphs c, e
Article 14:
    sub-paragraph b

The above-mentioned paragraphs and sub-paragraphs shall, in accordance with Article 3, paragraph 1, apply to the Sami language.

SLOVENIA

In accordance with Article 7, paragraph 5, of the Charter, the Republic of Slovenia will apply *mutatis mutandis* the provisions of Article 7, paragraphs 1 to 4, also to the romani language.

The Republic of Slovenia declares, that the Italian and Hungarian languages are considered as regional or minority languages in the territory of the Republic of Slovenia within the meaning of the European Charter for Regional or Minority Languages. In accordance with Article 2, paragraph 2, of the Charter, the Republic of Slovenia will apply to these two languages the following provisions of the Part III of the Charter:

Article 8
Paragraph 1, sub-paragraphs a (i, ii, iii), c (i, ii, iii), d (i, ii, iii), e (iii), f (iii, g, h, i); Paragraph 2
Article 9
Paragraph 1, sub-paragraphs a, b, c, d Paragraph 2, sub-paragraphs a, b c
Article 10
Paragraph; Paragraph 2; Paragraph 3;Paragraph 4; Paragraph 5;
Article 11
Paragraph 1, sub-paragraphs a (i), e (i); Paragraph 2; Paragraph 3
Article 12
Paragraph 1, sub-paragraphs a, d, e, f; Paragraph 2; Paragraph 3
Article 13
Paragraph 1; Paragraph 2
Article 14
Paragraph a; Paragraph b.

SWEDEN

Sami, Finnish and Meänkieli (Tornedal Finnish) are regional or minority languages in Sweden. Sweden"s undertakings pursuant to Article 2, paragraph 2 with respect to these languages are described in the appendix.
Romani Chib and Yiddish shall be regarded as non-territorial minority languages in Sweden when the Charter is applied

Appendix
The extent of Sweden's undertakings according to Part III of the European Charter for Regional or Minority Languages.
The followings paragraphs and sub-paragraphs under Article 8 shall apply to Sami, Finnish and Meänkieli:
 8.1.a.iii; 8.1.b.iv; 8.1.c.iv; 8.1.d.iv; 8.1.e.iii; 8.1.f.iii; 8.1.g; 8.1.h; 8.1.i; 8.2.;

The following paragraphs and sub-paragraphs under Article 9 shall apply to Sami, Finnish and Meänkieli:
 9.1.a.ii; 9.1.a.iii; 9.1.a.iv; 9.1.b.ii; 9.1.b.iii; 9.1.c.ii; 9.1.c.iii; 9.1.d; 9.2; 9.3

The following paragraphs and sub-paragraphs under Article 10 shall apply to Sami, Finnish and Meänkieli:
 10.1.a.iii; 10.1.a.v; 10.1.c.; 10.2.b.; 10.2.c.; 10.2.d.; 10.2.g.; 10.4.a.; 10.5

The following paragraphs and sub-paragraphs under Article 11 shall apply to Sami, Finnish and Meänkieli:
 11.1.a.iii; 11.1.d; 11.1.e.i; 11.1.f.ii; 11.2.
In addition, 11.1.c.i will apply with respect to Finnish.

The following paragraphs under Article 12 shall apply to Sami, Finnish and Meänkieli:

12.1.a; 12.1.b; 12.1.d; 12.1.f; 12.1.g; 12.2.

In addition, 12.1.e will apply to Sami, and 12.1.c and 12.1.h to Finnish and Sami. The following paragraphs under Article 13 shall apply to Sami, Finnish and Meänkieli:
13.1.a

The following paragraphs under Article 14 shall apply to Sami, Finnish and Meänkieli:
14.a; 14.b

This means that a total of 45 paragraphs or sub-paragraphs in part III of the Charter shall apply to Sami and Finnish, and 42 paragraphs or sub-paragraphs to Meänkieli.

SWITZERLAND

Declaration contained in the instrument of ratification deposited on 23 December 1997:

The Swiss Federal Council declares, in accordance with Article 3, paragraph 1, of the Charter, that in Switzerland Romansh and Italian are the less widely used official languages to which the following paragraphs chosen in accordance with Article 2, paragraph 2, of the Charter, shall apply:

a. Romansh
Article 8:
  Paragraph 1, sub-paragraphs a (iv), b (i), c (iii), d (iii), e (ii), f (iii), g, h, i
Article 9:
  Paragraph 1, sub-paragraphs a (ii), a (iii), b (ii), b (iii), c (ii); Paragraph 2, sub-paragraph a; Paragraph 3
Article 10:
  Paragraph 1, sub-paragraphs a (i), b, c; Paragraph 2, sub-paragraphs a, b, c, d, e, f, g; Paragraph 3, sub-paragraph b; Paragraph 4, sub-paragraphs a, c; Paragraph 5
Article 11:
  Paragraph 1, sub-paragraphs a (iii), b (i), c (ii), e (i), f (i); Paragraph 3
Article 12:
  Paragraph 1, sub-paragraphs a, b, c, e, f, g, h; Paragraph 2; Paragraph 3
Article 13:
  Paragraph 1, sub-paragraph d; Paragraph 2, sub-paragraph b
Article 14:
  sub-paragraph a; sub-paragraph b

b. Italian
Article 8:
  Paragraph 1, sub-paragraphs a (i), a (iv), b (i), c (i), c (ii), d (i), d (iii), e (ii), f (i), f (iii), g, h, I

Article 9:
   Paragraph 1, sub-paragraphs a (i), a (ii), a (iii), b (i), b (ii), b (iii), c (i), c (ii), d; Paragraph 2, sub-paragraph a; Paragraph 3
Article 10:
   Paragraph 1, sub-paragraphs a (i), b, c; Paragraph 2, sub-paragraphs a, b, c, d, e, f, g; Paragraph 3, sub-paragraphs a, b; Paragraph 4, sub-paragraphs a, b, c; Paragraph 5
Article 11:
   Paragraph 1, sub-paragraphs a (i), e (i), g; Paragraph 2; Paragraph 3
Article 12:
   Paragraph 1, sub-paragraphs a, b, c, d, e, f, g, h; Paragraph 2; Paragraph 3
Article 13:
   Paragraph 1, sub-paragraph d; Paragraph 2, sub-paragraph b
Article 14:
   sub-paragraph a; sub-paragraph b

FRAMEWORK CONVENTION FOR THE PROTECTION OF NATIONAL MINORITIES
Strasbourg, 1 February 1995 (ETS No. 157)

The member States of the Council of Europe and the other States, signatories to the present framework Convention, Considering that the aim of the Council of Europe is to achieve greater unity between its members for the purpose of safeguarding and realising the ideals and principles which are their common heritage;

Considering that one of the methods by which that aim is to be pursued is the maintenance and further realisation of human rights and fundamental freedoms;

Wishing to follow-up the Declaration of the Heads of State and Government of the member States of the Council of Europe adopted in Vienna on 9 October 1993;

Being resolved to protect within their respective territories the existence of national minorities;

Considering that the upheavals of European history have shown that the protection of national minorities is essential to stability, democratic security and peace in this continent;

Considering that a pluralist and genuinely democratic society should not only respect the ethnic, cultural, linguistic and religious identity of each person belonging to a national minority, but also create appropriate conditions enabling them to express, preserve and develop this identity;

Considering that the creation of a climate of tolerance and dialogue is necessary to enable cultural diversity to be a source and a factor, not of division, but of enrichment for each society;

Considering that the realisation of a tolerant and prosperous Europe does not depend solely on co-operation between States but also requires transfrontier co-operation between local and regional authorities without prejudice to the constitution and territorial integrity of each State;

Having regard to the Convention for the Protection of Human Rights and Fundamental Freedoms and the Protocols thereto;

Having regard to the commitments concerning the protection of national minorities in United Nations conventions and declarations and in the documents of the Conference on Security and Co-operation in Europe, particularly the Copenhagen Document of 29 June 1990;

Being resolved to define the principles to be respected and the obligations which flow from them, in order to ensure, in the member States and such other States as may become Parties to the present instrument, the effective protection of national minorities and of the rights and freedoms of persons belonging to those minorities, within the rule of law, respecting the territorial integrity and national sovereignty of states;

Being determined to implement the principles set out in this framework Convention through national legislation and appropriate governmental policies,

Have agreed as follows:

Section I

Article 1
The protection of national minorities and of the rights and freedoms of persons belonging to those minorities forms an integral part of the international protection of human rights, and as such falls within the scope of international co-operation.

Article 2
The provisions of this framework Convention shall be applied in good faith, in a spirit of understanding and tolerance and in conformity with the principles of good neighbourliness, friendly relations and co-operation between States.

Article 3
1. Every person belonging to a national minority shall have the right freely to choose to be treated or not to be treated as such and no disadvantage shall result from this choice or from the exercise of the rights which are connected to that choice.
2. Persons belonging to national minorities may exercise the rights and enjoy the freedoms flowing from the principles enshrined in the present framework Convention individually as well as in community with others.

Section II

Article 4
1. The Parties undertake to guarantee to persons belonging to national minorities the right of equality before the law and of equal protection of the law. In this respect, any discrimination based on belonging to a national minority shall be prohibited.
2. The Parties undertake to adopt, where necessary, adequate measures in order to promote, in all areas of economic, social, political and cultural life, full and effective equality between persons belonging to a national minority and those belonging to the majority. In this respect, they shall take due account of the specific conditions of the persons belonging to national minorities.
3. The measures adopted in accordance with paragraph 2 shall not be considered to be an act of discrimination.

Article 5
1. The Parties undertake to promote the conditions necessary for persons belonging to national minorities to maintain and develop their culture, and to preserve the essential elements of their identity, namely their religion, language, traditions and cultural heritage.
2. Without prejudice to measures taken in pursuance of their general integration policy, the Parties shall refrain from policies or practices aimed at assimilation of persons belonging to national minorities against their will and shall protect these persons from any action aimed at such assimilation.

Article 6
1. The Parties shall encourage a spirit of tolerance and intercultural dialogue and take effective measures to promote mutual respect and understanding and co-operation among all persons living on their territory, irrespective of those persons' ethnic, cultural, linguistic or religious identity, in particular in the fields of education, culture and the media.
2. The Parties undertake to take appropriate measures to protect persons who may be subject to threats or acts of discrimination, hostility or violence as a result of their ethnic, cultural, linguistic or religious identity.

Article 7
The Parties shall ensure respect for the right of every person belonging to a national minority to freedom of peaceful assembly, freedom of association, freedom of expression, and freedom of thought, conscience and religion.

Article 8
The Parties undertake to recognise that every person belonging to a national minority has the right to manifest his or her religion or belief and to establish religious institutions, organisations and associations.

Article 9
1. The Parties undertake to recognise that the right to freedom of expression of every person belonging to a national minority includes freedom to hold opinions and to receive and impart information and ideas in the minority language, without interference by public authorities and regardless of frontiers. The Parties shall ensure, within the framework of their legal systems, that persons belonging to a national minority are not discriminated against in their access to the media.
2. Paragraph 1 shall not prevent Parties from requiring the licensing, without discrimination and based on objective criteria, of sound radio and television broadcasting, or cinema enterprises.
3. The Parties shall not hinder the creation and the use of printed media by persons belonging to national minorities. In the legal framework of sound radio and television broadcasting, they shall ensure, as far as possible, and taking into account the provisions of paragraph 1, that persons belonging to national minorities are granted the possibility of creating and using their own media.
4. In the framework of their legal systems, the Parties shall adopt adequate measures in order to facilitate access to the media for persons belonging to national minorities and in order to promote tolerance and permit cultural pluralism.

Article 10
1. The Parties undertake to recognise that every person belonging to a national minority has the right to use freely and without interference his or her minority language, in private and in public, orally and in writing.
2. In areas inhabited by persons belonging to national minorities traditionally or in substantial numbers, if those persons so request and where such a request corresponds to a real need, the Parties shall endeavour to ensure, as far as possible, the

conditions which would make it possible to use the minority language in relations between those persons and the administrative authorities.
3. The Parties undertake to guarantee the right of every person belonging to a national minority to be informed promptly, in a language which he or she understands, of the reasons for his or her arrest, and of the nature and cause of any accusation against him or her, and to defend himself or herself in this language, if necessary with the free assistance of an interpreter.

Article 11
1. The Parties undertake to recognise that every person belonging to a national minority has the right to use his or her surname (patronym) and first names in the minority language and the right to official recognition of them, according to modalities provided for in their legal system.
2. The Parties undertake to recognise that every person belonging to a national minority has the right to display in his or her minority language signs, inscriptions and other information of a private nature visible to the public.
3. In areas traditionally inhabited by substantial numbers of persons belonging to a national minority, the Parties shall endeavour, in the framework of their legal system, including, where appropriate, agreements with other States, and taking into account their specific conditions, to display traditional local names, street names and other topographical indications intended for the public also in the minority language when there is a sufficient demand for such indications.

Article 12
1. The Parties shall, where appropriate, take measures in the fields of education and research to foster knowledge of the culture, history, language and religion of their national minorities and of the majority.
2. In this context the Parties shall *inter alia* provide adequate opportunities for teacher training and access to textbooks, and facilitate contacts among students and teachers of different communities.
3. The Parties undertake to promote equal opportunities for access to education at all levels for persons belonging to national minorities.

Article 13
1. Within the framework of their education systems, the Parties shall recognise that persons belonging to a national minority have the right to set up and to manage their own private educational and training establishments.
2. The exercise of this right shall not entail any financial obligation for the Parties.

Article 14
1. The Parties undertake to recognise that every person belonging to a national minority has the right to learn his or her minority language.
2. In areas inhabited by persons belonging to national minorities traditionally or in substantial numbers, if there is sufficient demand, the Parties shall endeavour to ensure, as far as possible and within the framework of their education systems, that persons belonging to those minorities have adequate opportunities for being taught the minority language or for receiving instruction in this language.

3. Paragraph 2 of this article shall be implemented without prejudice to the learning of the official language or the teaching in this language.

Article 15
The Parties shall create the conditions necessary for the effective participation of persons belonging to national minorities in cultural, social and economic life and in public affairs, in particular those affecting them.

Article 16
The Parties shall refrain from measures which alter the proportions of the population in areas inhabited by persons belonging to national minorities and are aimed at restricting the rights and freedoms flowing from the principles enshrined in the present framework Convention.

Article 17
1. The Parties undertake not to interfere with the right of persons belonging to national minorities to establish and maintain free and peaceful contacts across frontiers with persons lawfully staying in other States, in particular those with whom they share an ethnic, cultural, linguistic or religious identity, or a common cultural heritage.
2. The Parties undertake not to interfere with the right of persons belonging to national minorities to participate in the activities of non-governmental organisations, both at the national and international levels.

Article 18
1. The Parties shall endeavour to conclude, where necessary, bilateral and multilateral agreements with other States, in particular neighbouring States, in order to ensure the protection of persons belonging to the national minorities concerned.
2. Where relevant, the Parties shall take measures to encourage transfrontier cooperation.

Article 19
The Parties undertake to respect and implement the principles enshrined in the present framework Convention making, where necessary, only those limitations, restrictions or derogations which are provided for in international legal instruments, in particular the Convention for the Protection of Human Rights and Fundamental Freedoms, in so far as they are relevant to the rights and freedoms flowing from the said principles.

Section III

Article 20
In the exercise of the rights and freedoms flowing from the principles enshrined in the present framework Convention, any person belonging to a national minority shall respect the national legislation and the rights of others, in particular those of persons belonging to the majority or to other national minorities.

Article 21
Nothing in the present framework Convention shall be interpreted as implying any right to engage in any activity or perform any act contrary to the fundamental principles of international law and in particular of the sovereign equality, territorial integrity and political independence of States.

Article 22
Nothing in the present framework Convention shall be construed as limiting or derogating from any of the human rights and fundamental freedoms which may be ensured under the laws of any Contracting Party or under any other agreement to which it is a Party.

Article 23
The rights and freedoms flowing from the principles enshrined in the present framework Convention, in so far as they are the subject of a corresponding provision in the Convention for the Protection of Human Rights and Fundamental Freedoms or in the Protocols thereto, shall be understood so as to conform to the latter provisions.

Section IV

Article 24
1. The Committee of Ministers of the Council of Europe shall monitor the implementation of this framework Convention by the Contracting Parties.
2. The Parties which are not members of the Council of Europe shall participate in the implementation mechanism, according to modalities to be determined.

Article 25
1. Within a period of one year following the entry into force of this framework Convention in respect of a Contracting Party, the latter shall transmit to the Secretary General of the Council of Europe full information on the legislative and other measures taken to give effect to the principles set out in this framework Convention.
2. Thereafter, each Party shall transmit to the Secretary General on a periodical basis and whenever the Committee of Ministers so requests any further information of relevance to the implementation of this framework Convention.
3. The Secretary General shall forward to the Committee of Ministers the information transmitted under the terms of this Article.

Article 26
1. In evaluating the adequacy of the measures taken by the Parties to give effect to the principles set out in this framework Convention the Committee of Ministers shall be assisted by an advisory committee, the members of which shall have recognised expertise in the field of the protection of national minorities.
2. The composition of this advisory committee and its procedure shall be determined by the Committee of Ministers within a period of one year following the entry into force of this framework Convention.

Section V

Article 27
This framework Convention shall be open for signature by the member States of the Council of Europe. Up until the date when the Convention enters into force, it shall also be open for signature by any other State so invited by the Committee of Ministers. It is subject to ratification, acceptance or approval. Instruments of ratification, acceptance or approval shall be deposited with the Secretary General of the Council of Europe.

Article 28
1. This framework Convention shall enter into force on the first day of the month following the expiration of a period of three months after the date on which twelve member States of the Council of Europe have expressed their consent to be bound by the Convention in accordance with the provisions of Article 27.
2. In respect of any member State which subsequently expresses its consent to be bound by it, the framework Convention shall enter into force on the first day of the month following the expiration of a period of three months after the date of the deposit of the instrument of ratification, acceptance or approval.

Article 29
1. After the entry into force of this framework Convention and after consulting the Contracting States, the Committee of Ministers of the Council of Europe may invite to accede to the Convention, by a decision taken by the majority provided for in Article 20.d of the Statute of the Council of Europe, any non-member State of the Council of Europe which, invited to sign in accordance with the provisions of Article 27, has not yet done so, and any other non-member State.
2. In respect of any acceding State, the framework Convention shall enter into force on the first day of the month following the expiration of a period of three months after the date of the deposit of the instrument of accession with the Secretary General of the Council of Europe.

Article 30
1. Any State may at the time of signature or when depositing its instrument of ratification, acceptance, approval or accession, specify the territory or territories for whose international relations it is responsible to which this framework Convention shall apply.
2. Any State may at any later date, by a declaration addressed to the Secretary General of the Council of Europe, extend the application of this framework Convention to any other territory specified in the declaration. In respect of such territory the framework Convention shall enter into force on the first day of the month following the expiration of a period of three months after the date of receipt of such declaration by the Secretary General.
3. Any declaration made under the two preceding paragraphs may, in respect of any territory specified in such declaration, be withdrawn by a notification addressed to the Secretary General. The withdrawal shall become effective on the first day

of the month following the expiration of a period of three months after the date of receipt of such notification by the Secretary General.

Article 31
1. Any Party may at any time denounce this framework Convention by means of a notification addressed to the Secretary General of the Council of Europe.
2. Such denunciation shall become effective on the first day of the month following the expiration of a period of six months after the date of receipt of the notification by the Secretary General.

Article 32
The Secretary General of the Council of Europe shall notify the member States of the Council, other signatory States and any State which has acceded to this framework Convention, of:
   a. any signature;
   b. the deposit of any instrument of ratification, acceptance, approval or accession;
   c. any date of entry into force of this framework Convention in accordance with Articles 28, 29 and 30;
   d. any other act, notification or communication relating to this framework Convention.

In witness whereof the undersigned, being duly authorised thereto, have signed this framework Convention.

Done at Strasbourg, this 1st day of February 1995, in English and French, both texts being equally authentic, in a single copy which shall be deposited in the archives of the Council of Europe. The Secretary General of the Council of Europe shall transmit certified copies to each member State of the Council of Europe and to any State invited to sign or accede to this framework Convention.

CHART OF SIGNATURES AND RATIFICATIONS BY THE FRAMEWORK CONVENTION FOR THE PROTECTION OF NATIONAL MINORITIES
(Status as of October 2000)

States	Signature	Ratification	Entry into force
Albania	29/06/95	28/09/99	01/01/00
Austria	01/02/95	31/03/98	01/07/98
Bulgaria	09/10/97	07/05/99	01/09/99
Croatia	06/11/96	11/10/97	01/02/98
Cyprus	01/02/95	04/06/96	01/02/98
Czech Republic	28/04/95	18/12/97	01/04/98
Denmark	01/02/95	22/09/97	01/02/98
Estonia	02/02/95	06/01/97	01/02/98
Finland	01/02/95	03/10/97	01/02/98
Georgia	21/01/00		

Germany	11/05/95	10/09/97	01/02/98
Greece	22/09/97		
Hungary	01/02/95	25/09/95	01/02/98
Iceland	01/02/95		
Ireland	01/02/95	07/05/99	01/09/99
Italy	01/02/95	03/11/97	01/03/98
Latvia	11/05/95		
Liechtenstein	01/02/95	18/11/97	01/03/98
Lithuania	01/02/95	23/03/00	01/07/00
Luxembourg	20/07/95		
Malta	11/05/95	10/02/98	01/06/98
Moldova	13/07/95	20/11/96	01/02/98
Netherlands	01/02/95		
Norway	01/02/95	17/03/99	01/07/99
Poland	01/02/95		
Portugal	01/02/95		
Romania	01/02/95	11/05/95	01/02/98
Russia	28/02/96	21/08/98	01/12/98
San Marino	11/05/95	05/12/96	01/02/98
Slovakia	01/02/95	14/09/95	01/02/98
Slovenia	01/02/95	25/03/98	01/07/98
Spain	01/02/95	01/09/95	01/02/98
Sweden	01/02/95	09/02/00	01/06/00
Switzerland	01/02/95	21/10/98	01/02/99
The former Yugoslav Republic of Macedonia	25/07/96	10/04/97	01/02/98
Ukraine	15/09/95	26/01/98	01/05/98
United Kingdom	01/02/95	15/01/98	01/05/98

Non-member States of the Council of Europe:

Armenia	25/07/97	20/07/98	01/11/98
Azerbaijan	26/06/00 (a)	01/10/00	
Bosnia and Herzegovina	24/02/00 (a)	01/06/00	

RESERVATIONS AND (TERRITORIAL) DECLARATIONS
(Updated information available at http://conventions.coe.int/treaty)

AUSTRIA
Declaration contained in the instrument of ratification deposited on 31 March 1998:

The Republic of Austria declares that, for itself, the term 'national minorities' within the meaning of the Framework Convention for the Protection of National Minorities is understood to designate those groups which come within the scope of application of the Law on Ethnic Groups (*Volksgruppengesetz*, Federal Law Gazette No. 396/1976) and which live and traditionally have had their home in parts of the territory of the Republic of Austria and which are composed of Austrian citizens with non-German mother tongues and with their own ethnic cultures.

BULGARIA
Declaration contained in the instrument of ratification deposited on 7 May 1999:

Confirming its adherence to the values of the Council of Europe and the desire for the integration of Bulgaria into the European structures, committed to the policy of protection of human rights and tolerance to persons belonging to minorities, and their full integration into Bulgarian society, the National Assembly of the Republic of Bulgaria declares that the ratification and implementation of the Framework Convention for the Protection of National Minorities do not imply any right to engage in any activity violating the territorial integrity and sovereignty of the unitary Bulgarian State, its internal and international security.

DENMARK
Declaration contained in a Note Verbale dated 22 September1997, handed to the Secretary General at the time of deposit of the instrument of ratification, on 22 September 1997:

In connection with the deposit of the instrument of ratification by Denmark of the Framework Convention for the Protection of National Minorities, it is hereby declared that the Framework Convention shall apply to the German minority in South Jutland of the Kingdom of Denmark.

ESTONIA
Declaration contained in the instrument of ratification, deposited on 6 January 1997:

The Republic of Estonia understands the term 'national minorities', which is not defined in the Framework Convention for the Protection of National Minorities, as follows: are considered as 'national minority' those citizens of Estonia who - reside on the territory of Estonia - maintain longstanding, firm and lasting ties with Estonia - are distinct from Estonians on the basis of their ethnic, cultural, religious or linguistic characteristics; are motivated by a concern to preserve together their cultural traditions, their religion or their language, which constitute the basis of their common identity.

GERMANY
Declaration contained in a letter from the Permanent Representative of Germany, dated 11 May 1995, handed to the Secretary General at the time of signature, on 11 May 1995 and renewed in the instrument of ratification, deposited on 10 September 1997:

The Framework Convention contains no definition of the notion of national minorities. It is therefore up to the individual Contracting Parties to determine the groups to which it shall apply after ratification. National Minorities in the Federal Republic of Germany are the Danes of German citizenship and the members of the Sorbian people with German citizenship. The Framework Convention will also be applied to members of the ethnic groups traditionally resident in Germany, the Frisians of German citizenship and the Sinti and Roma of German citizenship.

Declaration contained in a letter from the Permanent Representative of Germany, dated 11 May 1995, handed to the Secretary General at the time of signature, on 11 May 1995

The Framework Convention contains no definition of the notion of national minorities. It is therefore up to the individual Contracting Parties to determine the groups to which it shall apply after ratification. National Minorities in the Federal Republic of Germany are the Danes of German citizenship and the members of the Sorbian people with German citizenship. The Framework Convention will also be applied to members of the ethnic groups traditionally resident in Germany, the Frisians of German citizenship and the Sinti and Roma of German citizenship.

LIECHTENSTEIN
Declaration contained in the instrument of ratification deposited on 18 November1997:

The Principality of Liechtenstein declares that Articles 24 and 25, in particular, of the Framework Convention for the Protection of National Minorities of 1 February1995 are to be understood having regard to the fact that no national minorities in the sense of the Framework Convention exist in the territory of the Principality of Liechtenstein. The Principality of Liechtenstein considers its ratification of the Framework Convention as an act of solidarity in the view of the objectives of the Convention.

LUXEMBOURG
Declaration contained in a letter from the Permanent Representative of Luxembourg, dated 18July1995, handed to the Secretary General at the time of signature, on 20 July 1995:

The Grand Duchy of Luxembourg understands by 'national minority' in the meaning of the Framework Convention, a group of people settled for numerous generations on its territory, having the Luxembourg nationality and having kept distinctive characteristics in an ethnic and linguistic way.

On the basis of this definition, the Grand Duchy of Luxembourg is induced to establish that there is no 'national minority' on its territory.

MALTA
Reservation and Declarations contained in the instrument of ratification, deposited on 10 February 1998:

The Government of Malta reserves the right not to be bound by the provisions of Article 15 insofar as these entail the right to vote or to stand for election either for the House of Representatives of for Local Councils.

The Government of Malta declares that Articles 24 and 25, in particular, of the Framework Convention for the Protection of National Minorities of 1 February 1995 are to be understood having regard to the fact that no national minorities in the sense of the Framework Convention exist in the territory of the Government of Malta. The Government of Malta considers its ratification of the Framework Convention as an act of solidarity in the view of the objectives of the Convention.

RUSSIA
Declaration contained in the instrument of ratification deposited on 21August 1998:

The Russian Federation considers that none is entitled to include unilaterally in reservations or declarations, made while signing or ratifying the Framework Convention for the Protection of National Minorities, a definition of the term 'national minority', which is not contained in the Framework Convention. In the opinion of the Russian Federation, attempts to exclude from the scope of the Framework Convention the persons who permanently reside in the territory of States Parties to the Framework Convention and previously had a citizenship but have been arbitrarily deprived of it, contradict the purpose of the Framework Convention for the Protection of National Minorities.

SLOVENIA
Declaration contained in a Note Verbale from the Permanent Representation of Slovenia, dated 23 March 1998, handed to the Secretary General at the time of deposit of the instrument of ratification, on 25 March 1998:

Considering that the Framework Convention for the Protection of National Minorities does not contain a definition of the notion of national minorities and it is therefore up to the individual Contracting Party to determine the groups which it shall consider as national minorities, the Government of the Republic of Slovenia, in accordance with the Constitution and internal legislation of the Republic of Slovenia, declares that these are the autochthonous Italian and Hungarian National Minorities. In accordance with the Constitution and internal legislation of the Republic of Slovenia, the provisions of the Framework Convention shall apply also to the members of the Roma community, who live in the Republic of Slovenia.

SWITZERLAND
Declarations contained in the instrument of ratification deposited on 21 October 1998:

Switzerland declares that in Switzerland national minorities in the sense of the framework Convention are groups of individuals numerically inferior to the rest of the population of the country or of a canton, whose members are Swiss nationals, have long-standing, firm and lasting ties with Switzerland and are guided by the will to safeguard together what constitutes their common identity, in particular their culture, their traditions, their religion or their language.

Switzerland declares that the provisions of the framework Convention governing the use of the language in relations between individuals and administrative authorities are applicable without prejudice to the principles observed by the Confederation and the cantons in the determination of official languages.

MACEDONIA (FYROM)
Declarations contained in the instrument of ratification, deposited on 10 April 1997. The Republic of Macedonia declares that:

The term 'national minorities' used in the Framework Convention for the Protection of National Minorities is considered to be identical to the term 'nationalities' which is used in the Constitution and the laws of the Republic of Macedonia.
The provisions of the Framework Convention for the Protection of National Minorities will be applied to the Albanian, Turkish, Vlach, Roma and Serbian national minorities living on the territory of the Republic of Macedonia.

PARLIAMENTARY ASSEMBLY RECOMMENDATION 1383 (1998) ON LINGUISTIC DIVERSIFICATION
Text adopted by the Assembly on 23 September 1998 (29th Sitting)

1. Europe's linguistic diversity is a precious cultural asset that must be preserved and protected.
2. Beyond the cultural and practical dimensions, a command of foreign languages is a decisive factor in understanding between peoples, tolerance of other communities, be they indigenous or foreign, and peace between nations, as well as being an effective barrier against the return of barbarity in its various guises.
3. Existing statistics show that a vast majority of pupils in Europe learn English, while other 'major' European languages such as French, German, Spanish and Italian lag far behind. Languages which are spoken by hundreds of millions of people in the world, such as Russian, Portuguese, Arabic and Chinese, have only a tiny place in school curricula. Moreover, the standard of teaching in these languages is not always satisfactory.
4. There is no disputing the importance of a lingua franca - nowadays English - in the context of globalisation created by telecommunications, tourism and trade. But a knowledge of English alone, seen as the international language of communication, appears insufficient if Europe is to stand its ground in the face of international economic competition and preserve its cultural diversity.
5. There should therefore be more variety in modern language teaching in the Council of Europe member states; this should result in the acquisition not only of English but also of other European and world languages by all European citizens, in parallel with the mastery of their own national and, where appropriate, regional language.
6. The new approach to modern languages in Europe's education systems should focus on the following objectives:
    i. a wider selection of languages to cater for the new needs generated by the development of international exchanges;
    ii. the teaching of languages of local minorities at school if there is sufficient demand;

iii. the acquisition of satisfactory skills in at least two foreign languages for all pupils by the time they leave school;
iv. the possibility of modern language learning as a lifelong activity;
v. the recognition of partial skills and learning ability;
vi. knowledge of the social, economic and cultural realities of the countries where the languages are spoken.

7. Consequently, the Assembly recommends that the Committee of Ministers:
   i. make linguistic diversification a priority of language policy. In practical terms, the Council for Cultural Co-operation (CDCC) should conduct, on a regular basis, comparative studies on linguistic diversification in its member countries, to serve as a basis for drawing up European policies on the matter. In order to avoid duplication, these studies should complement the work of the European Union's Eurydice office. The first study should be carried out within the framework of the conference on language learning policies, scheduled for 1999;
   ii. promote knowledge by students of at least two foreign languages by the time they leave school, with study of the second language beginning at secondary level;
   iii. involve the Parliamentary Assembly in the preparation of the European Year of Languages, which the Council for Cultural Co-operation plans to hold in 2001;
   iv. speed up work on 'threshold levels', the Common European Framework of Reference and the European Language Portfolio, and continue to provide expertise in drawing up national language policies;
   v. ensure that the work done by the CDCC in the fields of lifelong education and new technologies includes a linguistic dimension.

8. The Assembly also recommends that the Committee of Ministers invite member states:
   i. to promote the creation of regional language plans, drawn up in collaboration with elected regional representatives and local authorities, with a view to identifying existing linguistic potential and developing the teaching of the languages concerned, while taking account of the presence of non-native population groups, twinning arrangements, exchanges and the proximity of foreign countries;
   ii. to develop language co-operation agreements between border regions;
   iii. to promote distance education to make the major European languages accessible to all small schools and colleges and facilitate the development of less commonly taught languages;
   iv. to set up networks of schools and colleges to ensure diversity in the range of languages offered (including minority and less commonly taught languages);
   v. to promote and develop bilingual education and arrangements for pupils to be able to sit school-leaving exams wholly or partly in their chosen foreign language;
   vi. to extend arrangements for language study visits by:
       a. making them a compulsory feature of school education;
       b. making exclusively public funding the norm;

    c. allowing entire classes to participate in exchanges;
    d. making them an integral part of teacher training;
vii. to encourage member states to make wider use of foreign teachers, by developing extensive teacher exchange schemes between member states, underpinned by guarantees in relation to teachers' careers and conditions of employment;
viii. to ensure the supply of teachers of minority languages by means of a recruitment plan for each country, drawn up following a study of medium- and long-term requirements;
ix. to prioritise teaching methods geared to developing oral expression through the use of audiovisual materials and interactive media, setting up co-operation arrangements with educational television channels and promoting films on television and at the cinema in their original language;
x. to promote the creation of audiovisual materials in the different regional languages of each country, as well as the publication of newspapers and books in regional languages for the use of the general population;
xi. to promote a type of education that places greater emphasis on the culture and society of the countries concerned;
xii. to supervise the setting up and implementation of a licensing system for private language schools, to ensure that the language skills acquired are up to official standards.

THE EUROPEAN UNION

A ROUGH ORIENTATION THROUGH A DELICATE RELATIONSHIP: THE EUROPEAN UNION'S ENDEAVOURS FOR ITS MINORITIES

Gabriel von Toggenburg*

1. INTRODUCTION: IS MINORITY PROTECTION AN ISSUE IN THE EUROPEAN INTEGRATION PROCESS?

International organisations such as the OSCE, UN and in particular the Council of Europe have developed intensive activities concerning the issue of minorities. The European Union (EU), on the contrary, seems to be much less engaged in this field.[1] There are several interdependent reasons for this, the majority of them

---

* Researcher at the European Academy in Bozen/Bolzano and currently PhD-Candidate at the European University Institute in Florence.

[1] Of special importance for this topic are: Bruno de Witte, 'Politics versus Law in the EU's Approach to Ethnic Minorities', EUI working paper, RSC No 2000/4; Adam Biscoe, 'The European Union and Minority Nations', in Peter Cumper and Steven Wheatley (Eds.), *Minority Rights in the 'New' Europe* (1999); M. A. Martín Estébanez, 'The protection of national or ethnic, religious and linguistic minorities', in N.A. Neuwahl/A. Rosas (Eds.), *The European Union and Human Rights* (1995); Bruno de Witte, 'The European Community and its Minorities', in C. Brölmann et al. (Eds.), *Peoples and Minorities in International Law* (1993), pp. 167-185; Bruno de Witte, 'Surviving in Babel? Language Rights and European Integration', in Yoram Dinstein and Mala Tabory (Eds.), *The Protection of Minorities and Human Rights* (1992), pp. 277-300.

Remarks on minority aspects of the EU/EC are further to be found in Holger Kremser, 'Die Rechtsprechung des Europäischen Gerichtshofs zur Niederlassungsfreiheit und die Bedeutung für nationale Minderheiten', in D. Blumenwitz, G.H. Gornig and D. Murswiek, *Fortschritte im Beitrittsprozess der Staaten Ostmittel-, Ost- und Südosteuropas zur Europäischen Union* (1999), p. 51; Iván Gyurcsík, 'Basic Treaties, Minority Issues and the Enlargement of the European Union', Regio (1999); Franz Pan, *Der Minderheitenschutz im Neuen Europa und seine historische Entwicklung* (1998); Dietrich Murswiek, 'Der europäische Standart des Volksgruppen- und Minderheitenschutzes im Rahmen des Stabilitätspaktes von Paris. Voraussetzung für die Aufnahme ostmitteleuropäischen Staaten in die Europäische Union?', in D. Blumenwitz, G.H. Gornig and D. Murswiek (Eds.), *Der Beitritt der Staaten Ostmitteleuropas zur Europäischen Union und die Rechte der deutschen Volksgruppen und Minderheiten sowie der Vertriebenen* (1997), p. 145; Stefan Grigolli, *Sprachliche Minderheiten in Italien, insbesondere Südtirol, und in Europa* (1997), p. 60; Christian Scherer-Leydecker, *Minderheiten und sonstige ethnische Gruppen* (1997), p. 167; Rudolf Streinz, 'Minderheiten- und Volksgruppenrechte in der Europäischen Union', in D Blumenwitz and G. Gornig, *Der Schutz von Minderheiten- und Volks-*

S. Trifunovska (Ed.), *Minority Rights in Europe: European Minorities and Languages*
© 2000, T.M.C. Asser Press, The Hague, The Netherlands

resulting from the fact that the integration process has primarily been an economic project (despite the fact that it always had political aspects).[2] For this reason, the need to transfer powers to the European Community in order to intervene in political or cultural affairs by harmonising the public behaviour of the member States towards their linguistic or ethnic minorities, has never been felt.[3]

In addition to this (historical) explanation, it would be difficult to find a common denominator on the issue of minority protection in the EU framework. The fact that the EC is not a classic international but a supranational organisation implies that within European integration it is more difficult to escape to watered down solutions which stand somewhere between political and quasi-legal instruments.[4] Contrary to traditional international organisations, and apart from the requirement that every single EC act needs to be founded on a particular article in the EC Treaty (due to the so-called principle of enumerated powers), EC law also defines the legal forms and effects of the acts which may be adopted on the basis of an eventually introduced provision in Primary law.[5] Things might seem even more difficult for the member States if one considers that the European Court of Justice, acting as the engine-room of the integration process, may grant the provision agreed upon a meaning or a strength which was not expected by the States. Hence it may be said that in a supranational agglomeration, still equipped with the openness of a 'moving target',[6] an initial

---

Volksgruppenrechten durch die Europäische Union (1996), p. 11; Florence Benoit-Rohmer, *La question minoritaire en Europe: vers un système cohérent de protection des minorités nationales* (1996); Andrew Geddes, 'Immigrant and Ethnic Minorities and the EU's 'Democratic Deficit', *Journal of Common Market*, 33 (June 1995), No. 2, p. 197; Eckhard Klein, 'Überlegungen zum Schutz von Minderheiten und Volksgruppen im Rahmen der Europäischen Union', in *Festschrift für R. Bernhardt* (1995), p. 1211; Lucien Jacoby, *Die Tätigkeit der Europäischen Gemeinschaft für die Sprach- und Kulturminderheiten 1983-1989*, 1991. Others are quoted later on.

[2] The choice for economic and no political and cultural integration was most probably both of a strategic (it seemed politically more realistic to gradually create a political union through economic interdependencies) and a substantive (there was a fear of creating a sort of super-nation-state) nature. See Bruno de Witte, 'The impact of European Community rules on linguistic policies of the Member States', in F. Coulmas (Ed.) *Language Policy for the European Community* (1991), p. 165.

[3] It might be interesting for the reader to consult the *Package for Europe – Measures for Human Rights, Minority Protection, Cultural Diversity and Economic and Social Cohesion* (http://www.eurac.edu/publications/package.htm). Aim of this proposal by the European Academy (www.eurac.edu/fb2) was to use the scarce legal basis as good as possible for minority favouring measures. This bundle of measures was presented to the European Commission at end of 1998.

[4] This is what happens in the work of the traditional international organisations. See Hans-Joachim Heintze, 'Rechtliche oder politische Absicherung von Minderheitenrechten', in H.-J. Heintze (Ed.), *Moderner Minderheitenschutz* (1998).

[5] The 'Primary law' embodies all the different treaties, the general principles of Community law and customary law. 'Secondary law' comprises regulations, directives, decisions, procedural orders, programmes and so on.

[6] It was Walther Hallstein, President of the first 'High Authority' of the ECSC (then the equivalent to the Commission of the EEC), who described the integration process as a cyclist who has to cycle in order not to fall.

commitment to minority issues seems to be, politically speaking, more difficult than in a traditional international context.

In fact, the situation concerning minority issues is somewhat sobering: until the Amsterdam Treaty (signed on 2 October 1997 and entered into force on 1 May 1999), there had not been a single treaty provision dealing with the protection of minorities (apart from some indication in the Accession Treaties of the UK and Austria, Sweden, Finland, Norway).[7] This despite the fact that with the completion of the Single Market (1993) and the creation of the European Union (Treaty of Maastricht, 1992) the beginning of the last decade stands for a de-economisation of European integration. However, notwithstanding this development, there remains an evident lack of competence, i.e. a mandate provided by the Treaty's High Contracting Parties, regarding ethnic or linguistic minorities.

Looking at the interaction between the European integration process and the protection of minorities, it would be possible to make a division between the active behaviour of EC organs towards minorities on the one hand (let's call it 'positive approach') and the relation between EC law and national measures of minority protection on the other (let's call it 'negative approach'). This article attempts to exclusively analyse the development of activities in the field of minorities in the EC and EU ambit. Hence it will not speculate on the negative approach of this topic, i.e. on the issue whether in one way or another existing EC law and EC-principles hinder the national laws from protecting minorities. For the examination of the latter question it might be helpful to consider the recent judgements of the European Court of Justice in the cases *Bickel/ Franz* (24 November 1998)[8] and *Angonese* (6 June 2000).[9] There the Court checked

---

[7] See amongst different statements the answer of Commissioner Van den Broek relating to the written question E-2773/93 stating that 'the status of minorities and autonomous regions as such do not fall within the competencies of the Community'. This was also expressed by Delor in his response to the written question No. 3264/92 (see OJ 1993 No C 280, p. 28). Note that the Commission surprisingly states (and, indeed, incorrectly) in its report (at least in its German version) on 'the lesser used languages in the European Union' that rights of minorities 'were included', next to cultural diversity and subsidiarity in the Maastricht Treaty (representing 'different facets of one stone') (KOM (94) 602, 15.12.94).

[8] The judgement in this case C-274/96 was issued on 24 November 1998 (see under http://www.curia.eu.int/jurisp/cgi-bin/form.pl?lang=en). For comments see: Gabriel Toggenburg, Der EuGH und der Minderheitenschutz, *European Law Reporter*, Heft 1 (1999), p.11; Arthur Frei/Wolfgang Bauer, 'Ein Beitrag zum Urteil des Europäischen Gerichtshofes vom 24.November 1998 in der Rechtssache RS C-274/96, Bickel und Franz', *Informator* (Jänner 1999), S. 106; Meinhard Novak, 'EuGH: Gleichbehandlung bei der Gerichtssprache', *Europäische Zeitschrift für Wirtschaftsrecht* (Heft 3/1999), p. 82; Bruno de Witte, 'Free movement of Persons and Language Legislation of the Member States of the EU', *Academia*, No. 18, 1999, p. 1; Gabriel Toggenburg, 'Der Europäische Gerichtshof - unverhoffter Anwalt der Minderheiten Europas?', *Academia*, No. 18, 1999, p. 7; Andrea Gattini, 'La non discriminazione di cittadini comunitari nell'uso della lingua nel processo penale: il caso Bickel', *Rivista di diritto internazionale*, Vol. CXXXII (1999), p. 106; Rudolf Streinz, Gleichbehandlung bei der Gerichtssprache, *Europäische Zeitschrift für Wirtschaftsrecht*, Heft 10 (1999) 5, pp. 490 and 491; Elisabetta Palici di Suni Prat, 'L'uso della lingua materna tra tutela delle minoranze e parità di trattamento nel diritto comunitario', *Diritto comparato ed Europeo* (1999-I), p. 171; Barry Doherty, 'Bickel-Extending the Boundaries of European Citizenship?', *Irish Journal of European Law*, Vol. 8 (1999) Nos. 1 and 2, pp. 70-83;

regional provisions aiming at the protection of the German minority living in the Autonomous Province of Bozen (South Tyrol in Northern Italy) against Community law. Furthermore, in this context, it is essential to examine the attitude of Community Law regarding linguistic restraints (but, as said above, there is no space for all these reflections in this paper).

2. THE EUROPEAN PARLIAMENT'S MINORITY RELATED RESOLUTIONS

As already mentioned above, the activities of the EC relating to minorities are rather scarce. Measures which have been taken to date can be divided into four groups: (a) measures of a mainly political character, developed by the European Parliament and characterised by a normative approach; (b) measures undertaken by the European Commission, the Council (and the Parliament), characterised by a functional, i.e. financial approach; (c) measures taken within the framework of the EC/EU's foreign relations, which differ from the already mentioned two groups as they are not directed at the internal sphere of the EU (which does not, however, mean that they could not also have internal implications); and (d) not minority orientated policies and programme-type measures (not treated here), which still are relevant to minority issues. These include areas such as human rights policy, anti-racism policy, asylum policy, refugee policy, the attitude towards third-State nationals, the role of the regions in the EU, etc.

In conformity with its value-orientated role the European Parliament should be identified as the organ which has revealed the most intensive interest in minority issues. In fact the Parliament says, that it *'attaches great importance to the participation of cultural, racial and ethnic minorities in both social and political decision making processes'* and that Parliament itself should *'represent the cultural diversity of Europe'*.[10] To date several motions for resolutions dealing with the situation of minorities have been initiated within the European Parliament, though only a few of them have succeeded in being considered for further discussion. One has to bear in mind that the resolutions described in the following are of non-binding nature (due to this fact it was possible to legislate without referring to a specific competence basis) and therefore lack real practical effect.

Miele Bulterman, Case C-274/96, 'Criminal proceedings against Horst Otto Bickel and Ulrich Franz', *Common Market Law Review* Vol. 36 (1999), p. 1325; Peter Hilpold, 'Unionsbürgerschaft und Sprachenrechte in der EU – Das Vorabentscheidungsverfahren Bickel und Franz', *Juristische Blätter*, Heft 2 (February 2000), pp. 93-101.

[9] The Judgement in this case C-281/98 was issued on 6 June 2000 (see under http://www.curia.eu.int/jurisp/cgi-bin/form.pl?lang=en). For comments see: Gabriel Toggenburg, 'Horizontale Drittwirkung der Personenfreizügigkeit vor dem Hintergrund der Südtiroler Automomie', *European Law Reporter*, 7/8, 2000, pp. 242-247.

[10] See the resolution on 'racism, xenophobia and anti-semitism and on further steps to combat racial discrimination' (OJ 1999 no. C 98, p. 488).

2.1 The 1981 Resolution

The 1981 European Parliament **Resolution on a Community Charter of Regional Languages and Cultures and on a Charter of Rights of Ethnic Minorities**,[11] requested national, regional and local authorities to allow and promote the instruction of regional languages and cultures in official curricula from nursery school up to university level; to allow and to ensure sufficient access to local radio and television; and to ensure that individuals are allowed to use their own language in the field of public life and social affairs in their dealings with official bodies and in the courts (paragraph 1). The Resolution recommended, furthermore, that the regional funds should provide assistance for projects designed to support regional and folk cultures and regional economic projects (paragraphs 4 and 6). Finally, Parliament called on the Commission to review all Community legislation or practices which discriminate against minority languages (paragraph 5).

2.2 The 1983 Resolution

In 1983 Parliament passed a **Resolution on Measures in Favour of Linguistic and Cultural Minorities**.[12] Considering that some 30 million EU citizens have as their mother tongue a regional or a little spoken language, Parliament underlined the importance of the above-mentioned resolution of 1981, and again called upon the Commission to continue and intensify its efforts in this area; the Commission was asked to report the practical measures taken or due to be taken in the future to the Parliament. The resolution furthermore called upon the Council to ensure that the principles laid down are respected in practice.

2.3 The 1987 Resolution

A new **Resolution on the Languages and Cultures of the Regional and Ethnic in the European Community** (the so-called Kujpers Resolution) was adopted by the Parliament in 1987.[13] After regretting the lack of any progress in this matter, in this Resolution the Parliament provided different recommendations to the member States in the field of education, the mass media, cultural infrastructure, economic and social life as well as in the field of State administration and jurisdiction. In this last area the Parliament recommended in particular:

---

[11] Adopted by Parliament on 16 October 1981 on the basis of the so-called 'Arfé report' prepared by the Italian Rapporteur, Gaetano Arfé (OJ 1981 No. C 287, p. 106).

[12] Draft prepared by Gaetano Arfé and adopted by the European Parliament on 11 February 1983 (OJ 1983 No. C 68, p. 103).

[13] Draft prepared by Rapporteur Willy Kujpers and adopted by the European Parliament on 30 October 1987 (OJ 1987 No. C 318, p. 160).

to provide 'a direct legal basis for the use of regional and minority languages, in the first instance in the local authorities of areas where a minority group does exist',
to review 'national provisions and practices that discriminate against minority languages',
to require 'decentralised and central government services also to use national, regional and minority languages in the areas concerned' (paragraph 6).

It also officially recommended the recognition of surnames and place names expressed in a regional or minority language as well as the acceptance of place names and indications on electoral lists. Furthermore the measures should include:

'providing for the use of the regional and minority languages in postal concerns (postal services, etc.), [...] providing for consumer information and product labelling in regional and minority languages, providing for the use of regional languages for road and other public signs and street names' (paragraph 9).

The Parliament furthermore underlined the need for economic support and stressed its determination to ensure that at least ε 1,000,000 would be provided by the 1988 budget in favour of minority languages. It also stated that the Intergroup on Lesser Used Languages would be granted full status as an official Intergroup of the European Parliament.[14]

Further developments led to a report establishing a Charter of Rights for Ethnic Groups in 1988. Parliament never took a decision on this so-called 'Stauffenberg report',[15] as its term of office was running out. After the elections, the Parliament's Law Committee resumed work on a revised version of the Stauffenberg report and Count Stauffenberg's successor, Siegbert Alber presented the so-called 'Alber report' in 1993. This report incorporated much of the contents of the draft of the Federal Union of European Nationalities (FUEN).[16] As the Parliament wanted to observe which position the developments inside the Council of Europe (regarding a Charter on Regional and Minority Languages)[17] would take, it did not reach a decision on this revised report.

2.4 The 1994 Resolution

As a follow up the Parliament adopted, in 1994, a Resolution on Linguistic Minorities in the European Community on the basis of the so-called 'Killilea

---

[14] The Intergroup, consisting of MEPs and representing different minorities, was founded in 1980 with the task of spreading conscience on minority issues in all the political parties. From 1983 onwards it has been meeting on a regular basis. See the interview of its former president Joan Vallvé in *Academia* 18 (1999), p. 35 (see http://www.eurac.edu/Academia/index.asp). The current president is Eluned Morgan.

[15] PE 156.208.

[16] PE 204.838. The draft and a detailed collection of all the different sources of the Alber draft can be found in Christoph Pan, *Collection of Sources* (1994).

[17] See for this Convention: http://conventions.coe.int/treaty/EN/cadreprincipal.htm

report',[18] which again referred to the Arfé resolutions and pointed out that the member States should recognise their linguistic minorities and create the basic conditions for the preservation and development of these languages. The legal acts should

> 'at least cover the use and encouragement of such languages and cultures in the spheres of education, justice and public administration, the media, toponymics and other sectors of public and cultural life' (paragraph 4).

The Parliament, furthermore, called upon national governments and parliaments to sign and ratify the Council of Europe's Charter on Regional Languages, and recommended further financial support for the national Committees of the 'European Bureau for Lesser Used Languages' (EBLUL). It also called upon the European Commission to take account of the lesser used languages and their attendant cultures when elaborating various areas of Community policy. The Parliament desired the European Council and the Commission to

> 'ensure that adequate budgetary provision is made for the Community's programmes in favour of lesser used languages [...] and propose a multi-annual action programme in this field' (paragraph 11(b)).

The European Regional Development Fund should allocate for such purposes, and EC programmes for economic and social reconstruction should take due account of speakers of lesser used languages spoken in Central and Eastern European countries. Finally, the European Parliament specified that all these recommendations should also be applied to non-territorial autochthonous minorities (expressly mentioning the Roma and Sinti) which as such do not jeopardise the territorial integrity or public order of the member States.

2.5 The EP's mainstreaming approach

In documents treating human rights policy, cross-border co-operation, treaty revision or racism the Parliament usually mentions minority consciousness as an important aim. This goes also for the resolutions of the EP, in which the political situation of specific countries is commented.

In its **Resolution on human rights in the world in 1997 and 1998 and European Union human rights policy** the Parliament

> 'notes that many of the most violent conflicts around the world in recent years have involved problems related to minorities [...] Will draw up a definition of minority rights in order to lend greater weight to its policy [...] Calls for a redoubling of international efforts to end large scale discrimination against religious, national, linguistic or ethnic minorities and to help resolve inter-ethnic conflicts [...] Calls for greater recognition and protection of communal rights, and in particular of the rights of indigenous people [...] Calls for the

---

[18] See OJ 1994 No. C 61, p. 110.

strengthening of international monitoring mechanisms in relation to minority rights [...] Stresses the importance of EU support for the just treatment of minorities in Central and Eastern European countries, in strict observance of fundamental rights and freedoms and the principles of equality and citizenship and without undermining their identities, particularly in candidate countries'.[19]

In this context the Parliament uses a wide concept of minority as it says in its **Resolution on respect for human rights in the European Union** (1997) that an accession to the European Union is out of question for States

'which do not respect fundamental human rights, and calls on the Commission and Council to lay particular stress on the rights of minorities (ethnic, linguistic, religious, homosexual etc.) at the time of enlargement negotiations'.[20]

Another example of this mainstreaming approach is the **Resolution on racism, xenophobia and anti-Semitism and on further steps to combat racial discrimination** where the Parliament states that combating discrimination against immigrants and religious minorities is '*integral to any comprehensive policy against racism and xenophobia*'. Indeed there the Parliament says very clearly that it attaches great importance to '*the participation of cultural, racial and ethnic minorities in both social and political decision-making processes*'.[21] In its **Resolution on the role of public service television in a multi-media society** the Parliament calls on public service broadcasters '*to enact real equal opportunities to improve the representation of women and ethnic minorities in all television employment*'.[22] And in the Parliament's **Resolution on poor conditions in prisons in the European Union** special reference is made to '*particular groups requiring specific treatment: women, immigrants, homosexuals, and members of ethnic and religious minorities*'.[23]

In Resolutions on specific countries the Parliament stresses the importance of equal access for all sections of society to training and education (**Resolution on the political situation in South America**),[24] underlines the importance to guarantee equal rights to religious minorities (**Resolution on the violation of political and human rights in the Islamic Republic of Iran**)[25] and states that the only path to recognition of the international community and to a solution of a deep internal crisis is a meaningful political dialogue between the (Burma-) authorities and representatives of ethnic minorities (**Resolution on Burma, 1999**).[26]

---

[19] See OJ 1999 No. C 98, p. 270 (paras. 20-26).
[20] See OJ 1999 No. C 98, p. 279 (para. 10).
[21] See OJ 1999 No. C 98, p. 488 (reasoning point N).
[22] See OJ 1996 No. C 320, p. 180 (para. 27).
[23] See OJ 1996 No. C 32, p. 102 (para. 4).
[24] See OJ 1989 No. C 47, p. 28 (para. 10).
[25] See OJ, 1996 No. C 96, p. 295 (reasoning point G and para. 4).
[26] See OJ 1999 No. C 219, p. 405 (para. 6).

2.6 Resolutions regarding specific minorities

Last but not least one has to mention those EP-Resolutions which are treating one specific minority. Whereas the **Resolution on the situation of human rights and indigenous minorities in Argentina** (protesting against land allocation),[27] the **Resolution on the political rights of minorities in Albania** or the **Resolution on the protection of minority rights and human rights in Romania** (the latter being very detailed and aiming at the removal of specific national provisions which restrict the use of minority languages at school)[28] have mere external character, the **Resolution on discrimination on Roma** refers to an (also) EU-internal situation. In the latter the Parliament recognises the special Roma-culture and announces a special report *'as a matter of urgency'* and calls on the Commission to increase its efforts to help the Roma people *'to integrate in the societies in which they live and to contribute to that culture'*.[29]

3. OTHER EC MEASURES SUSTAINING MINORITIES AND MINORITY LANGUAGES

The second group of measures taken within the EU includes measures adopted by or in collaboration with other EC organs. Due to the lack of normative competence in the field of minority protection, it was not possible to create binding normative acts such as directives or regulations. Hence the approach was more of a mainstreaming one. This implies that the measures are of a technical nature (for example, providing for a budget sustaining minority-favouring institutions and/or activities) and it is thus only possible to provide an idea as to what has been done in this context.

Calls by the Parliament in the first Arfé Resolution soon produced results. In 1982 a non-profit organisation, the European Bureau for Lesser Used Languages (EBLUL), was founded. This Organization considers itself to be representative of the 50 million EU citizens who speak more than thirty different autochthonous languages. It seeks to promote and defend these regional or minority languages and the linguistic rights of those who speak them. The Bureau is independent, its members are volunteer associations and official institutions active in the promotion of minority languages throughout the EU. The members' associations are organised within 13 Member State Committees (Portugal and Greece are excepted). EBLUL is mainly funded by the European Commission.

---

[27] See OJ 1997 No. C 115, p. 171.
[28] See OJ 1995 No. C 249, p. 157.
[29] See OJ 1995 No. C 249, p. 156.

3.1 Financial support favouring minority protection

In 1982 the European Parliament established the B3-1006 budget line which provides funds for financing measures supporting lesser used regional or minority languages. This position has been renewed yearly[30] and the amount has been steadily increased (from 100,000 ECU in 1983 up to 4 million ECU in 1995-1996).[31] The 1999 *'support from the European Commission for measures to promote and safeguard regional or minority languages'* provides 2,250,000 ECU (OJ 1999 No. C 125, pp. 14-18). This support will be used for co-financing (up to 50%) of projects aimed at improving the quality of learning and the instruction of regional and/or minority languages as well as at preparing a future dissemination of information, experience and expertise in the field of regional/minority languages. The languages which may benefit from this budget are the indigenous languages traditionally spoken by part of the population in an EU Member State. Dialects, migrant languages and artificially created languages are excluded. 75-90 projects are expected to be co-financed by the 1999 budget.[32] In the quoted Communication the Commission seems to encounter possible reservations concerning competencies or political implications when stating that *'In consideration of member States' own powers and the principle of subsidiarity, any activity with a political or legislative impact is excluded'* (see end of page 14 of the quoted OJ).

There has been criticism[33] that there is no multi-annual action programme providing long-term financial support. The Commission is currently examining the feasibility of proposing such a programme.[34] For such a budget position the Commission will have to find an appropriate legal basis.[35]

---

[30] The budget line is in contrast to a multiannual programme and addendum which is annually appropriated by the European Parliament for a particular subject matter.

[31] Only the 1997 budget reduced the funds: only 3, 675 million ECU were distributed (see OJ 1997 No. C 178, p. 4).

[32] In 1995 and 1996 over 150 respective projects were co-financed. A description of the projects can be found in: Carys Wynne/Zoe Bray, *Compendium of projects promoting autochthonous minority languages in the European Union financed by the European Commission, 1995 and 1996.*

[33] See, for example, *Contact Bulletin* (Spring 1997) p. 6.

[34] The Commission's Communication in OJ 1999 No. C 125, p. 14.

[35] The budget line was not endowed with sufficient legal basis. Any Community expenditure requires a dual basis - the entry in the budget (which per se requires a Community competence in the respective field) and, as a general rule, the prior adoption of an act of secondary legislation authorising the expenditure in question. The only exception to the latter requirement concerns the funding of non-significant actions, namely pilot projects or preparatory actions. In that case, the legal basis lies in the Commission's power of initiative (see Art. 211 EC). In any other case the Commission would infringe Community Law (the principle of enumerated powers, Art. 7(1) EC). In fact, the 1998 Budget Line was suspended in May 1998 due to a ruling of the ECJ (Judgement of 12 May 1998 in Case C-106/96) underlining the mentioned legal situation and stating that the fact that projects are related to short-term activities, with a maximum duration of one year, which are not coordinated inter se and which entail considerably less expenditure than the pluri-annual programme does not automatically mean that they are 'non-significant' measures. The Commission must therefore clearly demonstrate that the planned measure is not significant.

3.2 Various studies on minority issues co-financed by the EC

Following Parliament's Kujpers Resolution, the European Commission and EBLUL started the establishment of the MERCATOR programme.[36] The MERCATOR network consists of four research institutions[37] which deal with general issues (interdisciplinary studies, seminars on the status of ethno-linguistic minorities), formation (studies on bilingualism and bilingual instruction), media and minority languages (establishment of a database and a MERCATOR media guide), and legislation (overall collection of language-related legal sources). Until 1994, the network was co-ordinated by EBLUL, since then by the European Commission.

In addition, a number of studies have been published by the EC: in 1984 the Commission published a study on the situation of the lesser used languages in the European Community,[38] in 1990 a study on the situation of linguistic minorities in Greece, Spain and Portugal,[39] and in 1992 the Commission (DG XXII) put a new study on the minority languages out to tender, highlighting the growing value of diversity for economic deployment and European integration. A network of researchers from important research institutions was established,[40] charged with elaborating a project aimed at providing a methodologically sound study permitting a comparative understanding of the current situation of the various language groups.[41] This project – known as EUROMOSAIC – in 1996 led to the publication of the EUROMOSAIC Report on the Production and Reproduction of the Minority Language Groups in the European Union.[42]

Especially the EU's eastern enlargement provided an impetus to look beyond the linguistic dimension of minorities in Europe, giving the minority question a clear political (and legal) dimension. This new approach, however seems to be limited to the minorities in Central and Eastern Europe. The European Commission (within the PHARE Programme) co-financed a Joint Programme

---

[36] Named after a famous cartographer of the sixteenth century who in his maps used the respective regional languages. Jens Woelk, 'Das Mercator-Netzwerk ist geknüpft', *Pogrom*, (August/September 1995) p. 36.

[37] University of Paris X-Nanterre; Fryske Akademy in Ljouwert/Leeuwarden, Friesland, www.fa.knaw.nl/mercator; University Wales at Aberystwyth, www.aber.ac.uk/~merwww; CIEMEN in Barcelona, www.troc.es/ciemen/mercator/index-gb.htm.

[38] 'Linguistic Minorities in the EC-countries' (summary published by the Office for Official Publications of the European Communities in 1990).

[39] 'Linguistic Minorities in the EEC: Spain, Portugal, Greece', Summary of the report by Miquel Siguan, Office for Official Publications (1990). See also the Working Paper of the Parliament on the 'Lesser used languages in Austria, Finland and Sweden', Education and Culture Series W-5, PE 167.009 (most of the working papers of the Parliament's Directorate-General for Research can be downloaded from the Parliament's web site).

[40] The Institut de Sociolinguistica Catalana (Barcelona), the Centre de recherche sur le plurilinguisme (Brussels) and the Research Centre Wales (Bangor).

[41] Normand Labrie, Peter H. Nelde and Peter J. Weber, 'Projet d'étude sur les langues moins répandues dans l'UE', *Europa Etnica* 2 (1994).

[42] Published by the Office for Official Publications of the European Communities, ISBN 92-827-5512-6.

entitled *'Minorities in Central European Countries'* together with the Council of Europe, which included seminars[43] on 'minorities and media', 'minorities and education', 'minorities and participation in decision-making processes'.[44]

3.3 The cultural dimension of EU as access road for minority favouring measures

The Treaty of Maastricht gave the process of European integration a clear transeconomic dimension by establishing a political Union. Within the context of minority rights, of special interest is Title IX-Culture (Article 128 TEC)[45], as it clearly emphasises the cultural dimension of the European integration and at the same time indirectly recognises that not a single Member State is culturally homogenous: The EC is asked to contribute to the flowering of the *'cultures of the member States, while respecting their national and regional*[46] *diversity'*.[47]

The cultural approach of the Community is designed to be a multi-political one as it shall *'take cultural aspects into account in its action under other provisions of the Treaty [...]'* (Article 151 paragraph 4 EC, ex-Article 128 paragraph 4 TEC). This kind of 'cultural impact assessment clause' establishes culture as an aspect which has to be respected by the Community *semper et ubique* thus providing a major role to this competence provision. It is interesting to note that this latter clause was then functionally specified as Amsterdam added *'[...] in particular in order to respect and to promote the diversity of its cultures'*.

Furthermore, one ought to draw attention to the changes inserted in the subvention provisions which allow, to a certain degree, the financial assistance to cultures by stating that *'aid to promote culture and heritage conservation where such aid does not affect trading conditions and competition in the Community to an extent that is contrary to the common interest'* can be considered compatible with the internal market.[48] Culture and other new Community

---

[43] Results of the seminar held in Brno (Slovenia) on 1-2 December 1997 were published by the Council of Europe in 1998 under the title 'Participation of national minorities in decision-making processes'.

[44] Other financed projects were regular meetings of representatives of Governmental Offices for National Minorities (Project MIN I) or various study visits for representatives of Offices for National Minorities to similar institutions in other countries (Project MIN II). See the Council of Europe's Final Report to the European Commission on the implementation of the Joint Programme with the Council of Europe entitled 'Minorities in Central European Countries' (April 1998).

[45] It has been argued that an incentive for the inclusion of competence in the field of culture in the Treaty (being the first change of the 'constitutional' treaties after the end of the Cold War) was the fear of a 'Balkanization' of Western Europe (see Adam Biscoe, loc. cit. n. 1, at p. 93).

[46] The term 'regional' diversity refers to cultures produced and cultivated by local groups, linguistic or ethnic minorities, having a regional importance, but it does not relate to an eventual linking to a sub-national administrative unit.

[47] Art. 151 para. 1 EC (ex i.e. before Amsterdam, Art. 128 para. 1 TEC).

[48] Art. 87 (2d) EC (ex Art. 92(3) TEC).

competencies such as education[49] opened up new legislative possibilities, or better still, gave them a solid basis, as one has to state that cultural measures had already been taken in times in which the integration process was formally limited to the economic dimension.[50]

A striking example of the fact that already during the pre-Maastricht period some cultural, and in this case minority protective measures were offered is the Council Directive dated back as far as 1977, referring to the education of the children of migrant workers (EU citizens) in their own mother tongue as well as studies on their home regions.[51] The exclusive legal basis for this Directive was Article 49 of the EC Treaty.[52] This act seems *prima facie* to be only remotely linked to the free movement of workers. It furthermore suggests that Articles 48 and 49 TEC not only push the member States into abolishing existing forms of discrimination which jeopardise the mobility of workers, but seems to function also as a basis for adopting affirmative actions on behalf of migrant workers in order to enhance the mobility. The Directive appears to express the view that the free movement of workers should not threaten the cultural identity of persons concerned (although on the other hand, linguistic variety existing within the Community may not impede this free movement).[53]

In the field of culture different programmes (some of them already in existence before Maastricht) provide financial support also for minority-relevant situations such as, for example, the translation and dissemination of works of contemporary literature in lesser used languages,[54] the conservation of regional culture,[55] its promotion[56] or research on minority languages.

---

[49] See Arts. 149 and 150 (ex Arts. 126 and 127 EC).

[50] Bruno de Witte, 'The Scope of Community Powers in Education and Culture in the Light of Subsequent Practice', in R. Bieber and G. Ress, *The Dynamics of EC Law* (1987), p. 261.

[51] Directive 77/486 of July 1977, OJ 1977 No. L 199, p. 32. In two subsequent reports the Commission stated that the Member States were not (properly) transposing the directives. (See the 1988 report in COM (88) 787 Final). The Directive was also incorporated in the Agreement on the European Economic Area (Annex V of the Treaty – OJ 1994 No. L001, p. 325). The interest of the Community in the field of education of children living under special conditions later found expression in the resolution of the Council of Ministers meeting of 22 May 1989 on school provision for children of occupational travellers (see OJ 1989 No. C 153, p. 1) mainly addressing children of the around 200,000 bargemen, showmen and circus-people, or the Resolution of the Council of Ministers of Education meeting on 22 May 1989 on school provision for Gypsy and Traveller children (see OJ 1989 No. C 153, p. 3). The Community programme COMENIUS (see OJ 1995 No. L 87) finances measures foreseen in Directive 77/486. See Léonce Bekemans and Yera Ortiz de Urbina, 'The teaching of immigrants in the European Union', PE 167.225, EP-Working Paper, Education and Culture Series.

[52] Now Art. 40 EC (regulating the mobility of workers). The Maastricht Treaty introduced a legal basis for such measures inserting the chapter 'Education, Vocational Training and Youth' in Arts. 126 (now 149) and 127 (now 150) TEC.

[53] See De Witte, 'The scope of ... ', loc. cit. n. 50, at p. 267.

[54] Community programme ARIANE (OJ 1997 No. L 291 and OJ 1999 No. L 57).

[55] This may be funded under the RAPHAEL programme (see OJ 1997 No. L 305).

[56] This may be funded under the KALEIDOSCOPE programme (see OJ 1996 No. L 99 and OJ 1999 No. L 57). ARIANE, RAPHAEL and KALEIDOSCOPE will be grouped together in the new programme CULTURE 2000 (see Commission Proposal COM (98) 266 final). These three

This changing legal background and political statements as e.g. the following made by President Prodi

> '[...] we must never forget that Europe is all about diversity. Therefore it needs us to respect and reap the rewards of diversity. European integration has always been about diverse peoples with varied cultures [...]. Diversity is one of Europe's greatest treasures [...].'[57]

show that diversity is perceived more and more as something which has to be protected and something, Europe has to be based upon. The political commitment to the concept of cultural diversity and its correlation with the protection of minorities results also from the following declaration of the entire Council:

> 'Europe, characterised by solidarity and a rich cultural mix, is founded on respect for diversity and on tolerance. All member States [...] are continuously striving to build and maintain a Europe based on [...] the diversity of its cultures and languages, a Europe where [...] rights of minorities are protected'.[58]

3.4 A hint at the regional dimension of both EU and minority issues

Regarding the regional dimension of the integration process, which has been enhanced in the Maastricht Treaty and which is often considered to be of significant importance for minorities,[59] one should not be too optimistic. The establishment of the Committee of the Regions and Local Authorities (CoR) indicates a specific commitment to the constantly growing role of the regions in Europe.[60] But COR holds a purely advisory status. It consists of both regional

---

programmes were administered by the Commission's DG X (Audio-visual, Information, Communication and Culture).

[57] Speech at the inauguration of the EMCR in Vienna, 7 April 2000.

[58] See 'Declaration by the Council and the representatives of the Governments of the Member States[...] on respecting diversity and combating racism and xenophobia', OJ 1998 No. C 001, p. 1. On the other hand diversity is not always meant to include minority cultures. This can be seen e.g. in the discussion regarding the inclusion of minority languages in the 'European Year of Languages' (see e.g. www.eurolang.net/news.asp?id=181).

[59] On relations between autonomy/region and minority rights see Javid Rehman, 'The Concept of Autonomy and Minority Rights in Europe', in P. Cumper and S. Wheatley, *Minority Rights in the 'New' Europe* (1999), p. 217; Daniel Thürer, 'Region und Minderheitenschutz - Aufbauelemente einer europäischen Architektur?', in U. Beyerlin, M. Bothe, R. Hofmann and E.-U. Petersmann, *Recht zwischen Umbruch und Bewahrung, Festschrift für R. Bernhardt* (1995) p. 1337; Stefan Oeter, 'Volksgruppen- und Minderheitenschutz durch Autonomieregelungen', in D. Blumenwitz, G.H. Gornig and D. Murswiek, *Der Beitritt ...*, op. cit. n. 1, pp. 163.

[60] CoR (see Artt. 263-265 EC, ex Art. 198a-c TEC) was inserted into the Maastricht Treaty mainly following the requests of the German *Länder*, the Belgian and Spanish regions/communities, the Assembly of the Regions and the Conference on a Europe of the Regions as it was supposed to provide a sort of power compensation: Some of the competence areas transferred via the Maastricht Treaty to the Community (culture, education) were, in some member States, dominated (in one way or another) by the respective regions. Despite the fact that the Maastricht Treaty furthermore opened the Council of the EU to members of regional governments (as long as they are 'authorised to commit the government of the Member State' (see Art.

and local level representatives, which are appointed by the Council upon the recommendation of national governments and must be consulted by the Council and Commission only in a restricted range of policy areas (including education, culture, economic and social cohesion). Nevertheless, one has to say that strong legislative and administrative powers of the regions in Europe (guaranteed through an effective insertion of regional interests in the legislative processes at the European level) as well as a widening of the subsidiarity principle established in Maastricht (which up to now only regulates the relationship between the national and the communitarian level – see Article 5 TEC), the flowering of regional cultures (through different EC financial programmes) and strong regional economies (through an effective EC regional policy)[61] tendentiously (!) favour minorities. The realisation of the Autonomy, Welfare and Culture-Protection triangle (AWCP conditions) in a given region may produce a situation in which the legal protection of minorities becomes less urgent. This, however, is valid above all for those minorities who build a majority in a geographical region which coincides with the administrative region gaining advantages from the above mentioned Community policies and institutions.[62] Anyway, there is no doubt that trans-regional co-operation favours minorities living in border areas. In fact the Parliament states in its **Resolution on cross-border and inter-regional co-operation** that *'co-operation between border regions can improve the opportunities for many European linguistic minorities to preserve and develop their culture, by helping to build structures which support the minority'*.[63]

3.5 Economic aspects

EU-politicians have realised that social exclusion, attendant problems and discrimination produce economic costs as these factors lead to unemployment, inadequate access to public and private services and wasted talents. On the other side surveys show that inclusion practised in companies fosters productivity.[64] In fact minorities seem to be perceived ever more as economic potential. A Commissioner stated that *'immigrants and ethnic minorities play an important role in Europe's economic development. Europe needs skill, talent, innovation and*

---

203 EC, ex Art. 146 TEC), this compensation does not seem to be satisfactory because of the above mentioned reasons.

[61] In 1995 the European Regional Development Fund (ERDF) included also a cultural dimension. Still, the indicators for the identification of problem areas are of an economic nature. For critical remarks regarding the minority protective effect of the Community's regional policy see: Biscoe, loc. cit. n. 1, at p. 92.

[62] Compare Bruno de Witte who states that 'regions may [...] correspond to any ethnically or linguistically defined territory or not, and minority areas may have regional autonomy or not, and this choice is still entirely left to the Member States' internal constitutional rules' (De Witte, *Politics versus ...*, op. cit. n. 1, at p. 16).

[63] See OJ 1997 No. C 167, p. 245.

[64] See Commissioner Diamantopoulou in her speech at the conference 'Immigration, Discrimination and the Far-Right Public Policy Breakfast', Brussels, 20 June 2000.

diversity. Immigrant and ethnic minority groups help provide these crucial qualities'.[65]

Anyway, the will to integrate minorities in the European economies is not limited to mere political statements. The Commission's Communication concerning the Structural Funds stresses that *'special attention should be given to the needs of [...] ethnic minorities [...] and to the development of appropriate preventive and active policies to promote their integration into the labour market'.*[66] Furthermore, there are efforts to *'raise awareness and capability'* in particular in minority groups for the opportunities offered by information society. Also the multi-annual programme to promote the linguistic diversity of the Community in the information society (MLIS) aims (also) at promoting a multilingual Europe and partly funds MELIN (Minority European Languages Information Network).[67]

Another example of the economic area can serve the initiative Ethnic Minority Business Network (EMBNET)[68] which is co-financed by the Commission and basically designed to augment the contribution of ethnic minority businesses (EMB) to local and national economies and to identify and transfer the best practices in the development and expansion of ethnic minority enterprises among EU member States.

4. MINORITY PROTECTION IN THE EUROPEAN COMMUNITY'S FOREIGN RELATIONS

4.1 Minority protection becoming part of EU's external habits

The impetus for using EC Foreign Trade to promote human rights in third States emerged quite immediately after the entry into force of LOMÉ I, when the European Parliament urged the Council – after the killing of several hundreds thousands people in Uganda – to suspend the flow of money directed towards this country. LOMÉ IV (1989) contained the first proper human rights clause in an EC agreement with third States. Since then different types of human rights clauses, varying in content as well as in enforcement, have been developed. Accordingly, in the period following May 1995, the agreements have contained

---

[65] See the speech by Padraig Flynn (European Commissioner for employment and social affairs under President Santer) delivered on 7 July 1998 (see Rapid file SPEECH/98/154). On the other hand compare 'The Damaging Impact of European Economic and Monetary Union upon Ethnic Minorities' under http://www.bullen.demon.co.uk/cibbb2.htm.

[66] See part II, point B of the quoted Communication (OJ 1999 No. C 267, pp. 2-21). The same is said in the Annex of the 1999 Employment Guidelines (see OJ 1999 No. C 69, pp. 2-8).

[67] See the Council Resolution on the employment and social dimension of the information society (OJ 2000 No. C 008, pp. 1-3). See also the web-sites: http://bangor.ac.uk/cyc/mlin/index.htm and www2.echo.lu/mlis

[68] For further information visit: http://www.embnet.com.

reference either to the Universal Declaration of Human Rights or, when the partner State is an OSCE State, to the OSCE principles.

The treatment of the Kurdish minority was, *inter alia*, the reason for which the European Parliament questioned Turkey's application for membership. An even more striking commitment regarding minorities was taken after the collapse of former Yugoslavia. The then twelve member States convened an international peace conference in The Hague, where they established the so-called Badinter Commission which was responsible for delivering expert opinions on legal questions arising from the dissolution of SFRY.[69] As a follow up to an expert opinion by this Commission, the EC member States agreed on a common position concerning the condition for the recognition of statehood: On 16 December 1991 the Foreign Ministers issued, within the framework of European Political Co-operation, a Declaration on the Guidelines on Recognition of New States in Eastern Europe and the Soviet Union and the Declaration on Yugoslavia. This recognition was made conditional upon amongst other things:

'guarantees for the rights of ethnic and national groups and minorities in accordance with the commitments subscribed to in the framework of the CSCE.'[70]

The EC thereby introduced[71] minority protection as a new element within the spectre of conditions for the recognition of statehood.[72]

The EC/EU has been subjected to criticism because the emphasis given to the minority issue in external relations presents a kind of double standard as the Community still ignores, at least formally, the issue of minority protection within its own borders.[73] Concern for minorities seems to be *'primarily an export article and not one for domestic consumption'*.[74]

---

[69] A. Pellet, 'The Opinions of the Badinter Arbitration Committee – A Second Breath for the Self-Determination of Peoples', *European Journal of International Law*, Vol. 3 (1992), p. 178.

[70] EC Bulletin 1991/12, p.119. Full text in C. Warbrick, 'Current Developments: Public International Law', *International and Comparative Law Quarterly*, Vol. 41 (1992), p. 473.

[71] The historical roots for this development may be seen in Art. 34 of the Berlin Treaty of 1878, which established the freedom of religious groups as quasi-conditio for the recognition of Bulgaria, Montenegro, Rumania and Serbia. See Peter Hilpold, 'Anerkennung der Neustaaten auf dem Balkan', *Archiv des Völkerrechts*, 31. Band, 4. Heft, p.401.

[72] The practice regarding this prerequisite was inconsistent as, for example, Croatia was recognised in 1992, although the Arbitration Committee had expressed reservations in regard to its minority protection laws, and, on the other hand, Macedonia was denied recognition thanks to Greece despite the fact that it complied with all the criteria (Bruno de Witte, Politics Versus Law in the EU's Approach to Ethnic Minorities, EUI working papers, RSC No. 2000/4, p. 5). On the politically special case of Macedonia (some provisions in the Guidelines on recognition were inserted only at a request by Greece, see Peter Hilpold, 'Völkerrechtsprobleme um Makedonien', *Recht in Ost und West* 4 (1998), p. 119, in: Dieter Blumenwitz/Gilbert H. Gornig/Dietrich Murswiek (Eds.), *Fortschritte im Beitrittsprozess der Staaten Ostmittel-, Ost- und Südosteuropas zur Europäischen Union* (1999).

[73] It should be pointed out, however, that ignoring the issue of minority protection also in Central and Eastern European States would be much more damaging. Besides, imposing duties on applicant states, which are not fulfilled by all of the Member States, is a frequent practice. A 'double standard' may also be found in EMU or in the Schengen system, since also in these

In fact minority protection is to be found in resolutions issued by the Joint Assembly of the Convention concluded between the African, Caribbean and Pacific States and the Community, in Agreements on partnership and co-operation, in Council regulations on assistance to and co-operation with developing countries in Asia and Latin America. Furthermore, minority protection is a general element of reports on third countries. The *'Guidelines for joint reports on third countries'* state that the *'situation of minorities'* is a point which has to be specified. These reports have to contain *'specific information on persecution for reasons of race, religion, nationality, membership of a particular social group or political opinion'*.[75]

4.2 The Pact on Stability in Europe

It was already in March 1992 that Balladur, the then French Prime Minister, proposed a sort of stability pact, which was to guarantee good neighbourliness and hence security in Central and Eastern Europe. The French initiative was taken up in December of the same year by the Council of the Community which decided to convene a conference. The scope of this initiative was to improve neighbourly relations by avoiding the issues of borders and by establishing minority rights, with the prospect of accession to the European Union as an incentive.[76] The 'Pact on Stability' was adopted at the conference held in Paris on 20-21 March 1995 by the representatives of 52 member States of the OSCE. [77] It consists of a mere Declaration and a list of 130 bilateral agreements, almost all of them already concluded before the signing of the Pact.[78] The role of the

---

contexts the applicant States have no possibility to opt out (in contrast to some of the Member State which gained such opting out options).

[74] De Witte, *Politics versus ...* , op. cit. no. 1, at p. 3. In this regard I recall Hans van den Broek, who could not really answer the written question E-0963/98 which asked whether the Commission is also that concerned about respect for minority languages in the Member States as it is concerned, for example, about the minority situation in Slovakia, and with which efforts it is considering to ensure respect for Basque, Occitan, Corsican, Breton and other minority languages. Van den Broek merely referred to the B3-1006 budget line (see OJ 1998 No. C 310, p. 150).

[75] Adopted by the Council on 20 June 1994, see OJ 1996 No. C 274, pp. 52-54.

[76] The Presidency Conclusions adopted in Brussels on 11 December 1993 stated that there were three reasons for the initiative: (a) the urgent need to reinforce stability in Europe; (b) the contribution of the Union to the efforts of the countries preparing for accession; and (c) the implementation of the common foreign and security policy (Stability Pact: Summary report, Annex I, para. 6; see Rapid file DOC/93/11). The Presidency Conclusions of Copenhagen of 21-22 June 1993 state in their para. 8 that 'the initiative is directed towards assuring in practice the application of the principles agreed by European countries with regard to respect for borders and rights of minorities' (see Rapid file DOC/93/3).

[77] It has been pointed out that one of the weaknesses of the Pact was the fact that the interested minority groups were neither invited to the negotiations of the Pact nor to the bilateral talks between governments (Kinga Gál, 'Bilateral Agreements in Central and Eastern Europe: A New Inter-State Framework for Minority Protection?', *ECMI Working Paper*, No. 4 (1999), p. 5).

[78] The splendid exception giving the Stability Pact great political importance was the treaty between Hungary and Slovakia signed in March 1995 (www.htmh.hu/dokumentumok/asz-sk-e.htm).

Union was that of initiator,[79] moderator[80] and finally that of sponsor for the Central and Eastern European States,[81] but it had no direct impact whatsoever on EU law and the Communities. After the Pact was signed, the OSCE became responsible for its implementation. The Pact showed that minority issues are of crucial importance for European politics and that in the view of the European Council the *'action in these areas [was] timely and appropriate'*.[82] The European Council saw in the Pact, despite its geographically open character, a means by which to exercise some influence on the candidate countries in the political sphere.[83]

4.3 Minority rights as accession criteria

At the meeting held in Copenhagen in June 1993, the European Council decided *'that the associated countries in Central and Eastern Europe that so desire shall become members of the European Union'* and established conditions to be fulfilled before accession. These conditions present an important element in the Union's Accession Strategy and form the basis for the first Opinions of the Commission on the candidate countries, for the Accession Partnerships as well as for the regular reports of the Commission on the progress of the candidates towards EU membership. Recent developments reveal that the criteria for minority protection are also becoming a crucial element of the EU's new policy towards South-Eastern Europe.[84]

---

[79] The instrument of CSFP 'joint action' was used for convening the inaugural conference.

[80] The Union wanted to 'encourage the parties to establish good neighbour agreements [...] and to undertake efforts to improve, *de jure* and *de facto*, the situation of national minorities [... to] encourage regional co-operation arrangements [...]' (Presidency Conclusions of Brussels of 10-11 December 1993, Annex I, para. 5 - role of the Union, see Rapid file DOC/93/11).

[81] Funds from the PHARE and TACIS Programmes for Democracy. See Biscoe, loc. cit. n. 1, at p. 98 and De Witte, *Politics versus* ... , op. cit. n. 1. See also Regulation No. 2760/98 of 18 December 1998 (OJ 1998 No. L 345, p. 49) which provides funds for cross-border cooperation such as 'cultural exchanges' and 'the development or establishment of facilities and resources to improve the flow of information and communications between border regions, including support for cross-border radio, television, newspaper and other media'.

[82] Presidency Conclusions of Copenhagen, 21-22 June 1993, para. 8 (see Rapid file DOC/93/3).

[83] The Pact has a 'geographically open and evolutionary character, with the possibility of focusing initially on those countries of Central and Eastern Europe which have the prospect of becoming members of the European Union and vis-à-vis which the Union has greater opportunities to exert its influence more effectively [...]. The objective [...] [is] to facilitate rapprochement between those states and the Union and their co-operation with it by helping them to fulfil the conditions listed by the European Council in Copenhagen' (Presidency Conclusions of Brussels, 10-11 December 1993, Annex I, para. 2(2)).

[84] The Commission is launching a new Stabilisation and Association process (Stability Pact). The Stabilisation and Association Agreements (SAAs), for which Bosnia and Herzegovina, Croatia, the Federal Republic of Yugoslavia, FYROM and Albania would be eligible, are supposed to be a new category in this process. Conditions for commencing negotiations on such SAAs are those set out in the Conclusions of the General Affairs Council of 29 April 1997. In its Communication on the Stabilisation and Association process for South Eastern Europe the

One of the political criteria of Copenhagen (beside democracy, rule of law and human rights) is that the candidate country demonstrates *'respect for and protection of minorities'*.[85] When, in July 1997, the Commission presented its Opinions[86] as to whether and to what degree the applicant States fulfilled the conditions for being admitted to accession negotiations, it discussed the respective minority situations in detail, using a broad definition of both minority groups as well as of minority protection.[87] In November 1998 the Commission issued its first regular report in which it analysed whether, in the light of the Copenhagen criteria, the reforms announced or indicated have in fact been implemented since July 1997. A so-called 'composite paper' contains a synthesis of this as well as further recommendations. In its part concerning minorities the Commission welcomes the developments in Latvia and regrets the situation in Estonia. The Commission underlines the discrimination against Roma taking place in Hungary, Slovakia, Bulgaria and the Czech Republic. The situation of the Hungarian minority in Romania is seen in a positive light, but some concerns are expressed about the Hungarians in Slovakia. The Commission concludes that *'overall, the problem of minorities continues to raise concerns in the perspective of enlargement'*.[88] On 13 October 1999 the Commission issued the second round of their regular reports for each candidate country.[89]

Finally, the Accession Partnerships (APs) adopted in 1998 indicated certain short-term and medium-term priorities including also minority items for each candidate state. Slovakia is requested to adopt legislation on the use of minority languages and Latvia and Estonia should facilitate the conditions for the naturalisation of non-citizens. In the medium term it is recommended that the Czech Republic, Hungary, Bulgaria and Romania improve the integration of the Roma population.[90] The new APs were issued on 13 October 1999.[91] Apart from

---

Commission announced that it will prepare regular reports on the developments in the countries in question (COM (1999) 235 final of 26 May 1999). The Commission Staff Working Paper of 17 May 1999 (SEC (99) 714) examines country by country whether or not they comply with the conditions set out in the Council Conclusions of 29 April 1999. One of the criteria is the 'Respect for and protection of minorities' (Stability Pact for the Balkans to be found on: http://195.13.20.69/lguide_stabpact.html

[85] Presidency Conclusions, Copenhagen European Council, 21-22 June 1993, para. 7(A iii). For a critical view on the use of this criteria: Dieter Blumenwitz, 'Die minderheitenschutzrechtlichen Anforderungen der EU ...', loc. cit. n. 1, p. 25.

[86] Published as Supplements to the Bulletin of the European Union, 1997.

[87] As pointed out by Bruno de Witte, the Commission maintained this approach in the case of Latvia and Estonia and made no distinction between citizens and non-citizens (De Witte, *Politics versus ...* , op. cit. n. 1, at p. 6).

[88] www.europa.eu.int/comm/dg1a/enlarge/report_11_98_en/index.htm.

[89] See under point B.1.2 (Human Rights and Protection of Minorities) for the new Commission's views on the respective minority-situations in the applicant States, http://europa.-eu.int/comm/enlargement/report_10_99/intro/index.htm.

[90] According to para. 14 of the Presidency Conclusions of Luxembourg of 12-13 December 1997, the Accession Partnership is the 'key feature of the enhanced pre-accession strategy' (for an enlightenment on the latter see the quoted conclusions; for the accession strategy see Annex IV of the Presidency Conclusions of Essen of 9-10 December 1994). In reality the 'Partnerships' are not

the above mentioned instruments, further mechanisms and *fora* of the enlargement process such as the *'structured relationship'* may be instrumentalised in order to exert delicate pressure on the candidate countries so that they fulfil the criteria defined in Copenhagen.[92]

According to these preliminaries one may conclude that the criteria of Copenhagen turned out to be a kind of 'structural principle' of the enlargement process. The Amsterdam Treaty transposed all the Copenhagen-criteria -except the one concerning minority protection- into Primary law. By doing so, the Treaty gave the criteria a clear legal quality and defined them as founding principles of the EU which are common to all the member States (internal dimension, Article 6 (1) TEC) and which are to be respected by any State applying for membership (external dimension, Article 49 TEC).[93] The fact that the minority clause was kept separate appears to indicate that its inclusion – whereby it would have assumed a clear binding force and an internal dimension – was not desired. Hence it is necessary to examine the expressiveness and the nature of a Copenhagen criterion which was not elevated to the nobility of Primary law.

It was, indeed, the first time that the Community established criteria for the accession of new member States by adopting Presidency Conclusions. In general, the regular conditions for accession are found in Primary Law (Article 49, formerly Article O TEU) and in the Accession Treaties which are to be signed by the member States and the acceding State (see Article 49 TEU). Furthermore, also the *aquis communautaire* is considered to be a condition for accession as the new member States have to comply with it. The reason for establishing 'additional' conditions for accession in Copenhagen was probably to give originally internal obligations (*aquis*) a more visible external direction (as they are directed towards the applicant States) without limiting the

---

a bilateral instrument (as the name would suggest), but mere communications of the Commission (see OJ 1998 No. C 202, pp.1-97). The system of Accession Partnership may be described as a three-level construction, having as its basis a general regulation (regulation no. 622/98, see OJ 1998 No. L 85) which states that the Council decides for each country on the principles, priorities, aims and conditions of the partnership. These statements are then respected in the Commission's communications. The Council's decisions are to be found in OJ 1998 No. L121, pp.16.

[91] See OJ 1999 No. L 335 from 28.12.1999 or: http://europa.u.int.comm/enlargemnt/docs.index.htm.

[92] For the concept of the 'structured relationship' see Annex II of the Presidency Conclusions of Copenhagen of 21-22.06.1993 and in more detail in Annex IV of the Presidency Conclusions of Essen of 9-10.12.1994. Legally, the strongest instruments are the Association Agreements as they are real bilateral treaties based on Art. 300 EC (ex Art. 228 TEC). The case of Slovakia shows that the Association Councils may also assume a role in minority issues: In April 1998 the EU ministers in the AC reiterated the demand for the urgent adoption of a new law on the use of minority languages (see Agence Europe, 29.04.1998, p.7).

[93] Art. 49 EU: 'Any European State which respects the principles set out in Art. 6(1) may apply to become a member of the Union [...]'.

Art. 6(1) EU: 'The Union is founded on the principles of liberty, democracy, respect for human rights and fundamental freedoms, and the rule of law, principles which are common to the Member States'.

Community organs and member States too much in their freedom to regulate accession to the Union: The Copenhagen criteria are not legally binding; they are merely of a political nature, being adopted in the conclusions of the European Council. Nevertheless, in a indirect sense they might be seen as legally binding in as far as they reflect already existing law.[94] Hence the question whether *'respect for and protection of minorities'* is part of the *aquis* or not, should indeed be raised. If no legal Community standard is identified, the standard applied in the course of eastern enlargement has to be of (more or less) political nature.[95]

5. ESTABLISHING NOLENS VOLENS MINORITY PROTECTION AS INTERNAL COMMON PRINCIPLE OF LAW?

Whereas various examples reveal that there are strong EC expressions of respect for minorities *inside* the Communitarian system, the measures undertaken are still limited to the non-legally binding resolutions and financial support for concrete measures and projects. Also in their *external* relations, the European Community, the Union (indeed, the CSFP provisions involve a programmatic indirect hint at the protection of minorities)[96] and individual member States (for example, within the framework of the Council of Europe) have revealed a substantial interest in the issue of minority protection. Since in international relations there is no duty of formal reciprocity which would prevent States from formulating rules of behaviour for other States without being prepared to follow such rules themselves, these activities (being mainly of a political character) have no direct impact on the EU internal legal system.

All this does not mean that EC law is not developing a non-written *'principle common to the laws of the member States'* as *'general principles of Community law'*.[97] Quite to the contrary, referring to the international treaties for the

---

[94] In my opinion the membership of a State violating the Copenhagen criteria would violate the existing Community and EU law, but the accession itself of such a State would not. Those who consider the criteria of Copenhagen as legally binding criteria which must be fulfilled before accession in order to avoid an illegitimate enlargement, will confront the interesting question whether and to what extent the criteria are justiciable. See Thomas Bruha/Oliver Vogt, 'Rechtliche Grundfragen der EU-Erweiterung', *Verfassung und Recht in Übersee* (VRÜ) 30 (1997), p. 477, especially at p. 490. In practical terms there is nearly no difference between these two views.

[95] See Boris Cilevics, 'A view of a Parliamentarian on the Role of Minority Issues in the Process Towards European Integration', *BalkanHR mailing list* (http://www.egroups.com/-message/balkanhr/559?source=1); compare also G. Toggenburg, Öster-reich Krise: Grenzen der Politik, Grenzen des Rechts - zu den juristischen Vehikeln eines politischen Konflikts (not yet published).

[96] Art. 11 EU defines as one objective of the CFSP to 'preserve peace and strengthen international security, in accordance with the principles of the United Nations Charter, as well as the principles of the Helsinki Final Act and the objectives of the Paris Charte'.

[97] See Arts. 6 (2) EU (ex Art. F (2) TEU) and 288 (2) EC (ex Art. 215 (2) TEC).

protection of human rights, the European Court of Justice never excluded the possibility of minority rights being declared general principles of Community law.[98] In the *Bickel/Franz* case the Court upheld that '*of course, the protection of such a minority may constitute a legitimate aim*' for State behaviour.[99] Furthermore the Court seemed to consider the possibility of accepting the protection of minorities as a ground for the justification of an infringement of the principle of non-discrimination on the grounds of nationality (which is, after all, one of the 'holy cows' of Community law). In any case, it should be pointed out that these judicial remarks are very far from a clear commitment on minority protection as a general principle of EC law. In addition, it should be kept in mind that legally minority protection is not clearly defined and it is not equally provided by all the member States.[100] This could constitute an argument against the establishment of EU/EC customary law,[101] but is not necessarily a compelling argument against the establishment of minority protection as a general principle of EC law: The exclusive competence of the Court to establish general principles of Community law in a process of comparing national laws does not require that the principles on the basis of which the Court defines the Communitarian principles must exist in all EU member States.[102] Until now the Court has not established such a principle relating to minority protection.

Despite single commitments and activities it would be possible to conclude that minority protection is not yet a part of the *aquis*, even if developments are currently moving in this direction. As a consequence, the EU has not been legally bound to establish minority protection as a criteria for accession and minority protection (which has always been considered as not completely covered by concepts such as democracy, rule of law, protection of human rights

---

[98] See, for example, Case C-4/73 [1974] ECR 0491; see also Barbara Brandtner and Allan Rosas, 'Human Rights and the External Relations of the European Community: 'An Analysis of Doctrine and Practice', *European Journal of International Law*, Vol. 9 (1998) No. 3, pp. 468-490.

[99] Case C-274/96, para. 29. See Toggenburg, Der EuGH ... , (1999), loc. cit. n. 8, p. 11.

[100] This can be illustrated by the reservation of the French Government to Art. 27 of the 1966 International Covenant on Civil and Political Rights which states that the French nation is one and is indivisible and that therefore there is no room for the existence of minorities in the sense of Art. 27. This issue re-emerged in 1999 during the discussion on whether or not to ratify the Council of Europe Charter on Regional and Minority Languages. The sensible stance of Greece regarding minority-issues is well known. The written question No. 1416/97 by Mr Kaklamanis to the Commission regarding Commission funding for ECMI (OJ 1998 No. C 21, p. 53) may serve as picturesque expression of this sceptical view.

[101] Customary law may be developed as Primary law (*consuetudo et opinio iuris sive necessitatis* of the Member States) or as Secondary law (in this case law may develop independently from the habitus of the member State, for example through the actions of the EC organs. This customary law has to comply with the principle of enumerated powers and is henceforth not of great assistance in our context).

[102] At least this is the case if one considers the mentioned Court competence on Art. 220 EC (ex Art. 164 TEC). This view corresponds in our eyes more to the supranational character of the Community. A contrary view seems adequate if one considers Art. 288 para. 2 EC (ex Art. 215 para. 2) TEC as the basis for competence. See also Niamh Nic Shuibhne, 'The Impact of European Law on Linguistic Diversity', *Irish Journal of European Law*, Vol. 5 (1996) No. 1, pp. 62-80, at p. 76.

and fundamental freedoms) is no legal condition for accession or membership. The role given to the criterion of minority protection will primarily depend on the political constellation dominating the respective phase of Eastern enlargement. Still, in political terms it seems quite impossible that in the future the EC will take essential retrograde steps as it has already devoted significant attention to its new approach towards minorities.

6. NEW PERSPECTIVES

6.1 Amsterdam's new Article 13 TEC: limits and perspectives

The Intergovernmental Conference working on the latest revision of the Treaties was subjected to subtle pressure to introduce a firmer foundation for social rights within the EU. The pressure deriving from the European Parliament was also directed at giving special attention to minorities.[103] Other proponents were independent EU Advisory Committees, different NGOs,[104] the European Trades Union Confederation and the Economic and Social Committee. The result of all this political input is Article 13 TEC whose possible scope is not yet easy to grasp. It reads as follows:

> 'Without prejudice to the other provisions of this Treaty and within its limits of the powers conferred by it upon the Community, the Council, acting unanimously on a proposal from the Commission and after consulting the European Parliament, may take appropriate action to combat discrimination based on sex, racial or ethnic origin, religion or belief, disability, age or sexual orientation.'

In addition to discrimination based on nationality, forbidden already by the old anti-discrimination clause in Article 12 TEC, the Amsterdam Treaty introduced in the new Article 13 TEC a provision for combating discrimination on the basis of eight further listed grounds. The main difference between Articles 12 and 13 TEC is that the latter has no direct effect, since without additional EC

---

[103] Parliament had two representatives in the Reflexion Group, Elmar Brok and Elisabeth Guigon, who insisted on the insertion of the minority issue in the Treaty (see the Dury/Maij Weggen report of 13.03.1996-PE 197.401, especially point 4.13): 'Europe's multiplicity is to be regulated paying attention to the particular protection of traditionally residing national minorities through the creation of Community legal standards in the framework of human rights, democracy and the rule of law' (motion for resolution of Bourlanges/Martin of 26.04.1995 (for the resolution see OJ 1995 No. C 151, p. 56)). Finally, a motion for a resolution by De Giovanni tried, unsuccessfully, to introduce in Art. 13 EC the majority voting procedure (02.06.1997, see PE 222.685).

[104] The most active was the Starting Line Group which received the backing of almost 300 organisations with their initiative Starting Line. ENAR (European Network Against Racism) provides on www.enar-eu.org/ a study on the Amsterdam Treaty 'Guarding standards – shaping the agenda'.

instruments based on Article 13 TEC the spirit of this Article would remain without any practical results.

Other differences between Articles 12 and 13 are less evident, but nevertheless puzzling. Especially the formulation in the first part of Article 13 gave rise to some insecurities as Article 12 TEC[105] uses, despite a similar content, a different formulation[106]: Concerning the field of application, Article 13 TEC uses the formula *'within the limits of the powers conferred by it'*. whereas Article 12 TEC uses *'within the scope of application of this Treaty'*. The difference in these two wordings suggests that the field of application of these two provisions must be different. Still, looking at the two phrases, it seems difficult to define where this difference should lie, as the limits of the single organs´ powers (competencies) are defined by the Treaty itself.[107] On the other hand, the jurisdiction of Article 12 TEC has been very expansive as far as the applicability of this article is concerned. Even situations not immediately linked to Community law have been viewed as *'governed by Community law'*.[108] It seems that only those issues which do not have a link to facts regulated by Community law and whose effects are limited to internal matters of the state remain outside the scope of Article 12 TEC. Such an interpretation leads to a scope which clearly exceeds the *'limits of powers conferred'* on the single organs. Indeed, once the Court has already drawn a distinction between the two concepts of 'competencies' and 'scope' suggesting that the latter is the wider one. So, it would be possible to conclude that the scope of Article 13 TEC is less broad than the one of Article 12 TEC. Measures embodied in Article 13 should be expressions of a competence which is expressly (even if only partly) delegated to the EC.[109]

The limitation on areas in which the Community has competence is crucial for the question whether legislation based on Article 13 TEC may also refer to non-EU citizens. Due to the fact that in practice it is non-EU nationals who are the main victims of ethnic discrimination, this topic has great political impact. In general the Community is not seen as having the competence to rule over third-

---

[105] Art. 12(1) TEC: 'Within the scope of application of this Treaty, and without prejudice to any special provisions contained therein, any discrimination on grounds of nationality shall be prohibited'.

[106] See on all these arising questions Mark Bell, 'The New Art. 13 EC Treaty: A Sound Basis для European Anti-Discrimination Law?', *Maastricht Journal*, Vol. 6, No. 1, (1999) p. 5. Bell as well as Lisa Waddington, 'Testing the Limits of the EC Treaty Article on Non-Discrimination', *Industrial Law Journal*, Vol. 28 (June 1999) No. 2, p. 133.

[107] This can be seen in Art. 7 TEC which says that 'each institution shall act within the limits of powers conferred upon it by this Treaty' (principle of enumerated powers).

[108] See, for example, case C-274/96 (Bickel/Franz), paras. 14, 15, or case C-186/87 (Cowan).

[109] This does not mean that Art. 13 will only become operative in those fields in which the Community has competence *expressis verbis*. According to Mark Bell, the logic prohibiting nationality discrimination, for example in housing (an area in which the EC has no express competence), may be extended to justify the Community establishing common rules against other forms of discrimination in housing: Discrimination in access to housing against ethnic minorities may seriously undermine their ability to migrate to another Member State in the 'freedom and dignity' which Regulation 1612/68 seeks to maintain (Mark Bell, loc. cit. n. 106, p. 18).

state nationals; also, non-EU citizens do not possess rights under Community Law and are reduced to an ignored 'Community minority'.[110] On the other hand, there are provisions which have been regarded as applying to third-State nationals (for example, Article 141 TEC and related secondary legislation) and arguments pleading for such a Community competence such as, for example, the internal market, if it is understood as implying such a power.[111] However, the fact that the Council did not insert an explicit reference to third-country nationals in Article 13 TEC as it had done in some other articles (for example in Article 137(3) TEC) could be interpreted as lack of political will to base legislation concerning third country nationals on Article 13 TEC. The Presidency conclusions of Tampere (European Council, 15 and 16 October 1999) show, quite on the contrary, that now there is a strong will to *'enhance non-discrimination in economic, social and cultural life'* in the treatment of third country nationals, to grant the latter *'rights and obligations comparable to those of EU citizens'* and to approximate their legal status to that of Member State's nationals.[112] Anyway, the first legislation issued on the basis of Article 13 EC (the so called Race Directive, see below) refers explicitly to third country nationals.

Despite the probably not so broad scope of Article 13 TEC and the lack of direct effect, the possibilities in both content and nature of the measures offered by Article 13 TEC should not be underestimated since they seem to exceed those offered by Article 12 TEC. Article 13 TEC reads that *'[...] the Council [...] may take appropriate action to combat discrimination'*. The word *'to combat'* has a broader meaning compared to the expression 'to prohibit' embodied in Article 12 TEC and thereby allows a plenty of actions directed against discrimination (such as action programmes for creating public awareness but probably even far-reaching ones such as pre-emptive measures). The presumption that Article 13 TEC could also be the legal basis for measures of positive discrimination[113] favouring ethnic minorities (as well as other groups which are subject to discrimination on the basis of grounds that are mentioned in Article 13 TEC)

---

[110] We may recall the protest of Member States when the 1990 Council Resolution on the fight against racism and xenophobia (OJ 1990 no C 157, p. 1) was initially planned to protect all persons on Community territory whether they were nationals of a member State or not.

[111] De Witte and there quoted references, 'The European Community ...', loc. cit. n. 1, at p. 183.

[112] See the heading *'fair treatment of third country nationals'* under point A.A 'A common EU Asylum and Migration Policy' in the Presidency conclusions. Under this perspective one should also observe the legislative process regarding the proposal for a Council Directive extending the freedom to provide cross-border services to third-country nationals established within the Community (OJ 1999/C 67/10) COM(1999) 3 final 1999/0013(CNS).

[113] An example is employment quotas where a specific number of positions are reserved for ethnic minorities. Such measures have been deployed in the USA, but are not familiar to the European tradition (an exception might be the Dutch law on the equal participation of foreigners in the labour market). See Mark Bell, 'European Union Anti-Discrimination Policy: From equal opportunities between women and men to combat racism', Parliament's working document, *Public Liberty Series*, LIBE 102 EN.

seems to go beyond the Article.[114] The latter merely wishes to combat discrimination (obviously without creating positive discrimination) and does not state as its aim the removal of the *de facto* differences. If the High Contracting Parties had other perspectives they could have used formulations similar to those which they have used in the context of gender discrimination.[115]

The term 'action' in Article 13 TEC is broader than the term 'rules' in Article 12 TEC, since actions may cover all the (also non-binding) legal instruments listed in Article 254 TEC as well as *sui generis* instruments which the EC regularly uses. Of course the fact that the actions have to be 'appropriate' may put considerable limits on both the content and form of such actions. Another hurdle will be the requirement of Council unanimity, which might be difficult to achieve in an area which is not undisputed. A current Commission proposal aims at amending Article 13 TEC during the current IGC so that measures to fight discrimination can be decided upon qualified majority.[116] A possible limitation could derive from the exclusively consultative role given to the European Parliament which is known to combat discrimination.

6.2 The Commission's Article 13-package

The future importance of Article 13 TEC has been announced early by the Commission as Padraig Flynn, the then Commissioner for Employment and Social Affairs, envisaged an anti-discrimination package based on Article 13 TEC.[117] On 30 November 1999 Ms Anna Diamantopoulou, new Commissioner for Employment and Social Affairs presented the definitive Commission proposal to the European Parliament. After the adoption of the proposal by the Commission Ms Diamantopoulou spoke of a *'milestone in the construction of a Social Europe'*. The Commission's package aims at creating a common level of protection against discrimination right across the EU hereby focusing on key areas in which discrimination occurs.

The package-proposal consists of a 'Council Directive establishing a general framework for equal treatment in employment', a 'Council Directive implementing the principle of equal treatment between persons irrespective of racial or ethnic origin' and a 'Council decision establishing a Community Action Programme to combat discrimination 2001-2006'. Whereas the Framework

---

[114] In the past, NGOs and Parliament sought the inclusion of the provisions on positive discrimination in the documents. Accordingly, in its resolution on the functioning of the TEU with a view to the 1996 IGC, the Parliament postulates that greater substance for the concept of EU citizenship should also be provided by 'the preservation of Europe's diversity through special safeguards for national minorities in terms of human rights, democracy and the rule of law' (see OJ 1995 No. C 151, p. 56).

[115] According to Art. 141 EC '[...] the principle of equal treatment shall not prevent [...] adopting measures providing for specific advantages in order to make it easier for the underrepresented [...] to [...] compensate for disadvantages [...]'.

[116] *Agence Europe*, 10. February, 2000, p. 6

[117] Speech given to a European Conference on Anti-Discrimination: 'Anti-Discrimination: the way forward', Vienna, 4 December 1998.

Directive (or Employment Directive as it is called by the Commission) refers to all grounds of discrimination listed in Article 13 TEC (leaving apart only gender-discrimination), the Race Directive focus on discrimination based on racial or ethnic differences. This is to explain by the fact that to the Commission it seemed politically possible to go further on racial discrimination than on other grounds of discrimination.[118]

Independent of the possible legislative outcome of the Commission's initiative, the impact of Article 13 TEC should be seen also from the perspective of law policy. As shown in previous chapters, the EC provides for the inclusion of measures favouring ethnic or linguistic minorities through instruments such as, for example, action programmes. This approach could intensify in the near future since now there is a specific reference in the Treaty. Given this new relevant reference in Primary Law, even the already mentioned possible establishment of a 'general principle of minority protection' in the jurisdiction of the European Court of Justice seems to become more likely.[119]

6.3 The Race Directive (June 2000)

This is not the right place to describe the entire Commission's 'package', but a few remarks regarding the so-called Race Directive should be made as the Council has already adopted the latter (in an amended form) at the end of June 2000.[120] The Race Directive applies a vast concept of discrimination as within the latter fall not only direct and indirect discriminations, but also 'harassment'. Harassment shall be deemed to be a discrimination, when '*an unwanted conduct related to racial or ethnic origin takes place with purpose or effect of violating the dignity of a person and of creating an intimidating, hostile, degrading, humiliating or offensive environment*' (see Article 2 paragraph 3). Also the scope of the Directive turned out to be a very wide one. Firstly the Directive applies to '*all persons*', hence also to legal persons and third country nationals (the directive emphasises that this is without prejudice to national provisions relating to the entry into and the residence of third country nationals and stateless persons on the territory of member States – see Article 3). Secondly the Directive

---

[118] See Kirsty Hughes replacing the responsible Commissioner in a speech for the conference 'Ethnic Minorities in Europe-rethinking and restructuring anti-discrimination strategies', Birmingham, 17-19 February 2000.

[119] See in this context: Liza Waddington, op. cit. n. 106, who quotes the Case C-249/96 (*Grant* v. *South-West Trains*) where the Court stated in paras. 44 and 45 that the general principles of Community law 'cannot have the effect of extending the scope of the Treaty provisions beyond the competences of the Community'. With this reasoning the Court felt unable to follow the Human Rights Committee in applying the right not to be discriminated against on the basis of gender also to homosexuals.

[120] Council Directive 2000/43/EC of 29 June 2000 implementing the principle of equal treatment between persons irrespective of racial or ethnic origin, see OJ No. L 180, 19.07.2000, pp. 22-26. For the development of this directive see also the respective opinions of the Committee of the Regions (12 April), the Parliament (18 May), the Economic and Social Committee (25 May) and the amended proposal of the Commission (COM(2000) 328 final, 31 May 2000).

goes far beyond the mere area of employment (contrary to the proposed Framework Directive), including also the access to all types and levels of vocational guidance and training, social protection (including social security and healthcare), education and furthermore the *'access to and supply of goods and services which are available to the public, including housing'* (see Article 3 paragraph 1). This is very important as decisions in loans, access to different sorts of services, scholarships and so on are areas where a marginalisation of individuals from ethnic minorities often occurs. Thirdly the Directive refers not only to national laws, regulations or administrative practice, but also to any provision contained in individual or collective contracts, agreements, internal rules of undertakings or non-profit associations (see Article 14).

Possible exceptions from this broad prohibition of ethnic and racial discrimination are reduced to *'genuine and determining occupational requirements'* which are necessary because of the special nature of a particular occupational activity. The Commission states in its Explanatory Memorandum that this *'genuine occupational qualification should be construed narrowly'* and that such cases will be *'highly exceptional'*.[121] The Directive states that the principle of equal treatment *'shall not prevent any Member State from maintaining or adopting specific measures to prevent or compensate for disadvantages linked to racial or ethnic origin'* (see Article 5). Hence the Directive itself may not be used as an argument against positive actions on the national level. Quite on the contrary the Directive is perceived as a set of *'minimum requirements'* (see Article 6). In order to assure an effective enforcement of the aims of the Directive, Article 7 obliges the member States to ensure that judicial, administrative and conciliation procedures are available to all persons who consider themselves victims of ethnic or racial discrimination, even after the relationship in which the discrimination is alleged to have occurred has ended. Also legal entities as e.g. associations, which have a legitimate interest in ensuring the enforcement of the Directive, may engage in any such procedure. Furthermore the Directive provides for a shift back of the burden of proof to the respondent (in proceedings in which it is for plaintiff – and not the Court – to investigate the facts of the case). The member States are bound to designate a body or bodies *'for the promotion of equal treatment of all persons without discrimination on the grounds of racial or ethnic origin'* (see Article 13). The competence of the latter authorities have to include at least: providing independent assistance to victims of discrimination in pursuing their complaints, conducting independent surveys, publishing independent reports and making recommendations.

The Race Directive is already in force and has to be complied with by 19 July 2003. member States have to communicate to the Commission by 19 July 2005, and every five years thereafter, all the information necessary for the Commission to draw up a report to the European Parliament and the Council on

---

[121] As example the Commission mentions the case of a dramatic performance where racial or ethnic origin is required for reasons of authenticity.

the application of the Race Directive (the report may also contain proposals to revise the latter).

6.4 **An open end**

On the basis of the evidence given I may conclude by stating that the issue of minority protection inside the EU-system is characterised by contradictions but also by a considerable potential of development. The last twenty years clearly show that the interest of the EC-organs in this topic has been considerably growing. Whereas the Pre-Maastricht period was dominated by documented interest of the European Parliament in the linguistic heritage of minorities, the process of Eastern enlargement has brought at stage the political dimension of minority protection. Maastricht finally gave birth to the concept of cultural diversity opening hereby new realms for minority-topics inside the EU. The latter aspect was reduced to the external sphere of the EU. The Post-Amsterdam development seems to foster the 'internalisation' of minority related topics. Article 13 TEC not only established the prohibition of minority-essential forms of discrimination, also the nearly immediate political use of this new legal competence basis is significant. Of course it has been argued that the latter fact is due to the Austrian crisis, but this crisis itself is (formally)[122] also an expression of an increasing 'internalisation' of minority protection in the EU-system. On the other hand a further formalisation of this internalisation process seems to be doomed to fail. This is the impression one may gain, looking at the rather probable breaking down of those efforts which aim at the introduction of a minority-paragraph in the Charter of Fundamental Rights.[123] Anyhow under the surface of daily policy the law is mushroom-like pathing its own way – time will show the outcome of this process.

---

[122] It can be recalled that the three 'wise men' who have to analyse the situation in Austria, are carrying out their task on the basis of a mandate issued by fourteen member States of the Union. This mandate states that the report to be drawn up has to cover (beside the political nature of the FPÖ) 'the Austrian Government's commitment to the common European values, in particular concerning the rights of minorities, refugees and immigrants'. On the Austrian crisis see in detail G. Toggenburg, Österreich Krise: Grenzen der Politik, Grenzen des Rechts ... , op. cit. n. 95).

[123] More than a dozen of proposals have been presented; the most detailed one was tabled by the International Institute for Right of Nationality and Regionality (May 2000 by D. Blumenwitz and M. Pallek). See: http://db.consilium.eu.int/df/default.asp?lang=en.

DOCUMENTS

JUDGEMENT OF THE EUROPEAN COURT
BICKEL/FRANZ v. ITALY case

24 November 1998[1]

(Freedom of movement for persons – Equal treatment – Language rules applicable to criminal proceedings)

In Case C-274/96,
REFERENCE to the Court under Article 177 of the EC Treaty by the Pretura Circondariale di Bolzano, Sezione Distaccata di Silandro (Italy), for a preliminary ruling in the criminal proceedings before that court against
Horst Otto Bickel,
Ulrich Franz,

on the interpretation of Articles 6, 8a and 59 of the EC Treaty,

THE COURT,
composed of: G.C. Rodríguez Iglesias, President, P.J.G. Kapteyn, J.-P. Puissochet, G. Hirsch and P. Jann (Presidents of Chambers), G.F. Mancini, J.C. Moitinho de Almeida, C. Gulmann, J.L. Murray, H. Ragnemalm (Rapporteur), L. Sevón, M. Wathelet and R. Schintgen, Judges,
Advocate General: F.G. Jacobs,

Registrar: H. von Holstein, Deputy Registrar,
after considering the written observations submitted on behalf of:

the Italian Government, by Professor Umberto Leanza, Head of the Legal Affairs Department of the Ministry of Foreign Affairs, acting as Agent, assisted by Pier Giorgio Ferri, Avvocato dello Stato,
the Commission of the European Communities, by Pieter van Nuffel, of its Legal Service, and Enrico Altieri, a national civil servant on secondment to that service, acting as Agents,

having regard to the Report for the Hearing,

after hearing the oral observations of Mr Bickel and Mr Franz, represented by Karl Zeller, of the Merano Bar; of the Italian Government, represented by Pier Giorgio Ferri; and of the Commission, represented by Pieter van Nuffel and Lucio Gussetti, of its Legal Service, acting as Agents, at the hearing on 27 January 1998,
after hearing the Opinion of the Advocate General at the sitting on 19 March 1998, gives the following

---

[1] Language of the case: Italian.

JUDGEMENT

1. By orders of 2 August 1996, received at the Court on 12 August 1996, the Pretura Circondariale, Sezione Distaccata di Silandro (District Magistrates' Court, Silandro Division), Bolzano, referred to the Court for a preliminary ruling under Article 177 of the EC Treaty a question on the interpretation of Articles 6, 8a and 59 of the EC Treaty.
2. That question was raised in criminal proceedings, brought against Mr. Bickel and Mr. Franz respectively.
3. Mr. Bickel is a lorry driver of Austrian nationality, resident at Nüziders in Austria. On 15 February 1994, while driving his lorry at Castelbello in the Trentino-Alto Adige Region of Italy, he was stopped by a *carabinieri* patrol and charged with driving while under the influence of alcohol.
4. Mr. Franz, a German national resident at Peissenberg in Germany, visited the Trentino-Alto Adige as a tourist. On 5 May 1995, in the course of a customs inspection, he was found to be in possession of a type of knife that is prohibited.
5. In each case, the accused made a declaration in the presence of the District Magistrate of Bolzano that he had no knowledge of Italian and, relying on rules for the protection of the German-speaking community of the Province of Bolzano, requested that the proceedings be conducted in German.
6. Article 99 of Presidential Decree No 670 of 30 August 1972 concerning the special arrangements for the Trentino-Alto Adige Region (GURI No 301 of 20 November 1972) provides that the German language is to have the same status there as Italian.
7. Under Article 100 of that decree, the German-speaking citizens of the Province of Bolzano (the area where most of the German-speaking minority live) are entitled to use their own language in relations with the judicial and administrative authorities based in that province or entrusted with responsibility at regional level.
8. Article 13 of Presidential Decree No 574 of 15 July 1988 (hereinafter 'Decree No 574/88') on the implementation of the special arrangements for the Trentino-Alto Adige with regard to the use of German or Ladin in relations between citizens and the public administration and in judicial proceedings (GURI No 105 of 8 May 1989) provides that the administrative and judicial authorities must, in their dealings with citizens of the Province of Bolzano and in documents concerning them, use the language of the person concerned.
9. Article 14 of Decree No 574/88 provides moreover that, in cases of *flagrante delicto* or arrest, the judicial or police authority must, before interviewing the person concerned or taking any other procedural step, ask him to state his mother tongue. If he is a German-speaker, the interview and all other steps in the procedure must be conducted in that language.
10. Lastly, pursuant to Article 15 of Decree No 574/88, the judicial authority responsible for drawing up a procedural document to be communicated to or served on a suspect or accused person must use that person's presumed language, which is determined on the basis of his known membership of a language group and other information which has come to light during the procedure. Within ten days of communication or service of the first procedural document, the suspect

or accused person may contest the language used by making a declaration in person or by arranging to have such a declaration submitted to the prosecuting authority. Where the latter option is exercised, the judicial authority must make sure that any documents already drawn up are translated and that all documents thereafter are drawn up in the language designated.

11. Since the national court was uncertain whether the rules of procedure applicable to the citizens of the Province of Bolzano must, under Community law, be extended to nationals of other Member States visiting the province, it decided to stay proceedings pending a preliminary ruling from the Court of Justice on the following question:

'Do the principle of non-discrimination as laid down in the first paragraph of Article 6, the right of movement and residence for citizens of the Union as laid down in Article 8a and the freedom to provide services as laid down in Article 59 of the Treaty require that a citizen of the Union who is a national of one Member State but is in another Member State be granted the right to have criminal proceedings against him conducted in another language where nationals of the host State enjoy that right in the same circumstances?'

12. By that question, the national court is essentially asking whether the right conferred by national rules to have criminal proceedings conducted in a language other than the principal language of the State concerned falls within the scope of the Treaty and must accordingly comply with Article 6 thereof. If so, the national court also asks whether Article 6 of the Treaty precludes national rules, such as those in issue, which, in respect of a particular language other than the principal language of the Member State concerned, confer on citizens whose language is that particular language and who are resident in a defined area the right to require that criminal proceedings be conducted in that language, without conferring the same right on nationals of other Member States travelling or staying in that area, whose language is the same.

The first part of the question

13. The first point to note is that in the context of a Community based on the principles of freedom of movement for persons and freedom of establishment, the protection of the linguistic rights and privileges of individuals is of particular importance (Case 137/84 *Mutsch* [1985] ECR 2681, paragraph 11).
14. Secondly, by prohibiting 'any discrimination on grounds of nationality', Article 6 of the Treaty requires that persons in a situation governed by Community law be placed entirely on an equal footing with nationals of the Member State (Case 186/87 *Cowan* [1989] ECR 195, paragraph 10).
15. Situations governed by Community law include those covered by the freedom to provide services, the right to which is laid down in Article 59 of the Treaty. The Court has consistently held that this right includes the freedom for the recipients of services to go to another Member State in order to receive a service there (*Cowan*, paragraph 15). Article 59 therefore covers all nationals of Member States who, independently of other freedoms guaranteed by the Treaty, visit another Member State where they intend or are likely to receive services. Such

persons – and they include both Mr Bickel and Mr Franz – are free to visit and move around within the host State. Furthermore, pursuant to Article 8a of the Treaty, '[e]very citizen of the Union shall have the right to move and reside freely within the territory of the Member States, subject to the limitations and conditions laid down in this Treaty and by the measures adopted to give it effect'.

16. In that regard, the exercise of the right to move and reside freely in another Member State is enhanced if the citizens of the Union are able to use a given language to communicate with the administrative and judicial authorities of a State on the same footing as its nationals. Consequently, persons such as Mr. Bickel and Mr. Franz, in exercising that right in another Member State, are in principle entitled, pursuant to Article 6 of the Treaty, to treatment no less favourable than that accorded to nationals of the host State so far as concerns the use of languages which are spoken there.

17. Although, generally speaking, criminal legislation and the rules of criminal procedure – such as the national rules in issue, which govern the language of the proceedings – are matters for which the Member States are responsible, the Court has consistently held that Community law sets certain limits to their power in that respect. Such legislative provisions may not discriminate against persons to whom Community law gives the right to equal treatment or restrict the fundamental freedoms guaranteed by Community law (see, to that effect, *Cowan*, paragraph 19).

18. Consequently, in so far as they may compromise the right of nationals of other Member States to equal treatment in the exercise of their right to move and reside freely in another Member State, national rules concerning the language to be used in criminal proceedings in the host State must comply with Article 6 of the Treaty.

19. Accordingly, the answer to the first part of the question referred for a preliminary ruling must be that the right conferred by national rules to have criminal proceedings conducted in a language other than the principal language of the State concerned falls within the scope of the Treaty and must comply with Article 6 thereof.

The second part of the question

20. In the submission of Mr. Bickel and Mr. Franz, if any discrimination contrary to Article 6 of the Treaty is to be avoided, the right to have proceedings conducted in German must be extended to all citizens of the Union, since it is already available to nationals of one of the Member States.

21. The Italian Government contends that the only nationals upon whom the right in question is conferred are those who are both residents of the Province of Bolzano and members of its German-speaking community, the aim of the rules in issue being to recognise the ethnic and cultural identity of persons belonging to the protected minority. Accordingly, the right of that protected minority to the use of its own language need not be extended to nationals of other Member States who are present, occasionally and temporarily, in that region, since provision has been

made to enable such persons to exercise the rights of the defence adequately, even where they have no knowledge of the official language of the host State.
22. The Commission points out that the right to have proceedings conducted in German is not accorded to all Italian nationals, but only to those who are resident in the Province of Bolzano and who belong to its German-speaking community. Accordingly, it is for the national court to determine whether the rules in issue genuinely give rise to discrimination on grounds of nationality, to identify the group of persons discriminated against and then to determine whether such discrimination is justifiable by reference to objective circumstances.
23. The documents before the Court show that the Italian rules restrict the right to have proceedings conducted in German to German-speaking citizens of the Province of Bolzano. It follows that German-speaking nationals of other Member States, particularly Germany and Austria – such as Mr Bickel and Mr Franz – who travel or stay in that province cannot require criminal proceedings to be conducted in German despite the fact that the national rules provide that the German language is to have the same status as Italian.
24. In those circumstances, it appears that German-speaking nationals of other Member States travelling or staying in the Province of Bolzano are at a disadvantage by comparison with Italian nationals resident there whose language is German. Whereas a member of the latter group may, if charged with an offence in the Province of Bolzano, have the proceedings conducted in German, a German-speaking national from another Member State, travelling in that province, is denied that right.
25. Even on the assumption that, as the Italian Government maintains, German-speaking nationals of other Member States who are resident in the Province of Bolzano may rely on the rules in issue and submit their pleadings in German – so that there is no discrimination on grounds of nationality as between residents of the region – Italian nationals are at an advantage by comparison with nationals of other Member States. The majority of Italian nationals whose language is German are in a position to demand that German be used throughout the proceedings in the Province of Bolzano, because they meet the residence requirement laid down by the rules in issue; the majority of German-speaking nationals of other Member States, on the other hand, cannot avail themselves of that right because they do not satisfy that requirement.
26. Consequently, rules such as those in issue in the main proceedings, which make the right, in a defined area, to have criminal proceedings conducted in the language of the person concerned conditional on that person being resident in that area, favour nationals of the host State by comparison with nationals of other Member States exercising their right to freedom of movement and therefore run counter to the principle of non-discrimination laid down in Article 6 of the Treaty.
27. A residence requirement of that kind can be justified only if it is based on objective considerations independent of the nationality of the persons concerned and is proportionate to the legitimate aim of the national provisions (see, to that effect, Case C-15/96 *Schöning-Kougebetopoulou* [1998] ECR I-47, paragraph 21).
28. However, it is clear from the order for reference that this is not the position in the case of the rules in issue.

29. The Italian Government's contention that the aim of those rules is to protect the ethno-cultural minority residing in the province in question does not constitute a valid justification in this context. Of course, the protection of such a minority may constitute a legitimate aim. It does not appear, however, from the documents before the Court that that aim would be undermined if the rules in issue were extended to cover German-speaking nationals of other Member States exercising their right to freedom of movement.
30. Furthermore, it should be recalled that Mr Bickel and Mr Franz pointed out at the hearing, without being contradicted, that the courts concerned are in a position to conduct proceedings in German without additional complications or costs.
31. Consequently, the answer to the second part of the question referred for a preliminary ruling must be that Article 6 of the Treaty precludes national rules which, in respect of a particular language other than the principal language of the Member State concerned, confer on citizens whose language is that particular language and who are resident in a defined area the right to require that criminal proceedings be conducted in that language, without conferring the same right on nationals of other Member States travelling or staying in that area, whose language is the same.

Costs

32. The costs incurred by the Italian Government and the Commission, which have submitted observations to the Court, are not recoverable. Since these proceedings are, for the parties to the main proceedings, a step in the proceedings pending before the national court, the decision on costs is a matter for that court.

On those grounds,

THE COURT,

in answer to the question referred to it by the Pretura Circondariale di Bolzano, Sezione Distaccata di Silandro, by orders of 2 August 1996, hereby rules:

1. The right conferred by national rules to have criminal proceedings conducted in a language other than the principal language of the State concerned falls within the scope of the EC Treaty and must comply with Article 6 thereof.

2. Article 6 of the Treaty precludes national rules which, in respect of a particular language other than the principal language of the Member State concerned, confer on citizens whose language is that particular language and who are resident in a defined area the right to require that criminal proceedings be conducted in that language, without conferring the same right on nationals of other Member States travelling or staying in that area, whose language is the same.

ORGANIZATION FOR SECURITY AND COOPERATION IN EUROPE

LINGUISTIC RIGHTS AND THE ORGANIZATION FOR SECURITY AND COOPERATION IN EUROPE

Edwin Bakker*

1. INTRODUCTION

Language is a vital and highly developed tool in human communication. Not only is it an instrument for communicating thoughts and ideas, it also forges cultural ties and economic relationships and records these in literature for future generations. Moreover, language plays a vital role in the development of groups of people with distinct identities, lifestyles, and a shared history. Arguably, language serves as a means of unifying a group and as a source of self-identification of the individual more than any other attribute of identity such as common traditions, religion, history or 'race'.

Stemming from the importance of language to the identity of groups and individuals, any threat to, disrespect for or attack upon the use of a language or its existence arouses strong emotions and constitutes a potential cause of dispute. Many of these disputes relate to the role of the modern State as a major purveyor of services and employment or economic opportunities, for which individuals intensely compete.[1] These services and opportunities are usually provided in the lingua franca or the official language of the State. Generally, this language is the mother tongue of the majority of its citizens.[2] Persons belonging to this group therefore have an enormous advantage over persons whose language is not the primary language of the State.[3] Hence, they aim to maintain or strengthen the official status or practical use of their language. Persons who speak a minority language seek to diminish disadvantages derived from limited or a total lack of knowledge of the State's primary language. These different interests regarding

---

* University Lecturer at the Peace Research Center of the University of Nijmegen, The Netherlands.
[1] Fernand de Varennes, *Language, Minorities and Human Rights*, The Hague: Kluwer Law International, 1996, page 1.
[2] Most States in Africa constitute an exception. In these States, the official language is often the language of the State of which they used to be a colony.
[3] Fernand de Varennes, op. cit. n. 1, p. 1.

S. Trifunovska (Ed.), Minority Rights in Europe: European Minorities and Languages
© 2000, T.M.C. Asser Press, The Hague, The Netherlands

the use and status of languages within a State often lead to serious disputes between representatives of minorities and representatives of the majority or the State over the linguistic rights of persons belonging to national minorities. Such disputes have become more recurrent following the end of the Cold War, particularly in Eastern Europe and the countries of the former Soviet Union.

2. INTERNATIONAL STANDARDS REGARDING LINGUISTIC RIGHTS

The disagreements over the use and status of minority languages are the cause of various, sometimes violent conflicts and threaten to continue to be so in the absence of a developed regime of respect for the linguistic rights of all.[4] The international community has partly responded to this threat by developing a number of standards concerning the linguistic rights of persons belonging to national minorities. The protection of these rights and minority language use is based on the two pillars of protection for national minorities: the right to non-discriminatory treatment in the enjoyment of all human rights; and the right to the maintenance and development of identity through the freedom to practice or use those special and unique aspects of their minority life – typically culture, religion, and language.[5] The objective of these specific standards has been to resolve and avoid language conflict. However, achieving a successful balance between the linguistic rights of communities, groups and persons who share the same State proves to be a matter of extraordinary complexity. Nonetheless, following the Universal Declaration of Human Rights, important steps were taken to attain a comprehensive set of international standards concerning minority language use.

The most relevant provisions in multilateral conventions, declarations and bilateral treaties, which pertain to linguistic rights of persons belonging to minorities can be divided into three groups: universal agreements, European agreements and special agreements, usually at the sub-regional and bilateral levels.

The following universal declarations and agreements contain provisions that have special relevance for the linguistic rights of persons belonging to national minorities:

- the 1948 Universal Declaration of Human Rights
- the 1958 International Labour Organization Convention No. 111 Concerning Discrimination in Respect of Employment and Occupation

---

[4] Donall O'Riagáin, 'The Importance of Linguistic Rights for Speakers of Lesser Used Languages', *International Journal on Minority and Group Rights*, Vol. 6 (1999) pp. 289-298, at p. 289.

[5] Cf. Report on the Linguistic Rights of Persons Belonging to National Minorities in the OSCE Area, III D, March 1999, reproduced in this publication.

- the 1966 International Covenant on Civil and Political Rights
- the 1989 Convention on the Rights of the Child
- the 1992 Declaration on the Rights of Persons Belonging to National or Ethnic, Religious and Linguistic Minorities

In Europe, the rights of persons belonging to regional and minority language groups have been addressed in an increasing number of multilateral treaties and conventions within the frameworks of the Council of Europe, the European Union and the Organization for Security and Cooperation in Europe (OSCE).[6] The most relevant with regard to linguistic rights are:

- the 1950 European Convention for the Protection of Human Rights and Fundamental Freedoms
- the 1982 Declaration on Freedom of Expression and Information
- the 1990 Document of the Copenhagen Meeting
- the 1992 European Charter for Regional or Minority Languages
- the 1995 Framework Convention for the Protection of National Minorities

Special agreements, concluded at sub-regional and bilateral levels include those post-First and Second World War treaties which address national minorities and are still in force, such as the 1923 Treaty of Lausanne between Greece and Turkey and the 1947 Treaty of Peace with Italy.[7] This group also includes the recently concluded bilateral agreements between OSCE participating States dealing with some of their linguistic minorities, such as between Hungary and the Slovak Republic (1995) and between Hungary and Romania (1996). An example of a sub-regional agreement that has special relevance for linguistic rights is the Convention on Guaranteeing the Rights of Persons Belonging to National Minorities adopted by the Commonwealth of Independent States in 1994.

3. THE OSCE AND LINGUISTIC RIGHTS

One international organization that has reacted to the growing awareness that language disputes will continue to cause conflicts in the absence of a developed regime of respect for the linguistic rights of all is the Organization for Security and Co-operation in Europe. This regional security organisation has been established as a primary instrument for early warning, conflict prevention, crisis management and post-conflict rehabilitation under Chapter VIII of the United

---

[6] At the Budapest Summit in December 1994, the decision was taken to rename the Conference on Security and Cooperation in Europe (CSCE) – that had formally opened in Helsinki in 1973 - as the Organization for Security and Cooperation in Europe.

[7] Cf. Report on the Linguistic Rights ... , op. cit. n. 5.

Nations Charter. Its approach to security is comprehensive and co-operative. It addresses a wide range of security-related issues including those related to national minorities and the linguistic rights of members of these groups.

The two main activities of the OSCE regarding these specific issues have been the following:

Firstly, the Organisation negotiated, formulated and elaborated a number of documents of relevance for the linguistic rights of persons belonging to national minorities; and

Secondly, it established the institution of the High Commissioner on National Minorities whose tasks include, *inter alia*, dealing with the issue of linguistic rights in cases of (potential) conflict affecting peace and stability between States.[8]

3.1 OSCE documents concerning linguistic rights

Although many universal and regional organisations have contributed to the current body of standards concerning the linguistic rights of persons belonging to national minorities, one could argue that significant attempts to create standards for the protection of persons belonging to national minorities that also involve linguistic rights have been those by the OSCE.

The development of standard setting started with the founding document of this Organisation, the 1975 Helsinki Final Act, which ended a long-standing taboo in East-West relations. By virtue of this Act, human rights became a legitimate subject of dialogue and a matter of legitimate concern to all participating States of the Conference on Security and Cooperation in Europe. A further elaboration of commitments and principles with regard to the rights of national minorities and the linguistic rights of persons belonging to these groups followed after the end of the Cold War. Since then, the OSCE has articulated, reiterated, and elaborated upon these rights according to international standards embodied in a number of documents, most notably in the 1990 Document of the Copenhagen Meeting of the Conference on the Human Dimension of the Conference on Security and Cooperation in Europe.

The Copenhagen Document contains the most comprehensive set of standards concerning the rights of persons belonging to national minorities adopted up to that time at the multilateral level.[9] The Document addresses a

---

[8] At the 1994 Budapest Summit, the OSCE Heads of State also established a Contact Point for Roma and Sinti Issues within the Office for Democratic Institutions and Human Rights. According to its mandate, the Contact Point serves as a clearing-house for the exchange of information on Roma and Sinti issues. Its activities with regard to linguistic rights only deal with those issues concerning persons belonging to the Roma and Sinti minorities in the different participating States.

[9] Cf. Asbjørn Eide, 'The Oslo Recommendations Regarding the Linguistic Rights of National Minorities: An Overview', *International Journal on Minority and Group Rights*, Vol. 6 (1999) No. 3, pp. 319-328, at p. 319.

number of issues, including non-discrimination, use of the mother tongue, and teaching of and in the mother tongue.

Although it is not a treaty, the Copenhagen Document has both political and legal significance due to its adoption by consensus by the OSCE participating States. According to the Report on the Linguistic Rights of Persons Belonging to National Minorities in the OSCE Area:

> 'its political significance lies in the willingness of OSCE States to accept that the protection afforded to national minorities - including those pertaining to linguistic rights - are worthy policy that contribute to the goals of the Organization in the human dimension: 'human rights, fundamental freedoms, democracy and the rule of law'. The OSCE has long held that violation of political commitments is as unacceptable as any violation of international law, and the OSCE is as concerned with violations of these instruments as with those of a legally binding nature. The importance of adherence to the Copenhagen Document has been repeatedly invoked in subsequent documents of the OSCE.'[10]

The Copenhagen Document also had an impact on developments both at the global and regional level. For instance, at the Vienna Meeting of the Heads of State of the Council of Europe in 1993, it was agreed to transform the commitments of the Copenhagen Document into legally binding obligations. This resulted in the adoption in 1994 of the Framework Convention for the Protection of National Minorities which is also open for signature to States that are not Member States of the Council of Europe. The Document has at the same time formed the basis for regulating minority questions in several bilateral agreements. At the global level, the Copenhagen Document influenced the final drafting of the United Nations Declaration on the Rights of Persons belonging to National or Ethnic, Religious or Linguistic Minorities.[11] Finally, the Document is one of the international instruments from which the Oslo Recommendations Regarding the Linguistic Rights of National Minorities were derived, discussed in more detail later on.

OSCE documents of less relevance to minority languages include the documents of the OSCE Summits in Paris (1990), Helsinki (1992), Budapest (1994) and Istanbul (1999) which reaffirm the conviction that friendly relations among peoples, as well as peace, justice, stability and democracy, require that, among others, the linguistic identity of national minorities be protected and conditions for the promotion of that identity be created. The need for effective implementation of relevant OSCE commitments is also expressed in these documents. The Istanbul Summit Declaration, for instance, emphasises the requirement that laws and policies regarding the linguistic rights of persons belonging to national minorities conform to applicable international standards. The Istanbul Declaration also commends the essential work of the High Commissioner on National Minorities and asserts that the participating States will increase their efforts to

---

[10] Op. Cit. Report on the Linguistic Rights ... , op. cit. n. 5.
[11] Asbjørn Eide, loc. cit. n. 9, at pp. 319-320.

implement the recommendations of the High Commissioner on National Minorities.

3.2 The OSCE High Commissioner on National Minorities and linguistic rights

3.2.1 *Mandate and general approach*

As a community of values, the OSCE has the obligation to offer assistance to all States which are in a transitional period, i.e. in the process of applying the full scope of these common values to their societies, and which are often going through a difficult period of political and economic transformation. The institution of the High Commissioner on National Minorities was established in 1992, during the early stages of this period. It was created largely in reaction to the situation in the former Yugoslavia which some feared would be repeated elsewhere in Eastern Europe and Central Asia. It was also believed that this and similar conflicts could undermine the promise of peace and prosperity as envisaged in the Charter of Paris for a New Europe adopted by the Heads of State and Government in November 1990. The High Commissioner on National Minorities was established to prevent this from occurring. According to his mandate the High Commissioner was to be an instrument of conflict prevention at the earliest possible stage, who could assist States, particularly those in transformation, to avoid or contain the destabilising and possibly violent effects of problems relating to national minorities.[12]

On 1 January 1993, Max van der Stoel took up his post as the first OSCE High Commissioner on National Minorities, initially for a period of three years.[13] Drawing on his experience as a former Foreign Minister of The Netherlands, Permanent Representative to the United Nations, and long-time human rights advocate, Max van der Stoel has turned his attention to minority-related disputes in the OSCE area, primarily in Eastern Europe and Central Asia. His focus has been on those disputes which, in his judgement, had the potential to escalate.[14] This resulted in the High Commissioner becoming involved in the following States: Albania, Croatia, Estonia, Hungary, Kazakstan, Kyrgyzstan, Latvia, Lithuania, the Former Yugoslav Republic of Macedonia, Romania, Slovakia and Ukraine. His involvement has focused primarily on those situations involving persons belonging to national or ethnic groups who constitute the numerical majority in one State but the numerical minority in another. These groups usually engage the interest of governmental authorities in each State, which

---

[12] Cf. Helsinki Document, II, CSCE High Commissioner on National Minorities, 1992.

[13] In December 1995, the OSCE Ministerial Council Meeting in Budapest decided to extend Mr. van der Stoel's mandate until 31 December 1998. In July 1998, it was decided to again prolong his mandate until December 1999. At the Istanbul Summit of December 1999 it was decided to ask Mr. van der Stoel to continue in office until the end of 2000.

[14] Cf. The Oslo Recommendations Regarding the Linguistic Rights of National Minorities & Explanatory Note, 1998.

constitutes a potential source of inter-State tension if not conflict.[15] The High Commissioner on National Minorities also paid special attention to the situation of the Roma and Sinti in the OSCE area who do not make up the majority in any of the States in which they live.

In addressing situations or tensions involving national minorities, the High Commissioner approaches the issues as an independent, impartial and co-operative actor. Endowed by his mandate, the High Commissioner has conducted on-site missions in the States mentioned above. In these cases, he has obtained first-hand information from the parties concerned. He has also been engaged in preventive diplomacy; trying to promote dialogue, confidence and co-operation between them. In cases where the international norms and standards to which all 55 OSCE participating States have committed themselves are not being met, he has issued several reports with recommendations to the Governments in question. These recommendations aim to persuade these Governments to change their policies. The High Commissioner tries to convince them by reminding them that peace and stability are, as a rule, best served by ensuring full rights to persons belonging to national minorities. It should be noted that the High Commissioner, as an impartial institution, also reminds persons belonging to these groups that they have duties as well as rights.[16]

3.2.2 Language-related issues

During the course of his activities over seven years, the High Commissioner has identified certain recurrent issues and themes which have become the subject of his attention in a number of States in which he has been involved. The right of persons belonging to national minorities to use their language in the private and public spheres is such an issue.[17] The High Commissioner deals with these issues on the basis of international human rights instruments that refer to linguistic rights in a number of different contexts. The content of these issues differs from State to State. Some of them have caused serious disputes or have even led to violent conflicts. According to the Report on the Linguistic Rights of Persons Belonging to National Minorities in the OSCE Area, problems have arisen where Governments have sought to limit the possibilities of persons belonging to minorities to speak their own language through national legislation or other practices, or have tolerated actions by others with such an effect.[18]

The HCNM has reacted to these problems in three different ways. First, he has been actively involved in a number of individual cases of disputes

---

[15] Cf. John Packer and Guillaume Siemienski, 'The Language of Equity: The Origin and Development of The Oslo Recommendations Regarding the Linguistic Rights of National Minorities', *International Journal on Minority and Group Rights* Vol. 6 (1999) pp. 329-350, at p. 330.

[16] Cf. High Commissioner on National Minorities, 1998, Speech delivered at the Bruno Kreisky Forum, 18/3/1998.

[17] Cf. John Packer and Guillaume Siemienski, loc. cit. n. 15, at p. 331.

[18] Cf. Report on the Linguistic Rights ... , op. cit. n. 5.

concerning linguistic rights. Second, he has conducted a survey among all States that participate in the OSCE on the linguistic rights of persons belonging to national minorities in order to provide Governments with an overview of the different options for fulfilling their commitments in this area. Third, he has requested key experts to elaborate two sets of recommendations, one on the educational rights of national minorities, and a second specifically dealing with the linguistic rights of persons belonging to national minorities.

3.2.3 *Dealing with individual cases*

In his work, the High Commissioner on National Minorities is confronted with language-related problems on a recurrent basis. These problems occur in almost all States in which the High Commissioner has been active since 1993. Where language issues have been acute or where the situation has been indicative of problems in this respect, the HCNM has met with local authorities, minority representatives and other parties concerned. In such cases, he has assisted these parties to address language-related problems. The HCNM has also issued a number of reports and letters that contain specific recommendations to Governments with regard to the linguistic rights of persons belonging to national minorities. Many of these recommendations deal with issues that relate to language requirements for obtaining citizenship, the use of minority languages in higher education, and the use of minority languages in official communications.

According to the 1999 Secretary General's Annual Report on OSCE Activities, during the course of 1999 the High Commissioner was involved in minority-related issues in Croatia, Estonia, Greece, Kazakhstan, Kyrgyzstan, Latvia, the former Yugoslav Republic of Macedonia, Romania, Slovakia and Ukraine. In all these cases the use and status of minority languages were of certain importance.

In Estonia the High Commissioner focused his attention in particular on the amendments to the language law. In a letter to the Foreign Minister he criticised the law, especially because it allowed intrusion into the private sphere which went beyond what international standards would allow. Other international organisations, such as the European Commission and the Council of Europe, expressed similar criticism. Subsequently, the Estonian Government promised to limit the impact of the new language law through implementation decrees. The High Commissioner acknowledged the effort to interpret the law narrowly and to implement its provisions with attention being paid to the justifications expressed in the law. At the same time he reiterated to the Estonian Government his recommendation to bring the law itself into conformity with international standards. The High Commissioner also organised a seminar on educational and linguistic rights in the capital Tallinn in co-operation with the Foundation on Inter-Ethnic Relations and the OSCE mission in the country.[19]

---

[19] Cf. Annual Report 1999 on OSCE Activities (1 December 1998 - 31 October 1999), para. 2, Report of the High Commissioner on National Minorities, 2.3, Estonia.

In Kazakhstan, the High Commissioner agreed with the Government to organise a seminar on the language policy of the Central Asian republic.[20]

In Latvia, the High Commissioner closely followed the development of the 1999 State Language Law. Upon his initiative, a group of experts met in Latvia in May 1999 with the responsible standing committee of the Latvian Parliament and discussed the latest draft law. In July, the Saeima (the Latvian Parliament) passed the draft. This draft, however, did not live up to the international standards which Latvia has subscribed to. Therefore, the High Commissioner appealed to the President not to promulgate the Law. She subsequently returned the Law to Parliament for further consideration.

As in Estonia, the High Commissioner organised a seminar on educational and linguistic rights in Riga in co-operation with the OSCE Mission and the Foundation on Inter-Ethnic Relations.[21]

In the former Yugoslav Republic of Macedonia, the High Commissioner presented a number of recommendations on a possible compromise solution concerning language education, particularly at the tertiary level. His recommendations included the creation of an Albanian-language university college for training teachers and of a private university for business and public administration with teaching in English, Macedonian and Albanian.[22]

In Romania, in 1999, the High Commissioner promoted dialogue on possibilities for changes to the Education Law that would permit improvements in the tertiary education available to the Hungarian minority in their mother tongue. This Education Law, which was subsequently adapted, did open up more opportunities for multicultural education.[23]

In Slovakia the High Commissioner and his experts were involved in discussions with the coalition Government on a new law on minority languages, after which a draft law was presented to Parliament. This draft was approved, but without any clear reference to the overriding character of this law in relation to the Law on the State Language, although the High Commissioner had advised such a clarification. Nevertheless, the Slovak Government subsequently assured the HCNM in writing that the law on minority languages constituted a *lex specialis* in respect of the Law on the State Language.[24]

Besides conducting on-site missions, issuing recommendations, and organising seminars, the High Commissioner has been involved in several studies and reports. One of these reports focuses on the linguistic rights of persons belonging to national minorities and the policies regarding these rights in the OSCE participating States.

---

[20] Idem, para. 2.5, Kazakhstan.
[21] Idem, para. 2.7, Latvia.
[22] Idem, para. 2.8, The former Yugoslav Republic of Macedonia.
[23] Idem, para. 2.9, Romania.
[24] Idem, para. 2.10, Slovak Republic.

4. SURVEY ON THE LINGUISTIC RIGHTS OF PERSONS BELONGING TO NATIONAL MINORITIES IN THE OSCE AREA

As part of the High Commissioner's mandate for conflict prevention and upon the suggestion of some States, a survey was conducted of OSCE State policies concerning linguistic rights. The aim of the analysis and comparison of the laws and policies of all the participating States, along with a consideration of the applicable legal standards, was to provide Governments with a sense of the numerous options for fulfilling their commitments in this area. A second objective was to provide governments with an understanding of those policies that fall short of those standards. In addition, such a study could heighten awareness among these States of the importance of this issue and the possibilities for the protection of linguistic rights as a means of ensuring human rights as well as peace and stability.[25]

In December 1996, the High Commissioner sent a questionnaire to the Ministers for Foreign Affairs of the OSCE participating States.[26] The questions related to four fundamental aspects of linguistic rights: the status of particular languages in the State; the extent of the rights of and possibilities for persons belonging to national minorities to use their language with the administrative and judicial authorities of the State; the role of minority languages in the educational curriculum; and the access for persons belonging to national minorities to public media in their language.

The survey led to the Report on the Linguistic Rights of Persons Belonging to National Minorities in the OSCE Area, which was published in March 1999. This Report reveals a range of practice by States with respect to the linguistic rights of persons belonging to national minorities. On the basis of these results, the report concludes that many States would be well served by setting their policies in this area through more official and legal methods. It stresses the importance of a legal framework for the protection of linguistic rights as a first step towards overcoming arbitrary interference with minority rights and full implementation of international standards. The responses to the survey also highlight the need for Governments to maintain close channels of communication with persons belonging to national minorities. In some States, according to the Report, mechanisms for ascertaining those needs are well established. But in many others, members of national minorities may be so isolated from channels of authority that the Government is unaware of what needs they have. Finally, the report concludes that some States need to be better aware of the content of the international standards concerning the linguistic rights of persons

---

[25] Cf. Report on the Linguistic Rights ... , op. cit. n. 5.
[26] All Governments to which the questionnaire was directed replied to it, with the exception of five States. Albania and Belgium did not respond. Iceland, Liechtenstein and Luxembourg stated that they did not have any national minorities and therefore did not provide answers to the questions.

belonging to national minorities. It states that foreign ministries should be cognisant of relevant international standards. Lawmakers and those in law-implementing agencies, however, may well be unfamiliar with these standards, including, in many respects, unfamiliarity as regards the inherent flexibility of such standards.[27]

The limited awareness of the content of international standards concerning linguistic rights is partly explained by the fact that their formulation sometimes remains rather general. Many standards also lack specificity with regard to their precise application in concrete situations. With this in mind, the High Commissioner on National Minorities concluded that - in addition to the survey - it would be useful to develop a set of guidelines concerning the linguistic rights of persons belonging to national minorities.[28]

4.1 Recommendations on the educational and linguistic rights of persons belonging to national minorities

In view of the need for guidelines, in the summer of 1996 the High Commissioner on National Minorities requested the Foundation on Inter-Ethnic Relations to consult a small group of experts of international repute so that their recommendations on an appropriate and coherent application of the linguistic rights of persons belonging to national minorities in the OSCE region could be received.[29] A similar request from the High Commissioner had previously resulted in the Hague Recommendations Regarding the Education Rights of National Minorities. Insofar as these recommendations comprehensively address the use of minority languages in the field of education, it was decided to exclude this issue from consideration by the experts who were to elaborate recommendations specifically on linguistic rights.[30] Their task was to interpret standards and to elaborate guidelines on an appropriate and coherent application of the linguistic rights of persons belonging to national minorities. The aim of the project was to clarify the existing standards and to provide a useful reference for the development of State policies and laws, which would contribute to an effective implementation of minorities' language rights.

According to the introduction to the subsequent Oslo Recommendations, the starting point for the consultations was:

'[...] to presume compliance by States with all other human rights obligations including, in particular, equality and freedom from discrimination, freedom of expression, freedom

---

[27] Cf. Report on the Linguistic Rights ... , op. cit. n. 5.

[28] Cf. John Packer and Guillaume Siemienski, loc. cit. n. 15, p. 336.

[29] The Foundation on Inter-Ethnic Relations is a non-governmental organisation established in 1993 to support specialised activities of the OSCE High Commissioner on National Minorities and liquidated in 2000. Its activities were incorporated into the High Commissioner's Office by means of a newly created 'project out'.

[30] Cf. The Oslo Recommendations Regarding the Linguistic Rights of National Minorities & Explanatory Note, Introduction, 1998.

of assembly and of association, as well as all the rights and freedoms of persons belonging to national minorities. It was also presumed that the ultimate object of all human rights is the full and free development of the individual human personality in conditions of equality. Consequently, it was presumed that civil society should be open and fluid and, therefore, integrate all persons, including those belonging to national minorities. Insofar as the use of language is also a fundamentally communicative matter, the essential social dimension of the human experience was also fully presumed.'[31]

The work of the experts resulted in February 1998 in the Oslo Recommendations Regarding the Linguistic Rights of National Minorities & Explanatory Note. These recommendations draw together the most prominent of those international standards which relate to language issues. Among these documents are the earlier mentioned Universal Declaration of Human Rights, the International Labour Organization Convention No. 111, the International Covenant on Civil and Political Rights, the Convention on the Rights of the Child, and the Declaration on the Rights of Persons Belonging to National or Ethnic, Religious and Linguistic Minorities. The recommendations are also derived from regional standards such as the earlier mentioned European Convention for the Protection of Human Rights and Fundamental Freedoms, the Declaration on Freedom of Expression and Information, the Document of the Copenhagen Meeting, the European Charter for Regional or Minority Languages, and the Framework Convention for the Protection of National Minorities.

The Oslo Recommendations are divided into sub-headings, corresponding to the language-related issues which arise in practice in cases in which the High Commissioner is involved. These are concrete issues concerning: names, religion, community life and non-governmental organisations, the media, economic life, administrative authorities and public services, independent national institutions, the judicial authorities, and deprivation of liberty. The Oslo Recommendations clarify how the principles of tolerance, coexistence and integration can be applied in relation to the use of language with regard to these specific issues. Many of the recommendations offer general examples of the effect of human rights in language matters. Written in straightforward language, the Recommendations are of considerable value for policy- and law-making as they show how these matters may be addressed in a way which provides for respect of and compliance with relevant international standards.[32] This particularly holds true for those States that have recognised the multilingual character of their population. For those States that still prefer to deny this characteristic or that remain unwilling to ensure linguistic rights, the Recommendations make it more difficult to assert that 'European standards' will be upheld by making use of the unclear situation that existed in this area.

---

[31] Idem.
[32] Fernand de Varennes, 'Equality and Non-discrimination: Fundamental Principles of Minority Language Rights', *International Journal on Minority and Group Rights*, Vol. 6 (1999) No. 3, pp. 307-318, at p. 311.

5. CONCLUDING REMARKS

Since the end of the Cold War, there has been an increase in the number of disputes relating to the use and status of minority languages. This has been particularly the case in Eastern Europe and Central Asia. As a pan-European Organization in which all European States, including the States of the former Soviet Union, participate (as well as, USA and Canada), the OSCE has recognised the importance of the development of international standards concerning the linguistic rights of persons belonging to national minorities in the prevention of disputes involving minority languages. Accordingly, the OSCE and its participating States have made a substantial contribution to the existing body of international standards by adopting the Copenhagen Document and other relevant documents. Through the institution of the High Commissioner on National Minorities, the OSCE has also been directly involved in managing language-related disputes and in preventing them from escalating. Moreover, through the work of the High Commissioner, the OSCE has embarked on an attempt to fill the gap between the more or less abstract international standards on the linguistic rights of persons belonging to national minorities and their full implementation in practice. The Oslo Recommendations in particular may prove to have contributed to an effective implementation of these standards by law-makers and by those involved in law-implementing agencies on the ground.

THE PROTECTION OF MINORITY LANGUAGE RIGHTS THROUGH THE WORK OF OSCE INSTITUTIONS

John Packer*

1. INTRODUCTION

This note is intended to provide a summary account of the work carried out by the institutions of the Organization for Security and Co-operation in Europe (OSCE) aiming at the protection of the linguistic rights of persons belonging to minorities through the course of 1998. It is not the intention of this note to recount relevant standards[1] nor to summarize various political discussions within the OSCE context which either directly or indirectly touch upon minority language rights.[2] Nor will this note describe or analyse the mentioned OSCE institutions, their particular mandates or motivations and rationale for addressing the specific matters.[3]

---

* Director, Office of the OSCE High Commissioner on National Minorities; from 1995 to early 2000, Mr. Packer was Senior Legal Adviser to the High Commissioner. The views expressed in this article are those of the author alone and do not necessarily reflect the views of the OSCE or any of its institutions. The author wishes to thank his colleagues from the OSCE institutions mentioned in this article for the information they provided, without which this article could not have been written.

[1] This has been done by others at various depths of analysis. See, e.g.: Patrick Thornberry, *International Law and the Rights of Minorities* (Oxford: Clarendon Press, 1991); Maria Amor Martín Estébanez, *International Organizations and Minority Protection in Europe* (Turku/Åbo: Åbo Akademi University Institute for Human Rights, 1996); Patrick Thornberry and Maria Amor Martín Estébanez, *The Council of Europe and Minorities* (Strasbourg: The Council of Europe, 1995); Fernand de Varennes, *Language, Minorities and Human Rights* (The Hague: Martinus Nijhoff Publishers, 1996); Athanasia Spiliopoulou Åkermark, *Justifications of Minority Protection in International Law* (Uppsala: Iustus Publishing Company, 1997); Alan Phillips and Allan Rosas (Eds.), *Universal Minority Rights* (Turku/Åbo: Åbo Akademi University Institute for Human Rights, 1995); and, for a brief overview of the specifically relevant standards together with some comments and a useful annotated bibliography, Pádraig Ó Riagáin and Niamh Nic Shuibhne, 'Minority Language Rights', *Annual Review of Applied Linguistics*, Vol. 17 (1997), pp. 11-29.

[2] Both general issues and specific situations are addressed in OSCE discussions on an on-going basis, whether through formal fora such as the weekly meetings of the Permanent Council or through informal contacts among diplomats and other governmental and non-governmental representatives. Beyond OSCE fora, discussions are pursued between the OSCE and other inter-governmental organizations and at international conferences at which the OSCE participates.

[3] Basic information on the OSCE, its institutions, their mandates and work is available from, e.g., the following: the Internet via the OSCE's web-site at www.osce.org; the OSCE Hand-

S. Trifunovska (Ed.), Minority Rights in Europe: European Minorities and Languages
© 2000, T.M.C. Asser Press, The Hague, The Netherlands

By providing an account of the relevant work actually carried out by OSCE institutions, it is intended that the reader will be able to understand better both the body of standards employed within the OSCE and the practical way in which the OSCE acts to give the agreed standards concrete meaning and effect in real situations. In this sense, the following account should be viewed as indicative of the overall OSCE approach to the protection of minorities, i.e. that the protection of minorities is a key element in the wider framework of contemporary European security which is grounded in the fundamental commitment of all OSCE participating States to free and open societies with market economies and democratic governance, including respect for human rights, under the rule of law.[4] As the principal OSCE institution mandated within the framework of 'comprehensive security' and 'co-operative security' specifically to prevent conflicts in situations involving minority issues, the High Commissioner on National Minorities (HCNM) has commented many times on the relevant conceptual and practical matters.[5] While the HCNM has substantially, evidently and consistently addressed the issues of minority language rights since he first took up his mandate in 1993,[6] it is important to note that other OSCE institutions

---

book and other relevant documentation (e.g. Fact Sheets, monthly Newsletter, etc.) published by the OSCE available from the OSCE's Documentation Section located at Rytirska 31, CZ-110 00 Prague, Czech Republic, e-mail: quest@osceprag.cz; and the OSCE Yearbooks prepared by the Institute for Peace Research and Security Policy at the University of Hamburg and published by Nomos Verlagsgesellschaft in Baden-Baden, Germany. In addition, useful compilations of documentation and analyses may be found, e.g., in the following: Arie Bloed (Ed.), *The Conference on Security and Co-operation in Europe: Analysis and Basic Documents, 1972-1993* (Dordrecht: Martinus Nijhoff Publishers, 1993); Arie Bloed (Ed.), *The Conference on Security and Co-operation in Europe; Basic Documents, 1993-1995* (The Hague: Kluwer Law International, 1997); Adam Daniel Rotfeld (Ed.), *From Helsinki to Budapest and Beyond; Analysis and Documents of the Organization for Security and Co-operation in Europe, 1973-1995* (London: Oxford University Press, 1996); Victor-Yves Ghebali, *L'OSCE dans l'Europe post-communiste, 1990-1996; Vers une identité paneuropéenne de sécurité* (Bruxelles: Etablissements Emile Bruylant, 1996); Michael Bothe, Natalino Ronzitti and Allan Rosas (Eds.), *The OSCE in the Maintenance of Peace and Security; Conflict Prevention, Crisis Management and Peaceful Settlement of Disputes* (The Hague: Kluwer Law International, 1997); and Jonathan Cohen, *Conflict Prevention in the OSCE; An Assessment of Capacities* (The Hague: Netherlands Institute of International Relations Clingendael, 1999).

[4] On OSCE values and the Organization's basic framework, see the two compilation of documents (all adopted by consensus) edited by Arie Bloed (op. cit. n. 3) together with the documents adopted by OSCE participating States at the subsequent Ministerial Council meetings in Copenhagen (1997) and Oslo (1998) as well as the Summit meetings in Lisbon (1996) and Istanbul (1999).

[5] See, e.g., the speeches of the HCNM available on the OSCE web-site or, in published form, the selection edited by Wolfgang Zellner and Falk Lange, *Peace and Stability through Human and Minority Rights* (Baden-Baden: Nomos Verlagsgesellschaft, 1999), and especially the HCNM's speech delivered at the London School of Economics and Political Science on 19 October 1999 in memory of Dr. Neelan Tiruchelvam entitled 'Human Rights, the Prevention of Conflict and the International Protection of Minorities: A Contemporary Paradigm for Contemporary Challenges'.

[6] See, e.g.: the description and analysis of the HCNM's activities on this and other issues in the Baltic States (especially Estonia and Latvia) in Rob Zaagman, 'Conflict Prevention in the Baltic States: The OSCE High Commissioner on National Minorities in Estonia, Latvia and

are also actively engaged in such matters within the context of their own mandates.

In order to avoid any misunderstanding about why or how OSCE institutions have become involved in such matters which often reach significantly into the otherwise internal affairs of participating States, it is important to underline that at the 1991 Moscow Meeting of the Conference on the Human Dimension of the then CSCE, all OSCE participating States voluntarily accepted that 'commitments undertaken in the field of the human dimension [in particular human rights, including minority rights] of the CSCE are matters of direct and legitimate concern to all participating States and do not belong exclusively to the internal affairs of the State concerned.'[7] Moreover, all OSCE participating States have bound themselves to respect not only express OSCE commitments, but all relevant international law irrespective of its source.[8] Further, the existence and functioning of any and all OSCE institutions is the product of consensus decision-making which, together with the principle of co-operative security, implies full participation and actual co-operation of all OSCE participating States: nothing in the OSCE context – neither standards nor institutions – is imposed.

The specific nature of language also warrants some preliminary remarks in order to clarify how this subject matter fits within the OSCE framework. Certainly, there is a vast literature on language and there are well-established professions which are dedicated to its analysis from both philological and socio-cultural perspectives.[9] But it is not for scientific or cultural reasons that the

---

Lithuania', ECMI Monograph # 1 (Flensburg: European Centre for Minority Issues, 1999); and the description of the HCNM's activities in the former Yugoslavia in John Packer, 'The Role of the OSCE High Commissioner on National Minorities in the Former Yugoslavia', *Cambridge Review of International Affairs*, Vol. XII, No. 2, 1999, pp. 169-184, especially at pp. 172-174 (regarding FYROM), pp. 174-176 (regarding Croatia), and 176-178 (regarding Kosovo).

[7] For the text of the Document of the Moscow Meeting, see Arie Bloed (Ed.), *The Conference on Security and Co-operation in Europe: Analysis and Basic Documents, 1972-1993* (Dordrecht: Martinus Nijhoff Publishers, 1993), pp. 605-629 at p. 606.

[8] It is to be noted that, beginning with Principle X of the *Helsinki Final Act* signed on 1 August 1975 by the Heads of State or Government of the then 35 participating States, all OSCE participating States have committed themselves to 'fulfill in good faith their obligations under international law, both those obligations arising from the generally recognized principles and rules of international law and those obligations arising from treaties or other agreements, in conformity with international law, to which they are parties'. It is also to be noted that a wide variety of relevant obligations arise from the fact that all OSCE participating States are members of the United Nations (with the exception of the Swiss Confederation which is, in any case, a party to numerous treaties elaborated within the UN context), 41 OSCE States are members of the Council of Europe, 16 OSCE States are members of the Central European Initiative, 15 OSCE States are members of the European Union, 12 OSCE States are members of the Commonwealth of Independent States, and 11 OSCE States are members of the Council of Baltic Sea States – all of which (not to mention sub-sub-regional organizations and arrangements or bilateral treaties) bind OSCE participating States to a fundamentally consistent body of essentially repeated obligations.

[9] As a short example directly related to the issues here in discussion, see Miklós Kontra, 'Some Reflections on the Nature of Language and Its Regulation', *International Journal on Minority and Group Rights*, Vol. 6 (1999) No. 3, pp. 281-288.

OSCE is engaged in language issues. As a *security* organization, the OSCE derives its interest in language issues from the fact that choices in the use of language – especially in the public sphere of governance – directly affect the enjoyment of not only culture but also access to important public goods (*inter alia*, services, facilities, employment and positions of prestige), not to mention participation in governance itself. Ó Riagáin and Nic Shuibhne capture a large part of the interest in and importance of minority language issues and rights as follows:

> 'Conceptually, the question of minority language rights can be located within the classic debates about the balancing of liberal freedom with the demands of a capitalist economy, of equity and efficiency. When a substantial minority of a population is denied full effective citizenship because of the language they speak, then language and language rights matter. The debate about minority language rights thus touches upon a range of other political controversies concerning multiculturalism [...], difference [...], recognition [...], presence [...], and citizenship [...].'[10]

For these and other reasons, concerns exist ranging from those of the Ulster Scots to the Crimean Tatars (as relatively small or even tiny linguistic groups) to those of so-called fragile majorities in the Baltic States, Central Asia or even powerful sub-State regions like Quebec. Such concerns have generated disputes sometimes manifesting bloody conflicts in the former Yugoslavia, Moldova and elsewhere. Clearly, human beings do not easily surrender their culture or their material interests, and insofar as language is of critical importance for both it will remain the source of significant disputes. As a matter of fact, disputes over language issues are real, intense, persistent and sometimes violent. As such, there is a clear need to address and resolve such issues generally and early.

2. THE WORK OF THE OSCE HIGH COMMISSIONER

The work of the HCNM is mainly conducted through quiet diplomacy such that only part of his activities and views are ever brought to public light. Certain especially relevant work of the HCNM in the period under consideration has been published and is reproduced in this compilation. Beyond these published materials, the HCNM has raised minority language issues in very many other aspects of his work including his on-going personal dialogues with various interlocutors, at seminars and round-tables conducted behind closed doors, through confidential exchanges of correspondence, in his periodic reports to the Chairperson-in-Office and the Permanent Council of the OSCE, in exchanges with inter-governmental organizations and in consultations with independent experts (linguists, jurists, pedagogues, political scientists, philosophers, sociologists, etc.). Various recurring issues (often those at the intersection of public and private affairs) have been addressed with a view to accommodating to

---

[10] Pádraig Ó Riagáin and Niamh Nic Shuibhne, loc. cit. n. 1, at p. 12.

the maximum extent the interests and desires of all. Since the material which is publicly available is reproduced in full in this compilation (except the HCNM's speeches), the following will offer just some comments aimed at situating the available material within the context of the HCNM's overall work.

2.1 Formal Exchanges of Letters

Since the daily focus of most of the HCNM's work is his engagement in the detailed treatment of specific issues within particular situations, it is appropriate to begin with some comments on the HCNM's specific recommendations as communicated through formal exchanges of letters with governments.[11] It is to be noted that such exchanges are not expressly prescribed in the HCNM's mandate, nor was it foreseen that these written exchanges would eventually become public (as they are, following some period for subsequent direct follow-up contacts, for domestic steps to be taken, and not before circulation and consideration behind the closed doors of the Permanent Council). However, this technique of formal written dialogue has become a principal element of the HCNM's method and is now established practice having never been contested by a participating State. It is also to be noted that these formal written exchanges are only one part of the HCNM's dialogue which normally follows considerable direct personal contacts in the form of visits, telephone conversations and other types of communication. Moreover, there are other written exchanges which may include specific recommendations but are not intended to be made public.

In the period under consideration, the HCNM completed and made publicly available one exchange with the Romanian Government, one exchange with the Latvian Government, three exchanges with the Slovak Government, and one exchange with the Estonian President. Together, they demonstrate the detailed analysis, generally legal in nature, which the HCNM applies to situations, aiming at politically possible (i.e. acceptable for the principal parties) solutions which are guided by applicable international norms and fall within the parametres of specific standards. They also demonstrate the level of engagement in rational dialogue of the problem-solving kind with assessments and recommendations being argued on the basis of facts, standards and political interests. In at least two cases (Romania and Slovakia), specific reference is made to the HCNM's co-operation with other international organisations (i.e. the Council of Europe and the European Commission).

With regard to the issues addressed, the exchange of letters with the Romanian Government concerns educational matters including access to tertiary education in the mother tongue of large minorities and curriculum content in

---

[11] Usually, according to protocol, the exchanges are conducted with Ministers for Foreign Affairs. But, as the herein published examples show, addressees may include other important personalities, such as Heads of Government and State, with sometimes copies being sent to other relevant Ministers (e.g., Ministers of Education) or addressed to them with copies being sent to the Minister for Foreign Affairs.

schools (regarding history) in addition to the language of instruction of certain subjects in schools. Educational matters were also addressed in the exchanges with the Slovak Government, specifically regarding efforts by a Slovak nationalist party to interfere with the right and opportunity of speakers of minority languages (in particular Hungarians) to receive instruction in their mother tongue, and the desire of ethnic Hungarians to have their children attending Hungarian-language schools receive their school certificates also in the Hungarian language, i.e. to receive at least bilingual certificates (as was the practice) rather than unilingual Slovak-language certificates (insofar as Slovak is the only State language). Other issues raised with the Slovak Government included: the use of minority languages in official communications with State bodies, agencies and services; the extent of cultural subsidies available to minorities (including for minority language publications and cultural productions); and the general regulation of language use in the State (i.e. the effects of, and relationship between, regulation of the Slovak language as the only State language and protection of minority languages). The HCNM's exchange with the Latvian Government focused on concerns about especially the Law on Citizenship and naturalization procedures in relation to the persistent problem of the huge number of Stateless persons in the country. Specifically, the HCNM sought to stimulate the stalled naturalization process by overcoming obstacles of language testing and procedural requirements (such as the so-called window system which restricted applicants according to date of birth) and also, through a greater pace of naturalizations, to promote social integration. Finally, in his appeal to the President of Estonia, the HCNM addressed the issue of linguistic requirements to stand for elected office, evidently impeding the accessibility of persons belonging to linguistic minorities and limiting the choice of the electorate. In this connection, it may be noted that a different, but related, issue regarding elections was raised with the Slovak Government which sought to fix electoral representation along ethnic lines which, in fact, reflected a linguistic nationalism whereby ethnicity was largely to be indicated by language.

While the arguments made in the exchanges of letters are to be evaluated on their own merits, some further comments are warranted. First, it is apparent from the tone of the letters that the exchanges were typically diplomatic – assistance-oriented on the part of the HCNM and generally co-operative on the part of the Governments. A notable exception on the part of a Government was the rather curt responses from the Slovak Minister for Foreign Affairs, Mrs. Kramplová, indicating the Meciar regime's limited interest in a serious dialogue and, moreover, its basic disregard for international standards or the concerns of minorities. Indeed, the marked difference in tone and depth between the responses from Mrs. Kramplová and the new Slovak Prime Minister, Mr. Mikulas Dzurinda (who succeeded Meciar in October 1998), is palpable and was further reflected in immediate positive steps taken by the Dzurinda Government (which includes an ethnic Hungarian coalition party). In the case of the President of Estonia's response to the HCNM, its tone is polite but in effect dismissive as the President had already acted contrary to the HCNM's specific recommendation and ultimately referred the matter, if contested under law, to the Council of Europe organs. The HCNM's exchanges of letters also reveal his attention to practical concerns such as financing (see his letter to the Romanian Government), his specifically preventive action (see his letter of 29 May 1998 to the Slovak Government seeking to stop adoption of damaging legislation), his attention to political timing (see his letter to the Latvian Government referring to the parliamentary programme and the possible effect of elections), and his effort to promote the further applicability of international law (see his letter of 4 November 1998 to the Slovak Government encouraging accession to the European Charter for Regional or Minority Languages).

Overall, the HCNM's exchanges of letters must be read in the wider context of then on-going dialogues (sometimes expressly mentioned in the letters) and the importance of then current events: none of the letter's is to be viewed as 'one-off'. Notwithstanding the availability of (not always accurate) press reports, the full stories have yet to be told, including the sometimes important interests and actions of third and fourth parties. In sum, however, the HCNM's exchanges of letters clearly indicate his practical, problem-solving, assistance-oriented approach as he raises issues and makes specific recommendations argued with precision and clarity. The exchanges also highlight the critical function of law (whether hard or soft) as the HCNM applies the standards voluntarily accepted by the State in question and sometimes interprets them in an effort to find solutions for specific issues.

2.2 General Recommendations

Aside from the HCNM's recommendations regarding specific issues in particular situations and addressed to individual States, the HCNM has tried to fill the need for guidelines accessible to policy- and law-makers *vis-à-vis* recurrent issues such as minority education and language rights. In connection with the last issue, the HCNM invited a group of internationally recognised independent experts to elaborate a set of general recommendations, for use in all OSCE participating States and beyond, which resulted in the Oslo Recommendations Regarding the Linguistic Rights of National Minorities published in February 1998.[12] The HCNM's initiative drew on the previous positive experience he had with another group of independent experts which resulted in The Hague Recommendations Regarding the Education Rights of National Minorities.[13] Since the story of the elaboration of the Oslo

---

[12] The full text of the Oslo Recommendations, together with Explanatory Note, is reproduced in this compilation.
[13] For the full text of The Hague Recommendations, together with Explanatory Note and supplemented with scholarly articles, see the special issue of the *International Journal on Minority and Group Rights*, Vol. 4 (1996/97) No.2.

Recommendations, together with some analysis, appears elsewhere,[14] only a few comments are warranted here. In particular, it is to be observed that the current era of transitional democracies and economies features societies and governments adopting new regimes where key notions, such as the distinction between the 'private sphere' and the 'public sphere' (as addressed in Recommendation 12 of the Oslo Recommendations), raise complex and difficult issues such as the legitimacy of purported public interests and, to the extent these may be established, their restriction proportionate to the aim sought. Indeed, these issues are still in the process of being fully worked out in the 'old' democracies. Nonetheless, they may be of added importance in situations of inter-ethnic tension amid fragile democratic institutions (including still weak judiciaries) such that regional peace and stability require resolution of these issues on an urgent basis. For example, there are intense specific disputes over the role of linguistic proficiency requirements affecting access to employment, or language requirements in the media (both public and private), not to mention the highly problematical question of the actual supervision and implementation of such requirements (i.e. to what extent and by what means may such requirements be imposed, and with what implications for, *inter alia*, the freedom of expression and the right to privacy?). Such issues test the meaning and limits of 'freedom' and challenge policy- and law-makers to find accommodations which respect both legitimate public interests and prerogatives on the one hand and the protection of human rights, including minority rights, on the other hand. Certainly, it is clear that the majority may not claim everything is 'public' which simply coincides with majoritarian interests or identity. The Oslo Recommendations aim, therefore, to assist States in finding appropriate accommodations consistent with existing international standards. Fully endorsed by the HCNM and available in several languages, they have been circulated widely, have been the subject of seminars organised by the HCNM, have been discussed in the Permanent Council and at the 1999 OSCE Summit Meeting in Istanbul, and have generally become a reference at least among OSCE participating States. And still there remains enormous scope to employ the Oslo Recommendations as a useful tool in various situations.

2.3 Survey of State Practice

Ó Riagáin and Nic Shuibhne have observed that so far 'scholarly debate over human rights has been dominated by normative theorists' and that '[l]ess work has been done in the area of assessing the operation of language rights legislation in practice', in particular that there is '[v]ery little research address[ing] the feasibility of official status, or assess[ing] the optimum means of state intervention.'[15] It was precisely because of the paucity of such research

---

[14] See the special issue of the *International Journal on Minority and Group Rights*, Vol. 6 (1999) No. 3.

[15] Pádraig Ó Riagáin and Niamh Nic Shuibhne, op. cit. n. 1, at pp. 21-22.

and available synthetic references that the HCNM undertook to survey the existing State practice in the OSCE area. While the results reflect only the official government responses (which reveal a considerable disparity in reporting and may well be challenged in terms of the veracity of certain claims and also effectiveness at the point of implementation), nonetheless the HCNM's survey is the first published compilation of at least what governments claim to be the case within their jurisdictions. The full texts of the replies are also publicly available, and form an Annex to the HCNM's Report.[16]

The HCNM's Report on the Linguistic Rights of National Minorities in the OSCE Area, reproduced in full in this compilation, is an analytical summary of the responses received from 51 of the 53 States surveyed.[17] With a questionnaire containing nine questions being sent out in mid-December 1996, responses were mainly received in the course of 1997 and 1998, indicating law and practices to the varying dates of submission. On request of the HCNM, analysis of the responses was made initially by Professor Steven Ratner of the University Texas School of Law (then working with the Office of the HCNM as Fulbright Senior Scholar in OSCE Studies) by grouping them not only according to the questions asked, but from the perspective of relevant international standards. In so doing, the HCNM intended both to indicate the range of existing practices and also to suggest which options or implied 'best' practices met or surpassed minimum international standards. In this way, it was hoped that OSCE participating States would see that virtually all States in fact address (one way or another, and to varying degrees) the issues surveyed and could draw upon the range of practices in developing or reforming their own policy, law and practice to the benefit of their populations and regional peace and stability.

3. THE WORK OF THE OSCE MISSIONS

With the support of in-puts from OSCE Mission Members submitted on the request of this author, concerns and activities of OSCE Missions in 1998 (and sometimes early 1999) in relation to minority language issues are summarised in the following sub-sections. In most cases, the Missions provided support to other OSCE institutions, especially the HCNM, by means of monitoring, maintaining direct contacts, and contributing analyses and performing tasks. Of course, first

---

[16] The Annex, running some 400 pages (not including a considerable number of attachments, such as legislation, submitted by States), is not reproduced in this compilation, but is available from the Office of the HCNM in The Hague.

[17] Questionnaires were addressed to all OSCE participating States except rump Yugoslavia (which may be considered either 'suspended' or 'non-recognised') and the Holy See. Responses were never received from Albania (which suffered significant domestic turmoil) and Belgium.

and foremost, OSCE Missions performed their functions according to their own specific mandates which to varying degrees include minority language issues.[18]

Bosnia and Herzegovina

It is to be underlined that the protection of minority language rights in Bosnia and Herzegovina suffers first of all from the general misunderstanding of the very notion 'minority'. Owing to the peculiar and pejorative (mis)understanding of the notion propagated under the Socialist Federal Republic of Yugoslavia,[19] factual and legal (according to international law) minorities in Bosnia and Herzegovina generally do not assert their rights to use 'their language' on the basis of affiliation with a minority, but on the basis of belonging to one of the 'constituent peoples'[20] of the fractured State. Nonetheless, issues of language use are raised – often aggressively – in reaction to actual or perceived discrimination and in relation to educational matters. Specifically, the language and script of instruction has remained a highly contentious issue which has largely hindered (in fact, precluded) integrated schools or classes and undermined efforts aimed at a comprehensive curriculum reform. Use of language in official communications, including documentation, and official settings (such as meetings) has been a constant source of disputes. Generally, politicians and private persons alike have used language as a means to accentuate differences and mediate access to public goods, including jobs and positions. The concerns of small linguistic groups, such as the Roma, have been ignored or trampled upon. While the OSCE Mission is aware of persistent problems and responds to certain of them, it along with other international actors have generally failed to move the society or government(s) forward in resolving these fundamental issues.

Croatia

The general status and protection of minorities in Croatia has been complicated by the unclear relationship between laws of the former Socialist Federal Republic of Yugoslavia, the former Socialist Republic of Croatia and the newly independent Republic of Croatia; in particular, it is not clear what rights may

---

[18] For a description and analysis of the concept and mandates of OSCE Missions, including accounts of the work of selected ones, see Allan Rosas and Timo Lahelma, 'OSCE Long-Term Missions', in Michael Bothe, Natalino Ronzitti and Allan Rosas (Eds.), op. cit. n. 3, pp. 167-190.

[19] For a brief account of the understanding and situation in the former Socialist Federal Republic of Yugoslavia, see Milan Paunović, 'Nationalities and Minorities in the Yugoslav Federation and in Serbia', in John Packer and Kristian Myntti (Eds.), *The Protection of Ethnic and Linguistic Minorities in Europe* (Turku/Åbo: Åbo Akademi University Institute for Human Rights, 1993), pp. 145-165.

[20] According to Article 1 of the Constitution of Bosnia and Herzegovina (Annex 4 to the Dayton Accords of December 1995), the State is composed of four 'constituent peoples': Bosniacs, Croats, Serbs, and Others. Aside from the evident difficulty in attributing membership in discrete and definitive terms with regard to the first three 'peoples', the fourth purported 'people' is without doubt highly problematical.

have been 'acquired' under the former regimes and remain to be protected under the new. Moreover, a part of Croatia (i.e. Eastern Slavonia) had been under temporary administration by the United Nations (i.e. UNTAES, which concluded its functions and departed Croatia on 15 January 1998) with specifically applicable agreements having been negotiated (e.g. the Erdut Agreement of 12 November 1995). In addition, the Italian and Hungarian minorities enjoy special protection under bilateral treaties concluded between Croatia and, respectively, Italy and Hungary.[21]

Under the Constitution and laws of the Republic of Croatia, minority languages (and their script) are protected, with a 1991 Constitutional Law on Human Rights and Freedoms and the Rights of National and Ethnic Communities and Minorities in the Republic of Croatia adding further guarantees, in particular the use of minority languages in official contacts where persons belonging to minorities constitute more than 50% of the population in a municipality, and also the use minority languages in official contacts at municipal level if the municipality so agrees. In addition, it is to be noted that Croatia is a party to the 1992 European Charter for Regional or Minority Languages specifying its application to the Czech, Hungarian, Italian, Ruthenian, Serbian, Slovak, and Ukrainian languages. With a view to clarifying the regulatory regime, a draft Law on Official Use of Minority Languages remained in parliament through 1998 and 1999 without much movement, indicating a fundamental lack of political will to bring legal clarity and make effective Croatia's constitutional and international commitments. Indeed, while this uncertainty has affected issues ranging from the use of minority languages before the judiciary, in public administration and education, the 1999 Telecommunications Law possibly constituted a step backwards as it contained no express protection for minority language programming while it stipulates that the language of broadcasting is 'the standard Croatian language'.

Estonia

While the OSCE Mission to Estonia has provided valuable support to the HCNM in his active engagement with minority language issues in Estonia, the Mission has also addressed language issues in the context of its own mandate. Language issues were and remain, in fact, the principal axis of inter-ethnic

---

[21] For a general treatment of contemporary bilateral treaty protections, see Arie Bloed and Pieter van Dijk (Eds.), *Protection of Minority Rights Through Bilateral Treaties; The Case of Central and Eastern Europe* (The Hague: Kluwer Law International, 1999), including treatment of bilateral treaties with Hungary by Patrick Thornberry, 'Hungarian Bilateral Treaties and Declarations', at pp. 127-161 (with the full texts of the 1992 and 1995 Hungarian-Croatian agreements at pp. 339-347). For a recent positive assessment of such bilateral arrangements, see Elizabeth F. Defeis, 'Minority Protections and Bilateral Agreements: An Effective Mechanism', *Hastings International and Comparative Law Review*, Vol. 22 (1999) Number 2, pp. 291-321. *Cf.* The skeptical assessment of Gudmundur Alfredsson, 'Identifying Possible Disadvantages of Bilateral Agreements and Advancing the "Most-Favoured-Minority Clause"', in Arie Bloed and Pieter van Dijk (Eds.), *supra*, pp. 165-175.

discourse (mainly dispute) often manifesting itself in conflicting claims and arguments regarding history, policy and law. Controversial amendments to the *Law on Language* adopted in late 1997 gave rise to several disputes, some of which remain unresolved. Of particular dispute was the tightening of the linguistic requirement to stand for elected office adopted pursuant to late 1998 legislative amendments which followed a 5 February 1998 decision of the Estonian Supreme Court which found the then existing law and practice to be unconstitutional on the grounds of being too broad and insufficiently prescribed by law. Another serious dispute concerns a 1997 amendment to the *Law on Basic and Upper-Secondary Schools* which prescribes universal Estonian-language instruction in the 2007/2008 academic year 'at the latest'. As was expected, the linguistic minorities (especially the Russian-speaking community) reacted with great consternation to this new legislation. For its part, the OSCE Mission followed and reported confidentially upon these developments, among others, acted to clarify facts, performed intermediary functions, and encouraged representatives of both majority and minority(ies) to moderate their rhetoric and modify policies and/or claims in seeking solutions.

Georgia

Similar to other newly independent States of the former Soviet Union, the factual situation in Georgia is such that a substantial part of the population (25-30%) does not speak Georgian as a mother tongue or to a high degree of proficiency. Moreover, minority language speakers are geographically concentrated, in particular in Abkazia, South Ossetia and Samtskhe-Javakheti. While the nationalist policies of the Gamzakhurdia period caused many persons belonging to minorities (e.g. Greeks, Russians, Germans and Jews) to depart Georgia, there still remain numerous minorities (45-50 registered groups) in substantial numbers. The only Constitutional recognition of minority language speakers is found in Article 8 – specifying Georgian as the State language, but also Abkhazian in the Abkhaz region[22] – and Article 38 which stipulates cultural equality and expressly provides for the free use by citizens of 'their language in private and public life'. Notwithstanding the geographic concentrations of some linguistic groups (*inter alia*, Ossetians, Armenians, Azeris), they enjoy no express constitutional guarantees.

To overcome the problem of insufficient knowledge of the State language (i.e. Georgian), minority language speakers have repeatedly expressed the wish for adequate educational opportunities to improve popular command of Georgian. This follows from limited opportunities (especially political ones) in the absence of a good command of the Georgian language. The Georgian *Law on Education* seeks to accommodate a balance between the need to know the State

---

[22] On the special situation in Abkhazia, see Jonathan Cohen (Ed.), 'A question of sovereignty: The Georgia-Abkhazia peace process', *Accord*, Issue 7 (London: Conciliation Resources, 1999).

language and also to maintain minority languages. However, practical opportunities to learn Georgian remain scarce in areas where minorities live compactly. Moreover, Russian remains the language of reference for scientific and international publications and other contacts throughout the country, even among Georgian-speakers.

In the period 1998-1999, attention was paid to the drafting of a law on the State language. In addition, practical problems such as the failure of many judges to pass mandatory Georgian language exams were seen to interfere with access to justice and the rule of law in some parts of the country. An especially acute problem has been the lack of educational materials, in particular textbooks, for minority language schools across the country. The serious economic constraints on the authorities, whether central or local, have made it difficult to overcome this practical problem.

Latvia

As in the case of other OSCE Missions, especially in Estonia, the Mission to Latvia provided significant support to the HCNM in his active engagement with minority language issues. It also carried out functions in the context of its own mandate. In terms of issues, principal attention was directed to the drafting of a new *State Language Law* which had passed its first reading in the Saeima (parliament) in May 1997 and was prepared for second reading only in the first part of 1998 after considerable consultations with representatives of, *inter alia*, the OSCE, Council of Europe and Council of Baltic Sea States. Through the remainder of 1998, the draft *State Language Law* drew the careful attention of the Mission and the international community in general as efforts were mounted (led by the HCNM) to persuade the Latvian authorities and parliamentarians to adopt a law which would fully conform with Latvia's international obligations and commitments. Parliamentary elections in the autumn of 1998 interrupted the process, but after the newly elected deputies took their seats in the Saeima work on the draft law continued (as it did through almost all of 1999).

The Mission also followed developments leading to adoption of a set of laws on education with significant effects for linguistic minorities who claim various important elements of the new legislation violate their rights and limit the maintenance and development of their culture. Also in relation to education, the Mission monitored implementation of *Minister of Education and Science Decree No. 175 of December 1996* controlling Latvian language proficiency requirements for teachers, carrying the prospect of numerous dismissals in minority-language schools or of non-Latvian-speaking teachers. Somewhat in balance of the implementation of Latvian language proficiency requirements in employment, the Mission monitored and encouraged the work of the National Programme for Latvian-Language Training, including efforts to find funding for this crucial programme. In a similar vein, the Mission monitored the work of the Naturalization Board and sought simplification and other improvements in the language tests for naturalization. Finally, following approval in October 1998 by the Cabinet of Ministers of the concept for a new Social Integration Programme for Latvia, the Mission promoted the concept and encouraged its full elaboration through public consultations with a view to eventual adoption of the whole Programme in 1999 and, ultimately, its effective implementation in the years thereafter.

Macedonia

The use of minority languages is amongst the most sensitive issues in the political life of the former Yugoslav Republic of Macedonia (FYROM). High on the domestic political agenda for several years has been the particular issue of access to higher education in the Albanian language, with a *Law on Higher Education* remaining to be debated in parliament – and put off again in 1998 due to parliamentary elections. Both constitutional and international legal protection of minority languages exists in FYROM, but its effective implementation and enjoyment has met legislative and administrative obstacles.

Aside from the dominant issue of higher education in the Albanian language, some other minority language issues were in dispute in the FYROM in 1998. Also at the level of higher education, there was a dispute at the Pedagogical Faculty of the principal university in Skopje as the Dean refused to implement a special law ensuring instruction in the Albanian language with a view to meeting the practical need to train a sufficient number of Albanian-language instructors to fill posts in Albanian-language schools throughout the country. Another educational issue arose in the village of Zhupa where parents from the Turkish minority sought to secure education for their children in the Turkish language but met resistance on the argument from the authorities that the children in question did not actually have a sufficient command of the Turkish language.[23] A more innocuous, but immediately political, issue arose when a court of registration refused to register an ethnic Albanian political party (the Party of Democratic Prosperity of Albanians, PDPA) partly on the ground that their party seal was bilingual – which was said to be unconstitutional since the State language is Macedonian written in the Cyrillic script. Aside from monitoring these cases, the OSCE Mission sought as appropriate to persuade the relevant authorities and actors to resolve matters according to applicable international standards.

---

[23] This situation raises complex issues of past discrimination constituting assimilation and, perhaps more fundamentally, the question of the criteria for membership of a minority and thereby access to enjoyment of minority rights, i.e. whether the State may unilaterally deny membership on the basis of some criterion such as linguistic inability or whether persons and communities enjoy a right to self-identification. On the still vexing problems in defining minorities and, therefore, the exact rights-holders of the catalogue of minority rights, see John Packer, 'Problems in Defining Minorities', in Deirdre Fottrell and Bill Bowring (Eds.), *Minority and Group Rights in the New Millennium* (The Hague: Kluwer Law International, 1999), pp. 223-274.

Moldova

There continued to be a great number of unsettled language issues in Moldova subsequent to independence, in particular stemming from the adoption on 31 August 1989 of Moldovan (in the Latin script) as the only State language in a country where over 35% of the population does not speak Moldovan and, moreover, where minority language speakers reside in compact areas in substantial numbers. Most spectacularly, this tension finds continuing expression in the situation in Transniestria (which has featured armed conflict) where the Russian-speaking majority rejects the authority of the Republic of Moldova and imposes its own de facto authority and administration in the Russian language – leaving Moldovan-speakers in the position of a vulnerable and unprotected minority in this region. More encouraging, however, is the substantial regional autonomy granted by law to areas inhabited mainly by minority language speakers, such as in Guagazia.

Even within the areas under its effective control, the Moldovan authorities have had difficulties imposing the use of the Moldovan language on both public administration and also popular use. The majority of press and printed material, in addition to popular radio and television broadcasting, remain in the Russian language which is spoken by the great majority of the population.[24] This has motivated legislative efforts to 'promote' Moldovan-language programming and material simply by means of prohibiting the use of other languages (or doing so in effect by prescribing the use *only* of the Moldovan language). One contentious example of such legislative efforts has been the *Law on Advertising* which effectively prohibits Russian-language (and other) advertising even in the commercial sphere. Naturally, such efforts have proved both inflammatory and ineffective. To counteract this kind of intrusion into the private commercial sphere and yet to promote the wider use of the Moldovan language, international attention has been drawn to the need to increase the popular proficiency and use of the Moldovan language.

Tajikistan

While Tajikistan is composed of significant ethnic and linguistic diversity, language issues have so far not become substantial obstacles in the aftermath of the civil war. Importantly, the Constitution guarantees minority language rights, including education, expressly for Tajik, Russian and Uzbek speakers, but also for the speakers of other languages in areas where they live in substantial numbers (e.g., Kyrgyz in Jirgatol and Murghob, and Turkman in Jilikul).

---

[24] A subsidiary, but not unimportant, problem is the fact that there is very little indigenous Moldovan language broadcast programming; it is mainly imported from Romania (the Moldovan and Romanian languages being very close if not essentially the same). This fact only adds interest to the pro-Moldovan language lobby and political forces to impose the Moldovan language by means of prohibiting the use of other 'foreign' languages. However, such a prohibition does not in fact substitute alternative programming or material, thus failing to satisfy popular demands.

Language rights include access to administrative services and courts in areas where minority language groups live in substantial numbers. State-owned media also reflects this diversity.

Nonetheless, linguistic minorities (especially the Russians and Uzbeks) have sought to improve and secure the protection and promotion of their linguistic identities by various means, including recognition of Russian as a second 'State language' and Uzbek as having some higher status than other minority languages. The normal democratic pursuit and consideration of these demands was interrupted in November 1998 by the aborted military coup led by Colonel Khudoiberdiev. In the circumstances, the OSCE Mission focused in 1998 on two issues: 1) the problem for young Turkmen conscripts in the Tajik Border Forces unit in Jilikul who had difficulty understanding Tajik (the command language), which led to the creation of an all-Turkmen platoon; and 2) the problem of finding sufficient educational materials, especially textbooks, in the Uzbek language for use in Uzbek language schools in Khatlon province, with the OSCE Mission facilitating the importation of some thousands of used textbooks.

Ukraine

Since its establishment in 1994, the OSCE Mission to Ukraine (now 'Project Co-ordinator in Ukraine') had a strong inter-ethnic component in its mandate including attention to linguistic issues within Ukraine as a whole and Crimea in particular. Again, a principal feature of the situation in the country and peninsula was the inversion of the linguistic hierarchy upon independence. A peculiar aspect of the situation in Ukraine (which prescribes Ukrainian as the only State language) is the situation in the Autonomous Republic of Crimea where the majority of the population speaks Russian and where the self-proclaimed 'indigenous people' of the peninsula (the Crimean Tatars) are a small minority. Consequently, there have been conflicting interests on all sides aimed at cultural recovery and language use through legal protection and promotion. Accordingly, guarantees have been achieved for the principal groups, to varying degrees.[25]

Through the course of 1998 and into 1999, the OSCE Mission's activities in the field of language use were focused on assisting constitutional dialogue between the Crimean authorities and minority representatives. This involved facilitation and monitoring of a variety of meetings of both governmental and non-governmental character. Issues in discussion included education (both public and private, and at all levels), media (both public and private) and the language of official contacts. Especially in Crimea, attention was paid to the position of the Russian-language as the language of the local majority with concerns over maintenance of its official status and protection against Ukrainianization of the peninsula. By contrast, the Crimean Tatars sought to establish

---

[25] On the situation in the Autonomous Republic of Crimea, see John Packer, 'Autonomy Within the OSCE: The Case of Crimea', in Markku Suksi, *Autonomy: Applications and Implications* (The Hague: Kluwer Law International, 1998), pp. 295-316.

their language as an official language for use throughout 'their' peninsula, and not merely in areas of their compact settlement. In addition, the Mission maintained a dialogue and advocated certain protections also for speakers of other languages (constituting 4-5% of the Crimean population) who held worries about threats to their national cultures and languages and sought to maintain Russian as the language of their inter-ethnic communication. Similarly, in Crimea the Ukrainian population (constituting a minority of 25%) expressed their interests in cultural recovery and language maintenance in the peninsula which, they and the Government in Kyiv stressed, is part of the unitary State of Ukraine. For its part, the Mission supported an integrative approach both in Crimea and Ukraine as a whole, and kept other OSCE institutions, as well as participating States, informed about developments.

Uzbekistan

The *Constitution of Uzbekistan* prescribes in Article 4 that Uzbek is the State language, but in the same Article obliges the State to 'ensure a respectful attitude toward the languages, customs and traditions of all nationalities and ethnic groups living on its territory, and create the conditions necessary for their development'. Especially the last part of this constitutional provision, together with the prescribed principle of non-discrimination (Article 18), implies far-reaching protections and also positive entitlements to promotion of minority languages. This liberal approach is also reflected in other provisions, such as the constitutional guarantee in Article 115 that 'all legal proceedings shall be conducted in Uzbek, Karakalpak, or in the language spoken by the majority of the people of the locality' and, moreover, that 'any person participating in court proceedings who does not know the language in which they are being conducted shall have the following right to be fully acquainted with the materials of the case, to have the services of an interpreter during the proceedings, and to address the court in his native language.' Such guarantees, at least as a matter of law, convey a liberal intention which is contradicted by other provisions such as the constitutional requirement (Article 90) that the President must have 'full command of the State language' and by the reality of public administration and other practices which fail to give practical effect to the express guarantees.

Notwithstanding the fact that the population of Uzbekistan is multi-ethnic and pluri-lingual, linguistic issues have not so far stood out as a major problem although there is real potential for disputes and even conflicts. The principal issue observed by the OSCE Mission in Tashkent is more the by-product of the linguistic transition which has followed independence as Russian has been replaced by Uzbek as the principal official language and, as such, non-Uzbek-speakers or those with poor command of Uzbek have claimed to suffer discrimination. Again, improvement in the popular proficiency in the Uzbek language would go a long way in diminishing sources of dispute and possible tension.

4. THE WORK OF THE OFFICE FOR DEMOCRATIC INSTITUTIONS AND HUMAN RIGHTS

Language issues have arisen in the work of the Office for Democratic Institutions and Human Rights (ODIHR) in the context of its work on elections and democratization. In relation to OSCE election-related commitments, as reflected principally in the 1990 Copenhagen Document,[26] there is no specific mention of language requirements, although issues arise in relation to the principle of non-discrimination, the freedom of expression and voter understanding of election processes and political platforms. In direct relation to these issues, the ODIHR Election Observation Handbook states that 'in multilingual societies, observers should note whether the election administration has made any effort to facilitate voting of those citizens who may not speak the language of the majority.' As such, ODIHR may assess language requirements concerning: design, print and dissemination of ballots; voter education/information campaigns; political party registration and promotion materials; and State language laws affecting voter/candidate registration.

In 1998, an example of an election-related case arose in the parliamentary elections in the Slovak Republic where a coalition party of ethnic Hungarians was prohibited from having its party logo (in the Hungarian language) appear on the ballot since the *Slovak Language Law* requires that the Slovak language must appear first in order before any other possible language. In early 1999, the 10 January presidential election in Kazakstan drew criticism from the ODIHR insofar as candidate registration required the passing of a Kazak language test which was considered to be arbitrary and gave rise to public mistrust of the process.[27] Also in early 1999, the ODIHR expressed concern about the effects of the recently amended *Estonian Election Law* tightening the language requirement for candidates thereby limiting the scope of democratic participation, specifically the right of citizens to seek office; the ODIHR Election Observation Mission also noted that regulations on language use interfered with the ability of some candidates to communicate with parts of the electorate by limiting the language on campaign posters and related materials only to the State language.[28]

In the context of democratization, ODIHR activities and projects have touched upon language issues. For example, ODIHR has sponsored the publication and distribution of the first Roma-Macedonian dictionary which was instrumental in fostering integration while contributing to the preservation of Roma identity. In Estonia, to facilitate social and economic integration, the ODIHR has sponsored an on-going Estonian-language training programme for

---

[26] For the full text of the Document of the Copenhagen Meeting of the Conference on the Human Dimension of the CSCE, adopted on 29 June 1990, see Arie Bloed (Ed., 1993), op. cit. n. 3, pp. 439-465, especially Chapter I of the Document (more especially paras. 5.1, 5.2 and 7 with all its sub-paragraphs) regarding elections at pp. 441-445.

[27] See report of the ODIHR Election Assessment Mission, 5 February 1999.

[28] See report of the ODIHR Election Observation Mission, 7 March 1999.

the widows and divorcees of former Soviet military officers who have remained in Estonia. More generally, the ODIHR has worked to ensure that basic human rights material is available, through translation and dissemination, in a variety of regional or minority languages.

5. THE WORK OF THE OSCE REPRESENTATIVE ON FREEDOM OF THE MEDIA

Since the Representative on Freedom of the Media, Mr. Freimet Duve from Germany, only took up his responsibilities in 1998, his office did not deal initially with the issue of minority languages in the media as a specific matter either in general or in a particular case.[29] However, there is no doubt that the freedom of the media extends to the language chosen as a vehicle of communication (whether in print or broadcast) – indeed, this aspect of freedom may well be absolute at least in the private sphere since it is difficult to imagine, according to the international standards (especially the freedom of expression), a legitimate public interest which would justify any restriction,[30] in this connection, an important distinction must be made between *language as a vehicle of communication* and *the content of any expression* however communicated.

In 1999, the Representative of Freedom of the Media did address the issue of the freedom of the use of (minority) languages in the predominant media, both broadcast and print, in Moldova and Ukraine. This followed from the adoption in Moldova of legislation prescribing a substantial amount of programming in the State language even in privately owned and operated media. In Ukraine, concern focused especially in geographical areas where the Russian-speaking minority predominates.

6. CONCLUSIONS

It is clear from the work of OSCE institutions acting alone or together that the protection of minority language rights is an important objective. It should be noted that generally good inter-institutional co-operation within the OSCE has extended to inter-organizational co-operation with other inter-governmental

---

[29] The activities and interests of the Representative on Freedom of the Media are reported publicly on an annual basis in *Freedom and Responsibility, Yearbook 1998/1999* and *1999/2000*, available through the OSCE secretariat in Vienna or the OSCE Documentation Section in Prague.

[30] On this question, see John Packer, 'United Nations Protection of Minorities in Time of Public Emergency: The Hard-Core of Minority Rights', in Daniel Prémont (Ed.), *Non-Derogable Rights and States of Emergency* (Brussels: Etablissements Emile Bruylant, 1996), pp. 501-522, arguing that there is essentially no basis for a derogation from certain minority rights (including, by extension, language as a vehicle of communication, as distinguished from its content, under either Article 19 of the *International Covenant on Civil and Political Right*s or Article 10 of the *European Convention on Human Rights*).

organizations, in particular (to varying degrees) the Council of Europe, the European Commission, the United Nations High Commissioner for Refugees, the United Nations Development Programme, and also to sub-regional organizations such as the Commissioner of the Council of Baltic Sea States. Such efforts and co-operation is necessary because of the continuing challenges manifested in many OSCE participating States.

There should be no doubt that a significant part of the contemporary challenge is due to the lingering effect of the European notion of the 'nation-State' with its ideal of the pure cultural-*linguistic* 'nation' or, at least, the dominant linguistic majority (which is titular to the State, e.g. Germans in Germany or Hungarians in Hungary). This Romantic ideal is often at the root of linguistic disputes as persons belonging to linguistic minorities seek equality both in law and in fact. The substantial distance between public policy and law (reflecting the nation-State ideal) on the one hand and the pluri-lingual reality of every State (to varying degrees) on the other hand demonstrates that most European States have yet to conform their thinking and governance to either the socio-cultural reality of their populations or to the international standards to which they are committed.

Extreme nationalism – *linguistic* nationalism – often underpinning policies and laws of not only inequality but actual prohibition still has considerable resonance among political leaders and voters in many parts of Europe (both among majority AND minority groups) which leads to separatist logic and objectives. Therefore, it is of critical importance that we sort out at popular and policy-making levels our understanding of the issues and relevant standards, so policy and law can be better devised and applied thereby reducing issues in tension and resolving – possibly even avoiding – disputes to the maximum extent possible. To this end, there is a key role for international standards to be applied under the rule of law, and where conflicts may be inevitable (e.g. in the field of public administration) for the standards to be applied carefully. In this connection, it is worth recalling, as Ó Riagáin and Nic Shuibhne put it, that 'both positive and negative elements [i.e. obligations of performance and forebearance] are essential prerequisites to effective enforcement of minority language rights.'[31] But beyond this, it is no doubt essential for there to be enlightened leadership on all sides supporting good governance responding to legitimate interests and desires beyond what the minimum international standards may require. Only then can we all come to know and enjoy the cultural richness and comparative advantages brought by diversity understood as a public asset rather than liability.

---

[31] Pádraig Ó Riagáin and Niamh Nic Shuibhne, loc. cit. n. 1, at p. 18.

DOCUMENTS

DOCUMENT OF THE COPENHAGEN MEETING OF THE CONFERENCE ON THE HUMAN DIMENSION OF THE CSCE

Copenhagen, 5 June- 29 July 1990

[Extracts]

IV

30. The participating States recognize that the questions relating to national minorities can only be satisfactorily resolved in a democratic political framework based on the rule of law, with a functioning independent judiciary. This framework guarantees full respect for human rights and fundamental freedoms, equal rights and status for all citizens, the free expression of all their legitimate interests and aspirations, political pluralism, social tolerance and the implementation of legal rules that place effective restraints on the abuse of governmental power.
They also recognize the important role of non-governmental organizations, including political parties, trade unions, human rights organizations and religious groups, in the promotion of tolerance, cultural diversity and the resolution of questions relating to national minorities.
They further reaffirm that respect for the rights of persons belonging to national minorities as part of universally recognized human rights is an essential factor for peace, justice, stability and democracy in the participating States.

31. Persons belonging to national minorities have the right to exercise fully and effectively their human rights and fundamental freedoms without any discrimination and in full equality before the law.
The participating States will adopt, where necessary, special measures for the purpose of ensuring to persons belonging to national minorities full equality with the other citizens in the exercise and enjoyment of human rights and fundamental freedoms.

32. To belong to a national minority is a matter of a persons individual choice and no disadvantage may arise from the exercise of such choice.
Persons belonging to national minorities have the right freely to express, preserve and develop their ethnic, cultural, linguistic or religious identity and to maintain and develop their culture in all its aspects, free of any attempts at assimilation against their will. In particular, they have the right.

   32.1.– to use freely their mother tongue in private as well as in public;
   32.2.– to establish and maintain their own educational, cultural and religious institutions, organizations or associations, which can seek voluntary fi-

nancial and other contributions as well as public assistance, in conformity with national legislation;

32.3.– to profess and practice their religion, including the acquisition, possession and use of religious materials, and to conduct religious educational activities in their mother tongue;

32.4.– to establish and maintain unimpeded contacts among themselves within their country as well as contacts across frontiers with citizens of other States with whom they share a common ethnic or national origin, cultural heritage or religious beliefs;

32.5.– to disseminate, have access to and exchange information in their mother tongue;

32.6.– to establish and maintain organizations or associations within their country and to participate in international non-governmental organizations.

Persons belonging to national minorities can exercise and enjoy their rights individually as well as in community with other members of their group. No disadvantage may arise for a person belonging to a national minority on account of the exercise or non-exercise of any such rights.

33. The participating States will protect the ethnic, cultural, linguistic and religious identity of national minorities on their territory and create conditions for the promotion of that identity. They will take the necessary measures to that effect after due consultations, including contacts with organizations or associations of such minorities, in accordance with the decision-making procedures of each State.

Any such measures will be in conformity with the principles of equality and non-discrimination with respect to the other citizens of the participating State concerned.

34. The participating States will endeavour to ensure that persons belonging to national minorities, notwithstanding the need to learn the official language or languages of the State concerned, have adequate opportunities for instruction of their mother tongue or in their mother tongue, as well as, wherever possible and necessary, for its use before public authorities, in conformity with applicable national legislation.

In the context of the teaching of history and culture in educational establishments, they will also take account of the history and culture of national minorities.

35. The participating States will respect the right of persons belonging to national minorities to effective participation in public affairs, including participation in the affairs relating to the protection and promotion of the identity of such minorities.

The participating States note the efforts undertaken to protect and create conditions for the promotion of the ethnic, cultural, linguistic and religious identity of certain national minorities by establishing, as one of the possible means to achieve these aims, appropriate local or autonomous administrations corresponding to the specific historical and territorial circumstances of such minorities and in accordance with the policies of the State concerned.

36. The participating States recognize the particular importance of increasing constructive co-operation among themselves on questions relating to national minorities. Such co-operation seeks to promote mutual understanding and confidence, friendly and good-neighbourly relations, international peace, security and justice.
Every participating State will promote a climate of mutual respect, understanding, co-operation and solidarity among all persons living on its territory, without distinction as to ethnic or national origin or religion, and will encourage the solution of problems through dialogue based on the principles of the rule of law.

37. None of these commitments may be interpreted as implying any right to engage in any activity or perform any action in contravention of the purposes and principles of the Charter of the United Nations, other obligations under international law or the provisions of the Final Act, including the principle of territorial integrity of States.

38. The participating States, in their efforts to protect and promote the rights of persons belonging to national minorities, will fully respect their undertakings under existing human rights conventions and other relevant international instruments and consider adhering to the relevant conventions, if they have not yet done so, including those providing for a right of complaint by individuals.

39. The participating States will co-operate closely in the competent international organizations to which they belong, including the United Nations and, as appropriate, the Council of Europe, bearing in mind their on-going work with respect to questions relating to national minorities.
They will consider convening a meeting of experts for a thorough discussion of the issue of national minorities.

40. The participating States clearly and unequivocally condemn totalitarianism, racial and ethnic hatred, anti-semitism, xenophobia and discrimination against anyone as well as persecution on religious and ideological grounds. In this context, they also recognize the particular problems of Roma (Gypsies).
They declare their firm intention to intensify the efforts to combat these phenomena in all their forms and therefore will

    40.1.– take effective measures, including the adoption, in conformity with their constitutional systems and their international obligations, of such laws as may be necessary, to provide protection against any acts that constitute incitement to violence against persons or groups based on national, racial, ethnic or religious discrimination, hostility or hatred, including anti-semitism;

40.2.— commit themselves to take appropriate and proportionate measures to protect persons or groups who may be subject to threats or acts of discrimination, hostility or violence as a result of their racial, ethnic, cultural, linguistic or religious identity, and to protect their property;

40.3.— take effective measures, in conformity with their constitutional systems, at the national, regional and local levels to promote understanding and tolerance, particularly in the fields of education, culture and information;

40.4.— endeavour to ensure that the objectives of education include special attention to the problem of racial prejudice and hatred and to the development of respect for different civilizations and cultures;

40.5.— recognize the right of the individual to effective remedies and endeavour to recognize, in conformity with national legislation, the right of interested persons and groups to initiate and support complaints against acts of discrimination, including racist and xenophobic acts;

40.6.— consider adhering, if they have not yet done so, to the international instruments which address the problem of discrimination and ensure full compliance with the obligations therein, including those relating to the submission of periodic reports;

40.7.— consider, also, accepting those international mechanisms which allow States and individuals to bring communications relating to discrimination before international bodies.

THE OSLO RECOMMENDATIONS REGARDING THE LINGUISTIC RIGHTS OF NATIONAL MINORITIES AND EXPLANATORY NOTE

February 1998

INTRODUCTION

In its Helsinki Decisions of July 1992, the Organization for Security and Cooperation in Europe (OSCE) established the position of High Commissioner on National Minorities to be 'an instrument of conflict prevention at the earliest possible stage'. This mandate was created largely in reaction to the situation in the former Yugoslavia which some feared would be repeated elsewhere in Europe, especially among the countries in transition to democracy, and could undermine the promise of peace and prosperity as envisaged in the Charter of Paris for a New Europe adopted by the Heads of State and Government in November 1990.

On 1 January 1993, Mr. Max van der Stoel took up his duties as the first OSCE High Commissioner on National Minorities (HCNM). Drawing on his considerable personal experience as a former Member of Parliament and Foreign Minister of The Netherlands, Permanent Representative to the United Nations, and long-time human rights advocate, Mr. Van der Stoel turned his attention to the many disputes between minorities and central authorities in Europe which had the potential, in his view, to escalate. Acting quietly through diplomatic means, the HCNM has become involved in the following States: Albania, Croatia, Estonia, Hungary, Kazakstan, Kyrgyzstan, Latvia, the Former Yugoslav Republic of Macedonia, Romania, Slovakia and Ukraine. His involvement has focused primarily on those situations involving persons belonging to national/ethnic groups who constitute the numerical majority in one State but the numerical minority in another (usually neighbouring) State, thus engaging the interest of governmental authorities in each State and constituting a potential source of inter-State tension if not conflict. Indeed, such tensions have defined much of European history.

In addressing the substance of tensions involving national minorities, the HCNM approaches the issues as an independent, impartial and cooperative actor. While the HCNM is not a supervisory mechanism, he employs the international standards to which each State has agreed as his principal framework of analysis and the foundation of his specific recommendations. In this relation, it is important to recall the commitments undertaken by all OSCE participating States, in particular those of the 1990 Copenhagen Document of the Conference on the Human Dimension which, in Part IV, articulates detailed obligations relating to national minorities. It is also important to note that all OSCE States are bound by United Nations obligations relating to human rights, including minority rights, and that the great majority of OSCE States are also bound by the standards of the Council of Europe.

After five years of intense activity, the HCNM has been able to identify certain recurrent issues and themes which have become the subject of his attention in a number of States in which he is involved. The linguistic rights of national minorities, i.e. the right of persons belonging to national minorities to use their language in the private and public spheres, is such an issue. International human rights instruments refer to this right in a number of different contexts. On the one hand, language is a personal matter closely connected with identity. On the other hand, language is an essential tool of social organisation which in many situations becomes a matter of public interest. Certainly, the use of language bears on numerous aspects of a State's functioning. In a democratic State committed to human rights, the accommodation of existing diversity thus becomes an important matter of policy and law. Failure to achieve the appropriate balance may be the source of inter-ethnic tensions.

It is with this in mind that, in the summer of 1996, the HCNM requested the Foundation on Inter-Ethnic Relations to consult a small group of internationally recognised experts with a view to receiving their recommendations on an appropriate and coherent application of the linguistic rights of persons belonging to national minorities in the OSCE region. A similar request from the HCNM had previously resulted in the elaboration of **The Hague Recommendations Regarding the Education Rights of National Minorities and Explanatory Report**.[1] Insofar as **The Hague Recommendations** address comprehensively the use of the language or

---

[1] Copies of The Hague Recommendations Regarding the Education Rights of National Minorities and Explanatory Report (October 1996) are available in several languages from the Foundation on Inter-Ethnic Relations.

languages of national minorities in the field of education, it was decided to exclude this issue from consideration of the experts.

The Foundation on Inter-Ethnic Relations — a non-governmental organisation established in 1993 to carry out specialised activities in support of the HCNM — facilitated a series of consultations of experts from various pertinent disciplines, including two meetings in Oslo and one in The Hague. Among the experts consulted were jurists specialising in international law, as well as linguists, advocates and policy analysts specialising in the situations and needs of minorities. Specifically, the experts were:

Professor Gudmundur Alfredsson, Co-Director, Raoul Wallenberg Institute (Sweden); Professor Asbjørn Eide, Senior Fellow, Norwegian Institute of Human Rights (Norway); Ms. Angelita Kamenska, Senior Researcher, Latvian Centre for Human Rights and Ethnic Studies (Latvia); Mr. Dónall Ó Riagáin, Secretary General, European Bureau of Lesser Used Languages (Ireland); Ms. Beate Slydal, Advisor, Norwegian Forum for the Freedom of Expression (Norway); Dr. Miquel Strubell, Director, Institute of Catalan Sociolinguistics, Government of Catalonia (Spain); Professor György Szepe, Department of Language Sciences at Janus Panonius University (Hungary); Professor Patrick Thornberry, Department of Law, Keele University (United Kingdom); Dr. Fernand de Varennes, Director of the Asia-Pacific Centre for Human Rights and the Prevention of Ethnic Conflict (Australia); Professor Bruno de Witte, Faculty of Law, University of Maastricht (The Netherlands); Mr. Jean-Marie Woehrling, Institut de droit local alsacien-mosellan (France).

Insofar as existing standards of minority rights are part of human rights, the starting point for the consultations was to presume compliance by States with all other human rights obligations including, in particular, equality and freedom from discrimination, freedom of expression, freedom of assembly and of association, as well as all the rights and freedoms of persons belonging to national minorities.

It was also presumed that the ultimate object of all human rights is the full and free development of the individual human personality in conditions of equality. Consequently, it was presumed that civil society should be open and fluid and, therefore, integrate all persons, including those belonging to national minorities. Insofar as the use of language is also a fundamentally communicative matter, the essential social dimension of the human experience was also fully presumed.

The resultant **Oslo Recommendations Regarding the Linguistic Rights of National Minorities** attempt to clarify, in relatively straight-forward language, the content of minority language rights generally applicable in the situations in which the HCNM is involved. In addition, the standards have been interpreted in such a way as to ensure their coherence in application. The Recommendations are divided into sub-headings which respond to the language related issues which arise in practice. A more detailed explanation of the Recommendations is provided in an accompanying Explanatory Note wherein express reference to the relevant international standards is to be found. It is intended that each Recommendation is read in conjunction with the specifically relevant paragraphs of the Explanatory Note.

It is hoped that these Recommendations will provide a useful reference for the development of State policies and laws which will contribute to an effective implementation of the language rights of persons belonging to national minorities, especially in the public sphere.

Although these Recommendations refer to the use of language by persons belonging to national minorities, it is to be noted that the thrust of these Recommendations and the international instruments from which they derive could potentially apply to other types of minorities. The Recommendations which follow below are meant to clarify the existing body of rights. They are not meant to restrict the human rights of any person or groups of persons.

THE OSLO RECOMMENDATIONS REGARDING THE LINGUISTIC RIGHTS OF NATIONAL MINORITIES

NAMES

1. Persons belonging to national minorities have the right to use their personal names in their own language according to their own traditions and linguistic systems. These shall be given official recognition and be used by the public authorities.
2. Similarly, private entities such as cultural associations and business enterprises established by persons belonging to national minorities shall enjoy the same right with regard to their names.
3. In areas inhabited by significant numbers of persons belonging to a national minority and when there is sufficient demand, public authorities shall make provision for the display, also in the minority language, of local names, street names and other topographical indications intended for the public.

RELIGION

4. In professing and practicing his or her own religion individually or in community with others, every person shall be entitled to use the language(s) of his or her choice.
5. For those religious ceremonies or acts pertaining also to civil status and which have legal effect within the State concerned, the State may require that certificates and documents pertaining to such status be produced also in the official language or languages of the State. The State may require that registers pertaining to civil status be kept by the religious authorities also in the official language or languages of the State.

COMMUNITY LIFE AND NGOs

6. All persons, including persons belonging to national minorities, have the right to establish and manage their own non-governmental organisations, associations and institutions. These entities may use the language(s) of their choosing. The State may not discriminate against these entities on the basis of language nor shall it unduly restrict the right of these entities to seek sources of funding from the State budget, international sources or the private sector.

7. If the State actively supports activities in, among others, the social, cultural and sports spheres, an equitable share of the total resources made available by the State shall go to support those similar activities undertaken by persons belonging to national minorities. State financial support for activities which take place in the language(s) of persons belonging to national minorities in such spheres shall be granted on a non-discriminatory basis.

THE MEDIA

8. Persons belonging to national minorities have the right to establish and maintain their own minority language media. State regulation of the broadcast media shall be based on objective and non-discriminatory criteria and shall not be used to restrict enjoyment of minority rights.
9. Persons belonging to national minorities should have access to broadcast time in their own language on publicly funded media. At national, regional and local levels the amount and quality of time allocated to broadcasting in the language of a given minority should be commensurate with the numerical size and concentration of the national minority and appropriate to its situation and needs.
10. The independent nature of the programming of public and private media in the language(s) of national minorities shall be safeguarded. Public media editorial boards overseeing the content and orientation of programming should be independent and should include persons belonging to national minorities serving in their independent capacity.
11. Access to media originating from abroad shall not be unduly restricted. Such access should not justify a diminution of broadcast time allocated to the minority in the publicly funded media of the State of residence of the minorities concerned.

ECONOMIC LIFE

12. All persons, including persons belonging to national minorities, have the right to operate private enterprises in the language or languages of their choice. The State may require the additional use of the official language or languages of the State only where a legitimate public interest can be demonstrated, such as interests relating to the protection of workers or consumers, or in dealings between the enterprise and governmental authorities.

ADMINISTRATIVE AUTHORITIES AND PUBLIC SERVICES

13. In regions and localities where persons belonging to a national minority are present in significant numbers and where the desire for it has been expressed, persons belonging to this national minority shall have the right to acquire civil documents and certificates both in the official language or languages of the State and in the language of the national minority in question from regional and/or local public institutions. Similarly regional and/or local public institutions shall keep the appropriate civil registers also in the language of the national minority.

14. Persons belonging to national minorities shall have adequate possibilities to use their language in communications with administrative authorities especially in regions and localities where they have expressed a desire for it and where they are present in significant numbers. Similarly, administrative authorities shall, wherever possible, ensure that public services are provided also in the language of the national minority. To this end, they shall adopt appropriate recruitment and/or training policies and programmes.
15. In regions and localities where persons belonging to a national minority are present in significant numbers, the State shall take measures to ensure that elected members of regional and local governmental bodies can use also the language of the national minority during activities relating to these bodies.

INDEPENDENT NATIONAL INSTITUTIONS

16. States in which persons belonging to national minorities live should ensure that these persons have, in addition to appropriate judicial recourses, access to independent national institutions, such as ombudspersons or human rights commissions, in cases where they feel that their linguistic rights have been violated.

THE JUDICIAL AUTHORITIES

17. All persons, including persons belonging to a national minority, have the right to be informed promptly, in a language they understand, of the reasons for their arrest and/or detention and of the nature and cause of any accusation against them, and to defend themselves in this language, if necessary with the free assistance of an interpreter, before trial, during trial and on appeal.
18. In regions and localities where persons belonging to a national minority are present in significant numbers and where the desire for it has been expressed, persons belonging to this minority should have the right to express themselves in their own language in judicial proceedings, if necessary with the free assistance of an interpreter and/or translator.
19. In those regions and localities in which persons belonging to a national minority live in significant numbers and where the desire for it has been expressed, States should give due consideration to the feasibility of conducting all judicial proceedings affecting such persons in the language of the minority.

DEPRIVATION OF LIBERTY

20. The director of a penal institution and other personnel of the institution shall be able to speak the language or languages of the greatest number of prisoners, or a language understood by the greatest number of them. Recruitment and/or training programmes should be directed towards this end. Whenever necessary, the services of an interpreter shall be used.
21. Detained persons belonging to national minorities shall have the right to use the language of their choice in communications with inmates as well as with others. Authorities shall, wherever possible, adopt measures to enable prisoners to

communicate in their own language both orally and in personal correspondence, within the limitations prescribed by law. In this relation, a detained or imprisoned person should, in general, be kept in a place of detention or imprisonment near his or her usual place of residence.

EXPLANATORY NOTE
TO THE OSLO RECOMMENDATIONS REGARDING THE LINGUISTIC RIGHTS OF NATIONAL MINORITIES

GENERAL INTRODUCTION

Article l of the **Universal Declaration of Human Rights** refers to the innate dignity of all human beings as the fundamental concept underlying all human rights standards. Article 1 of the **Declaration** states 'All human beings are born free and equal in dignity and rights...' The importance of this article cannot be overestimated. Not only does it relate to human rights generally, it also provides one of the foundations for the linguistic rights of persons belonging to national minorities. Equality in dignity and rights presupposes respect for the individual's identity as a human being. Language is one of the most fundamental components of human identity. Hence, respect for a person's dignity is intimately connected with respect for the person's identity and consequently for the person's language.

In this context, the **International Covenant on Civil and Political Rights** is of considerable importance. Article 2 of the **Covenant** requires States to ensure that the human rights of all individuals within their territory and subject to their jurisdiction will be ensured and respected 'without distinction of any kind such as [...] language [...]'. Article 19 of the **Covenant** guarantees freedom of expression which, as it is formulated in the **Covenant**, not only guarantees the right to impart or receive information and ideas of all sorts, regardless of frontiers, but also guarantees the right to do so in the medium or language of one's choice. The imparting and receiving of information also suggests people acting in community. In this context, Articles 21 and 22 of the **Covenant** guaranteeing the freedoms of peaceful assembly and association may be especially relevant.

Similarly, in Europe the freedom of expression stipulated in Article 10 of the **European Convention for the Protection of Human Rights and Fundamental Freedoms** shall be, according to Article 14 of the same convention, 'secured without discrimination on any ground such as [...] language [...]'. With expressed reference to both the **Universal Declaration of Human Rights** and the **European Convention for the Protection of Human Rights and Fundamental Freedoms**, the Council of Europe's **Declaration on Freedom of Expression and Information** affirms 'that the freedom of expression and information is necessary for the social, economic, cultural and political development of every human being, and constitutes a condition for the harmonious progress of social and cultural groups, nations and the international community'. In this connection, the freedoms of peaceful assembly and association as guaranteed by Article 11 of the **European Convention for the Protection of Human Rights and Fundamental Freedoms** are important.

Within the context of the Organization for Security and Cooperation in Europe (OSCE), the same fundamental ideas of freedom of expression, assembly and association are enumerated in paragraphs 9.1-9.3 of the **Document of the Copenhagen Meeting of the Conference on the Human Dimension**.

In the **Charter of Paris for a New Europe**, the Heads of State and Government of the OSCE participating States 'affirm that, without discrimination, every individual has the right to: [...] freedom of expression, freedom of association and peaceful assembly, [...].'

Article 27 of the **International Covenant on Civil and Political Rights** is another key provision which has direct bearing on the linguistic rights of national minorities. It affirms that 'persons belonging to [...] minorities shall not be denied the right, in community with the other members of their group, to [...] use their own language'.

Similarly, Article 2(1) of the **UN Declaration on the Rights of Persons Belonging to National or Ethnic, Religious and Linguistic Minorities** proclaims the right of persons belonging to national minorities to 'use their own language, in private and in public, freely and without interference or any form of discrimination'. Article 10(1) of the Council of Europe's **Framework Convention for the Protection of National Minorities** stipulates that States will recognise the right of persons belonging to national minorities 'to use freely and without interference his or her minority language, in private and in public, orally and in writing.'

Although the instruments refer to the use of minority languages in public and in private, these same instruments do not precisely delimit the 'public' as opposed to the 'private' spheres. Indeed the spheres may overlap. This may well be the case, for example, when individuals acting alone or in community with others seek to establish their own private media or schools. What might begin as a private initiative may become the subject of legitimate public interest. Such an interest may give rise to some public regulation.

The use of minority languages 'in public and in private' by persons belonging to national minorities cannot be considered without making reference to education. Education issues as they relate to the languages of national minorities are treated in detail in **The Hague Recommendations Regarding the Education Rights of National Minorities** which were developed for the benefit of the OSCE High Commissioner on National Minorities by The Foundation on Inter-Ethnic Relations in collaboration with experts of international repute in the fields of both international human rights and education. **The Hague Recommendations** were developed with a view to facilitating a clearer understanding of the international instruments pertaining to the rights of persons belonging to national minorities in this area which is of such vital importance to the maintenance and development of the identity of persons belonging to national minorities.

International human rights instruments stipulate that human rights are universal and that they must be enjoyed equally and without discrimination. Most human rights, however, are not absolute. The instruments do foresee a limited number of situations in which States would be justified in restricting the application of certain rights. The restrictions permitted by international human rights law can be invoked in life-threatening emergencies and in situations which pose a threat to the rights and freedoms of others, or in situations which threaten public morals, public health, national security and the general welfare in a democratic society.[2] In human rights law, restrictions on freedoms are to be interpreted restrictively.

The rights of persons belonging to national minorities to use their language(s) in public and in private as set forth and elaborated in **The Oslo Recommendations Regarding the Linguistic Rights of National Minorities** must be seen in a balanced context of full participation in the wider society. The Recommendations do not propose an isolationist approach, but rather one which encourages a balance between the right of persons belonging to national minorities to maintain and develop their own identity, culture and language and the necessity of ensuring that they are able to integrate into the wider society as full and equal members. From this perspective, such integration is unlikely to take place without a sound knowledge of the official language(s) of the State. The prescription for such education is implied in Articles 13 and 14 of the **International Covenant on Economic, Social and Cultural Rights** and Articles 28 and 29 of the **Convention on the Rights of the Child** which confer a right to education and oblige the State to make education compulsory. At the same time, Article 14(3) of the **Framework Convention for the Protection of National Minorities** provides that the teaching of a minority language 'shall be implemented without prejudice to the learning of the official language or the teaching in this language.'

NAMES

1. Article 11(1) of the **Framework Convention for the Protection of National Minorities** stipulates that persons belonging to national minorities have the right to use their first name, their patronym and their surname in their own language. This right, the enjoyment of which is fundamental to one's personal identity, should be applied in light of the circumstances particular to each State. For example, public authorities would be justified in using the script of the official language or languages of the State to record the names of persons belonging to national minorities in their phonetic form. However this must be done in accordance with the language system and tradition of the national minority in question. In view of this very basic right relating closely to both the language and the identity of individuals, persons who have been forced by public authorities to give up their original or ancestral name(s) or whose name(s) have been changed against their will should be entitled to revert to them without having to incur any expenses.
2. Names are an important element of corporate identity as well, especially in the context of persons belonging to national minorities acting 'in community'. Article 2(1) of the **UN Declaration on the Rights of Persons Belonging to National or Ethnic, Religious and Linguistic Minorities** proclaims the right of persons belonging to national minorities to 'use their own language, in private

---

[2] The above mentioned limitations are included, e.g., in the following provisions:
Art. 30 **Universal Declaration of Human Rights**
Art. 19(3) **International Covenant on Civil and Political Rights**
Art. 10(2) **European Convention for the Protection of Human Rights and Fundamental Freedoms**.

and in public, freely and without interference or any form of discrimination'. Article 10(1) of the **Framework Convention for the Protection of National Minorities** stipulates that States will recognise the right of persons belonging to national minorities to 'use freely and without interference his or her minority language, in private and in public, orally and in writing.' Article 27 of the **International Covenant on Civil and Political Rights** declares that 'persons belonging to [...] minorities shall not be denied the right, in community with other members of their group [...] to use their own language'. A person's right to use his or her language in public, in community with others and without any interference or any form of discrimination is a strong indication that legal entities such as institutions, associations, organisations or business enterprises established and run by persons belonging to national minorities enjoy the right to adopt the name of their choice in their minority language. Such a corporate name should be recognised by the public authorities and used in accordance with the given community's language system and traditions.

3. Article 11(3) of the **Framework Convention** states that 'in areas traditionally inhabited by substantial numbers of persons belonging to a national minority, the Parties shall endeavour [...] to display traditional local names, street names and other topographical indications intended for the public also in the minority language when there is sufficient demand for such indications'. Refusal to recognise the validity of historic denominations of the kind described can constitute an attempt to revise history and to assimilate minorities, thus constituting a serious threat to the identity of persons belonging to minorities.

RELIGION

4. Article 27 of the **International Covenant on Civil and Political Rights** affirms that 'In those States in which ethnic, religious or linguistic minorities exist, persons belonging to such minorities shall not be denied the right, in community with the other members of their group [...] to profess and practice their own religion, or to use their own language.' Article 3(1) of the **UN Declaration on the Rights of Persons Belonging to National or Ethnic, Religious and Linguistic Minorities** stipulates that 'Persons belonging to minorities may exercise their rights [...] individually as well as in community with other members of their group, without any discrimination.'

Religious belief and its practice 'in community' is an area of great importance to many persons belonging to national minorities. In this context it is worth noting that the right to one's own religion is unlimited and guaranteed by Article 18(1) of the **International Covenant on Civil and Political Rights** and Article 9(1) of the **European Convention for the Protection of Human Rights and Fundamental Freedoms.** However, the freedom to manifest one's religion and beliefs, including public worship, is subject to a number of limitations listed in subsidiary paragraphs of the same articles. These limitations must be prescribed by law and relate to the protection of public safety, order, health, morals and the protection of the fundamental rights and freedoms of others. They must be reasonable and proportional to the end sought, and States may not invoke them with a view to stifling the legitimate spiritual, linguistic or cultural aspirations of persons belonging to national minorities.

In minority contexts, the practice of religion is often especially closely related to the preservation of cultural and linguistic identity. The right to use a minority language in public worship is as inherent as the right to establish religious institutions and the right to public worship itself. Hence, public authorities may not impose any undue restrictions on public worship nor on the use of any language in public worship, be it the mother tongue of the national minority in question or the liturgical language used by that community.

5. Religious acts such as wedding ceremonies or funerals may also constitute legal civil acts determining civil status in certain countries. In such cases, public interest must be taken into consideration. Keeping in mind the principle that administrative considerations should not prevent the enjoyment of human rights, public authorities should not impose any linguistic restrictions on religious communities. This should apply equally to any administrative functions which religious communities assume and which may overlap with civil jurisdiction. The State may, however, require the religious community to record legal civil acts for which it has authority also in the official language or languages of the State so that the State may perform its legitimate regulatory and administrative tasks.

COMMUNITY LIFE AND NGOs

6. The collective life of persons belonging to national minorities, their acting 'in community' as stated by the international instruments, finds its expression in numerous activities and areas of endeavour. Not least of these is the life of their non- governmental organisations, associations and institutions whose existence is usually vital for the maintenance and development of their identity and is generally seen as beneficial and conducive to the development of civil society and democratic values within States.

Articles 21 and 22 of the **International Covenant on Civil and Political Rights** and Article 11 of the **European Convention for the Protection of Human Rights and Fundamental Freedoms** guarantee the right of persons to peaceful assembly and the freedom of association. The right of persons to act 'in community' with other members of their group - their right to establish and manage their own non-governmental organisations, associations and institutions - is one of the hallmarks of an open and democratic society. Article 27 of that same **Covenant** affirms that 'Persons belonging to [...] minorities shall not be denied the right, in community with the other members of their group, to [...] use their own language'. As a rule, therefore, public authorities should not be involved in the internal affairs of such entities 'acting in community', nor may they impose any limits on them, other than those permitted under international law. Article 17(2) of the **Framework Convention for the Protection of National Minorities** similarly engages States 'not to interfere with the right of persons belonging to national minorities to participate in the activities of non-governmental organisations, both at the national and international levels'.

Article 2(1) of the **International Covenant on Civil and Political Rights** stipulates that each State undertakes 'to ensure to all individuals within its territory and subject to its jurisdiction the rights recognised in the present **Covenant**, without distinction of any kind such as [...] language'. In line with this standard, States may not discriminate against NGOs on the basis of language nor impose any undue language requirements on them. This having been said, public authorities may require that such organisations, associations and institutions conform to the requirements of domestic law on the basis of a legitimate public interest, including the use of the official language(s) of the State in situations requiring interface with public bodies.

With regard to resources, paragraph 32.2 of the **Copenhagen Document** states that persons belonging to national minorities have the right 'to establish and maintain their own educational, cultural and religious institutions, organisations or associations, which can seek voluntary financial and other contributions as well as public assistance, in conformity with national legislation.' Accordingly, States should not prevent these entities from seeking financial resources from the State budget and from public international sources as well as from the private sector.

7. With regard to State financing of non-governmental activities in, among others, the social, cultural or sports fields, application of the principles of equality and non-discrimination requires that the public authorities provide an appropriate share of funding to similar activities taking place in the language of the national minorities living within their borders. In this context, Article 2(1) of the **International Covenant on Civil and Political Rights** stresses not only that there will be no distinction based on language in the treatment of individuals, but stipulates in Article 2(2) that States are required to 'take the necessary steps [...] to adopt such legislative or other measures as may be necessary to give effect to the rights recognised in the [...] Covenant'. Furthermore, Article 2(2) of the **International Covenant on the Elimination of Racial Discrimination,** (which seeks to eliminate any distinction, exclusion, restriction, or preference based on race, colour, descent, or national or ethnic origin) stipulates that 'States Parties shall, when the circumstances so warrant, take, in the social, economic, cultural and other fields, special and concrete measures to ensure the adequate development and protection of certain racial groups or individuals belonging to them, for the purpose of guaranteeing them the full and equal enjoyment of human rights and fundamental freedoms [...]' Insofar as language is often a defining criterion of ethnicity as protected by the aforementioned convention, minority language communities may also be entitled to the benefits of such 'special and concrete measures'.

At the European level, paragraph 31 of the **Copenhagen Document** stipulates that 'States will adopt, where necessary, special measures for the purpose of ensuring to persons belonging to national minorities full equality with the other citizens in the exercise and enjoyment of human rights and fundamental freedoms'. Paragraph 2 of Article 4 of the **Framework Convention for the Protection of National Minorities** obligates the States Parties 'to adopt, where necessary, adequate measures in order to promote, in all areas of economic, social, political and cultural life, full and effective equality between persons belonging to a national minority and those belonging to the majority'; paragraph 3 of the same Article further specifies that such 'measures adopted in accordance with paragraph 2 shall not be considered to be an act of discrimination.' Moreover, Article 7(2) of the **European Charter for Regional or Minority Languages** stipulates that 'the adoption of special measures in favour of regional or minority languages aimed at promoting equality between the users of the languages and the rest of the population or which take account of their specific conditions is not considered to be an act of discrimination against the users of more widely used languages.' In this context, therefore, public authorities should provide an equitable share of resources from the State budget to the activities of persons belonging to national minorities in, among others, the social, cultural and sports related fields. Such support can be made available through subsidies, public benefits and tax exemptions.

THE MEDIA

8. Article 19 of the **International Covenant on Civil and Political Rights**, which guarantees the right to hold opinions as well as the right to express them, is a fundamental point of reference regarding the role and place of media in democratic societies. While Article 19(1) provides that 'everyone shall have the right to hold opinions without interference', Article 19(2) proceeds to guarantee to everyone the freedom 'to seek, receive and impart information and ideas of all kinds, regardless of frontiers, either orally, in writing or in print, in the form of art, or through the media of his choice.' Article 10 of the **European Convention for the Protection of Human Rights and Fundamental Freedoms** guarantees the right to freedom of expression in a similar way. The member States of the Council of Europe reiterated in Article I of the **Declaration on the Freedom of Expression and Information** 'their firm attachment to the principles of freedom of expression and information as a basic element of democratic and pluralist society'. On this basis, States declared in the same instrument [at II] that 'in the field of information and mass media they seek to achieve [...] d. The existence of a wide variety of independent and autonomous media, permitting the reflection of diversity of ideas and opinions'.

Article 9(1) of the **Framework Convention for the Protection of National Minorities** states clearly that persons belonging to national minorities are free 'to hold opinions and to receive and impart information and ideas in the minority language, without interference by public authorities and regardless of frontiers...' Further on, the same provision engages States to 'ensure, within the framework of their legal systems, that persons belonging to a national minority are not discriminated against in their access to the media.' Article 9(3) of the **Framework Convention** stipulates that States 'shall not hinder the creation and the use of printed media by persons belonging to national minorities.' The same provision requires that 'in the legal framework of sound radio and television broadcasting, [States] shall ensure, as far as possible [...] that persons belonging to national minorities are granted the possibility of creating and using their own media.' It is also to be noted that media may constitute entities of the kind foreseen in *inter alia*, paragraph 32.2 of the **Copenhagen Document** which provides for the right of persons belonging to national minorities to 'establish and maintain their own educational, cultural and religious institutions, organisations or associations [...].' Even though the media are not cited expressly in this standard, the media often plays a fundamental role in the promotion and preservation of language, culture and identity.

Although there can be no doubt that persons belonging to national minorities have the right to establish and maintain private media, it is also true that this right is subject to the limitations provided by international law as well as such legitimate requirements of the State regarding the regulation of the media. Article 9(2) of the **Framework Convention** makes this very clear by underlining that the freedom of expression referred to in article 9(1) of the **Convention** 'shall not prevent Parties from requiring the licensing, without discrimination and based on objective criteria, of sound radio and television broadcasting, or cinema enterprises.' Regulatory requirements, where justified and necessary, may not be used to undermine the enjoyment of the right.

9. The issue of access to publicly funded media is closely linked with the concept of freedom of expression. Article 9(1) of the **Framework Convention** stipulates that the freedom of expression of persons belonging to national minorities includes the freedom to impart information and ideas in the minority language, without interference by public authorities, and goes on to say that 'members of minorities shall not be discriminated against in their access to the media.' Article 9(4) of the **Framework Convention** stipulates that 'Parties shall adopt adequate measures in order to facilitate access to the media for persons belonging to national minorities.' This implies that a national minority consisting of a substantial number of members should be given access to its fair share of broadcast time, on public radio and/or television, with the numerical size of the minority in question having a bearing on its share of broadcast time.

Numerical strength and concentration, however, cannot be seen as the only criteria when judging the amount of broadcast time to be allocated to any given national minority. In the case of smaller communities, consideration must be given to the viable minimum of time and resources without which a smaller minority would not meaningfully be able to avail itself of the media.

Moreover, the quality of the time allotted to minority programming is an issue that needs to be approached in a reasonable, non-discriminatory manner. The time-slots allotted to minority language programming should be such as to ensure that persons belonging to a national minority can enjoy programming in their language in a meaningful way. Hence, public authorities should ensure that this programming is transmitted at reasonable times of the day.

10. In an open and democratic society the content of media programming should not be unduly censored by the public authorities. The freedom of expression as guaranteed by Article 19(1) of the **International Covenant on Civil and Political Rights** and Article 10(1) of the **European Convention for the Protection of Human Rights and Fundamental Freedoms** is important in this regard. Any restrictions which might be imposed by the public authorities must be in line with Article 19(3) of the **Covenant** which stipulates that these restrictions 'shall only be such as are provided by law and are necessary a) For the respect of the rights and reputations of others, b) For the protection of national security or of public order (*ordre public*), or of public health and morals.' Article 10(2) of the **European Convention for the Protection of**

Human Rights and Fundamental Freedoms stipulates almost identical restrictions on any interference by public authorities with the enjoyment of freedom of expression.

Mechanisms should be put in place to ensure that the public media programming developed by or on behalf of national minorities reflects the interests and desires of the community's members and is seen by them as independent. In this context, the participation of persons belonging to national minorities (acting in their private capacity) in the editorial process would go a long way in ensuring that the independent nature of the media would be preserved and that it would be responsive to the needs of the communities to be served.

In line with the principle of equality and non-discrimination, the composition of public institutions should be reflective of the populations they are designed to serve. This also applies to public media. Article 15 of the **Framework Convention** engages States to 'create the conditions necessary for the effective participation of persons belonging to national minorities in cultural, social and economic life and in public affairs, in particular those affecting them.' Article 2 of **International Labour Organisation Convention No. 111 Concerning Discrimination in Respect of Employment and Occupation** is more explicit in committing States to 'pursue a national policy designed to promote [...] equality of opportunity and treatment in respect of employment and occupation, with a view to eliminating any discrimination in respect thereof.' The non-discriminatory hiring of persons belonging to national minorities to work in the media will contribute to the representativity and objectivity of the media.

11. In keeping with the spirit of Articles 19(2) of the **International Covenant on Civil and Political Rights** and Article 9(1) of the **Framework Convention for the Protection of National Minorities** and of the principle of non-discrimination, access to programming in the language of persons belonging to a national minority, transmitted from another State or from the 'kin-State', should not justify a diminution of programme time allotted to the minority on the public media of the State in which its members live.

Transfrontier access to information and media networks is a fundamental element of the right to information which, in the context of accelerated technological progress, is of growing importance. Consequently, when cable licensing is involved, for example, it is not legitimate for a State to ref??use to license television or radio stations based in a kin-State when the desire for access to these stations has been clearly expressed by the national minority concerned. This right applies not only to cable media but also to electronic information networks in the language of the national minority.

As a general matter, the member States of the Council of Europe resolved in Article III(c) of the **Declaration on the Freedom of Expression and Information** 'to promote the free flow of information, thus contributing to international understanding, a better knowledge of convictions and traditions, respect for the diversity of opinions and the mutual enrichment of cultures'. In relation to media contacts across frontiers, States should conform their policies to the spirit of this provision.

ECONOMIC LIFE

12. International instruments make little reference to the rights of persons belonging to national minorities in the field of economic activity. International instruments do, however, refer to the right of persons belonging to national minorities to use their language in public and in private, freely and without any form of discrimination, orally and in writing, individually and with others. Article 19(2) of the **International Covenant on Civil and Political Rights** and Article 10(1) of the **European Convention for the Protection of Human Rights and Fundamental Freedoms** guarantee freedom of expression with respect not only to ideas and opinions which may be transmitted to others (i.e. the content of communications), but also to language as a medium of communication. These rights, coupled with the right to equality and non-discrimination, imply the right of persons belonging to national minorities to run their businesses in the language of their choice. In view of the importance to private entrepreneurs to be able to communicate effectively with their clientele and to pursue their initiatives in fair conditions, there should be no undue restrictions on their free choice of language.

    Article 11(2) of the **Framework Convention** stipulates that 'every person belonging to a national minority has the right to display in his or her minority language, signs, inscriptions and other information of a private nature visible to the public.' In the **Framework Convention** the expression 'of a private nature' refers to all that is not official. Hence, the State may not impose any restrictions on the choice of language in the administration of private business enterprises.

    Notwithstanding the above, the State may require that the official language or languages of the State be accommodated in those sectors of economic activity which affect the enjoyment of the rights of others or require exchange and communication with public bodies. This follows from the permissible restrictions on freedom of expression as stipulated in Article 19(3) of the **International Covenant on Civil and Political Rights** and Article 10(2) of the **European Convention for the Protection of Human Rights and Fundamental Freedoms.** While the limited permissible restrictions expressed in the aforementioned articles could justify restrictions on the content of communications, they would never justify restrictions on the use of a language as a medium of communication. However, protection of the rights and freedoms of others and the limited requirements of public administration may well justify specific prescriptions for the additional use of the official language or languages of the State. This would apply to sectors of activity such as workplace health and safety, consumer protection, labour relations, taxation, financial reporting, State health and unemployment insurance and transportation, depending on the circumstances. On the basis of a legitimate public interest, the State could, in addition to the use of any other language, also require that the official language or languages of the State be accommodated in such business activities as public signage and labelling – as expressly stated in paragraph 60 of the **Explanatory Report to the Framework Convention for the Protection of National Minorities.** In sum, the State could never prohibit the use of a language, but it could, on the basis of a legitimate public interest, prescribe the additional use of the official language or languages of the State.

In keeping with the logic of legitimate public interest, any requirement(s) for the use of language which may be prescribed by the State must be proportional to the public interest to be served. The proportionality of any requirement is to be determined by the extent to which it is necessary. Accordingly, for example, in the public interest of workplace health and safety, the State could require private factories to post safety notices in the official language or languages of the State in addition to the chosen language(s) of the enterprise. Similarly, in the interest of accurate public administration in relation to taxation, the State could require that administrative forms be submitted in the official language or languages of the State and that, in the case of an audit by the public authorities, relevant records be made available also in the official language or languages of the State; the latter eventuality would not require that private enterprise maintain all records in the official language or languages of the State, but only that the burden of possible translation rests with the private enterprise. This is without prejudice to the possible entitlement of persons belonging to national minorities to use their language(s) in communications with administrative authorities as foreseen in Article 10(2) of the **Framework Convention for the Protection of National Minorities**.

ADMINISTRATIVE AUTHORITIES AND PUBLIC SERVICES

13/14/15. OSCE Participating States are committed to taking measures which will contribute to creating a dynamic environment, conducive not only to the maintenance of the identity of persons belonging to national minorities (including their language) but also to their development and promotion. As a consequence, these States have undertaken to respect 'the right of persons belonging to national minorities to effective participation in public affairs' as outlined in paragraph 35 of the **Copenhagen Document**. Article 10(2) of the **Framework Convention for the Protection of National Minorities** expressly requires States to 'make possible the use of minority languages in communications with administrative authorities.' Paragraph 35 of the **Copenhagen Document** also makes reference to the possibility of creating an environment that would be conducive to the participation of national minorities in public affairs, in their own language, by establishing 'appropriate local or autonomous administrations corresponding to the specific historical and territorial circumstances of minorities in accordance with the policies of the State concerned'. Article 15 of the **Framework Convention** engages States to 'create the conditions necessary for the effective participation of persons belonging to national minorities in cultural, social and economic life and in public affairs, in particular those affecting them.' These provisions engage public authorities to enable persons belonging to national minorities to deal with local authorities in their language or to receive civil certificates and attestations in their own language. In line with the principles of equality and non-discrimination, these provisions also imply a dynamic participatory relationship wherein the language of the minority may be a full-fledged vehicle of communication in local political life and in the interface between citizens and public authorities including in the provision of public services.

The ethnic representativity of administrative institutions and agencies designed to serve the population is usually reflective of a pluralistic, open and non-discriminatory society. In order to counter the effects of past or existing discrimination within the system, Article 2 of **International Labour Organisation Convention No. 111 Concerning Discrimination in Respect of Employment and Occupation** requires States to 'pursue a national policy designed to promote [...] equality of opportunity and treatment in respect of employment and occupation, with a view to eliminating any discrimination in respect thereof.'

When designing and implementing programmes and services intended to serve the public, it is reasonable to expect that governments committed to the principles outlined above should take into consideration the expressed desires of persons belonging to national minorities as well as the principle of numerical justification. Where the need is expressed and the numbers are significant, equity requires that taxpayers belonging to national minorities have access to services also in their own language. This is particularly so in the case of health and social services which affect the quality of peoples' lives in an immediate and fundamental manner.

In line with the principles of equality and non-discrimination, administrative authorities are expected to deal with persons belonging to national minorities in an inclusive and equitable manner. States must recognise the demographic realities of the regions under their jurisdiction. Above all, States should not seek to avoid their obligations by changing the demographic reality of a region. Specifically Article 16 of the **Framework Convention** engages States to refrain from measures which might arbitrarily alter the proportion of the population in areas inhabited by persons belonging to national minorities with the objective of restricting the rights of these minorities. Such measures could consist of arbitrary expropriations, evictions, expulsions as well as the arbitrary redrawing of administrative borders and census manipulation.

INDEPENDENT NATIONAL INSTITUTIONS

16. Human rights acquire real meaning for their intended beneficiaries when the public authorities of the State establish mechanisms to ensure that the rights guaranteed in international conventions and declarations, or in domestic legislation, are effectively implemented and protected. As a complement to judicial procedures, independent national institutions usually provide quicker and less expensive recourses and are as such more accessible.

Discrimination as referred to in the **Convention on the Elimination of Racial Discrimination** is not defined according to criteria relating strictly to race. Article 1(1) of the **Convention** stipulates that the concept of racial discrimination shall mean 'any distinction, exclusion, restriction or preference based on race, colour, descent or national or ethnic origin which has the purpose or effect of nullifying or impairing the recognition, enjoyment or exercise, on an equal footing, of human rights and fundamental freedoms in the political, economic, social, cultural or any other field of public life.' Article 6 of the **Convention** declares that 'State Parties shall assure to everyone within their jurisdiction effective protection and remedies, through the competent national tribunals and other State institutions against any acts of racial discrimination which violate his human rights and fundamental freedoms contrary to this Convention...' In this context, the establishment by States of independent national institutions that can act as mechanisms of redress and compensation, such as the institution of ombudsperson or a human rights commission is a measure of a given State's democratic and pluralistic nature. Accordingly, and with reference to **United Nations resolution 48/134 of 20 December 1993**, the Council of Europe has encouraged, in **Committee of Ministers Recommendation No. R(97)14 of 30 September 1997**, the establishment of 'national human rights institutions, in particular human rights commissions which are pluralist in their membership, ombudsmen or comparable institutions.' Such mechanisms of redress should be made available also to persons belonging to national minorities who consider that their linguistic and other rights have been violated.

JUDICIAL AUTHORITIES

17/18. International law requires public authorities to ensure that all persons who are arrested, accused and tried be informed of the charges against them and of all other proceedings in a language they understand. If need be, an interpreter must be made available to them free of charge. This standard of due process of law is universal in its application and does not relate to the linguistic rights of national minorities as such. Rather, the underlying principles are those of equality and non-discrimination before the law. Respect for these principles is particularly vital in relation to criminal charges and proceedings. As a consequence, Article 14(3)(a) of the **International Covenant on Civil and Political Rights** requires that everyone charged with a criminal offence shall 'be informed promptly and in detail in a language which he understands of the nature and cause of the charge against him'. Article 6(3)(a) of the **European Convention for the Protection of Human Rights and Fundamental Freedoms** stipulates the same requirement in almost identical language. In addition, Article 5(2) of the aforementioned convention stipulates the same requirement in relation to arrest. Furthermore, Article 14(3) of the **International Covenant on Civil and Political Rights** stipulates the entitlement of everyone 'in full equality' [...] '(e) to examine, or have examined, the witnesses against him and to obtain the attendance and examination of witnesses on his behalf under the same conditions as witnesses against him'. In this connection, Article 14(3)(f) of the **International Covenant on Civil and Political Rights** and Article 6(3)(e) of the **European Convention for the Protection of Human Rights and Fundamental Freedoms** guarantee the right of everyone 'to have the free assistance of an interpreter if he cannot understand or speak the language used in court.' While these guarantees concerning expressly the use of language are prescribed specifically in relation to criminal procedures, it follows from the fundamental guarantee of equality before courts and tribunals, as stipulated in the first sentence of Article 14(1) of the **International Covenant on Civil and Political Rights**, that legal proceedings of all kinds are to be considered more perfectly fair to the extent that the conditions are more strictly equal. This determination, which applies equally with respect to the choice of language for proceedings as a whole, should guide States in the development of their policies concerning the equal and effective administration of justice.

More generally, Article 7(1) of the **European Charter for Regional or Minority Languages** declares that States shall base their policies, legislation and practice on such objectives and principles as 'the recognition of the regional or minority languages as an expression of cultural wealth [...]' and 'the need for resolute action to promote regional or minority languages in order to safeguard them'. Article 7(4) of the **European Charter** stipulates that 'in determining their policy with regard to regional and minority languages, [...] Parties shall take into consideration the needs and wishes expressed by the groups which use such languages.' Moreover, Article 15 of the **Framework Convention** engages States to 'create the conditions necessary for the effective participation of persons belonging to national minorities in cultural, social and economic life and in public affairs, in particular those affecting them.' If one considers the abovementioned standards while taking into consideration the importance, in democratic societies, of effective access to justice, it is reasonable to expect that States should, so far as possible, ensure the right of persons belonging to national minorities to express themselves in their language in all stages of judicial proceedings (whether criminal, civil or administrative) while respecting the rights of others and maintaining the integrity of the processes, including through instances of appeal.

19. Insofar as access to justice is vital to the enjoyment of human rights, the degree to which one may participate directly and easily in available procedures is an important measure of such access. The availability of judicial procedures functioning in the language(s) of persons belonging to national minorities, therefore, renders access to justice more direct and easy for such persons.

On this basis, Article 9 of the **European Charter for Regional or Minority Languages** provides that, to the extent feasible and pursuant to the request of one of the affected parties, all judicial proceedings should be conducted in the regional or minority language. The Parliamentary Assembly of the Council of Europe, has come to the same conclusion in Article 7(3) of its **Recommendation 1201** which provides that 'In regions in which substantial numbers of a national minority are settled, the persons belonging to a national minority shall have the right to use their mother tongue in their contacts with the administrative authorities and in proceedings before the courts and legal authorities.' Accordingly, States should adopt appropriate recruitment and training policies for the judiciary.

DEPRIVATION OF LIBERTY

20. Rule 51, paragraphs 1 and 2, of the **United Nations Standard Minimum Rules for the Treatment of Prisoners** as well as Rule 60, paragraphs 1 and 2 of the **European Prison Rules of the Council of Europe** stress the importance of the

right of the incarcerated to be understood by the prison administration as well as the importance for the prison administration to be understood by the inmate population. These provisions do not relate to minority rights as such. However, taken into consideration along with the expressed desire of affected populations, their numerical strength and the principle of equality and non-discrimination, the aforementioned provisions are even more compelling in regions or localities where persons belonging to national minorities are present in significant numbers.

21. Rule 37 of the **United Nations Standard Minimum Rules for the Treatment of Prisoners** as well as Article 43(1) of the **European Prison Rules of the Council of Europe** uphold the right of prisoners to communicate with their families, reputable friends and persons or representatives of outside organisations. In view of the importance of such human rights as freedom of expression and the right to use one's language in public and in private, it is incumbent upon authorities to respect these rights within the limitations prescribed by law even in penitentiary institutions. As a rule, prisoners should be able to communicate in their own language both orally with other inmates and with visitors and also in personal correspondence. Nevertheless, certain human rights and freedoms of persons detained for criminal acts may legitimately be restricted or suspended for reasons of public security in conformity with the limitations prescribed by the international instruments. As a practical matter, enjoyment of the linguistic rights of detained persons may be best facilitated by their detention in a place where their language is usually spoken.

CORRESPONDENCE OF THE OSCE HIGH COMMISSIONER ON NATIONAL MINORITIES WITH SOME OSCE COUNTRIES

Letter of the OSCE High Commissioner on National Minorities, Max van der Stoel, to the Romanian Minister of Foreign Affairs, Andrei Plesu and response of the Romanian Minister of Foreign Affairs to the High Commissioner

The Hague, 2 March 1998
Ref. 730/98

Dear Mr. Minister,

Please allow me to thank you, once more, for the hospitality you offered to me during my recent visit to your country. I should also like to express my gratitude for the effective help the staff of your Ministry provided in arranging my programme.

During the various meetings I had, the question of how to meet requests by minorities for tertiary education in their mother language frequently came up. In this respect I was informed about the progress made at the Babes-Bolyai University in Cluj towards the development of a multicultural structure aiming at the development of three lines of study programmes in Romanian, Hungarian and German. I express the hope that the Government will do what it can to stimulate this process and to ensure that other universities will follow a similar course. It can, however, only come to full fruition if the universities will be granted additional financial resources for this purpose, while it will also be necessary to allow more decentralisation in the system of tertiary education in general.

In the discussion regarding the development of a multicultural structure in the field of tertiary education, the point has frequently been made that the intellectual and cultural development of majorities and minorities should not take place in isolation. In this connection I have noted that the Senate, debating the revision of the Law on Education of 1995, has adopted an article formulated in such a way that it would be impossible to create an independent state-funded tertiary education institution with tuition in a minority language, while in the version of the article laid down in Government Decree 36/1997 of 10 July 1997 such a possibility is kept open.

I should like to make the following comments. In recognizing that the multicultural system being developed in the Babes-Bolyai University in Cluj (and hopefully in future also in other universities) has many advantages insofar as it meets a number of the cultural and educational needs of minorities while, at the same time, ensuring that students following separate courses in their mother language nonetheless study together at the same university, it would in my view not be desirable to include in the revised Law on Education a provision excluding the possibility of a state-funded university with education in a minority language. It would be preferable to create a commission of independent experts which could analyse whether there would be such a need for one or more minorities. If this commission would come to the conclusion that the preservation of the cultural identity of a minority would require such an institution, it could also analyse the question whether such a separate institution could restrict itself to a limited number of subjects. It might perhaps be of use to ask experts of the Council of Europe to provide information about the way similar problems have been solved in other European States.

In the discussion on this subject, I noted that sometimes insufficient attention has been paid to the fact that, in case the Government would come to the conclusion that a separate state funded institution in a minority language would be needed, a separate law would be needed to create it. If such a system would come into being, it would of course have to be open for any student, irrespective of his or her ethnicity. The development of forms of cooperation with other state universities would in my view also need special attention.

Permit me finally, Mr Minister, to make two remarks about the content of Decree 36/1997 regarding the revision of the Law on Education. Article 120(2) refers to the teaching of the history of the 'Romanians'. Considering the multi-ethnic character of Romania, I wonder whether it would not be preferable to refer to the history of 'Romania'. I also should like to recall paragraph 34 of the Document of the Copenhagen meeting of the Conference on the Human Dimension of the CSCE of 1990 to which Romania, like all other OSCE States, has subscribed. It states that in the school curriculum, States will also take account of 'the history and culture of national minorities'. I would suggest a provision would be added to Article 120 stating that this subject will be taught in the minority language.

I look forward with great interest, Mr Minister, to your reply to these recommendations. I have taken the liberty of sending a copy of this letter to the Minister of Education, Mr Marga.

Yours sincerely,
Max van der Stoel

* * *

March 30, 1998

Dear Mr. High Commissioner,

I am writing to you, in answer to your letter dated earlier this month. It is, indeed, with great pleasure that I recall the visit you paid to Romania in February, and particularly, the fascinating discussions we had over lunch at the Diplomatic Club.

As you certainly are well aware, debates on the revision of the 1995 Law on Education (Government Decree 36/1997) are still under way in Parliament, and for the time being, at least, it is difficult to foresee what the result of these debates will be. In any case, copies of your letter have been sent to the Presidents of the Senate and Chamber of Deputies, and certainly Minister Marga is familiar with your recommendations.

The Ministry of National Education, and Romanian authorities as a whole, attach particular importance to the process of decentralization of administration in general and of education institutions, in particular, which will also mean greater freedom in managing financial resources.

As for creating new opportunities of tertiary education for national minorities, the Government of Romania, within which the political party of ethnic Hungarians (UDMR) plays a considerable role, has most clearly expressed its willingness to look into the most adequate ways and means to achieve this, taking into consideration authentic needs and requests. We are confident that legislation to be passed in the field will make it possible.

Certainly, a commission of independent experts can be useful in defining the specific needs of one minority or another, and it is an option we are generally open to. We would, however, be careful so as not to give the wrong signal within or outside the country, especially since we believe that this is a question that can be solved together with our Hungarian colleagues.

Thanking you once again for your interest and contribution to the issue of national minorities in Romania, and looking forward to continuing the fruitful cooperation with the institution that you represent, I remain,

Sincerely yours,
Andrei Gabriel PLESU
Minister of Foreign Affairs

Letter of the Head of Government Working Group concerning the Amendments to the Citizenship Law of the Republic of Latvia to the OSCE High Commissioner on National Minorities, Response of the High Commissioner addressed to the Latvian Prime Minister, Guntars Krasts

Riga, April 24, 1998

On the Proposals of the Working Group Concerning
the Amendments to the Citizenship Law

Honorable Mr. M. van der Stoel,

As it was agreed between You and Prime Minister, I am sending to you proposals – concerning amendments to the Citizenship, Education and Languages Laws.

Following version have been prepared and agreed by the parliamentarian working group of granting citizenship to children of stateless persons:

The law shall be supplied with Article 3¹ as follows:
'Article 3¹, The citizenship of a child born in Latvia after August 21, 1991

1. a child born in Latvia after August 21, 1991 in accordance with the order stated in this law has rights to gain the citizenship of Latvia coming into age of 16, if

both of parents are citizens of former USSR, or if one of them is the citizen of the former USSR but the other is stateless or unknown and who are no citizens (residents) of any other state and who at the moment of submitting the application permanently reside in Latvia for no less than 5 years;
2. a child born in Latvia after August 21, 1991 in accordance with the order stated in this law has rights to gain the citizenship of Latvia coming into age of 16, if both of parents are stateless, or one of them is stateless but the other is unknown and who are no citizens (residents) of any other state and who at the moment of submitting the application permanently reside in Latvia for no less than 5 years;
3. if a child wishes to gain citizenship of Latvia in accordance with the order stated in Paragraph 1 and 2 of this Article at the same time when submitting the application for granting citizenship of Latvia he/she shall submit one of the following documents:

1. a document confirming that a parson applying has gained special or industrial education (industrial secondary school, industrial high school, industrial school) with the Latvian language as a language of tuition;
2. a document confirming in accordance with the order stated in the Articles 19 and 20 of this law that a person applying knows the Latvian language.'

The Government working group have prepared following version of granting citizenship to children of stateless persons:

'Article 31. The citizenship of a child born in Latvia after August 21, 1991

1. a juvenile born in Latvia after August 21, 1991 and who is less than 16 years old is the citizen of Latvia if:
   1. it is claimed by both parents who at the moment of submitting the application permanently reside in Latvia for no less than 5 years and who are citizens (residents) of any other state;
   2. it is claimed by one of the parents who brings up the juvenile alone or the adopter who at the moment of submitting the application permanently resides in Latvia for no less than 5 years and who are no citizen (resident) of any other state;

2. a juvenile whom in accordance with the Paragraph 1 of this Article the citizenship is asked for shall reside in Latvia permanently and he/she must not be the citizen of any other state since birth;
3. a person is considered to be one of the parents bringing up a child alone:

   1. a mother n case there is no record on father in the birth certificate;
   2. one of the parents in case the other has been deprived of the authority of parents;
   3. one of the parents in case the other in accordance with the law has been 4. proclaimed man-hunted and has been hunted for at least one year;
   4. one of the parents in case the other is admitted missing;
   5. one of the parents in case the other is dead;

6. one of the parents in case the marriage is divorced.

(2)[4] a juvenile, if persons who are authorized to submit the application for granting the citizenship to a child has not submitted it, coming into age of 16 has rights to gain the citizenship of Latvia in accordance with the order stated in this Article submitting one of the following documents:

1. a document confirming that a person applying has gained special or industrial education (industrial secondary school, industrial high school, industrial school) with the Latvian language as a language of tuition;
2. a document confirming in accordance with the order defined in the Articles 19 and 20 of this law that a person applying knows the Latvian language.

(2)[5] persons who are authorized to submit application for granting the citizenship to a child when submitting the application in addition provide with the pledge confirmed in accordance with the order defined by the Cabinet of Ministers to promote the integration of a child in Latvia and the mastering of the Latvian language as an official language of the state, to promote the education and to cultivate the loyalty of a child of the Republic of Latvia.'

The group of experts turns your attention to the fact that accepting the parliamentarian version together with the cancellation of naturalization 'windows' children of stateless persons can gain the citizenship together with their parents in accordance with naturalization since the moment of birth till becoming 16 years old. Besides, such children shall not pass any test stated by the Law on Citizenship as well as they shall not pay the naturalization free. Furthermore, these children, in case their parents are not willing to undergo naturalization, can gain the citizenship independently coming into the age of 16 in accordance with lightened regulations without passing tests of the Constitution of Latvia Republic, national anthem, the knowledge of the history if they have gained professional education in the Latvian language or in case they have passed the test of the knowledge of Latvian in accordance with the order stated in the Articles 19 and 20 of the Law on Citizenship.

It must be emphasized that for those children who have gained general education in the Latvian language in accordance with the Paragraphs 1-3 of the Article 2 of the Law on Citizenship the citizenship of Latvia can be gained in the order of registration without passing any tests. For that reason, in order to promote the realization of the process of the integration of society and learning of the state language the Government experts propose to add the following supplement, to the project of the Law on Education:

Article 27 shall be supplied with the paragraph 6 as follows:
'6. Learning of the state language.'

Article 31 shall be supplied with the new Section 5 as follows:
'5. In the programs of basic education for ethnical minorities the bilingual education shall be performed and the level of the knowledge of the state language shall be

provided to the extend to create the possibility to continue the education in the state language.'

The supplement to the Article 27 of the project provides the contents of the preparatory educational program with the regulation on the mastering of the state language but the amendment to the Article 31 of the project supplies the programme of basic education for [ethnical] minorities with the regulation that a person gaining the basic education achieves the level of the state language that provides the possibility to continue education in the state language.

The project of the law on the state language shall be supplied with the standards stating that in all educational institutions the learning of the state language shall be provided in such level that holders of school completion certificate can work in any profession or hold any position in the Republic of Latvia.

Consequently, the Article 12 of the project of the law on the state language shall be supplied with the new Section 3 as follows:

'The rights to obtain the education in the state language are guaranteed in the Republic of Latvia. In schools of other language of tuition, also in private schools and in educational institutions sponsored by foreign countries the mastering of the state language shall be provided according to the state standards of the school education in the Latvian language that would grant the possibility to holders of school completion certificate to study in any secondary and higher educational establishment as well as hold any position in the Republic of Latvia.'

I am asking your opinion on the versions prepared by the parliamentarian and government working groups till April 27 of this year.

The matter is so urgent due to the fact that the Government of Latvia will review the matter in the meeting of the Cabinet of Ministers on April 28 of this year.

Sincerely yours,

Juris Vinkelis
Head of Government Working Group

* * *

The Hague, 30 April 1998

Reference No 984/98/L

Dear Mr. Krasts,

Thank you for the letter of 24 April in which Mr Vinkelis sent the two variants of proposals of the Government Working Group concerning the Amendments to the Citizenship Law. Allow me, as requested by you, to submit some comments on the Working Group's proposals. I will restrict my comments only to the second variant prepared by the Government Working Group, since the proposals in the first variant do not, I regret, comply in any way with my original Recommendations regarding children of stateless parents.

First of all, I welcome the basic underlying principle that citizenship should be granted to children who were born in Latvia since 21 August 1991, who are under 16 years of age, and whose parents are stateless and have been resident in Latvia for no less than 5 years. I would emphasise, however, that while I understand, on the one hand, the logic of making amendments not only to the Citizenship Law to introduce these new provisions, but also to incorporate amendments to the drafts in the new Education Law and Language Law, it must be taken into account that the adoption of these laws might turn out to be protracted processes.

It would seem highly unlikely that either the new Language Law or Education Law will be adopted by the Saeima before the Summer. There even appears to be a distinct possibility that the final version of these laws can only be decided upon by parliament after the elections. I assume, therefore, that the coming into force of the legislation regarding the conferral of citizenship on children of stateless parents according to the formula I have proposed will not be made dependent on the adoption or entering into force of the text you have sent me. As we discussed before, it might meet little international understanding if Latvia, after having agreed to fulfil my recommendation regarding children of stateless parents in Latvia, would subsequently delay its implementation.

I note and welcome from the proposals of the Government Working Group the endeavor to relax citizenship requirements for children. However, what it is necessary to retain in the new law is the _right_ of stateless children born in Latvia to be conferred citizenship _unconditionally_ (i.e. without language, educational, or other requirements). In my view, it is not only a legal obligation on the Republic of Latvia to conform its Citizenship Law with this requirement of international law, but such a step would also contribute significantly to promoting social integration within the country. Insofar as the Republic of Latvia does of course have a legitimate interest also in ensuring that everyone within the State has an adequate knowledge of State language, it is to be stressed that the State is in a position to achieve this through control of the school curriculum and education system in general. That is to say, the State is able to prescribe for all children the learning of the state language. The main point I would make here is that meaningful Integration of non-Latvian youths into society, as it seems to me, will be achieved through both the granting of citizenship and a good grounding in the Latvian language through the education system. The two processes go hand in hand. In this respect, I recall that the only persons who could benefit from the proposed change in the Citizenship Law will reach the age of 7 after 21 August of this year. As such, they are all to be subject to the full education system of Latvia.

If I may return, Mr. Prime Minister, to the specifics of the proposals of the Government Working Group, while I welcome the possibility of children as of age 16 (Para. 4, on page 3) to apply on their own for citizenship (in case the person authorized to apply on their behalf before they have reached that age has failed to do so), this nevertheless must not be made dependent on conformity with any other conditions. It should be entirely sufficient for them to submit an application. Consequently, sub paras 1 & 2 of Para. 4 should be deleted. Furthermore, on the same basis, I recommend to delete Para. 5 as well. To reiterate, the concerns embodied in these aforementioned paragraphs will in any event be met through the education process to which all children are subject.

I have taken note of the particular changes of the Education law and Language law which the government intends to submit to the Saeima. In my view these proposals have to be seen against the background of the general policy of Latvia aimed at ensuring that all citizens have an adequate knowledge of the state language. I note that this general policy is in conformity with the 1990 OSCE Human Dimension Copenhagen Document, which refers in Para. 34 to the need for persons belonging to national minorities to learn the official language of the State concerned. At the same time, the OSCE Copenhagen Document requires that '[...] (t)he participating States will endeavour to ensure that persons belonging to national minorities [...] have adequate opportunities for instruction of their mother tongue or in their mother tongue [...]'. This clearly points towards the need for balance, and I would expect that the specific content of Latvian language education would and should respect the right of persons belonging to a national minority to learn their own language as well.

These would be some initial comments, Mr Prime Minister, to the proposals which I received from the Government Working Group. I would be happy to provide further details, if required, as well as comments on any subsequent draft proposals.

With best wishes,
Yours sincerely,
Max van der Stoel
OSCE High Commissioner on National Minorities

[c.c. Mr Juris Vinkelis/Head of Government Working Group]

Letter of the OSCE High Commissioner on National Minorities, Max van der Stoel, to the Minister of Foreign Affairs of the Slovak Republic, H.E. Ms. Zdenka Kramplová and Response of the Slovakian Minister of Foreign Affairs to the High Commissioner

Ref. no. 1026/98

29 May 1998

Dear Madam Minister,

Please permit me to draw your attention to two draft laws presently under consideration in the Parliament of the Republic of Slovakia.

First, with regard to the draft Law on Local Elections which has been recently introduced into Parliament by the Government, I have serious concerns about its essential thrust and effects. As I understand the bill, its main aim is to fix the electoral representation along ethnic lines. I believe this is generally undesirable and would in its effects violate the fundamental principle of democracy, i.e. that 'the will of the people shall be the basis of the authority of government' as expressed in Article 21(3) of the Universal Declaration of Human Rights. More particularly, the effects of the draft Law would be to interfere, on the one hand, with the will of the people to elect representatives of their choosing without unjustifiable constraints and, on the other hand, with the right to stand for office without discrimination nor unjustified interference with one's private life.

The principle expressed in Article 21(3) of the Universal Declaration of Human Rights has further specification in Article 25(b) of the International Covenant on Civil and Political Rights which provides for the right 'to vote and to be elected at genuine periodic elections [...], guaranteeing the free expression of the will of the electors'. The principle of free elections protects the right of eligible voters not to be pressured or impermissibly influenced in forming and expressing their will. Eligible voters should be able freely to choose among various alternatives, e.g. parties, programmes, candidates. In my view, the condition of relevant nationality required for eligibility to hold a seat in the municipal council as prescribed in amended paragraph 1 of Article 51 of the draft law means that only candidates with the relevant nationality can be elected. Therefore, the effect of the draft Law is to prevent electors from being able to vote for a candidate who would have an ethnicity different from that attached to the mandates on the basis of the ethnicity of the incumbent. This is a serious and unjustifiable limitation on the possible alternatives for the electorate. The implication also follows that the essential choice will not be between candidates from political parties or programmes, but between ethnicities/nationalities.

While the effect of the draft Law clearly limits the choices available to the electorate, it also entails a serious interference to the right to be elected without discrimination as guaranteed in several international instruments to which the Slovak Republic is a State Party, including: Article 25(b) of the International Covenant on Civil and Political Rights in conjunction with Article 2 of the Covenant; Article 5(c) of the International Convention on the Elimination of All Forms of Racial Discrimination; and Article 3 of Protocol No. 1 to the Council of Europe Convention for the Protection of Human Rights and Fundamental Freedoms, read in conjunction with Article 14 of the Convention; and Paragraph 7(5) of the Copenhagen Document of the CSCE Conference on the Human Dimension. In exercising one's right to be elected (or to vote), no citizen may be hindered or restricted in law or in fact for reason of race, colour, religion, birth, political or other opinion, [...] national or ethnic origin, sex, property or other status. The requirement of indication of ethnic origin for purposes of the municipal elections would, in my view, represent an impermissible restriction to the right to be elected without any distinction as to ethnic origin.

The requirement of the draft Law that candidates must indicate their ethnicity in registration forms, ballots, etc. in cases where the individual does not wish to express his or her ethnical/national origin, will in fact deprive persons who do not wish publicly to identify their ethnicity of the opportunity to stand for office in municipal elections. In this connection, one should bear in mind that membership of an ethnic group has an important subjective element. If individuals wish to express or renounce their association with a group, they must be free to do so. Compelling an individual to be associated or to express association with a minority culture would violate the right to privacy.

In sum, the draft Law violates a number of international principles and specific standards concerning free elections and individual human rights.

Turning to the second issue upon which I wish to address you, it has come to my attention that a bill has been presented to Parliament by some members of the Slovak National Party, which, among other things, aims at modifications regarding the language of instruction in Hungarian language schools. In this respect, I have noted the statement of Prime Minister Meciar that he considers the law to be unconstitutional. On my part I would express the hope that the law will not be adopted at all. It clearly intends to impose the concept of the so-called alternative school. However, your Government, in its Policy statement of April 1994, stated that the right to choose the language of teaching would be respected. Regarding the preferences of the Hungarian minority, a survey of the views of the parents in 1995 showed that an overwhelming majority of the parents rejected this concept. The comment of your predecessor Mr Juray Schenk in his letter of October 1995 was '[...] this was a free decision of the majority of parents and will be respected as such'. Against this background I express the hope that your Government will try to convince Parliament not to adopt this law.

These, Madame Minister, were the matters I wish to address you upon at this time.

Yours sincerely,
Max van der Stoel

* * *

Bratislava, 13 July 1998
No.: 200.414198 - KAMI (Unofficial translation)

Dear Commissioner,

Thank you for your interest in the development of the legislative process connected with the preparation of amendment of several laws.

In connection with the draft Law on Local Elections I have the honour to inform you that this draft law has already been adopted in the National Council of the Slovak Republic. It can also be said that through this law the Slovak Republic safeguards the right of 'the national minorities to govern the affairs they are concerned with.

As for the draft amendment of the School Law presented by the Group of deputies of' the Slovak National Party, I have the honour to inform you that the Committee on Constitutional and Legal Matters of the National Council of the Slovak Republic on 9 June 1998 did not recommend the adopting of this bill and eventually at the Parliamentary session on 2 July 1998 the Parliament did not even pass it.

As regards the alternative education I would like to inform you that it bears no relationship to the draft amendment of the School Law. It is a form of bilingual education based on the freedom of choice. The expression alternative education is chosen deliberately so as to emphasize the opportunity of an alternative, i.e. the free choosing and decision of parents on whether to put their children in schools with bilingual teaching, in Slovak language as well (at least some subjects, i.e. Slovak, geography and history). By claiming that the majority rejected this system, the rights of parents who made use of this opportunity do not cease to exist. If the state does not give its citizens the opportunity to choose freely, but on the contrary, through its passivity actually creates conditions for a forced assimilation of Slovak and other non-Hungarian citizens in ethnically mixed regions, it would severely violate the rights of a number of citizens who want to learn their mother tongue and national language on an appropriate level, what is a right guaranteed also by the Constitution and international regulations.

Sincerely,

Minister of Foreign Affairs of the Slovak Republic
Zdenka Kramplová

Letter of the OSCE High Commissioner on National Minorities, Max van der Stoel, to the Minister of Foreign Affairs of the Slovak Republic, H.E. Ms. Zdenka Kramplová of 24 July 1998, and Response of the Slovakian Minister of Foreign Affairs to the High Commissioner of 10 August 1998

Ref. no. 1069/98

24 July 1998

Dear Madam Minister,

Thank you for your letter of 13 July in reply to my letter of 29 May 1998. I have noted with regret that, contrary to the usual practice, you have not taken a position regarding the objections I had formulated against a number of provisions of the then draft Law on Local Elections. I equally regret that this Law has been adopted without the amendments required to ensure that the Law would be in conformity with international standards accepted by Slovakia.

Regarding the remarks in your letter concerning the concept of alternative education, I want to make it clear that I do respect the right of those favouring an alternative schooling to opt for such schooling. On the other hand, I am also of the opinion that the system of alternative education cannot be imposed on parents who object it. I was pleased to note that the Parliament of Slovakia, by rejecting the legislative proposals which the Slovak National Party had proposed in order to impose this system, has decided in favour of the freedom of parents to choose the school system they prefer.

Yours sincerely,

Max van der Stoel

* * *

Bratislava, 10 August 1998

Dear High Commissioner,

I wish to thank you for your continuing interest in further details concerning some national legal standards in the Slovak Republic. Simultaneously permit me to express my surprise in connection with your putting in doubt the compatibility of the amendment of the Act on elections into self-governing bodies of municipalities with the system of valid legal standards which envisage the commitments of the Slovak Republic resulting from international treaties.

The main significance of the amendment is to ensure the legal guarantee for the equal participation of persons belonging to national minorities and ethnic groups in the representative corps of municipalities. In conformity with the general acknowledged principle of subsidiarity the Slovak Republic attaches due importance to the application of the principle of equality already on the level of the basic degree of territorial self-government, i.e. municipalities. That was the reason why there was set up a specific legal system for electing the deputies of municipality representation in municipalities where the population consists of representatives of both minority and majority nations. Through this measure the Slovak republic legally guarantees the participation of persons belonging to national minorities and ethnic groups in the administration of public affairs. In this way, the possibility of discrimination is excluded.

In connection with the question of alternative educational system I have the honour to repeatedly assure you that its basis is the application of the principle of voluntary approach. The very title of the abovementioned system of education was used with the aim to emphasize the right of the parents to freely choose one of the two alternatives, i.e. to put their children into a bilingual school or leave them at school with education in their mother tongue. In this way the Slovak Republic confirmed that it accepted and utilizes the bilingual system of education which belongs to standard forms of education at schools where the language of education is that of national minorities in all European states.

Yours sincerely

(Signature)

[Zdenka Kramplová]

Letter of the OSCE High Commissioner on National Minorities, Max van der Stoel, to the Prime Minister of the Republic of Slovakia, Mr. Mikulas Dzurinda, and Response of the Slovakian Prime Minister to the High Commissioner

4 November 1998

Dear Mr Prime Minister,

As I stated in my letter of congratulations to you of 30 October 1998, I am looking forward to an early and fruitful dialogue with your government aimed at resolving the differences of views which had arisen between the previous government and my office regarding a number of questions relating to national minorities. In order to facilitate the preparation of such a dialogue, permit me to list these questions in the remarks which follow.

Before doing so, however, I should like to express my great appreciation for the fact that parliament, on the proposal of your government and following the ruling on this subject of the Constitutional Court of 15 October 1998, has acted so quickly to abolish the new Law on Local Elections which was adopted by parliament in its previous composition in June of this year and to adopt again, apart from some technical changes, the text of the old law. As I wrote to the previous Foreign Minister on 29 May 1998, the new law violated a number of international principles and specific standards concerning free elections and individual human rights.

As to the list of items I would hope to discuss with your government, I should like to mention in the first place the question of the use of minority languages in official communications. Section 12 of the Law on the State Language of the Slovak Republic has declared null and void the Slovak National Council Law no. 428/1990 on the official language of the Slovak Republic. This meant i.a. that section 6 paragraph 2 of that law ('of persons belonging to a national minority constitute at least 20% of the population of a town or village, they have the right to use their language in such towns or villages in official communications') was no longer valid. At the same time, Section 3 paragraph 5 of the Act of the National Council of the Slovak Republic no. 270/1995 on the State Language of the Slovak Republic in association with the provisions contained in Section 12 of the aforesaid Act is not in harmony with Article 34 paragraph 2(6) of the Constitution of the Slovak Republic to the extent that it applies to those citizens of the Slovak Republic who belong to national minorities or ethnic groups'. My suggestion to introduce legislation on the subject was not heeded by the previous government. I express the hope that the question can be discussed again with representatives of your government.

As far as the Law on the State Language in general is concerned, I would suggest a discussion on the question whether a number of its provisions are compatible with international standards accepted by Slovakia.

It also seems to me that it would be desirable to draft a law on minority languages as a counterpart to the Law on the State Language. I am aware that several existing laws contain provisions regarding minority languages. I therefore suggest that references to these provisions will be included in such a law.

Another subject to which I should like to draw your attention is the question of school certificates. As you are aware, these certificates were always issued in both the state language and the minority language until an administrative decision ended this practice. I express the hope that your government will decide to return to the old practice. While, according to the Law on the State Language, the certificates have to be issued in the state language, there is to my knowledge no provision prohibiting its issuance in a minority language as well.

Regarding minority languages, I also express the hope that government and parliament will agree to the accession of Slovakia to the European Charter for Regional or Minority Languages.

As you may know, a joint team of experts of the Council of Europe, the OSCE and European Commission twice had meetings with governmental experts in Bratislava in the course of this year. Though no major progress was made, a practical result was that a useful inventory has been made of the several of the problem I have mentioned above. I express the hope, therefore, that you will agree to the same formula regarding the future dialogue on these issues.

Finally, I should like to draw your attention to the question of cultural subsidies for national minorities. On 2 July 1996, Decree no. 193/1996 which regulated the distribution of cultural subsidies was annulled. The new system gave the Ministry of Culture the right to decide on applications for subsidies. The way this system functions is far from transparent; in fact, there have been clear indications of arbitrariness in the decision-making process. I hope very much to discuss these issues, together with some other questions regarding minority cultural institutions, with the Minister of Culture.

These, Mr Prime Minister, were the points I wanted to bring to your attention. I am looking forward with great interest to your reply.

Yours sincerely,
Max van der Stoel

* * *

Predseda vlády Slovenskej republiky [President of the Slovak Government]

Bratislava, 12 November 1998

Excellency,

Allow me first to express my high appreciation of your letter from 4 November 1998 and assure you that the Government of the Slovak Republic has a firm interest to solve any open questions on the issue of national minorities, as soon as possible.

Concerning the abolition of the amended law on local elections I would like to inform you that the Government of the Slovak Republic decided to postpone the elections for a later date – 18 and 19 December 1998 – they will be implemented under the provision of the original law from 1990.

The basis for the new approach to the solution of issues related to national minorities are included in the Program Thesis from 27 October 1998 of the SDK-

SDL-SMK-SOP coalition. Please, let me inform me about those of them which reflect the pertinent subject:

Chapter I – State, Constitution, Legislation
The government will evaluate the level of the guaranteed rights of national minorities in relation to international obligations, to which the Slovak Republic is bound. Based on this analysis the decision about the preparation of a constitutional law on the position of national minorities will be taken.

The government will adopt laws to implement basic rights and liberties, including the rights of national minorities, wherever it is foreseen in the Constitution of the Slovak Republic.

A new concept for the solution of problems of the Roma minority has to be worked out.

Chapter XII – Education
Reestablishment of methodical centres for schools with education in Hungarian or the languages of other national minorities.

Establishment of a Section for education in minority language in the Ministry of Education.

Return to bilingual school certificate and pedagogic documentation.
The government will guarantee the improvement of the education level of citizens belonging to national minorities on the level of the state average and will solve the preparation of teachers for schools educating in minority languages, priests, employees in the sphere of minority culture by establishing an appropriate institutional level within the existing universities.

To guarantee the conditions for a normal functioning of the minority school system.

Chapter XIII – Culture
Enhancing the further development of the culture of national minorities and Slovaks living abroad.

A new system of financing national minorities, fixing the share in the budget of the Ministry of Culture dedicated to financing minority cultures.

Adjusting the funding of the theatres of the Hungarian and the Roma minorities up to the level of other theatres.

Establishing the Section of minority cultures in the Ministry of Culture

The adoption of a law on the use of minority languages.

To create the conditions for broadcasting in minority languages in the Slovak TV a Slovak Radio according to Art. 9 of the Framework Agreement.

Chapter XV – Foreign Affaires
Solve some questions concerning minorities in line with the international obligations of the Slovak Republic excluding any type of territorial autonomy.

Adopt the European Charter for Regional or Minority Languages.

Excellency, I hope, that the above quoted commitments of the governing coalition will give you a clear picture of the new approach towards national minorities in Slovakia, as a result of the Change, for which the majority of our citizens voted in the recent elections. I would highly appreciate further consultations on this very important issue to Slovakia. We regard the rapid solution of the open questions concerning national minorities in our country as our contribution to build an inclusive type of society and thus extend the zone of peace and stability in Central Europe, which is an important element of the European integration process in this part of our continent.

With best regards,
Mikuláš Dzurinda

Letter of the OSCE High Commissioner on National Minorities, Max van der Stoel to the President of the Republic of Estonia, Lennart Meri, and Response of the Estonian President to the High Commissioner

19 December 1998

Excellency,

I have the honour to address you with regard to the adoption by the Riigikogu on 15 December 1998 of an amendment to the Estonian Laws on Parliamentary Elections, Local Elections and the State Language according to which 'knowledge of written and spoken Estonian' would be required in order to be a member of the Riigikogu or a local governmental council.

As you know, I issued a statement recently confirming my intention not to come forward with new proposals regarding the Law on Citizenship after adoption by the Riigikogu of the recent amendments to that Law in relation to otherwise Stateless children. I wish to reiterate that this is still my intention. However, the issue at hand relates to the use of language, about which I have made a number of recommendations in the past. It is against this background that I should like to submit to you the following considerations.

In my view, the amendment to the Estonian Laws on Parliamentary Elections, Local Elections and the State Language is in accord neither with the Estonian Constitution nor with Estonia's international obligations and commitments. Moreover, I believe that promulgation of the law amending the Laws on Parliamentary Elections, Local Elections and the State Language would not constitute a constructive contribution to the national integration process.

With regard to the law applicable in Estonia, the amendment in question is in my view not compatible with specific requirements of the Constitution which, *inter alia*, stipulates no linguistic requirements as a condition to vote or to stand for office. Moreover, the Constitution stipulates the supremacy of international treaties binding on Estonia over Estonian laws which contradict such obligations. This leads me to draw your attention to the requirements of Article 3 of Protocol 1 of the **European Convention on Human Rights** and Article 25 of the **International Covenant on Civil and Political Rights** which stipulate that the will of the people (i.e. the citizenry) is to be the basis of government. It is to be noted that Article 3 of Protocol 1 of the European Convention on Human Rights is to be read in conjunction with Article 14 of the same Convention which forbids discrimination on the basis of language. Article 25 of the **International Covenant on Civil and Political Rights** is even more explicit in providing as follows:

> 'Every citizen shall have the right and the opportunity, without any of the distinctions mentioned in article 2 and without unreasonable restrictions:
> a. To take part in the conduct of public affairs, directly or through freely chosen representatives;
> b. To vote and to be elected at genuine periodic elections which shall be by universal and equal suffrage and shall be held by secret ballot, guaranteeing the free expression of the will of the electors;
> c. To have access, on general terms of equality, to public service in his country.'

The distinctions mentioned in Article 2, referred to above, are as follows:

> '1. Each State Party to the present Covenant undertakes to respect and to ensure to all individuals within its territory and subject to its jurisdiction the rights recognized in the present Covenant, without distinction of any kind, **such as** race, colour, sex, **language**, religion, political or other opinion, national or social origin, property, birth or other status.' [emphasis added]

It is clear from the above that there is to be absolutely no distinction regarding the language of a candidate for election, nor any 'unreasonable restriction'; in relation to this last point, it is further to be noted that only prescription of a minimum age, legal competence, non-incarceration and non-judicial service are generally accepted as the very few reasonable restrictions.

The rationale for the above-noted absolute entitlement to stand for office to be enjoyed by citizens (without unreasonable restriction) is rooted in the essence of the democratic process, i.e. that the will of people should be the basis of government. In a representative democracy, there should be no mediation of the will of the people, i.e. they should be essentially free to decide among themselves who they would wish to elect, and each citizen should be equally free to present themselves for election. Linguistic or other proficiency is fundamentally irrelevant to this process or objective. Should the electorate so choose, they should be free to elect persons who may enjoy their confidence but who may not in the opinion of others possess relevant or desirable skills or abilities, much less purported 'proficiencies'. The critical matter is that the elected person is deemed by the electorate (through the secret ballot) to represent them. There is no other matter of relevance. To require anything more would be to interfere with the basic democratic process and undermine the will of the people as the basis of government.

Aside from the above-described essential and substantive aspect of representative democracy, the notion of prescribing a specific 'proficiency' is evidently highly problematical from the perspective of procedure. In my view, any system to fix and measure 'proficiency' will ultimately be arbitrary and subject of abuse. This would be in contradiction to the democratic objective.

Permit me to note that the above arguments are not merely academic. By way of citing more extreme examples, the current Minister of Education in the United Kingdom, Mr. David Blunkett, is blind; as such he is unable to read or write in the English language. As another example, a current Member of Parliament in Canada is deaf; as such, he is unable to read or write in either of the official languages, nor is his spoken 'proficiency' necessarily at the highest level (he is provided with a signer to assist him in his work as Member of Parliament). In neither of the two aforementioned cases may it be said that the elected persons de not serve their electorate, the citizenry at large or the State: in each case they have been specifically elected by their immediate constituents according to the constituency system. Indeed, in the British case, the person has been included within the government and accorded Ministerial responsibilities. By reference to these extreme cases, it is evident *a fortiori* that 'proficiency' in the State language cannot be a requirement for public service as an elected representative and that to require such could interfere with the will of the people being the basis of government.

Allow me, Mr. President, also to draw your attention to the requirements of the Council of Europe's Framework Convention for the Protection of National Minorities which provides in Article 4 that the State Parties are 'to adopt, where necessary, adequate measures in order to promote, in all areas of economic, social, **political** and cultural life, full and effective equality between persons belonging to a national minority and those belonging to the majority. In this respect, they shall take due account of the specific conditions of the persons belonging to national minorities.' In addition, Article 15 of the same Convention provides that 'The Parties shall create the conditions necessary for the effective participation of persons belonging to national minorities in cultural, social and economic life and in **public affairs**, in particular those affecting them.' In my view, excluding such persons without 'proficiency' in the Estonian language would in effect exclude them from the possibility to participate in the most fundamental aspects of political life and public affairs, i.e. to stand for elected office.

Finally, as High Commissioner on National Minorities of the Organisation for Security and Cooperation in Europe, permit me to draw your attention also to the requirements of (among other relevant OSCE documents) the 1990 Copenhagen Document through which Estonia has committed itself to the principle of fully democratic elections and to ensure the effective participation of persons belonging to national minorities in public decision-making processes. In my view, to exclude persons without 'proficiency' in the Estonian language from holding elected office would be in contradiction with Estonia's OSCE commitments.

As a consequence of the above arguments, I appeal to you not to promulgate the amendments in question as adopted by the Riigikogu. In so doing, I wish to stress that maintaining the fully open and democratic nature of the Estonian political institutions in no way undermines the preservation and protection of the Estonian language. I am confident that the Republic of Estonia possesses, within the wide scope of its sovereignty, the means to protect, promote and develop the use of the Estonian language — including through prescription of the Estonian language as the language of Parliament and public administration in general. I am fully committed to supporting the Republic of Estonia in this objective.

Yours respectfully,

Max van der Stoel,
OSCE High Commissioner on National Minorities

* * *

Kadriorg, January 12, 1999

Dear High Commissioner,

Thank you for your letter of December 19, 1999. As has been true so often before, we in Estonia appreciate the attention you have devoted to the development of our legal system. And as you also know, our government has worked very hard to make all 29 of the changes in the Estonian legislation that you earlier indicated we needed to make in order to be in full compliance with European norms.

Of the many points in your letter concerning the amendments to the Estonian electoral law, which I promulgated on December 31, 1999, I would like to comment three:

First, you note that 'there should be no mediation of the will of the people, i.e. they should be essentially free to decide among themselves who they would wish to elect'. I completely agree and believe the actions of the Estonian parliament in the past and with these amendments fully conform with the wishes of the Estonian electorate.

In fact, these amendments do not create any impediment to anyone wishing to run for office, as they do not impose any preliminary control of a candidate's qualifications. Rather, these amendments constitute a necessary safeguard for elected persons. As you, I am sure, well know, a general requirement for elected officials to know Estonian language has existed long before the present amendments were adopted. The present amendments should ensure that this requirement will not be abused and will provide proper recourse to courts for elected officials who believe that their rights have not been respected.

Second, you suggest that 'within the scope of its sovereignty' Estonia has the means necessary 'to protect, promote and develop the use of the Estonian language'. I am confident that we do but only if we ensure that the elected officials will in fact speak Estonian. As you know, our historical experience has created a very different situation here than is the case in many other countries, and consequently, we believe that the steps we have taken are fully justified.

And third, you argue that the amendments in question do not conform to the Estonian Constitution, which as you correctly point out, stipulates that Estonian legislation must be in conformity with the international treaties to which Estonia is a signatory. However, the Estonian Supreme Court has in fact stated that Articles 6, 51 (1), 52 (1), and 55 of the Constitution do justify enactment of requirements of knowledge of the Estonian language for candidates to Parliament or to local assemblies. Article 6 of the Constitution, as you will recall, states that the Estonian language is the state language of Estonia.

Dear High Commissioner,

As you yourself well know, due process is guaranteed in Estonia. Thus, should any one individual believe that his or her rights have been infringed upon by these amendments, he or she will, of course, have recourse to all court instances of the Republic of Estonia. More importantly, individuals' rights are protected also by the provisions of the European Convention on Human Rights, which are applicable in this case. Therefore, a decision made by the Estonian courts can ultimately be contested in the European Court of Human Rights.

Through this transparent and fair mechanism all questions related to the conformity of the recent amendments with the international obligations of Estonia can find an answer, while avoiding any premature debates on this issue of legal matter.

Finally, I would like to recall that here is widespread agreement both in Estonia and in the international community that the legislative framework of integration is nearly complete. I believe you will agree with me on this matter. It is time now to concentrate all our efforts on the practical aspects of integration, to keep the process on track and to avoid false signals.

Sincerely Yours,

Lennart Meri

COUNCIL OF THE BALTIC SEA STATES

PROTECTION OF RIGHTS OF PERSONS BELONGING TO MINORITIES IN THE BALTIC SEA STATES

Ole Espersen[*] and Hanne Fugl[**]

The profound political upheavals in the Baltic Sea area in 1989-91 put the question of human rights and the protection of minority rights high on the European and Baltic agenda. The new political reality also made it not only possible but also necessary to change the structures of co-operation in the region. The demands for change were many and originated not only within inter-regional co-operation but were also seen from a broader European perspective.

It was in this political context that the Council of the Baltic Sea States (CBSS) was established in 1992. The Council in 1994 decided to appoint a Commissioner who was charged with promoting democratic development and the protection of human rights, including the rights of persons belonging to minorities.

1. NEW CONDITIONS FOR EUROPEAN CO-OPERATION

During the 1990s, existing organisations and mechanisms for international co-operation experienced a dramatic expansion of activities and renewed challenges, unknown for several decades.

The Council of Europe was first to feel the demands from the emergence of the new European States. The organisation witnessed a rapid increase of membership and consequently an increasing responsibility for the protection of human rights and support to new member countries in establishing democratic institutions and to democratise those already in existence. Special focus was also drawn to the particular problems of persons belonging to minorities.

The OSCE experienced a similar development. Membership was quickly expanded as was the organisation's task of monitoring human rights and finding responses to the many national and ethnic conflicts following the disintegration of the Soviet Union. Steps had already been taken to renew the organisation by

---

[*] Commissioner of the Council of the Baltic Sea States on Democratic Institutions and Human Rights, including the Rights of Persons belonging to Minorities.
[**] Assistant to the Commissioner of the Council of the Baltic Sea States.

S. Trifunovska (Ed.), Minority Rights in Europe: European Minorities and Languages
© 2000, T.M.C. Asser Press, The Hague, The Netherlands

means of three meetings on the human dimension in Paris, Copenhagen and Moscow in the years 1989-91 and the establishment of the Office of Democratic Institutions and Human Rights (ODIHR) in Warsaw.

The European Union also reacted to the persistent demands from the new democracies for trade, association and membership. Negotiations on accession to the European Union have started with a number of Central and Eastern European States.

2. SUB-REGIONAL CO-OPERATION

The profound changes in the European political picture and the resulting strain on existing institutions has inspired the development of sub-regional structures of co-operation. In particular within the OSCE, efforts to diversify co-operation have been pronounced. From the OSCE summit meeting in Prague in December 1994 and from the implementing meeting of the Human Dimension in Warsaw in October 1995 came clear calls for promoting sub-regional organisations of co-operation. Among such organisations one could mention the Council of the Baltic Sea States, the Barents/Euro-Arctic Council, the Central European Initiative and the Black Sea Economic Co-operation.

3. THE COUNCIL OF THE BALTIC SEA STATES (CBSS)

The CBSS was formed in March 1992 in Copenhagen at a conference of Ministers for Foreign Affairs. The CBSS consists of the following members: Denmark, Estonia, Finland, Germany, Iceland, Latvia, Lithuania, Norway, Poland, Russia, Sweden and the European Commission. The meeting of the Ministers for Foreign Affairs drew up the so-called Copenhagen Declaration of 5 March 1992 containing the objectives and mandate of the Council. The CBSS aims to strengthen existing co-operation between the Baltic Sea States and to reinforce co-operation and co-ordination on such central issues as democratic stability, development of infrastructure, trade and economy, protection of the environment and other issues of vital importance to the Baltic Sea States.

The objectives of the CBSS build directly on the principles of the Human Dimension of the OSCE in recognising that stability and democracy in the region presupposes the protection of the security, freedom and dignity of the individual.

The Council meets annually at the level of Ministers for Foreign Affairs, and takes all substantial decisions by consensus. In between meetings of the Council, business is conducted by a Committee of Senior Officials (CSO) consisting of high-ranking officials from the Foreign Ministries of the member States. The CBSS established a permanent secretariat in Stockholm in October 1998. The Council has established three working groups: Assistance to Democratic

Institutions, Nuclear Safety and Economic Co-operation. Since the establishment of the CBSS the heads of State have met at two summits. The first one was held in Visby, Sweden on 3-4 May 1996 and the second in Riga, Latvia on 22-23 January 1998.

4. THE COMMISSIONER

Already during the founding meeting in March 1992, the Council discussed the possibility of appointing a Commissioner for Human Rights. After thorough debate, the Council at its meeting in Tallinn in 1994 decided to establish a post for an initial 3-year period as Commissioner of the Council of the Baltic Sea States on Democratic Institutions and Human Rights, including the Rights of Persons belonging to Minorities. This somewhat unwieldy title was the result of a compromise between those States which wanted to include the collective rights of minorities in the purview of the Commissioner, and those who resisted this idea, pointing to existing institutions in the OSCE. The Council laid down the mandate of the Commissioner and appointed Professor Ole Espersen, from Denmark, as the first Commissioner. Denmark has accepted to the host the institution with offices in Copenhagen. The Office of the Commissioner is financed partly through contributions from member States and partly by the Danish Government as host country. The Council decided in 1997 to prolong the mandate of the Commissioner until 1 October 2000.

5. THE MANDATE

The mandate charges the Commissioner with promoting democratic development and the protection of human rights, including the rights of persons belonging to minorities, in member States and thereby to promote the implementation of recognised international human rights standards.

The mandate makes specific reference to principles and rules in the UN World Declaration of Human Rights, standards of the Council of Europe, including the Helsinki Final Act, the Paris Charter for a new Europe, the Helsinki Document of 1992, the Copenhagen Document of 1993 and other relevant documents of the OSCE and the CBSS. However, the mandate does not contain any restrictions as to what principles and standards may be invoked by the Commissioner. Thus, the Commissioner is not limited in his activities to instruments which are legally binding on the member States.

While the Commissioner on the one hand enjoys considerable discretion in his application of standards and instruments of international law, he is, on the other hand, not able to make decisions which are binding on member

States. The recommendations of the Commissioner are advisory and their implementation depends on national governments and parliaments. The mandate has equipped the Commissioner with the possibility of referring a matter to the Council at his own discretion, if he believes that it warrants the attention and possibly the action of the Council as such.

6. CO-OPERATION WITH OTHER INSTITUTIONS

The mandate stipulates that the Commissioner co-operates with and avoids unnecessary duplication of activities with other international organisations, including the Council of Europe, the OSCE and the UN system. Of particular importance to the work of the Commissioner are the Human Rights organs within the Council of Europe, the OSCE's Office for Democratic Institutions and Human Rights (ODIHR) and the OSCE High Commissioner on National Minorities. The Commissioner has also co-operated with the European Centre for Minority Issues (ECMI) in Flensburg, Germany. The Commissioner is a member of the Advisory Council of the ECMI. The Commissioner is furthermore a boardmember of the European Monitoring Centre on Racism and Xenophobia.

Unlike, for example, the Council of Europe, the Commissioner's duties do not include a systematic monitoring of the implementation of human rights instruments, and member States have not assumed any obligation of periodic reporting to the Commissioner as they have otherwise done in the case of various international conventions. In this area the Commissioner therefore co-operates with the Council of Europe and the UN-system, in particular with respect to exchange of information.

Another important area mentioned in the mandate is the obligation of the Commissioner to co-operate with institutions for the protection of human rights in the member States, including ombudsmen, administrative entities, NGOs and private organisations, like human rights institutions and centres.

7. A REGIONAL OMBUDSMAN

The Commissioner's area of work includes three main functions: (1) Studying and reporting on matters covered by the mandate and making recommendations to the member States of the CBSS; (2) Providing expert opinion on human rights in member States; (3) Receiving communications from individuals, groups or organisations based on which the Commissioner may decide to make recommendations to governments.

The Commissioner may receive and treat individual complaints within the framework of his mandate. The treatment of complaints is confidential and the Commissioner is free to choose if and how he wishes to proceed with a case.

The Commissioner will, as a general rule, desist from taking any steps in a case as long as it is subject to court proceedings or pending before any other national instance of appeal.

The right of individuals to address communications to the Commissioner means, in effect, that the Commissioner functions as a kind of regional ombudsman, and that based on his treatment of complaints he may submit recommendations to member States in the same manner as national ombudsmen would normally do. The number of individual complaints has markedly increased over time.

8. SURVEYS AND EXPERT OPINIONS

The Commissioner initiates surveys on human rights issues in member States in such a way that all member States are normally included. The surveys, including recommendations, are submitted to the Council of the Baltic Sea States and the Commissioner may discuss the implementation of his recommendations with member States. To date, 13 surveys have been completed, while 3 more are pending. Three of the completed surveys were published in 1998.

In the field of minority issues, four surveys should namely be mentioned. The latest is the survey on 'Rights of Non-citizens, Residing Legally in the Member States of the CBSS - Part II: Freedom of Association, Right of Access to Civil Service and other Special Posts or Work' which was made public in April 1998. The survey is a follow-up to the survey entitled 'Rights of Non-citizens, Residing Legally in the Members States of the CBSS. Part I, Voting Rights and The Right to Stand for Public Office', completed in February 1996.

Part II from 1998 examines the legal position of non-citizens residing legally in a member State with respect to formation of organisations, participation in political organisations and employment in the civil service and in other special posts.

In the survey an overview of the legal situation in member States is presented and some considerations regarding the elimination of possible discrimination between citizens and non-citizens in the areas of membership and founding of associations and political organisations are put forward.

The survey comprises several recommendations. It recommends that all member States, as a general rule, should secure the right to freedom of association to everyone – citizens as well as non-citizens.

Concerning the participation of non-citizens in political organisations those member States of the CBSS who have not yet done so are recommended to sign and ratify the Council of Europe Convention on the Participation of Foreigners in Public Life at Local Level.

It is also recommended that all member States allow non-citizens to take part in political organisations under the same conditions as citizens. The Commissioner underlines that in his opinion it is not consistent with the contemporary perception of human rights in a democracy to restrict the right of resident non-citizens to form and take part in political associations.

Member States which as a general rule reserve posts as civil servants and other posts in the civil service for citizens only, are recommended to consider whether it is in all cases necessary and in the interest of the State to make such reservations.

Furthermore, it is recommended that member States review their legislation in order to identify existing obstacles for non-citizens to take up gainful employment and to reappraise the justification of the rules in the light of international standards and policies for eliminating discrimination and promoting the integration of non-citizens into society.

Two other surveys also deal with the protection of the rights of minorities:

1. Some problems related to the Extent of the Right to Freedom of Expression (Racism, etc.), February 1996.
2. Criteria and Procedures for Obtaining Citizenship in the CBSS Member States, April 1996.

The Commissioner follows up on the implementation of all surveys on a regular basis. This is mostly done during official visits to the CBSS member countries and through regular correspondence with relevant authorities.

The above description shows that the mandate of the Commissioner does not limit the scope of activities to receiving communications from individuals, groups or organisations, but also calls for taking initiatives related to human rights problems, for example in surveys. Some of these initiatives touch in part or in whole on problems facing groups of individuals or minorities.

Besides the continuous efforts to inform other relevant actors on the 'minority scene' about pertinent activities, the Commissioner's newsletter 'Mare Balticum' should be mentioned. It was launched in 1996 and deals in concise form with important events and questions relating to democratic institutions and human rights protection in member States and makes the major activities of the Commissioner known. All ten issues of 'Mare Balticum' have in one way or another dealt with the issue of the protection of minority rights.

9. COUNCIL OF EUROPE FRAMEWORK CONVENTION FOR THE PROTECTION OF NATIONAL MINORITIES

The Commissioner in 1998 recommended that a conference on the implementation of the Council of Europe Framework Convention for the Protection of National Minorities should be held. This conference was organised by the ECMI and took place on 14 June 1998 in Flensburg. The aim of the conference was to discuss the political, legal and financial aspects of implementation.

The Commissioner has made a special effort to promote one of the recommendations from the conference: 'All countries of Europe should ratify or accede to the Framework Convention for the Protection of National Minorities. The States Parties should refrain from reservations and interpretative declarations. In this context it should be recalled that "the existence of minorities is a question of fact, not of law"'.

In June 1997, the Commissioner sent letters to all CBSS Ministers for Foreign Affairs underlining the importance of the Framework Convention, as it is the first legally binding multilateral instrument devoted to the protection of national minorities. The letter also emphasised how important it is that States should refrain from making any reservation or declaration to the Framework Convention which might weaken or limit the scope of the instrument which in itself contains rather vaguely defined objectives and principles.

At the Council of Europe seminar, 'From Paper to Practice', held in Strasbourg on 28 October 1998 an assistant to the Commissioner made a reference to one of the other recommendations of the Flensburg Conference; that it would be desirable if the Council of Europe prepared a handbook on the Framework Convention. It was with great satisfaction that the Commissioner noted that the Council intends to publish two handbooks on this issue and that one of them will focus on the involvement of NGOs in the implementation process.

10. THE COMMISSIONER'S ACTIVITIES IN THE FIELD OF LANGUAGE ISSUES

In Estonia the Commissioner has had contacts with the government on the amendments to the Law on Language passed by the Estonian Parliament in November 1997. The amendments were closely related to the Local Government Council Election Act. Accordingly, the Government was authorised to establish the required level of language proficiency for, *inter alia*, Members of Parliament, members of town councils, public service employees, employees of institutions, business associations, non-profit organisations or foundations and self-employed entrepreneurs. The law authorised the Government to draw up regulations for the fulfilment of the language proficiency requirements.

Although the application of the legal provisions had yet to be determined, the Commissioner was concerned that the law left wide discretionary powers in the hands of the Government on issues involving important questions of freedom of expression and assembly affecting very large groups in society. The Commissioner consequently communicated these concerns to the President of the Republic of Estonia.

The President returned the law to Parliament for reconsideration on the grounds that it gave the Executive disproportionally extensive powers, but the law was nevertheless re-adopted by Parliament without amendment. The

President subsequently brought the Law before the Supreme Court contesting its constitutionality. On 5 February 1998 the Court ruled in favour of the President.

Amendments to the Riigikogu Election Act, the Local Government Council Election Act and the Language Act, were passed on 15 December 1998.

In early 1999 the Commissioner voiced his concern that the adopted amendments seemed to be a pre-electoral selection of candidates which restricts both a citizen's right to stand for office and the right of the electorate to vote for whomever they please. This poses a problem, *inter alia*, vis-à-vis the International Covenant on Civil and Political Rights, Article 25, which constitutes a binding reference to non-discrimination in the citizens' exercise of their political rights. Another important aspect, from the point of view of the principle of the rule of law, concerns the question of how it is envisaged that these new language requirements will be enforced.

In relation to Latvia the Commissioner has presented his views on the Draft on the State Language Law on several occasions during 1998.

In his contacts with the Latvian Parliament (the Saeima) and the Ministry of Foreign Affairs the Commissioner has voiced concern, primarily with reference to the freedom of expression. He has also pointed at the importance of honouring the general principles of the rule of law with regard to the practical understanding and implementation of a law.

The handling of the Draft on the Law on the State Language could not be concluded by the 6th Saeima. Consequently, the Draft was introduced to the 7th Saiema after the national elections in early October, 1998.

At the end of 1999 the final draft law was adopted. It is to a large extent a 'framework law' and several governmental decrees have been issued to regulate the use of languages.

The Commissioner has leant his support to the recommendations of the OSCE High Commissioner on National Minorities, concerning the language issue in both Latvia and Estonia. The conclusions of the High Commissioner have in general been that the laws essentially are in conformity with international obligations and he expresses the hope that the administration will respect these obligations.

11. CONCLUSION – PROTECTION OF RIGHTS OF MINORITIES AND HUMAN RIGHTS IN THE BALTIC SEA AREA

It is obvious that there are significant differences between the countries in the CBSS, both in terms of past history, population, minority groups, the degree of homogeneity of languages, governance, parliamentary traditions and legislation. The experience of each country in establishing democratic institutions and protecting human rights are often very different, just as practical approaches in this respect vary considerably. This is to a high degree the case for minority issues.

Against this background it can hardly be avoided that a considerable part of the Commissioner's activities have been devoted to the situation in the Baltic States, Russia and to some extent in Poland.

It would be a misconception, however, to believe that there are no problems in, for example, the Nordic countries and that no more could be done to fortify the protection of human rights and to raise their visibility. On several occasions the Commissioner has raised questions of human rights with precisely these countries, e.g. with respect to citizenship legislation, asylum procedures and visa regulations. All issues highly relevant for the 'new' minorities of migrants, who are usually not accepted as minorities in the legal sense of the word .

The Commissioner has continuously placed particular emphasis on the fact that the issues raised are of concern to all or at least several member States. This has also been done by stressing the CBSS as a co-operative structure where experience, legislation and measures may serve as points of mutual consideration and inspiration.

During the past few years significant progress has been made concerning minority and human rights in the Baltic Sea area. This is perhaps best underlined by the fact that serious conflicts have happily been avoided, although tensions and adversities among groups from different ethnic backgrounds continue to exist. Legislation and administrative practice is gradually removing the insecure position of citizens and residents - although the process in the eyes of many is too slow. Legislation has been adopted on the establishment of democratic institutions, which are now operative in almost all countries in the form of ombudsmen, constitutional courts, advisory councils and national human rights institutions. Hard work has been done in Parliaments and Governments adapting national legislation to the requirements of international conventions.

The integration of all CBSS member States into the human rights system of the Council of Europe is now virtually complete, and this will make the mechanisms for the protection of human rights more effective. Concurrently, there is a process of establishing democratic institutions and national mechanisms for complaints. There has been a considerable growth of NGOs within all areas of civil society, and many of these are already part of the social and political life of their countries and have formed international networks.

Many problems obviously remain unsolved, and it is worth underlining that an effective protection of the rights of minorities is hardly a situation which any country will obtain once and for all. It is a dynamic process which at all times demands vigilance and adaptation to development. Even though it can be difficult in a period of economic and political transition, further actions still need to be taken in the CBSS member countries. One of them is to ratify and implement the Framework Convention for the Protection of National Minorities. Thus it is not least within the field of minority rights that we can expect to see changes take place in the years to come in the Baltic Sea area.

CENTRAL EUROPEAN INITIATIVE

ACTIVITIES OF THE CENTRAL EUROPEAN INITIATIVE IN THE FIELD OF MINORITIES

Snežana Trifunovska[*]

The Central European Initiative (CEI) is a relatively recent, post-Cold War forum for discussion, consultation and co-operation among a number of countries in Central and Eastern Europe. It started its activities in 1989 and aims to strengthen the process of integration in Europe, to promote co-operation between its member States and to support those participating States which are EU candidates in their approach to the EU. As of April 1997 there were 16 countries participating in CEI. These are: Albania, Austria, Belarus, Bosnia and Herzegovina, Bulgaria, Croatia, the Czech Republic, Hungary, Italy, Macedonia, Moldova, Poland, Romania, the Slovak Republic, Slovenia and Ukraine.

CEI has no strict institutional structure but works in a flexible manner and is guided in its work by the 'Guidelines for Activities and Rules of Procedure of the Central European Initiative' (adopted in Warsaw on 7 October 1995).

Annual meetings are held on the level of the Heads of Government and also on the level of Ministers for Foreign Affairs. There is also a Committee of National Coordinators which holds regular meetings. In addition, there are special meetings of sectoral ministers as well.

Members of Parliament of both the member States and Associated countries meet within the framework of the CEI Parliamentary Conference and Committee.

As a supporting institutional structure there is the Secretariat for CEI projects at the European Bank for Reconstruction and Development (EBRD) in London, as well as the CEI Centre for Information and Documentation in Trieste.

Substantial work is on a regular basis done by a number of Working Groups established for different fields of activities like: (1) agriculture; (2) civil protection; (3) combating organized crime; (4) culture and education; (5) energy with a subgroup on environment and transport; (6) human dimension; (7) human resource development and training; (8) migration (9) minorities; (10) reconstruction and rehabilitation of Bosnia and Herzegovina and Croatia; (11) science and technology; (12) small and medium-sized enterprises; (13) tourism;

---

[*] Senior University Lecturer of the Law Faculty of Nijmegen, The Netherlands.

S. Trifunovska (Ed.), Minority Rights in Europe: European Minorities and Languages
© 2000, T.M.C. Asser Press, The Hague, The Netherlands

(14) transport; and (15) youth affairs. Working groups meet at the senior official or ministerial level.

All CEI structures work in closed sessions and a more extensive and concrete information is not available to wider public.

1. ACTIVITIES IN THE FIELD OF MINORITIES

The issue of minorities was included in the work of the CEI in order to give political cooperation a higher profile within the CEI. It was expected that a positive solution to the problem of national minorities at the regional level could offer a model to be applied within a greater European framework.[1]

The Working Group on the Protection of Minorities was created in 1990 and presents a diplomatic conference meeting twice a year in different places and upon the invitation of a participating State. It works in closed sessions in which the participants consult and exchange views and experiences.

Although there is no monitoring and/or supervisory mechanism, the Working Group follows up the implementation of the Instrument for the Protection of Minority Rights which was approved by the Ministers for Foreign Affairs of the CEI countries at their meeting in Turin, on 18-19 November 1994. This Instrument presents a major achievement by the Working Group.

In addition, the CEI Working Group on Minorities organizes a number of discussion forums. One of the more recent activities was a Symposium held in Gorizia on 28 November 1998, on the status of minorities in CEI member States.[2] During the Symposium concrete experiences and results achieved in inter-ethnic relations in the regions such as South Tyrol and Transilvania, were presented. Within the framework of the established cooperation, representatives of the Council of Europe dealing with the issues of minorities were also present at the Symposium.

The last regular meeting of the Working Group was held in Geneva, in May 2000,[3] when at the same time a joint meeting was organized with the Working Group on Minorities of the UN Sub-Commission for the Promotion and Protection of Human Rights. On that occasion special attention was paid to the present status and future application of the CEI Instrument for the Protection of Minority Rights.

One of the more significant endeavours of the Working Group relates to the workings of the Stability Pact for South Eastern Europe, for which the Working Group is preparing a contribution with respect to the situation of the Roma population; the effective participation of minorities; and transfrontier contacts.

---

[1] http://www.ceinet.org/minority.html

[2] The Symposium was organized in cooperation with the Institute of International Sociology of Gorizia (ISIG), and with the Italian Ministry of Foreign Affairs.

[3] The next meeting is supposed to take place in Budapest in the autumn of 2000.

The implementation report of the Working Group will be based on the contributions provided by the CEI member States.

Since 1998 there has been a joint Hungarian-Romanian co-chairmanship of the Working Group.

2. A BRIEF SURVEY OF THE CEI INSTRUMENT FOR THE PROTECTION OF MINORITY RIGHTS

The Instrument consists of 27 articles dealing with minority rights and guarantees which the States signatories of the Instrument should provide to their citizens who belong to national minorities. It contains a definition of a 'national minority' in Article 1 paragraph 1. The emphasis in the definition is placed on three elements, as follows:

- the numerical inferiority of the minority group in relation to the rest of the population of a State;
- the existence of ethnic, religious or linguistic characteristic; and
- the existence of the will to safeguard the group's culture, traditions, religion or language.

It is a free choice of individuals to belong to a national minority (Article 2). However, States will recognize the existence of national minorities as such and will consider them to be integral part of the society in which they live (Article 1 paragraph 1).

States should provide guarantees that minorities shall exercise fully and effectively their human rights and fundamental freedoms, individually or in common with others to be guaranteed by States, as well as the right of persons belonging to minorities to preserve their identity and to maintain their culture (Articles 3 and 4). In accordance with this, States should refrain from any policies aimed at assimilation of persons belonging to minorities against their will, and have a duty to protect these persons against such acts or activities and will take effective measures to provide for protection against acts of and/or incitement of violence against persons or groups which is based on national, racial, ethnic or religious discrimination, hostility or hatred, including anti-Semitism (Articles 6 and 8).

The Instrument deals with the issue of minority languages in Articles 10-15 and 18-19. Persons belonging to a national minority have the right to use their language freely, in private and public, orally and in writing. In dealings with the public authorities the own language will be used in the areas in which the number of persons belonging to a national minority reaches a significant level and wherever possible. There is also a corresponding provision according to which in areas populated with a majority population belonging to a minority group, States will promote the knowledge of the minority language among officials of the local and decentralised State administrative offices.

In the field of education, the Instrument provides for the right of persons belonging to a national minority to learn their own language and receive education in that language. It will be the task of the State to establish the appropriate types and levels of education in minority languages depending on the size and concentration of a minority group in a certain area. Similarly, States guarantee the right of persons belonging to a national minority to avail themselves of the media in their own language.

In exercising religious freedoms, persons belonging to a minority group may use their own language in worshiping, teaching, religious practice and observance.

The Instrument also deals with the right to use the surname and the first name in the mother tongue of the persons belonging to a minority group which includes the right to official acceptance and registration of such names and surnames.

Finally, in areas where there is a significant number of persons belonging to a national minority, States may allow the display of bilingual or plurilingual local names, street names and other topographical signs. Privately signs can be displayed, as well as inscriptions or other similar information of a private nature and should not be subject to any restrictions other than those generally applied in the field.

The CEI Instrument for the Protection of Minority Rights has been signed by Austria, Bosnia and Herzegovina, Croatia, Italy, Hungary, Macedonia and Poland. The Government of the Republic of Slovenia had announced that the signature of the document would take place in May, 1996.[4]

As pointed out above, the CEI Instrument is a document of major significance for the protection of minorities in the CEI geographic area. It is complementary to the other international, OSCE and the Council of Europe documents relevant for the protection of minorities and as such it strengthens the endeavours of the CEI States in the field of minority protection within their territory and more broadly in the region.

---

[4] No available information on the date of signature of the States signatories.

DOCUMENTS

CEI INSTRUMENT FOR THE PROTECTION OF MINORITY RIGHTS

Turin, 19 November 1994

The Member States of the Central European Initiative signatory hereto,

- recognising that the questions relating to national minorities can only be resolved satisfactorily in a truly democratic political framework which is based on the rule of law and guarantees full respect for human rights and fundamental freedoms, equal rights and status for all citizens,
- reaffirming that the protection of national minorities concerns only citizens of the respective state, who will enjoy the same rights and have the same duties of citizenship as the rest of the population,
- convinced that national minorities form an integral part of the society of the States in which they live and that they are a factor of enrichment of each respective State and society,
- bearing in mind that a very effective remedy to achieve stability in the region are good relations between neighbours, and being conscious of the need to avoid any encouragement of separatist tendencies of national minorities in the region,
- confirming that issues concerning the rights of persons belonging to national minorities are matters of legitimate international concern and consequently do not constitute exclusively an internal affair of the respective State,
- considering that respect for the rights of persons belonging to national minorities, as part of universally recognised human rights, is an essential factor for peace, justice, stability and democracy in the States,
- convinced that the international protection of the rights of persons belonging to national minorities, as enshrined in the present Instrument, does not permit any activity, which is contrary to the fundamental principles of international law and in particular of sovereignty, territorial integrity and political independence of States,
- recognising the particular importance of increasing constructive co-operation among themselves on questions relating to national minorities, and that such co-operation seeks to promote mutual understanding and confidence, friendly and good-neighbourly relations, international peace, security and justice,
- expressing their condemnation of aggressive nationalism, racial and ethnic hatred, anti-Semitism, xenophobia and discrimination against any person or group and of persecution on religious and ideological grounds

have agreed as follows:

Article 1
States recognise the existence of national minorities as such, considering them integral parts of the society in which they live and guarantee the appropriate conditions for the promotion of their identity.

For the purpose of this Instrument the term "national minority" shall mean a group that is smaller in number than the rest of the population of a State, whose members being nationals of that State, have ethnical, religious or linguistic features different from those of the rest of the population, and are guided by the will to safeguard their culture, traditions, religion or language.

Article 2
To belong to a national minority is a matter of free individual choice and no disadvantage shall arise from the exercise or non-exercise of such a choice.

Article 3
States recognise that persons belonging to national minorities have the right to exercise fully and effectively their human rights and fundamental freedoms, individually or in common with others, without any discrimination and in full equality before the law. Those persons shall be able to enjoy the rights foreseen by the present Instrument individually or in common with others and to benefit from the measures ensuring those rights.

Article 4
States guarantee the right of persons belonging to national minorities to express, preserve and develop their ethnic, cultural, linguistic or religious identity and to maintain and develop their culture in all its aspects.

Article 5
The adoption of special measures in favour of persons belonging to national minorities aimed at promoting equality between them and the rest of the population or at taking due account of their specific conditions shall not be considered as an act of discrimination.

Article 6
States shall take effective measures to provide protection against any acts that constitute incitement to violence against persons or groups based on national, racial, ethnic or religious discrimination, hostility or hatred, including anti- Semitism;

Article 7
States recognise the particular problems of Roma (Gypsies). They undertake to adopt all the legal administrative or educational measures as foreseen in the present Instrument in order to preserve and to develop the identity of Roma, to facilitate by specific measures the social integration of persons belonging to Roma (Gypsies) and to eliminate all forms of intolerance against such persons.

Article 8
Without prejudice to democratic principles, States, taking measures in pursuance of their general integration policy, shall refrain from pursuing or encouraging policies aimed at the assimilation of persons belonging to national minorities against their will and shall protect these persons against any action aimed at such assimilation.

Article 9
In case of modification of administrative, judicial or electoral subdivisions States should take into account that such modifications, among other criteria, will respect the existing rights of the persons belonging to national minorities and the exercise of those rights. In any case, they should consult, according to national legislation, with the populations directly affected before adopting any modification in the matter.

Article 10
Any person belonging to a national minority shall have the right to use his or her language freely, in public as well as in private, orally and in writing.

Article 11
Any person belonging to a national minority shall have the right to use his or her surname and first names in his or her language and the right to official acceptance and registration of such surname and names.

Article 12
Whenever in an area the number of persons belonging to a national minority reaches, according to the latest census or other, methods of ascertaining its consistency, a significant level, those persons shall have the right, wherever possible, to use, in conformity with applicable national legislation, their own language in oral and in written for, in their contacts with the public authorities of the said area. These authorities may reply as far as possible, in the same language.

Article 13
In conformity with their national legislation States may allow, where necessary through bilateral agreements with other interested States, in particular with neighbouring States, the display of bilingual or pluri-lingual local names, street names and other topographical indications in areas where the number of persons belonging to a national minority reaches, according to the latest census or other methods of ascertaining its consistency, a significant level. The display of signs, inscriptions or other similar information of private nature also in the minority language should not be subject to specific restrictions, other than those generally applied in this field.

Article 14
Any person belonging to a national minority, exercising religious freedom, shall have the right to use his or her own language in worship, teaching, religious practice or observance.

Article 15
Whenever the number of persons belonging to a national minority reaches, according to the latest census or other methods of ascertaining its consistency, the majority of the population in an area, States will promote the knowledge of the minority language among officers of the local and decentralised State administrative offices. Endeavours should be made to recruit, if possible, officers, who, in addition to the knowledge of the official language, have sufficient knowledge of the minority language.

Article 16
States recognise the right of persons belonging to national minorities to establish and maintain their own cultural and religious institutions, organisations or associations, which are entitled to seek voluntary financial and other contributions as well as public assistance, in conformity with national legislation.

Article 17
States recognise the right of persons belonging to national minorities to establish and maintain their own private pre-schools, schools and educational establishments and possibly obtain their recognition in conformity with the relevant national legislation. Such establishments may seek public financing or other contributions.

Article 18
Notwithstanding the need to learn the official language of the State concerned, every person belonging to a national minority shall have the right to learn his or her own language and receive an education in his or her own language. The States shall endeavour to ensure the appropriate types and levels of public education in conformity with national legislation, whenever in an area the number of persons belonging to a national minority, according to the latest census or other methods of ascertaining its consistency, is at a significant level. In the context of the teaching of history and culture in such public educational establishments, adequate teaching of history and culture of the national minorities should be ensured.

Article 19
States guarantee the right of persons belonging to a national minority to avail themselves of the media in their own language, in conformity with relevant State regulations and with possible financial assistance. In case of TV and radio in public ownership, the States will assure, whenever appropriate and possible, that persons belonging to national minorities have the right of free access to such media including the production of such programmes in their own language.

Article 20
States shall guarantee the right of persons belonging to national minorities to participate without discrimination in the political, economic, social and cultural life of the society of the State of which they are citizens and shall promote the conditions for exercising those rights.

Article 21
States shall allow persons belonging to a national minority to establish political parties.

Article 22
In accordance with the policies of the States concerned, States will respect the right of persons belonging to national minorities to effective participation in public affairs, in particular in the decision-making process on matters affecting them. Therefore, States note the efforts undertaken to protect and create conditions for the promotion of the ethnic, cultural, linguistic and religious identity of certain national minorities by adopting appropriate measures corresponding to the specific circumstances of such minorities as foreseen in the CSCE documents.

Article 23
Every person belonging to a national minority, while duly respecting the territorial integrity of the State, shall have the right to have free and unimpeded contacts with the citizens of another country with whom this minority shares ethnic, religious or linguistic features or a cultural identity. States shall not unduly restrict the free exercise of those rights. Furthermore, States will encourage transfrontier arrangements at national, regional and local levels.

Article 24
Any person belonging to a national minority shall have an effective remedy before a national judicial authority against any violation of rights set forth in the present Instrument, provided that those rights are enacted in national legislation.

Article 25
In any area where those who belong to a national minority represent the majority of the population, States shall take the necessary measures to ensure that those who do not belong to this minority shall not suffer from any disadvantage, including such that may result from the implementation of the measures of protection foreseen by the present Instrument.

Article 26
None of these commitments shall be interpreted as implying any right to engage in any activity in contravention of the fundamental principles of international law and, in particular, of the sovereign equality, territorial integrity and political independence of States. Nothing in the present Instrument shall affect the duties related to persons belonging to national minorities as citizens of the States concerned.

Persons belonging to national minorities will also respect, in the exercise of their rights, the rights of others, including those of persons belonging to the majority population of the respective State or to other national minorities.

Article 27

This Instrument shall not prejudice the provisions of domestic law or any international agreement which provide greater protection for national minorities or persons belonging to them.

Done in one copy at Turin this 19th day of November 1994 in the English language.

Part Three

National Activities and Documents

INTRODUCTORY REMARKS

States are free to adopt national legislation which is most suitable for their particular minority situation. In this respect factors such as the size of the minority group(s), their ethnic, linguistic, religious and/or cultural characteristics, the historical background which brought about their formation (migration movements, changes of boundaries, etc.), the political and economic strength and the capacity of the respective State to provide for the necessary rights and to meet the needs of minorities, as well as the variety of claims which minorities might have, should be taken into consideration. As a result of the impact which the above-mentioned factors have on minority legislation, there appear to be, sometimes substantial, differences in the level and form of the protection of different minority groups within a country, as well as differences between various countries.[1] This is the rule from which no exception can be made. So, what can be observed is, on the one hand, different minority situations in each of the European, i.e. OSCE States, and, on the other, different situations with respect to the national minority legislation, i.e. documents and measures adopted by the States in which the respective minorities live. The 1999 Report on the Linguistic Rights of Persons belonging to National Minorities in the OSCE Area, prepared by the OSCE High Commissioner on National Minorities, confirms the complexity of the existing minority situations within the OSCE participating States and the (sometimes substantial) differences among them.

The existing variety and complexity of minority situations has been one of the major reasons for the inclusion of a separate chapter on national activities and documents of the OSCE participating States (excluding the USA and Canada) in this publication. The 1999 Report of the High Commissioner on National Minorities provides an analysis of the laws, policies and practices of the OSCE States with respect to minority languages aimed at revealing 'the range of existing practice among OSCE participating States'. However, as pointed out in Chapter II.4 of the Report 'it does not provide for an independent examination of the actual practices within the State, nor an evaluation of the specific context within which laws and policies have been adopted and are applied in each State'. By taking this into consideration, and intending to be complementary to the Report, Part Three of the Yearbook includes information, which is additional to the Report of the High Commissioner.

---

[1] This is what is called the 'sliding-scale' approach with respect to the linguistic rights of minorities, which is discussed in more detail in this publication by Fernand de Varennes.

S. Trifunovska (Ed.), *Minority Rights in Europe: European Minorities and Languages*
© 2000, T.M.C. Asser Institute, The Hague, The Netherlands

Information included

The primary intention of Part Three is to provide an overview of the current situation with respect to the legal obligations of the countries included relevant for the protection of minority languages, rather than a critical analysis. Accordingly, most of the attention has been devoted to the collection and reproduction of relevant legal documents/texts.

The survey on national legislation and documents is in most cases divided into three and sometimes into four sections:

(a) The section on the demographic situation includes information on the population composition and size of the main minority groups – notwithstanding their constitutional status – in the countries covered by the survey. It should serve as an indication with respect to demographic complexity and does not pretend to be absolutely precise as regards the figures included. As is well known, there are sometimes substantial discrepancies between the official information and that provided by other sources, such as experts, minority organizations, etc. Moreover, population composition and size is in a continuous process of change and it is therefore very difficult in practice to establish the exact situation. The same could also be said with respect to the information on the languages spoken officially or unofficially. In some cases it might be viewed as being misleading or incorrect; it is simply to be noted that this information has been reproduced from the sources indicated in this introduction.

(b) The section on international legal obligations includes a survey of the legal obligations of States with respect to a number of selected United Nations documents and relevant binding documents of the Council of Europe. From the human rights documents adopted under the auspices of the United Nations, only those major documents to which reference was made in the 1999 Report of the High Commissioner on National Minorities (section III (B)) have been included. This section also includes reference to relevant bilateral treaties, though sometimes, and in absence of more complete information, certain bilateral treaties are only indicated. It should be pointed out that the survey does not provide expressly for OSCE commitments, as all the States included are participating in the OSCE process (except the then suspended Federal Republic of Yugoslavia) and as such are bound by the OSCE documents.

(c) The section on national legislation consists mainly of excerpts from the legal (and political) documents, which are of major significance for minority languages:

- Firstly, it includes in all cases (when possible) the constitutional provisions referring to linguistic rights; not all the constitutions of the OSCE participating States contain provisions on languages. The UNESCO web site[2] provides a list of countries with and without such constitutional provision(s). In this respect, it should be pointed out that the current situation seems quite satisfactory as there are only a few OSCE participating States which contain no provisions on the use of languages in their constitutions,[3] among these being also those which have declared that they do not have any minorities on their territory; and
- Secondly, it includes laws and other documents, which are relevant for the use of languages in general, and of minority languages in particular. The intention has been to reproduce the texts of the relevant laws whenever possible, in order to enable readers to use the original legal texts instead of a description of the laws and regulations. When this has not been possible (mostly because of the unavailability of the texts) other sources indicating the legal documents have been used. The legislative documents included in this section have been reproduced without any grammatical changes having been made.

(d) Finally, in some cases there is a special chapter containing additional information concerning national laws and/or comments on developments, laws, practice, statistics, etc.

Sources used

For the preparation of Part Three of this publication information from various sources has been used. Information and direct assistance were provided by a number of Ministries of Foreign Affairs of the OSCE States. Though our gratitude has already been given in the Foreword to this volume, we would like once more to thank to Ministries of Foreign Affairs of the Republic of Croatia, the Czech Republic, Denmark, Finland, France, Georgia, Hungary, Iceland, Ireland, Kazakhstan, Latvia, Liechtenstein, Lithuania, Malta, Portugal, Romania, the Slovak Republic, Spain and Switzerland, as well as to the Ministry of Interior of the German Federal Republic. We are also grateful to the Ministries of Foreign Affairs of Liechtenstein, Iceland and Malta who informed us that there are no minorities in their territory in the sense of the Framework Convention for the Protection of National Minorities.

In addition to the above-mentioned information, in preparing Part Three the following sources were used:

---

[2] http://www.unesco.org/most/ln2.nat.htm

[3] These are: the Czech Republic, Denmark, Iceland, Latvia, The Netherlands, San Marino and the United Kingdom.

- Facts on National Minorities in the Republic of Macedonia, Ministry of Foreign Affairs of the Republic of Macedonia, April 1997
- Legislative Acts of the CIS and the Baltic States on Citizenship, Migration, and Related Matters, International Organization for Migration (IOM), Moscow & Helsinki (1996)
- Report No. J/3670 of the Government of the Republic of Hungary to the National Assembly on the situation of national and ethnic minorities living in the Republic of Hungary, Appendix I
- *World Directory of Minorities*, Edited by Minority Rights Group, Minority Rights Group International, 1997

Reports submitted (until September 2000) in accordance with Article 25 paragraph 1 of the Council of Europe's Framework Convention for the Protection of National Minorities:

- Croatia – received on 16 March 1999
- Cyprus – received on 1 March 1999
- Czech Republic – received on 1 April 1999
- Denmark – received on 6 May 1999
- Estonia – received on 22 December 1999
- Finland – received on 16 February 1999
- Germany – received on 24 February 2000
- Hungary – received on 21 May 1999
- Italy – received on 3 May 1999
- Liechtenstein – received on 3 March 1999
- Malta – received on 27 July 1999
- Moldova – received on 29 June 2000
- Romania – received on 24 June 1999
- Russian Federation – received on 8 March 2000
- San Marino – received on 4 May 1999
- Slovak Republic – received on 3 February 1999
- Ukraine – received on 2 November 1999
- United Kingdom – received on 26 July 1999

In the absence of State reports shadow reports for some of the countries were used, like, for example, for Albania (1999), Bosnia and Herzegovina (1999), Bulgaria (1999) and Macedonia (1999). These reports were in most cases prepared by the Helsinki Committees of the respective countries.

The periodic reports of States submitted under Article 9 of the International Convention on the Elimination of All Forms of Racial Discrimination to the Committee on the Elimination of Racial Discrimination:

- Czech Republic – CERD/C/372/Add.1, 14 April 2000
- Denmark – CERD/C/362/Add. 1, 12 July 1999
- Finland – CERD/C/363/Add.2, 16 May 2000
- Netherlands – CERD/C/362/Add.4, 6 July 1999
- Slovak Republic –CERD/C/328/Add.1, 14 December 1999
- Slovenia – CERD/C/352/Add.1, 2 May 2000
- Sweden – CERD/C/362/Add.5, 25 November 1999
- United Kingdom – CERD/C/338/Add.12, 25 April 2000
- Uzbekistan – CERD/C/327/Add.1, 9 May 2000

Internet sources:

http://www.unesco.org/most/htm
http://www.president.az/azerbaijan/const.htm
http://www.iom.ch/mgrationweb/legislat…azerbaijan
http://www.iom.ch/migrationweb/legisat…estonia/estonia
http://www.riga.lv/minelres/archive
http://www.meh.hu/nekh/Angol/report.htm
http://www.tol.cz/week.html
http://www.ecri.coe.fr/en/03/03/30e03033001.htm
http://www.vm.ee/welcome.html
http://www.osi.hu/fmp/laws/
http://www.angelfire.com/sd/tadjikistanupdate/culture.html
http://www.ceinet.org/minority.html
http://www.president.az/azerbaijan/const.htm
http://www.hrw.org/hrw/press98/feb/fe-turk.htm
http://www.ecri.coe.fr
http://www.armeniaemb.org/geninfo/constitution.htm
http://www.andorra.ad/consel/constituk.htm
http://server.parliament.ge/
http://www.bsos.umd.edu/cidcm/mar/gabkhaz.htm
http://win.relcom.kz/kzcourt/con.htm
http://www.richmond.edu/~jpjones/confinder/moldova3.htm
http://www.websp.com/~ethnic/new/rschools.htm
http://www.troc.es/ciemen/mercator/index-gb.htm
http://www.ecostan.org/Laws/turkm/turkmenistancon.html

REPORT ON THE LINGUISTIC RIGHTS OF PERSONS BELONGING TO NATIONAL MINORITIES IN THE OSCE AREA

Of the OSCE High Commissioner on National Minorities, Max van der Stoel

The Hague, March 1999

I. INTRODUCTION

Under the terms of the 1992 Helsinki Document of the Conference on Security and Cooperation in Europe, the High Commissioner on National Minorities is 'an instrument of conflict prevention at the earliest possible stage.' His specific mandate is to serve as a mechanism of early warning as well as early action for those 'national minority issues which [...] have the potential to develop into a conflict' within the CSCE (now-OSCE) area. Through sustained consultations with and recommendations to governments of OSCE participating States and in coordination with the Chairman-in-Office and other mechanisms of the OSCE, the High Commissioner attempts to resolve minorities problems in a number of countries.

Since the entry into office of the current High Commissioner in January 1993, he has found that the issue of linguistic rights for persons belonging to national minorities has assumed great importance in many OSCE States. This stems from the centrality to the identity of many persons belonging to national minorities of their ability to use their own language freely. For most minorities, language, as much as if not more than any other attribute of identity (such as common religion or history), serves as a means of unity of the group and source of self-identification of the individual. The enjoyment and preservation of the minority culture turns upon the freedom to transmit ideas, customs, and other indicia of culture in the original language of the minority. Their ability to speak that language generally distinguishes them from the majority group in OSCE States.

Each State within the OSCE faces a different set of issues concerning linguistic rights, and no two States have adopted the exact same set of policies. Governments within the OSCE have recognized in a number of ways the importance of linguistic rights for the enjoyment of minority rights. Some have taken special measures to protect and promote minority languages used in their territories. Problems have arisen, however, where governments have sought to limit the possibility of persons belonging to minorities to speak their own language through national legislation or other practices, or have tolerated actions by others with such an effect.

The tensions created by situations in which persons belonging to national minorities are not afforded sufficient rights have prompted the High Commissioner to involve his office in a number of linguistic-related issues as part of his conflict-prevention mandate. Governments that enact or tolerate such policies and practices generally justify them based on the view that the majority language, often adopted as the official or State language, is an important unifying factor in the State and use of competing languages would prevent or disrupt national unity. This argument is especially used when the national minorities, together or separately, constitute a significant proportion of the overall population. Yet international law does provide a variety of rights to national minorities to use their language without interference. The OSCE has itself articulated, reiterated, and elaborated upon these rights in a number of important documents, most notably in the 1990 Document of the Copenhagen Meeting of the Conference on the Human Dimension. States may protect those rights through numerous different approaches.

As part of the High Commissioner's mandate for conflict prevention and at the suggestion of some States, it was determined in 1996 that a comprehensive approach to the issue of linguistic rights would be useful. An analysis and comparison of the laws and policies of all the participating States, along with consideration of the applicable legal standards, would, it was hoped, provide governments with a sense of the numerous options for fulfilling their commitments in this area as well as an understanding of those policies that fall short of those standards. Such a study could heighten awareness among governments of the importance of this issue and the possibilities for protection of linguistic rights as a means of ensuring domestic tranquility and human rights. The result was a decision to conduct a survey of OSCE State policies regarding linguistic rights and compile the results in a public report of the High Commissioner.

II. THE PROCESS OF GATHERING INFORMATION

The High Commissioner's mandate (paragraph 23) authorizes him to collect and receive information regarding the situation of national minorities from any source, other than those that practice or publicly condone terrorism or violence. After consultation with experts in the area of linguistic rights, it was determined that a series of nine questions would be posed to OSCE participating States.[4] These questions appear in the Appendix to this report and are also repeated

---

[4] The government of the Federal Republic of Yugoslavia (Serbia-Montenegro) was not surveyed because of the suspension of its membership in the Organization; the Holy See was not sent the questionnaire because of its unique political status and the extraordinarily small number of permanent residents.

before the analytical summary of responses that appears in Part IV of this report. The questions seek information on four fundamental aspects of linguistic rights:

- the status of particular languages in the State;
- the extent of the rights of and possibilities for persons belonging to national minorities to use their language with administrative and judicial authorities of the State;
- the role of minority languages in the educational curriculum, in particular the extent to which students have the opportunity to learn minority languages and cultures and the extent to which they may receive their education in their minority language; and
- the access for persons belonging to national minorities to public media in their language.

By letter dated 10 December 1996, the High Commissioner sent the questionnaire to the Ministers of Foreign Affairs of the OSCE participating States. Most replies were received in the first half of 1997, with a smaller number arriving in the fall of 1997. In some situations, the High Commissioner sent reminders to governments that had not responded. All governments to which the questionnaire was directed have replied to it, with the exception of two States, Albania and Belgium. In addition, three States – Iceland, Liechtenstein, and Luxembourg – having stated that they did not have any national minorities, did not provide answers to the questions. (Other States asserting that they lacked national minorities chose to answer some or all of the questions nonetheless.) The full text of the replies of the 51 responding States are reproduced in the Annex to this report, which is published as a separate volume.

The analysis and comparisons that follow are based solely upon the responses of governments to this survey. Non-governmental sources were not consulted, and official governmental sources were not examined unless they were included as annexes to the responses provided by governments. As a result of this methodological decision, the High Commissioner has had to take account of five factors inherent in the form of information-gathering used here:

1. The demographic aspects of each State with respect to the presence of minorities varies significantly across OSCE participating States, including with respect to the number of persons belonging to national minorities, the number of minority groups, and their geographic concentration. One confronts a range of situations, from multilingual States whose linguistic groups are not regarded as minorities, to States with only a small number of persons belonging to national minorities, to those with many such persons and minority groups. In addition, States face different economic situations which can affect their policies in this area. The questions were worded

broadly enough to cover all OSCE participating States, although the answers reflect the range of their situations.

2. Different States provided significantly varying levels of responsiveness and detail in their replies to the questionnaire. These ranged from the three States noted above that stated only that they lacked any national minorities or national minority languages, to substantial responses describing laws, policies, and practices in great detail, sometimes with accompanying documentation.[5] Some States chose to combine their answers to several questions; some chose to answer some but not all questions. Obviously, the description of a government's policies is only as complete and accurate as that provided in its official response. As a result, perfect comparisons are impossible.

3. Apart from the varying level of detail, the range of options and practices undertaken by States necessitates some generalizations and groupings for comparative purposes. Such groupings do not always reflect differences among States, but they are necessary in order to provide some useful form of comparative analysis. To gain a complete picture of the responses of the States, readers are thus encouraged to refer to the full text responses published in the Annex to this report.

4. The analysis is limited to the laws, policies, and practices of the State as reported by its government. It does not provide an independent examination of the actual practices within the State, nor an evaluation of the specific context within which laws and policies have been adopted and are applied in each State. Although the High Commissioner has focussed on such issues in particular States within the OSCE as part of his conflict-prevention function, it is not the purpose of this study to assess the compatibility of each State's domestic law and practice with international standards. (Indeed, although OSCE commitments are shared by all OSCE participating States, specific legal obligations may vary according to the treaties to which each State is party.) Rather, as noted, the aim of this study is to reveal the range of existing practice among OSCE participating States and offer general commentary on it.

5. The results discussed in this report are current as of the date of the reply received, in most cases the first half of 1997. Because of the constraints of

---

[5] In this context, it should be noted that two States did not answer the questions specifically, but rather attached reports they had previously prepared for other purposes: Luxembourg, which attached its 1996 report to the UN Committee on the Elimination of Racial Discrimination, and United States of America, which attached its 1994 report to the UN Human Rights Committee. These reports have been examined and in some cases provide answers to the questions in the questionnaire.

time and the desire to avoid another round of requests to capitals, no updates were sought from governments. It is thus recognized that certain of the practices as described in this report may no longer reflect governmental policy. The High Commissioner is, of course, aware of legislative reforms under way in a number of States.

III. OVERVIEW OF INTERNATIONAL STANDARDS REGARDING LINGUISTIC RIGHTS

The linguistic rights of persons belonging to national minorities are the subject of a variety of international instruments. This section of the report describes those instruments in general insofar as they concern linguistic rights. These provisions will be examined in more detail in the context of the discussion of the individual questions.

A. OSCE Instruments

The most significant attempt to create standards for the protection of persons belonging to national minorities that also involve linguistic rights is the 1990 Document of the Copenhagen Meeting of the Conference on the Human Dimension. As examined further below, the Copenhagen Document addresses a number of issues, including non-discrimination, use of the mother tongue, and education of and in the mother tongue. Although not a treaty, the Copenhagen Document has both political and legal significance due to its adoption by consensus by the OSCE participating States. Its political significance lies in the willingness of OSCE States to accept that the protections afforded to national minorities – including those pertaining to linguistic rights – are worthy policy that contribute to the goals of the Organization in the human dimension: 'human rights, fundamental freedoms, democracy and the rule of law.'[6] The OSCE has long held that violation of political commitments is as unacceptable as any violation of international law, and the OSCE is as concerned with violations of these instruments as with those of a legally binding nature. The importance of adherence to the Copenhagen Document has been repeatedly invoked in subsequent documents of the OSCE. The Helsinki Final Act also includes a duty to uphold international law.

B. Treaties

In addition to the standards declared by the OSCE, OSCE participating States may be parties to one or more of three distinct groups of treaties, with legally

---

[6] 1991 Document of the Moscow Meeting of the Conference on the Human Dimension, para. 1.

binding obligations: universal agreements; European agreements; and special agreements, usually at the subregional and bilateral levels, that address minority issues. The principal <u>universal agreements</u> are the International Covenant on Civil and Political Rights ('ICCPR')[7] and the International Covenant on Economic, Social and Cultural Rights ('ICESCR'),[8] both concluded in New York in 1966. While their focus is not upon minority rights in particular, a number of their provisions have special relevance for linguistic rights of persons belonging to national minorities. Fifty-one OSCE States are parties to the ICCPR; the same 51 are also parties to the ICESCR.[9]

The principal <u>European agreements</u> are the 1950 Convention for the Protection of Human Rights and Fundamental Freedoms ('ECHR')[10] and the 1995 Framework Convention for the Protection of National Minorities ('Framework Convention'), both concluded under the auspices of the Council of Europe.[11] The former parallels in many respects the ICCPR, while the latter is the first modern pan-European convention aimed specifically at the protection of persons belonging to national minorities and contains a number of articles related to linguistic rights. Forty OSCE States are parties to the ECHR;[12] 23 OSCE States are parties to the Framework Convention.[13]

The third set of agreements are <u>special agreements</u> between European States that are not meant to be adopted at a pan-European or universal level. These include those post-World War I and II treaties still in force that address national minorities, such as the 1923 Treaty of Lausanne between Greece and Turkey[14] and the 1947 Treaty of Peace with Italy.[15] Equally significant are recent treaties between various neighboring States in the OSCE that contain provisions on minorities.[16] Some of these treaties, e.g., Romania-Hungary and Slovakia-

---

[7] 999 UNTS 171.

[8] 993 UNTS 3.

[9] All States except Andorra, Holy See, Kazakhstan, and Turkey.

[10] ETS No. 5, 213 UNTS 221.

[11] ETS No. 157. Also of significance is the 1992 European Charter for Regional or Minority Languages. It is to be noted that 'the Charter's overriding purpose is cultural [and it] sets out to protect and promote regional or minority languages, not linguistic minorities.' Council of Europe, European Charter for Regional or Minority Languages, Explanatory Report, paras. 10-11.

[12] Albania, Andorra, Austria, Belgium, Bulgaria, Croatia, Cyprus, Czech Republic, Denmark, Estonia, Finland, France, Germany, Greece, Hungary, Iceland, Ireland, Italy, Latvia, Liechtenstein, Lithuania, Luxembourg, Malta, Moldova, Netherlands, Norway, Poland, Portugal, Romania, Russian Federation, San Marino, Slovakia, Slovenia, Spain, Sweden, Switzerland, the former Yugoslav Republic of Macedonia, Turkey, Ukraine, and United Kingdom.

[13] Armenia, Austria, Croatia, Cyprus, Czech Republic, Denmark, Estonia, Finland, Germany, Hungary, Italy, Liechtenstein, Malta, Moldova, Romania, Russian Federation, San Marino, Slovakia, Slovenia, Spain, the former Yugoslav Republic of Macedonia, Ukraine, and United Kingdom.

[14] 28 LNTS 11.

[15] 49 UNTS 3.

[16] A representative sample may be found in Fernand de Varennes, *Language, Minorities and Human Rights* (1996), pp. 352-80.

Hungary, include by incorporation Council of Europe Recommendation 1201 on an Additional Protocol to the ECHR on the Rights of National Minorities (although the Recommendation itself was rejected by the Council of Europe Committee of Ministers). Also of note is the Agreement Establishing the Commonwealth of Independent States[17] and the 1994 CIS Convention Guaranteeing the Rights of Persons Belonging to National Minorities.

These three groups of international agreements do not exhaust the applicable treaty law on linguistic rights. A number of other conventions contain general provisions on minority rights, including the 1960 UNESCO Convention Against Discrimination in Education,[18] the 1958 International Labor Organization Convention (No. 111) concerning Discrimination in respect of Employment and Occupation,[19] the 1965 International Convention on the Elimination of All Forms of Racial Discrimination,[20] and the 1989 Convention on the Rights of the Child.[21]

C. Customary International Law

Equally binding upon States is customary international law, which is relevant insofar as it pertains to protection of persons belonging to national minorities. Customary law refers to those rules backed by the consistent practice of States with the requisite understanding by them that the behavior is legally required (opinio juris).[22] In the area of human rights, a number of norms, including some that affect minorities, are regarded as customary international law. It is worth noting, for instance, that the UN Human Rights Committee established under the ICCPR has stated that the right of minorities to enjoy their own culture, profess their own religion, or use their own language represents customary international law.[23] It is less clear, however, whether any of the more detailed OSCE standards or regional practices represent custom as well.

D. Other Documents

Alongside the standards noted above are other significant documents that seek to protect linguistic rights, though without creating any binding legal obligations

---

[17] 8 December 1991, 31 ILM 138 (1992). See especially Art. 3.
[18] 429 UNTS 93.
[19] 362 UNTS 31.
[20] 660 UNTS 195.
[21] G.A. Res. 44/25, 20 November 1989, UN GAOR, 44th Sess., Supp. No. 49, at 166, UN Doc. A/44/49 (1989).
[22] North Sea Continental Shelf (FRG/Den., FRG/Neth.), 1969 ICJ 3, 45.
[23] UN Human Rights Committee, General Comment No. 24, Issues relating to reservations made upon ratification or accession to the Covenant or the Optional Protocols thereto, or in relation to declarations under Article 41 of the Covenant, 4 November 1994, para. 8, in Report of the Human Rights Committee, UN GAOR, 50th Sess., Supp. No 40, Annex V, at 124, UN Doc. A/50/40 (1995).

upon States. At the universal level, the UN General Assembly adopted in 1992 the Declaration on the Rights of Persons Belonging to National or Ethnic, Religious and Linguistic Minorities ('1992 UN Declaration'), which sets forth some detailed provisions that attempt to address many issues related to minorities that are not covered by the ICCPR or ICESCR.[24] Within Europe, at the subregional level, the 16 States of the Central European Initiative have elaborated an Instrument for the Protection of Minority Rights.[25]

At the European level, the High Commissioner has attempted to provide guidance to States on desirable policy through the convening of two conferences of independent experts on minority rights who provided a series of recommendations. The 1996 Hague Recommendations Regarding the Education Rights of National Minorities and the 1998 Oslo Recommendations Regarding the Linguistic Rights of National Minorities attempt to elaborate upon the various existing legal and other documents to provide clear guidance to States on how to implement OSCE minority commitments.[26] Although these Recommendations are formally non-governmental in origin and have not been accepted by States through the mechanisms of the OSCE, they nonetheless have been presented to participating States by the High Commissioner as a point of reference and have generally been received positively by them.

E. Basic Purposes of Protection of Linguistic Rights

The protection of linguistic rights for persons belonging to national minorities is based on the two pillars of protection for national minorities found in the international instruments above: the right to non-discriminatory treatment in the enjoyment of all human rights; and the right to the maintenance and development of identity through the freedom to practice or use those special and unique aspects of their minority life – typically culture, religion, and language.

The first protection can be found, for instance, in paragraph 31 of the Copenhagen Document, Articles 2(1) and 26 of the ICCPR, Article 14 of the ECHR, Article 4 of the Framework Convention, and Article 3(1) of the 1992 UN Declaration. It ensures that minorities receive all of the other protections without

---

[24] UNGA Res. 47/135, 18 December 1992, UN GAOR, 47th Sess., Supp. No. 49, at 210, UN Doc. A/47/49 (1992).

[25] Albania, Austria, Bosnia and Herzegovina, Bulgaria, Belarus, Croatia, Czech Republic, Hungary, Italy, the former Yugoslav Republic of Macedonia, Moldova, Poland, Romania, Slovakia, Slovenia, and Ukraine.

[26] Foundation on Inter-Ethnic Relations, The Hague Recommendations Regarding the Education Rights of National Minorities & Explanatory Note (1996); Foundation on Inter-Ethnic Relations, The Oslo Recommendations Regarding the Linguistic Rights of National Minorities & Explanatory Note (1998). Both documents are available in a number of different languages from the Foundation's office in The Hague. For a history of The Hague Recommendations and further views on the relevant standards, see 4(2) International Journal of Group & Minority Rights (1996/97).

regard to their ethnic, national, or religious status;[27] they thus enjoy a number of linguistic rights that all persons in the State enjoy, such as freedom of expression and the right in criminal proceedings to be informed of the charges against them in a language they understand, if necessary through an interpreter provided free of charge.

The second pillar, encompassing affirmative obligations beyond non-discrimination, appears, for example, in paragraph 32 of the Copenhagen Document, Article 27 of the ICCPR, Article 5 of the Framework Convention, and Article 2(1) of the 1992 UN Declaration. It includes a number of rights pertinent to minorities simply by virtue of their minority status, such as the right to use their language.[28] This pillar is necessary because a pure non-discrimination norm could have the effect of forcing persons belonging to minorities to adhere to a majority language, effectively denying them their rights to identity by treating them just like any member of the majority.[29]

Both the rights of non-discrimination and of the maintenance and development of identity serve to advance the primary function of human rights law, respect for human dignity. As most clearly stated in the first article of the Framework Convention, 'The protection of national minorities and of the rights and freedoms of persons belonging to national minorities forms an integral part of the international protection of human rights [...]'[30] Linguistic rights, and minority rights in general, help ensure that minorities are able to realize and enjoy rights that the majority might be able to enjoy on its own, or subject only to the protection of the general human rights instruments.[31]

The right to maintain and develop one's identity does not come without certain responsibilities upon persons belonging to minority groups. One important duty, expressed in Article 20 of the Framework Convention and

---

[27] Paragraph 31 of the Copenhagen Document states:
'Persons belonging to national minorities have the right to exercise fully and effectively their human rights and fundamental freedoms without any discrimination and in full equality before the law.'
Article 2(1) of the ICCPR states:
'Each State Party to the present Covenant undertakes to respect and to ensure to all individuals within its territory and subject to its jurisdiction the rights recognized in the present Covenant, without distinction of any kind, such as race, colour, sex, language, religion, political or other opinion, national or social origin, property, birth or other status.'

[28] For instance, Article 27 of the ICCPR States:
'In those States in which ethnic, religious or linguistic minorities exist, persons belonging to such minorities shall not be denied the right, in community with other members of their group, to enjoy their own culture, to profess and practise their own religion, or to use their own language.'

[29] See Patrick Thornberry, International Law and the Rights of Minorities (1991) p. 394.

[30] See also Framework Convention, Arts. 22-23 (noting that nothing in the Framework Convention shall limit the human rights ensured under domestic law or, for parties to the European Convention on Human Rights, under that treaty).

[31] See Francesco Capotorti, Study on the Rights of Persons belonging to Ethnic, Religious and Linguistic Minorities (1991), at 40-41; John Packer, 'On the Content of Minority Rights', in J. Räikkä (Ed.) *Do We Need Minority Rights?* (1996) pp. 121, 146-49.

Article 8(2) of the 1992 UN Declaration, is that persons belonging to minorities are not entitled to exercise their special rights, including linguistic rights, in a way that impedes the human rights of others, whether of the majority or of other minorities (or even members of their own minority). Second, the extent to which the government is obligated to take affirmative steps to foster minority identity is the subject of some uncertainty. Certainly governments are obligated to take affirmative steps to eliminate discrimination against minorities in the enjoyment of fundamental human rights.[32] But the legal standards also take into account other factors that might affect a State's ability to assist minority groups. Financial constraints may, for instance, limit a government's ability to offer education in a minority language to all persons belonging to minorities. The details of this issue are discussed further below.

IV. ANALYSIS OF THE RESPONSES OF GOVERNMENTS TO THE QUESTIONNAIRE

A. Presence of State and Official Languages and Languages with Special Status

QUESTION 1: Which languages have 'State' or 'official' status in your country? Please also provide relevant information on any other languages which may have special status in your country.

1. International Standards

None of the universal or regional instruments discussed above contains any authoritative definition of 'State' or 'official' language.[33] Indeed, the terms are sometimes used interchangeably by States. States may also use the former term to refer to the historic, national language (often originating in or unique to the country) and the latter term to refer to a language from another State that has been so utilized in every day life that it is now accepted as a formal means of communication by the government with its citizens. Moreover, there are no international standards on whether States must adopt more than one official language to respond to the needs of persons belonging to national minorities

---

[32] See UN Human Rights Committee, General Comment No. 23, Article 27 of the International Covenant on Civil and Political Rights, para. 6.2, 8 April 1994, in Report of the Human Rights Committee, UN GAOR, 49th Sess., Supp. No. 40, Annex V, at 107, UN Doc. A/49/40 (1994).

[33] The European Charter for Regional or Minority Languages does not define these terms, though it does define in Article 1(a) 'regional or minority languages' as languages

'i. traditionally used within a given territory of a State by nationals of that State who form a group numerically smaller than the rest of the State's population; and

ii. different from the official language(s) of that State.'

(and indeed there is no obligation to have an official language), and there is no internationally accepted definition of languages with special status. Rather, the standards address particular needs of the national minority to communicate with others in their group and with those outside their group.

2. Questionnaire Results

Of the 51 States returning the questionnaire, three (Hungary, Sweden, and United States of America) responded that they had no official or State languages; while the Czech Republic said the term was not defined, although the status of Czech as the official language was implicit in some laws.[34] Three States (Greece, Liechtenstein, and Luxembourg) did not answer the question. Of the remaining States, 34 stated that they had only one official language; eight stated that they had two languages;[35] and two States (Switzerland and Bosnia and Herzegovina) stated that they had three or more official languages. At the same time, it may be underlined that 22 of the 34 States noting that they have only one official language give special status for languages other than the official one. And in some of those cases, the governments specifically indicated that the other language was an 'official' language in a particular region of the country.[36] Two States with two official languages also indicated that they give special status to others.[37] As a result, only 12 States responding to the question have stated that they have one language without granting special status for others.[38]

3. Analysis of Results

The lack of international standards in this area makes finding a benchmark for comparisons difficult. It would seem commendable that relatively few States with one official language do not grant a special status for others. In some cases, this may reflect a genuine lack of persons speaking other languages; in others, it

---

[34] United States of America responded that certain of its States had laws mandating an official language, some of which were being challenged in court.

[35] Belarus (Belarussian and Russia); Canada (English and French); Cyprus (Greek and Turkish); Finland (Finnish and Swedish); Ireland (Irish as first official language, English as second official language); Kazakhstan (Kazak as the State language, Russian as an official language); Malta (Maltese as national language, English as an official language); and Norway (Norwegian and Sami).

[36] Croatia (other, unspecified languages in certain local units); Denmark (Greenlandish and Faroese official on those islands); Georgia (Abkhazian official in Abkhazia); Italy (French, German, and Slovenian official in three different regions); Moldova (Gagauzian and Russian official in Gaugazia); Russian Federation (national languages official in seven republics); Slovenia (Italian and Hungarian official in certain areas); Spain (Catalan, Gallego, Euskera, Valenciano official in each of four Autonomous Communities). A number of other States noted that second languages have *de jure* special status in certain regions without calling them 'official.'

[37] Canada (Aboriginal) and Finland (Sami).

[38] Andorra, Bulgaria, Estonia, France, Iceland, Monaco, Poland, Portugal, Romania, San Marino, Turkey, and Uzbekistan.

may represent a governmental policy to channel all official communication through the official language(s), even though this might potentially interfere with the linguistic rights of persons belonging to national minorities. To the extent that States have decided to adopt more than one official language, or to give special status to other languages, in the whole country or in particular regions, this will certainly contribute to the protection of the linguistic rights of persons speaking those languages. In such States, the persons will likely be more able to freely communicate with governmental officials, understand official documents, see their children educated in the minority language, and obtain access to the media in their language. The consequence may well be greater protection against discrimination. In any case, it is clear that most States give (in various ways and to varying degrees) official status to more than one language.

B. Use of Minority Languages in Official Communications

QUESTION 2: May persons belonging to national minorities use their own language in their contacts with administrative authorities and public services throughout your country? Is this a matter of right under national law in territories in which the minority language is traditionally used by a substantial part of the local population?

QUESTION 3: May persons belonging to national minorities use their own language in judicial proceedings and other contacts with judicial authorities throughout your country? Is this a matter of right under national law in territories in which the minority language is traditionally used by a substantial part of the local population?

1. *International Standards*

The ability of persons belonging to national minorities to communicate with governmental officials and bodies in their own language is an essential linguistic right. It both ensures that they will be able to understand governmental policies that affect them and express their views to appropriate governmental instrumentalities. It also permits such persons to become actively involved in the civil life of the country in order to create a pluralistic and open society, where members of minority groups feel integrated without having to sacrifice their identity.[39] The questions posed to governments focus on administrative bodies as well as judicial authorities; moreover, governments were specifically asked whether this possibility is a matter of right (i.e. legal entitlement) under national

---

[39] See, e.g., de Varennes, supra note 13, at 176-78.

law in areas where the language is traditionally used by a substantial part of the local population.

The international standards derive from a number of instruments. As a starting point, paragraph 34 of the Copenhagen Document expresses a clear standard that all OSCE States have accepted:

> The participating States will endeavour to ensure that persons belonging to national minorities, notwithstanding the need to learn the official language or languages of the State concerned, have adequate opportunities for instruction of their mother tongue or in their mother tongue, as well as, wherever possible and necessary, for its use before public authorities, in conformity with applicable national legislation.

With respect to communication with administrative authorities, the 23 OSCE States that are parties to the Framework Convention[40] have a legal obligation under Article 10(2) thereof:

> In areas inhabited by persons belonging to national minorities traditionally or in substantial numbers, if those persons so request and where such a request corresponds to a real need, the Parties shall endeavour to ensure, as far as possible, the conditions which would make it possible to use the minority language in relations between those persons and the administrative authorities.

In addition, some States have obligations in this area under bilateral treaties with neighbors.[41]

Both the Copenhagen Document and the Framework Convention express the same idea: where national minorities need to communicate with governmental institutions in their own language, typically though not exclusively in those regions where they are concentrated or have lived traditionally, the government should make every effort to make this possible. Both instruments recognize that the government might well not be able to accommodate every such person in every situation, and that financial constraints may come into play.[42] It would also seem that, where such constraints exist, the government should focus on those institutions of most importance to the local populations, e.g., taxing authorities, police, health and safety officials, and emergency services.

---

[40] See supra note 10.

[41] See, e.g., Treaty on Good Neighbourliness and Friendly Cooperation between the Slovak Republic and the Republic of Hungary [hereinafter Slovakia-Hungary Treaty], 19 March 1995, Art. 15(2)(g):

'persons belonging to the Hungarian minority in the Slovak Republic and those belonging to the Slovak minority in the Republic of Hungary shall [...] have the right, in conformity with the domestic legislation and with the international commitments undertaken by the two parties, to use their minority language in contacts with administrative authorities, including public administration, and in court proceedings [...].'

[42] See Council of Europe, Explanatory Report on the Framework Convention for the Protection of National Minorities, paras. 64-66; Oslo Recommendations, Explanatory Note, at 29.

With regard to communication with judicial authorities, the international instruments are more sweeping in their provisions. Most notably, States parties to the ICCPR, ECHR, and Framework Convention are legally obligated to ensure that individuals facing criminal charges – whether or not members of national minorities – are informed of the charges against them in their own language and are provided with an interpreter at no cost if they cannot understand the language used in court.[43] This important right is closely linked with the special concern of human rights law for persons deprived of their liberty. With respect to non-criminal court proceedings, the OSCE has not itself promulgated standards to this effect, although bilateral treaties incorporating Council of Europe Recommendation 1201 provide for the right to use the mother tongue in all court proceedings,[44] while the Oslo Recommendations support such an entitlement.[45]

2. Questionnaire Results

With respect to communications before <u>administrative authorities</u>, the questionnaire reveals a wide variety of stated policies, ranging from total insistence upon use of one official language through legally guaranteed free interpretive services for persons using minority languages. Analysis of the results is encumbered by the variety of completeness to the answers. Most States, for example, in discussing the ability to 'communicate' did not explain whether this included the possibility to receive responses from the government in the minority language, or interpreted or translated into the minority language. The answers may nonetheless by grouped into six categories.

In the <u>first category</u> is one State that stated that it does not allow such communication: France. A <u>second category</u> encompasses those States that did not indicate whether or not they allow such communication: Armenia, Belarus, Bulgaria, Kyrgyzstan, Poland, Tajikistan, and Turkey. (This group might also include those States that responded that they have no national minorities – Cyprus, Iceland, Liechtenstein, Luxembourg, and San Marino.)

A <u>third group</u> said that they allow communications, but only in those languages that have been designated official languages for the State as a whole: Canada (right to communicate in either English or French 'wherever there is significant demand,' with variations among different provinces); Ireland (right to communicate in English or Irish); Malta (Maltese and English); Norway (Sami in administrative areas of the Sami language); and Switzerland (right to communicate in any official language with federal authorities, but only in the

---

[43] See ICCPR, Art. 14(3); ECHR, Arts. 5(2), 6(3); Framework Convention, Art. 10(3).
[44] See Slovakia-Hungary Treaty, Art. 15(2)(g).
[45] Oslo Recommendations, paras. 18-19 (recommending free interpretation and consideration of all judicial proceedings in the minority language in regions where minorities live in significant numbers and wish it).

official language(s) of the canton or the commune with cantonal or communal authorities, respectively).

A fourth group said that they allow communications, but only in certain designated minority languages and/or in certain designated regions of the country: Austria (Slovene and Croat in regions with mixed populations); Finland (Sami in the Sami homeland); Germany (Sorbian in Sorbian areas); Greece (Turkish); Italy (French in Valle d'Aosta, German in Alto Adige, and Slovene in parts of Friuli-Venezia Giulia); Latvia (Russian); Netherlands (Frisian in Friesland); Russian Federation (the official language of the particular constituent republic of the administrative authorities); Slovenia (Italian and Hungarian in regions with 'original' minorities of those nationalities); Spain (regional language in each of four Autonomous Communities); United Kingdom (Welsh in Wales, Gaelic in Scotland, and Irish in Northern Ireland); and United States (Native American languages).

A fifth group of States responded that they permitted such communications without limiting it to designated languages but constraining it by proportion of the population: Croatia (in municipalities where minorities are a majority of the population); Estonia (in localities where half the permanent population belongs to a minority); Lithuania (in regions 'densely populated' by minority); Moldova (in localities with 'compact' population);[46] the former Yugoslav Republic of Macedonia (in localities where a minority constitutes the majority or is present 'in considerable numbers'); and Turkmenistan ('where the majority of the population is of another ethnic group').

A sixth group simply responded affirmatively to the question without noting any restrictions to certain languages, regions, or proportions. Those States were: Andorra (which noted that replies will only be in Catalan), Bosnia and Herzegovina, Czech Republic, Denmark, Georgia, Greece, Hungary, Kazakstan, Monaco (noting foreign nationals can 'very often' use their own language), Portugal ('possibility of requesting' an interpreter), Romania, Slovakia, Sweden, Ukraine, and Uzbekistan. Except for the special federal provisions regarding Native American languages, the United States of America's reply indicated that its policy varies by States.

Beyond these six categories, some States noted that administrative authorities are obligated to reply to persons wishing to use the minority language in that language: Estonia; Italy (requirement of bilingual civil servants in Alto Adige and Valle d'Aosta); Norway (Sami only); Malta; and United Kingdom (Welsh only). Other States (e.g., Finland for the Sami language) stated that public notices must be published in the minority language; or stated that the minority language might be used for local self-government (Russian Federation and the former Yugoslav Republic of Macedonia).

As for whether those States that provide such rights do so by law, the answer seems to be yes in most States. Some States made reference to provisions of

---

[46] Moldova noted that it also allows such communication in Gagauzia.

their constitution (Austria, Croatia, Estonia, Finland, Slovakia, and Switzerland); while many mentioned specific statutes (Canada, Croatia, Czech Republic, Estonia, Finland, Germany, Hungary, Latvia, Lithuania, Moldova, Netherlands, Norway, Romania, Russian Federation, Slovenia, Spain, the former Yugoslav Republic of Macedonia, Ukraine, and Uzbekistan).

With respect to the possibility to communicate with judicial authorities in the national minority language, responses were far more consistent; each State that answered the question stated that it provided some possibility to communicate. Again, however, the answers are not complete in that they do not usually indicate whether the person may simply speak his or her language; whether the proceedings will be interpreted into that language, or documents translated; or whether the full proceedings will be conducted in the language. In addition, Armenia, Cyprus, Iceland, Kyrgyzstan, Liechtenstein, Luxembourg, and San Marino did not answer this question.

A first group gave affirmative answers without qualification in terms of the particular language, region, or court at issue: Azerbaijan, Belarus, Bosnia and Herzegovina, Czech Republic, Georgia, Greece, Hungary, Kazakstan, Latvia, Lithuania, Malta, Moldova, Poland, Romania, Russian Federation, Slovakia, Slovenia, Sweden, Tajikistan, the former Yugoslav Republic of Macedonia, Turkmenistan, United Kingdom, and Uzbekistan. A second group, comprised of Canada, Ireland, and Switzerland, noted that proceedings can take place only in an official language.

A third group stated that they limited the possibility to communicate in judicial proceedings in the minority language to certain minorities or regions: Austria (Slovene and Croat in regions with mixed populations); Germany (Sorbian in Sorbian regions); Italy (French in Valle d'Aosta, German in Alto Adige, and Slovene in parts of Friuli-Venezia Giulia); Netherlands (Frisian in Friesland); Norway (Sami administrative areas); Slovenia (Italian and Hungarian in regions with 'original' minorities of those nationalities); Spain (four regional languages in their respective Autonomous Communities); and Ukraine (where the minority language is 'traditionally used by a substantial part of the local population'). In addition, some of the States in the previous two groups stated that they also provide interpretive services for any person not speaking the language of the court, at least for criminal cases (e.g., Germany and Netherlands).

A fourth group specified that the rights applied in only certain types of proceedings, such as criminal proceedings or those at the federal level: Bulgaria (criminal only), Canada (at the discretion of the provinces for provincial civil proceedings); Denmark (civil proceedings or some criminal cases only if the court has knowledge of the language); Estonia (only criminal cases); Finland ('general administrative courts'); Norway (national courts only);[47] and United States of America (federal and State criminal courts).

---

[47] As noted above, Norway also allows for use of Sami in Sami courts.

Beyond these four categories, some States replied specifically that proceedings themselves might be held in a minority language: Belarus (where 'spoken by a substantial part of the location population of a region'); Latvia (if accepted by the parties, their lawyers, and the prosecutor); Russian Federation (in the language of a constituent republic or of a minority 'compactly residing in some locality'); Slovenia (in Italian and Hungarian 'if the party uses the Italian or Hungarian language'); Spain (in the four Autonomous Communities 'provided that none of the parties objects' because it does not understand the language); Tajikistan ('the language of the majority of the population of the particular locality'); United Kingdom (in Welsh in Wales); and Uzbekistan (also noting that proceedings themselves are held in Uzbek, Karakalpak, or the 'language of the majorities of that territory').

As with the question of access to administrative authorities, most States provided for access to judicial authorities by law. Some States made reference to their constitution (Austria, Azerbaijan, Estonia, Georgia, Lithuania, Romania, Tajikistan, the former Yugoslav Republic of Macedonia, and Uzbekistan). Most States mentioning specific laws noted that it was required in their codes of criminal or civil procedure (Bulgaria, Canada, Czech Republic, Denmark, Estonia, Finland, Hungary, Lithuania, Norway, Slovakia, Slovenia, the former Yugoslav Republic of Macedonia, and Uzbekistan); while a handful referred to language laws (Belarus, Lithuania, Moldova, Netherlands, Russian Federation, Turkmenistan, and Uzbekistan). Two States made reference to special treaties governing this issue: Germany to the 1990 Unification Treaty, and Turkey to the 1923 Treaty of Lausanne. In addition, Germany, Malta, and Switzerland made reference to the requirements of the European Convention on Human Rights (see above).

3. Analysis of Results

With respect to the question of administrative authorities, the responses of nearly all those States answering the question suggest that their stated policies do conform to the standards in the Copenhagen Document – that minorities must 'have adequate opportunities [to use their mother tongue] [...] wherever possible and necessary [...] in conformity with applicable national legislation.' The exceptions would be States that do not allow communication in the minority language; and any of the numerous States limiting the right to communicate in the minority language to certain persons (designated by language, minority, location, or proportion of the population – the third, fourth, and fifth groups above) if, in those States, it was 'possible and necessary' to provide 'adequate opportunities' beyond those they have provided. Nevertheless, in a great many States, minority languages may be used for contacts with administrative authorities where the minority has resided traditionally or constitutes a substantial part of the local population.

Of the 23 States that are parties to the Framework Convention,[48] all 20 that answered the question[49] provided responses that, if matched in practice, suggest a high degree of consistency with Article 10(2) of the Convention quoted above. The critical language in the Convention is that States 'shall endeavour to ensure, as far as possible,' conditions for use of the language '[i]n areas inhabited by persons belonging to national minorities traditionally or in substantial numbers, if those persons so request and where such a request corresponds to a real need.' Some of the 20 States would appear to have implemented this provision in a way that it applies to specific languages or regions (e.g., Germany, Italy, and United Kingdom). Others have used a proportional threshold that resembles the Convention language (Estonia, Moldova, and the former Yugoslav Republic of Macedonia). It should be pointed out that, whatever groups or thresholds these States may have chosen, their obligation is a broad one, concerning any regions inhabited by minorities 'traditionally or in substantial numbers' where there is a 'real need.'

Although neither the Copenhagen Document, Framework Convention, nor other OSCE standards specify that the ability to communicate with administrative authorities must be guaranteed by law, it is to be noted that fewer than half the OSCE States responded that their laws provide for such an ability. It is to be hoped that legislation will be forthcoming to provide these rights in all OSCE participating States.

The practice described by governments for the possibility to communicate with judicial authorities seems more consistent with that envisaged by the relevant international standards than that for the ability to communicate with administrative authorities. The overwhelmingly positive answers to the question regarding judicial authorities seems related to the clear obligations upon States under the ICCPR and the ECHR regarding interpretation in criminal trials for defendants who do not 'understand or speak the language used in court.' It is to be hoped that the many States responding without further elaboration that they permit communication with judicial authorities in the minority language in fact provide the interpretation in both directions required by the ICCPR and the ECHR.

As noted above, the question posed to governments concerns not simply the right to interpretation in the case where a criminal defendant cannot understand or speak the language, but two broader categories: (a) in all judicial proceedings; and (b) even where the person understands the official language but wishes to use the national minority language. If the affirmative responses to the question posed mean that persons belonging to national minorities may use their language in regions where they represent a significant portion of the local population, and may do so in all judicial proceedings, then this would be along the lines of that proposed in the Oslo Recommendations. Some of the States effectively stated

---

[48] See supra note 10.
[49] Armenia, Cyprus, and San Marino did not answer the question.

that they have gone beyond these Recommendations, towards the conduct of proceedings in minority languages mentioned in the European Charter for Regional or Minority Languages.[50] Finally, some States specifically mentioned the ways they are making possible the use of minority languages with administrative and judicial authorities, e.g., Italy's use of bilingual civil servants in some regions.

C. Teaching of and in Minority Languages

QUESTION 4: Which minority languages are taught in your country? At which levels of education are they taught (i.e. primary, secondary, vocational teacher training, university)? Are these taught only in some localities? If so limited, by what criteria are the localities defined in which such education is available?

QUESTION 5: Do persons belonging to national minorities enjoy the right to education in their language, i.e. the whole or significant parts of their education in their own language? If is limited, please indicate which subjects are taught in the minority languages and which subjects are required to be taught in the State or official language(s) at each level of education. Please also indicate whether the right is enjoyed throughout your country. If it is enjoyed in only some localities, by what criteria are the localities defined in which such education is available?

1. *International Standards*

Questions 4 and 5 address two important issues: (1) the teaching of minority languages to members of the national minority and others wishing to learn it; and (2) the teaching in minority languages of the educational curriculum to members of the national minority. The willingness of States to provide these two opportunities is important to the protection of minority rights in a number of senses.

First, the fulfilment of the basic human right of persons belonging to national minorities to 'use their language' (ICCPR, art. 27) naturally depends upon their ability to know the language. As stated in The Hague Recommendations, 'the right of persons belonging to national minorities to maintain their identity can only be fully realised if they acquire a proper knowledge of their mother tongue

---

[50] The European Charter lists among its menu of options (Art. 9) the obligation to ensure that persons involved in any judicial proceedings have the possibility to use their minority language even if they are able to communicate in the majority language.

during the educational process.'[51] Although the oral aspect of the language may be passed on within a family, the written and literary aspects require the active commitment of educational institutions. Adults, moreover, may need to learn through adult education.

Second, the teaching of the minority language to persons who are not members of the minority can contribute to greater communication, and thus understanding, between the majority and the minorities. For example, if the various rights discussed above concerning the possibility to communicate with administrative and judicial authorities in the national minority language are to be fully realized, then the language will need to be taught outside the minority group. The Council of Europe has recently recognized the importance of knowledge of more than one language as a means of inter-cultural communication, understanding, and tolerance.[52]

Third, although language courses provide a necessary component for learning the language and maintaining identity as a person belonging to a national minority, the language can often be fully learned only if a broader part of the curriculum is taught in the national language. Fourth, for those persons who have learned the national minority language at home and have not yet learned the majority or official language, some component of the education in the minority language has been shown by research to assist in education.

The international standards with respect to education derive from a variety of documents addressing different facets of the educational process. The Copenhagen Document states in paragraph 34: 'The participating States will endeavour to ensure that persons belonging to national minorities, notwithstanding the need to learn the official language or languages of the State concerned, have adequate opportunities for instruction of their mother tongue or in their mother tongue [...].' More broadly, the Framework Convention states in Article 14 that every person belonging to a national minority 'has the right to learn his or her minority language,' further specifying:

> In areas inhabited by persons belonging to national minorities traditionally or in substantial numbers, if there is sufficient demand, the Parties shall endeavour to ensure, as far as possible and within the framework of their educational systems, that persons belonging to those minorities have adequate opportunities for being taught the minority language or for receiving instruction in this language.

These terms also appear in the 1992 UN Declaration and certain bilateral treaties.[53] Detailed recommendations for implementing these standards are found in the 1996 Hague Recommendations, which specify the need for education in minority languages at the primary, secondary, vocational, and tertiary levels.

---

[51] The Hague Recommendations, para. 1.
[52] Council of Europe Committee of Ministers, Recommendation No. R (98) 6 Concerning Modern Languages, 17 March 1998.
[53] 1992 UN Declaration, Art. 4(3); Slovakia-Hungary Treaty, Art. 15(2)(g).

Beyond these standards, other standards apply to the establishment of private schools, an issue considered in Question 7 below.

These instruments, and in particular the Framework Convention, suggest certain affirmative steps that the State must take in the area of minority language education. At the same time, the phrase 'endeavour to ensure as far as possible [...] adequate opportunities' provides States with flexibility over this issue. In particular, the drafters took cognizance of the financial and administrative difficulties involved in such education.[54] Thus, there are no detailed requirements regarding the levels at which such instruction must take place or, in the case of instruction in the language, the courses in which it should be used, although The Hague Recommendations elaborate upon desirable policies for implementing the commitments in the Copenhagen Document and the Framework Convention. Moreover, States are not specifically required to provide both education of the language and education in it; nevertheless, the two terms are not, as noted above, mutually exclusive.[55]

2. Questionnaire Results

As a methodological matter, it should be noted that the responses of States are often difficult to compare for these two questions, as many States, in answering both questions, did not distinguish between education of and education in the language. Some referred to only one or the other. The matter is further confused because, in many situations, teaching in the national minority language will include teaching of the minority language. However, the former will not include the latter with respect to persons who wish to be taught the minority language but are not placed in classes in the minority language, typically persons who are not members of the national minority (e.g., a non-Frisian citizen of the Netherlands seeking to learn Frisian). In addition, and quite significantly, many did not specify whether the opportunities they said they were providing for education were within the public schools, or rather through private schools. Finally, some States did not distinguish between languages of national minorities and foreign languages, i.e. languages not traditionally spoken within the country, instead grouping them together as all languages different from the majority language.

With regard to education of the minority language, all States responding to this question seem to allow the teaching of languages of national minorities.[56] The number of such languages taught varied significantly, apparently depending on the number of national minorities in the State and the number of persons using the language. In many States, at least several languages are taught, for

---

[54] Framework Convention, Explanatory Report, paras. 75-76.
[55] Id., para. 77.
[56] States not responding to this question were: Cyprus, Iceland, Liechtenstein, Luxembourg, Portugal, San Marino, and United States of America.

example: Armenia (Russian, Kurdish, Jewish,[57] Greek, and Polish); Austria (Slovene, Croat, Czech, and Slovak); Bulgaria (Hebrew, Armenian, Romani, and Turkish); Czech Republic (Slovak, Polish, German, Romani, Hungarian, and Ukrainian); France (Breton, Basque, Occitan, Corsican, and Catalan); Germany (Danish, Sorbian, Frisian, and Romani); Slovakia (Hungarian, Ukrainian, German, and Ruthenian); and Spain (Euskera, Galician, Valencian, and Catalan). In some States the number of languages taught was quite large: eight in Belarus, Latvia, and Moldova; 11 in Lithuania; 12 in Croatia and Hungary; 14 in Kazakstan; 15 in Romania; and 18 in Ukraine. A small group of States taught only official languages of the State (along with key foreign languages) due to the way in which their polities address the question of national minorities: Canada, Ireland, and Switzerland.

In terms of the <u>levels of education</u>, it is difficult to discern many patterns among the responses. Many States responded that they teach a variety of languages at the primary level, but fewer at the secondary or university level. In some cases, however, it is unclear whether they are referring to education <u>in</u> the minority language (e.g., transition classes for students who have only spoken the minority language at home) or the teaching <u>of</u> the minority language as a separate course. A number of States seemed to provide for greater levels of education for one or more national minority languages than for others: Russian in Armenia; German in Denmark; Russian in Estonia; Russian, Polish, Belarussian, and Ukrainian in Lithuania; Hungarian and German in Romania; Hungarian and Ukrainian in Slovakia; and Welsh and Gaelic in United Kingdom.

With respect to the <u>locations</u> in which minority languages are taught, most States did not provide detailed answers on this issue, and many of the answers seem to refer to teaching in minority languages, rather than teaching of minority languages. Some States limit the teaching of some or all minority languages to particular regions where minorities live, e.g.: Austria (Slovene in Carinthia, and Croatian and Hungarian in Burgenland); Finland (Sami in their homeland); Georgia (Abkhaz in Abkhazia); Germany (Sorbian in Free State of Saxony and <u>Land</u> Brandenburg); Greece (Turkish in Thrace); Italy (Slovenian in Slovenian regions of Friuli-Venezia Giulia); Netherlands (Frisian in Friesland); Russian Federation (in autonomous republics and 'localities of compact residence of minorities'); Slovenia (areas of 'traditional settlement and autochthonous origin of national minorities' defined by statute); and Spain (four languages of Autonomous Communities in those regions). Others set more general limitations: Poland (at the request of parents in primary schools, at the request of students in secondary schools, as well as 'regions inhabited by dense concentrations of a given minority for generations or as a result of the latest political events and contemporary historical processes (displacements in the

---

[57] A number of States used the term 'Jewish' without specifying whether it referred to Hebrew or Yiddish.

post-war period)'); and Romania ('where there is a significant number of pupils' belonging to national minorities).

As for teaching in minority languages, it appears again that every State responding to the question grants the right for some teaching in the minority language, although whether these take place in public or private schools is unclear from most responses.[58] A few patterns nonetheless emerge. First, all 14 States of the former Soviet Union (in addition to Russia) provide for significant teaching in Russian. Some of these States' responses suggest that Russian is the second language of instruction for students (e.g., Kazakhstan, Kyrgyzstan, and Turkmenistan); other responses suggest that students have the option to go to a Russian language school or a mixed-language school (e.g., Estonia, Georgia, Latvia, and Lithuania). Second, most other States provide opportunities to learn in more than one minority language, although in many cases the number of languages in which students may learn appears smaller than the number of languages students may learn as separate subjects.

The geographic regions in which students may learn in these languages generally correspond to the regions where they may learn the language themselves, usually the regions in which minorities are most concentrated, though in some cases it is more confined. Some States specified that the establishment of classes depended upon demand and the number of pupils needed for a class (e.g., the former Yugoslav Republic of Macedonia and United Kingdom); others stated that they put more emphasis on the right of the parents to decide the language in which their children will be educated (Slovakia). The three countries that stated that they offered curricula only in the official language(s) (Canada, Ireland, and Switzerland) had different approaches to the issue, each taking account of the demographic patterns of people speaking the various languages.

Finally, the range of subjects available in the national minority language varied considerably. In some cases, the entire curriculum was in the minority language through separate classes or schools (Czech Republic, Estonia, Latvia, and Lithuania); in some it was only part of the curriculum (Sorbian and Frisian alongside German in parts of Germany; German and French alongside Italian in Italy; equal numbers of Polish and minority language classes in Poland); and in some it was a small amount of class time (three to five lessons per week in the mother tongue in Denmark). United States of America stated that non-English-speaking students had the right to equal educational opportunities and that the government provided grants for bilingual instruction.

Some States specified particular courses or types of courses to be taught in the official language: Latvia replied that it requires at least two subjects from first to ninth grade, and three from 10th to 12th grade, be taught in Latvian 'in

---

[58] The same States that did not respond to Question 4 did not respond to Question 5, with the exception of United States of America, which made some reference to the issue in its 1994 report to the UN Human Rights Committee provided as its response.

humanitarian or exact sciences;' and Romania replied that Romanian history, literature, and geography must be taught in Romanian. At least one State, Croatia, stated that it combined several options: some schools all in the minority language, some in which the natural sciences are taught in Croatian and the arts and social studies in the minority language, and some with the basic curriculum in Croatian and additional classes in the minority language. Austrian law guarantees members of the Slovene, Croat, and Hungarian minorities in Carinthia and Burgenland the individual right to use their language as the language of instruction or learn it as a compulsory subject, and also offers possibilities for such instruction in other areas of the country based on demand.

3. Analysis of Results

The most immediate conclusion to be drawn from the results is simply to point out the numerous approaches of OSCE States to the issue of education of and in minority languages. Whether with respect to the number of languages or the places, levels, or subjects taught, States have adopted a wide variety of approaches, sometimes offering different possibilities within the same State. Certainly the responses indicate a level of sensitivity to the needs of persons belonging to national minorities with respect to their language. Most States provided extensive lists of languages offered as an indication of their concern over this issue. However, the data alone do not indicate whether the governments are adequately responding to the desires of minorities.

Beyond this general point, several other conclusions are possible. First, the answers suggest that States need to consider the differences between teaching of minority languages and teaching in minority languages more explicitly in their educational policy. Although the OSCE standards only require that one of these forms of education be provided, the overarching goal remains the creation of conditions favorable to the maintenance and development of the identity of persons belonging to national minorities. Education in the minority language may go far in accomplishing this goal. However, education of the minority language also for persons not belonging to the minority has, as noted above, the important beneficial result of fostering tolerance and communication.

Second, the experiences of some States show that it is possible to provide the teaching in minority languages even when the number of persons belonging to national minorities is small.

Third, the answers suggest that States need to carefully consider the range of options available to them to balance the teaching of the minority languages with that of the main or official languages. The range of answers shows that it may be unwise to make a priori conclusions about which courses must be taught in one language and which in the other. Much should depend on the views of the persons belonging to minorities themselves, although obviously the State has an interest in fostering understanding by all its citizens of the main or official languages.

Fourth, the answers suggest that some States might wish to consider the differences between the language of national minorities and truly foreign languages. Although the latter may be taught as a means of integration between the State and its neighbors or important economic partners, teaching the former is aimed at fostering understanding within the State.

D. Inclusion of National Minority Perspectives in the General School Curriculum

QUESTION 6: To what extent is the culture, history, religion and belief of national minorities taught in the general curriculum?

1. International Standards

The teaching of the culture, history, religion, and beliefs of persons belonging to national minorities in the general curriculum has two facets: first, it ensures that minority students will be exposed to formal education that takes into account their own experiences and perspectives, just as the students of the majority are. But second and more important, it entails the teaching of these subjects to the student population at large, in particular students who are not members of the minority and would thus have no other obvious place in which to learn about them. Such knowledge is critical for building a tolerant, multi-ethnic society – one resistant to strains of ethnic hatred that so often stem from ignorance of, or misinformation propagated about, minority cultures.[59] Knowledge and understanding are thus prerequisites to internal stability and social harmony.

The pertinent international standards in this area are fairly recent. As a general matter, Article 29(1) of the UN Convention on the Rights of the Child stipulates that 'the education of the child shall be directed to [...] (d) The preparation of the child for responsible life in a free society, in the spirit of understanding, peace, tolerance, equality of sexes, and friendship among all peoples, ethnic, national and religious groups and persons of indigenous origin.' Paragraph 34 of the Copenhagen Document states: 'In the context of the teaching of history and culture in educational establishments, they [the participating States] will also take account of the history and culture of national minorities.' Article 12 of the Framework Convention obligates States to, 'where appropriate, take measures in the fields of education and research to foster knowledge of the culture, history, language and religion of their national minorities and of the majority.' Article 4(4) of the 1992 UN Declaration states: 'States should, where appropriate, take measures in the field of education, in order to encourage knowledge of the history, traditions, language and culture of the minorities existing within their territory. Persons belonging to minorities

---

[59] See Framework Convention, Explanatory Report, para. 71.

should have adequate opportunities to gain knowledge of the society as a whole.' Finally, The Hague Recommendations spell out the details of these obligations by urging '[s]tate educational authorities [to] ensure that the general compulsory curriculum includes the teaching of the histories, cultures and traditions of their respective national minorities.'[60]

These international standards thus envisage a two-way process of learning – with persons in the majority learning about minorities, and persons in the minority learning about the majority. Because the latter is generally easier to ensure, as persons in the minority will be exposed in many contexts to the culture of the majority, the question focuses on the extent to which the participating States are fostering the learning about minorities by persons in the majority. It is to be noted that the question refers to 'culture, history, religion, and belief of national minorities.' The question was meant to be inclusive and encourage States to report all measures taken to teach about their national minorities to the student body at large through the general curriculum.

2. Questionnaire Results

The replies to the questionnaire reveal some clear patterns. First, the vast majority of States responding to this question asserted that they do teach about one or more of their national minorities in the curriculum.[61] The only exceptions were: Armenia, which said it taught about them only at the university level and in Sunday schools; Georgia, which said it taught about them only in special societies; and Malta, which said its schools 'concentrate on Maltese culture.'

Second, and somewhat militating against the promising results suggested by the first pattern, a significant number of States – 15 – responded in a way that indicates that the minority cultures are not taught in the general curriculum as that term is usually understood, i.e. the curriculum or curricula for all students, both members of the majority and minorities. Instead, for these States, the minority cultures were taught only to the members of the minorities (or only to students attending the schools where the teaching is done in the minority language). States responding in this way were: Azerbaijan, Belarus, Bosnia and Herzegovina, Bulgaria, Croatia, Germany (Danish and Sorbian traditions only in specific Lander, though Roma culture taught throughout the country), Italy,

---

[60] The Hague Recommendations, para. 19. They also recommend other measures to promote dialogue: encouragement of members of the majority to learn minority languages, involvement of minority groups in preparation of curricula, and establishment of centers of minority language education. Id. paras. 19-21.

[61] States not responding to the question were Cyprus, France, Greece, Iceland, Liechtenstein, Portugal, San Marino, Tajikistan, and United States of America. In addition, Canada responded that this was a matter for provincial authorities; Monaco responded that it followed the French curriculum with the addition of materials on Monagesque culture; and Russian Federation noted that protection and development of national and regional cultures is part of the State education policy, but did not provide further details about its curricula.

Kazakstan, Moldova, Netherlands, Romania, the former Yugoslav Republic of Macedonia, Ukraine, United Kingdom, and Uzbekistan. The same result – teaching about minority cultures only in certain areas and not in the general curriculum – would appear to apply for those States responding that they had a national educational curriculum (without stating that it included study of minority cultures) but noting that different regions could devote a proportion of class hours to local issues, including local minorities: Finland, Ireland, Latvia, and Spain. The total number of States whose responses to the question suggest lack of teaching in the national curriculum is thus 21 (if Germany is not included as it does teach about the Roma in the general curriculum).

Third, 16 States offered answers suggesting the presence of a program of teaching about their own national minorities in the general curriculum: Austria, Czech Republic, Denmark, Estonia, Germany (Roma only), Hungary, Kyrgyzstan, Lithuania, Norway, Poland, Slovakia, Slovenia, Sweden, Switzerland, Turkey, and Turkmenistan. Some of these States mentioned particular minorities that were studied in these classes: Estonia (Baltic Germans), Lithuania (Jews, Tatars, and Karaites), and Sweden (Sami).

Fourth, a number of States mentioned that they offered courses teaching tolerance and inter-cultural understanding generally. In some States, these appeared to be instead of courses about their national minorities, and in others in addition to such courses: Austria, Czech Republic, Luxembourg, Netherlands, and United Kingdom.

Fifth, States had differing approaches to the teaching of minority religion, with certain States pointing out that they did not teach it and others that they did. Belarus and the former Yugoslav Republic of Macedonia indicated that religious study was not included in the public school curriculum; and Hungary, Kyrgyzstan, Sweden, and Switzerland noted that they taught history and culture of national minorities, but did not mention minority religion. Croatia, Denmark, Finland, Latvia, Poland, Romania, Slovakia, and Uzbekistan stated that minority religion was taught, although, as noted above, many of these States taught these religions only to members of the minority group (often as religious instruction per se at the wish of the parents) and not in the general curriculum as instruction about the religion(s) of the national minorities.

Finally, the responses from the relatively few States describing the levels at which minority cultures are taught reveal different methods. Some stated that such studies begin at the primary level (Czech Republic, Kyrgyzstan, and Slovenia); others noted these issues were taught in secondary schools (Austria, Denmark, Turkmenistan, and Uzbekistan).

3. Analysis of Results

The results of the questionnaire are thus somewhat disappointing in terms of the reported practices of States. Fewer than one-third of the States responded affirmatively that they teach about minority cultures in the general curriculum (although, as noted, some States did not answer the question). This suggests that, although States are providing minorities with opportunities to learn about their own culture, most are not instructing the student body at large about the minorities in a way that will help foster a spirit of understanding, tolerance, and national unity. Failure to follow through on teaching about national minorities to the broader student body may undercut the efforts to provide minorities with education about their own culture, in that a heightened sense of minority identity by these persons will be met only by continued ignorance or misunderstanding by the majority culture. The practice by some States in teaching tolerance is welcome.

The cause of this problem is likely complex. The responses of States to the question suggest that some are unaware that the standards discussed above concern education in the general curriculum, and not just education for the minority students. They may thus be assuming that they have fulfilled their OSCE and other commitments in the area of minority rights by adding minority cultural studies to the curricula of minority schools or of schools in regions with significant numbers of persons belonging to national minorities. Beyond this, some may be addressing other priorities within their educational system. It is nonetheless to be hoped that States view inter-cultural understanding and dialogue as a priority in and of itself and devote the necessary resources to this goal.

As for the levels at which such courses should be taught, there is no specification in the international standards, and the number of States responding to this question is too small to reveal any clear patterns. Nonetheless, the process of creating understanding between persons belonging to minority and majority cultures is one that should begin at a young age. Just as it is assumed that persons belonging to the minority population will be learning the culture of the majority from an early age, so it is to be hoped that persons belonging to the majority can begin to learn about the cultures of national minorities at a young age and create the potential for greater tolerance.

Finally, as for teaching about the religion of national minorities in the general curriculum, the standards do not require that students be given any formal lessons about the religion of the minority. They are not, moreover, meant to override any policies separating church and State and certainly not to override the rights of students to practice their own religion without coercion from other faiths. Rather, religion is included only as a facet of creating an understanding of minority cultures. Thus, to give one obvious example, the Croatian majority in Croatia would need to have some understanding of the Eastern Orthodox religion in order generally to understand the culture of the Serb minority in Croatia. Where the national minority is not religiously distinct, for instance the French minority in Italy, then teaching about the religion would presumably be unnecessary.

E. Implementation of the Right to Establish Private Schools

QUESTION 7: In which ways has your country implemented the right to establish privately administered educational institution for persons belonging to national minorities? Are such institutions entitled to receive public funding?

1. *International Standards*

The ability of persons belonging to national minorities to establish private schools is another important component of the realization of linguistic and other rights of national minorities. Such schools either represent a substitute for the public schools or serve as important supplements to the public schools for additional education in minority languages and culture. The ability of persons belonging to national minorities to establish private schools is not meant to challenge the legitimacy of the public school system, but to create additional options for them to learn their culture and language while still satisfying the basic educational requirements of the State.

The international standards in this regard reflect the balance between the needs of minorities and the legitimate policies of the State regarding educational standards and the use of public funding. Thus, paragraph 32.2 of the Copenhagen Document states that minorities have the right 'to establish and maintain their own educational, cultural and religious institutions, organizations or associations, which can seek voluntary financial and other contributions as well as public assistance, in conformity with national legislation.' Article 13(3) of the International Covenant on Economic, Social and Cultural Rights provides:

> The States Parties to the present Covenant undertake to have respect for the liberty of parents and, when applicable, legal guardians to choose for their children schools, other than those established by the public authorities, which conform to such minimum educational standards as may be laid down or approved by the State and to ensure the religious and moral education of their children in conformity with their own convictions.

Article 13(1) of the Framework Convention states: 'Within the framework of their educational systems, the Parties shall recognise that persons belonging to a national minority have the right to set up and to manage their own private educational and training establishments.' In addition, certain bilateral agreements provide for these rights as well.[62]

Thus, the international standards provide minorities with the right to establish private schools, but not the right to exemption from national standards of education nor the right to public funding. Nevertheless, as noted in The Hague

---

[62] See, e.g., Slovakia-Hungary Treaty, Art. 15(2)(e).

Recommendations, the State may not, in the name of educational standards, impose unduly burdensome legal and administrative requirements on minority private schools (para. 9). Nor may it interfere with these schools' ability to receive funding from private sources at home and abroad (para. 10).

2. Questionnaire Results

Every State answering this question noted that national minorities have the right to establish private schools.[63] Seven noted that this right was written in or derived from their constitution (Andorra, Armenia, Austria, Germany, Netherlands, Switzerland, and United States of America); while six noted that the right was specifically guaranteed in law (Andorra, Croatia, Estonia, Latvia, the former Yugoslav Republic of Macedonia, and United Kingdom). Armenia, Austria, and Turkey noted that such schools were guaranteed under special treaties to which they were parties – the CIS Convention Guaranteeing the Rights of Persons Belonging to National Minorities, the Treaty of St. Germain, and the Treaty of Lausanne, respectively. Nevertheless, some States replied that they had no private schools especially for minorities (Armenia, Hungary, Malta, Norway, Poland, and Turkmenistan); and others replied that such schools were quite uncommon, often due to the prevalence of attendance at public schools (Belarus, Finland, Moldova, and the former Yugoslav Republic of Macedonia). Some also said minority schools only existed at certain levels: Azerbaijan (university level); Denmark (elementary level); Moldova (secondary and college); Tajikistan (elementary level); the former Yugoslav Republic of Macedonia (secondary level); and Uzbekistan (elementary level).

Many States responding to the question noted that minority schools would have to meet certain standards set by the State and would then receive a license or other form of <u>accreditation</u>. Some noted specific requirements for receipt of such a license, e.g., teaching on the level of or equivalent to that in the State schools (Denmark, Sweden). Switzerland stated that such schools might be required to use the official language. It is unclear, however, whether these standards apply to all private schools established by minorities or just those that are meant to serve as substitutes for, rather than supplements to, the public schools.

With regard to <u>funding</u>, answers were somewhat less uniform. The following States said such schools were entitled to public funding: Austria, Canada, Czech Republic, Denmark, Estonia, Finland, Georgia, Germany, Hungary, Ireland, Italy, Kazakhstan, Latvia, Lithuania, Moldova, Netherlands, Norway, Poland, Romania, Russian Federation, Slovakia, Slovenia, Sweden, Switzerland (except primary schools), Turkey, and United Kingdom. Monaco and Spain stated private schools do not receive public funding, and United States of America said

---

[63] Bulgaria, Cyprus, France, Greece, Iceland, Kyrgyzstan, Liechtenstein, Luxembourg, Portugal, and San Marino did not respond to the question.

that its constitutional separation of church and State set strict limits on such funding. Of those States that did provide funding, some stated that funding depended on attendance thresholds (Denmark, Ireland, and Slovakia); others said it was contingent upon meeting certain educational standards (Czech Republic, Lithuania, Netherlands, Norway, Romania, and Russian Federation). Latvia stated that it would provide public funding only if school courses were in Latvian, with exceptions possible for bilingual preschools and elementary schools. (Other States may well contain similar requirements in their standards without mentioning them in the response to the questionnaire.) Finally, a number of States noted certain limits on public funding of private schools: Denmark (75 percent of costs); Latvia (80 percent of employees' wages and benefits); Poland (50 percent of costs); while others noted that funding was unrestricted (Lithuania, Slovakia).

3. Analysis of Results

It appears that every OSCE participating State responding to the question has acknowledged the right of minorities to establish private schools, and in most States such schools exist, although the questionnaire results do not make clear whether these are regular day schools or supplementary schools. While only a minority of States responded that such a right was enshrined in their constitution or law, it might well be the case that the number is significantly higher. In either case, it would seem a positive step for those States that do not yet have legal provisions guaranteeing the right of minorities (and others) to establish private schools to codify this right as soon as possible.

As for accreditation, none of the responses provided by States suggested requirements that would be unduly burdensome or discriminate against minority schools, although most States did not provide the detailed contents of their accreditation standards. It bears repeating that such standards must not discriminate against minority schools or constitute de facto barriers to their operation. It would seem in this context that the standards, if any, required for schools supplementing the regular schools (e.g., after-school and weekends) should not be nearly as high as those for private schools that will be the main educational institution for the student.

Regarding funding, it is to be welcomed that so many States do provide some funding for such schools. Such funding can help minority schools meet the standards that States have set for their educational quality and thus, in effect, help ensure the continued operation of the schools. Conditioning funding upon a minority school's previously attaining the State schools' standards may thus, as a de facto matter, amount to a denial of funding. Funding initially conditioned upon attendance would seem a better way of linking it to minority interest; future funding could be conditioned on meeting the educational standards.

F. Access to Public Media

QUESTION 8: In which ways and to what extent, do persons belonging to national minorities have access to public media in their language? For example, do they enjoy access to and time on public electronic media channels (television and radio) to produce and transmit programmes in their language?

1. *International Standards*

The right of persons belonging to minorities to receive and impart information to each other depends in great part on access to media outlets. This right derives from the basic human right to seek, receive, and impart information specified in Article 19 of the ICCPR and Article 10 of the ECHR. Under these conventions, the choice of language employed cannot per se be a legitimate basis for any governmental restrictions on communication. Minority language newspapers, radio and television broadcasts, and, increasingly, electronic fora (e.g., worldwide web sites) are all possible avenues for communication. These media are especially important when minorities are scattered across large regions. International standards dealing specifically with access to the media for minorities are somewhat limited in nature. The only multilateral instrument addressing the issue expressly is the Framework Convention, which states in Article 9(3):

> The Parties shall not hinder the creation and the use of printed media by persons belonging to national minorities. In the legal framework of sound radio and television broadcasting, they shall ensure, as far as possible, and taking into account the provisions of paragraph 1 [regarding the right to receive and impart information without discrimination], that persons belonging to national minorities are granted the possibility of creating and using their own media.

In addition to this provision, bilateral treaties contain similar requirements.[64]

Several aspects of this provision should be noted. First, the Framework Convention prohibits States from hindering the creation and use of media. Second, it requires States to grant minorities the possibility to use their own media, though subject to two limitations – (a) that States may provide that such use be undertaken within the legal framework of their broadcasting laws; and (b) that States ensure this opportunity 'as far as possible.' The second clause recognizes that there are technical factors affecting the ability of a State to grant members of minority groups the possibility to create and use certain media, notably radio and TV, where frequencies might be limited.[65]

---

[64] See, e.g., Slovakia-Hungary Treaty, Art. 15(2)(g).
[65] See Framework Convention, Explanatory Report, para. 61.

Third, the reference to paragraph one of Article 9 and its standards of non-discrimination suggests that, in addition to the positive obligation to provide access, any access should not discriminate among languages and thus not restrict the enjoyment of minority rights.[66] This means that any distinctions among programming for different languages should be based on objective factors such as demand and technical limitations, and not prejudice against a linguistic group. It would also imply that governments should not restrict or censor the content of minority programming except to the limited extent permissible for the media generally (e.g., incitement to racial hatred, obscenity, etc.).[67]

The Framework Convention does not address public funding of media, either through access to State radio or television or government grants to minority media. The Oslo Recommendations, however, suggest that minorities should have access to broadcast time on publicly funded media and not merely the right to establish private stations. At the same time, the Recommendations recognize that access must be commensurate with the size and concentration of the group.[68]

The Framework Convention also does not directly address access by minority groups to broadcasts from other States in the minority language. Paragraph 32.4 of the Copenhagen Document and Article 17(1) of the Framework Convention require States to respect the rights of persons belonging to national minorities to establish and maintain free and peaceful contacts across frontiers. It may be especially important for the maintenance and development of identity for such persons to have access to the usually more developed and fuller programming available from the kin State. In any event, consistent with the principle of non-discrimination, such access should not be denied based solely upon the language of the communication, a principle also reflected in the Oslo Recommendations.[69]

2. *Questionnaire Results*

Most States responding to the question addressed both print media and electronic media, although some focussed exclusively on the latter.[70] Ten States discussing <u>newspapers</u> noted that a wide variety of national minorities had their own newspapers or periodicals, in most cases in their own languages:[71] Armenia (Russian, Ukrainian, Kurdish, and Jewish); Azerbaijan (Kurdish, Lezgi, Talysh, Russian, and Georgian); Belarus (Tatar, Jewish, Ukrainian, and Polish);

---

[66] See Oslo Recommendations, para. 8.
[67] Id. para. 10.
[68] Id. para. 9.
[69] Id. para. 11.
[70] Cyprus, Iceland, Liechtenstein, Luxembourg, Portugal, and San Marino did not answer the question.
[71] Some States listed the languages, while others listed the minority groups.

Bulgaria (Turkish, Russian, Armenian, Wallachian, and Jewish); Croatia (Italian, Czech, Slovak, Hungarian, Ruthenian, Ukrainian, Serb, German, Austrian, Jewish, Albanian, Roma, Montenegrin, and Macedonian); Kazakstan (Russian, German, Uighur, Korean, Ukrainian, Kurdish, and Uzbek); Latvia (Russian, Belarussian, Lithuanian, Liv, Jewish, and Estonian); Lithuania (Russian, Polish, Belarussian, Ukrainian, German, Yiddish, English, and French); Ukraine (Russian, Armenian, Romanian, Jewish, Bulgarian, Polish, and Tatar); and Uzbekistan (Russian, Tajik, Kazak, Tatar, Kyrgyz, and Turkmen). Some States noted the presence of many newspapers or magazines in a small number of languages: Azerbaijan (20 in Russian); Estonia (12 in Russian); Greece (10 in Turkish); and Turkey (eight in Armenian). And nine States added that they provide State subsidies to newspapers or magazines: Germany, Hungary, Norway, Poland, Romania, Sweden, the former Yugoslav Republic of Macedonia, Ukraine, and United Kingdom.

As for broadcast media, all responding States noted that they provided access to such media for minorities, with the exception of Andorra, which stated that the only public media programming was the national news. The number of languages broadcast was, not surprisingly, somewhat smaller than the number of languages for printed media, but 16 States nonetheless reported offering radio or TV broadcasting in at least several minority languages: Azerbaijan, Croatia, Czech Republic, France, Germany, Italy, Kazakstan, Kyrgyzstan, Lithuania, Moldova, Poland, Romania, Slovakia, Sweden, the former Yugoslav Republic of Macedonia, and Uzbekistan. In addition, many States noted that they freely allowed broadcasts from neighboring countries where the language is the majority language (e.g., the Baltic States from Russian Federation, Sweden from Finland, Greece from Turkey).

Nevertheless, the responses revealed certain differences and patterns. First were large differences with respect to the number of hours or programs offered in the minority language, although many States did not specify the amount of programming. States whose responses noted a relatively high amount of minority language programming – greater than two hours per day per language – were: Estonia (Russian); Slovenia (Italian and Hungarian); the former Yugoslav Republic of Macedonia (Albanian and Turkish); and United Kingdom (Welsh); although other States may meet this threshold as well. Some reported a rather small amount of programming, e.g., Moldova (30-45 minutes per month, with more for Ukrainian). In addition, Canada and Switzerland provide a full range of radio and television programming in the official languages (although Switzerland has more limited programming for Romansch).

Second, States differed in terms of their provision of access through public media versus private media (though some did not distinguish between the two in their answers). Some States with official stations mentioned that they have laws specifying that broadcasts should address the concerns of national minorities or that minorities should have access to State media: Croatia, Hungary, Latvia,

Lithuania, Poland, and Russian Federation (although the Croatian and Latvian laws also restrict the amount of broadcast time in minority languages to a certain percentage of air time). Many noted that they provided access to State TV and radio for some programming and noted that private stations could also broadcast or were broadcasting in minority languages: Canada, Estonia, Hungary, Italy, Latvia, Lithuania, Russian Federation, Slovakia, the former Yugoslav Republic of Macedonia, and United Kingdom. Others noted that the stations were government stations, though they included both national and regional stations: Austria, Croatia, Czech Republic, Finland, Moldova, Norway, Romania, and Ukraine. (It would appear that some stations mentioned by other States are also public stations.) Several States mentioned that the media was private, though it broadcast minority language programming in any case: Germany, Sweden, Switzerland. These three States also have press laws or contracts with the private companies mandating that programming take account of the different language groups in the country. United States of America has a law allowing for the provision of grants to organizations producing radio and TV programs in Native American languages.

Third, and relatedly, is the question of editorial control over the content of minority language broadcasts on government channels. While a small number of States suggested that the broadcast units were independent of government control (Finland for Sami and Swedish broadcasts; Czech Republic; the three States noted above which have exclusively private broadcasters; and United States of America), a large number did not specify, leaving the impression that the government might restrict the amount and determine or censor the content of such broadcasts. A small number noted that a member of the minority has the right to sit on a broadcast regulation board which might or might not have the power to regulate content (Croatia, Germany, and Hungary), although it is possible that other States might utilize this method as well.

Fourth, and also related to the question of independence and content of broadcasts, is the question of broadcasts about minorities versus broadcasts by minorities in their own language. Several States noted that they provide a periodically scheduled official broadcast about minorities in their country or otherwise provided news about minority groups (Croatia, Kyrgyzstan, and Poland) and it seems likely that other States provide this type of programming as well.

3. Analysis of Results

The results of the questionnaire provide some welcome results with respect to access by minorities to media in their own language. As an initial matter, the results suggest that printed media is flourishing in the OSCE region. Although only nine States responded that they provided subsidies to the printed media, it is our sense that the number is larger, a trend which is to be encouraged.

The great variety in broadcast programming opportunities across OSCE States is welcome, with many States providing access to government channels and some even guaranteeing it in legislation. As for those States providing relatively few hours of programming in minority languages, the issue for them regarding the international standards is whether they are adequately responding to a real demand by minority groups in light of the technical limitations on the State. It would seem that those States providing only a short broadcast each day in a minority language may well be in a position to expand the number of hours, especially if the production is left to members of minority groups rather than through hiring of new professionals for State TV or radio. Permitting a minority group to establish its own private TV or radio station, as many States have done, is in many cases not a substitute for access to State TV or radio, which is likely to have more sophisticated broadcasting mechanisms and be received by a greater number of residents of the State. It is to be welcomed that the three States with exclusively private stations that responded to this question have legal guarantees that programs will be made for minority communities.

Regarding editorial control, the responses from governments suggest that much of the minority language programming is provided on government stations. Although most States did not directly address the question of editorial control, it is important that such control be left with the minority groups. Any other policy would undermine not only the OSCE standards with respect to access to the media but other important international legal principles regarding freedom of expression. The presence of minorities on oversight bodies is a welcome trend in this direction, in that it helps stations remain aware of the need for minority language programming, but it should not be viewed as interchangeable with editorial freedom. Finally, as for programming about minorities, such programs, if they accurately reflect minority (rather than simply government) perspectives, may enhance awareness of minority cultures and concerns throughout the country; yet they should not be viewed as a replacement for programs prepared by minority groups and broadcast in their own language.

None of the States addressed the question of computer-related media. It is to be hoped that all States in the OSCE respect the right of minority groups to establish worldwide web sites free of government restrictions (except those permitted by international human rights standards).

G. Other Protections for Minorities

QUESTION 9: In relation to the use and development of their language(s), what additional rights, if any, are enjoyed in your country by persons belonging to national minorities?

1. Questionnaire Results

Most States provided a response to this question, although a number of them referred to minority rights generally rather than the use and development of language. Some noted the presence of special associations, schools, institutes, cultural centers, theatres, festivals, and other activities by and for minorities, some of which receive government funding; some also noted the presence of various autonomy regimes.

Four groups of responses are of particular note. First, regarding the right to use names, Italy stated that regional statutes allow for place name identification in minority languages; Slovakia stated that persons belonging to national minorities have the legal right to use minority languages for personal and place names; and the former Yugoslav Republic of Macedonia noted that such persons have the right to use their languages for identification cards and birth/death/marriage registries.[72]

Second, two States address the rights of civil servants to use and speak minority languages: Canada, which stated that federal employees have the right to work and be supervised in their own language, coupled with a formal complaint mechanism in the event of violations; and Lithuania, which noted that the amount of Lithuanian required of civil servants varied with their level of responsibility, and that only new employees must pass language examinations immediately, whereas there is no fixed deadline for incumbents.

Third, a few States highlighted the existence of government bodies or advisory groups that protect the rights of minorities to use their languages: Austria has established Ethnic Advisory Councils; Lithuania noted several special governmental structures to protect minorities; Switzerland noted that the Chamber of Cantons provided representation for different language groups, that the composition of the Federal Council strove to include representation of all four language groups, and that the Federal Court included persons who spoke all four languages; and United Kingdom noted various government bodies to hear minority views.

Fourth, Croatia and Moldova added that they had central libraries for national minorities financed by the State.

---

[72] Czech Republic noted the presence of bilingual signs in regions of high minority concentration, although not provided by law.

2. Analysis of Results

All of the additional rights noted by States are welcome additions to those in the responses to the other questions. The use of minority languages for identification cards, government registries, and place names is welcome and conforms to the requirements of Article 11 of the Framework Convention, which gives persons belonging to national minorities the right to official recognition of their name in the minority language and commits governments to endeavor to display names in the minority language in regions traditionally inhabited by substantial numbers of minorities.[73] It is hoped that all OSCE participating States – in particular those parties to the Framework Convention – are similarly offering such opportunities for use of names in minority languages. The flexibility shown by a number of States regarding language requirements for public employees is also noteworthy. The Canadian plan, with its rights for persons to speak and use their own language (i.e. choosing one of the two official languages), goes very far and follows that State's commitment to official bilingualism; the Lithuanian plan, while more modest, is a creative way of accommodating civil servants who speak only a minority language while working towards the State's goal of knowledge of Lithuanian for new civil servants with significant levels of responsibility.

The creation of institutions within States to address minority concerns directly is also important. Such bodies can act as a check on majoritarian trends within the government and help prevent discrimination against minorities. Such bodies must have significant independent authority guaranteed by law to ensure that they will be more than merely symbolic. In addition, the creation of libraries dedicated to minority culture and literature can be an important method of maintaining group consciousness and identity. It is obviously important that such libraries receive adequate funding.

V. CONCLUSIONS

As might be expected, the survey results reveal a broad range of practices by States with respect to the linguistic rights of persons belonging to national minorities. Indeed, in addition to a first set of differences – those between States' responses to a particular question – one confronts a second set of differences – those between a State's response to one question (e.g., use of language with governmental authorities) and the same State's response to another question (e.g., teaching of minority cultures). Many of these differences are due to basic demographic facts: States with large numbers of persons speaking minority languages or a large number of minority languages, or both, will usually have a broader range of programs to protect linguistic rights than

---

[73] See also Oslo Recommendations, paras. 1-3.

those with only small pockets of minorities. The differences may also be traced, however, to other factors, such as the economic development of the country and consequently the resources available for minority programs; and the degree of rootedness of concepts of democracy and human rights, including minority rights. These factors are more changeable and suggest the possibility of real improvement regarding the enjoyment of linguistic rights in those areas where States are currently not meeting OSCE and other international standards. Nevertheless, many of these States are already making positive efforts to improve the enjoyment of linguistic rights.

The results suggest several general conclusions as well as more specific recommendations. First, it would seem that some States need to be better aware of the content of the international standards in these various areas. Although foreign ministries may be cognizant of relevant international standards, lawmakers and those in law-implementing agencies may well be unfamiliar with them, including with their flexibility in many respects. The standards themselves are the result of compromise and aim to protect the linguistic rights of persons belonging to national minorities while respecting certain objective limits upon the State, e.g., financial and infrastructural.

Second, the results suggest that many States would be well served by setting their policies in this area through more official and legal methods, i.e. legislation. A legal framework for protection of linguistic rights is a crucial first step to overcoming arbitrary interference with minority rights and full implementation of international standards. This is not to say that an all-encompassing law on languages is necessary or even desirable; indeed, many States appear to have good track records regarding respect for the international standards without such language laws, and the existence of such a law is certainly not sufficient to protect linguistic rights.

Third, and especially important, the responses highlight the need for governments to maintain close channels of communication with persons belonging to national minorities. Many of the international standards turn on an assessment of the genuine needs of minorities, to which governments must respond. In some States, mechanisms are well established for ascertaining those needs. But in many others, members of national minorities may be sufficiently isolated from channels of authority – sometimes due to the very language differences at issue here – that the government is not aware of what schools, media, access to interpreters, or other needs they have. A prerequisite to successful implementation of the standards is thus efficient lines of communication between minorities and decisionmakers. This requires a willingness on both sides to cooperate, even if ultimately the burden will fall upon governments to meet the standards.

Beyond these general points, the answers of States to the individual questions suggest a number of specific recommendations, some of which appear earlier in this report:

1. States with official languages should endeavor to extend some form of <u>status or recognition to non-official languages</u> where those languages are spoken by large numbers of people. Most States have already done this in some form, although the practical implications of such status for minorities vary significantly across States. It is important that such status will result in the enjoyment of linguistic rights.

2. With respect to access to <u>administrative and judicial authorities,</u> many States should consider more legal protections in this area. Many members of minority groups may not speak the official language well, and, even if they do, may consider it an important part of their minority identity to be able to use the minority language in communication with governmental authorities. Those States that limit such communications by region or proportion should consider that, in so doing, they may well be failing to address adequately the rights of minorities throughout the country. States should make available adequate resources (e.g., interpreters, translators, bilingual civil servants) to ensure that persons belonging to national minorities are adequately understood and may receive a reply in their own language.

3. States should give closer attention to the <u>teaching of and in minority languages</u>. It is often unclear how much minority languages are taught outside the regions where minority populations are most concentrated. States should create a flexible policy that responds to the different needs of persons belonging to national minorities and local conditions. Moreover, States need to ensure that minorities are closely involved in the decisions to set up classes taught in those languages, so that the needs of the pupils and their parents are reflected in the curricula.

4. Similarly, there is clearly a sense from the responses that most States are not <u>teaching about minority cultures in the general curriculum</u>. As noted earlier, States need to include such teaching in order to increase inter-ethnic understanding and dialogue, key ingredients for a democratic and tolerant society. Special courses that teach tolerance, already included in the curricula in some States, are also useful. They can serve as a form of transition to full teaching about their minority cultures and also advance the important goal of sensitizing students to foreign cultures that do not qualify as national minorities, e.g., recent immigrants or refugees resident in the country.[74] The

---

[74] See Copenhagen Document, para. 36 (Each participating State will promote a climate of mutual respect, understanding, co-operation and solidarity among all persons living on its territory, without distinction as to ethnic or national origin or religion [...]').

Council of Europe is now taking a proactive role in providing ideas for curricula in these areas.[75]

5. Although <u>private schools</u> appear to be flourishing in the OSCE region, it is important that States ensure that no discriminatory treatment is given with respect to establishment or accreditation of such schools. In particular, when such schools are to serve as substitutes for regular schools, States should ensure that the conditions for their operation are impartial.

6. Finally, with respect to access to the media, States should consider all available options for <u>increasing the amount of programming in minority languages</u> to match the needs of the minority population. New technologies, allowing minorities to produce their own broadcasts, the broadcasting of foreign programs, and other methods can be used to expand the hours devoted to minority programming.

Because of the centrality of language to ethnic identity, the process of ensuring the linguistic rights of minorities is critical to the advancement of minority rights overall and human rights generally. The OSCE documents set important and reasonable standards for States to meet. Additional bilateral and multilateral treaties set higher legally binding obligations for some States. All deserve respect and compliance in order to create pluralistic and democratic societies throughout the OSCE region.

It is hoped that, in their policy- and law-making, OSCE participating States will draw from the variety of options and the best practices known in this field and apply these in their specific situations as may be appropriate.

Appendix

Questionnaire Sent to Governments

Question 1: Which languages have 'State' or 'official' status in your country? Please also provide relevant information on any other languages which may have special status in your country.

Question 2: May persons belonging to national minorities use their own language in their contacts with administrative authorities and public services throughout your country? Is this a matter of right under national law in

---

[75] See Michael Byram & Geneviève Zarate, *Young people facing difference: Some proposals for teachers*, Council of Europe Council for Cultural Cooperation Education Committee, 1995

territories in which the minority language is traditionally used by a substantial part of the local population?

Question 3: May persons belonging to national minorities use their own language in judicial proceedings and other contacts with judicial authorities throughout your country? Is this a matter of right under national law in territories in which the minority language is traditionally used by a substantial part of the local population?

Question 4: Which minority languages are taught in your country? At which levels of education are they taught (i.e. primary, secondary, vocational, teacher training, university)? Are these taught only in some localities? If so limited, by what criteria are the localities defined in which such education is available?

Question 5: Do persons belonging to national minorities enjoy the right to education in their language, i.e. the whole or significant parts of their education in their own language? If it is limited, please indicate which subjects are taught in the minority languages and which subjects are required to be taught in the State or official language(s) at each level of education. Please also indicate whether the right is enjoyed throughout your country. If it is enjoyed in only some localities, by what criteria are the localities defined in which such education is available?

Question 6: To what extent is the culture, history, religion, and belief of national minorities taught in the general curriculum?

Question 7: In which ways has your country implemented the right to establish privately administered educational institutions for persons belonging to national minorities? Are such institutions entitled to receive public funding?

Question 8: In which ways, and to what extent, do persons belonging to national minorities have access to public media in their language? For example, do they enjoy access to and time on public electronic media channels (television and radio) to produce and transmit programmes in their language?

Question 9: In relation to the use and development of their language(s), what additional rights, if any, are enjoyed in your country by persons belonging to national minorities?

SURVEY OF NATIONAL ACTIVITIES AND DOCUMENTS

ALBANIA

I. Demographic situation

Population (1992): Total 3,400,000. Minority groups: Greeks 59,000 (1.8%); Macedonians 4,700 (0.19%).

Other estimates: Greeks 150,000 (4.4%); Roma up to 100,000 (2.9%); Vlachs 35,000-50,000 (1-1.5%); Macedonians 40,000 (1.2%); South Slavs up to 40,000 (1.2%). However, according to some other estimates the figures are much lower: Greeks: 70,000; Macedonians 6,000; Montenegrins 2,000.

Languages: Albanian, Greek, Romani, Aromanian.

II. International obligations

Pursuant to Article 126 of the 1998 Albanian Constitution any international agreement that has been ratified by the Republic of Albania constitutes, after its publication in the official journal, a part of the internal legal system. It is implemented directly except in cases when the treaty is not self-executing and its implementation requires issuance of a law. A ratified international agreement has supremacy over national laws not compatible with it.

United Nations
- International Covenant on Civil and Political Rights (accession 4 October 1991)
- Not a party to the First Optional Protocol
- International Covenant on Economic, Social and Cultural Rights (accession 4 October 1991)

Council of Europe
- Member of the Council of Europe (13 July 1995)
- Party to the ECHR (signature 13 July 1995, ratification 2 October 1996)
- Not a party to the Charter for Regional and Minority Languages
- Framework Convention for the Protection of National Minorities (signature 29 June 1995, ratification 28 September 1999, entry into force 1 January 2000)

Bilateral treaties
- 1997 – with Greece, a treaty of cooperation and friendship which led to an agreement on the issue of Greek language education in Albania

III. National legislation

Constitution (4 August 1998)

Article 14
1. The official language in the Republic of Albania is Albanian.

Article 18
2. No one may be unjustly discriminated against for reasons such as gender, race, religion, ethnicity, language, political, religious or philosophical beliefs, economic condition, education, social status, or ancestry.

Article 20
1. Persons who belong to national minorities have the right to exercise in full equality before the law the human rights and freedoms.
2. They have the right freely to express, preserve and develop their ethnic, cultural, religious and linguistic identity, to study and to be taught in their mother tongue, as well as unite in organisations and societies for the protection of their interests and identity.

Article 28
1. Everyone whose liberty has been taken away has the right to be notified immediately, in a language that he understands, of the reasons for this measure, as well as the accusation made against him.
Every person whose liberty has been taken away shall be informed that he has no obligation to make a declaration and has the right to communicate immediately with a lawyer, and he shall also be given the possibility to realise his rights.

Article 31
During a criminal proceeding, everyone has the right:
    c) to have the assistance without payment of a translator, when he does not speak or understand the Albanian language; [...]

IV. Developments/events/comments

Education
The Decision of the Council of Ministers of the Republic of Albania of 1994 (No. 396) provides for the right of persons belonging to minorities to have education in their mother tongue for eight years. In addition, Article 10 of the

Law on the Educational System (No. 7152 (21 June 1995)) enables persons belonging to minorities to study and to be taught in their mother tongue.

Media
There are three newspapers published in the Greek language in southern Albania, while local radio broadcasts some Greek-language programmes.

Labour
Article 9 paragraphs (1) and (2) of the 1995 Labour Code (No. 7961/1995) prohibits every type of discrimination in employment or professional life. 'Discrimination' means any distinction, exclusion or preference that is based on, *inter alia*, race, color, sex, age, religion, political conviction and national origin. Distinctions, exclusions or preferences that reflect requirements for a specific position are not considered to be discriminatory.

National bodies
Under the authority of the Minister for Foreign Affairs a Government Office for National Minorities was established in 1993. Amongst its tasks, it implements fundamental political orientation for recognition and full respect of minority rights, brings concrete problems or minority complaints to the attention of the Government, develops cultural, linguistic, religious and ethnic identity of minorities and promotes better inter-ethnic understanding.

ANDORRA

I. Demographic situation

Population: Total 64,000. Minority groups: Andorrans 11,860 (18.4%); Portuguese 7,035 (10.9%); French 4,685 (7.3%).

Languages: Andorran, Spanish.

II. International obligations

Pursuant to Article 3, paragraphs 3 and 4, of the 1993 Constitution the universally recognized principles of public international law are incorporated into the legal system of Andorra. Treaties and international agreements take effect in the legal system from the moment of their publication in the Butlletí Oficial del Principat d'Andorra and cannot be amended or repealed by law.

United Nations
- Not a party to the International Covenant on Civil and Political Rights
- Not a party to the First Optional Protocol
- Not a party to the International Covenant on Economic, Social and Cultural Rights

Council of Europe
- Member of the Council of Europe (10 October 1994)
- Party to the ECHR (signature 10 November 1994, ratification 22 January 1996)
- Not a party to the Charter for Regional and Minority Languages
- Not a party to the Framework Convention for the Protection of National Minorities

III. National legislation

Constitution (28 April 1993)

Article 2
1. Catalan is the official language of the State.

ARMENIA

I. Demographic situation

Population: Total 3,400,000. Minority groups: Kurds 60,000 (1.7%); Russians 15,000-20,000 (0.4-0.6%).

Other estimates (1989): Armenian 93%, Azeri 3%, Russian 2%, other (mostly Yezidi Kurds) 2%.

Languages: Armenian, Russian.

II. International obligations

Pursuant to Article 6 of the 1995 Constitution international treaties that have been ratified are constituent parts of the legal system of Armenia. If norms provided by these treaties are contrary to those provided by the laws of the Republic, then the norms provided in the treaty shall prevail.

United Nations
- International Covenant on Civil and Political Rights (accession 23 June 1993)
- First Optional Protocol (accession 23 June 1993)
- International Covenant on Economic, Social and Cultural Rights (accession 13 September 1993)

Council of Europe
- Special Guest status to the Parliamentary Assembly (since 26 January 1996)
- Not a party to the Charter for Regional and Minority Languages
- Framework Convention for the Protection of National Minorities (signature 25 July 1997, ratification 20 July 1998, entry into force 1 November 1998)

III. National legislation

Constitution (5 July 1995)

Article 12
The State language of the Republic of Armenia is Armenian.

Article 15
Citizens, regardless of national origin, race, sex, language, creed, political or other persuasion, social origin, wealth or other status, are entitled to all the rights and freedoms, and subject to the duties determined by the Constitution and the laws.

Article 37
Citizens belonging to national minorities are entitled to the preservation of their traditions and the development of their language and culture.

Law of the Republic of Armenia on Language (Adopted on 17 April 1993, entered into force on 18 April 1993)

The present Law shall establish the principal tenets of the policy on language of the Republic of Armenia, shall govern a status of language, language relations between bodies of State authority and administration, enterprises, institutions and organizations.

Article 1 – Policy on Language of the Republic of Armenia
The Armenian language which spheres of life of the Republic shall be the State language of the Republic of Armenia. The literary Armenian language shall be the official language of the Republic of Armenia.

The Republic of Armenia shall promote preservation and dissemination of the Armenian language among Armenians residing outside its borders.

The Republic of Armenia shall promote unification of orthography of the Armenian language.

The Republic of Armenia on its territory shall guarantee the free usage of languages of national minorities.

Article 2 – Language of Education
The literary Armenian language shall be the language of teaching and education in the educational and teaching systems on the territory of the Republic of Armenia.

In communities of national minorities in the Republic of Armenia the general education may be organized in their native language in accordance with the State program and with the State patronage and compulsory teaching of the Armenian language.

On the territory of the Republic of Armenia a specialized educational institution in a foreign language may be established only by the Government of the Republic of Armenia upon the agreement of the standing committee on education, science, language and culture of the Supreme Soviet of the Republic of Armenia.

The entrance examination on the Armenian language and teaching of the Armenian language shall be obligatory at all secondary specialized, vocational and higher education institutions of the Republic of Armenia. The entrance examinations and education for repatriates, refugees, non-Armenians and aliens residing on the territory of the Republic of Armenia shall be organized in the manner established by the Government of the Republic of Armenia.

Article 3 – Language obligations of citizens
The officials and citizens of the Republic of Armenia working in certain spheres of service shall be obliged to know the Armenian language.

The Armenian language shall be the language of official statements of persons representing the Republic of Armenia, if it does not contradict the order accepted in that international institution.

In the official conversation citizens of the Republic of Armenia shall be obliged to ensure the purity of the language.

Article 4 – Language rights and obligations of institutions
The enterprises, institutions and organizations located on the territory of the Republic of Armenia shall communicate with State bodies, enterprises,

institutions, organizations and citizens of other countries in a mutually acceptable language.

The State bodies, enterprises, institutions and organizations of the Republic of Armenia shall be obliged:

a. to conduct the office work in the Armenian language;
b. to ensure simultaneous translation of statements in other languages into Armenian at congresses, sessions, meetings, symposia, during public statements, official and other public events;
c. to design signboards, letterheads, labels, post stamps, seals, international mail envelopes in the Armenian language accompanied, where necessary, by translation into other languages.

The foreign State bodies, enterprises, institutions and organizations located on the territory of the Republic of Armenia shall supply the documents that are subject to the State control, with translation into Armenian.

The organizations of national minorities residing on the territory of the Republic of Armenia shall design their documents, letterheads, seals in the Armenian language with parallel translation into their language.

Article 5 – Implementation of the State policy on language
The Government of the Republic of Armenia, local bodies of State authority and administration as well as the duly authorized State body shall implement the State policy on language in accordance with the legislation of the Republic of Armenia.

The Republic of Armenia shall encourage publications, press as well as preparation of textbooks, training appliances, scientific, methodical, reference, popular scientific literature in the Armenian language.

The legislation of the Republic of Armenia shall establish responsibility for violation of the requirements of the present Law.

IV. Developments/events/comments

At the Round Table meeting organized by the Union of Nationalities of Armenia on 21 July 2000, ethnic minorities claimed that they are experiencing serious problems in preserving their language and culture, problems which stem from the difficult socio-economic situation in the country. With respect to the Kurdish language it was pointed out that textbooks have not been published for almost two decades. Besides, lessons in the national language and literature available during the period of Soviet rule were now missing from schools in Kurdish villages.

AUSTRIA

I. Demographic situation

Population: Total 7,900,000. Minority groups: Former Yugoslavs 197,886 (2.5%); Turks 70,000 (0.9%); Other Central and Eastern Europeans 45,000 (0.6%); Roma 20,000-25,000 (0.15-0.30%); Burgenland Croats 19,109 (0.24%); Carinthian Slovenes 14,850 (0.19%); Styrian Slovenes 1,695 (0.02%); Burgenlands Hungarians 10,000 (0.13%); Jews 8,000 (0.1%); Czechs 8,000 (0.1%).

Languages: German.

II. International obligations

Article 9, paragraph 1 of the 1929 Constitution stipulates that the generally recognized rules of international law are regarded as integral parts of federal law. Pursuant to Article 16 (Implementation of Treaties), paragraph 1, federal units (States) are bound to take measures which become necessary within their autonomous sphere of competence for the implementation of international treaties. In case a federal unit fails to comply punctually with this obligation, the competence for such measures, particularly the issuing of the necessary laws, passes to the Federation.

United Nations
- International Covenant on Civil and Political Rights (signature 10 December 1973, ratification 10 September 1978)
- First Optional Protocol (signature 10 December 1973, ratification 10 September 1978)
- International Covenant on Economic, Social and Cultural Rights (signature 10 December 1973, ratification 10 September 1978)

Council of Europe
- Member of the Council of Europe (16 April 1956)
- ECHR (signature 13 December 1957, ratification 3 September 1958)
- European Charter for Regional and Minority Languages (signature 5 November 1992)
- Framework Convention for the Protection of National Minorities (signature 1 February 1995, ratification 31 March 1998, entry into force 1 July 1998)

Other international treaties
- 1919 – Treaty of St. Germain-en-Laye (Articles 66 and 67)
- 1955 – The Vienna State Treaty (Articles 6-8)

III. National legislation

Constitution (of 1929, status as on 1 July 1983)

Article 8
Without prejudice to the rights provided by federal law for linguistic minorities, German is the official language of the Republic.

Article 14
(6) Public schools are those schools which are established and maintained by authorities so required by law. The Federation is the authority so required by law in so far as legislation and execution in matters of the establishment, maintenance, and dissolution of public schools are the business of the Federation. The State or, according to the statutory provisions, the County, or a County Association is the authority so required by law in so far as legislation or implementing legislation and execution in matters of establishment, maintenance and dissolution of public schools are the business of the State. Admission to public school is open to all without distinction of birth, sex race, status, class, language and religion, and in other respects within the limits of the statutory requirements. The same applies analogously to kindergartens, centres, and student hostels.

IV. Developments/events/comments

The 1919 Treaty of St. Germain stipulates in Articles 66 and 67 that all Austrian citizens are equal before the law and enjoy the same civil and political rights without regard to their race, language or religion. Notwithstanding the introduction of an official language by the Austrian Government, non-German speaking Austrian citizens will be offered adequate facilities for the use of their language, verbally and in writing before the courts. Austrian citizens who belong to a racial, religious or linguistic minority shall enjoy the same treatment and the same guarantees, in law and in fact, as all other Austrian citizens.

In a similar way Article 8 the 1955 Treaty of Vienna guarantees all citizens the right to be elected to public office without regard to race, sex, language, religion or political opinion.

Federal Act on the Legal Status of Ethnic Groups in Austria
The legal status of ethnic groups in Austria is regulated in more detail by the Ethnic Groups Act enacted on 7 July 1976 (No. 396/1976). It stipulates in Section 1 paragraph 1, that the ethnic groups in Austria and their members enjoy the protection of the law; the preservation of the ethnic groups and the security of their existence are guaranteed. Their languages and ethnic characteristics shall be respected. According to paragraph 2, ethnic groups within the meaning of this Act are those groups of Austrian nationals with non-German mother tongues and

their own ethnic characteristics who have their residence and homes in parts of the Federal territory.

Topographic names
In an agreement with the Main Committee of the *Nationalrat* and after consulting the *Land* concerned, the Federal Government shall determine by ordinance the areas where, on account of a relatively high number (one quarter) of the members of an ethnic group who reside in the *Land*, that the topographical terminology shall be bilingual (Section 2, paragraph 1(ii), of the 1976 Ethnic Groups Act).

National bodies
Generally, responsibility for ethnic minorities is in the hands of the Federal Chancellery. In addition, the Federal Ministry of Education and Cultural Affairs deals with matters of minority education. By the Federal Government Ordinance of 18 January 1977, Ethnic Advisory Councils have been established for the Croat, Slovene, Hungarian, Czech, Slovak and Roma ethnic groups. Some of the main tasks of the Ethnic Advisory Councils is to advise the Federal Government and the Federal Ministers in matters concerning respective ethnic groups; to safeguard and represent the overall interests of the ethnic groups; and to make proposals for the improvement of the situation of ethnic groups and their members.

AZERBAIJAN

I. Demographic situation

Population: Total 7,300,000. Minority groups: Russians 440,000 (6.0%); Talysh 300,000 (4.2%); Lezgins 290,000 (4.0%); Kurds 200,000 (2.8%); Armenians 100,000 (1.4%).

Other estimates (census 1989): Azerbaijanis 82.7%, various ethnic groups (Lezgins, Avars, Talysh, Tsakhurs, Kurds, Udis, Russians, Ukrainians, Armenians, Tatars, Georgians and Belarusians) 17.3%.

Languages: Azeri, Russian.

II. International obligations

Articles 148 and 151 of the 1995 Constitution stipulate that international treaties to which Azerbaijan is a party are an inalienable part of the legislative system of the Azerbaijani Republic. In case of conflict between national legal acts and international treaties, international treaties will have supremacy and be applied.

United Nations
- International Covenant on Civil and Political Rights (accession 13 August 1992)
- Not a party to the First Optional Protocol
- International Covenant on Economic, Social and Cultural Rights (accession 13 August 1992)

Council of Europe
- Azerbaijan has had special observer status in the Council of Europe as of June 1996
- Not a party to the ECHR;
- Not a party to the Charter for Regional and Minority Languages
- Framework Convention for the Protection of National Minorities (accession 26 June 2000)

III. National legislation

Constitution (12 November 1995)

Article 21
The Azerbaijan language shall be the State language of the Azerbaijan Republic.

The Azerbaijan Republic shall ensure the development of the Azerbaijan language.

The Azerbaijan Republic shall guarantee the free use and development of other languages spoken by the population.

Article 25
Every person shall be equal to the law and court.

Men and women shall have equal rights and freedoms.

Every person shall have equal rights and freedoms irrespective of race, nationality, religion, sex, origin, property status, social position, convictions, political party, trade union organisation and social unity affiliation. Limitations or recognition of rights and freedoms because of race, nationality, social status, language origin, convictions and religion shall be prohibited.

Article 44
Every person shall have the right to preserve national/ethnic identity.
No one can be deprived of the right to change national/ethnic identity.

Article 45
Every person shall have the right to use Native Language. Everyone shall have the right to be raised and get an education, be engaged in creative activities in Native language.
No one can be deprived of the right to use Native Language.

The Law on the State Language in the Republic of Azerbaijan (Adopted on 22 December 1992, entered into force on 31 December 1992)

Believing that the usage of the Turkic language as the State language is one of the principal conditions for the sovereignty of the Republic of Azerbaijan, it shall take care of its application, preservation and development and shall encourage the Azerbaijanis residing abroad to get education in the native language and to meet their national and cultural requirements.

The present Law shall establish a legal status of the Turkic language on the territory of the Republic of Azerbaijan.

The present Law shall not govern the usage of any languages in private, unofficial relations.

I. General Provisions

Article 1
The Turkic language shall be the State language of the Republic of Azerbaijan. The work in all State bodies of the Republic of Azerbaijan shall be conducted in the Turkic language. The Turkic language as the State language of the Republic shall be applied in all spheres of political, economic, public, scientific and cultural life and it shall function as a means of interethnic communication on the territory of the Republic.

Representatives of other nationalities shall be encouraged and assisted to study the Turkic language.

Article 2
The legal status and sphere of application of the language in the Republic of Azerbaijan as well as the principles of the usage of languages of peoples residing on its territory shall be established by the supreme State authorities of the Republic of Azerbaijan.

II. The Right of Citizens to Choose a Language

Article 3
Citizens of the Republic of Azerbaijan shall be guaranteed the freedom to choose a language of teaching.

Nationalities and ethnic groups compactly residing on the territory of the Republic of Azerbaijan shall be granted the right to establish, by means of the State bodies of the Republic, pre-school institutions in the native language as well as general secondary schools or separate classes and groups in the native language at various educational institutions.

The study, as an obligatory discipline, of the Turkic language which is the State language of the Republic of Azerbaijan shall be provided in educational institutions with teaching in another language.

Article 4
Replies to suggestions, applications, and complaints of citizens of the Republic of Azerbaijan filed to State bodies, shall be in the State language of the Republic of Azerbaijan.

Article 5
The legal proceedings and notary actions shall be in the Turkic language. The participants in a case who do not know the language in which the proceedings are carried out shall be ensured the right to be acquainted with the materials of the case, to participate in the court proceedings through an interpreter as well as to make statements in the native language.

Article 6
Official documents identifying a person or information therein (passport, labor book, military card, school-leaving certificate, diploma, birth, marriage, death certificates etc.) shall be filled up in the Turkic language.

Article 7
Workers of the service sphere (trade, medical service, transport, customer service, long-distance communications etc.) shall use in working hours the State language of the Republic of Azerbaijan.

The evasion from customer service under the pretext of lack of knowledge of the language shall be inadmissible.

III. A Language to be used in the Work of State Bodies, Enterprises and Organizations

Article 8
Sessions of the Supreme Soviet of the Republic of Azerbaijan shall be in the Turkic language. Peoples' deputies of other ethnicity in the Republic of Azer-

baijan in case of lack of knowledge of the State language of the Republic of Azerbaijan shall be granted the right to make statements in the other language.

The drafts of laws and of other legal acts submitted for consideration by the Supreme Soviet of the Republic of Azerbaijan, by its commissions shall be presented in the State language of the Republic of Azerbaijan.

Article 9
The laws and other legal acts adopted by the National Assembly of the Republic of Azerbaijan and by its commissions and by the President of the Republic of Azerbaijan, shall be published in the Turkic language.

Article 10
Official publications of acts of State authority and administration bodies of the Republic of Azerbaijan and of the autonomous republic of Nakhichevan, shall be issued in the State language of the Republic of Azerbaijan.

Article 11
The documentation related to elections of the President of the Republic of Azerbaijan, of the Supreme Soviet and local Soviets shall be prepared in the State language of the Republic of Azerbaijan and shall be submitted to the Central electoral commission in that language.

Article 12
The office work at the enterprises, institutions, and organizations being a State property of the Republic of Azerbaijan, shall be in the Turkic language.

The texts of letterheads, stamps and signboards with names of ministries, institutions, enterprises, organizations of the Republic of Azerbaijan and of autonomous republic of Nakhichevan shall be produced in the Turkic language.

Article 13
The Turkic language and the accepted international language shall be used in the operator's communications, documentation and reference information in order to ensure the safe and uninterrupted functioning of the energy and transport systems (principal railway, air, sea, pipe transport etc.).

Article 14
The State language of the Republic of Azerbaijan shall be used in the military forces, internal and border guard troops of the Republic of Azerbaijan.

IV. Language in Information and Names

Article 15
Besides the State language, other languages may be used in the mass media on the territory of the Republic of Azerbaijan.

Printed announcements, communications, advertisements and other visual information may be produced in the State language of the Republic and, where necessary, at the same time in the accepted international language.

Labels of the goods produced in the Republic of Azerbaijan, names of industrial and alimentation goods, instructions for the goods shall be produced in the Turkic language and, where necessary - in the accepted foreign language.

Article 16
The names of settlements, administrative units and other geographic entities on the territory of the Republic of Azerbaijan shall be written in the State language, their writing on maps shall be established in accordance with the special reference books approved by the State.

Article 17
The names of State authority bodies, ministries, State committees and departments, enterprises, organizations and their subdivisions shall be written in the Turkic language.

Article 18
The proper name of a citizen of the Republic of Azerbaijan of Azerbaijanian ethnicity shall be composed of a name, patronymic and family name (patrimonial name). The patronymic shall be used together with the words 'ogly' and 'guyzy'. Every citizen of the Republic of Azerbaijan shall have the right to have a family name in accordance with his national affiliation.

The present Law shall not govern the writing of names and family names of representatives of other nationalities residing on the territory of the Republic.

V. Responsibility for Violation of the Law on the State Language

Article 19
The officials of all State bodies, enterprises, institutions and organizations in case of being guilty of violation of the Law on the State language shall be called to account in accordance with the legislation of the Republic of Azerbaijan.

IV. Developments/events/comments

Education
In areas with a high proportion of persons belonging to minorities the teaching of the mother tongue and of national history and culture is provided in two-hour weekly instruction introduced in schools. Such instruction is provided in Lezgin, Tati, Talysh and other languages.

Within the Ministry of Education a council has been created with the task of preparing and publishing curricula, manuals and textbooks for the teaching of minority languages. Financing for these publications is mostly provided by the

State funds. In 1997 textbooks and alphabets financed by the State were published in Russian, Talysh, Kurdish, Lezgin, Tsakhur and Tatar.

BELARUS

I. Demographic situation

Population: Total 10,150,000. Minority groups: Russians 1,342,100 (13.2%); Poles 417,700 (4.1%); Ukrainians 291,000 (2.9%); Jews 111,900 (1.1%); Others 84,000 (0.8%).

Languages: Belarusian, Russian.

According to the 1995 census the Belarusian-speaking community can be considered as a minority in Belarus as only 45% speak Belarusian.

II. International obligations

According to Article 8, paragraph 1 of the 1994 Constitution, the Republic of Belarus recognizes the supremacy of the universally acknowledged principles of international law and ensures that its laws comply with such principles.

United Nations
– International Covenant on Civil and Political Rights (ratification 12 November 1973)
– First Optional Protocol (accession 30 September 1992)
– International Covenant on Economic, Social and Cultural Rights (signature 19 March 1968, ratification 12 November 1973)

Council of Europe
– Not member of the Council of Europe[1]
– Not a party to ECHR

---

[1] The special guest status granted to the Belarusian Parliament on 16 September 1992, allowed a parliamentary delegation to attend sessions of the Parliamentary Assembly. However, on 13 January 1997 the special guest status was suspended because of the way in which the new legislature had come into being, thereby depriving it of democratic legitimacy, as the new Belarus constitution, in the view of the Council of Europe's Venice Commission, did not respect minimum democratic standards and violated the principles of separation of powers and the rule of law.

- Not a party to the European Charter for Regional and Minority Languages
- Not a party to the Framework Convention for the Protection of National Minorities

Bilateral agreements
- 1992 – with Poland

III. National legislation

Constitution (Adopted on 15 March 1994)

Article 17
1. The official language of the Republic of Belarus shall be Belarusian.
2. The Republic of Belarus shall safeguard the right to use the Russian language freely as a language of inter-ethnic communication.

Article 50
3. Everyone shall have the right to use his native language and to choose the language of communication. In accordance with law, the State shall guarantee the freedom to choose the language of education and teaching.

Law of the Republic of Belarus on National Minorities in the Republic of Belarus (Adopted and entered into force on 11 November 1992)

Article 2
The citizens of the Republic of Belarus who consider themselves as national minorities should observe the Constitution of the Republic of Belarus, its laws, contribute to the preservation of State sovereignty and territorial integrity of the Republic, respect traditions of citizens of any ethnicity residing in the Republic, their language and culture.

Article 5
The Republic of Belarus, respecting the human rights, shall guarantee the citizens of the Republic of Belarus who consider themselves as national minorities, equal political, economic and social rights and freedoms, including:

b. the right to learn and use the native language;
c. the right to print and distribute information on their native language;
e. the right to worship any religion, to perform national and ritual ceremonies in their native language.

Article 7
The Republic of Belarus in accordance with the legislation shall contribute to the creation of material conditions for the advance of education and cultures of

national minorities by allocating necessary financial means from the State budget.

Article 9
Public and cultural organizations of national minorities can form on their own means cultural and educational institutions.

Article 12
The citizens of the Republic of Belarus of any ethnicity shall enjoy protection of the State on equal footing.

Law of the Republic of Belarus on the Press and Other Mass Media (N 3515-XII of January 13, 1995)

Article 6. Language of Mass Media
Periodic printed editions and other mass media of the Republic of Belarus shall execute their activities in the State languages, as well as in other languages in accordance with the Constitution of the Republic of Belarus and the legislation in force.

Distortion of generally accepted norms of the language used shall not be allowed.

IV. Developments/events/comments

Education
Two official languages, Belarusian and Russian, are included in the school programme, but Russian prevails in education being the language of instruction to 59.4% of all students, and in Minsk only this percentage is 79%.

In September 1998 about 200 parents and public activists rallied in Minsk city centre to protest against the increasing use of Russian as primary language in public education. 'Only 30% of the country's students can go to schools where the primary language is Belarusian,' stated Alexander Sidyaka, deputy chief of the Belarusian Language Association, which organized the rally. In 1996 President Alexander Lukashenko made Russian an official language, along with Belarusian, which is difficult for Belarusian speakers to understand. Demonstrators claimed that the authorities harassed parents whose children went to Belarusian-language schools and forcefully transferred such schools to Russian-language education. In 1992 up to 70% of the nation's students went to schools where the primary teaching language was Belarusian.

In October 1998 several hundred people staged a rally in defence of the Belarusian language in the centre of Minsk. According to the rally organizers, the number of children entering schools teaching in Belarusian fell from 70% in 1991 to about 30% in 1998. In Minsk, only 7.3% of the total number of children who reached school age went to Belarusian-language schools in 1997 and by 1998 this had fallen to 4.7%.

National bodies
There is the Committee of the Republic of Belarus for Religious and National Affairs which possesses the rights of a Ministry in the respective issues. In addition, there is the Coordinating Council for Minorities established by the Cabinet of Ministers in January 1995. Among the main tasks of the Council is the coordination of activities of ministries and other central administrative bodies, the development of culture and education of minorities, developing ties between Belarus and the States which are the historic motherland of minorities, etc.

BELGIUM

I. Demographic situation

Population: Total 9,900,000. Minority groups: Flemings 5,500,000 (55.0%); Walloons 3,200,000 (32.0%); Italians 241,006 (2.4%); Moroccans 135,464 (1.4%); Germans 100,000 (1.0%); French 91,444 (0.9%) Turks 79,460 (0.8%); Jews 35,000-40,000 (0.3-0.4%); Luxembourgers 24,000-39,000 (0.2-0.4%); Roma 10,000-15,000 (0.1-0.15%); Other new minorities 230,000 (2.3%).

Languages: Flemish, French, German.

II. International obligations

The current Belgian Constitution does not contain any articles providing for the supremacy of international obligations in case of inconsistency with national obligations. Article 169 only contains a provision for ensuring that international and supranational obligations are respected.

United Nations
- International Covenant on Civil and Political Rights (signature 10 December 1968, ratification 21 April 1983)
- First Optional Protocol (accession 17 May 1994)
- International Covenant on Economic, Social and Cultural Rights (signature 10 December 1968, ratification 21 April 1983)

Council of Europe
- Member of the Council of Europe (5 May 1949)
- ECHR (signature 4 November 1950, ratification 14 June 1955)
- Not a party to the European Charter for Regional and Minority Languages
- Not a party to the Framework Convention for the Protection of National Minorities

III. National legislation

Constitution (of 7 February 1831 as revised to 17 February 1994)

Article 2
Belgium is made up of three Communities: the French Community, the Flemish Community, and the German-speaking Community.

Article 4
1. Belgium has four linguistic regions: the French-speaking Region, the Dutch-speaking Region, the bilingual Region of Brussels-Capital, and the German-speaking Region.
2. Each commune of the Kingdom is part of one of these linguistic regions.
3. The limits of the four linguistic regions can only be changed or modified by a law adopted by majority vote in each linguistic group in each House, on the condition that the majority of the members of each group are gathered together and from the moment that the total of affirmative votes given by the two linguistic groups is equal to at least two thirds of the votes expressed.

Article 30
The use of languages current in Belgium is optional; only the law can rule on this matter, and only for acts of the public authorities and for legal matters.

Article 43
1. For cases determined by the Constitution, the elected members of each House are divided into a French linguistic group and a Dutch linguistic group, in the manner determined by law.
2. The senators referred to in Article 67 (1)(2,4,7) make up the French linguistic group of the Senate. The senators referred to in Article 67 (1)(1,3,6), make up the Dutch linguistic group of the Senate.

Article 54
1. With the exception of budgets and laws requiring a special majority, a justified motion, signed by at least three-quarters of the members of one of the linguistic groups and introduced following the introduction of the report and prior to the final vote in a public session, can declare that the provisions

of a draft bill or of a motion are of a nature to gravely damage relations between the Communities.
3. This procedure can only be applied once by the members of a linguistic group with regard to the same bill or motion.

Article 129
1. The French and Dutch Community Councils rule by decree, in as much as each is concerned, excluding the federal legislator, on the use of language for:
   1. administrative matters;
   2. education in those establishments created, subsidised, and recognised by public authorities;
   3. social relations between employers and their personnel, in addition to corporate acts and documents required by law and by regulations.

2. These decrees have force of law in French-language and in Dutch-language regions respectively except as concerns:
   – those communes or groups of communes contiguous to another linguistic Region and in which the law prescribes or allows use of another language than that of the Region in which they are located. For these communes, a modification of the rules governing the use of languages as described in (1) may take place only through a law adopted by majority vote as described in Article 4, last paragraph;
   – services the activities of which extend beyond the linguistic Region within which they are established;
   – federal and international institutions designated by law, the activities of which are common to more than one Community.

Article 136
1. There are linguistic groups within the Brussels-Capital Regional Council, and among the governing bodies, qualified with respect to Community issues; their composition, functioning, and responsibilities and, without prejudice to Article 175, their financing, are regulated by a law adopted by majority vote as described in Article 4, last paragraph.

Article 138
1. The French Community Council, on one hand, and the Walloon Regional Council and the French linguistic group of the Brussels-Capital Regional Council, on the other hand, may decide of common accord and each by decree, that the Walloon Regional Council and Government in the French-language Region, and the Brussels-Capital Regional Council and its governing bodies in the bilingual Region of Brussels-Capital may exercise, in full or in part, the responsibilities of the French Community.

2. These decrees are adopted by a two-thirds majority vote within the French Community Council, and by absolute majority within the Walloon Regional Council and by the French linguistic group within the Brussels-Capital Regional Council, provided that a majority of the Council members or of the members of the linguistic group concerned are present. They may settle the financing of the responsibilities which they designate, in addition to transfers of personnel, of assets, of rights and of obligations which may concern them.

Article 139
1. Upon request by their respective Governments, the German-speaking Community Council and the Walloon Regional Council may, by decree, decide of common accord that Walloon Regional responsibilities may be exercised in whole or in part by the German-speaking Community Council and Government in the German-language Region.

BOSNIA AND HERZEGOVINA

I. Demographic situation

Population (census 1991): Total 4,380,000. Minority groups: Muslims 1,900,000 (43.7%); Serbs 1,400,000 (31.4%); Croats 756,000 (17.3%); 'Yugoslavs' 240,000 (5.5%); Roma and others 100,000 (2.1%).

Other estimates: Roma 100,000 (2.3%).

Languages: Bosnian, Croatian, Serbian.

II. International obligations

Article 2, paragraph 2, of the Constitution of Bosnia and Herzegovina stipulates that the rights and freedoms set forth in the European Convention for Human Rights and Fundamental Freedoms and its Protocols shall apply directly in Bosnia and Herzegovina and shall have priority over all other laws.

United Nations
– International Covenant on Civil and Political Rights (succession 1 September 1993)
– First Optional Protocol (signature 1 March 1995, ratification 1 March 1995)

- International Covenant on Economic, Social and Cultural Rights (succession 1 September 1993)

Council of Europe
- Special guest status to the Parliamentary Assembly (28 January 1994)
- Not a party to ECHR
- Not a party to the Charter for Regional or Minority Languages
- Framework Convention for the Protection of National Minorities (24 February 2000 accession)

III. National legislation

Bosnia and Herzegovina is composed of two entities: the Federation of Bosnia and Herzegovina and the Republic of Srpska.

Constitution of Bosnia and Herzegovina (The Constitution was adopted at the Dayton Peace Conference on 21 November 1995 as Annex 4 of the Dayton Peace Accords, and entered into force with its signature in Paris on 14 December 1995).

Article I
7. There shall be a citizenship of Bosnia and Herzegovina, to be regulated by the Parliamentary Assembly, and a citizenship of each Entity, to be regulated by each Entity, provided that:
   (b) No person shall be deprived of Bosnia and Herzegovina or Entity citizenship arbitrarily or so as to leave him or her stateless. No person shall be deprived of Bosnia and Herzegovina or Entity citizenship on any ground such as sex, race, colour, language, religion, political or other opinion, national or social origin, association with a national minority, property, birth or other status.

Article II
4. The enjoyment of the rights and freedoms provided for in this Article or in the international agreements listed in Annex I to this Constitution shall be secured to all persons in Bosnia and Herzegovina without discrimination on any ground such as sex, race, colour, language, religion, political or other opinion, national or social origin, association with a national minority, property, birth or other status.

Constitution of the Federation of Bosnia and Herzegovina

Article 6
1. The official languages of the Federation shall be the Bosniac and the Croatian language. The official script will be the Latin alphabet.
2. Other languages may be used as means of communication and instruction.

Constitution of Republika Srpska

Article 7
The Serbian language of *iekavian* and *ekavian* dialect and the Cyrillic alphabet shall be in official use in the Republic, while the Latin alphabet shall be used as specified by the law.

In regions inhabited by groups speaking other languages, their languages and alphabet shall also be in official use, as specified by law.

IV. Developments/events/comments

As a consequence of the ethnic cleansing which occurred in the recent past, apart from the so-called 'classical minorities', a category of 'new minorities' has been created which includes members of the three constitutional peoples of Bosnia and Herzegovina (Croats, Bosniacs and Serbs) who do not constitute a majority in the entity in which they live. As such, newly created minorities are considered as second-category citizens and are deprived of a number of their human rights, including their political and linguistic rights.

Practice
Persons belonging to minorities can use their language in everyday communication. Besides, the right of any individual belonging to a national minority to use his/her mother tongue in court proceeding is guaranteed, and an interpreter will be provided for this purpose. Education is exclusively in the official languages defined in the entity constitutions. There are no TV or radio broadcasts in minority languages.

BULGARIA

I. Demographic situation

Population (census 1992): Total 8,490,000. Minority groups: Turks 800,000 (9.4%); Roma 313,000 (3.7%); Others (including Russians, Armenians and Macedonians) 102,600 (1.2%).

Other estimates: Slav-speaking Muslims 250,000 (2.9%); Macedonians 250,000 (2.9%); Roma 577,000-600,000.

Languages: Bulgarian, Turkish, Macedonian.
In an official publication published in 1994 by the National Institute of Statistics there are, according to the 1992 census, about 31 various ethnic groups which speak 25 different languages not including those belonging to the groups 'other' and 'undeclared'.

II. International obligations

Article 5, paragraph 4, of the 1991 Constitution determines that any international instruments which have been ratified by the constitutionally established procedure, promulgated, and having entered into force with respect to the Republic of Bulgaria, shall be considered part of the domestic legislation of the country. They shall supersede any domestic legislation stipulating otherwise.

United Nations
- International Covenant on Civil and Political Rights (signature 8 October 1968, ratification 21 September 1970)
- First Optional Protocol (accession 26 March 1992)
- International Covenant on Economic, Social and Cultural Rights (signature 8 October 1968, ratification 21 September 1970)

Council of Europe
- Member (7 May 1992)
- ECHR (signature 7 May 1992, ratification 7 September 1992)
- Not a party to the Charter for Regional or Minority Languages
- Framework Convention for the Protection of National Minorities (signature 9 October 1997, ratification 7 May 1999, entry into force 1 September 1999)

Other treaties
- 1878 – Treaty of Berlin
- 1919 – Treaty of Neuilly-sur-Seine (Section I, Articles 49-57)

III. National legislation

The Constitution of Bulgaria does not mention minorities but only (in Article 36 paragraph 2) 'citizens whose mother tongue is not Bulgarian'.

Constitution (12 July 1991)

Article 3
Bulgarian is the official language of the Republic.

Article 36
1. Every citizen has the right and the obligation to study and use the Bulgarian language.
2. Citizens, for whom the Bulgarian language is not the mother tongue, will have the right to study and use their own language alongside the duty to study the Bulgarian language.
3. Cases where only the official language is to be used will be determined by law.

IV. Developments/events/comments

Education
Article 8 paragraph 2 of the Law on National Education provides for the right of students whose mother tongue is not Bulgarian to study their own language in the municipal schools. The 1994 Decree on Studying the Mother Tongue in Municipal Schools in the Republic of Bulgaria (No. 183) stipulates further in Article 1 paragraph 1 that students whose mother tongue is not Bulgarian can receive instruction in that language from the first to the eighth grade as a facultative subject.

The teaching of the Roma language has been allowed since 1992. A special 1994 decree extends this right for children from the first to the eighth grade.

Media and culture
Bulgarian citizens of Turkish, Russian, Armenian, Wallachian, Jewish, and Macedonian origin as well as Roma, have their own periodicals and newspapers published in Bulgarian as well as in their own language. The Government does not provide any subsidies for broadcasts or publications in the languages of ethnic groups, except for Turkish-language programmes on the National Radio. There is a half-hour programme twice a day in the Turkish language.

There are a number of societies and associations for Bulgarian citizens belonging to various ethnic, religious and linguistic groups. Among them, one could mention the cultural organization of Karachans and the cultural society of and for the Armenian theatre which is currently being revived.

Judicial procedures
The Judiciary Act (Article 105, paragraph 1), Code of Civil Procedure (Article 5, and the Code of Criminal Procedure (Article 11, paragraph 1) stipulate that the language used in courts will be Bulgarian. In cases where persons participating in proceedings do not speak Bulgarian, the court will appoint an interpreter. However, Articles 17 and 35 of the Law on the Supreme Administrative Court require that all complaints and protests be drafted in Bulgarian. The Law on the Execution of Sentences stipulates in Article 33, paragraph 1 (b), that the conversation during visits paid to detainees shall be conducted in Bulgarian. In case the detainee or his or her visitors do not speak Bulgarian, the administration shall appoint an interpreter at their own expense. This might be a problem in cases when the detainee or his/her visitor does not speak Bulgarian.

National bodies
In December 1997 the National Council on Ethnic and Demographic Issues (NCEDI) was established by Decree No. 449 of the Council of Ministers. It is a body for consultation, cooperation and coordination between governmental organs and non-governmental organizations which deal with demographic issues and migration, as well as with the promotion and protection of tolerance and understanding between Bulgarian citizens belonging to different ethnic and religious groups.

Under the auspices of the President of the Republic there is a Public Council on Ethnic issues and on the Situation of Bulgarians Abroad, which consists of intellectuals and public figures involved in the field and which mostly gives opinions on concrete issues.

CROATIA

I. Demographic situation

Population (census 1991)[2]: Total 4,500,000.[3] Minority groups: Serbs 581,663 (12.16%); Muslims 43,469 (0.91%); Slovenian 22,376 (0.47%); Hungarian

---

[2] The last census was held in 1991 under the auspices of the former Socialist Federal Republic of Yugoslavia. Despite the initiatives of the Croatian Government to conduct a new census, it is the opinion of the international community that, while some of the population movements as a result of the war on the territory of the former Yugoslavia still exist, it is premature to carry out a new population census until the situation normalizes.

[3] This is the estimated total population of the Republic of Croatia on 30 June 1997. The figure includes all persons who have resided in the Republic of Croatia for one or more years (also

22,355 (0.47%); Italian 21,303 (0.45%); Czech 13,086 (0.27%); Albanians 12,032 (0.25%); Others (6.92%).

Languages: Croatian, Serbian, Hungarian.

II. International obligations

Pursuant to Article 134 of the 1990 Constitution, international agreements concluded and ratified by Croatia in accordance with the Constitution and published in the Official Gazette, are incorporated into its domestic legal order and are superior in terms of their legal effect.

United Nations
- International Covenant on Civil and Political Rights (succession 12 October 1992)
- First Optional Protocol (accession 12 October 1995)
- International Covenant on Economic, Social and Cultural Rights (succession 12 October 1992)

Council of Europe
- Member (6 November 1996)
- ECHR (signature 6 November 1996, ratification 5 November 1997)
- Charter for Regional or Minority Languages (signature 5 November 1997, ratification 5 November 1997, entry into force 1 March 1998)
- Framework Convention for the Protection of National Minorities (signature 6 November 1996, ratification 11 October 1997, entry into force 1 February 1998)

Bilateral agreements
- 1975 – with Italy, Osimo Agreement, concluded by the former Socialist Federal Republic of Yugoslavia to which Croatia succeeded
- 1992 – with Hungary, Treaty on friendly relations and cooperation
- 1992 – with Hungary, Protocol on the principles of cooperation and guarantees for national minorities
- 1992 – with Italy and Slovenia, Memorandum on mutual understanding between Croatia, Italy and Slovenia on the protection of rights of the Italian minority in Croatia and Slovenia
- 1995 – with Hungary, Agreement on the protection of the rights of the Croat minority in the Republic of Hungary and the Hungarian minority in the Republic of Croatia

---

refugees) and excludes persons absent from the Republic of Croatia for one or more years (persons working abroad and members of their families living with them abroad).

- 1996 – with Italy, Agreement on the Rights of Minorities
- 1996 – with the Federal Republic of Yugoslavia, Agreement on the normalization of relations

Other agreements
- 1996 – The Principle Agreement on Eastern Slavonia, Baranja and West Srijem
- 1997 – Proclaimed Letter of Intention of the Republic of Croatia on the completion of the peaceful reintegration of Eastern Slavonia, Baranja and West Srijem, under Interim Administration

Both documents were adopted with the participation of the international community.

III. National legislation

Constitution (of 1990 as amended on 15 December 1997)

Article 1 amending Chapter I – Historical Foundations – Paragraph 3
The Republic of Croatia constitutes itself as a national State of the Croatian people and as a State of the members of autochthonous national minorities: Serbs, Czechs, Slovaks, Italians, Hungarians, Jews, Germans, Austrians, Ukrainians, Ruthenians and others who are its citizens and who are guaranteed equality with the citizens of Croatian nationality and the exercise of national rights in accordance with the demographic standards of the United Nations Organisations and the free world countries.

Article 12
1. The Croatian language and the Latin script shall be in official use in the Republic of Croatia.
2. In individual local units another language and the Cyrillic or some other script may, along with the Croatian language and the Latin script, be introduced into official use under conditions specified by law.

Article 14
1. Citizens of the Republic of Croatia shall enjoy all rights and freedoms, regardless of race, colour, sex, language, religion, political or other opinion, national or social origin, property, birth, education, social status or other properties.

Article 15
1. Members of all nations and minorities shall have equal rights in the Republic of Croatia.

2. Members of all nations and minorities shall be guaranteed freedom to express their nationality, freedom to use their language and script, and cultural autonomy.

Article 17
1. During a state of war or an immediate danger to the independence and unity of the Republic, or in the event of some natural disaster, individual freedoms and rights guaranteed by the Constitution may be restricted. This shall be decided by the Croatian Sabor by a two-thirds majority of all representatives or, if Croatian Sabor is unable to meet, by the President of the Republic.
2. The extent of such restrictions shall be adequate to the nature of the danger, and may not result in the inequality of citizens in respect of race, colour, sex, language, religion, national or social origin.

Article 24
2. The arrested person shall be immediately informed in a way understandable to him of the reasons for arrest and of his rights determined by law.

Constitutional Law on Human Rights and Freedoms and the Rights of National and Ethnic Communities or Minorities in the Republic of Croatia
(as adopted in 1991 and amended in March 1992)

Article 7
Members of all ethnic or national communities or minorities in the Republic of Croatia shall be entitled to the free use of their language and alphabet, both publicly and privately.

In those municipalities where members of a national or ethnic community or minority represent the majority of the total population, the alphabet and language of that national or ethnic community or minority will be officially used together with the Croatian language and the Latin alphabet.

Article 8
Local self-governing units may decide to use two or more languages and alphabets officially, taking into account the number of the members and interests of the national or ethnic communities or minorities.

Article 14
Members of ethnic and national communities or minorities living in the Republic of Croatia will be educated in kindergartens and schools in their own language and alphabet, with programmes adequately presenting their history, culture and science, if such a wish is expressed.

Education in the part of the school programme from paragraph 1 of this Article not related to the students' national affiliation shall be provided in the range and content regulated by the competent bodies of the Republic of Croatia.

The part of the programme related to the national affiliation of the students will be designated by the bodies from Paragraph 2 of this Article, following the suggestions from the Office of Inter-Ethnic Relations of the Government of the Republic of Croatia.

Article 15
In towns and other populated areas outside the special statute districts (Article 21 of this Constitutional Law), where national and ethnic communities or minorities represent a relative majority of the population, and if the numbers of students justify this, separate education institutions of school departments will be established with classes held in the language and alphabet of the particular national or ethnic community or minority, if such a wish is expressed.

In cases when such schools or school departments cannot be established according to the criteria stated in Paragraph 1 of this Article, owing to the small number of students, instruction in the subjects which are related to the national affiliation of the students (language, literature, history, etc.) will be carried out within a separate school department by teachers of the same national affiliation, if such a wish is expressed by the student's parents.

In towns and populated areas outside the territories of special statute municipalities from which the native population of other ethnic and national communities or minorities was banished into parent country, or the policy of forced migration into parent countries was pursued, during and after World War II, teaching a foreign language can be introduced as an optional subject, beginning with the fourth grade of elementary education until the end of secondary education, that foreign language being the language of that ethnic and national community, regardless of the percentage of the total population that that ethnic and national community or minority represents in that region.

In towns and populated areas outside the territories of special statute districts, in order to protect the collective rights of autochthonous ethnic and national communities or minorities, steps for special protection for taking part in public affairs shall be taken, as well as in education, culture, spiritual and religious life, and in access to the public media, regardless of their share in the total population.

Measures from paragraph 4 of this Article shall be pursued until the re-establishment of the system of proper institutions aimed at fostering and promoting national particularities and culture and educational institutions of the minority communities in their former scope.

Article 16
Besides municipal funds, the Republic of Croatia shall provide adequate funding for the realisation of the programmes enumerated in Article 14 of this Law.

Article 17
Members of national and ethnic communities or minorities may establish private kindergartens, schools and other educational institutions.

IV. Developments/events/comments

The practice of officially using minority languages is currently being implemented in 43 municipalities with respect to the Italian language, in 9 municipalities with respect to the Czech language, in 6 municipalities with respect to Slovak, in 4 municipalities with respect to Ruthenian, in 2 municipalities with respect to Ukrainian and in 36 municipalities with respect to the Hungarian language. In accordance with Article 6 of the Basic Agreement on the Region of Eastern Slavonia, Baranja and Western Sirmium of 12 November 1995, the right to the official use of the Serbian language has also been provided for the Croatian Danubian Region, Knin and Banovina.

Judicial proceedings
With respect to judicial proceedings the official language in Croatia is the Croatian language and Latin script as prescribed by Article 12 of the Constitution. However, in criminal cases according to the 1997 Law on Criminal Procedure there is an express obligation for the authorities to provide a free of charge interpreter for defendants whose language is not Croatian. Pursuant to the 1991 Law on Civil Procedure parties to the proceedings as well as other participants have the right to use their own language when participating in the hearing and when verbally undertaking other procedural matters before the court as well as the right to free interpretation. Moreover, a draft law on the official use of languages and scripts of national minorities in the Republic of Croatia before the public administration, courts, public and other legal services vested with legal authority is in the process of being prepared. In addition, the validity of legal instruments and documents in minority languages are recognized in criminal, civil, administrative procedures by virtue of being incorporated into the Law on Criminal Procedure, the Law on Civil Procedure and the Law on Administrative Litigation respectively.

Education
Schools attended by pupils belonging to national minorities have their own special curricula which are complementary to the normal ones and which are designed to teach history, geography, art and music in their respective languages. Curricula prepared for members of the Italian, Hungarian, Czech, Slovak, Ruthenian, Ukrainian and Serb ethnic and national communities or minorities have been adopted at elementary school level. The form of instruction and the application of various curricula are determined by the specific characteristics of each ethnic and national community. They are prepared by experts belonging to the respective ethnic and national communities or

minorities, and who submitted their proposals for approval to the governmental body of the Republic of Croatia responsible for the National Curriculum. Currently four types of curricula are in use. In practice, some national minorities (e.g. Italians) choose curricula taught wholly in their native language, whereas others prefer curricula designed for the promotion of their native language, history, culture (e.g. Ruthenians and Ukrainians), although all of them have equivalent legal options.

The production costs and the retail price of textbooks in minority languages are covered by the State budget. Most textbooks are translated from Croatian into the respective minority languages, the majority are printed as original copies whilst a smaller proportion are imported from other countries of origin.

Media
Pursuant to Article 56 of the Law on Telecommunications, Croatian Radio and Television (HRT) is obliged to respect human dignity and fundamental human rights in its programmes and to promote understanding for members of ethnic and national communities or minorities. For the purpose of protecting the interests of ethnic and national communities or minorities as well as religious communities, the Croatian State Parliament appoints two representatives to the HRT Council of Croatian Radio and Television, one from an ethnic and national community or minority and the other from a religious community.

In addition, HRT has an editorial staff dedicated to producing specialist programmes for the members of ethnic and national communities or minorities. 'Prizma' is a multinational magazine, a regular weekly 60-minute programmes prepared in Zagreb in cooperation with all regional studios, dedicated to a particular region with a high concentration of members of ethnic and national communities and minorities. In late 1997, Danube Television Station began to broadcast from its studios in Vukovar and Beli Manastir a number of programmes including the news in Serbian for the Serb community living in the region. In forthcoming county chronicles there will be news for members of ethnic and national communities or minorities in their respective mother tongue.

Ethnic and national communities or minorities also participate in the production of programmes in their mother tongue for local radio and TV stations.

Several newspapers, monthlies, almanacs, as well as children's literature are published in respective minority languages by all the national communities through their own publishing houses.

Citizenship
The knowledge of the Croatian language and Latin alphabet is one of the requirements for acquiring Croatian citizenship by naturalization (Article 8, paragraph 1(4) of the 1991 Law on Croatian Citizenship).

National bodies

There is a Committee on Human Rights and the Rights of Ethnic and National Communities or Minorities, established by the House of Representatives. It consists of 15 representatives of national minorities with its main task being to participate in the process of elaborating legislation concerning ethnic and national communities or minorities.

In addition there is the institution of the Ombudsperson for minority and/or human rights established in 1992. His/her main tasks consist of the protection of constitutional and legal rights of citizens in proceedings before government administration bodies vested with public powers.

The Ministry of Public Administration, the Ministry of Education and Sports and the Ministry of Justice, have special tasks with respect to the implementation of the existing legislation relevant for minorities in respective fields. The Ministry of Justice is responsible for issues concerning the use of minority languages before judicial bodies.

There is also the Governmental Office for Ethnic and National Communities or Minorities which is a subsidiary body of the Croatian Government. It has primary responsibility in the implementation of the cultural autonomy of ethnic and national communities or minorities. Its main tasks are, *inter alia*, to propose measures for the protection of national, cultural, and religious rights of minorities; to monitor the implementation of international conventions concerning inter-ethnic relations; to propose the implementation of particular models for the establishment of inter-ethnic relations; to organize projects involving minorities; to advise the Government on minority draft legislation and policy; and to organize the training of members of minorities. Communities or minorities covered by the activities of the Governmental Office are: Serbs, Italians, Czechs, Slovaks, Germans, Austrians, Jews, Slovenes, Albanians, Muslims, Montenegrins, Macedonians, Hungarians, Roma, Ruthenians and Ukrainians.

The Council of Ethnic and National Communities or Minorities was established by a decision of representatives of ethnic and national communities or minorities in June 1997. It is a coordinating and advisory body of representatives from minority associations with the task of monitoring and implementing the policy of maintaining and promoting the protection of ethnic and national communities or minorities. In addition, it considers minority problems, takes specific standpoint on the draft laws which are relevant for minorities, submits opinions and cooperates with all State authorities on the issues of minorities.

CYPRUS

I. Demographic situation

Population: Total 756,000. Minority groups: Turkish Cypriots 136,000 (18.0%); Maronites 11,000 (1.4%); Armenians, Latin-Cypriots and British (combined) 18,900 (2.9%); Roma 500-1,000 (0.07-0.13%).

Other estimates (situation as of 1986): total 741,000; Greek Cypriots 621,800 (83.9%); Turkish Cypriots 89,200 (12.0%); Armenians 2,500 (0.4%); Maronites 4,500 (0.6%); Latins 700 (0.1%); foreign nationals (mainly British, Greek, other Europeans and Arabs) 22,300 (3.0%).

Languages: Greek, Turkish.

II. International obligations

Article 169 of the 1960 Constitution stipulates that by publication in the Official Gazette of the Republic of Cyprus, international legal instruments are incorporated into municipal law and have, from that date, superior force to any municipal law. Such instruments are directly applicable in the Republic and can be invoked before and directly enforced by the Courts and administrative authorities. In case an international treaty does not contain self-executing provisions, the legislature has a legal obligation to adopt the necessary legislation in order to harmonize municipal law with that treaty.

United Nations
- International Covenant on Civil and Political Rights (signature 19 December 1966, ratification 2 April 1969)
- First Optional Protocol (signature 19 December 1966, ratification 15 April 1992)
- International Covenant on Economic, Social and Cultural Rights (signature 9 January 1967, ratification 2 April 1969)

Council of Europe
- Member (24 May 1961)
- ECHR (signature 16 December 1961, ratification 6 October 1962)
- Charter for Regional or Minority Languages (signature 12 November 1992)
- Framework Convention for the Protection of National Minorities (signature 1 February 1995, ratification 4 June 1996, entry into force 1 February 1998)

III. National legislation

The Constitution does not make any reference to 'minorities' or 'national minorities', and neither it nor any other national legal document contain a definition of the term 'national minority'. Instead, it uses the term 'communities' and 'religious groups'.

Constitution (6 August 1960)

Article 2
For the purposes of this Constitution:
1. the Greek Community comprises all citizens of the Republic who are of Greek origin and whose mother tongue is Greek or who share the Greek cultural traditions or who are members of the Greek Orthodox Church;
2. the Turkish Community comprises all citizens of the Republic who are of Turkish origin and whose mother tongue is Turkish or who share the Turkish cultural traditions or who are Moslems.

Article 3
1. The official languages of the Republic are Greek and Turkish.
2. Legislative, executive and administrative acts and documents shall be drawn up in both official languages and shall, where under the express provisions of this Constitution promulgation is required, be promulgated by publication in the official Gazette of the Republic in both official languages.
3. Administrative or other official documents addressed to a Greek or a Turk shall be drawn up in the Greek or the Turkish language respectively.
4. Judicial proceedings shall be conducted or made and judgements shall be drawn up in the Greek language if the parties are Greek, in the Turkish language if the parties are Turkish, and in both the Greek and the Turkish languages if the parties are Greek and Turkish. The official language or languages to be used for such purposes in all other cases shall be specified by the Rules of Court made by the High Court under Article 163.
5. Any text in the official Gazette of the Republic shall be published in both official languages in the same issue.
6. 1) Any difference between the Greek and the Turkish texts of any legislative, executive or administrative act or document published in the official Gazette of the Republic, shall be resolved by a competent court.
   2) The prevailing text of any law or decision of a Communal Chamber published in the official Gazette of the Republic shall be that of the language of the Communal Chamber concerned.
   3) Where any difference arises between the Greek and the Turkish texts of an executive or administrative act or document which, though not published in the official Gazette of the Republic, has otherwise been published, a statement by the Minister or any other authority concerned

as to which the text should prevail or which should be the correct text shall be final and conclusive.
4) A competent court may grant such remedies as it may deem just in any case of a difference in the texts as aforesaid.
7. The official languages shall be used on coins, currency notes and stamps.
8. Every person shall have the right to address himself to the authorities of the Republic in either of the official languages.

Article 11
4. Every person shall be informed at the time of his arrest in a language which he understands of the reasons for his arrest and shall be allowed to have the services of a lawyer of his own choosing [...]
6. The judge before whom the person arrested is brought shall promptly proceed to inquire into the grounds of the arrest in a language understandable by the person arrested and shall, as soon as possible and in any event not later than three days from such appearance, either release the person arrested on such terms as he may deem fit or where the investigation into the commission of the offence for which he has been arrested has not been completed remand him in custody and may remand him in custody from time to time for a period not exceeding eight days at any one time;

Article 12
5. Every person charged with an offence has the following minimum rights:
   a) to be informed promptly and in a language which he understands and in detail of the nature and grounds of the charge preferred against him; [...]
   e) to have the free assistance of an interpreter if he cannot understand or speak the language used in court.

Article 28
2. Every person shall enjoy all the rights and liberties provided for in this Constitution without any direct or indirect discrimination against any person on the ground of his community, race, religion, language, sex, political or other convictions, national or social descent, birth, colour, wealth, social class, or on any ground whatsoever, unless there is express provision to the contrary in this Constitution.

Article 30
3. Every person has the right [...]
   (e) to have free assistance of an interpreter if he cannot understand or speak the language used in court.

Article 171
1. In sound and vision broadcasting there shall be programmes both for the Greek and the Turkish Communities.

2. The time allotted to programmes for the Turkish Community in sound broadcasting shall be not less than seventy-five hours in a seven day week, spread to all days of such week in daily normal periods of transmission:
   - provided that if the total period of transmissions has to be reduced so that the time allotted to programmes for the Greek Community should fall below seventy-five hours in a seven day week, then the time allotted to programmes for the Turkish Community in any such week should be reduced by the same number of hours as that by which the time allotted to programmes for the Greek Community is reduced below such hours;
   - provided further that if the time allotted to programmes for the Greek Community is increased above one hundred and forty hours in a seven day week, then the time allotted to programmes for the Turkish Community shall be increased in the ratio of three hours for the Turkish Community to every seven hours for the Greek Community.
3. In vision broadcasting there shall be allotted three transmission days to the programmes for the Turkish Community of every ten consecutive transmission days and the total time allotted to the programmes for the Turkish Community in such ten transmission days shall be in the ratio of three hours to seven hours allotted to programmes for the Greek Community in such ten transmission days.
4. All official broadcasts in sound and vision shall be made both in Greek and Turkish and shall not be taken into account for the purposes of calculating the time under this Article.

Article 180
1. The Greek and the Turkish texts of this Constitution shall both be originals and shall have the same authenticity and the same legal force.

Article 189
Notwithstanding anything in Article 3 contained, for a period of five years after the date of the coming into operation of this Constitution:
   a) All laws which under Article 188 will continue to be in force may continue to be in the English language.
   b) The English language may be used in any proceedings before any court of the Republic.

IV. Developments/events/comments

Education
The members of all communities may use their own language in private and in public. They can also learn and be taught in their mother tongue. The Ministry of Education and Culture provides subsidies for cultural activities, including publications, performances, libraries, etc.

The Government assigns public educational officers to Armenian schools and private schools attended by Maronites, for the purpose of teaching the Greek language.

Media
There are special programmes broadcast on the radio in the Greek and Turkish languages as well as in Armenian and English. There are also Turkish and English TV programmes.

Judicial procedures
Every person charged with an offence has the right to be informed promptly and in a language in which he/she understands. An interpreter will be provided free of charge if he or she cannot understand or speak the language used in court. In addition, Article 3(1) of the 1981 Prison Regulations, does not allow any discrimination on the grounds of race, colour, sex, language, religion etc.

National bodies
The Council of Ministers has established a National Institution for the Protection of Human Rights whose function is, *inter alia*, to hear complaints regarding the violation of human rights

CZECH REPUBLIC

I. Demographic situation

Population (census of 1991): Total 10,300,000. Minority groups: Moravians 1,360,000 (13.0%); Slovaks 309,000 (3.0%); Poles 60,000 (0.6%); Germans 50,000 (0.6%); Silesians 44,000 (0.4%); Roma 33,000 (0.3%); Others 137,000 (1.3%).

Other estimates: Roma up to 300,000 (2,9%).

Languages: Czech, Slovak, Polish and German.

II. International obligations
According to Article 10 of the 1993 Constitution, ratified and promulgated international accords on human rights and fundamental freedoms, to which the

Czech Republic has committed itself, are immediately binding and are superior to other laws.

United Nations
- International Covenant on Civil and Political Rights (succession 22 February 1993)
- First Optional Protocol (succession 22 February 1993)
- International Covenant on Economic, Social and Cultural Rights (succession 22 February 1993)

Council of Europe
- Member (30 June 1993)
- ECHR (signature 21 February 1991, ratification 18 March 1992)
- Not a party to the Charter for Regional or Minority Languages
- Framework Convention for the Protection of National Minorities (signature 28 April 1995, ratification 18 December 1997, entry into force 1 April 1998)

Bilateral agreements
- 1991 – with Poland, on cultural and scientific cooperation
- 1992 – with Poland, on good neighbour relations, solidarity and friendly cooperation
- 1992 – with Germany, on good neighbour relations and friendly cooperation
- 1993 – with Slovakia, on good neighbourliness, friendly relations and cooperation
- 1994 – with Poland, on cross-border cooperation

Other agreements
- 1919 – Treaty of St.-Germain-en-Laye (Articles 8 and 9)

III. National legislation

Constitution (1993)

[The Constitution does not contain any provisions on languages.]

Charter on Fundamental Rights and Freedoms (1993)

Article 3
1. Fundamental rights and freedoms shall be secured to all, irrespective of sex, race, skin colour, language, belief or religion, political or other convictions, national or social origin, membership of a national or ethnic minority, property, birth or position of any kind.

Article 25

Citizens who constitute a national or ethnic minority are guaranteed all-round development, in particular, the right to develop, together with other members of the minority, their own culture, the right to disseminate and receive information in their native language, and the right to associate in national associations. Detailed provisions shall be set down by law.

Citizens belonging to national and ethnic minority groups are also guaranteed, under the conditions set down by law:
  a. the right to education in their own language
  b. the right to use their own language when dealing with officials
  c. the right to participate in the resolution of affairs that concern national and ethnic minorities.

Second Periodic Report of the Czech Republic on the Convention on the Elimination of All Forms of Racial Discrimination (in the period 1993-1996)

7.12. The right to use one's mother tongue

276. The Charter (Article 25) safeguards the right to use mother language in official communication subject to the rules specified by law. Under Law No. 71/1967 on administrative procedure, administrative authorities are required to give all persons participating in administrative procedure equal opportunities to effectively assert their rights and interests; which means that the right of persons who are not proficient in Czech to use their own language is a general procedural principle.

277. The right to use minority language in communication with law enforcement authorities and in judicial proceedings is fully guaranteed and specified by the Code of Civil Procedure, Code of Criminal Procedure and by the Law on the Constitutional Court.

278. The operative Czech legislation does not determine the official language. In consequence, individual minority languages may be deemed equal with the Czech language in the administrative as well as judicial procedure. This situation has created problems especially in the Český Těšín area, where the Polish population insists on using the Polish language in communication with the local authorities. In the absence of any specific guidelines, the authorities are making every effort to comply with such requirements.

279. In the sphere of judicial practice, the right to use one's own language is not subject to any restrictions.

280. The right to use minority language in private and in public is safeguarded by the Charter (Article 25). Inscriptions of a private nature (e.g. shop-signs, etc.) are not subject to any legislative or executive restrictions. Official local names in the Czech Republic are subject to Ordinance No. 97/1961 Coll. on local names, street names and house numbers, as amended by the subsequent regulations. Pursuant to the relevant decision of the Ministry of

the Interior, official local names are determined by the Statistical Lexicon of Municipalities. The use of local names in a minority language is covered by any specific Regulation nevertheless the aforesaid Ordinance does not rule it out. The same applies to other topographical indications.
281. The practice of using signs and inscriptions in the Polish language is widespread in the Český Těšin area (shops, restaurants, etc.) and the Polish language is used in public according, to the needs of the Polish minority.
282. Requirements concerning the use of bilingual local names and other topographical indications have been tabled above all by the Polish population in the area of Český Těšin. They demand that Polish local names and other topographical indications should be used side by side with their official Czech versions in areas traditionally inhabited by Poles. This problem is now on the agenda of the Council for Nationalities of the Government of the Czech Republic, Ministry of the Interior and other competent local authorities.

IV. Developments/events/comments

The Ministry of Culture and the Ministry of Education, Youth and Sports are responsible for promoting the conditions which are necessary for the preservation and development of cultural traditions, identity and language. For this purpose the State provides grants.

With respect to the use of languages there is no law which defines the official language or the language of communication, although some laws specify the use of the Czech language in certain situations (such as, for example, the judiciary, registries, defence acts, etc.). In some cases law allows the use of the Slovak language, although in practice it is used without limitation, also in official communications. The Charter of Fundamental Rights and Freedoms guarantees the use of languages by persons belonging to national minorities in the Czech Republic in official communications (Article 25, paragraph 2). According to Article 198 of the 1995 Criminal Code anyone who publicly defames a nation or its language, a race or a group of inhabitants commits a criminal offence.

Media
Both the Laws on the Czech Radio and on Television expressly guarantee the access of national minorities to the media. The Czech Radio has four independent national minority departments (Polish, Slovak, Romany and German) and also broadcasts regular programmes for citizens from the Hungarian, German, Polish, Romany, Slovak, Ukrainian, Croatian, Vietnamese and Jewish communities. In addition to the wok of the minority departments Television broadcasts programmes for and on national minorities in the Czech Republic.

With respect to publications, there are a number of national minority periodicals (three for the Slovak minority; six for the Polish; two for the

German; three for the Roma; one for the Hungarian and one for the Ukrainian minority).

Judicial procedures

According to the Report submitted by the Czech Republic pursuant to Article 25, paragraph 1 of the Framework Convention, the use of languages of the national minorities in administrative proceedings is insufficiently defined. The parties to the proceedings are guaranteed equal rights and duties, and consequently the right to speak their mother tongue. However, the 1967 Law on Administrative Proceedings, as amended, does not define the right of a party in the proceedings to use his or her mother tongue without having to bear the costs of exercising this right, as the State does not cover such costs.

Under Article 2 (14) of the 1991 Law on Criminal Court Proceedings, as amended, every person has the right to use his or her mother tongue before law enforcement authorities. Law enforcement authorities shall conduct proceedings and proclaim their rulings in the Czech language. For parties not speaking Czech an interpreter shall be provided. Similarly, the 1993 Law on the Constitutional Court, as amended, provides in Article 33, paragraph 1, that the proceedings before the Constitutional Court shall take place in the Czech language. Persons may use their language in verbal proceedings or other personal communication. An interpreter will be provided for the parties who communicate or testify before the Constitutional Court in a language other than Czech. The Court does not have an obligation to do this for testimony given in the Slovak language.

In civil procedure the parties to the proceedings have the right to use their mother tongue (Article 18 of the 1992 Law on Civil Rules of Court, as amended).

Education

In addition to the Charter of Fundamental Rights and Freedoms, there is the 1984 Act on the System of Primary, Secondary and Higher Vocational Schools, as amended (No. 29/1984) and the 1990 Act on State Administration and Local Self-Government in Education, as amended (No. 564/1990) which contain provisions on the education of persons belonging to national minorities in their mother tongue.

The right to receive instruction in one's mother tongue is exercised in three ways: schools in which subjects are taught in the language of a national minority; schools in which a minority language is an optional subject; and dislocated classes in which subjects are taught in the language of a national minority. A fully developed school system with subjects taught in the minority language only exists in the areas with a concentrated Polish minority (Karvina and Frydek-Mistek). For the Slovak and German minorities dispersion is a problem for the establishment of clearly defined educational programmes.

Employment
The Preamble of the 1990 Employment Act states that citizens shall have the right to employment irrespective of race, skin colour, sex, language, religion or other convictions, membership of a political party or movement, nationality, ethnic or social origin, property, state of health or age.

Names and surnames
The 1949 Law on Registries, as amended, provides for the writing of names according to the linguistic usage of foreigners and accordingly also persons belonging to minorities. There is a provision requiring the change of feminine surnames by adding the suffixes '-ova' or by changing 'y' into 'a'. This requirement is considered to be a discriminatory restriction of the linguistic rights of female persons belonging to minorities. A new law expected to enter into force in 2000 will alter this requirement and make it dependent upon the request of a person, whether a foreigner or a member of a national minority.

Topographic and other signs
There is no prohibition on using bilingual topographic signs, especially in the Tesin area in Silesia populated by the Polish minority. However, there are no bilingual names of municipalities, cities, streets or local structures on official display. For the time being, it is only the Polish minority which is demanding bilingual toponyms, as other minorities are mostly dispersed throughout the country.

The display of signs, inscriptions and other information of a private nature is not prohibited.

National bodies
The Council for National Minorities, established in 1994, serves as a State office and its Chairman has the rank of Minister without portfolio. Its main tasks are to participate in the preparation of Governmental measures affecting the rights of national minorities, to give opinions on draft laws, to prepare recommendations for the Government and Ministers concerning minorities and to cooperate with regional self-governing bodies. It consists of 12 representatives from national minorities, 6 representatives from the State administration, 1 representative from the Chamber of Deputies and 1 representative from the President's Office. A representative from the Senate has guest status.

In addition, there is also an Inter-ministerial Commission for Roma, established in 1997. Its Chairman also has the rank of Minister without portfolio. Among other tasks, the Commission reviews draft materials on Governmental measures concerning the Roma community, evaluates the effectiveness of Governmental and ministerial measures with regard to the Roma, collects data on the status and development of the Roma community and informs the Roma on State assistance afforded to their community.

A number of consultative bodies have been established: at the Ministry of Culture – the Consultative Committee for Issues Concerning the Cultures of

National Minorities; at the Ministry of Education, Youth and Sports – the Consultative Committee for Issues Concerning the Educational System of National Minorities; and at the Ministry of Labour and Social Affairs – the Committee of the Ministry of Labour and Social Affairs for the Realization of Measures Promoting Employment of persons who Face Difficulties on the Labour Market with Special Attention to the Romany Population.

Within the framework of the Chamber of Deputies of the Czech Parliament, there is also the Subcommittee for National Minorities and the Subcommittee for the Application of the Charter of Fundamental Rights and Freedoms which act as petition committees of the Chamber of Deputies.

DENMARK

I. Demographic situation

Minority groups in Denmark are registered in the Danish National Registrar according to citizenship, parents' citizenship and place of birth. They are not registered according to the criteria of ethnicity, religion or language.

Out of a total population of 5,294,860, there are 249,628 non-citizens. Statistics dating from 1 January 1998 reveal the following groups of non-citizens: Turks 37,519; Ex-Yugoslavs 33,931; Stateless 9,902; Iranians 6,844; Iraqis 9,419; Pakistanis 6,934; Lebanese 4.421; Somalis 11.890; Vietnamese 5.228; Sri Lankans 5,409.

There is no record of the size of the German minority in Denmark, mainly residing in Southern Jutland along the border with Germany. It is estimated, however, that the German minority comprises around 20,000 people.

Other estimates: Faroese 48,000 (0.9%); Inuit (Greenlanders) 45,000 (0.9%); Asians 38,000 (0.7%); Turks 30,000 (0.6%); Germans of South Jutland 5,000-20,000 (0.1-0.4%); Jews 7,000 (0.1%); Roma 1,500-2,000 (less than 0.1%); Other new minorities 70,000 (1.3%).

Languages: Danish, Greenlandic and Faroese.

II. International obligations

Whereas Section 19 of the 1953 Constitution deals with the authority of the King with respect to foreign affairs it does not contain any provision establishing the primacy of international obligations in the national legal system. Denmark has a 'dualist' system under which, prior to adhering to international agreements, Denmark needs to ensure that its domestic law is in conformity with the agreement in question. All Danish authorities, including Parliament, the judiciary and administrative authorities, have an obligation to ensure compliance with the human rights principles contained in the Constitution and international instruments ratified by Denmark. Individual conventions may be transformed into domestic law.

United Nations
- International Covenant on Civil and Political Rights (signature 20 March 1968, ratification 6 January 1972)
- First Optional Protocol (signature 20 March 1968, ratification 6 January 1972)
- International Covenant on Economic, Social and Cultural Rights (signature 20 March 1968, ratification 6 January 1972)

Council of Europe
- Member (5 May 1949)
- ECHR (signature 4 November 1950, ratification 13 April 1953)
- Charter for Regional or Minority Languages (signature 5 November 1992, ratification 8 September 2000)
- Framework Convention for the Protection of National Minorities (signature 1 February 1995, ratification 22 September 1997, entry into force 1 February 1998)

III. National legislation

Constitution (5 June 1953)

[Contains only a non-discrimination clause in Article 70.]

Home Rule Act of the Faroe Islands No. 137 (adopted on 23 March 1948)[4] (Faroe Islands and Greenland are self-governing communities within the Danish State).

Section 11
Faroese is recognised as the principal language, but Danish is to be learnt well and carefully, and Danish may be used as well as Faroese in public affairs.

When cases of appeal are submitted all Faroese documents shall be accompanied by a Danish translation.

---

[4] The population of the Faroe Islands are not characterized as a Danish minority and the Faroese language is therefore not considered to be a minority language.

The Greenland Home Rule Act No. 577 (Adopted on 29 November 1878)[5]

Section 9
1. Greenlandic shall be the principal language. Danish must be thoroughly taught.
2. Either language may be used for official purposes.

Declaration on the general rights of the German minority in South Jutland
(Approved by the Danish Parliament on 19 April 1955)

I
Under Danish law – the Basic Law of the Kingdom of Denmark of 5 June 1953 and other legislation – every citizen and thus also every member of the German minority regardless of the language which he uses shall enjoy the following rights and freedoms:
12. the right to equal treatment pursuant to which no one may be disadvantaged or favoured because of his parentage, his language, his origin, or his political opinions.

II
2. Members of the German minority and their organizations may not be hindered from speaking and writing the language of their choice. The use of the German language in courts and administrative agencies shall be governed by the relevant legal provisions.

IV. Developments/events/comments

Education
In the Danish-German border region the German minority, similar to the Danish minority south of the border, are entitled to establish their own schools, where teaching is conducted in both languages so that the children become bilingual. The schools receive grants from the Danish (and the German for the Danish minority in Germany) authorities, and examinations taken at these schools qualify for admission to higher education in both countries.

Schools established by the German minority in Denmark are subsidised by the Danish State in accordance with the Act on Free Schools and Private Elementary Schools.

In addition to the above minority, 41,833 children of immigrants and refugees were enrolled in the Danish Folkeskole (municipal primary and lower secondary schools) on 1 October 1997, corresponding to 7.8% of all pupils. The largest groups are from Turkey, the Middle East, Bosnia, Pakistan and Somalia. They are all non-Danish-speaking, i.e. they have a mother tongue other than

---

[5] The population of Greenland are also not characterized as a Danish minority and the Greenlandic language is therefore not considered to be a minority language.

Danish. According to the regulations in force, non-Danish-speaking children are entitled to 3 to 5 hours teaching in their mother tongue per week in the 1st to 9th grades. There are plans to extend this provision to the pre-school class from 1999.

Immigrants and refugees are entitled to establish their own schools in accordance with the Act on Free Schools and Private Elementary Schools, and under this act they receive grants for running the schools. These schools also offer teaching in the mother tongue and often also teaching in the pupils' religion. Apart from a few international schools, the language of teaching is Danish.

There are no special provisions for minorities in higher education.

Administrative and judicial procedures
It follows from the rules contained in the Danish Public Administration Act (Fory-alltningsloven) that the Danish administrative authorities are under a general obligation to ensure that minorities are able to understand and to be understood by persons in matters which are to be considered by the authority concerned. Depending on the circumstances, an administrative authority must therefore provide persons who apply to the authority and who have not mastered the Danish language with the assistance of interpreters and translations. This applies to foreign as well as Danish citizens.

According to section 149 of the Danish Administration of Justice Act the language of the courts is Danish. As far as possible the interrogation of persons who have not mastered the Danish language takes place with the assistance of an interpreter. In civil proceedings an interpreter may not be called in cases where none of the parties requests interpretation and the court is of the opinion that it has sufficient knowledge of the foreign language. This also applies to criminal proceedings outside the oral pleadings at the High Courts. Documents, which are not drawn up in Danish, shall be accompanied by a translation, which, upon the request of the court or the opposite party shall be certified by a translator. Translation is not necessary, however, if both parties agree to this and the court is of the opinion that it has sufficient knowledge of the foreign language.

Employment opportunities
Insufficient knowledge of the Danish language may cause problems as far as the employment of the unemployed persons with an ethnic background is concerned, and it presents a barrier to labour market integration.

National bodies
The Board for Ethnic Equality was established in June 1993 with the task of providing advice on questions of discrimination and ethnic equality. Under the 1997 Act on the Board for Ethnic Equality, its position has been strengthened in several ways.

In addition, there is a Secretariat for the German Minority which handles relations with Parliament and the Government in Copenhagen. It was set up by the Danish Government in 1983, as the number of votes cast for the Schleswig Party, the party of the German minority, was no longer sufficient to give the minority a seat in the Danish Parliament (*Folkrtinget*). The head of this Secretariat is elected by the German minority.

Cases
In a judgement delivered in 1997 the Western High Court found that a previous judgement of a district court should be overturned as the accused, who was an Iranian citizen living in Denmark, had not been assisted by an interpreter at the district court's hearing of the case. The matter was thus referred back to the district court for a new hearing. The High Court referred to Article 6, paragraph 3, e, of the European Convention on Human Rights on the right to have the free assistance of an interpreter if the person charged with a criminal offence cannot understand or speak the language used in court.

Home Rule Act of the Faroe Islands (No. 137, 23 March 1948)
As the population of the Faroe Islands are not characterised as a Danish minority the Faroese language is therefore not considered to be a minority language. The Home Rule Act of the Faroe Islands, which has the status of a self-governing community, recognises in Section 11 Faroese as the principal language, although Danish should be thoroughly learnt. Both Danish and Faroese may be used in public affairs. When cases are submitted all Faroese documents shall be accompanied by a Danish translation.

The Greenland Home Rule Act (No. 577, 29 November 1878)
The population of Greenland are also not considered to be a minority and the Greenlandic language is therefore also not considered to be a minority language. Section 9 of the Greenland Home Rule Act confirms that Greenlandic is the principal language in Greenland and that Danish must be thoroughly taught. Either language may be used for official purposes.

Declaration on the General Rights of the German Minority in South Jutland
The Declaration on the General Rights of the German Minority in South Jutland approved by the Danish Parliament on 19 April 1955 confirms that under Danish law – the Basic Law of the Kingdom of Denmark of 5 June 1953 and other legislation – every citizen and thus also every member of the German minority regardless of the language which he/she uses shall enjoy, *inter alia*, the right to equal treatment pursuant to which no one may be placed at a disadvantage or favoured because of his parentage, his language, his origin, or his political opinions. Accordingly, members of the German minority and their organizations may not be hindered from speaking and writing the language of their choice. The use of the German language in courts and administrative agencies shall be governed by the relevant legal provisions.

ESTONIA

I. Demographic situation

Population (1999): Total 1,445,580. Minority groups: Russians 406,049 (28.08%); Ukrainians 36,659 (2.5%); Belarusians 21,363 (1.4%); Finns 21,363 (1.4%); (Smaller population of Jews, Tatars, Germans, Latvians, Poles, Lithuanians and others 25,956 (1.7%)).

Languages: Estonian, Russian.

II. International obligations

Article 3 of the Estonian Constitution stipulates that generally recognized principles and rules of international law are an inseparable part of the Estonian legal system and, according to Article 123, paragraphs 1 and 2, the Republic of Estonia shall not conclude international treaties which are in conflict with the Constitution. If Estonian laws or other acts are in conflict with treaties ratified by Parliament, the articles of the international treaty shall be applied. As an inseparable part of the internal legal system the provisions of international treaties may be directly referred to.

United Nations
- International Covenant on Civil and Political Rights (accession 21 October 1991)
- First Optional Protocol (accession 21 October 1991)
- International Covenant on Economic, Social and Cultural Rights (accession 21 October 1991)

Council of Europe
- Member (14 May 1993)
- ECHR (signature 14 May 1993, ratification 16 April 1996)
- Not a party to the Charter for Regional or Minority Languages
- Framework Convention for the Protection of National Minorities (signature 2 February 1995, ratification 6 January 1997, entry into force 1 February 1998)

III. National legislation

Constitution (28 June 1992)

Article 6
The official language of Estonia shall be Estonian.

Article 12
1. All persons shall be equal before the law. No person may be discriminated against on the basis of nationality, race, colour, gender, language, origin, religion, political or other beliefs, financial or social status, or other reasons.

Article 21
1. Any person who is deprived of his or her liberty shall be informed promptly, in a language and manner which he or she understands, of the reason for the arrest, and of his or her rights, and shall be given the opportunity to notify his or her immediate family of the arrest [...]
2. No person may be held in custody for more than 48 hours without specific permission by a court. Such a decision shall be promptly made known to the person in custody in a language and in a manner he or she understands.

Article 37
4. All persons shall have the right to instruction in Estonian. Educational institutions established for ethnic minorities shall choose their own language of instruction.

Article 51
1. All persons shall have the right to address State or local government authorities and their officials in Estonian, and to receive answers in Estonian.
2. In localities where at least half of the permanent residents belong to an ethnic minority, all persons shall have the right to receive answers from State and local government authorities and their officials in the language of that ethnic minority.

Article 52
1. The official language of State and local government authorities shall be Estonian.
2. In localities where the language of the majority of the population is other than Estonian, local government authorities may use the language of the majority of the permanent residents of that locality for internal communication, to the extent and in accordance with procedures established by law.
3. The use of foreign languages, including the languages of ethnic minorities, by State authorities and in court, and pre-trial proceedings shall be established by law.

Law on Cultural Autonomy for National Minorities (Adopted on 26 October 1993 by the *Riigikogu* (State Assembly). Based on the same basic ideas and principles as the Law on Cultural Autonomy for National Minorities of 12 February 1925)

Article 4
Members of a national minority have the right:
4. to use their mother tongue in dealings within the limits established by the Language Law;
5. to publish ethnic language publications;
6. to circulate and exchange information in their mother tongue.

Article 8
1. The national register contains the following information regarding a person:
   3) ethnicity and mother tongue;

Article 24
Institutions of cultural autonomy are:
1. educational institutions providing intensive training in the ethnic language or ethnic culture-school institutions and schools;

Law on Estonian Language Requirements for Applicants for Citizenship
(enacted in the *Riigikogu* on 10 February 1993, entered into force on 25 February 1993)

Article 1 – Task of the Law
1. Proceeding from Paragraph 3 of Article 6 of the Law on Citizenship, this Law shall establish the requirements for knowledge of the Estonian language for applicants for citizenship by naturalization.
2. For the purposes of the Law, knowledge of the Estonian language shall be defined as a general (not scientific) knowledge of the Estonian language.

Article 2 – Estonian Language Knowledge Requirements
Applicants for citizenship should:
1. have a listening comprehension of general information (announcements, warnings, news, reports of events and explanations of occurrences) and official statements. The applicant may fail to comprehend some details and relations between sentences;
2. be able to hold a conversation and to speak on a given topic, using negative and affirmative forms, using questions, commands, prohibitions and wishes, expressing opinions, assumptions and explanations, and using various verb tenses correctly. The applicant's conversation must be comprehensible but he or she may hesitate to find the correct word, may repeat or rephrase ideas and may make grammatical errors;

3. be able to read and comprehend texts written in everyday language (public notices, lists, news, newspaper and magazine articles, sample forms, catalogues, instruction manuals, traffic information, tests, records, regulations, etc.). The applicant may have difficulty in comprehending uncommon words or complicated sentence structures;
4. be able to compose standard applications in writing, be able to fill out applications and other forms and be able to compose a curriculum vitae.

Article 3 – Assessment of Estonian Knowledge
1. The knowledge of the Estonian language of an applicant for citizenship shall be assessed through an examination, for which the procedures, requirements and recommended content shall be established by the Government of the Republic.
2. The following applicants for citizenship shall be exempt from the obligation of taking an examination:
   1. persons who have obtained primary, general, secondary or higher education in the Estonian language;
   2. persons who have obtained an employment-related knowledge of the language, attested by an E or F category certificate, obtained in accordance with procedures established by the Government of the Republic;
   3. The Government of the Republic may establish simplified Estonian language examination requirements for persons born before January 1, 1930, as well as for category I invalids and those category II invalids, who are considered to be permanent invalids and who are unable to complete an examination in accordance with the general requirements due to the state of their health.

Article 4
The present law shall enter into force as of the day of its proclamation.

Law on Language (Adopted on 21 February 1995, unofficial translation)

CHAPTER I – General Provisions

Article 1 – The status of the Estonian language:
1. The State language of Estonia shall be the Estonian language.
2. The basis of the official use of the Estonian language, in the context of the present Law, shall be the standard of the Estonian written language according to the procedures determined by the Government of the Republic.

Article 2 – A foreign language:
1. Every other language besides the Estonian language shall be a foreign language in the context of the present Law.

2. The language of a national minority shall be a foreign language which Estonian citizens belonging to a national minority have historically used in Estonia as their mother tongue.

Article 3 – Language of administration:
1. The language of administration in a State institution, a local government and in its institutions (referred to as local government), as well as the language of service and command in the Estonian defence forces, shall be the Estonian language. Exceptions shall be determined in Chapters 2, 3 and 4 of the present Law.
2. Language use in pre-trial proceedings and trial proceedings shall be determined in applicable laws.

Article 4 – The right to use the Estonian language:
1. Everyone shall have the right to use the Estonian language in dealing with administration in State institutions, local government, and cultural autonomy bodies, as well as in institutions, enterprises and organisations.
2. All employees of institutions, enterprises and organisations must be guaranteed work-related, Estonian-language information.

Article 5 – Requirements for knowledge and usage of the Estonian language:
Requirements for the knowledge and usage of the Estonian language by employees of State institutions and local governments, as well as of institutions, enterprises and organisations, in work-related dealings with the public shall be determined by the Government of the Republic.

Article 6 – Acquirement of education in the Estonian language and in a foreign language:
State institutions and local governments shall guarantee the opportunity to acquire Estonian-language education, according to the procedures prescribed in law, in all the educational institutions belonging to them, as well as the opportunity to acquire a foreign-language education, according to the procedures prescribed by law.

CHAPTER 2 – The Use of Foreign Languages in State Institutions and Local Governments

Article 7 – Demands made of employees regarding the knowledge and use of the Estonian language:
If the language of a national minority is, together with the Estonian language, the language of internal administration in local government, the employees must have a knowledge of the Estonian language within the requirements determined

by the Government of the Republic for the knowledge and usage of the Estonian language.

Article 8 – Administration in a foreign language:
Persons who do not have knowledge of the Estonian language may also use, in their spoken communication with employees of State institutions and local governments, a foreign language which these employees know, if there is mutual agreement. If there is no mutual agreement, the communication shall be conducted with the mediation of an interpreter, with the expenses being borne by the person who lacks the knowledge of the Estonian language.

Article 9 – The language of foreign communication:
State institutions and local governments, as well as their employees, shall have the right to use in their foreign communications a language which is suitable to both parties.

Article 10 – The right to use the language of a national minority:
1. Everyone in a local government unit, where at least half of the permanent residents are of a national minority, shall have the right to receive replies in the language of this national minority, as well in the Estonian language, from the State institutions which operate on the territory of the applicable local government unit, and from the applicable local government, as well as from their officials.
2. A permanent resident of a local government unit shall be a person who is legally in Estonia and who lives in the local government unit for at least 183 days per year, whereby his or her absence from the local government unit must not exceed 90 consecutive days.

Article 11 – Use of the language of a national minority as a language of administration:
The internal language of administration in a local government unit, where the language of the majority of the permanent residents is not the Estonian language, may be, as well as the Estonian language, the language of the national minority which comprises the majority of the permanent residents of the local government unit, according to a proposal by the council of the applicable local government, and to a decision by the Government of the Republic.

Article 12 – The language of correspondence:
Correspondence with State institutions and other local governments by local governments shall be conducted in the Estonian language, where the language of internal administration, together with the Estonian language, is the language of the national minority.

Article 13 – Language for seals, rubber stamps, letterheads, advertisements, invitations and announcements:
1. The seals, rubber stamps and letterheads in a local government where, together with the Estonian language, the language of administration is the language of the national minority, must be in the Estonian language.
2. The invitations, advertisements and announcements in the local governments noted in Paragraph 1 of the present Article must be in the Estonian language, to which the local government may add a translation into the applicable language of the national minority.

CHAPTER 3 – The Use of the Language of a National Minority in the Cultural Autonomy

Bodies of a National Minority

Article 14 – The language of the cultural autonomy bodies of a national minority:
1. The cultural autonomy bodies of a national minority may use, as the language of internal administration, the language of its national minority.
2. Communication by the cultural autonomy bodies, both with State institutions as well as with their local governments where the language of the national minority is not in use as the language of internal administration, shall be conducted in the Estonian language.

Article 15 – Language for seals, letterheads, advertisements, announcements and rubber stamps in the cultural autonomy bodies of a national minority:
1. The seals of the cultural autonomy bodies must be in the Estonian language.
2. Official letterheads, advertisements, announcements and rubber stamps must be in the Estonian language, to which the cultural autonomy bodies may add a translation into the language of the applicable national minority.

CHAPTER 4 – Use of Language in Other Fields

Article 16 – The right of the consumer to Estonian-language information:
A consumer of goods and services shall have the right to Estonian-language information and service, in accordance with the Law on Consumer Protection (RT I 1994, 2, 13).

Article 17 – The language of reporting:
Reporting by institutions, enterprises and organisations which are registered in Estonia shall be conducted in the Estonian language, according to the procedures prescribed by law.

Article 18 – The use of foreign languages in other fields:
The use of foreign languages for the transfer of information to the consumers of services and goods, as well as in work-based communication, shall be conducted according to the procedures determined by the Government of the Republic.

CHAPTER 5 – Names, Designations and Information

Article 19 – The language for a place name:
1. Estonian place names shall be in the Estonian language. Exceptions which can be justified historically or culturally may be allowed for place names.
2. Every Estonian place shall have only one official name. The basic form of an Estonian place name shall be written in the Estonian-Latin script. Estonian place names shall be written in the language of a national minority, which uses a different alphabet, according to transcription rules determined by the standards of the written language.

Article 20 – Writing the name of an Estonian citizen:
The official form of the name of an Estonian citizen shall be written in Estonian-Latin letters. The names of Estonian citizens shall be written in languages using other alphabets, according to the transcription rules determined by the standards of the written language.

Article 21 – The designation of an institution, enterprise or organisation:
1. The designation of an Estonian institution, enterprise or organisation shall be entered into registries in the Estonian language, to which the keeper of the registry may add a translation into a foreign language, according to the determined procedures. The names which are part of these designations shall not be translated.
2. The seals, rubber stamps and letterheads of an institution, enterprise of organisation which is registered in Estonia shall be in the Estonian language. In foreign communication, the institution, enterprise or organisation may add a translation into a foreign language.

Article 22 – The international form of a name:
1. The international Latin-letter form of a name of an Estonian place, citizen, item, enterprise, institution or organisation shall be same as the name used in Estonia.
2. The writing of names, as determined in paragraph 1 of the present Article, in a language which uses another alphabet, shall implement the transcription rules which are determined in the standards for the written language.

Article 23 – The language of information:
1. Public signs, signposts, advertisements, announcements and advertising shall be in the Estonian language, except in the cases determined in Articles 13, 15

and 18 of the present Law, and except in the organisation of international events.
2. The provisions in the present Article shall not apply to the representations of foreign countries.

Article 24 – The language of State registration signs:
The letter combinations of State registration signs may contain only Latin letters.

Article 25 – Translation of the spoken text of a foreign language of an audio-visual work, or a transmission or program transmitted by a broadcasting organisation:
1. In making public an audio-visual work, an Estonian-language translation must be added to the foreign-language-spoken text.
2. The foreign-language spoken texts transmitted by radio or television stations, which possess a broadcasting license in Estonia, must be provided with an Estonian-language translation, except for language instruction transmissions, or radio transmissions and programs directed at a foreign language listener.

Article 26 – The use of Riigikogu as the name of the Estonian legislative body:
1. The Riigikogu, as the name of the Estonian legislative body, shall not be translated.
2. Riigikogu shall be written, as in the Estonian language, in foreign languages which use the Latin alphabet, and in languages using other alphabets, according to the transcription rules determined in the standards for the written language.
3. The term 'parliament' may be use instead of, or in addition to, Riigikogu as the unofficial name of the Estonian legislative body, in both the Estonian language and in foreign languages.

CHAPTER 6 – Final Provisions

Article 27 – Consequences of violating the Law:
Violators of the present Law, and other legal acts associated with it, shall be administratively prosecuted, according to the procedures prescribed by law.

Article 28 – Checking the fulfilment of the Law:
Abidance by the present Law shall be checked according to the procedures determined by the Government of the Republic.

Article 29 – Amendments to legal acts:
The Estonian SSR Law on Language (ENSV Teutaja 1989, 4, 60; RT I 1993, 20, 352; 1994, 49, 804) shall be declared null and void.

(1) The following amendments shall be made in the Law on Local Government Organisation (RT I 1993, 37, 558; 1994, 12, 200; 19, 340; 72, 1263; 84, 1475):

1) Paragraph 8 of Article 23 shall be amended and worded as follows:
   (8) The ordinances and decisions of the Council, as well as the minutes of the sessions, shall be formulated and made public in the Estonian language. In local government units, where the language of the majority of the permanent residents is not the Estonian language, the minutes of the sessions of the Council may be prepared in the language of the national minority which forms a majority of the permanent residents in the given local government unit, but an Estonian-language translation must be added to these.

2) Paragraph 2 of Article 41 shall be amended and worded as follows:
   (2) The use in local governments of foreign languages, including the languages of national minorities, shall be determined by the Law on Language.

Article 30 – Coming into force of the Law:
The present Law shall come into force on April 1, 1995.

IV. Developments/events/comments

Education
As stipulated under current legislation the language of instruction in public educational institutions is Estonian, but it can also be some other language. Russian is the main minority language used in education, and in fact there is currently no other minority language of instruction than Russian. (During the period 1992-1998 there was a class in the Ukrainian language in the Tallinn Secondary School; however, it ceased to exist due to a lack of interest among Ukrainian parents). In 1998/99 there were 110 schools teaching in the Russian language and 18 mixed Estonian-Russian language schools (out of a total of 722 schools). Currently the educational system is being reformed with the primary objective being to integrate minority language schools into the unified Estonian educational system.

At the same time there are a number of Sunday schools organized by national cultural societies for the teaching of the mother tongue, culture and history. Azerbaijanis, Latvians, Jews, Poles and Tatars operate such Sunday schools.

There are also language schools and courses organized by the Romania-Moldova and the Uzbek Cultural Society, as well as the Swedish language school organized by the Virumaa Swedes.

Funding for education in minority languages is provided from different sources i.e. the State budget, local budgets, membership fees and donations from various organizations and enterprises.

Judicial procedures
Although in principle the language of criminal proceedings is Estonian, it is possible to use another language if the parties and the court so agree. Parties and other persons involved in criminal proceedings are allowed to submit petitions, give statements and provide testimony in their own language, or with the aid of an interpreter or translator at the expense of the State (Section 16 and 89 (I) of the 1995 Code on Criminal Procedure). Free assistance by an interpreter is also provided in administrative proceedings if necessary (Section 351 (3) of the 1992 Code of Administrative Offences).

Whereas the provision dealing with the use of languages other than Estonian in civil proceedings is quite similar to the one dealing with criminal procedure, there is the burden of having to pay the fees of the interpreters and translators (not those employed at the court in question) (Sections 7(1) and 53 (1) of the 1998 Code of Civil Procedure).

At the courts of first instance in the regions with a non-Estonian majority, criminal proceedings are usually conducted in the Russian language.

Employment
The 1992 Employment Act prohibits illegal preferences and restriction of rights on grounds of sex, ethnicity, colour, race, native language, social origin, etc. However, it is not contrary to the provision of the Act establishing a prohibition on illegal preferences to require language skills necessary for the work and to pay compensation for proficiency in languages.

Personal names
Members of national minorities can use personal names in their minority language. Officially names must be written in Estonian Latin letters. Russian personal names in the Cyrillic alphabet shall be transcribed or transliterated according to an alphabet table.

Topographic names
In addition to Article 19 (1) of the Language Law, Article 14 (1) of the 1997 Place Names Act also provides that place names in Estonia shall be in Estonian except in cases which are historically justified. One of the exceptions is based on the language of the long-term inhabitants of a place, long-term in this respect being from 27 September 1939. A place may have a traditional foreign language name as its main name or in parallel with an Estonian language name.

Media
Estonian legislation expressly guarantees the access of national minorities to the media, and the State may not interfere with the planning of radio and TV

programmes, neither can it take decisions on the content of articles in the press. There are 15 different Russian language newspapers, and 5 different TV channels broadcasting in the Russian language.

Bodies

The Presidential Roundtable on National Minorities was founded in 1993. It is a permanent forum for the representatives of ethnic minorities' associations and political parties. Within the framework of its mandate it makes proposals and recommendations on issues relating to minorities, and comments on relevant draft laws. The objective of the Roundtable is to elaborate recommendations and proposals concerning, *inter alia*, the resolution of questions related to the learning and use of the Estonian language and the preservation of the cultural and ethnic identity of ethnic minorities residing in Estonia.

There is also a Governmental Commission of Experts established in 1997, with the task of dealing with questions relating to the Estonian demographic situation and the integration of ethnic minorities into Estonian society. It makes various proposals to the Government.

During the same year (1997) a Cultural Council of National Minorities was established under the Ministry of Culture with the task of coordinating the cultural activities of minorities and participating in decision-making with respect to the cultural aspects of minorities in Estonia.

Events

On 19 November 1997 the Estonian Parliament (by 45 votes in favour and 6 against) adopted amendments to the Law on Language, which have established restrictions to the right to vote in the Estonian Republic.

The adopted changes in the Law on Language establish where knowledge of the State language is necessary and the list of persons and legal entities which should have such knowledge. Among them are the following:
- members of Parliament;
- members of local government;
- workers and employees of commercial and non-profit associations;
- employees of NGOs.

In addition, one of the amendments establishes a special governmental institution to deal with the control and examination of the level of language skills.

Cases

In 1997 two cases were instigated against two local government deputies accusing them for inappropriate knowledge of the State language as required by the 1995 Law on Language. The cases were initiated by the Department of State Language and the National Election Committee. Both cases were grounded on the same legal basis. However, whereas in one of the cases the court decided in favour of the deputy in question, in the other case the decision was negative. In the first case the court found that legislation currently in force delegates to the

Government of the Republic the right to identify the level of language proficiency of the representatives of legislative power. In case of a municipal council, language requirements have to be determined by the Local Governments Election Act. Considering that the claim was about violations of the constitutional right to participate in the elections, the court rejected the claim of the National Election Committee and at the same time proposed to the National Court to declare unconstitutional a number of Estonian legal acts relevant for the matter.

In the other case the court was of the opinion that by lacking the knowledge of Estonian, the deputy violated Article 3(3) of the Local Governments Election Act, which requires a proficient knowledge of a deputy in oral and written Estonian. In the appeal procedure the National Court rejected the claim of the deputy.

FINLAND

I. Demographic situation

Population (1997): Total 5,147,349. Minority groups: Swedish speakers 295,000 (5.8%); Åland Islanders 25,000 (0.5%); Russian speakers 15,000-20,000 (0.3-0.4%); Sami 6,400-7,000 (0.1%); Roma 6,000 (0.1%); Others including Jews, Tatars and Old Russians.

Languages: Finnish and Swedish. Less than 50% of the Sami minority, which totals about 6,400 persons, still speaks the Sami language.

II. International obligations

According to Article 95 of the 1999 Constitution there are three ways in which international conventions can be implemented (conventions are not directly applicable and require a special procedure). Firstly, their incorporation into the legal system either by an Act of Parliament or by Decree; secondly, by harmonizing domestic law with the convention in question; and thirdly, by inserting special clauses in national legislation explicitly referring to an international convention. In some cases an international convention can even have precedence over national law.

United Nations
- International Covenant on Civil and Political Rights (signature 11 October 1967, ratification 19 August 1975)
- First Optional Protocol (signature 11 December 1967, ratification 19 August 1975)
- International Covenant on Economic, Social and Cultural Rights (signature 11 October 1967, ratification 19 August 1975)

Council of Europe
- Member (5 May 1989)
- ECHR (signature 5 May 1989, ratification 10 May 1990)
- Charter for Regional or Minority Languages (signature 5 November 1992, ratification 9 November 1994, entry into force 1 March 1998)
- Framework Convention for the Protection of National Minorities (signature 1 February 1995, ratification 3 October 1997, entry into force 1 February 1998)

Regional treaties
At the regional level Finland is a party to agreements concluded between the Nordic Countries (Sweden, Denmark, Norway, Iceland and Finland) which also provide for the right of citizens of a Nordic Country to use their own language in the other Nordic Countries.

Bilateral treaties
With respect to bilateral treaties, of significance is the Agreement on the Foundations of Relations concluded with the Russian Federation which provides support for the preservation of the identity of Finns and Finno-Ugric peoples and nationalities in Russia and, correspondingly, of persons of Russian-origin in Finland.

III. National legislation

Constitution (of 11 June 1999, entered into force on 1 March 2000)

Chapter 2 – Basic rights and liberties

Section 6 – Equality
2. No one shall, without an acceptable reason, be treated differently from other persons on the ground of sex, age, origin, language, religion, conviction, opinion, health, disability or other reason that concerns his or her person.

Section 17 – Right to one's language and culture
1. The national languages of Finland are Finnish and Swedish.
2. The right of everyone to use his or her own language, either Finnish or Swedish, before courts of law and other authorities, and to receive official documents in that language, shall be guaranteed by an Act. The public

authorities shall provide for the cultural and societal needs of the Finnish-speaking and Swedish-speaking populations of the country on an equal basis.
3. The Sami, as an indigenous people, as well as the Roma and other groups, have the right to maintain and develop their own language and culture. Provisions on the right of the Sami to use the Sami language before the authorities are laid down by an Act. The rights of persons using sign language and of persons in need of interpretation or translation aid owing to disability shall be guaranteed by an Act.

Section 51 – Languages used in parliamentary work
1. The Finnish or Swedish languages are used in parliamentary work.
2. The Government and the other authorities shall submit the documents necessary for a matter to be taken up for consideration in the Parliament both in Finnish and Swedish. Likewise, the parliamentary replies and communications, the reports and statements of the Committees, as well as the written proposals of the Speaker's Council, shall be written in Finnish and Swedish.

Section 121 – Municipal and other regional self-government
3. Provisions on self-government in administrative areas larger than a municipality are laid down by an Act. In their native region, the Sami have linguistic and cultural self-government, as provided by an Act.

Language Act (148/1922)

1. General provisions

Section 1 (10/1975):
1. The national language of Finland, Finnish or Swedish, or both Finnish and Swedish, shall be used before courts and other State authorities, as well as before the authorities of the municipalities, the other autonomous districts and the joint municipal organisations, as provided by this Act. The language or languages used shall be determined on the basis of the language of each administrative district, autonomous district, corresponding community or joint municipal Organisation, as well as of the parties to the matter.
2. Separate provisions shall be enacted on the right to use the Sami language before the authorities. (517/1991)

Section 2 (10/1975):
1. An administrative district or an autonomous district that comprises only one municipality shall be unilingual, if its entire population uses the same language or if the number of the inhabitants using the other language is less than eight per cent of the total number of inhabitants. The district shall be bilingual if the number of the inhabitants using the other language equals or

exceeds the said percentage, or is at least 3000. The same provision shall apply to an administrative district smaller than a municipality.
2. An administrative district or an autonomous district that comprises several municipalities, as well as a joint municipal Organisation, shall be unilingual if all the member municipalities are unilingual. The language or languages used in each municipality shall be correspondingly used in a district with unilingual member municipalities with different languages or with bilingual member municipalities.
3. Every ten years the Council of State shall determine on the basis of the official statistics those administrative districts and autonomous districts that shall be unilingual and those that shall be bilingual in accordance with the provisions above. A bilingual municipality shall not be determined to be unilingual unless the number of the inhabitants using the other language has fallen to six per cent or less of the total.
4. For a special reason the Council of State can, on the proposal of the municipal council or also otherwise after having obtained an opinion from the municipality, determine a municipality to be bilingual for the following ten-year period, even if it would be unilingual according to the provisions above in this section.
5. When the boundaries of administrative districts or autonomous districts are changed, the languages of the new districts shall at the same time be determined in accordance with the provisions of paragraphs (1) - (4). Also in this situation the Council of State shall have the right referred to in paragraph (4).

2. Language of the Parties to a Matter and Language of Official Documents

Section 3:
1. The language of the district or one of the languages of a bilingual district shall be used before a court and another State authority. However, a Finnish citizen shall have the right to use his own language, Finnish or Swedish, in a matter to which he is a party and in a matter in which he is being heard. Also, a municipality and another autonomous community, a joint municipal organisation, a religious community, a Finnish association, a cooperative, a company, a partnership, a foundation and an institution shall have the right to use the language in which its minutes are kept and an educational institution the language it uses for education. (10/1975)
2. If a document submitted to a court or to another State authority has been written, contrary to the provisions of paragraph (1), in the other national language, the authority shall obtain a valid translation the expense of the submitting party. However, the authority shall obtain the translation on its own expense, if it is to see to the interpretation in the matter in accordance with section 22 of the Administrative Procedure Act (598/1982). (599/1982)

Section 4:
1. When a State attorney, a public prosecutor or another State official is pursuing an action as a part of his official duties, he shall use the language of the defendant, if he is required to know this language.
2. If necessary, interpretation shall be resorted to in an oral hearing of a matter before a court or when a matter is considered by the police.

Section 5 (141/1935):
1. In a unilingual administrative district a court and another authority shall issue its documents in the language of the district.
2. However, the Council of State, a Ministry, a central administrative board, a court and a County Government shall be obliged to enclose a valid translation to its documents if the original document should according to section 6 be issued in the other language and a party to the matter, who according to section 3 has the right to use the other language than that used in the administrative district, has requested a translation.

Section (141/1935):
1. In a bilingual administrative district a court and another authority shall issue its documents in the language of the party or the parties to the matter or in the language agreed on by the parties.
2. If the parties have used different languages and they do not agree on the document language, the following provisions shall apply:
   1) In a criminal matter the language of the defendant shall be used.
   2) In another matter and in a criminal matter with defendants using different languages the language of the majority of the population of the administrative district shall be used, unless the authority, with regard to the rights and interests of the parties, decides otherwise.

Section 7:
Before municipal authorities and the authorities of other autonomous districts the language or, if the district is bilingual, one of the languages of the district shall be used. The provisions of section 5(1) and section 6 shall also apply with regard to these authorities.

Section 8:
1. A higher court and another higher authority shall in each case issue its documents in the language used, in accordance with this Act, by the lower authority concerned.
2. A party to a matter who according to section 5(2) has the right to request that a valid translation be enclosed to a document shall have the same right with regard to the documents of a higher court and a higher authority.

Section 9 (141/1935):
If a unilingual municipality or other autonomous community is officially requested to issue an opinion or to give an explanation in a matter in which the other language than that of the municipality or community is used, the documents shall be sent to the municipality or community as a translation officially certified by the authority concerned. The same provision shall apply to a document issued in such a matter.

Section 10 (141/1935):
1. Announcements, notifications, proclamations and the other comparable documents issued by a court, another State authority or an authority of a municipality or another autonomous district and intended for public notice shall in an unilingual administrative district or autonomous district be written in the language of the district and in a bilingual administrative district or autonomous district in both the national languages.
2. The official notices and proclamations issued in a bilingual district by a District Court, a judge, a County Government, a District Registry, a department of a branch office of a District Registry of an official of one of the above and relating to the rights of a private individual may be drawn up only in the language of the majority of the population, unless otherwise requested by the petitioner. (201/1996)

3. Language Used within the Administration

Section 11:
1. A court and another State authority in a unilingual administrative district shall use the language of the district in its internal affairs.
2. In this Act the language used in internal affairs means the language used in such minutes and other documents that are not to be given to a private party to a matter, in the correspondence between authorities and in official diaries.

Section 12 (10/1975):
A court and another State authority in a bilingual administrative district or exercising jurisdiction over bilingual municipalities or unilingual municipalities with different languages shall use the language of the majority of the administrative district in its internal affairs. However, in a matter where the documents are to be issued in the language of the minority the language of the documents shall be used, unless there are special reasons for using the language of the majority. If a language other than that of the documents has been used, a valid translation of the documents relating to the matter shall without delay be enclosed to the documents, if a party to the matter so requests. This provision shall not apply to documents obviously irrelevant to the decision in the matter.

Section 13 (141/1935):
1. In a matter where documents are to be issued, a higher authority shall communicate with a lower authority in the language that the latter is to use in accordance with section 12 and with an unilingual municipality or other autonomous district and their authorities in the language of the municipality or district. (10/1 975)
2. Regardless of the provision of paragraph (1) a lower authority may not refrain from complying with an order issued in the other language, if the authority is required to know this language.

Section 14:
1. An authority whose activities concern only one language group shall use the language of this group in its internal affairs.
2. The administrative organs and officials of unilingual education and instruction institutions of the State or a municipality shall also use the language of the institution even if it were located in a municipality using the other language.

Section 15:
1. The provisions of sections 11, 12 and 14 shall apply also to the authorities of municipalities and other autonomous districts. In addition, in bilingual districts these authorities shall comply with the provision of section 13(I) in their correspondence with authorities subordinate to them.
2. However, in a matter where the documents are to be issued in the language of the minority of the municipality, a valid translation shall without delay be enclosed to the minutes of the municipal authority, if a party to the matter or a member of the municipality so requests. (10/1975)
3. Also, the provision in paragraph (1) shall not preclude the right of the council of an autonomous district to decide that the minutes be kept in both languages.

Section 16 (141/1935):
1. A member of a collegiate body with jurisdiction over a bilingual administrative district, bilingual municipalities or unilingual municipalities with different languages shall in discussions and in opinions to be entered in the minutes have the right to use the language, Finnish or Swedish, he deems appropriate.
2. The members of the councils of autonomous districts and the members of general committees and boards shall have the same right. If a member of a council does not understand a statement given in the other language, it shall be briefly interpreted to him, if he so requests.

4. Miscellaneous Provisions

Section 17 (141/1935):
1. The provisions of this Act on the language of State authorities shall apply also to the language of the parties to a matter, the language of official documents and the language used within the administration in the Cathedral Chapters, Vicar's offices and other authorities of the Evangelical Lutheran Church, unless the matter by its nature is to be deemed an internal matter of the Church under the Church Act. The provisions on municipalities and other autonomous communities shall apply correspondingly to the parishes of this Church. Also, parishes formed on the basis of language shall remain unilingual regardless of the language of the people of the district.
2. Provisions on the official language of the Greek Orthodox Church shall be issued by Decree.

Section 17a (10/1975):
The provisions of this Act on the language of municipal authorities shall apply also to the language of the parties to a matter, the language of official documents and the language used within the administration in the authorities of joint municipal organisations.

Section 17b (368/1995):
A State enterprise and a service-providing company controlled by the State, one or more bilingual municipalities or several unilingual municipalities with different languages shall serve the public and provide information both in Finnish and in Swedish, unless this is unnecessary or, when assessed as a whole, unreasonable from the point of view of the company.

Section 18 (141/1935):
Separate provisions shall be enacted on the official language of the authorities of State Universities and institutions of higher education and on the language used in instruction and examinations there.

Section 19:
1. This Act shall apply to military authorities. Their administrative districts shall be deemed unilingual, if the rank and file of the units subordinate to them have been assembled in order to set up an unilingual unit and bilingual, if the rank and file have been assembled regardless of mother tongue or if the activities of the authorities concern units of different languages.
2. The command language of the Armed Forces shall be Finnish.

Section 20 (141/1 935):
1. Regardless of the provisions of section 2(2), the State Railway administrative districts shall for the part of each stopping place be deemed to use the language or languages of the stopping place.
2. Stopping places shall be unilingual, if the municipalities immediately surrounding them are unilingual, and bilingual, if the municipalities immediately surrounding them are bilingual or unilingual with different languages.

Section 21 (10/1975):
The law proposals and reports prepared and published by a Ministry, a State committee, a commission or another corresponding body shall be published in Finnish and, unless especially persuasive reasons otherwise warrant, in full, in part or as a synopsis also in Swedish, as decided by the competent Ministry with regard to the importance of the matter to the Swedish-speaking population and to other circumstances.

Section 22:
1. The provisions on the authorities in bilingual administrative districts shall apply to Finnish missions abroad. They shall apply also to consulates headed by a Consul by career.
2. Provisions on the use of a language other than Finnish or Swedish in missions and consulate shall be issued by Decree.

Section 23:
1. A document issued as a valid translation in accordance with this Act shall be considered equal to the original.
2. If a State authority is to give or send a party to the matter a translation of a document or if internal documents of the authorities are to be translated in accordance with section 12, the costs of the translation shall be covered by the State. The costs arising from the translation referred to in section 1 5(l) and (2) and the interpretation referred to in section 16(2) shall be covered by the autonomous community or the joint municipal Organisation. (10/1975).

Section 24:
This Act shall not apply to official correspondence addressed to foreign States or foreign citizens or to documents intended to be used abroad; however, the provisions of sections 5 and 6 shall be complied with also in connection with such documents, unless they are issued in a foreign language or in both the national languages.

Section 25:
Further provisions on the implementation of this Act shall be issued by Decree.

Section 26:
This Act shall enter into force on 1 January 1923.

Act on the Autonomy of Åland (16 August 1991/1144)

Chapter 6 – Language provisions

Section 36 - Official language:
The official language of Åland shall be Swedish. The language used by the State and Åland officials and in the municipal administration shall be Swedish.

The official language of the Åland Delegation shall be Swedish. The opinions and decisions of the Supreme Court referred to in this Act shall be written in Swedish.

The provisions of this Act on the language used in State administration shall also apply, where appropriate, to the officials of the Evangelical Lutheran Church, unless otherwise provided by the Church Code.

Section 37 - Right to use Finnish:
In a matter concerning himself a citizen of Finland shall have the right to use Finnish before a court and with other State officials in Åland.

Section 38 - Language of correspondence:
Letters and other documents between Åland officials and the State officials in Åland shall be written in Swedish. The same provision shall apply also to correspondence between the said authorities and the Åland Delegation, on one hand, as well as the Council of State, the officials in the central government of Finland and the superior courts and other State officials to whose jurisdiction Åland or a part thereof belongs, on the other hand.

However, a treaty referred to in section 59 that is submitted for approval of the Legislative Assembly may be sent to Åland in the original language, if the treaty by law is not to be published in Swedish. A document referred to in section 59 a that is notified to Åland may be sent to Åland in the original language, if it has not yet been translated into Swedish. (31 December 1994/1556)

Section 39 – Translations:
On the request of a party, the courts and the County Government of Åland shall enclose a Finnish translation in their documents.

If a document submitted to a court or another State official is written in Finnish, the official shall see to its translation into Swedish, if necessary.

A private party in Åland shall have the right to receive an enclosed Swedish translation with his copy of the document in matters that are considered by a State official in the State, referred to in section 38, paragraph 1, and on which the document shall according to general language legislation be written in Finnish.

Section 40 - Language of education:
The language of education in schools maintained by public funds or subsidised from the said funds shall be Swedish, unless otherwise provided by an Act of Åland.

Section 41 - Proficiency in Finnish:
A graduate of an educational institution in Åland may, as further provided by Decree, be admitted to a State-maintained or State-subsidised Swedish or bilingual educational institution and be graduated therefrom, even if he does not have the proficiency in Finnish required for admittance and graduation.

Section 42 - Linguistic proficiency of State officials:
Provisions on the linguistic proficiency of a State official in Åland shall be issued by Decree with the consent of the Government of Åland.
    The State shall organise training in Swedish for the persons in its service in Åland.

Section 43 - Information and regulations issued in Swedish:
The Council of State shall take measures to have the necessary product and service information distributed to the consumers in Åland in Swedish, where possible.
    The Council of State shall also see to the availability in Swedish of the regulations to be followed in Åland.

Act on the Use of the Sami Language before the Authorities (8 March 1991/516)

Chapter 1 – General Provisions

Section 1:
[Amended – 1726/95]

Section 2:
In this Act, a Sami means a person who considers himself a Sami, provided that he himself or at least one of his parents or grandparents learnt Sami as his first language.
    The Sami domicile area means the municipalities of Enontekiö, Inari and Utsjoki as well as the area of the reindeer-grazing association of Lapland situated in the municipality of Sodankylä.

Section 3:
The authorities and agencies to which this Act shall apply are the following:
1. the courts of law and regional and local State authorities whose jurisdictional or administrative areas cover all or part of the Sami domicile area;

2. the County Government of Lapland and the bodies functioning in connection therewith;
3. [amended – 1726/95]
4. the Chancellor of Justice and the Parliamentary Ombudsman;
5. the Consumer Ombudsman and the Consumer Complaint Board, the Equality Ombudsman and the Council for Equality as well as the Data Protection Ombudsman and the Data Protection Board;
6. the Social Security Institution and the Farmers' Pension Institution; as well as
7. administrative State authorities which handle appeals brought in matters that have been initiated before said authorities.

This Act shall also apply to administrative matters handled in accordance with the Reindeer Husbandry Act (1990/848) and the Reindeer Husbandry Decree (1990/883) by State authorities and public-law associations whose administrative or functional areas cover all or part of the Sami domicile area.

Sections 5, 11 through 13 and 12 through 20 shall apply also to other State authorities than those referred to in paragraphs 1 and 2 above.

Section 4:
This Act shall apply to the authorities of the municipalities and joint municipal organisations as provided in sections 14 through 16.

It may be stipulated by decree that this Act shall apply to the handling of administrative matters also where these matters are to be handled by a public-law association or agency other than one referred to in Section 3, paragraph 1 or 2, or by a State-controlled limited company or a private body.

Chapter 2 – Language Rights

Section 5:
A Sami whose residence referred to in the Population Registration Act (1969/141) is in Finland may have the Sami language entered in the population Register as his native language.

Section 6:
In a matter regarding himself or in a matter in which he is heard, a Sami may use the Sami language before an authority or agency referred to in Section 3, paragraphs 1 and 2.

An organisation or a foundation which keeps its records in the Sami language as well as an educational institution whose instruction is given in the Sami language shall have a corresponding right to use the Sami language in accordance with paragraph 1.

Section 7:
In a matter which may be handled at the initiative of an authority, a State civil servant or employee shall, upon the request of a Sami party, use the Sami language in the Sami domicile area if the State civil servant or employee is required to know this language.

Section 8:
Upon his request, a Sami party shall, free of charge, receive a translation in the Sami language of a decision Issued if the qualifications required by law or otherwise of a civil servant or employee of an authority referred to in section 3, paragraph 1 or 2 do not include a knowledge of the Sami language. The translation shall be attached to the decision.

If the qualifications required by law or otherwise of a civil servant or employee of an authority referred to in section 3, paragraph 1 or 2 include a knowledge of the Sami language and if the matter is being handled by said civil servant or employee, a Sami party shall, upon request, receive the decision issued in the Sami language. A Sami party shall, however, only receive a Sami translation of a document where there are several concerned parties and they cannot agree on the use of the same language.

Section 9:
Public notices, announcements and proclamations or other documents issued to the public by an authority or agency referred to in section 3, paragraphs 1 and 2 as well as road and other signs and forms meant for the use of the public, together with any instructions regarding their use, shall, in the Sami domicile area, be drafted and issued also in the Sami language.
[Amendment – 888/1996]

Section 10:
Within the Sami domicile area and, when the matter especially concerns the Samis, also outside the Sami domicile area, a member of a State committee or board or other corresponding collegiate State administrative body has the right to use the Sami language In the discussions of the administrative body as well as in a statement issued for the record.

If a member of an administrative body referred to in paragraph 1 does not understand the language used in the discussion or a statement, he shall, upon request, be given a short interpretation of the discussion or statement.

Section 11:
Any public notices, announcements and proclamations or other documents as well as road and other signs and forms meant for the use of the public, together with any instructions regarding their use, referred to In section 9, paragraph 1 and drafted and issued by other State authorities and agencies than those referred to In section 3, paragraphs 1 and 2, shall, in the Sami domicile area, be available

also in the Sami language if they mainly concern the Samis or if other specials reasons therefore exist.

Section 12:
Any Acts or decrees or decisions of the Council of State or the ministries published in the Collection of Finnish Statutes as well as other decisions, public notices and proclamations to be published in the Collection of Finnish Statutes as well as rules to be published in a collection of rules by an authority which especially relate to the Samis shall, by decision of the Council of State or the ministry issuing the decision or rule, be published also in a translation in the Sami language.

Any Bills and reports or their summaries, prepared by a ministry or a State commission, committee or other corresponding body, which shall be published, shall, upon the decision of the ministry, be published also in the Sami language if they especially relate to the Samis or if other special reasons therefor exist.

Section 13:
A State authority, whose work relates to the Samis only, may, in addition to Finnish, use the Sami language as its internal working language.

Chapter 3 - Rules applicable to municipal authorities and the authorities of other autonomous bodies

Section 14:
The provisions of sections 6 through 8 and section 9, paragraph 1 on State authorities and agencies and their civil servants or employees shall also apply to the authorities of the Enontekiö, Inari, Utsjoki and Sodankylä municipalities and the authorities of joint municipal organisations with one or more of the above municipalities as member.

The notification cards prepared for elections and consultative referenda shall, however, not be drafted In the Sami language.

The provisions of section 10 on the right of a member of a committee and a board and a collegiate body to use the Sami language shall be applied also to a member of a municipal or joint municipal council, executive council or other corresponding body.

Section 15:
A municipality or joint municipal organisation referred to in section 14, paragraph 1 may, in addition to the internal official language of the municipality, use also the Sami language in any minutes of meetings and other documents which are not issued to a private party as well as in any correspondence between authorities and official books and records.

If the share of the Sami population in the population of the municipality exceeded one third on the first day of the preceding year, also the Sami language shall be used in the minutes, documents, correspondence and official books and records referred to in paragraph 1.

Section 16:
The provisions of this Act on the language(s) to be used by State authorities or agencies shall he applied to the language(s) to be used by the parties in the Cathedral Chapter of the Oulu Diocese of the Evangelical-Lutheran church and the offices of the parishes covering all or part of the Sami domicile area unless a matter, by its nature, is to be deemed an internal matter of the church under the Church Act (1964/635), as well as in the office of the Oulu Cathedral Chapter of the Greek-Orthodox church.

The provisions of this Act on municipalities or joint municipal organisations shall respectively be applied to the Enontekiö, Inari, Utsjoki and Sodankylä parishes of the Evangelical-Lutheran church unless a matter, by it nature, is to be deemed an internal matter of the church under the Church Act, as well as to the Lapland parish of the Greek-Orthodox church.

Chapter 4 - Interpretation and translation

Section 17:
When the Sami language in used orally under this Act, the authority or agency shall obtain an interpretation if the civil servant, officer or employee handling the matter does not know the Sami language.

Section 18:
Where an authority or agency, under this Act, shall issue a document also in a translation in the Sami language, it shall be entitled to have the document translated into the Sami language by the Office of the Sami Language referred to in section 21 if the translation cannot otherwise be appropriately acquired. The authority and agency shall have a corresponding right to a Finnish translation of a document in the Sami language.

Section 19:
If a State authority or agency shall issue a decision or document to a party In the Sami language or in a translation in the Sami language or if it shall have something interpreted in or from the Sami language, the State shall bear the costs of having the document drafted or translated in the Sami language or for the interpretation. The costs for the drafting or translation of a decision or document, or for the interpretation, referred to in section 14, paragraph 1, section 15, paragraph 2 and section 16 shall be borne by the autonomous community or joint municipal organisation.

Section 20:
If a document filed with an authority or agency of the State, municipality or other autonomous community or joint municipal organisation is drafted in the

Sami language even though the party concerned does not have the right to use the Sami language, the authority or agency shall have the document translated in the language used by the authority or agency at the expense of the party concerned.

Chapter 5 - Miscellaneous provisions

Section 21:
[Amended – 1726/95]

Section 22:
A public office of a Sami-language assistant may be established in the County Government as well as in a regional or local State authority. The services of the assistant shall be provided free of charge.

Section 23:
A civil servant or employee of a State authority or agency all of whose official area is situated in the Sami domicile area shall, in accordance with further provisions to be issued by decree, be entitled to paid leave of absence in order to acquire a knowledge of the Sami language necessary for him to carry out his official duties.

A civil servant or employee of a State authority or agency part of whose official area is situated in the Sami domicile area shall, in accordance with further provisions to be issued by decree, be entitled to paid leave of absence referred to in paragraph 1.

Section 24:
When appointing a civil servant or employee of a regional or local State authority or agency whose official area covers all or part of the Sami domicile area or a civil servant or employee of the County Government of Lapland or when engaging a private-law employee to work with said authority or agency, a knowledge of the Sami language shall be deemed a special merit even if it is not included in the qualifications for the office, job or task.

When appointing persons to said offices or tasks, the authorities referred to in paragraph 1 shall, by means of the measured referred to in section 25 and otherwise, ensure that its personnel includes a sufficient number of people knowing the Sami language.

Section 28:
The right of the Samis to receive comprehensive-school education and other instruction and day care in their native language as well as the teaching of the Sami language shall be governed by special provisions thereon.

Section 29:
Further provisions on the implementation of this Act shall be issued by decree.

Chapter 6 – Entry into force

Section 30:
This Act shall enter into force on 1 January 1992.

Measures necessary for the implementation of this Act may be taken prior to its entry into force.

This Act shall be published in the Collection of Finish Statutes also in a translation in the Sami language.

IV. Developments/events/comments

At present there are 389 Finnish speaking, 5 Swedish-speaking and 42 bilingual municipalities (this is the case when more than 8% of the population speak another official language of the country) and in addition all the 16 municipalities of the Åland Islands are Swedish speaking. Every ten years the Government determines which municipalities are monoglot and which are bilingual.

Notwithstanding the extensive legislation there are in practice some problems relating to the implementation of linguistic rights mainly due to the deficiency of language skills among public officials, and also because of prejudice towards minorities and misunderstanding. For these reasons it is possible that correspondence between different authorities and Swedish-speaking municipalities takes place only in Finnish.

Judicial and administrative procedures
In proceedings before a court or other authority everyone has the right to use his own language, and to obtain documents from the bodies in charge in that language. According to the Decree on the Implementation of the Language Act interpretation will be arranged in a criminal matter initiated by a public prosecutor if a party is not able to speak Finnish or Swedish.

Based on a newspaper article of 9 September 1996 according to which the Swedish-speaking Finns had difficulties in using their own language in criminal proceedings, the Parliamentary Ombudsman initiated an investigation which resulted in a proposal to the Government on 24 April 1998 concerning the measures necessary to improve the status of the Swedish language in criminal proceedings. A working group set up with the task of dealing with the proposal was expected to finish its work by the end of 1999.

In addition, due to the fact that the Act on the Use of the Sami Language before Authorities does not sufficiently ensure the preservation of the Sami language, as it is often based on interpretation and translation, a separate working group has been set up by the Ministry of Justice. It has the task of drafting a proposal aimed at amending the existing Law.

Under the Administrative Procedure Act (No. 589/1996) a public authority involved in an administrative procedure should arrange for interpretation and translation when a party is not able to speak the language officially used before that authority.

Education

The Comprehensive Schools Act (628/1998), the Upper Secondary Schools Act (629/1998) and the Act on Vocational Training (630/1998) provide for the Finnish, Swedish and Sami languages to be taught as the mother tongue. In addition, the Roma language or some other languages of the student may be taught as the mother tongue. It is also possible for the immigrant children to be taught in their native language.

According to Section 13 of the Comprehensive Schools Act (No. 628/1998), in municipalities in which both Finnish and Swedish are spoken, there is a duty on the part of the municipality to arrange comprehensive school education for both language groups. For the Sami and Roma education can be provided in their own languages as a matter of free choice on the part of the parents or custodians. As from 1 January 1999 the State pays the costs of education in comprehensive schools, upper secondary schools and in vocational training aimed at ensuring that education is provided in the Sami language and that the Sami language is taught in the Sami Homeland. With respect to the Roma language the State subsidises 86% of the costs of teaching in the mother tongue.

Names and signs

Neither the use of surnames and first names in minority languages nor signs, inscriptions or other information of a private nature displayed in public in minority languages is in any way prohibited.

Public announcements (street and road signs, official decisions, notification and information signs emanating from the public authorities) will be written either in one or in two languages (Finish and Swedish or Finish and Sami)

Media

For the Swedish-speaking population there are specific TV programmes and two nation wide channels in addition to local radio stations. The Sami people have their own radio channel with 40-hours a week broadcasting time. Once a week there is also a radio news broadcast in the Roma language as well as in Russian.

In addition, for the Swedish-speaking population there are several newspapers and magazines published in Swedish, and the Roma have three newspapers (two published by a national Roma association and one by the National Board of Education), although there are all published in Finnish and contain only some articles in the Roma language.

National bodies

There are several advisory bodies dealing with human rights and minority issues. The Advisory Board for Ethnic Relations (formerly the Advisory Board for Refugee and Migrant Affairs – PAKSI) is basically concerned with ethnic relations and the prevention of racism. There is also an Advisory Board for Sami

Affairs with the duty to coordinate and prepare matters concerning the Sami people and it is subordinated to the Ministry of Justice. Concerning the issued of Roma there is an Advisory Board for Roma Affairs – in charge of monitoring the living conditions of Roma, taking initiatives and promoting the status of the Roma language and culture, and it is subordinated to the Ministry of Social Affairs and Health; as well as the Roma Language Board – established in 1997 to study and develop the Roma language as well as to provide advice in the use of the Roma language.

FRANCE

I. Demographic situation

Population (1994): Total 57,400,000. Minority groups: Occitan speakers 2,000,000 (3.5%); Alsatians 1,5-2,000,000 (2.6-3.5%); Bretons 700,000 (1.2%); Portuguese 650,000 (1.1%); Algerians 614,000 (1.1%); Moroccans 572,000 (1.0%); Jews 500,000-700,000 (0.9-1.2%); Roma 280,000-340,000 (0.5-0.6%); Italians 252,000 (0.4%); Asians 227,000 (0.4%); Spanish 216,000 (0.4%); Tunisians 208,000 (0.4%); Catalans 200,000 (0.35%); Turks 198,000 (0.34%); Corsicans 170,000 (0.3%); Basques 80,000 (0.14%); Flemings 80,000 (0.14%); Former Yugoslavs 52,000 (less than 0.1%); Germans 52,000 (less than 0.1%); Poles 40,000 (less than 0.1%); Luxembourgers 40,000 (less than 0.1%); Others including sub-Saharan Africans 200,000 (on estimated 0.35%).

Languages: French, Breton, Corsican, Catalan, Basque, German, Occitan, Flemish, Arabic and Berber.

II. International obligations

Article 55 of the 1958 French Constitution determines that duly ratified or approved treaties or agreements shall, upon their publication, override laws, subject, as regards each agreement or treaty, to its application by the other party.

United Nations
– International Covenant on Civil and Political Rights (accession 4 November 1980)[6]

---

[6] France made a reservation to Article 27 as follows: '(8) In the light of Article 2 of the Constitution of the French Republic, the French Government declares that Article 27 is not applicable as far as the Republic is concerned'.

- First Optional Protocol (accession 17 February 1984)
- International Covenant on Economic, Social and Cultural Rights (accession 4 November 1980)

Council of Europe
- Member (5 May 1949)
- ECHR (signature 4 November 1950, ratification 3 May 1974)
- Charter for Regional or Minority Languages (signature 7 May 1999)
- Not a party to the Framework Convention for the Protection of National Minorities

III. National legislation

Constitution (of 4 October 1958, as modified up to 25 June 1992)

Article 2
The language of the Republic shall be French.

GEORGIA

I. Demographic situation

Population (1995)[7]: Total 5,600,000. Minority groups: Armenians 437,211 (8.1%%); Russians 341,720 (6.3%); Azeris 307,556 (5.7%); Ossetians 164,055 (3.0%); Greeks 100,324 (1.9%); Ukrainians 52,443 (0.7%); Kurds 33,333 (0.6%); Jews 24,795 (0.5%)

There are also other ethnic minorities living in the country as well as 94 nationalities.

Languages: Georgian, Mingrelian, Svan, Armenian and Russian.

---

[7] Because of the serious social and economic crisis during the period between 1990-1995, thousands of members of ethnic minorities, along with the Georgian population, left Georgia. There is, however, a lack of any systematic information and of accurate statistics in this regard. As pointed out by the Georgian Ministry of Foreign Affairs large-scale sociological surveys indicate that the emigration process was not caused by discrimination in general, or discrimination towards minorities in particular, but was rather due to economic reasons (lowering of living standards) and, absence concerning the optimism in future.

II. International obligations

Article 6, paragraph 2, of the 1995 Constitution establishes that the legislation of Georgia corresponds with the universally recognized norms and principles of international law. International treaties and agreements concluded with and by Georgia, as long as they do not contradict the Constitution, take precedence over domestic normative acts. Further on, in Article 7 the State recognizes and defends universally recognized human rights and freedoms as eternal and supreme values. The people and the State are bound by these rights and freedoms as well as by current legislation for the exercise of the State power.

United Nations
– International Covenant on Civil and Political Rights (accession 3 May 1994)
– First Optional Protocol (accession 3 May 1994)
– International Covenant on Economic, Social and Cultural Rights (accession 3 May 1994)

Council of Europe
– Member (27 April 1999)
– ECHR (signature 27 April 1999, ratification 20 May 1999)
– Not a party to the Charter for Regional or Minority Languages
– Framework Convention for the Protection of National Minorities (signature 21 January 2000)

III. National legislation

Constitution (24 August 1995)

Article 8
The State language of Georgia is Georgian; in Abkhazia, Abkhazian is also the State language.

Article 14
Everyone is born free and is equal before the law, regardless of race, skin colour, language, sex, religion, political and other beliefs, national, ethnic and social origin, property and title of nobility or place of residence.

Article 38
1. Citizens of Georgia are equal in social, economic, cultural and political life regardless of national, ethnic, religious or language origin. According to universally recognised principles and norms of international law all have the right to develop their culture freely without any discrimination and interference. They may use their language in private and public life.

Article 85
2. Jurisdiction is exercised in the State language. Persons not having command of the legal language of the court are provided with interpreters. In the regions where the population does not have a command of the State language, the State provides teaching in the State language and explanations of matters pertaining to its jurisdiction.

The Law on Georgian Citizenship (Adopted on 25 March 1993)

Article 4 – Equality of Georgian Citizens:
Georgian citizens shall be equal under the law irrespective of origin, social and property status, racial and national affiliation, sex, education, language, religion and political beliefs, occupation, place of residence and other circumstances.

Article 26 – Conditions for admission to the citizenship of Georgia:
Under the present Law, to the citizenship of Georgia shall be admitted an adult alien or a stateless person who:
    b. knows, within established minimum, the Georgian or Abkhasian language;

The Law on the Legal Status of Aliens (Adopted on 3 June 1993)

Article 13 – Right to enjoy Cultural Values:
In the Republic of Georgia aliens shall have the right to enjoy cultural values on equal terms with Georgian nationals.
In the Republic of Georgia aliens shall be guaranteed the right to use their native language, the right to protection and development of national culture and traditions, unless it interferes with national interests of the Republic of Georgia, legitimate interests and rights of persons residing there.

IV. Developments/events/comments

Draft Law on the State Language
It is expected that the draft Law on the State Language which is currently in preparation, will serve as a basis for the language policy of Georgia and will solve a number of problems now encountered in practice, as there is no special legislation dealing with the use of minority languages in public and in official matters (in courts, contacts with authorities, etc.).[8] In this sense, the Law on Self-Government adopted in 1997 did not pay the necessary attention to the issue of the use of language(s) which could have prevented serious conflicts caused by language issues.

---

[8] However, according to Article 82(2) of the Constitution and Article 135 of the Code of Criminal Procedure, a member of an ethnic minority has the right to a translator.

Correspondence in some regions is still carried out in Russian. For the Georgian State reinforcing the Georgian language as a State language in such territories has high priority. There is, however, a balance in this respect: the policy of reinforcing the Georgian language must include careful attention aimed at the preservation and development of minority languages.

Georgia is currently making an effort to reconciliate the conflicts in the existing autonomous regions. Within the framework of a supposed federalisation in which Abkhazian and (possibly) Ossetian autonomies would enjoy a specific political status, the Abkhazian and Ossetian languages would enjoy the status of one of the State languages - together with Georgian.

Media
On 15 August 1999, the first issue of a Kurdish-language newspaper, the monthly 'Glavezh', was published in Georgia. It is of a political nature and will focus on Yezid religious teaching, Kurdish culture, folk traditions, education, history, language, etc.

Education and culture
Article 4 of the 1997 Law on Education provides that, pursuant to the recommendations of local authorities, the State will create all necessary conditions for providing all the citizens of Georgia who have a native language other than Georgian, with the possibility of obtaining primary and secondary education in their mother tongue.

Despite the difficult economic situation and the austere budget, the whole infrastructure of the cultural autonomy of minorities (schools, cultural and educational institutions, the press, theatres) is being maintained. There are around 500 secondary schools with instruction in minority languages - Russian, Azeri, Armenian and Ossetian. At some schools, lessons are provided in the Greek, Jewish (Ivrit) and Kurdish languages on a facultative basis.

The State Pedagogical University trains specialists for Russian, Armenian and Azeri schools. Newspapers are published in the same languages (Russian, Armenian and Azeri). There are two State Russian drama companies, an Armenian drama company, as well as numerous amateur associations and folk theatres (Greek, Kurdish, Azeri, Ossetian and others).

GERMANY

I. Demographic situation

Population (1994): Total 81,100,000. Minority groups: Turks and Kurds 1,600,000 (2.0%); former Yugoslavs 956,000 (1.2%); Italians 568,000 (0.7%); Greeks 324,000 (0.4%); Poles 324,000 (0.4%); Roma/Gypsies/Sinti 110,000-130,000 (0.1-0.2%); Others 2,000,000 (2.5%): Jews 60,000-70,000, Danes 50,000-60,000, Frisians 52,000, Sorbs 40,000-45,000, Vietnamese 40,000, Spanish, Tunisians, Portuguese and Mozambican

Languages: German.

II. International obligations

The 1995 Constitution establishes in Article 25 that the general rules of public international law constitute an integral part of federal law. They take precedence over statutes and directly create rights and duties for the inhabitants of the federal territory.

United Nations
- International Covenant on Civil and Political Rights (signature 9 October 1968, ratification 17 December 1973)
- First Optional Protocol (accession 25 August 1993)
- International Covenant on Economic, Social and Cultural Rights (signature 9 October 1968, ratification 17 December 1973)

Council of Europe
- Member (13 July 1950)
- ECHR (signature 4 November 1950, ratification 5 December 1952)
- Charter for Regional or Minority Languages (signature 5 November 1992, ratification 16 September 1998, entry into force 1 January 1999)
- Framework Convention for the Protection of National Minorities (signature 11 May 1995, ratification 10 September 1997, entry into force 1 February 1998)[9]

Bilateral agreements
- 1991 – with Poland
- 1992 – with Hungary, Treaty on friendly cooperation and partnership in Europe

---

[9] The German Government, acting in agreement with the *Länder*, made an Interpretative Declaration on the Convention's scope of application in Germany. For the text of the Declaration see Part Two, Documents of the Council of Europe.

- 1992 – with Hungary, Joint Statement on assistance for the German minority in Hungary and for the teaching of German as a foreign language
- 1992 – with Czech Republic, on good neighbour relations and friendly co-operation

III. National legislation

Constitution (of 23 May 1949 as amended up to 1995)

Article 3
3. No one may be prejudiced or favoured because of his sex, his parentage, his race, his language, his homeland and origin, his faith or his religious or political opinions.

Constitution of the Land of Brandenburg

Article 25
7. The Sorbs have the right to he preservation and promotion of the Sorbian language and culture in public life and to have these imparted in schools and child day-care centres.
8. In the settlement area of the Sorbs, the Sorbian language shall be included in the marking of public identification signs for buildings and places [...]

Constitution of the Free State of Saxony

Article 6
1. The citizens of Sorbian ethnic origin living in the *Länder* are members of the State's population who enjoy equal rights. The *Länder* guarantees and protects the right to the preservation of their identity and to the cultivation and development of their traditional language, culture and tradition, especially by schools, pre-school facilities and cultural institutions.

Treaty on the Establishment of German Unity (31 August 1990)

Article 35
Regarding Article of the Unification Treaty, the Federal Republic of Germany and the German Democratic Republic declare the following:
3. Members of the Sorbian people and their organisations enjoy the freedom to cultivate and preserve the Sorbian language in public life.

IV. Developments/events/comments

In the respective areas where they are spoken, the minority languages – Danish, High Sorbian and Low Sorbian, North Frisian and Saterland Frisian – are protected by at least 35 specific undertakings under Part III of the European

Charter on Regional or Minority Languages. In addition, the protection afforded by Part III of the Charter extends to the regional language of Low German in five *Länder* in northern Germany. Protection of Romany, the minority language of the German Sinti and Roma, in the entire Federal territory and of the regional language Low German in the *Länder* of Brandenburg, North Rhine/Westphalia and Saxony-Anhalt, can only be provided under Part II of the Charter, which covers the objectives of, and principles for, the policies to be applied to regional or minority languages. However, in an agreement with the *Länder*, the Federal Government has, as a voluntary commitment by the Federal Republic, complied with specific provisions of Part III of the Charter, with which German law and German administrative actions already accord.

Education
(a) Danish minority
A Danish Schools Association (*Dansk Skoleforening for Sydslesvig*) in South Schleswig runs 53 different schools (primary and secondary schools, four *realskoler* and a grammar school) and 63 kindergartens. The language of instruction is Danish except for the main subject of German. In the final classes and courses, however, technical terms are also provided in German, especially in mathematics, science and economics. This is to make it easier for the pupils to work or study at German-speaking companies and universities. The school-leaving qualifications are recognized in both Germany and Denmark.

According to the Education Act of Schleswig-Holstein, all Danish minority schools must be approved and given financial support by the Danish Schools Association. The private Danish schools must meet the same criteria as those required for State schools. Schleswig-Holstein provides a contribution for each pupil in order to meet personnel and running costs. This contribution amounts to 100% of the costs incurred in keeping one pupil at a comparable State school during the previous year.

In the kindergartens Danish is also used as a working language. The Danish minority has its own Central Danish Library for South Schleswig (*Dansk Centralbibliotek for Sydslesvig*).

(b) Sorbian minority
The Schools Act for the Free State of Saxony of 3 July 1991 provides for the right of pupils to learn the Sorbian language, and in some schools to be taught selected subjects – for all year-groups – in Sorbian. Under the Schools Act of the *Land* of Brandenburg of 12 April 1996 (Section 4, paragraph 2), the promotion of knowledge and understanding of the Sorbian (Wendish) culture are specific tasks for the schools. In the settlement areas of the Sorbs, pupils have the right to learn the Sorbian language and to be taught in the Sorbian language in subjects and year-groups to be specified. The Saxon Act on Child Day-Care Institutions of 10 September 1993 provides the legal basis for the teaching and fostering of the Sorbian language and culture in Sorbian and bilingual child day-care centres in the German-Sorbian area.

Participation in language instruction is voluntary. At present, Sorbian is taught as a subject in 74 publicly maintained schools, and at 13 of these schools instruction is given in the vernacular. A total of some 5,000 pupils take part in Sorbian-language education. In these 13 schools, a number of subjects are taught in Sorbian. There is one Sorbian grammar school in Bautzen (High Sorbian) and in Cottbus (Low Sorbian). Two other grammar schools – in Hoyerswerda – offer Sorbian language courses. Adult education centres in the German-Sorbian area also offer Sorbian language courses. The training of teachers in Sorbian as a school subject and of students of the Sorbian language and culture (*Sorabists*) is offered by the Institute for the study of Sorbian Language and Culture at Leipzig University. Sorbian is the colloquial language in 15 day-care centres in an area with a high percentage of the Sorbian population. In addition, there are some 25 bilingual child day-care centres

(c) The Frisians in Germany
In some private schools for the Danish minority and the public schools in the North Frisian region instruction is given in the Frisian language. These are mostly optional courses in the third and fourth grades. For some years, a start has been made with the introduction of Frisian in some nursery schools. There are now more than 20 nursery schools in Nordfriesland where children are instructed in the Frisian language.

(d) The German Sinti and Roma
The children of German Sinti and Roma grow up in the bilingual environment of Romany and German and, as a general rule, have a command of both languages. None of the Schools Acts of the *Länder* provide for instruction in the Romany language within the State school system. On account of the abuse of so-called scientific research into the ethnic group – including research into Romany – during the era of National Socialism and the subsequent genocide of Sinti and Roma, the Central Council takes the view that this language should only be passed on within the ethnic group itself and be taught by teachers belonging to that ethnic group. Thus the native language of Romany is, for the major part, kept up by oral tradition within the families and the ethnic group.

However, the Central Council also advocates some form of in-school supplementary instruction for interested children of the German Sinti and Roma, which would deal with school subjects in the Romany language and thus increase the proficiency of those children in Romany. Further, it advocates language courses for children on a private basis and within the framework of adult education, to be taught by teachers belonging to that ethnic group. The wide dispersion, also in conurbation, of the places of residence of the Sinti and Roma makes it difficult, or in some cases even impossible, to provide specific complementary courses where instruction is given in Romany.

Therefore, the use of the Romany language within the public school system is limited to pilot schemes for Roma children (often of foreign origin) who live in close proximity to each other. The Central Council of German Sinti and Roma attaches great importance to maintaining the unrestricted use, as previously, of the existing State-supported and officially recognised school and educational system by the children of the ethnic group. Therefore, it rejects separate schools for Roma or school classes only for Sinti and Roma. It is obviously the wish of parents to send their German Sinti and Roma children to ordinary local schools or secondary schools.

Special opportunities to promote scholastic development as regards Sinti and Roma children, with the inclusion of their cultural traditions and their language, have materialised in some of the *Länder* of the Federal Republic of Germany within the framework of local projects. Thus, for instance, in Hamm and in Cologne, material for instruction and regional follow-up training has, with the involvement of the locally resident Sinti and Roma, been developed to provide information on the culture complex and the history of the Sinti and Roma, designed to reinforce the mutual relationship between the ethnic group and the school during lessons.

Media
The Danish minority has a bilingual daily newspaper *Flensborg Avis*, however can also make use of the Danish press which is available to it.

The Sorbian press is of particular importance for the preservation of the Sorbs' national identity. Among others, there is a daily publication in High Sorbian, *Serbbske Nowiny*, a weekly in Low Sorbian, *Nowy Casnik*, and the monthly cultural periodical, *Rozhlad*, a professional journal for Sorbian teachers. Also scientific and cultural books in Sorbian as well as textbooks, new and classical Sorbian fiction and poetry, literature for young people, children's books and picture books are published with governmental financial support.

With respect to Roma the Berlin-based radio station SFB 4 *Multikuli* broadcasts a 15-minute programme twice a month in Romany.

Names
In July 1997 a Minorities Name Alteration Act was adopted, thereby allowing any person belonging to an ethnic minority to change his/her name into the minority language or to use a phonetical transcript of his/her name in the minority language or to adopt a name which was formerly used in the language of that minority.

National bodies
The Federal Ministry of the Interior is responsible for legislation on minorities as well as for its implementation. Within the Ministry a division for 'Minority Law Issues and Affairs of German Minorities' exists. Federal units, like Schleswig-Holstein and/or Brandenburg, have also appointed special commissioners to deal with minority issues in respective *Länder*.

GREECE

I. Demographic situation

Population: Total 10,500,000. Minority groups: Albanians 200,000-300,000 (1.9-2.9%); Vlachs 200,000 (1.9%); Arvanites 200,000 (1.9%); Slavo-Macedonians 200,000 (1.9%); Roma 160,000-200,000 (1.5-1.9%); Turks 50,000 (0.5%); Pomaks 30,000 (0.3%); Other new minorities 200,000-300,000 (1.9-2.9%).

Languages: Greek.

II. International obligations

As stipulated in Article 28, paragraph 1, of the 1975 Constitution, the generally recognised rules of international law, as well as international conventions as of the time they are sanctioned by statute and become operative according to their respective conditions, shall be an integral part of domestic Greek law and shall prevail over any contrary provision of the law. The rules of international law and of international conventions shall be applicable to aliens only under the condition of reciprocity.

United Nations
- International Covenant on Civil and Political Rights (accession 5 May 1997)
- First Optional Protocol (accession 5 May 1997)
- International Covenant on Economic, Social and Cultural Rights (accession 16 May 1985)

Council of Europe
- Member (9 August 1949)
- ECHR (signature 28 November 1950, ratification 28 November 1974)
- Not a party to the Charter for Regional or Minority Languages
- Framework Convention for the Protection of National Minorities (signature 22 September 1997)

Bilateral treaties
- 1997 – with Albania, Treaty on cooperation and friendship which led to an agreement on the issue of Greek language education in Albania

Other treaties
- 1923 – Treaty of Lausanne (Section III, Articles 37-45)

III. National legislation

Constitution (11 June 1975)

Article 3
The text of the Holy Scripture shall be maintained unaltered. Official translation of the text into any other form of language, without prior sanction by the Autocephalous Church of Greece and the Great Church of Christ in Constantinople is prohibited.

Article 5
All persons living within the Greek territory shall enjoy full protection of their life, honour and freedom, irrespective of nationality, race or language and of religious or political beliefs. Exceptions shall be permitted only in cases provided for in international law.

HUNGARY

I. Demographic situation

Population (Census 1990): Total 10,374,823. Minority groups: Roma 143,000 (1.3%); German 31,000 (0.3%); Croat 13,700 (0.1%); Slovak 10,500 (0.1%); Others 33,300 (0.3%).
A total of 232,751 persons reported minority affiliation, and 137,724 stated that their native language was one of the national or ethnic minority languages. Estimates from researchers and minority organizations indicate that the true number of national and ethnic minorities is greater: individual groups are considered to comprise from a few thousand persons up to nearly half a million.

Other estimates: Roma 250,000-800,000 (2.4-7.8%); Slovaks 120,000 (1.2%); and Jews 100,000 (1%).

According to some other sources, the total number of persons belonging to national or ethnic minorities in Hungary is 835,000-1,083,950 out of which there are: Roma 400,000-600,000; Germans 200,000-220,000; Slovaks 100,000-110,000; Croats 80,000-90,000.

Languages: Hungarian, Romany, German, Slovak, Serbo-Croat.

II. International obligations

International treaties which have been accepted by Hungary represent the second regulatory level with regard to minority rights. Pursuant to Article 7 of the Hungarian Constitution '[t]he legal system of the Republic of Hungary adopts the generally accepted regulations of international law, and provides for harmonisation of both Hungarian law and all international legal documents.'

United Nations
- International Covenant on Civil and Political Rights (signature 25 March 1969, ratification 17 January 1974)
- First Optional Protocol (accession 7 September 1988)
- International Covenant on Economic, Social and Cultural Rights (signature 25 March 1969, ratification 17 January 1974)

Council of Europe
- Member (6 November 1990)
- ECHR (signature 6 November 1990, ratification 5 November 1992)
- Charter for Regional or Minority Languages (signature 5 November 1992, ratification 26 April 1995, entry into force 1 March 1998)
- Framework Convention for the Protection of National Minorities (signature 1 February 1995, ratification 25 September 1995, entry into force 1 February 1998)

Bilateral treaties
- 1991 – with Ukraine, Treaty on good neighbourliness and cooperation
- 1992 – with Ukraine, Statement on the principles of cooperation in the field of minority rights
- 1992 – with Slovenia, Agreement on the rights of the Slovene national minority in the Republic of Hungary and the rights of the Hungarian ethnic community in the Republic of Slovenia
- 1992 – with Slovenia, Treaty on friendship and cooperation
- 1992 – with Croatia, Treaty on friendly relations and cooperation
- 1992 – with Croatia, Protocol on the principles of cooperation and guarantees for national minorities
- 1992 – with Germany, Treaty on friendly cooperation and partnership in Europe
- 1992 – with Germany, Joint Statement on assistance for the German minority in Hungary and for the teaching of German as a foreign language
- 1995 – with Croatia, Agreement with Croatia on the protection of the rights of the Croat minority in the Republic of Hungary and the Hungarian minority in the Republic of Croatia
- 1995 – with Slovakia, Treaty on neighbourly relations and friendly cooperation

- 1996 – with Romania, Treaty on understanding, cooperation and neighbourliness

Other treaties
- 1920 – Treaty of Trianon (Peace Treaty between the Allied and Associated Powers and Hungary), (Section VI, Articles 54-60)

III. National legislation

Constitution (20 August 1949, updated to 1996)

Article 68
2. The Republic of Hungary shall provide for the protection of national and ethnic minorities and ensure their collective participation in public affairs, the fostering of their cultures, the use of their native languages, education in their native languages and the use of names in their native languages.

Article 70A
1. The Republic of Hungary shall respect the human rights and civil rights of all persons in the country without discrimination on the basis of race, colour, gender, language, religion, political or other opinion, national or social origins, financial situation, birth or on any other grounds whatsoever.
2. Any discrimination against people as defined in par. 1 shall be severely prosecution.
3. The Republic of Hungary shall assist the realisation of equality before the law through measures aimed at preventing inequalities of opportunity.

Act on the Rights of National and Ethnic Minorities (No. LXXVII of 1993)

Chapter 2 - Individual Minority Rights

Article 11
A person belonging to a minority has the right to respect family traditions, to cultivate family relationships, to celebrate family festivals in his/her mother tongue, and to require that the religious services associated with these festivals be performed in his/her mother tongue.

Article 12
1. A person belonging to a minority has the right to choose the first name of his/her child freely, to have the first and last name of his/her child registered under the conventions governing the writing of the mother tongue, and to indicate the names in official documents as long as this complies with applicable provisions. If the names are not registered using Latin characters, it is compulsory to give the phonetic representation of the names with Latin letters.

2. If requested, the registration of births and the compilation of other personal documents – as listed in paragraph 1 – may also be bilingual.

Article 13
Persons belonging to a minority have the right to
a. learn, foster, enrich and pass on their mother tongue, history, culture and traditions;
b. participate in education and cultural development in their mother tongue;
c. protect any personal data related to their minority status as determined by a separate Act.

Chapter 3 – Rights of Minorities as Communities

Article 18
1. Public service television and radio stations – as provided for in a separate Act – will ensure that national and ethnic minority programmes are produced and broadcast on a regular basis.
2. On territories inhabited by minorities, the government – through international contracts – will promote the reception of radio and television programmes from the kin State.
3. Minority communities have the right to
a. initiate the creation of the necessary conditions for kindergarten, primary, secondary and higher education in the mother tongue or 'bilingually' (i.e. in the mother tongue and in Hungarian);
b. establish a national educational, training, cultural and scientific institutional structure of their own within the boundaries of existing laws.
4. The Republic of Hungary – within the framework of its laws – guarantees the rights of minority communities to hold their own events and celebrate their own festivals free from disturbance, to preserve and maintain their architectural, cultural and religious relics, to preserve, foster and pass on their traditions, and to use their cultural symbols.

Chapter 6 – The Cultural and Educational Self-Governance of Minorities

Article 42
In accordance with this Act the following languages are deemed languages used by minorities: Bulgarian, Gypsy ('Romani' and 'Beás'). Greek, Croatian, Polish, German, Armenian, Romanian, Ruthenian, Serbian, Slovakian, Slovenian and Ukrainian.

Article 43
1. The State recognises the mother tongues of minorities as a factor contributing to community cohesion and supports their teaching – where requested – in educational institutions which are not under the authority of settlement-level

minority self-governments in accordance with the provisions of paragraphs 2 and 4, and Articles 44-49.
2. In accordance with the decision of their parents or guardian, children will be and may be educated in their mother tongue, 'bilingually' (in their mother tongue and in Hungarian), or in Hungarian.
3. The education of minorities in their mother tongue or 'bilingually' may be provided in minority kindergartens, schools, or in classes or groups within schools, according to the capacity and requirements at a self-level.
4. At the request of the parents or legal representatives of eight students belonging to the same minority group, it is compulsory to establish and run a minority class or group.

Article 44
The extra costs of minority education in the mother tongue or 'bilingually' as provided for in Article 43 – in line with the provisions of the law – are to be met by the State or self-government.

Article 45
1. In the course of the legal regulation of education and higher education, the choice of content and structure of educational activity and the supervision of such activity, in line with this Act, must be harmonised with those educational interests which are the prerequisites of the educational and cultural autonomy of minorities.
2. To relieve the disadvantages of the Gypsy minority in the field of education specific educational conditions may be introduced.
3. In educational institutions established in accordance with Article 43 (3)-(4) it will be ensured that students acquire a knowledge of their people, the history of their minority and its motherland, as well as its cultural traditions, and values.

Article 46
1. Self-and minority governments will co-operate in assessing the demand for minority education and in the organisation of such education.
2. It is the duty of the State to train native teachers to provide education in the mother tongue or 'bilingually' to minorities.
3. The State will ensure, through international agreements, that members of minorities participate in full-time and part-time training, further training, and scientific training at foreign institutions which teach in the relevant minority language and foster that culture.
4. To act in accordance with the provisions of paragraph 2 the State shall support the employment in Hungary of visiting lecturers from the mother country or from the linguistic region of the minority concerned.
5. If persons belonging to minorities pursue their studies in countries where there are universities, colleges and other educational institutions which run

their courses in the mother tongue of that person and cultivate the culture of the community s/he belongs to, the degrees, diplomas and other certificates the students is awarded there – within the authority of applicable laws and international agreements – must be considered equivalent to the appropriate degrees, diplomas and certificates obtained in the Republic of Hungary.

Article 47
A settlement-level minority self-government or minority self-government may assume control of an educational institution from another authority only if it can ensure the maintenance of the same standards of education. The amount of State subsidies granted to the institution transferred may not be reduced as a result of the transfer.

Article 48
1. Those who do not belong to the minority concerned may only study in educational institutions for minorities if the institutions still have places available after satisfying the needs of the minority. The admission of students (enrolment) will occur on the basis of regulations made public in advance.
2. The teaching of the Hungarian language – providing as many classes necessary and at the standard necessary to acquire the language – will also be ensured in educational institutions for minorities.
3. In settlements where the Hungarian population – or the population of another national or ethnic minority – is in a numerical minority, the mother tongue or bilingual education of children whose mother tongue is Hungarian or the other language will be guaranteed by the settlement government – in accordance with the provisions of the law.

Article 49
1. Minority organisations may engage in public educational activities – within the framework of applicable legislation – and may establish institutions, which may maintain international relations, for such purposes.
2. The national council has the right to establish and maintain a minority theatre, museum/exhibition hall, public collection with a country-wide coverage, a library, publishing house, and a national cultural, arts, and scientific institute. It may apply for budget support to run these programmes.
3. A minority library system will ensure that the minority has access to the literature of it-s mother tongue.
4. In settlements where no settlement-level minority self-government has been established, it is the responsibility of the settlement government to provide the minority population with library material in their mother tongue.
5. The right of acquisition of minority public collections does not extend to documents which must be transferred to archives in accordance with effective legislation governing archives.

Article 50
1. The State guarantees the compilation of textbooks and the provision of equipment necessary for minority education.
2. The State supports
   a. the collection of material monuments of minority cultures, the establishment and enrichment of public collections;
   b. the publication of books by minorities and the publication of their periodicals;
   c. the publication of acts and announcements of public interest in the mother tongues of the minorities;
   d. the performance of ceremonies related to the family rites of minorities in their mother tongue, and the religious activities of churches in the mother tongue of minorities.

Chapter 7 – Language Use

Article 51
1. In the Republic of Hungary everybody may freely use his/her mother tongue wherever and whenever s/he wishes to do so. The conditions of the language use of minorities – in cases provided for by a separate law – must be guaranteed by the State.
2. In the course of civil or criminal proceedings, or in administrative procedures the use of the mother tongue is ensured by the applicable procedural acts.

Article 52
1. In the National Assembly, MPs belonging to minorities may also use their mother tongue.
2. On the board of representatives of the self-government, a minority representative may also use his/her mother tongue. If the contribution is made in the language of a minority, the Hungarian translation of the contribution or a summary of its contents will be included in the minutes of the meeting.
3. If, from among the population of a settlement, there are people who belong to a minority, the minutes and resolutions of the board of representatives may also be recorded or worded in the mother tongue of the given minority – as well as appearing in Hungarian. In the event of disputes over the interpretation, the Hungarian version is deemed to be authentic.

Article 53
At the request of the minority self-government operating on the territory under its authority, the settlement government must ensure that
   a. the announcement of its regulations and the publication of its announcements are made in the language of the minority – in addition to the Hungarian language;

b. the forms used in the course of administrative procedures are also available in the language of the minority;
c. signs bearing the names of places and streets, public offices, and companies undertaking public services, or announcements relating to their operations – in addition to the Hungarian wording and lettering, with the same content and form – may also be read in the mother tongue of the minority.

Article 54
In settlements where there are people who belong to minorities, the self-authorities will ensure that in the course of filling vacancies in self-civil or public services, candidates with a knowledge of the mother tongue of the given minority will be employed, provided that these people meet the general professional requirements.

Chapter 8 – Assistance to Minorities, the Financial Management and Property of Minority Governments

Article 55
1. The State shall financially contribute to the enforcement of the rights of minorities in accordance with the provisions of paragraphs 2-4.
2. To the extent specified in the prevailing Central Budget Act, the State shall
   a. provide additional standard assistance for the kindergarten education of minorities, and for their mother tongue (bilingual) schooling
   b. the National Assembly shall ensure, in a proportion specified by itself, the operation of the governments of national or ethnic minorities, and support the operation of national or ethnic civil organisations.
3. A public foundation shall be established to help preserve the identity of self-minorities, foster and pass on their traditions, preserve and develop their mother tongues, preserve their intellectual and material monuments, and promote activities aimed at diminishing the cultural and political disadvantages which derive from the fact that they belong to minorities.

Act on Public Schooling (LXXIX of 1993)

In order to provide for right to education as defined in the Constitution of the Republic of Hungary on the basis of equal opportunities, the enforcement of the principles of freedom of conscience and religious liberty, of the education of patriotism in public education, the implementation of the education of the native languages for the national and ethnic minorities, of academic freedom and the freedom of teaching, definition of the rights and obligations of children, students and parents in relation to public education as well as the governance and operation of a public education system providing up-to-date knowledge, the Parliament adopts the following decision:

Section 5
The languages to be used in education in kindergartens, education and teaching in schools and in education in student hostels are the Hungarian language as well as the languages of the national and ethnic minorities. Children, students of national or ethnic minorities may receive education in kindergartens, education and teaching in schools and education in student hostels in their respective native languages or in their native languages and in Hungarian or solely in Hungarian - on the basis of the choice specified in the Act on the rights of national and ethnic minorities. Education and teaching may also be conducted in different languages, in part or in full.

Section 9
5. In the matricular examination (secondary final exam) students account for their knowledge of mandatory and optional subjects. The mandatory subjects are as follows: Hungarian language and literature, history, as well as, for those receiving national or ethnic minority teaching the native language and the literature thereof as well as – unless otherwise provided for by law – mathematics, and, except for those receiving national or ethnic minority teaching, a foreign language. In some subjects the matricular examination may be taken in accordance with two sets of criteria, of different standards.

Section 48
1. The pedagogical programme of each school defines the following aspects:
   a. the goals of education and teaching in the school,
   b. the local syllabus of the school, in the framework of which:
   – the subjects taught at the various year (grades) of the school, the mandatory and the obligatory activities and the numbers of hours of each, the prescribed curriculum and the related requirements,
   – the principles governing the selection of textbooks, teaching aids and tools to be applied,
   – the criteria for entering the next grade of the school,
   – the requirements and forms of reporting, giving account of the knowledge gained,
   – the criteria for the evaluation and grading of the behaviour and diligence of students and – within the statutory limits – the form of the evaluation and grading of the behaviour and diligence of the students,
   – in the case of national and ethnic minority education and teaching the curriculum of the native language, history, geography, culture and national awareness, of the given national or ethnic minority,
   – the curriculum for students participating in national or ethnic minority education and teaching at school for the studying of the Hungarian language and culture; for the students not belonging to national or ethnic minorities the curriculum required for learning of the culture of the national and ethnic minority or minorities living in the municipality.

Government Decree on the National Curriculum (No. 130/1995. (X.26.))

Educational segments of the National Curriculum (NC) and proposed ratios:

1. Native language and literature (Hungarian language and literature; minority language and literature)

Specific principles of education of national and ethnic minorities:
National and ethnic education functions within the framework of the Hungarian education system. Consequently, it must provide equivalent basic education with the same contents, values and the same potential for further development, and it must also offer equal opportunities. Therefore the requirements stated within the NC are also applicable to the education of national and ethnic minorities.

A special objective of the education of minorities is to retain and strengthen the identity of the minority. Within this framework the aims of education include the following:
- through the development of verbal and written understanding and the use of a given minority to promote the acquisition of the given native language at the level of an educated public language,
- teaching and maintaining of folk poetry, music, fine arts, customs and traditions,
- teaching of historical traditions, native language culture, adequate knowledge of the land and its peoples,
- by emphasising the values of different cultures, acceptance and recognition of otherness and tolerance,
- teaching culture and history of the mother country,
- equalisation of social disadvantages suffered by the Gypsies and their integration into society,
- the requirements and forms of reporting, giving account of the knowledge gained, the criteria for the evaluation and grading of the behaviour and diligence of students and – within the statutory limits – the form of the evaluation and grading of the behaviour and diligence of the students,
- in the case of national and ethnic minority education and teaching the curriculum of the native language, history, geography, culture and national awareness, of the given national or ethnic minority,
- the curriculum for students participating in national or ethnic minority education and teaching at school for the studying of the Hungarian language and culture; for the students not belonging to national or ethnic minorities the curriculum required for learning the culture of the national and ethnic minority or minorities living in the municipality.

Within the framework of minority education the minority native language of all thirteen minorities living in Hungary may be taught as a second language and used as the language of education.

The teaching and education of national minorities should be aimed at the objective that, in accordance with the various pedagogical stages and educational types, it should offer a language teaching phase in which, based on the language of the minority as a second language, the level of knowledge may be achieved on which the bilingual education and native education may be based.

Knowledge of the people is a subject material, containing the most important information about the culture, history and traditions of each minority group, and related to the educational fields of the NC. The language training, bilingual, native language, catching-up courses for the Gypsies and inter-cultural educational programmes must include teaching about the people of minorities. This knowledge of the people may be integrated into the NC educational segments, into the catching-up courses for the Gypsies or inter-cultural educational programmes, or may also be taught as an independent subject.

The objective of education in the native language is to provide a valuable, full minority education. In this education type the language of teaching is the native language of the minority. Within the native minority education teaching of the Hungarian language as the second language must be guaranteed.

The objective of bilingual minority education is to develop well-balanced bilingual skills. In the bilingual minority education the languages of education are the minority native language and the Hungarian language. The educational segments taught in the language of the minority are specified in the local curriculum of the schools. In this educational type at least half of the educational subject material of the NC must also be taught in the language of the minorities.

The objective of minority language education is to make sure that students, whose dominant language is Hungarian, can acquire their native language as the second language. In this type of education the language of education is the Hungarian language and, from the first year, the education of the minority language takes place taking into account the curricular requirements of live foreign languages, included in the NC. The pedagogical programme of schools may include other live foreign languages in addition to the minority native language.

[...] In minority schools the community's native language and literature must be taught in the relevant native language, based on a separate programme approved by the Minister of Culture and Public Education, while the Hungarian language and literature must be taught as a foreign language, in compliance with the provisions of the NC.

Government Decree on the education requirements in the primary training of teachers, tutors and kindergarten teachers (No. 158/1994. (X1.17.))

Section 2
2. Faculties preparing for the acquisition of teacher's, tutor's certificate
    b. 'nationality teachers' faculty'

(in compliance with the provisions in section 42, of Act LXXVII/1993. on the rights of national and ethnic minorities, specifying the language used by the minorities),
the certificate of which entities the bearer to perform educational work in all the educational areas (subjects), in the Hungarian language, in the 1st to 4th grades of school education, as well as to teach the subjects taught in the language used by the minority (in 1st to 6th grade minority native language education, in 1st to 4th grades environmental studies, music and physical education, in the language used by the minority.

4. Faculties preparing for the acquisition of kindergarten teacher's certificate
    b. 'nationality kindergarten teachers' faculty'
    (in compliance with the provisions in section 42, of Act LXXVII/1993. on the rights of national and ethnic minorities, specifying the language used by the minorities),
    the certificate of which entities the bearer to educate children in kindergartens in the Hungarian and minority languages.

Training requirements for the nationality teachers' faculty

The faculty: nationality teacher (Croatian, German, Romanian, Serbian, Slovak, Sloven)

2. The training objective: to train teachers who possess thorough knowledge, skills and abilities and are capable of teaching and training all educational areas from 1st to 4th grades and teaching the minority language from 1st to 6th grades of primary schools.
Nationality teachers as intellectuals of their nationality possess up-to-date general knowledge, social sensitivity, language skills to learn the culture of their native language, responsibility for the community and acceptance of tasks, demand and capability for permanent education, respect for universal human and national, nationality values and moral standards; they possess the practical skills and abilities required for the education in the native language of the nationality and to increase the national and nationality identity.
3. Level of qualifications
    3.1. A nationality teacher's certificate may be obtained within the framework of college education.
    3.2. Training period: four curricular years, with 3,200 hours on daily courses.
    3.3. Qualifications specified in the certificate: nationality teacher.

The certificate of a nationality teacher entities the bearer to perform educational work in all the educational areas (subjects), in the Hungarian language, in the 1st to 4th grades of school education, as well as to teach the subjects taught in the language used by the minority (Croatian, German,

Romanian, Serbian, Slovak, Sloven) (in 1st to 6th grade minority native language education, in 1st to 4th grades environmental studies, music and physical education, taught in the language used by the minority).

Training requirements for the nationality kindergarten teachers' faculty

1. The faculty: nationality kindergarten teacher (Croatian, German, Romanian, Serbian, Slovak, Sloven)
2. The training objective: to train teachers who possess thorough general and technical education, highly developed kindergarten pedagogy skills, self-knowledge and human knowledge, a child-centred and emotional nature and are capable of developing and educating children in kindergartens in co-operation with the families and social environment, inter-mediating universal and national interests and moral standards, as well as performing the tasks of minority language training.
Minority kindergarten teachers should possess the pedagogical skills required for modern general, special and minority language teaching and intensification of national and rationality identity, and should apply those in a creative way.
They should possess a high level of language skills, sensitivity for the society, awareness of community tasks, and demand and capability for permanent education.

IV. Developments/events/comments

There is a broad network of various legal documents relating to the use of minority languages. In principle minority languages can be used in public and private life. In addition to the major document regulating the issue of minorities, the Act LXXVII/1993 on the rights of minorities which provides for individual and collective rights for minorities in Hungary, there are a number of documents regulating specific aspects and including provisions on minority languages.

Personal names
The Law Decree No. 17 of 1982 on registers, on the procedure of weddings and on the use of personal names in Sections 22 and 27 provides for a possibility for the bride and the bridegroom to use their own respective native languages during the wedding ceremony. Where the bride or the groom or a witness or either of them does not speak Hungarian, or if the registrar does not speak the foreign language spoken by the bride, the groom or the witness, an interpreter shall be employed. The interpreter shall be provided by the marrying couple.

The family and the Christian name(s) to be entered in the register are the ones borne by the person concerned, at the time of birth, marriage or death. Only such given names (no more then two) may be entered in the register, in the sequence specified by the parents that are contained in the Magyar Utónévkönyv (Hungarian Book of Given Names) supplemented by the names used by national/ethnic minorities – unless otherwise provided by law – matching the sex of the child. Citizens belonging to the national/ethnic minorities living in Hungary or those speaking the languages of such minorities may bear the given names customary in their respective minorities, without an obligation to evidence their belonging to such minorities.

Education
Basic documents regulating to the issue of education in minority languages are Act LXXVII of 1993 on the Rights of the National and Ethnic Minorities and Act LXXIX of 1993 on Public Education. In addition, there are a number of decrees regulating specific aspects of education and the use of minority language(s), such as Decree No. 130/1995. (X.26.) on the National Curriculum.

Starting from the kindergartens throughout all higher educational levels, the learning of native and minority languages for those belonging to national minorities is provided for by the existing educational system.

According to the Decree of the Minister of Culture and Public Education No. 24/1997. (VI.5.) on the issue of the examination procedures of the core educational examinations members of Hungarian nationality and ethnic minorities, must take an examination in four compulsory and two selected subjects. Amongst the compulsory subjects are the Hungarian language and literature and native language and literature (Section 3 paragraphs 1 and 2 (a and d). The examination taken in nationality and ethnic minority languages must be taken in the language of the national or ethnic minority in at least two subjects, including the subjects of the native language (minority) and literature (Section 3, paragraph 9).

Similarly, the Government Decree No. 100/1997.(VI.13.) on the issue of the examination procedures of the secondary final examination provides in Section 6(4) that subject to the examination rules, for those participating in minority education native language and literature shall be part of mandatory examinations.

There are various rules concerning the use of native as well as the official, Hungarian, language for those receiving education, examination and qualifications for drivers of road vehicles, (Section 9(3) of the Decree of the Minister of Transport, Telecommunications and Water Management No. 2011992. (Vil.21.)), and those servicemen in the Armed Forces (Section 56(2g) of the Armed Forces Act No. CX of 1993 on national defence.)

With respect to the use of the Slovak language, at this moment there are 4 nurseries with Slovak as the language of tuition, and 65 schools with bilingual activities.

National bodies
An Office for National and Ethnic Minorities was established in 1990. It is an independent State administrative body with national authority, operating under the supervision of the Ministry of Justice and responsible for co-ordinating the implementation of the Government's objectives. The Office analyses minority

policy and drafts minority policy concepts. It is also charged with facilitating the exchange of views and information between the government and the minority organisations.

Judicial procedures
According to Section 7 of Act No. IV of 1972 on the courts and Section 8 of Act No. 1 of 1973 on justice and punishment, the official language in court and criminal proceedings is Hungarian, but no disadvantage may be suffered by anyone who lacks the command of the language. Accordingly, everyone is entitled to use one's own language in written and oral proceedings. Where a person whose native language is other than Hungarian intends to use his/her native language, an interpreter shall be employed (Section 80(1)).

In the procedure on punitive sanctions and measures the accused is entitled to be informed in his/her native language or any other spoken language known by him/her of the provisions concerning his/her rights and obligations and may not be discriminated, for not speaking Hungarian. The native language may also be used in the process of effecting of the penalty.

In addition, there are strict rules established by Decree No. 1911995. (XII.13.) of the Minister of the Interior on procedures in detention rooms at police stations. It provides in Section 2(8) that at the time of admission to the detention room, the detained is entitled to learn in writing or, if justified, verbally, in his native language or another language known by him of his rights and responsibilities and the manner in which they shall be exercised. In the case of detention, the institution in question shall ensure that the detained persons should be able to learn of the provisions concerning their rights and responsibilities in their native language or other languages known by them. The fact that this information has been presented and acknowledged must be stated in writing.

Act 111 of 1952 on the Use of the Mother Tongue in the Code of Civil Procedure, stipulates in Section 8 that the language of legal proceedings is Hungarian and at the same time it provides for the possibility for everyone to speak his/her own mother tongue. Nobody may be disadvantaged because of not knowing Hungarian.

Similarly, Section 2(5) of Act No. IV of 1957 on General rules of proceedings in State administration provides that in the proceedings of public administration everyone is entitled to use his/her own native language both in writing and orally. Nobody shall be prejudiced because of his/her lack of command of the Hungarian language.

Elections and Parliamentary proceedings
Candidates representing a minority may request the writing of their names on the voting card in their native language.

Members, belonging to minorities, delegated to the election body, may take an oath or pledge in their respective native languages.

In Parliamentary proceedings the language of the sittings is Hungarian. If the mother tongue of a Member is not Hungarian, he or she may also speak in his/her mother tongue. For the Member with a non-Hungarian mother tongue a continuous interpretation, as well as translation of documents, shall be provided, if so requested.

Culture
According to Section 9 of Act V of 1976 on culture and adult education referring to cultural development the State provides for cultural possibilities for Hungarian citizens belonging to national and ethnic minorities by supporting the free cultivation of their national/ethnic culture in their respective native languages.

Aimed at maintaining the cultural identity of minority groups, public libraries take into account the composition of the affected group of citizens from the aspect of occupation, education, age and native language. National minorities' basic libraries assist in deciding on the provision of literature to the population belonging to various national and ethnic minorities in their own respective languages.

Media
Among the programmes which may be sponsored in public service broadcasting and public broadcasting, Act I of 1996 on Radio and Television Broadcasting includes in Section 25 the programmes presented in the mother tongues of national and ethnic minorities, and presenting the life and culture of national and ethnic minorities.

It is the obligation of public service broadcasters to foster the culture and mother tongue of the national and ethnic minorities living in Hungary, and to provide information in their mother tongues on a regular basis. There is nation wide broadcasting or, with regard to the geographical location of the minority, regional or local broadcasting of television programmes which provide subtitles in minority language(s), or there is also multilingual broadcasting. The national self-governments of national and ethnic minorities, or in the absence thereof their national organizations, shall decide independently upon the utilisation of broadcasting time made available to them by the public service broadcaster. The public service broadcaster is obliged to take their decision into consideration, although this may not affect the contents of the programme and the editing of broadcasts.

Finally, a Board, referred to by Act I of 1996 on Radio and Television Broadcasting, authorises a non-profit company owned exclusively by the self-government of national and ethnic minorities, as a non-profit-oriented broadcaster, to broadcast in the interest of enforcing the rights of the national and ethnic minorities, at least four and at most eight hours per week, without inviting a tender, if the needs of the national and ethnic minorities in respect of the provision of information in their mother tongue cannot otherwise be satisfied in the area of reception defined by the invitation to tender.

With respect to newspapers it should be pointed out that at least one nationally distributed newspaper per minority receives full State support for publication purposes. In 1998 financial support was given to 17 nationally distributed newspapers representing 13 minorities.

ICELAND

I. Demographic situation

According to the information which we received from the Icelandic Ministry of Foreign Affairs, in Iceland there are no minority groups as defined by international conventions on the rights of minority groups, ethnic, religious or linguistic, and therefore in Icelandic legislation there is no law relating to such groups.

Languages: Icelandic.

II. International obligations

United Nations
- International Covenant on Civil and Political Rights (signature 30 December 1968, ratification 22 August 1979)
- First Optional Protocol (accession 22 August 1979)
- International Covenant on Economic, Social and Cultural Rights (signature 30 December 1968, ratification 22 August 1979)

Council of Europe
- Member (9 March 1950)
- ECHR (signature 4 November 1950, ratification 29 June 1953)
- Charter for Regional or Minority Languages (signature 7 May 1999)
- Framework Convention for the Protection of National Minorities (signature 1 February 1995)

IRELAND

I. Demographic situation

Population: Total 3,500,000. Minority groups: Protestants 115,404 (3.3%); Travellers 22,000-28,000 (0.6-0.8%)

Languages: English, Irish.

II. International obligations

Article 29, paragraph 3, of the 1990 Constitution of the Republic of Ireland states that Ireland accepts the generally recognized principles of international law as its rule of conduct in its relations with other States. Paragraph 6 of the same Article establishes that no international agreement shall be part of the domestic law of the State save as may be determined by Parliament. As the Irish system is clearly 'dualist' it must ensure that its domestic law is in conformity with the agreement in question. In some cases this means that the entire contents of an international agreement are transposed into domestic law by providing that the agreement shall have the force of law within the State. This applies equally to human rights treaties. The provisions of human rights instruments cannot, therefore, be invoked before and directly enforced by the Courts.

United Nations
- International Covenant on Civil and Political Rights (signature 1 October 1973, ratification 8 December 1989)
- First Optional Protocol (accession 8 December 1989)
- International Covenant on Economic, Social and Cultural Rights (signature 1 October 1973, ratification 8 December 1989)

Council of Europe
- Member (5 May 1949)
- ECHR (signature 4 November 1950, ratification 29 June 1953)
- Not a party to the Charter for Regional or Minority Languages
- Framework Convention for the Protection of National Minorities (signature 1 February 1995, ratification 7 May 1999, entry into force 1 September 1999)

III. National legislation

Constitution (1 July 1937)

Article 8
1. The Irish language as the national language is the first official language.
2. The English language is recognised as a second official language.

3. Provision may, however, be made by law for the exclusive use of either of the said languages for any one or more official purposes, either throughout the state or in any part thereof.

Article 18

7. Before fore each general election of the members of the Seanad Eireann to be elected from panels of candidates, five panels of candidates shall be formed in the manner provided by law containing respectively the names of persons having knowledge and practical experience of the following interests and services, namely:
   (i) national language and culture, literature, art, education and such professional interests as may be defined by law for the purpose of this panel;

Article 25

4. 3 Every bill shall be signed by the President in the text in which it was passed or deemed to have been passed by both Houses of the Oireachtas, and if a bill is so passed or deemed to have been passed in both the official languages, the President shall sign the text of the bill in each of those languages.
   4 Where the President signs the text of a bill in one only of the official languages, an official translation shall be issued in the other official language.
   5 As soon as may be after the signature and promulgation of a bill as a law, the text of such law which was signed by the President or, where the President has signed the text of such law in each of the official languages, both the signed texts shall be enrolled for record in the office of the Registrar of the Supreme Court and the text, or both texts, so enrolled shall be conclusive evidence of the provisions of such law.
   6 In case of conflict between the texts of a law enrolled under this section in both the official languages, the text in the national language shall prevail [...]
5. 1 It shall be lawful for the Taoiseach, from time to time as occasion appears to him to require, to cause to be prepared under his supervision a text, in both official languages, of this Constitution as then in force embodying all amendments theretofore made therein...
   4 In case of conflict between the texts of any copy of this Constitution enrolled under this section, the text in the national language shall prevail.

Employment Equality Bill (1998)

Article 36
1. Nothing in this Part or *Part II* shall make unlawful the application of any provision (whether in the nature of a requirement, practice or otherwise) such as is mentioned in *subsection (2)* with respect to
    (a) holding office under, or in the service of, the State (including the Garda Síochána and the Defence Forces) or otherwise as a civil servant, within the meaning of the Civil Service Regulation Act, 1956,
    (b) officers or servants of a local authority, for the purpose of the Local Government Act, 1941, a harbour authority, a health board or vocational education committee, or
    (c) teachers in primary and post-primary schools.
2. The provisions referred to in *subsection (1)* are those relating to all or any of the following:
    (a) residence;
    (b) citizenship;
    (c) proficiency in the Irish language.
3. Nothing in this Part or Part II shall make it unlawful to require, in relation to a particular post
    (a) the holding of a specified educational, technical or professional qualification which is a generally accepted qualification in the State for posts of that description, or
    (b) the production and evaluation of information about any qualification other than such a specified qualification.
4. Nothing in this Part or Part II shall make unlawful for a body controlling the entry to, or carrying on of, a profession, vocation or occupation to require a person carrying on or wishing to enter that profession, vocation or occupation to hold a specified educational, technical or other qualification which is appropriate in the circumstances.
5. Nothing in this section shall render lawful discrimination on the gender ground.

IV. Developments/events/comments

While the Irish language is the first official language of the State (the other language being English), it is used as a vernacular only by a minority of the population as a whole (30% according to the 1986 census), particularly in a number of areas officially designated as Irish-speaking districts, known collectively as '*the Gaeltacht*'. The Irish language is a Celtic language, closely related to Scottish Gaelic, Welsh and Breton.

A Government Minister is charged with the promotion of the cultural, social and economic welfare of those designated areas and with encouraging the preservation of Irish as a vernacular language. He also heads a Government

Department which, *inter alia*, promotes a number of schemes designed to help foster the Irish language not only in the *Gaeltacht* but also in the country in general.

One of the two statutory bodies under the aegis of the Minister, Bord na Gaeilge, is charged with the promotion of Irish as a living language throughout the country. While most of its work is of an advisory nature, it provides grants for Irish language nursery schools, magazines and a weekly newspaper in the Irish language.

In 1970 the Government accepted a scheme proposed by RTÉ for the provision of a Radio service for the Gaeltacht and Irish speakers in general. In connection with the establishment of Radio na Gaeltachta, a committee was appointed under Section 21 of the Broadcasting Authority Act.

An Irish language television service, Teilifís na Gaeilge, commenced services on 31 October 1996. It is intended that the service will operate as a separate statutory entity, but until such time as the necessary legislation can be put in place, RTÉ has been charged with the establishment, programming and initial operation of the service.

ITALY

I. Demographic situation

Population (1996): Total 58,500,000. Minority groups: Sardinians 1,600,000 (2.7%); Friulians 600,000 (1.0%); South Tyrolese German speaking 303,000 (0.5%); Roma/Gypsies 90,000-100,000 (0.15-0.17%); Slovenes 100,000 (0.17%); Moroccans 100,000 (0.17%); Albanians 100,000 (0.17%); Franco-Provençal-speaking Aostans 75,000 (0.13%).

In addition, Occitans (50,000), Tunisians (46,575), Filipinos (40,292), Jews (32,000), Ladins (30,000), and Greeks (10,000-12,000), amount to less than 0.1 per cent, whereas French-speaking Aostians and Croatians, other new minorities including Cape Verdeans, Eritreans, Somalis and Ethiopians (600,000) amount to 1 per cent of the total population.

Languages: Italian, German, French, Greek, Albanian, Slovene, Sardinian, Friulian, Occitan.

II. International obligations

Article 10, paragraph 1, of the 1947 Constitution states that the legal system of Italy shall conform to the generally recognized principles of international law.

United Nations
- International Covenant on Civil and Political Rights (signature 18 January 1967, ratification 15 September 1978)
- First Optional Protocol (signature 30 April 1976, ratification 15 September 1978)
- International Covenant on Economic, Social and Cultural Rights (signature 18 January 1967, ratification 15 September 1978)

Council of Europe
- Member (5 May 1949)
- ECHR (signature 4 November 1950, ratification 26 October 1955)
- Charter for Regional or Minority Languages (signature 27 June 2000)
- Framework Convention for the Protection of National Minorities (signature 1 February 1995, ratification 3 November 1997, entry into force 1 March 1998)

Bilateral agreements
- 1975 – Osimo Agreement, with the former Socialist Federal Republic of Yugoslavia, succeeded by Slovenia and Croatia
- 1992 – with Croatia and Slovenia, Memorandum on mutual understanding between Croatia, Italy and Slovenia on the protection of rights of the Italian minority in Croatia and Slovenia
- 1996 – with Croatia, Agreement on the rights of minorities

III. National legislation

Constitution (Adopted on 22 December 1947)

Article 3
All citizens are invested with equal social status and are equal before the law, without distinction as to sex, race, language, religion, political opinions and personal or social conditions.

Article 6
The Republic shall safeguard linguistic minorities by means of special provisions.

KAZAKSTAN

I. Demographic situation

Population (1994): Total 16,900,000. Minority groups: Russians 5,769,000 (34%); Ukrainians 820,000 (4.8%); Germans 575,000 (3.4%); Uzbeks 372,400 (2.2%). There are also some smaller minority groups such as Tatars, Belarusians, Uighurs, Koreans, Poles, Jews, Greeks, Meskhetian, Turks and others.

Languages: Kazak, Russian, Uzbek.

II. International obligations

According to Article 4, paragraph 3, of the 1995 Constitution international treaties ratified by the Republic of Kazakstan shall have priority over its laws and will be directly implemented except in cases where the application of an international treaty shall require the promulgation of a law.

United Nations
- Not a party to the International Covenant on Civil and Political Rights
- Not a party to the First Optional Protocol
- Not a party to the International Covenant on Economic, Social and Cultural Rights

Council of Europe
- Not member of the Council of Europe
- Not a party to the Charter for Regional or Minority Languages
- Not a party to the Framework Convention for the Protection of National Minorities

Bilateral agreements
- 1995 – with the Russian Federation, Treaty on the legal status of the citizens of the Russian Federation, permanently residing in the territory of the Republic of Kazakstan, and the citizens of the Republic of Kazakstan permanently residing in the territory of the Russian Federation

III. National legislation

Constitution (30 August 1995)

Article 7
1. The State language of the Republic of Kazakstan shall be the Kazak language.

2. In State institutions and local self-administrative bodies, the Russian language shall be officially used on equal grounds along with the Kazak language.
3. The State shall promote conditions for the study and development of the languages of the people of Kazakstan.

Article 14
2. No one shall be subject to any discrimination for reasons of origin, social, property status, occupation, sex, race, nationality, language, attitude towards religion, convictions, place of residence, or any other circumstances.

Article 19
2. Everyone shall have he right to use his native language and culture, to freely choose the language of communication, education, instruction, and creative activities.

Article 41
2. A citizen of the Republic shall be eligible for the office of the President of the Republic of Kazakstan if he is by birth not younger than 35 and not older than 65, and has a perfect command of the State language and has lived in Kazakstan for not less than 15 years.

Article 93
With the purpose of implementation of Article 7 of the Constitution, the Government, local representative and executive bodies must create all necessary organizational, material and technical conditions for fluent and free-of-charge mastery of the State language by all citizens of the Republic of Kazakstan in accordance with a special law.

Decree by the President of the Republic of Kazakhstan having the force of law on the Legal Status of Aliens in the Republic of Kazakhstan (Adopted on 19 June 1995)

Article 3 – Principles of the Legal Status of Aliens in the Republic of Kazakhstan
Aliens in the Republic of Kazakhstan shall be equal before the law, irrespective of origin, social and property status, race and ethnicity, sex, education, language, religion, occupation.

IV. Developments/events/comments

Although the Kazak language is the State language, Russian is a popular working language in official institutions and a language of communication. The State Committee on Languages established in 1994 that out of 55,008 State organizations of the Republic, only 16.6% used both Kazak and Russian languages, while 70.3% used only Russian. In the 1992 Decision on the Implementation of the State Programme for Development of the Kazak and other Ethnic Languages in the Republic of Kazakhstan until the year 2000, the Cabinet of Ministers introduced several measures aimed at improving the use of Kazak as the State language (it imposed an obligation on regional and city governments to guarantee the use of Kazak as the State language; to present a timetable for introducing Kazak in official documentation; to employ Kazak translators in official institutions and to renew the nationwide teaching of Kazak).

Education
The 1992 Law on Education provides for an obligation on educational institutions to take part in active learning, use and development of the Kazak language as a State language throughout the whole territory of the Republic, as well as to grant free learning of the Russian language. In cases of numerous and densely residing ethnic minorities there is a possibility for the establishment of State-supported educational institutions with a native language of instruction. In other cases of non-numerous and dispersed residing minorities, Sunday schools and extra-curricular activities may be founded.

In the sphere of education, among the total number of 1533 pre-school institutions there are 1097 teaching in the mother tongue; 2 in Uigurs; 3 in Uzbeks; 1 in Korean; 3 in German; 2 in Ukrainian; and 425 pre-school institutions with mixed languages.

Judicial proceedings
Both Kazak and Russian are official languages in the courts. However, the language of the majority residing in the given locality may also be used.

KYRGYZSTAN

I. Demographic situation

Population (1994): Total 4,430,000. Minority groups: Russians 757,500 (17.1%); Uzbeks 612,000 (13.8%); Ukrainians 80,000 (1.8%); Tatars 60,000 (1.3%); Kazakhs 41,500 (0.9%); Uighurs 40,000 (0.9%); Germans 35,000 (0.8%); also Dungans, Tajiks and Jews.

Languages: Kyrgyz, Russian, Uzbek.

II. International obligations

Article 12, paragraph 3, of the Constitution of the Kyrgyz Republic states that international treaties and other norms of international law, which have been ratified by the Kyrgyz Republic, shall be a constituent and directly applicable part of Kyrgyz legislation.

United Nations
- International Covenant on Civil and Political Rights (accession 7 October 1994)
- First Optional Protocol (accession 7 October 1994)
- International Covenant on Economic, Social and Cultural Rights (accession 7 October 1994)

Council of Europe
- Not a member of the Council of Europe
- Not a party to the Charter for Regional or Minority Languages
- Not a party to the Framework Convention for the Protection of National Minorities

Bilateral treaties
- 1995 – with the Russian Federation, Treaty on the legal status of the citizens of the Russian Federation, permanently residing in the territory of the Kyrgyz Republic, and the citizens of the Kyrgyz Republic permanently residing in the territory of the Russian Federation

III. National legislation

Constitution (of 5 May 1993, as amended in 1996)

Article 5
1. The State language of the Kyrgyz Republic shall be the Kyrgyz language.
2. The Kyrgyz Republic guarantees the preservation, equal and free development and functioning of the Russian language and all the other languages, used by the population of the Republic.
3. Infringement upon citizens' rights and freedoms based upon lack of knowledge or command of the State language is not allowed.

Article 15
3. All persons in the Kyrgyz Republic shall be equal before the law and the court. No one may be exposed to any discrimination, infringement of rights and freedoms, on the motives of origin, sex, race, nationality, language, creed, political and religious convictions or by any other public or personal conditions or circumstances.

Law on the Citizenship of the Kyrgyz Republic (Adopted on 18 December 1993)

Article 21 – Acquisition of Citizenship as a Result of Admission to Citizenship
Foreign citizens and stateless persons may, upon their applications, be admitted to the citizenship of the Kyrghyz Republic following all the indicated requirements:
5. knowledge of the State language in the volume established by legislation in force; the States shall create conditions for learning the State language

Law on the Legal Status of Aliens in the Kyrgyz Republic (Adopted on 14 December 1993)

Article 3 – Principles of the Legal Status of Aliens in the Kyrgyz Republic
Aliens in the Kyrgyz Republic shall enjoy the same rights and freedoms and shall perform the same duties as citizens of the Kyrgyz Republic unless the present Law and other legislative acts of the Kyrgyz Republic provide for otherwise.

Aliens in the Kyrgyz Republic shall be equal before the law irrespective of origin, social and property status, race and ethnicity, sex, education, language, religion, occupation and other circumstances.

IV. Developments/events/comments

Since 1991 there has been massive emigration among the Russian-speaking population, the major reason for this being the language issue which emerged in a new post-Soviet socio-political context and which is less advantageous for Russian speakers. As a consequence, the percentage of the Russians decreased from 21.5% in 1989 to 15.7% in 1996, of the Ukrainians from 2.5% to 1.7%, and of the Belarusians from 0.2% to 0.16%. During the last few years the emigration from Kyrgyzstan has also decreased as a result of various measures to reintroduce the Russian-speaking population into all areas of Kyrgyz society.

The 1989 Law of the Kyrgyz SSR on the State Language deals with the rights and freedoms of citizens concerning languages. The Kyrgyz language has the status of the State language. However, Chapter II of the Law establishes that 'every citizen has a right of free choice of language' and that 'in Kyrgyzstan the free development of languages of all other nationalities inhabiting the Republic shall be guaranteed'. Russian is a 'language of inter-ethnic communication' and can be used along with Kyrgyz in the public sphere, in enterprises, institutions, education, science and culture, as well as in the administration of justice. However, in those entities where the majority are Russian speakers and where the use of Russian is inevitable, such as in health care, technical sciences, etc., it has the status of an official language.

A resolution on the entry into force of the Law of the Kyrgyz SSR on State Language, adopted by the Supreme Soviet of the Kyrgyz SSR in 1989, obliges the Council of Ministers to allocate special funds for the necessary financing arrangements, foreseen by the language policy, to create conditions for learning the State language, to start issuing documents in the State language, etc.

By an addendum to the 1998 Decree on the Concept of the Development of the State Language of the Kyrgyz Republic, the President of the Kyrgyz Republic introduced a new concept which includes special strategies and priorities for the development of the State language.

In May 2000 the Parliament of the Kyrgyz Republic decided Russian language to be assigned the status of official language in the Republic. It can be expected that this measure will, *inter alia*, assist in prevention of further out-migration of ethnic Russians.

National bodies
In 1998 a special agency for the promotion of the use of the State language was created. The National Commission on the State Language functions under the auspices of the President of the Republic.

LATVIA

I. Demographic situation

Population: Total 2,413,103 (100%, with Latvian citizenship 73.3%); Latvians 1,383,355 (57.33%); Russians 718,725 (29.78%); Belarusians 100,173 (4.15%); Ukrainians 65,226 (2.70%) Poles 61,122 (2.53%); Lithuanians 34,156 (1.42%); Jews 11,252 (0.47%); Gypsies 8,050 (0.33%); Germans 3,525 (0.15%); Tatars 3,270 (0.14%); Estonians 2,729 (0.11%); Armenians 2,642 (0.11%); Moldavs 1,915 (0.08%); Azerbaijanis 1,703 (0.07%); Georgians 1,035 (0.04%); Others 14,225 (0.59%).

Other estimates: Russians 849,300 (33.1%); Belarusians 105,100 (4.1%); Ukrainians (3%); Poles 57,200 (2.2%); Lithuanians 33,200 (1.3%); Jews 13,284 (0.5%) and smaller populations of Armenians, Azeris, Bulgarians, Estonians, Georgians, Germans, Livs, Roma, Tatars, Uzbeks and Yakuts.

Languages: Latvian, Russian.

II. International legal obligations

The Declaration on the Renewal of Independence of Latvia of 4 May 1990, recognizes in Section 1 the supremacy of the fundamental principles of international law over national law and re-establishes the authority of the Constitution of the Republic of Latvia adopted on 15 February 1922 (Section 3). At the same time the Declaration reaffirms in Section 8 the guarantee to 'citizens of the Republic of Latvia and those of other nations permanently residing in Latvia social, economic, and cultural rights, as well as those political rights and freedoms which are defined in international human rights instruments. To apply these rights also to those citizens of the USSR who express the desire to continue living in the territory of Latvia.'

The Latvian Constitution establishes in Article 89 that the State recognizes and protects fundamental human rights in accordance with the Constitution, the laws and international agreements binding upon Latvia.

United Nations
- International Covenant on Civil and Political Rights (accession 14 April 1992)
- First Optional Protocol (accession 22 June 1994)
- International Covenant on Economic, Social and Cultural Rights (accession 14 April 1992)

Council of Europe
- Member (10 February 1995)
- ECHR (signature 10 February 1995, ratification 27 June 1997)
- Not a party to the Charter for Regional or Minority Languages
- Framework Convention for the Protection of National Minorities (signature 11 May 1995)

III. National legislation

Constitution (of 15 February 1922 as amended on 23 October 1998, unofficial translation)

Article 4:
The State language in the Republic of Latvia shall be Latvian. The national flag of the Latvian State shall be red with a white stripe.

Article 77
If Saeima has amended the second, third, fourth or seventy-seventh Article of the Constitution, such amendments, in order to acquire the force of Law, shall be submitted to the referendum.

Chapter VIII – Fundamental Human Rights

Article 91
All persons in Latvia are equal before the Law and the Courts. The human rights shall be exercised without any discrimination.

Article 114
Persons belonging to ethnic minorities, have the right to preserve and develop their language, their ethnic and cultural particularity.

State Language Law (adopted by the Saeima on 9 December 1999)

The Saeima has adopted and the President of the State has proclaimed the following law:

Article 1
The purpose of this Law shall be to ensure:
1. the preservation, protection and development of the Latvian language;
2. the preservation of the cultural and historical heritage of the Latvian nation;
3. the right to use the Latvian language freely in any sphere of life in the whole territory of Latvia;
4. the integration of national minorities into Latvian society while respecting their right to use their mother tongue or any other language;
5. the increase of the influence of the Latvian language in the cultural environment of Latvia by promoting a faster integration of society.

Article 2
1. This Law shall regulate the use and protection of the State language at State and municipal institutions, courts and agencies belonging to the judicial system, as well as at other agencies, organisations and enterprises (or companies), in education and other spheres.
2. The use of language in private institutions, organisations and enterprises (or companies) and the use of language with regard to self-employed persons shall be regulated in cases when their activities concern legitimate public interests (public safety, health, morals, health care, protection of consumer rights and labour rights, workplace safety and public administrative supervision) (hereafter also: legitimate public interests) and shall be regulated to the extent that the restriction applied to ensure legitimate public interests is balanced with the rights and interests of private institutions, organisations, companies (enterprises).
3. The Law shall not regulate the use of language in the unofficial communication of the residents of Latvia, the internal communication of national and ethnic groups, the language used during worship services,

ceremonies, rites and any other kind of religious activities of religious organisations.

Article 3
1. In the Republic of Latvia, the State language shall be the Latvian language.
2. In the Republic of Latvia every person has the right to file applications and communicate in the State language at agencies, voluntary and religious organisations, enterprises (or companies).
3. The State shall ensure the development and use of the Latvian sign language for communication with the deaf.
4. The State shall ensure the preservation, protection and development of the Latgalian written language as an historically-established variety of the Latvian language.

Article 4
The State shall ensure the protection, preservation and development of the Liv language as the language of the indigenous population (autochtons).

Article 5
For the purpose of this Law, any other language used in the Republic of Latvia, except the Liv language, shall be regarded as a foreign language.

Article 6
1. Employees of State and municipal institutions, courts and agencies belonging to the judicial system, State and municipal enterprises, as well as employees in companies in which the State or a municipality holds the largest share of the capital, must know and use the State language to the extent necessary for the performance of their professional and employment duties.
2. Employees of private institutions, organizations, enterprises (or companies), as well as self-employed persons, must use the State language if their activities relate to legitimate public interests (public safety, health, morals, health care, protection of consumer rights and labour rights, workplace safety and public administrative supervision).
3. Employees of private institutions, organizations and enterprises (or companies), as well as self-employed persons who, as required by law or other normative acts, perform certain public functions must know and use the State language to the extent necessary for the performance of their functions.
4. Foreign specialists and foreign members of an enterprise (or company) administration who work in Latvia must know and use the State language to the extent necessary for the performance of their professional and employment duties, or they themselves must ensure translation into the State language.

5. The required level of the State language proficiency of the persons referred to in paragraphs 1, 2 and 3 of this Article, as well as the assessment procedure of their State language proficiency, shall be set by the Cabinet of Ministers.

Article 7
1. The State language shall be the language of formal meetings and other business meetings held by State and municipal institutions, courts and agencies belonging to the judicial system, State or municipal enterprises and companies in which the State or a municipality holds the largest share of the capital. If the organizers consider it necessary to use a foreign language during the meeting, they shall provide translation into the State language.
2. In all other cases when a foreign language is used at formal meetings and other business meetings, the organizer shall provide translation into the State language if so requested by at least one participant of the meeting.

Article 8
1. At State and municipal institutions, courts and agencies belonging to the judicial system, State and municipal enterprises, as well as in companies in which the State or a municipality holds the largest share of the capital, the State language shall be used in record-keeping and all documents. Correspondence and other types of communication with foreign countries may be conducted in a foreign language.
2. Employees of private institutions, organizations, enterprises (or companies), as well as self-employed persons, shall use the State language in record-keeping and documents if their activities relate to legitimate public interests (public safety, health, morals, health care, protection of consumer rights and labour rights, workplace safety and public administrative supervision).
3. Private institutions, organizations and enterprises (or companies), as well as self-employed persons who perform public functions as required by law or other normative acts shall use the State language in record-keeping and documents which are required for performing their functions.
4. Statistical reports, annual reports, accountancy documents and other documents which, according to law or other normative acts, are to be submitted to the State or municipal institutions shall be in the State language.

Article 9
Contracts of natural and legal persons about the provision of medical and health care services, public safety and other public services in the territory of Latvia shall be in the State language. If the contracts are in a foreign language, a translation into the State language shall be attached.

Article 10
1. Any institution, organization and enterprise (or company) shall ensure acceptance and review of documents prepared in the State language.

2. State and municipal institutions, courts and agencies belonging to the judicial system, as well as State and municipal enterprises (or companies) shall accept and examine documents from persons only in the State language, except for cases set forth in paragraphs 3 and 4 of this Article and in other laws. The provisions of this Article do not refer to the statements of persons submitted to the police and medical institutions, rescue services and other institutions when urgent medical assistance is summoned, when a crime or other violation of the law has been committed or when emergency assistance is requested in case of fire, traffic accident or any other accident.
3. Documents submitted by persons in a foreign languages shall be accepted if they are accompanied by a translation verified according to the procedure prescribed by the Cabinet of Ministers or by a notarized translation. No translation shall be required for documents issued in the territory of Latvia before the date on which this Law comes into force.
4. Documents received by State and municipal institutions, organizations and enterprises (or companies) from foreign countries may be accepted and reviewed without a translation into the State language.

Article 11
1. Events organized by State and municipal institutions, courts and agencies belonging to the judicial system, State and municipal enterprises, as well as by companies in which the State or a municipality holds the largest share of the capital, shall be conducted in the State language. Should a foreign language be used, translation into the State language shall be provided by the organizer.
2. In events taking place in the territory of Latvia in which foreign natural and legal persons participate and in which institutions mentioned in paragraph 1 of this Article participate in the organizing, one of the working languages shall be the State language, and the organizer shall ensure translation into the State language. In cases stipulated by the Cabinet of Ministers, the State Language Centre may exempt the organizer from this requirement.
3. Taking into account the purpose of this Law and the basic principle of language use as provided by Article 2 of this Law, the Cabinet of Ministers may determine cases when, in serving legitimate public interests, organizers of other events taking place in the territory of Latvia may be obliged to ensure translation of the event into the State language.
4. Use of language in meetings, marches and pickets is provided for by the Law on Meetings, Marches and Pickets.

Article 12
In the structural units of the National Armed Forces, only the State language shall be used except for cases when other laws and international treaties concluded by the Republic of Latvia, as well as international treaties on the

participation of the National Armed Forces in international operations or exercises, stipulate otherwise.

Article 13
Legal proceedings in the Republic of Latvia shall be conducted in the State language. The right to use a foreign language in court is prescribed by the laws regulating court functions and procedures.

Article 14
The right to receive education conducted in the State language is guaranteed in the Republic of Latvia. The use of the State language in education is prescribed by the laws regulating education.

Article 15
Research papers qualifying for a scientific degree shall be submitted in the State language or in a foreign language accompanied by a translation of a comprehensive summary in the State language. Research papers may be publicly presented in the State language or in a foreign language if the author agrees and if the relevant council that confers scientific degrees approves.

Article 16
The language of mass media broadcasts is regulated by the Law on Radio and Television.

Article 17
1. Feature films, videofilms or their excerpts shown in public shall be provided with a voice-over, dubbed in the State language or shown with the original sound track and subtitles in the State language while observing accepted norms of the literary language.
2. In the cases mentioned in this Article, subtitles in a foreign language are also permissible. Subtitles in the State language shall be placed in the foreground and shall not be smaller in size or less complete in content than the subtitles in the foreign language.

Article 18
1. In the Republic of Latvia, place names shall be created and used in the State language.
2. The names of public institutions, voluntary organizations and enterprises (or companies) founded in the territory of Latvia shall be created and used in the State language except for cases prescribed by other laws.
3.1 The names of events mentioned in Article 11 of this Law shall be created and used in the State language except for cases prescribed by other laws.
4. In the territory of the Liv Shore, the place names and the names of public institutions, voluntary organizations, enterprises (or companies), as well as

the names of events held in this territory, shall be created and used also in the Liv language.
5. Creation and use of designations shall be prescribed by the Cabinet of Ministers regulations.

Article 19
1. Personal names shall be reproduced in accordance with the Latvian language traditions and shall be transliterated according to the accepted norms of the literary language while observing the requirements of paragraph 2 of this Article.
2. In a person's passport or birth certificate, the person's name and surname reproduced in accordance with Latvian language norms may be supplemented by the historical form of the person's surname or the original form of the person's name in another language transliterated in the Latin alphabet if the person or the parents of a minor so desire and can provide verifying documents.
3. The spelling and the identification of names and surnames, as well as the spelling and use in the Latvian language for personal names from other languages, shall be prescribed by the Cabinet of Ministers regulations.

Article 20
1. The text on stamps and seals, except those mentioned in paragraph 3 of this Article, shall be in the State language if stamps and seals are used on documents which, according to this Law or other normative acts, shall be in the State language.
2. Texts on letterheads, except those mentioned in paragraph 3 of this Article, shall be in the State language if the letterheads are used on documents that, according to this Law or other normative acts, shall be in the State language.
3. The text on stamps and seals, as well as the text on letterheads of State and municipal institutions, courts and agencies belonging to the judicial system, State and municipal enterprises and companies in which the State or a municipality holds the largest share of the capital, shall be only in the State language except for the cases referred to in paragraph 4 of this Article. This provision applies also to private institutions, organizations, enterprises (or companies), as well as to self-employed persons who under law or other normative acts perform certain public functions, if the performance of these public functions involves the use of stamps, seals or letterheads.
4. The Cabinet of Ministers shall determine cases in which the institutions and persons mentioned in paragraph 3 of this Article may use also foreign languages along with the State language in creating and using stamps, seals and letterheads.
5. If a foreign language is used along with the State language in the texts on stamps, seals and letterheads, the text in the State language shall be in the

foreground and shall not be smaller in size or less complete in content than the text in a foreign language.

Article 21
1. Information intended for the public provided by State and municipal institutions, courts and agencies belonging to the judicial system, State and municipal enterprises and companies in which the State or a municipality holds the largest share of the capital shall be only in the State language except for cases provided for by paragraph 5 of this Article. This provision shall apply also to private institutions, organizations, enterprises (or companies), as well as to self-employed persons who under law or other normative acts perform certain public functions, if the performance of these functions involves the providing of information.
2. Information on labels and markings on goods manufactured in Latvia, user instructions, inscriptions on the manufactured product and on its packaging or container shall be in the State language. In cases when a foreign language is used along with the State language, the text in the State language shall be placed in the foreground and shall not be smaller in size or less complete in content than the text in the foreign language. These requirements do not apply to goods meant for export.
3. If the markings, user instructions, warranties or technical certificates of imported goods are in a foreign language, a translation of the above information in the State language shall be attached to every imported item.
4. Information on signs, billboards, posters, placards, announcements and any other notices shall be in the State language if it concerns legitimate public interests and is meant to inform the public in places accessible to the public, except for cases provided by paragraph 5 of this Article.
5. Taking into account the purpose of this Law and the basic principle of language use as provide by Article 2 of this Law, the Cabinet of Ministers shall determine cases when the use of a foreign language along with the State language is permissible in information intended to inform the public in places accessible to the public.
6. The Cabinet of Ministers shall also determine the cases when the institutions and persons mentioned in paragraph 1 of this Article may provide information in a foreign language and set the procedure for using the languages in information mentioned in paragraphs 1, 2, 3, and 4 of this Article.
7. If a foreign language is used along with the State language in information, the text in the State language shall be in the foreground and shall not be smaller in size or less complete in content than the text in the foreign language.

Article 22
1. Standardized terminology shall be used in specialized teaching materials, in technical documents and office documents. The creation and use of terms shall be prescribed by the Terminology Commission of the Latvian Academy of Sciences (hereafter, the Terminology Commission). New terms and their definition standards may be used in official communications only after their approval by the Terminology Commission and publication in the newspaper 'Latvijas Vçstnesis'.
2. The Statutes of the Terminology Commission shall be approved by the Cabinet of Ministers.

Article 23
1. In official communications, the Latvian language shall be used in accordance with the norms of the literary language.
2. The norms of the Latvian literary language shall be codified by the Commission of the Latvian Language Experts of the State Language Centre.
3. The Statutes of the Commission of the Latvian Language Experts and the norms of the Latvian literary language shall be approved by the Cabinet of Ministers.

Article 24
1. It shall be the duty of State and municipal institutions to provide material resources for the research, cultivation and development of the Latvian language.
2. The State shall ensure the formulation of the State language policy which shall include scientific research, protection and teaching of the Latvian language; which shall augment the role of the Latvian language in the national economy; and which shall promote individual and public awareness of the language as a national value.

Article 25
Persons who have violated the provisions of this Law shall be held liable in accordance with the procedure set by law.

Article 26
1. The State Language Centre shall monitor the observance of this Law in the Republic of Latvia.
2. The State Language Centre shall be subordinate to the Ministry of Justice, and Statutes of the Centre shall be approved by the Cabinet of Ministers.

Transitional Provisions
1. This Law shall come into force on 1 September 2000.

2. When this Law comes into force, the Law on Languages of the Republic of Latvia (Latvian SSR Supreme Council and Government Reporter, 1989, No. 20) shall become null and void.
3. By 1 September 2000, the Cabinet of Ministers shall adopt the regulatory acts referred to in this Law and shall approve the Statutes of the Commission of the Latvian Language Experts and the Statutes of the Terminology Commission.

The President of the State: V.Vîîe-Freiberga
Riga, 21 December 1999

Education Law (29 October 1998, unofficial translation)

Article 2 – Objective of the Law:
The objective of this law is to provide every resident of Latvia with possibilities to develop his/her mental and physical potential for the formation of independent and developed personality, conscientious and responsible member of the society and the democratic State of Latvia [...]

Article 3 – Right to Education:
Every citizen of the Republic of Latvia and a person who is entitled to the alien's passport issued by the Republic of Latvia, a person who has received a permanent residence permit, as well as citizens of European Union countries who have received temporary residence permits as well as their children shall have equal rights to acquire education irrespective of his/her economic or social status, race, ethnicity, sex, religious or political convictions, health condition, occupation and the place of residence.

Article 9 – Language of acquiring of education:
1. At State and municipal education institutions education shall be acquired in the State language.
2. Education may be acquired in another language:
   1) at private education institutions;
   2) at State or municipal education institutions which implement minority education programs. The Ministry of Education and Science shall determine the subjects of these programs which have to be taught in the State language;
   3) at education institutions prescribed by special laws.
3. Every person to be educated, in order to acquire primary or secondary education, shall learn the State language and take examinations of the State language to the extent and in accordance with a procedure set by the Ministry of Education and Science.

4. Examinations for professional qualification shall be taken in the State language.
5. Papers necessary for qualifying for an academic degree (Bachelor's or Master's degree) and a scientific degree (Ph.D.) shall be written and presented in the State language, except for cases provided for by other laws.
6. Raising of professional qualification and changing of a profession which is financed from the State or a municipal budget, shall be in the State language.

Article 38 – Types of Education Programs:
1. Types of education programs are as follows: general, vocational and academic, further education and interest education programs.
2. Special types of education programs are:
    1) programs of national minority education;
    2) programs of special education;
    3) programs of social corrective education;
    4) education programs for adults.

Article 41 – Minority Education Programs:
1. Education institutions shall prepare education programs for national minorities in accordance with State standards of education, using as a basis the model general education programs which have been approved by the Ministry of Education and Science.
2. Minority education programs shall include in addition the content necessary for acquiring the respective ethnic culture and for the integration of minorities in Latvia.
3. The Ministry of Education and Science shall determine the subjects for study in minority education programs which are to be taught in the State language.

IV. Developments/events/comments

Cultural autonomy
The Latvian Law on the Unrestricted Development and Right to Cultural Autonomy of Latvia's Nationalities and Ethnic Groups, entered into force on 19 March 1991, guarantees to all nationalities and ethnic groups in the Republic of Latvia the rights to the cultural autonomy and self-administration of their culture.

Equality
The Constitutional Law on the Rights and Obligations of a Citizen and a Person of 10 December 1991 reaffirms that all persons in Latvia are equal under the law regardless of race, nationality, sex, language, party affiliation, political and religious persuasion, social, material and occupational standing and origin (Article 12).

In 1998 the Latvian Government prepared a conceptual paper entitled 'The Integration of Society in Latvia – Framework Document for a National Programme' aimed at supporting social cohesion in Latvia. The Document emphasises that the integration of society means mutual agreement and cooperation between various groups and individuals within the framework of a common nation. The basis for this is loyalty to the Latvian State and the willingness to accept Latvian as the State language and respect for Latvian and minority languages and cultures. It has been considered that the majority of non-citizens have not become integrated into Latvian society specifically because of the language barrier, and this is the basis for divisions within the population of Latvia. According to the Framework Document one of the most prominent demonstrations of social division is the parallel existence of the Latvian and Russian language school systems.

In July 1994 the Latvian Government requested assistance from the United Nations Development Programme (UNPD) in drafting a comprehensive Latvian-language training programme for non-Latvian-speaking residents which would reflect, *inter alia*, the need to introduce a new subject – Latvian as a Second Language – and the need to pay most attention to using the language rather than acquiring knowledge of the language and literature.

With respect to language the Framework Document emphasises that Latvian fluency is a 'crucial prerequisite for the integration of society'. Although, as an objective, the prestige of the Latvian language must be enhanced, the preservation of Latvia's national minority languages must also be supported.

New Language Law
On 9 December 1999 the Latvian Parliament (Saeima) adopted the new State Language Law, to enter into force in September 2000. At the same time the Cabinet of Ministers has prepared the draft Regulations on the implementation of the State Language Law – 8 out of 10 documents to be adopted before 1 September 2000, according to the State Language Law, while two more drafts (regulations on usage of language in public information and on writing personal names) are still to be finalised. The main issues concerning national minorities as embodied in the Regulations are the following:
- the right of inspectors from the State Language Centre to visit all public and private institutions, business enterprises and NGOs, to invite all persons for the Latvian language command examination to the Centre, and to annul State language proficiency certificates even if a person has received it in full accordance with the procedure envisaged by law;
- new Regulations envisage 6 categories of State language proficiency instead of the existing 3 categories. '3 B' category (the highest) requires that a person must know Latvian at a level 'equal to the mother tongue', including phraseologisms and dialectisms. This category is necessary, for example, for members of all elected bodies including municipal councils (also in villages), heads of State institutions, rectors and deans of higher educational

institutions, philosophers and historians, editors, secretaries, lawyers and notaries, prosecutors and judges etc. – including even chairpersons of political parties and NGOs (clearly in contradiction with the declared respect for freedom of language use in the private sphere). This in practice means that all these positions and professions will be reserved for Latvian native speakers only, and persons belonging to national minorities, if their mother tongue is not Latvian, will not be able to work in these professions;
- if the State language proficiency certificate has been lost, it cannot be renewed ('a duplicate cannot be issued'); and
- public events, organized by private persons, enterprises or associations, must be translated into the State language, if (a) persons representing the Latvian State, municipal or judicial institutions/enterprises take part in these events, or (b) the agenda includes items related to participants' property or commercial activities, and (c) all open cultural events, including explicitly mentioned theatre performances, concerts, circus shows, opera, ballet or pantomime.

Education

Education in minority languages is a precondition for the maintenance of the cultural identities of national minorities in Latvia. The Government of Latvia continues to facilitate education in minority languages even where the small numbers of pupils make such efforts uneconomical. State-financed secondary education is available in eight minority languages: Russian, Polish, Jewish, Ukrainian, Estonian, Lithuanian, Roma (Gypsy) and Belarusian. State-financed tertiary education is provided in Latvian (during the first year of studies – also in Russian). A number of private educational institutions with language(s) of instruction other than Latvian exist and they may receive financial assistance from the State. In some minority schools the language of instruction is mostly Latvian or Russian. The distribution of State and municipal schools by language of instruction at the beginning of the 1997-1998 school year was as follows: 719 Latvian, 199 Russian, 149 mixed, and 70 other.[10]

The new Law on Education of October 1998 formally permits the use of minority languages in education. However, the Ministry is authorised to decide which subjects are taught in the State language and which are taught – in the minority language. The education development concept elaborated and adopted by the Ministry, and reportedly approved by the Government, envisages the elimination of schools with instruction in minority languages as soon as the necessary number of teachers able to teach in the State language has become available. The Integration Programme contains the same approach to the problem. In fact, minority schools are viewed as a kind of anomaly which Latvians have to put up with, as switching to teaching only in the State language is technically impossible. Many Russian NGOs have argued strongly against this concept.

---

[10] Framework Document for a National Programme (1998).

It seems that striving to switch to Latvian as the sole language of instruction is the main reason behind the growing demands for the State language proficiency: teachers either have to pass the test and to teach their subject in Latvian or to lose their jobs. At the same time, the number of minority students trained in their mother tongue is continuously reducing: in 1990, 157,199 students were taught in Russian, in 1995 this number decreased to 131,645, and in 1998 to 119,195. This does not seem to be primarily a result of the Russian emigration. Figures for first-grade pupils reveal a similar decrease: in 1990, 22,489 children entered Latvian-language schools, 19,020 Russian-language schools, and 51 started education in other languages. In 1998 the respective figures were the following: 24,025; 9,165; and 286. Taking into account the negative natural increase in all ethnic groups in Latvia, the figures reveal an articulate assimilation trend, and many NGO activists claim that this assimilation is far from always being voluntary.

One of the points of concern expressed by the UN Committee on the Elimination of Racial Discrimination concerning Latvia's 1999periodic report was that instruction in minority languages might be reduced in the near future. In that sense the Committee recommended maintaining the possibility to receive an education in the languages of various minority groups or to study those languages, as well as to use one's mother tongue in private and in public.

Media
Approximately 50% of all the newspapers and magazines registered in Latvia are in languages other than Latvian and their number is not limited by any legal act in Latvia. According to the Law on Radio and Television, 20% of all the transmissions on the second distribution network of Latvian Radio and Television may be transmitted in minority languages (transmissions on the first and second distribution network are permitted to public broadcasters – Latvian Radio and Latvian Television, but permission for transmissions on the second distribution network may also be issued to other broadcasters).

Judicial procedures
Both the Code on Criminal Procedure and the Civil Law admit the use of language other than Latvian. Article 16 of the Code on Criminal Procedure stipulates that the legal procedure in a criminal case takes place in the Latvian language, but that other languages may also be admitted if the prosecutor and the participants in the procedure agree. For a person who takes part in the case but does not have command of the language of the proceedings, the court, judge, prosecutor and investigation institution provide the right to submit applications, to present evidence, to lodge appeals, to become acquainted with all case documents as well as to speak in court in the language in which this person has command and to use the assistance of an interpreter in the order provided by this Code. Procedural documents that are to be handed to the accused, defendant or other participants in the proceedings who do not have command of the language

of the proceedings must be translated into the language these persons understand.

Similarly Article 9 of the Civil Law provides that the legal procedure in the Republic of Latvia takes place in the State language unless the court admits other languages of legal procedure if the parties, their representatives, and the prosecutor agree. For a person who takes part in the case but does not have command of the language of the proceedings the court provides the right to get acquainted with the case documents and to take part in the action of the court with the assistance of interpreters as well as to speak court in the language which this person understands.

Language requirements in the Citizenship Law
The Law on the Citizenship of the Republic of Latvia, which was adopted on 22 July 1994 and entered into force on 25 August 1994, establishes that Latvian citizenship shall be granted to those persons who are registered in the Residents' Registry and have fulfilled cumulatively a number of conditions, *inter alia*, command of the Latvian language (Article 12, paragraph 1 (2)). The Law further provides a special procedure for testing the command of the Latvian language by commissions established by the Cabinet of Ministers. A person shall be considered to have command of the Latvian language if he/she completely understands information of an everyday and official nature; can freely talk, carry on a conversation and answer questions on topics of an everyday nature; can read freely and understand any texts of an everyday nature, laws and other normative acts and other instructions of an everyday nature and can write a composition on a topic from everyday life. Some categories like individuals who have graduated from secondary schools, vocational schools, higher educational establishments with Latvian language teaching, 1st category of invalids whose invalidity has no term limits, as well as 2nd and 3rd category optic, hearing and speech invalids, are exempted.

LIECHTENSTEIN

I. Demographic situation

Population (1994): Total 30,000. Minority groups: Swiss 4,500 (15.0%); Walsers 2,500 (8.3%); Austrians 2,100 (7.0%); Germans 1,200 (4.0%).

By a letter dated 24 June 1998, the Office for Foreign Affairs of the Principality of Liechtenstein informed us that

- in accordance with Article 2, paragraph 2, and in accordance with Article 3, paragraph 1 of the European Charter for Regional Minority Languages of 5 November 1992, there are no regional or minority languages in the sense of the Charter in the territory of the Principality of Liechtenstein at the time of ratification.
- Articles 24 and 25, in particular, of the Framework Convention for the protection of National Minorities of 1 February 1995 are to be understood having regard to the fact that no national minorities in the sense of the Framework Convention exist in the territory of the Principality of Liechtenstein.[11]

Languages: German.

II. International obligations

United Nations
- International Covenant on Civil and Political Rights (accession 10 December 1998)
- First Optional Protocol (accession 10 December 1998)
- International Covenant on Economic, Social and Cultural Rights (accession 10 December 1998)

Council of Europe
- Member (13 November 1978)
- ECHR (signature 23 November 1978, ratification 8 September 1982)
- Charter for Regional or Minority Languages (signature 5 November 1992, ratification 18 November 1997, entry into force 1 March 1998)
- Framework Convention for the Protection of National Minorities (signature 1 February 1995, ratification 18 November 1997, entry into force 1 March 1998)

III. National legislation

Constitution (6 October 1921)

Article 6
The German language is the national and official language.

---

[11] For the text of the declarations see: Part Two, chapter reproducing documents of the Council of Europe.

LITHUANIA

I. Demographic situation

Population: Total 3,704,000. Minority groups: Russians 304,800 (8.2%); Poles 256,600 (7.0%); Belarusians 54,500 (1.5%); Ukrainians 36,900 (1.0%); Jews 5,200 (0.1%); Others (Armenians, Azeris, Germans, Karaini, Latvians, Moldovans, Roma, Tatars and Uzbeks) 24,900 (0.7%).

Languages: Lithuanian (official), Polish and Russian.

II. International obligations

Article 138, paragraph 3, of the 1992 Lithuanian Constitution establishes that international agreements which are ratified by the Parliament of the Republic of Lithuania shall be the constituent part of the legal system of the Republic of Lithuania. According to Article 12 of the 1991 Law on International Treaties, international treaties of the Republic of Lithuania shall have the force of law on the territory of the Republic of Lithuania.

United Nations
– International Covenant on Civil and Political Rights (accession 20 November 1991)
– First Optional Protocol (accession 20 November 1991)
– International Covenant on Economic, Social and Cultural Rights (accession 20 November 1991)

Council of Europe
– Member (14 May 1993)
– ECHR (signature 14 May 1993, ratification 20 June 1995)
– Not a party to the Charter for Regional or Minority Languages
– Framework Convention for the Protection of National Minorities (signature 1 February 1995, ratification 23 March 2000, entry into force 1 July 2000)

Bilateral agreements
– 1994 – with Poland

III. National legislation

Constitution (25 October 1992)

Article 14
Lithuanian shall be the State language.

Article 29
A person may not have his rights restricted in any way or be granted any privileges on the basis of his or her sex, race, nationality, language, origin, social status, religion, convictions, or opinions.

Article 37
Citizens who belong to ethnic communities shall have the right to foster their language, culture and customs.

Article 45
Ethnic communities of citizens shall independently administer the affairs of their ethnic culture, education, organisations, charity, and mutual assistance. The State shall support ethnic communities

Article 117
In the Republic of Lithuania, court trials shall be conducted in the State language.
Persons who do not speak Lithuanian shall be guaranteed the right to participate in investigation and court proceedings through an interpreter.

Law on State Language (Adopted on 31 January 1995)

Article 1
This Law shall regulate the use of the State language in public life of Lithuania, protection and control of the State language, and the responsibility for violations of the Law on the State language.
The Law shall not regulate unofficial communication of the population and the language of events of religious communities as well as persons belonging to ethnic communities.
Other laws of the Republic of Lithuania and legal acts adopted by the Seimas of the Republic of Lithuania shall guarantee the right of persons, belonging to ethnic communities, to foster their language, culture and customs.

Article 17
In the Republic of Lithuania public signs shall be in the State language.
Seals, stamps, letterheads, plaques, signs in offices and other places of enterprises, institutions and organizations of the Republic of Lithuania, as well as names of goods and services provided in Lithuania and their descriptions, must be in the State language.

Article 18
Names of organisations of ethnic communities, their informational signs may be rendered in other languages along with the State language.

The format of signs in other languages cannot be larger than that of signs in the State language.

Law on Ethnic Minorities (Adopted on 23 November 1989)

Preamble
The Republic of Lithuania shall guarantee to all its citizens regardless of ethnicity, equal political, economic, and social rights and freedoms, shall recognise its citizens, ethnic identity, the continuity of their culture, and shall promote ethnic consciousness and the expression thereof.

People of all ethnic groups residing in Lithuania must observe the Fundamental Law of the Republic of Lithuania and other laws, protect Lithuania's State sovereignty and territorial integrity, contribute to the establishment of an independent, democratic State in Lithuania, and respect Lithuania's State language, culture, traditions, and customs.

Article 1
The Republic of Lithuania, adhering to the principles of ethnic equality and humanism, shall guarantee to all ethnic minorities residing in Lithuania the right to freely develop, and shall respect every ethnic minority and language.

Any discrimination with regard to race, ethnicity or nationality, language or anything else related to ethnicity shall be prohibited and punished under the procedures provided by the laws of the Republic of Lithuania.

Article 2
The State shall provide equal protection for all, the citizens of the Republic of Lithuania, regardless of ethnicity.

The Republic of Lithuania, taking into account the interests of all ethnic minorities shall guarantee them the right under the law and the procedures thereunder:
- to obtain aid from the State to develop their culture and education;
- to have schooling in one's native language, with provision for pre-school education, other classes, elementary and secondary school education, as well as provision for groups, faculties and departments at institutions of higher learning to train teachers and other specialists needed by ethnic minorities (amended on January 29, 1991);
- to have newspapers and other publications and information in one's native language;
- to profess any or no religion, and to perform religious or folk observances in one's native language;
- to form ethnic cultural organisations;
- to establish contact with persons of the same ethnic background abroad;
- to be represented in government bodies at all levels on the basis of universal, equal, and direct suffrage; and

— to hold any post in the bodies of State power or government, as well as in enterprises, institutions or organisations.

The Law on the Legal Status of Foreigners in the Republic of Lithuania
(Adopted on 4 September, 1991)

Article 23
Foreigners staying in the Republic of Lithuania shall enjoy the same rights to cultural properties of the Republic of Lithuania.

Foreigners shall be guaranteed the rights to use their native language, to protect and foster their culture and traditions.

The Law on Education (Adopted on 25 June 1991)

Article 10 – Language of Instruction:
The language of instruction in Lithuanian schools of, the Republic of Lithuania shall be Lithuanian.

In the numerous close communities of ethnic minorities, the State will either provide or support pre-schools and schools or classes of general education in the native language. The parent or guardian may choose the pre-school or school of general education according to its language of instruction.

For small ethnic minorities who do not comprise a close community, compulsory or optional classes as well as Sunday schools aimed at learning or improvement of the native language may be established. The State schools of general education may establish separate classes, optional classes, or Sunday school classes for small ethnic minorities who do not comprise a close community but would like to learn or improve their native language.

In non-Lithuanian educational institutions, Lithuanian language and literature shall be taught in Lithuanian. If the parents or children so desire conditions shall be provided to study other subjects in the Lithuanian language as well.

All secondary schools of general education must ensure command of the Lithuanian language in accordance with the standards established by the Ministry of Culture and Education.

The opportunity to have instruction in the Lithuanian language shall be provided throughout the territory of the Republic of Lithuania.

Article 26 – The Organization of the Educational Process:
Educational institutions of the Republic of Lithuania shall function according to plans and programs approved by the Ministry of Culture and Education, or in coordination with the order established by the Ministry. The contents and methods of teaching must correspond to the given tasks of educational institutions, as well as to the needs of society.

At educational institutions, it shall be prohibited to propagandise hostility (racial, ethnic, religious or social), or superiority which runs counter to the universally recognized principles of international law and humanism.

Schools of general education of ethnic minorities may be supplemented by the elements of ethnic culture.

At secondary schools of general education, languages other than Lithuanian shall be taught depending on the preference of the parents and the capacity of the school.

Militaristic subjects shall not be taught at a school of general education.

The Law on Fundamentals of Protection of the Rights of the Child (Adopted on 14 March 1996)

Article 4 – General Provisions in Protection of the Rights of the Child:
3. every child shall enjoy equal rights with other children and can not be discriminated against for reasons of his parents' or other legal child representatives' gender, age, nationality, race, language, religion, convictions, social, monetary and family position, state of health or any other circumstances;

Article 17 – Rights of Children Belonging to Ethnic Communities (Minorities) of the Republic of Lithuania:
Children belonging to ethnic communities (minorities) of the Republic of Lithuania shall have the right to develop their own language, culture, customs and traditions. This right shall be ensured by the Constitution of the Republic of Lithuania, laws and other legal acts.

Article 34 – General Provisions of Rights of the Child to Education:
1. The child shall have the right to an education, which would develop his general cultural knowledge, intellect, abilities, views, moral and social responsibility, and would create conditions for development of his personality.
2. Every child must be assured the opportunities of learning to respect his parents, educators, teachers, other people, his native language, the State language and culture and other languages and cultures and nature, of preparing for an independent existence and work and of becoming a useful member of society.

The Law on Courts (Adopted on 31 May 1994)

Article 8 – The Language of Court Proceedings:
Court proceedings in the Republic of Lithuania shall be conducted in the State language.

Persons who do not know the Lithuanian language shall be guaranteed the right to participate in court proceedings through the interpreter. This right shall also be guaranteed to persons who do not know the Lithuanian language and wish to speak during court proceedings in their native language or any other language designated by them.

The costs of interpreter's services shall be covered from the State budget.

Law on the Provision of Information to the Public (Adopted on 2 July 1996)

Article 11 – Language in which Public Information shall be Presented:
1. Public information shall be presented and disseminated in the State language or some other language pursuant to the provisions of the Law on State Language.
2. Public information producers must show concern for the culture of the language.

IV. Developments/events/comments

Use of minority languages
The Law on State Language of 1995, while regulating the use of State language in public life, its protection and control, does not apply to informal communication and does not impose the language on the events of NGOs, religious communities as well as persons belonging to national minorities.

According to the amendments to the Law on National Minorities adopted in 1991, upon the proposal of Polish MPs and NGOs, in local institutions and organizations of administrative territorial units with a dense population of a particular national minority, the (local) language of national minority can be used along with the State language. In such administrative territorial units, signs can be in both Lithuanian and the (local) language of a national minority.

Moreover, according to the 1995 Decision on 'Temporary Rules of Audio and Written Information and Other Public Signs' of the Commission of the State Language, 'when information is given in places with dense (compact) population of national minority or is related to the activity of national minorities, the language of those minorities may be used along with the State language.'

Persons belonging to national minorities are granted an interpreter free of charge in both civil and criminal court procedures, as the procedure should be conducted in the State language.

Education in minority languages
According to legislation, national minorities in Lithuania enjoy the right to be taught their mother tongue and their history.

In the academic year 1997/1998 in ten major towns and twenty-three municipalities there were 232 schools of general education with a non-Lithuanian language of instruction, comprising 69,777 pupils (12.8% of the total number of pupils in the country). Among them, there were 49,347 pupils with

Russian language of instruction (9.5%), 20,263 pupils with Polish language of instruction (3.72%) and 167 pupils with Belarusian language of instruction.

Among the schools with a non-Lithuanian language of instruction in the academic year 1997/1998 there were 80 schools teaching in Russian, 63 in Polish and 1 in Belarusian. Mixed schools are as follows: 24 Lithuanian and Russian, 10 Lithuanian and Polish, 37 Russian and Polish, 1 Russian and Belarusian, 15 Lithuanian, Russian and Polish. Ukrainian classes operate in a secondary school in Vilnius. A Jewish school was opened in 1989 in Vilnius and a German school was opened in 1992 in Klaipdda. The Polish, Belarusian, Ukrainian, German, Jewish, Armenian, Karaites and Tatar minorities have their own Sunday schools.

There are two private schools with a Russian language of instruction (in Vilnius and Klaipäda) and there are private Polish, Jewish pre-school institutions. In 1996, a religious Jewish school was opened.

Pupils at the national minority schools study from textbooks in their mother tongue which are free of charge. Textbooks are published in Russian and Polish by a special State publishing house. Textbooks are also purchased from abroad.

State support for education in national minority languages is approximately 50 million Litas per year.

Media

In 1998 there were 56 periodicals in the languages of national minorities: 43 periodicals in Russian, 7 in Polish, 4 in German. Tatar and Greek ethnic communities issue their publications in other languages (Lithuanian, Russian) with paragraphs in their native languages.

Lithuanian National (Public) Television and Radio broadcast programmes in the languages of national minorities. Radio programmes broadcast one-hour daily news coverage in Russian, a half-hour programme in Polish, a half-hour programme twice a month in Ukrainian, and a half-hour programme once a week in Belarusian. TV programmes include a daily ten-minute news bulletin in Russian; once a week a Russian programme ('Teleartel'); a Polish programme ('Rozmowy Wilenskie'); an Ukrainian programme ('Trembita'); and twice a month a ten-minute programme in Belarusian. There is also a Jewish programme ('Menora').

In addition, there are programmes in the languages of national minorities broadcasted by private and foreign stations. The private Polish radio station 'Znad Wilii' broadcasts 24 hours a day.

Citizenship

The Lithuanian Law on Citizenship entered into force on 11 December 1991 and in Article 12 it states that a person requesting Lithuanian citizenship should, among other conditions, also pass the examination in the Lithuanian language (i.e. can speak Lithuanian). The Lithuanian Government established the procedure for the provision of examination certificates relating to Lithuanian language proficiency (as well as on the fundamentals of the Constitution of the

Republic of Lithuania). This requirement applies to all persons except those over the age of 65 or to Group I or II invalids or to persons suffering from a serious chronic mental disease. It is also possible that the President of the Republic may grant citizenship of the Republic of Lithuania to citizens of foreign States who have made contributions to Lithuania without applying the conditions for the granting of citizenship as provided under Article 12 of the Law (Article 16).

LUXEMBOURG

I. Demographic situation:

Population (1993): Total 395,000. Minority groups: Portuguese 42,650 (10.8%); Italians 19,850 (0.5%); Others (French, Belgians, Germans and Roma/Gypsies).

Languages: Letzeburgish, French, German.

II. International obligations

Pursuant to Article 37, paragraph 1, of the Constitution the Grand Duke concludes treaties. These do not enter into effect until they have been sanctioned by law and published in the manner laid down for the publication of laws.

United Nations
- International Covenant on Civil and Political Rights (signature 26 November 1974, ratification 18 August 1983)
- First Optional Protocol (accession 18 August 1983)
- International Covenant on Economic, Social and Cultural Rights (signature 26 November 1974, ratification 18 August 1983)

Council of Europe
- Member (5 May 1949)
- ECHR (signature 4 November 1950, ratification 3 September 1953)
- Charter for Regional or Minority Languages (signature 5 November 1992)
- Framework Convention for the Protection of National Minorities (signature 20 July 1995)

III. National legislation:

Constitution (Adopted on 17 October 1868)

Article 29
The law will determine the use of languages in administrative and judicial matters.

MACEDONIA (The Former Yugoslav Republic of)

I. Demographic situation

Population (1994): Total 1,937,000. Minority groups: Albanians 443,000 (23%); Turks 77,000 (4.0%); Roma 44,000 (2.3%); Serbs 39,000 (2.0%); Others 46,000 (2.4%). Other estimates: Roma - 200,000 (10.3%).

Languages: Macedonian, Albanian, Turkish.

II. International obligations

Article 118 of the 1992 Macedonian Constitution states that international agreements ratified in accordance with the Constitution are part of the internal legal order and cannot be changed by law.

United Nations
– International Covenant on Civil and Political Rights (succession 18 January 1994)
– First Optional Protocol (succession 12 December 1994)
– International Covenant on Economic, Social and Cultural Rights (succession 18 January 1994)

Council of Europe
– Member (9 November 1995)
– ECHR (signature 9 November 1995, ratification 10 April 1997)
– Charter for Regional or Minority Languages (signature 25 July 1996)
– Framework Convention for the Protection of National Minorities (signature 25 July 1996, ratification 10 April 1997, entry into force 1 February 1998)

III. National legislation

Constitution (17 November 1991)

Article 7
1. The Macedonian language, written using its Cyrillic alphabet, is the official language in the Republic of Macedonia.
2. In the units of local self-government where the majority of the inhabitants belong to a nationality, in addition to the Macedonian language and Cyrillic alphabet, their language and alphabet are also in official use, in a manner determined by law.
3. the units of local self-government where there is a considerable number of inhabitants belonging to a nationality, their language and alphabet are also in official use, in addition to the Macedonian language and Cyrillic alphabet, under conditions and in a manner determined by law.

Article 48
2. The Republic guarantees the protection of the ethnic, cultural, linguistic and religious identity of the nationalities.
4. Members of the nationalities have the right to instruction in their language in primary and secondary education, as determined by law. In schools where education is carried out in the language of a nationality, the Macedonian language is also studied.

Article 54
2. The restriction of freedoms and rights cannot discriminate on grounds of sex, race, color of skin, language, religion, national or social origin, property or social status.

IV. Developments/events/comments

Bodies
According to Article 78 of the Macedonian Constitution the Assembly has established a Council for Inter-Ethnic Relations which consists of the President of the Assembly and two members each from among the Macedonians, Albanians, Turks, Vlachs and Romas, as well as two members from the ranks of other nationalities in Macedonia. The Council considers issues of inter-ethnic relations in the Republic, undertakes appraisals and makes proposals for the solution of existing problems. The Assembly is obliged to take into consideration the Council's appraisals and proposals and to take decisions in this respect.

Census Law
As provided by Article 35 of the 1994 Law on the Census of the Population, Households, Dwellings and Agricultural Holdings in the Republic of

Macedonia, the census taker shall be obliged to inform the persons that they have the right to freely choose to use the official Macedonian language or the language of the national minority to which the person belongs (Albanian, Turkish, Vlach, Romany or the Serbian languages. In such a case the bilingual forms are filled in the language which represents that person's choice.

Local self-government and topographical names
According to Article 89 of the 1995 Law on Local Self-Government, during sessions of the Council, of local self-government and of other organs of self-government units where citizens belonging to minorities are the majority or amount to a significant number, in addition to the Macedonian language and the Cyrillic alphabet, the language and the alphabet of the national minority which is in majority shall also be in official use. In such case documents will also be published in the official and minority language(s). This rule is also followed in public services, public institutions and public enterprises where citizens belonging to a national minority are the majority. Article 90 of the same Law further stipulates, that in units of local self-government where persons belonging to a national minority are in majority, the names of towns, the names of public services and institutions, the names of enterprises and of other public enterprises which have been established by the unit of local self-government in question shall be written in both the Macedonian language and its alphabet and in the language and alphabet of the national minority which represents the majority. However, the names of institutions representing culture or art, the sole purpose of which is the development and promotion of the cultural and educational aims of the national minorities, in addition to the Macedonian language, shall also be written in the language and alphabet of the national minority regardless of the number of citizens belonging to the national minority in the unit of local self-government.

Personal names
The personal name of a child shall be registered in the Macedonian language and in its Cyrillic alphabet, while the names of persons belonging to national minorities shall also be entered in the language and alphabet of the national minorities (Article 9 of the 1995 Law on Identity Cards).

Education
For the members of national minorities instruction in primary schools is conducted in their language and alphabet (although they do study the Macedonian language as well) in the manner specified by the 1995 Act on Primary Education (Article 8). For that purpose pedagogical documentation shall be kept and issued, in addition to Macedonian, also in the language and alphabet of the national minority in question; whereas pedagogical records shall be kept and issued in the language and alphabet of instruction (Article 81).

Similar provisions are contained in the 1995 Act on Secondary Education (Articles 4 and 73).

Articles 1 and 2 of the 1997 Act on Languages of Instruction at the Pedagogical Faculty 'St. Climent Ohridski' in Skopje stipulate that instruction for groups studying pre-school education and class instruction shall be conducted in both the Macedonian language and in the languages of the national minorities (in subjects contained in educational curricula and programmes, with the exception of subjects relating to the Macedonian language and culture).

According to the official statistics, in 1990/91 the situation with respect to languages of instruction was as follows:

- Macedonian primary schools: 828 (18,8051 children); secondary schools 90 (67,975 students);
- Albanian primary schools: 279 (71,121 children); secondary schools 5 (2,535 students);
- Turkish primary schools: 55 (5,432 children); secondary schools 2 (186 students); and
- Serbian primary schools: 15 (1,209 children); no secondary schools.

Albanian-language Tetovo University
Since 1994 a prolonged discussion has been taking place with respect to the claim of the Albanian minority to legalize the Albanian-language Tetovo University. On 25 July 2000 the Macedonian Parliament adopted the Law on Higher Education. The provisions of the Law give the possibility for higher education in the languages of the national minorities of Macedonia. The Law also allows for the establishment of the private university in Tetovo. The adoption of the Law on Higher Education represents an important measure in promoting the peaceful coexistence of different ethnic groups in the country, and presents a compromise between the claim of the Albanian minority for a State-run Albanian university and the refusal of the Macedonian Government to agree to this.

Judicial procedure
In criminal proceedings the Macedonian language and Cyrillic are in official use (Article 6 of the 1997 Criminal Procedure Act). However, citizens belonging to a national minority have the right to use their own language and alphabet. The court shall provide an interpreter for such persons free of charge. Also other parties, witnesses and participants in the court proceedings have the right to the assistance of an interpreter free of charge. Documents can also be submitted in the language and alphabet of the nationality to which participants in the proceedings belong (for foreign citizens the principle of reciprocity shall be applied). Summonses, decisions and other court documents shall be written in both Macedonian and the language of the nationality to which persons taking part in the proceedings belong (Articles 8 and 9).

Media
Macedonian Radio broadcasts on a daily basis 15 hours of programmes in the languages of national minorities. Macedonian Radio broadcasts 570 minutes daily in Albanian and 270 minutes daily in Turkish. In the Vlach and the Roma languages there are 120 minutes of programmes per week. Since 1995 Macedonian Television has expanded the programme in the Albanian language from 1 to 2 hours daily. There is a one-hour programme in the Turkish language and half an hour a week is broadcast in Vlach, Roma and Serbian languages. In addition, 120 hours of normal scheduled programmes (documentaries) on Macedonian Television are broadcast in the languages of the national minorities.

In the autumn of 1999 a 40-part children's television drama series started on Macedonian State TV. It is aimed at bridging the gap between Macedonian and Albanian 10-year olds who are taught in their own languages in separate classrooms. The series focuses on language and customs and provides and opportunity, *inter alia*, to learn a basic vocabulary and everyday phrases in Macedonian and Albanian. The producer is the US Children's Television Workshop.

MALTA

I. Demographic situation

Population (1994): Total 359,000.

Languages: Maltese, English.

By a letter dated 1 July 1998 the Maltese Ministry for Foreign Affairs and the Environment informed us that in Malta no national minorities in the sense of the Framework Convention of the Council of Europe exist. At the time of ratifying the Convention Malta declared that this was being done as an act of solidarity with the objectives of the Convention.

II. International obligations

United Nations
- International Covenant on Civil and Political Rights (accession 12 September 1990)
- First Optional Protocol (accession 12 September 1990)

- International Covenant on Economic, Social and Cultural Rights (signature 22 October 1968, ratification 13 September 1990)

Council of Europe
- Member (29 April 1965)
- ECHR (signature 12 December 1966, ratification 23 January 1967)
- Charter for Regional or Minority Languages (signature 5 November 1992)
- Framework Convention for the Protection of National Minorities (signature 11 May 1995, ratification 10 February 1998, entry into force 1 June 1998)

III. National legislation

Constitution (1964)

Article 5
1. The national language of Malta is the Maltese language.
2. The Maltese and the English languages and such other languages as may be prescribed by Parliament, by a law passed by not less than two-thirds of all the members of the House of Representatives, shall be the official languages of Malta and the Administration may for all official purposes use any of such languages:
   Provided that any person may address the Administration in any of the official languages and the reply of the Administration thereto shall be in such language.
3. The language of the courts shall be the Maltese language:
   Provided that Parliament may make such provision for the use of the English language in such cases and under such conditions as it may prescribe.
4. The House of Representatives may, in regulating its own procedure, determine the language or languages that shall be used in parliamentary proceedings and records.

Article 35
2. Any person who is arrested or detained shall be informed, at the time of his arrest or detention, in a language that he understands, of the reasons for his arrest or detention:
   Provided that if an interpreter is necessary and is not readily available or if it is otherwise impracticable to comply with the provisions of this subsection at the time of the person's arrest or detention, such provisions shall be complied with as soon as practicable.

Article 75
Save as otherwise provided by Parliament, every law shall be enacted in both the Maltese and English languages and, if there is any conflict between the Maltese and the English texts of any law, the Maltese text shall prevail.

MOLDOVA

I. Demographic situation

Population (1992): Total 4,300,000. Minority groups: Ukrainians 600,000 (13.9%); Russians 562,000 (13.0%); Gagauz 153,000 (3.5%); Bulgarians 88,000 (2.0%); Jews 66,000 (1.5%); Others 71,000 (1.6%).

Languages: Moldavian/Romanian, Russian.

II. International obligations

According to Article 4, paragraph 2, of the 1994 Constitution whenever discrepancies occur between conventions and treaties signed by the Republic of Moldova and its own national laws, priority shall be given to international regulations.

United Nations
– International Covenant on Civil and Political Rights (accession 26 January 1993)
– Not a party to the First Optional Protocol
– International Covenant on Economic, Social and Cultural Rights (accession 26 January 1993)

Council of Europe
– Member (13 July 1995)
– ECHR (signature 13 July 1995, ratification 12 September 1997)
– Not a party to the Charter for Regional or Minority Languages
– Framework Convention for the Protection of National Minorities (signature 13 July 1995, ratification 20 November 1996, entry into force 1 February 1998)

III. National legislation

Constitution (29 July 1994)

Article 10
2. The State recognizes and guarantees all its citizens the right to preserve, develop and express their ethnic, cultural, linguistic and religious identity.

Article 13
1. The national language of the Republic of Moldova is Moldovan, and its writing is based on the Latin alphabet.

2. The Moldovan State acknowledges and protects the right to preserve, develop and use the Russian language and other languages spoken within the national territory of the country.
3. The State will encourage and promote studies of foreign languages enjoying widespread international usage.
4. The use of languages in the territory of the Republic of Moldova will be established by organic law.

Article 16
2. All citizens of the Republic of Moldova are equal before the law and the public authorities, without any discrimination as to race, nationality, ethnic origin, language, religion, sex, political choice, personal property or social origin.

Article 35
2. The State will enforce under the law the right of each person to choose his/her language in which teaching will be effected.
3. In all forms of educational institutions the study of the country's official language will be ensured.

Article 78
2. Any citizen of the Republic of Moldova over 35 years of age that has been living in the country for at least 10 years and speaks the State language can run for the office of President of the Republic of Moldova. The appropriate organic law shall determine the manner of selecting the candidates aspiring to this office.

Article 118
1. Legal cases will be heard in the Moldovan language.
2. Those persons who do not know or are unable to speak Moldovan have the right to take knowledge of all documents and items on file and to talk to the court through an interpreter.
3. In accordance with the law legal hearings may also be conducted in a language that is found to be acceptable by the majority of the persons participating in the hearing.

Law on the Moldavian Soviet Socialist Republic on the Functioning of Languages on the Territory of the Moldavian SSR (Adopted on 1 September 1989, entering into force stage by stage)

Confirmation by the Constitution (Basic Law) of the Moldavian Soviet Socialist Republic of the status of the Moldavian language as a State language shall be aimed at promoting the full sovereignty of the Republic and creating necessary guarantees for its comprehensive and overall application in all spheres of political, economic, social and cultural life. The Moldavian SSR shall encourage Moldavians residing outside the territory of the Republic, and taking into account the reality of the Moldavian-Romanian language identity, and also Romanians residing on USSR territory to obtain education and meet their cultural needs in their native language used under the conditions of equality of all citizens before the Law.

For the purpose of State protection and development of the Gagauz language the Moldavian SSR shall create the necessary guarantees for the successive expansion of its social functions.

The Moldavian SSR shall ensure on its territory the conditions for the use and development of the Russian language as a language of inter-ethnic communication in the USSR, as well as languages of people of other nationalities residing in the Republic.

Chapter 1 – General provisions

Article 1

In accordance with the Constitution (Basic Law) of the Moldavian SSR the Moldavian language shall be a State language of the Moldavian SSR and shall be applied on the basis of the Latin script. The Moldavian language as a State language shall be applied in all spheres of political, economic, social and cultural life, and shall function therefore as a language of inter ethnic communication on the territory of the Republic.

The Moldavian SSR shall guarantee free teaching of the State language to all residents of the Republic at the level necessary to perform professional functions.

Article 2

The State, Gagauz or Russian languages shall be the languages of official communication in the public life at places of residence of the majority of the population of the Gagauz nationality.

Article 3

The Russian language as a language of inter ethnic communication in the USSR shall be applied on the territory of the Republic along with the Moldavian language as a language of inter ethnic communication; it ensures the real national-Russian and Russian-national bilingualism.

Article 4

The Moldavian SSR shall guarantee the usage of Ukrainian, Russian, Bulgarian, Hebrew, Yiddish, Gypsy languages and languages of other ethic groups residing on the territory of the Republic to meet their national and cultural needs.

Article 5
The present Law shall not regulate the usage of languages in private relations, professional activity of the railway and air transport (with the exception of servicing passengers), as well as in military units and institutions within the jurisdiction of the USSR Ministry of Defence, in military units of the USSR KGB and the USSR Ministry of Interior.

Chapter 2 – Rights and Guarantees for a citizen to choose a Language

Article 6
In relations with the bodies of the State authority, State administration and public organizations, as well as with enterprises, institutions and organizations located on the territory of the Moldavian SSR the language for oral and written communication – Moldavian or Russian – shall be chosen by a citizen. In localities inhabited by people of Gagauz nationality a right of a citizen to use in these relations the Gagauz language as well, shall be guaranteed. In localities where the majority of the population are of Ukrainian, Russian, Bulgarian or any other ethnicity, the native or another acceptable language shall be used for communication.

Article 7
For the high level administrative officials, for the officials of bodies of State authority, State administration and public organizations, as well as for officials of enterprises, institutions and organizations, who due to their professional duty communicate with citizens (public health, public education, culture, mass media, transportation, communication, trade, service sphere, housing and communal services, organs providing for the law and order, emergency and rescue services, etc.), irrespective of ethnic belonging, for the purpose of assurance of a citizen's right to choose a language, the requirements with respect to the knowledge of the Moldavian, Russian and, in localities inhabited by people of the Gagauz nationality, Gagauz languages at the communication level sufficient to perform professional duties shall be established. The volume and level of the knowledge of languages shall be defined under the procedure established by the Council of Ministers of the Moldavian Republic in accordance with the legislation in force.

Article 8
At the congresses, sessions, plenary sessions, conferences, meetings, rallies and other actions organized in the Moldavian SSR the choice of a language by their participants shall not be limited.

Chapter 3 – Languages used in bodies of State authority, State administration and public organizations, in enterprises, institutions and organizations

Article 9
The working language in bodies of State authority, State administration and public organizations shall be the State language introduced stage by stage. Translation or interpretation into Russian shall be provided.

The language for office work in bodies of the State authority, State administration and public organizations shall be the State language. If necessary, the documents shall be translated into Russian.

In localities inhabited by people of the Gagauz nationality the working language and the language for office work in the bodies of State authority, State administration and public organizations shall be the State, Gagauz or Russian languages.

The language for meetings and office work in the bodies of State authority, State administration and public organizations in localities where the majority of the population are of Ukrainian, Russian, Bulgarian or another ethnicity shall be the State, native or another acceptable language.

Article 10
The acts of the bodies of the State authority, State administration and public organizations shall be drawn up and submitted in the State language with the subsequent translation into the Russian language, in localities inhabited by people of the Gagauz nationality – in the State language, Gagauz or Russian language with the subsequent translation. The acts of the local bodies of State authority, State administration and public organizations in the territories where the majority of population is of Ukrainian, Russian, Bulgarian or another ethnicity, may be submitted in the native or another acceptable language with the subsequent translation into the State language.

Article 11
In the written communication of the bodies of the State authority, State administration and public organizations to a citizen, the Moldavian or Russian language shall be used, in localities inhabited by people of the Gagauz nationality – the Moldavian, Gagauz or Russian language. Upon issuance of documents the Moldavian or Russian language, or the Moldavian and Russian languages shall be used upon a citizen's choice, in localities inhabited by people of the Gagauz nationality – the Moldavian, Gagauz or Russian language, or the Moldavian Gagauz and Russian languages.

The bodies of the State authority, State administration and public organizations, enterprises, institutions and organizations shall accept and consider documents submitted by citizens in the Moldavian or Russian language, in localities inhabited by the people of the Gagauz nationality – in the

Moldavian, Gagauz or Russian language. The translation into the Moldavian or Russian language should be attached to documents submitted in other languages.

Article 12
Office work in enterprises, institutions and organizations located on the territory of the Moldavian SSR, shall be carried out in the State language. Technical standard documentation may be used in the original language.
With due regard for the demographic situation, production process requirements, office work in the enterprises, institutions and organizations specified by the Council of Ministers of the Moldavian SSR upon the proposals of the district and city Soviets of people's deputies may be carried out also in the Russian or another acceptable language. Correspondence among the enterprises, organizations and institutions located on the territory of the Republic shall be effected in the State language and the language for the office work.

Article 13
Correspondence among the bodies of the State authority, State administration and public organizations, as well as between them and the enterprises, institutions and organizations located on the territory of the Moldavian SSR shall be effected in the State language or another acceptable language.

Article 14
Documentation and other information forwarded outside the territory of the Moldavian SSR shall be drawn up in the Russian or another acceptable language.

Chapter 4 – The language for proceedings in criminal, civil and administrative cases, for arbitration, notarial deeds, bodies for registration of acts of civil status

Article 15
The proceedings in criminal, civil and administrative cases in the Moldavian SSR shall be effected in the State language or in the language acceptable for the majority of persons participating in them.

The participants in a case who do not know the language in which the proceedings are effected, shall be ensured the right to be acquainted with the materials of the case, to participate in the court and investigation proceedings through an interpreter, as well as the right to make a statement and to give a testimony in the native language.

The investigation and court documents in accordance with the procedure established by the legal procedure shall be handed over to the accused, defendant and to other persons participating in a case after being translated into a language they know.

Article 16
The bodies of the State arbitration shall carry out their activities in the State language or in the language acceptable for the parties in a dispute.

Article 17
Notary work in the State notary's offices and executive committees of the district, city, town and village Soviets of people's deputies, as well as office work in the bodies for registration of acts of civil status of the Moldavian SSR shall be effected in the State or Russian language.

In the executive committees of the local Soviets of people's deputies the documents shall be drawn up in the State language and upon citizens' wish – in the Russian language as well; in the notary's offices and bodies for registration of acts of civil status – in the State and Russian languages.

Chapter 5 – Language in public education, science and culture

Article 18
The Moldavian SSR shall guarantee the right to have a pre-school, general secondary, specialized secondary, vocational training and high education in the Moldavian and Russian languages and shall create conditions for the exercise of the right of the citizens of other nationalities residing in the Republic to the upbringing and education in the native language (the Gagauz, Ukrainian, Bulgarian, Hebrew, Yiddish and other languages)

Article 19
The pre-school institutions and schools providing general education shall be opened in accordance with the single language principle.

Office work, meetings, audio and visual information shall be carried out in them in the language of upbringing and education. The pre-school institutions and schools providing general education on the principle of bilingualism shall be opened in those localities where the number of children and students does not allow to open pre-school institutions and schools providing general education in accordance with the single language principle. Meetings and audio and visual information shall be carried out in them on equal grounds in the relevant languages of upbringing and education, and office work – in the State language.

Article 20
In the specialized secondary, vocational training and high education institutions education shall be guaranteed in the State and Russian languages to acquire professions necessary to the Moldavian SSR. To meet economic cultural requirements of the Republic, groups of students studying in the languages applied on the territory of the Moldavian SSR (the Gagauz, Ukrainian, Bulgarian, Yiddish and other languages) shall be established. In special national

groups the teaching of specialized disciplines shall be carried out in the native language of pupils and students.

Article 21
In educational institutions of all levels the study of the Moldavian language as a discipline – in the classes and groups providing education in the Russian or other languages (for students of Gagauz and Bulgarian nationality within the volume necessary to communicate) and of the Russian language – in classes and groups providing education in the Moldavian and other languages shall be guaranteed.

Pupils and students graduating from the educational institution shall pass the final examination in the Moldavian or Russian language accordingly; that creates conditions for the expansion of the areas of communication in the whole territory of the Republic.

Article 22
The Moldavian SSR shall create the necessary conditions for the development of the Moldavian and Gagauz national science and culture, as well as for scientific and cultural activities in other languages which are applied in the Republic. Defence of these shall be carried out in the Moldavian, Russian or other languages determined by the relevant specialized council.

Article 23
Scientific and practical conferences, symposia and seminars, other meetings at the republican level shall be held in the State language (with the translation into Russian), and the meetings at the Union level – in the Russian language.

Chapter 6 - Languages in names and information

Article 24
Localities and other geographic entities in the territory of the Moldavian SSR shall have a single official name in its initial Moldavian and, accordingly, Gagauz forms (without translation and adaptation) subject to historical traditions of a given locality. The correct writing of the names of localities and other geographical entities shall be established in accordance with the special reference books.

The names of squares, streets lanes, city districts shall be formed in the State language without translation (in localities inhabited by people of the Gagauz nationality – in the Gagauz language), and in rural areas where the majority of the population is of Ukrainian, Russian or Bulgarian ethnicity – in the acceptable language.

Article 25
The names of ministries, State committees and departments, enterprises, institutions and organizations and their structural units shall be formed in the

State language with the translation into the Russian language, and in localities inhabited by people of the Gagauz nationality – in the Gagauz language as well. The names cited in quotation marks shall not be translated but transcribed.

Article 26
The proper name of a citizen of the Moldavian SSR of Moldavian ethnicity shall be composed of a name (or several names) and family name (single or double). The family name shall not be altered by gender; the patronymic shall be used without suffixes. When translating the Moldavian names and family names into other languages the specificity of their writing in the Moldavian language shall remain without adaptation.

The spelling of names and family names of representatives of other nationalities residing in the Republic shall not be regulated by the present Law.

Article 27
The official letterheads, texts of seals, stamps and postmarks shall be produced in the State and Russian languages, in the relevant localities – in the State, Gagauz and Russian languages.

Forms (cards) used in the social sphere (telegraph services, saving banks, institutions providing consumer services to the population, etc.) shall be produced in the State and Russian languages (in the relevant localities – in the State, Gagauz and Russian languages) and shall be filled upon the wish of a citizen in one of the languages of a form (card).

Article 28
Signs with the names of the bodies of State authority, State administration and public organizations, enterprises, institutions and organizations, sign-boards with the names of squares, streets, lanes, localities and other geographic entities shall be produced in the State and Russian languages, in the relevant localities – in the State, Gagauz and Russian languages and shall be placed in the left side (on the top) in the State language and in the right side (below) in the Russian language, in the relevant localities – in the left side (on the top) in the Gagauz language, in the centre (below) in the State language, in the right side (lower) in the Russian language.

Article 29
The texts of public announcements, notifications, advertisements and other visual information shall be designed in the State language with the translation, if necessary, into the Russian language, in the relevant localities – in the State, as well as in the Gagauz and Russian language.

Names of the goods and products, labels (tags) of the goods, marking, instructions for goods produced in the Republic, as well as any visual information presented to the population of the Republic shall be designed in the State and Russian languages.

In all occasions the texts of the visual information shall be written in the order provided for in the Article 28 of the present Law. Print of the texts in the State language should not be of a smaller size than in the other languages.

In the rural areas where the majority is population of the Ukrainian, Russian or Bulgarian ethnicity, the visual information may be designed in the relevant languages.

Chapter 7 - State protection of languages

Article 30
The heads of the bodies of the State authority, State administration and public organizations, as well as of the enterprises, institutions and organizations located in the territory of the Moldavian SSR, shall bear personal responsibility for the non-observance of the legislation in force.

Article 31
The propaganda of animosity, neglect of languages of other nationalities, creation of obstacles for the functioning of the State language and other languages in the territory of the Republic, as well as infringement upon the right of the citizens on language grounds shall entail the responsibility in accordance with the procedure established by the legislation

Article 32
Control over the observance of the legislation on the functioning of languages in the territory of the Moldavian SSR shall be carried out by the Supreme Soviet of the Moldavian SSR through a specially established Commission, and in districts (cities) – the relevant Soviets of people's deputies of the Moldavian SSR.

IV. Developments/events/comments

On 31 August 1989 a Law on the Status of the State Language of the Moldavian SSR was adopted, along with the Law of the Moldavian SSR on the Functioning of Languages on the Territory of the Moldavian SSR on 1 September 1989. The latter deals with the use of languages in bodies of State authority, State administration and public organizations, in enterprises, institutions and organizations; in proceedings in criminal, civil and administrative cases, for arbitration, notarial deeds, bodies for registration of acts of civil status; in public education, science and culture; and in names and information.

MONACO

I. Demographic situation

Population (1994): Total 30,000. Minority groups: Monegasque 4,600 (15.3%); Italians 4,600 (15.3%).

Languages: French, Italian, English, Monegasque

II. International obligations

United Nations
- International Covenant on Civil and Political Rights (signature 26 June 1997, ratification 28 August 1997)
- Not a party to the First Optional Protocol
- International Covenant on Economic, Social and Cultural Rights (signature 26 June 1997, ratification 28 August 1997)

Council of Europe
- Not a member of the Council of Europe
- Not a party to the Charter for Regional or Minority Languages
- Not a party to the Framework Convention for the Protection of National Minorities

III. National legislation

Constitution (24 December 1922)

Article 8
The French language is the official language of the State.

THE NETHERLANDS

I. Demographic situation

Population (1994): Total 15,200,000. Minority groups: Frisians 700,000 (4.6%); Indonesians 240,000-295,000 (1.6-1.9%); Turks 203,000 (1.3%); Surinamese 200,000 (1.3%); Moroccans 157,000 (1.0%); Moluccans 40,000 (0.3%);

Roma/Gypsies/Sinti 35,000-40,000 (0.2-0.3%); Jews 25,000 (0.16%); Chinese 20,000 (0.14%).

Some other sources indicate that in 1997 a total of 2,677,000 persons belonged to an ethnic minority (17.2%).

Languages: Dutch, Frisian.

II. International obligations

According to Articles 93 and 94 of the 1983 Constitution provisions of treaties and of resolutions by international institutions, which may be binding on all persons by virtue of their contents shall become binding after they have been published. Statutory regulations in force within the Kingdom shall not be applicable if such application is in conflict with provisions of treaties that are binding on all persons or of resolutions by international institutions.

United Nations
- International Covenant on Civil and Political Rights (signature 25 June 1969, ratification 11 December 1978)
- First Optional Protocol (signature 25 June 1969, ratification 11 December 1978)
- International Covenant on Economic, Social and Cultural Rights (signature 25 June 1969, ratification 11 December 1978)

Council of Europe
- Member (5 May 1949)
- ECHR (signature 4 November 1950, ratification 31 August 1954)
- Charter for Regional or Minority Languages (signature 5 November 1992, ratification 2 May 1996, entry into force 1 March 1998)
- Framework Convention for the Protection of National Minorities (signature 1 February 1995)

III. National legislation

[There is no provision in the Constitution of the Kingdom of Netherlands on languages]

IV. Developments/events/comments

Education
The main language of instruction in schools and universities is Dutch. However, pupils and students at all levels of education can opt to spend more time learning their mother tongue, whereas children in secondary schools have the opportunity

to choose to study their own language rather than another subject in the educational programme.

Judicial and administrative procedures
The 1992 General Administrative Law Act (Algemene wet bestuursrecht) stipulates in Article 2:6 that administrative bodies use the Dutch language unless otherwise provided by law. Another language can be used if this is more appropriate. The Act also contains detailed provisions on the use of the Frisian language in administrative matters (Articles 2:7-2.12).

National bodies
There is a Minister for Urban Policy and Integration of Ethnic Minorities who is in charge of the coordination policy on the integration of ethnic minorities. In addition, there is an Ombudsman for minority and/or human rights issues or a Parliamentary Committee for petitions to which every individual in the Netherlands may submit complaints. Neither the Ombudsman nor the Lower House Petitions Committee specifically deal with minorities. The Equal Treatment Commission deals with complaints relating to discrimination, including discrimination against persons belonging to minorities.

NORWAY

I. Demographic situation

Population: Total 4,300,000 (1994); Sami 60,000-100,000 (1.4%-2.3%); new minorities 100,000 (2.3%); a small Roma/Gypsy, Jewish and Finnish-speaking population .

Some other sources indicate that the numbers of persons with an immigrant background in Norway have risen to a total of 244,705 persons, or 5.5% of the total population.

Languages: Norwegian; Sami.

II. International obligations

Article 26, paragraph 2, and Article 110C of the 1814 Constitution stipulates that treaties on matters of special importance, and, in all cases, treaties whose implementation, according to the Constitution, necessitates a new law or a decision by Parliament, are not binding until Parliament has given its consent thereto. It is the responsibility of the authorities of the State to respect and ensure human rights. Specific provisions for the implementation of treaties thereon shall be determined by law.

United Nations
- International Covenant on Civil and Political Rights (signature 20 March 1968, ratification 13 September 1972)
- First Optional Protocol (signature 20 March 1968, ratification 13 September 1972)
- International Covenant on Economic, Social and Cultural Rights (signature 20 March 1968, ratification 13 September 1972)

Council of Europe
- Member (5 May 1949)
- ECHR (signature 4 November 1950, ratification 15 January 1952)
- Charter for Regional or Minority Languages (signature 5 November 1992, ratification 10 November 1993, entry into force 1 March 1998)
- Framework Convention for the Protection of National Minorities (signature 1 February 1995, ratification 17 March 1999, entry into force 1 July 1999)

III. National legislation

Constitution (17 May 1814)

Article 92
Only Norwegian citizens, men and women, who speak the language of the country, shall be appointed to official posts of the State, [...]

Article 110A
The State authorities have a duty to create conditions in order to make the Sami population able to secure and develop its language, culture and social life.

IV. Developments/events/comments

Sami Act of 1987
In addition to the Constitution, the 1987 Sami Act is the most relevant document containing the Norwegian policy towards the Sami. It emphasizes the responsibility of the State to create conditions enabling the Sami people to preserve and to develop their language, culture and way of life. This Act, *inter alia*, contains provisions on the establishment of an administrative area for the Sami language in which certain rights and duties concerning the use of the Sami language in public affairs shall apply.

Education
In cooperation with the Sami Parliament in 1997 a Sami curriculum was implemented for primary and lower secondary schools, which is comparable to the national curriculum, but is based on the Sami culture. Since the introduction of the Sami curriculum the number of pupils choosing Sami-language education has been increasing.

The 1998 Education Act passed by the Storting (entry into force on 1 August 1999) provides the Sami Parliament with the authority to decide in educational matters and assures all Sami pupils throughout Norway the right to language education in their own language in primary and secondary schools (attended by 33,100 pupils during the 1997/98 school year). If at least 10 pupils in the community speak Sami, the pupils belonging to the Sami minority have the right to receive all education in their mother tongue.

In 1996 the right to three hours a week tuition in Finnish was introduced upon the condition that there are at least three pupils who require such tuition.

Media
Annually there are 1,359 hours of radio programmes and 34 hours of TV programmes in the Sami language provided by the Norwegian Broadcasting Corporation. In addition there are six local radio stations broadcasting in the Sami language. The Sami population also have three newspapers and one periodical publication (in 1997).

For other immigrant communities there are 10 local radio stations and 11 newspapers published in languages of the immigrant population (five in Urdu, two in Hindi, one each in Tamil, Finnish, Polish and Chinese).

POLAND

I. Demographic situation

Population (1994): Total 38,654,561. Minority groups: Germans 750,000-1,100,000 (1.9-2.8%); Ukrainians 350,000-500,000 (0.9-1.3%); Belarusians 200,000-300,000 (0.51-0.8%); Others Roma (15,000), Lithuanians (10,000-30,000), Slovaks (10,000-20,000), Czechs (5,000), Greeks and Macedonians (2,000) (less than 0.1%).

Languages: Polish.

II. International obligations

Article 87 of the 1997 Constitution provides that sources of universally binding law of the Republic of Poland shall be: the Constitution, statutes, ratified international agreements, and regulations. At the same time, according to Article 91 paragraph 1, after the promulgation of an international agreement in the Journal of Laws of the Republic of Poland, such an agreement shall constitute part of the domestic legal order, meaning that Polish citizens may refer to norms contained in the ratified international treaties and the courts are obliged to apply them. In the case of a conflict of norms, international agreements have precedence over a statutory norm.

United Nations
- International Covenant on Civil and Political Rights (signature 2 March 1967, ratification 18 March 1977)
- First Optional Protocol (accession 7 November 1991)
- International Covenant on Economic, Social and Cultural Rights (signature 2 March 1967, ratification 18 March 1977)

Council of Europe
- Member (29 November 1991)
- ECHR (signature 26 November 1991, ratification 19 January 1993)
- Not a party to the Charter for Regional or Minority Languages
- Framework Convention for the Protection of National Minorities (signature 1 February 1995)

Bilateral agreements
- 1991 – with the Czech and Slovak Federation (both the Czech Republic and Slovakia are successors to the Treaty)
- 1991 – with the Federal Republic of Germany
- 1992 – with the Russian Federation
- 1992 – with Belarus
- 1992 – with the Czech Republic, on good neighbour relations, solidarity and friendly cooperation
- 1994 – with the Czech Republic, on cross-border cooperation
- 1994 – with Lithuania

III. National legislation

Constitution (2 April 1997)

Article 27
Polish shall be the official language in the Republic of Poland. This provision shall not infringe upon national minority rights resulting from ratified international agreements

Article 35
1. The Republic of Poland shall ensure Polish citizens belonging to national or ethnic minorities the freedom to maintain and develop their own language, to maintain customs and traditions, and to develop their own culture.
2. National and ethnic minorities shall have the right to establish educational and cultural institutions, institutions designed to protect religious identity, as well as to participate in the resolution of matters connected with their cultural identity.

Article 233
2. Limitation of the freedoms and rights of persons and citizens only by reason of race, gender, language, faith or lack of it, social origin, ancestry or property shall be prohibited.

IV. Developments/events/comments

The Act on the Use of the Polish Language, which was approved by the Sejm in 1999 acknowledges that the official language in Poland is Polish. The use of minority languages is be regulated by a separate act, i.e. a 1998 Draft Law on National Minorities. The later also includes a chapter on the use of minority languages providing for the freedom to use one's own language in private and public affairs; to use one's own name as it is spelled and pronounced in the minority language; to display in one's own minority language information of a private nature visible to the public; as well as the right to study one's own native language and to be instructed in it (Articles 8-12).

Administrative and judicial procedures
In administrative and judicial procedures Polish laws ensure the possibility of translation for non-Polish defendants and for the use of an interpreter. However, whether non-Polish-speaking participants in proceedings also include members belonging to a Polish minority is not quite clear.

Places-names and topographical signs
None of the legal acts and documents in force in Poland allow for displaying place-names and topographical signs in a minority language. It seems that this

situation will remain in the future as the possibility of displaying bilingual names of villages and places is not under consideration by the Polish authorities.

Education

According to the 1991 Act on the Educational System, persons belonging to minorities have the right to learn and to obtain instruction in their own language. Three types of schools may be organized for learning one's own language: (a) schools with additional classes in the native language in question (on, for example, Polish literature and history); (b) bilingual schools (kindergartens) in which both Polish and the minority language are equally taught; (c) schools which provide for obligatory lessons in the native language; and (d) additional native language study organized for pupils from different schools.

There are a multitude of problems with respect to education in minority languages, one of the most significant being the lack of textbooks and teachers who are adequately trained

PORTUGAL

I. Demographic situation

Population (1994): Total 9,800,000. Minority groups: Azoreans 350,000 (3.6%); Madeirans 300,000 (3.0%); Africans 45,000 (0.5%); Roma/Gypsies 40,000-50,000 (0.4-0.5%); Brazilians 11,000 (0.1%); Asians 4,000 (less than 0.1%).

Languages: Portuguese.

II. International obligations

Article 8 of the 1976 Constitution states that the rules and principles of general or ordinary international law are an integral part of Portuguese law. Rules provided for in international conventions duly ratified or approved, following their official publication, apply under municipal law as long as they remain internationally binding with respect to the Portuguese State. Rules laid down by the competent organs of international organizations to which Portugal belongs, apply directly under municipal law insofar as the constitutive treaties provide to that effect.

United Nations
- International Covenant on Civil and Political Rights (signature 7 October 1976, ratification 15 June 1978)
- First Optional Protocol (signature 1 August 1978, ratification 3 May 1983)
- International Covenant on Economic, Social and Cultural Rights (signature 7 October 1976, ratification 31 July 1978)

Council of Europe
- Member (22 September 1976)
- ECHR (signature 22 September 1976, ratification 9 November 1978)
- Not a party to the Charter for Regional or Minority Languages
- Framework Convention for the Protection of National Minorities (signature 1 February 1995)

III. National legislation

Constitution (2 April 1976)

Article 9
The basic tasks of the State are:
(f) To secure training on and constant valorization of the Portuguese language, to defend its use and promote its international circulation.

Article 13
2. No one is privileged, favored, injured, deprived of any right, or exempt from any duty because of his ancestry, sex, race, language, territory of origin, religion, political or ideological convictions, education, economic situation, or social condition.

Article 74
3. In the implementation of its educational policy it is a State duty to:
(h) Secure for emigrants' children the teaching of the Portuguese language and access to Portuguese culture.

ROMANIA

I. Demographic situation

Population (census 1992): Total 20,352,980 (89.4%); Magyars 1,620,199 (7.1%); Gypsies 409,723 (1.8%); Germans 119,436 (0.5%); Others 257,064 (1.2%); Not declared 1,047 (under 0.1%);

Other estimates: Roma up to 1,800,000 (7.9%).

Languages: Romanian, Hungarian, German, Romani, Ukrainian (Ruthene), Lipovan (Russian).

II. International obligations

International treaties ratified by the Romanian Parliament are part of national law. According to Article 20 of the Romanian Constitution constitutional provisions concerning citizens' rights and liberties shall be interpreted and enforced in conformity with the Universal Declaration of Human Rights and the Covenants and other treaties to which Romania is a party. In case of inconsistencies between the covenants and treaties on fundamental human rights and internal laws, the international regulations will have priority.

United Nations
- International Covenant on Civil and Political Rights (signature 27 June 1968, ratification 9 December 1974)
- First Optional Protocol (accession 20 July 1993)
- International Covenant on Economic, Social and Cultural Rights (signature 27 June 1968, ratification 9 December 1974)

Council of Europe
- Member (7 October 1993)
- ECHR (signature 7 October 1993, ratification 20 June 1994)
- Charter for Regional or Minority Languages (signature 17 July 1995)
- Framework Convention for the Protection of National Minorities (signature 1 February 1995, ratification 11 May 1995, entry into force 1 February 1998)

Bilateral treaties
- 1996 – with Hungary, Treaty with Romania on understanding, cooperation and neighbourliness
- 1997 – with Ukraine, Treaty on the relations of neighbourliness and cooperation

Other treaties
- 1923 – Treaty of Lausanne (Section III, Articles 37-45)
- 1920 – Treaty of Trianon (Section VI, Articles 47, 54-60)

III. National legislation

Constitution (8 December 1991)

Article 4 – Unity of people and equality among citizens:
2. Romania is the common and indivisible homeland of all its citizens, without any discrimination on account of race, nationality, ethnic origin, language, religion, sex, opinion, political adherence, property or social origin.

Article 6 – Right to identity:
1. The State recognises and guarantees the right of persons belonging to national minorities, to the preservation, development and expression of their ethnic, cultural, linguistic and religious identity.
2. The protecting measures taken by the Romanian State for the preservation, development and expression of the identity of the persons belonging to national minorities shall conform to the principles of equality and non-discrimination in relation to the other Romanian citizens.

Article 13
In Romania, the official language is Romanian.

Article 23
5. Any person detained or arrested shall be promptly informed, in a language he understands, of the grounds for his detention or arrest, and notified of the charges against him, as soon as practicable; the notification of the charges shall be made only in the presence of a lawyer of his own choosing or appointed ex officio.

Article 32 – Right to education:
2. Education of all grades shall be in Romanian. Education may also be conducted in a foreign language of international use, under the terms laid down by law.
3. The right of persons belonging to national minorities to learn their mother tongue and their right to be educated in this language are guaranteed; the ways to exercise these rights shall be regulated by law.

Chapter VI – Juridical Authority

Article 127 – Right to have an interpreter:
1. Procedure shall be conducted in Romanian.

2. Citizens belonging to national minorities, as well as persons who cannot understand or speak Romanian have the right to take cognisance of all acts and files of the case, to speak before the Court and formulate conclusions, through an interpreter; in criminal trials, this right shall be ensured free of charge.

Article 148
1. The provisions of this Constitution with regard to the national, independent, unitary and indivisible character of the Romanian State, the Republican form of government, territorial integrity, independence of the judiciary, political pluralism and official language shall not be subject to revision.

IV. Developments/events/comments

Education
Persons belonging to minorities have the right to study and receive instruction in their mother tongue at all levels and in all forms of education. The 1995 Law on Education provides for the possibility to establish classes, sections or schools teaching in minority languages, which will not prejudice the learning of the official language. Pupils belonging to national minorities shall be granted, upon request and according to the legal provisions, instruction in the mother tongue and literature, as well as the history and traditions of the respective national minority, as a subject of study. Upon request the history and traditions of national minorities shall be taught in the mother tongue at the secondary level of education. In vocational, technical, economic, administrative, agricultural, forestry as well as in post-secondary education training is provided in Romanian, ensuring however, as far as possible, the learning of specialist terminology in the mother tongue. It is also possible, upon request and in accordance with the Law, to establish in public university education, sections and groups with tuition in the mother tongue in order to train the necessary staff for teaching and cultural-artistic activities. Although the Law provides that entrance and graduation examinations are taken at all levels of education in Romanian, it is also possible for them to be taken in the mother tongue in schools, classes, and specialist groups in which teaching is provided in the respective mother tongue.[12]

On request and under the terms of the Law, the study of the mother tongue and additional literature shall be provided in schools with Romanian as the teaching language to those pupils belonging to national minorities. The study of the mother tongue shall begin in the first class of primary school, but can also commence later by joining the ongoing programme if knowledge at the respective level can be proved by taking a written and oral language test.

One of the reasons why Romania has refused to establish a university in Hungarian is the absence of international standards in the field, as none of the existing international agreements to which Romania is a party, include the

---

[12] Law on Education No. 84/1995, Chapter XII.

establishment of State universities in the mother tongue as one of their standards.[13]

In the letter addressed to the Romanian Minister for Foreign Affairs, the High Commissioner on National Minorities[14] expressed the view that the revised Law on Education should not contain a provision excluding the possibility of a State-funded university with education in a minority language. At the same time he suggested setting up a commission of independent experts which could analyse whether there would be such a need for one or more minorities.

Judicial procedures

In addition to Article 127 of the Constitution, the Law on Local Public Administration[15] provides that in territorial-administrative units where national minorities represent a significant part of the population, decisions (of the local councils) shall be publicly announced to the citizens in their own languages.

In addition, there is the right of citizens belonging to national minorities to address the authorities of the local public administration in their mother tongue, whereas petitions which can be submitted may be written in their own language and accompanied by a translation in the Romanian language. The services of an interpreter shall be used in case the representative or the employee of the public authority does not know the language of the respective minority.

National bodies

Established in 1993 by the Romanian Government, the Council for National Minorities consists of representatives of both national minorities and some ministries. Its aim is 'to keep itself informed about and settle specific problems of persons belonging to national minorities' (Article 1 of the Rules of Procedure, approved by the Council in 1993).

RUSSIAN FEDERATION

I. Demographic situation

Population (1992): Total 148,100,000. Minority groups: Tatars 5,522,000 (3.7%); Ukrainians 4,363,000 (2.9%); Chuvash 1,774,000 (1.2%); Baskirs 1,345,000 (0.9%); Belarusians 1,206,000 (0.8%); Moldovans 1,073,000 (0.7%); Chechens 899,000 (0.6%); Germans 842,000 (0.6%); Others 7,762,000 (5.2%).

---

[13] Council of Europe, Romania, Shadow Report: October 1999, ACFC/INF(98)1.
[14] Letter of the OSCE HCNM dated 2 March 1998 (Ref. 730/98).
[15] No. 69/November 26,1991 modified and complemented by Law No. 24/April 12, 1996.

Languages: Russian, others.[16]

II. International obligations

Article 15 paragraph 4, of the 1993 Constitution stipulates that the commonly recognized principles and norms of international law and the international treaties of the Russian Federation shall be a component part of its legal system. If an international treaty of the Russian Federation stipulates rules other than those stipulated by law, the rules of the international treaty shall apply.

United Nations
- International Covenant on Civil and Political Rights (signature 18 March 1968, ratification 16 October 1973)
- First Optional Protocol (accession 1 October 1991)
- International Covenant on Economic, Social and Cultural Rights (signature 18 March 1968, ratification 16 October 1973)

Council of Europe
- Member (28 February 1996)
- ECHR (signature 28 February 1996, ratification 5 May 1998)
- Not a party to the Charter for Regional or Minority Languages
- Framework Convention for the Protection of National Minorities (signature 28 February 1996, ratification 21 August 1998, entry into force 1 December 1998)

Bilateral agreements
- 1992 – with Poland
- 1995 – with Kazakstan
- 1995 – with Kyrgyzstan
- 1995 – with Turkmenistan

III. National legislation

Constitution (12 December 1993)

Article 19
2. The State shall guarantee the equality of rights and liberties regardless of sex, race, nationality, language, origin, property or employment status, residence, attitude to religion, convictions, membership of public associations or any other circumstance. Any restrictions of the rights of citizens on social, racial, national, linguistic, or religious grounds shall be prohibited.

---

[16] Though there are major minority groups living in Russia which have their own languages other than Russian, the available sources make reference only to 'Russian and other languages'.

Article 26
2. Everyone shall have the right to use his native language and to freely choose the language of communication, education, training and creative work.

Article 29
2. Propaganda or inciting social, racial, national, or religious hatred and strife is impermissible. The propaganda of social, racial, national, religious, or linguistic supremacy is forbidden.

Article 68
1. The State language of the Russian Federation throughout its territory shall be the Russian language.
2. The republics shall have the right to institute their own State languages. They shall be used alongside the State language of the Russian Federation in bodies of State power, bodies of local self-government and State institutions of the republics.
3. The Russian Federation shall guarantee all its peoples the right to preserve their native language and to create the conditions for its study and development.

IV. Developments/events/comments

One of the principles embodied in the Concept of the State National Policy approved by the Decree of the President of the Russian Federation of 15 June 1996, is the prohibition of any forms of restrictions on the rights of citizens on the grounds of social, racial, national, linguistic or religious affiliation. It also determines the principle that the development of national cultures and languages of the peoples of the Russian Federation.

Laws and regulations
On 24 July 1998 the Federal Law on the Languages of the Peoples of the Russian Federation was enacted. Each citizen of the Russian Federation is allowed to use the language he or she knows, and those who do not know the State – Russian – language or the language of the republic,[17] can use the language which they know at meetings, conferences, assemblies of State bodies, organizations, enterprises and institutions.

In the highest legislative bodies the working language is Russian. However, in their work deputies have the right to use the State languages of the republics and, if necessary, any other language spoken in Russia with its interpretation into the State language.

In addition, the Federal Law on the Guarantees of the Rights of Indigenous Small Peoples of the Russian Federation stipulates the right of Small Peoples to

---

[17] There are 89 constituent entities in the Russian Federation: 21 republics, 6 krais, 49 oblasts, 2 cities of federal significance, 1 autonomous oblast and 10 autonomous okrugs.

preserve and develop native languages, to receive and disseminate information in native languages and to establish mass media aimed at preserving and developing their culture and identity.

In areas with a compact residence of national minorities there are a number of republican laws.

Judicial procedure(s)

Judicial proceedings are in the Russian language or in the language of autonomous units (republics, oblasts, okrugs) or in the language of the majority of the population of the area in which the proceedings are taking place (Article 17 of the Code of Criminal Procedure (CCP) of the RSFSR). Statements and evidence can be given orally or in writing in the native language for which purpose a translator or interpreter shall be provided (Article 8 of the CCP). A defendant who does not know the language of the court proceedings will be provided with an interpreter. In the case of non-compliance with this provision the sentence may be repealed.

In general, the person not speaking the official language of civil proceedings, irrespective of in which capacity he or she participates in the proceedings (suspect, accused, victim, witness, civil claimant and/or defendant), will be afforded the same rights as in criminal proceedings.

Geographic names

Geographic names, inscriptions and signs can be written in the native languages of the persons making up a compact group in the areas of their residence.

Personal names

The law does not impose any limits on the rights of persons to use their surnames, first and second names in their mother tongue. Identification documents, civil registrations and other documents are issued in the State language of the republic, if so allowed by the republic's rules, together with the State language of the Russian Federation.

Media

There are more than 400 newspapers and magazines published in 59 languages of the peoples of Russia, whereas radio programmes are broadcast in 43 languages and TV programmes in 33 national languages. A number of regional TV and radio companies broadcast their programmes also in their national languages. In these cases the costs are covered by local budgets and partly through sponsors and contributions from public associations.

Education

The Law on the Languages of the Peoples of the Russian Federation provides for the rights of national minorities to preserve and develop their native languages and to receive instruction in those languages, whereas the Law on Education in the Russian Federation specifies in more detail the possibility to receive basic general education in the native language. The Ministry of Education is responsible for providing conditions for and support to all the languages of the peoples of the country as languages of education and learning. Except for peoples of the North, the constitutive units of the Russian Federation are competent in terms of decision-making with respect to educational programmes, textbooks, teacher training etc.

There is currently primary education available in 38 languages, whereas 75 different languages, including the languages of national minorities, are taught in 9,000 secondary schools throughout the country.

Education in native languages is financed by the Federal budget and other resources.

Events
In September 1997 the Chechen Parliament declared Chechen as the sole official language of the Chechen Republic. Before the declaration of independence, Russian was together with Chechen the official language of the Republic.

SAN MARINO

I. Demographic situation

Population: Total 25,000 all belonging to the same ethnic group.

Languages: Italian.

II. International obligations

According to Article 1 of Law No.59 of 8 July 1974 entitled 'Declaration on Citizens' Rights and Fundamental Principles of San Marino Constitutional Order', the Republic of San Marino implements the rules of general international law as an integral part of its constitutional order, rejects war as a means to settle disputes between States, adheres to the international conventions on human rights and freedoms and reasserts the right to political asylum.

United Nations
– International Covenant on Civil and Political Rights (accession 17 October 1985)
– First Optional Protocol (accession 17 October 1985)

- International Covenant on Economic, Social and Cultural Rights (accession 17 October 1985)

Council of Europe
- Member (16 November 1998)
- ECHR (signature 16 November 1988, ratification 22 March 1989)
- Not a party to the Charter for Regional or Minority Languages
- Framework Convention for the Protection of National Minorities (signature 11 May 1995, ratification 5 December 1996, entry into force 1 December 1998)

SLOVAK REPUBLIC

I. Demographic situation

Population (census 1994): Total 5,356,207. Minority groups: Hungarians 568,714 (10.6%); Roma 83,988 (1.6%); Czechs 51,293 (1.0%); Ruthenians 17,277 (0.3%); Ukrainians 14,314 (0.3%); Moravians, Silesians 6,361 (0.1%); Germans 5,380 (0.1%); Croats 4,000 (0.07%); Jews 3,500 ((0.06%); Poles 3,039 (0.05%); Russians 1,624 (0.02%); Bulgarians 1,400 (0.01%); Others 6,814 (0.1%).

According to some sources Slovakia has the highest proportion of Roma population in Europe, currently estimated at around 500,000 (CERD-/C/328/Add.1, of 14 December 1999, paragraph 10).

Languages: Slovak, Hungarian, Romani, German and Ruthene/Ukrainian.

II. International obligations

According to Article 11 of the Slovak Constitution international instruments on human rights and freedoms ratified by the Slovak Republic and promulgated under statutory requirements shall take precedence over national laws provided that the international treaties and agreements guarantee greater constitutional rights and freedoms.

United Nations
- International Covenant on Civil and Political Rights (succession 28 May 1993)

- First Optional Protocol (succession 28 May 1993)
- International Covenant on Economic, Social and Cultural Rights (succession 28 May 1993)

Council of Europe
- Member (30 June 1993)
- ECHR (signature 21 February 1991, ratification 18 March 1992)
- Not a party to the Charter for Regional or Minority Languages
- Framework Convention for the Protection of National Minorities (signature 1 February 1995, ratification 14 September 1995, entry into force 1 February 1998)

Bilateral treaties
- 1991 – with Poland
- 1993 – with Czech Republic, on good neighbourliness, friendly relations and co-operation
- 1995 – with Hungary, on neighbourly relations and friendly cooperation

III. National legislation

Constitution (3 September 1992)

Article 6
1. Slovak is the official language of the Slovak Republic.
2. The use of languages other than the official language in official communications shall be determined by law.

Article 12
2. Fundamental rights shall be guaranteed in the Slovak Republic to every person regardless of sex, race, colour, language, faith, religion, political affiliation or conviction, national or social origin, nationality or ethnic origin, property, birth or any other status, and no person shall be denied their legal rights, discriminated or favoured on any of these grounds.

Article 26
5. Government authorities and public administration shall be obligated to provide reasonable access to the information in the official language of their work. The terms and procedures of execution thereof shall be specified by law.

Article 34
1. Citizens of national minorities or ethnic groups in the Slovak Republic shall be guaranteed their full development, particularly the rights to promote their cultural heritage with other citizens of the same national minority or ethnic

group, receive and disseminate information in their mother tongue, form associations, and create and maintain educational and cultural institutions. Details thereof will be determined by law.
2. In addition to the right to learn the official language, the citizens of national minorities or ethnic groups shall, under conditions defined by law, also be guaranteed:
   a) the right to be educated in a minority language,
   b) the right to use a minority language in official communications,
   c) the right to participate in decision-making in matters affecting the national minorities and ethnic groups.

Article 47
2. Every person shall have the right to counsel from the outset of proceedings before any court of law, or a governmental or public authority as provided by law [...]
4. A person who claims not to know the language used in the proceedings under section 2 of this Article shall have the right to an interpreter.

IV. Developments/events/comments

The Slovak legal system does not provide a definition of national minority.

The system of legislative acts that currently relate to the protection of minorities is made up of a total of 26 legal documents, including the Constitution. A large number of these documents deal with the right of minorities to use their mother tongue. In 1999 the Law on the Use of Languages of National Minorities was adopted (No. 184/1999).

The right to use one's mother tongue at home and privately is guaranteed and is not regulated by any legislation. Some sociological surveys reveal that about 70% of the Hungarian minority use their mother tongue at home.

Personal names
The Act on Names and Surnames provides that any person born on Slovak territory may be given, in the manner and under conditions stipulated in Section 1, more than one name including foreign names, but not more than three names.[18] With respect to the surname of a female person other than of Slovak ethnic origin or nationality, it is possible to record it without the Slovak orthographic ending for female gender where the parents express such a wish. This will also be possible if a female person makes such a request at the time of recording an act of marriage in the book of marriages and if a female person makes such a request in connection with recording the decision on the change of surname pursuant to a separate law.

---

[18] No. 300/1993 Coll., Section 2, paragraph 1.

Place-names
In areas traditionally inhabited by a substantial number of persons belonging to minorities (at least 20% of the population) place-names shall be displayed in the national minority languages on free-standing traffic signs which mark the beginning and the end of the municipality.[19]

Education
Article 34, paragraph 2(a) of the Slovak Constitution provides that citizens of national minorities or ethnic groups shall, under provisions determined by law, be guaranteed the right to be educated in a minority language.

Of significance is also the Act on the System of Elementary and Secondary Schools according to which education and training will be provided in the Slovak language, but citizens of Czech, Hungarian, German, Polish and Ukrainian (Ruthenian) ethnic origin (nationality) shall to the extent necessary for the interest of their national development, also be guaranteed the right to education in their language.[20] The schools inspectorate is in charge of overseeing the implementation of the rights to and the conditions for education in minority languages and in the official language, as well as of the use of official language in the activities of schools, educational establishments and of the State school administrative bodies.[21]

Three ways of educating pupils at schools with instruction in the languages of ethnic minorities have been created:

- schools where instruction is exclusively in the language of the ethnic minority (the Hungarian ethnic minority) with the State language being a compulsory subject. These are mostly primary schools and high schools,
- schools where instruction is bilingual, i.e. in the mother tongue and in the State language (Ukrainian and German ethnic minorities), and
- schools where the mother tongue is taught as one of the subjects and other subjects are taught in the State language (partially Ukrainian, German, Roma and Ruthenian ethnic minorities).

The choice of any of these 'systems' depends on the free decision of the pupils' parents or legal custodians. The schools, as an integral constituent part of the education system of the Slovak Republic, are funded by the State budget. There are legal possibilities or also establishing private or religious schools in addition to the State schools.

At the university level students belonging to ethnic minorities have an option to choose to study the mother tongue or to study selected subjects bilingually

---

[19] Act on the Names of Municipalities in National Minority Languages, No. 191/1994 Coll., Section 1(1).
[20] No. 29/1984 Coll., Section 3(1).
[21] Decree of the Ministry of Education, Youth and Sports of the Slovak Republic on School Inspection, No. 293/1991 Coll., Section 6(1e).

(Pedagogical University in Nitra, Pedagogical Faculty and Philosophy Faculties of the P.J. Šafárik University in Prešov and the Faculty of Philosophy of Comenius University in Bratislava). For example, the revitalisation of German and Roma education systems is an expression of optimising the conditions for the free development of the identity of members of ethnic minorities in the Slovak Republic. In favourable conditions created in this manner, a codification of the Ruthenian language has occurred in the recent past and a concept for educating children of Ruthenian ethnicity has been developed.

With respect to Roma, of significance is an 'Alternative Programme for Teaching Roma Children with Special Emphasis on Improving their Slovak Language Skills' which starts during the third year of elementary schools, a scheme which was experimentally launched in September 1996. For the third and fourth grades of elementary schools the Ministry of Education in 1995 approved the publication of the textbook entitled 'Amari Alphabet – Our Alphabet' in the Roma and Slovak languages.

Cultural activities and information in minority languages
There were 149 minority associations active in Slovakia in 1998 (63 associations representing citizens with a Hungarian background, 59 Roma, 17 Ruthenian or Ukrainian, 4 German, 2 Croatian, 1 Polish, 1 Bohemian, 1 Moravian and 1 association representing citizens of Bulgarian ethnic origin).

There are a number of legal acts which provide for the right to receive and disseminate information in minority languages. In accordance with Article 34 (1) of the Slovak Constitution the Act on the Operation of Radio and Television Broadcasting (No. 268/1993 Coll.) provides in Section 9, paragraph 2(c) that the 'ex lege' operators have an obligation to produce an important proportion of programmes with the objective of preserving and developing the cultural identity of the nation, national minorities and ethnic groups of the Slovak Republic. In that sense Slovak Radio contributes to the development of national culture and cultures of national minorities living in the Slovak Republic and to conveying the cultural values of other nations.[22] Slovak Television secures, through television broadcasting in minority languages, the implementation of interests of national minorities and ethnic groups living in Slovakia. By broadcasting Slovak Television contributes to the development of national culture and cultures of national minorities living in Slovakia and to conveying the cultural values of other nations.[23]

In 1997 Slovak Radio provided in total 29,111 hours of broadcasting (SKK 26,412,642) and television 48 hours for members of national minorities (SKK 9,626,000). After the parliamentary elections in 1998 Slovak Television presented some plans for increased broadcasting time in minority languages. There are plans to have 10 minutes daily broadcasting for the Hungarian and Ruthenian minorities and to extend the broadcasting time in minority languages

---

[22] Act on Slovak Radio, No. 270/1993 Coll., Section 3(3).
[23] Act on Slovak Television No. 271/1993 Coll., Section 3 (3) respectively Section 6 (j).

to 1 hour at the weekends. In addition, there should be 30 minutes of broadcasting for the Roma minority at least once a month, and there are some proposals to broadcast in Czech, German, Serbo-Croatian and Bulgarian, whereas broadcasting for the Jewish community which is perceived more as a 'religious minority' remains an open issue.

Official communications
Based on Article 34, paragraph 2(b) of the Constitution everyone has the right to use his/her mother tongue in proceedings before the court,[24] in civil proceedings[25] and before the competent criminal authorities.[26] The use of one's mother tongue in oral hearings or other personal interviews is also provided in proceedings before the Constitutional Court. Such incurred costs will be borne by the Constitutional Court.[27]

Penal Code and the Code of Criminal Procedure
Section 198 paragraph 1 of the Slovak Penal Code determines the accountability of any person who publicly defames any nation, its language or any race.

Any person who declares that he or she does not speak the language of the proceedings has the right to use his/her mother tongue before bodies active in criminal proceedings and the right to an interpreter (Section 2, paragraph 14).

Employment
The 1996 Employment Act, the 1965 Labour Code as amended and the 1998 Social Security Act provide guarantees for the right to work, to free choice of employment, to just and favourable conditions of work, to protection against unemployment, to equal pay for equal work and to just and favourable remuneration. These rights are guaranteed to all without distinction as to race, colour, language, faith and religion, political affiliation or other conviction.

Bodies
There is no Government office for national minorities, although within some Ministries departments dealing with the issues of minorities have been established. There is, however, the Council for Nationalities of the Government of the Slovak Republic, created in 1995. Members of the Council are representatives of 11 cultural associations representing national minorities, officials of six departments and experts of the Academy of Science and scientific institutes. The Council advises the Government on draft legislation relating to minorities and serves as a forum for discussion and dialogue between the Government and minorities.

---

[24] Act on the Judiciary No. 335/91 Coll., Section 7(3).
[25] Code of Civil Procedure No. 70/1992, Section 18.
[26] Act on Criminal Court Proceedings, No. 158/1992, Section 2 (14).
[27] Act on the Organization of the Constitutional Court, proceedings before the Court and the Status of its Judges, No. 38/1993 Coll., Section 23.

SLOVENIA

I. Demographic situation

Population (census 1991): Total 2,000,000. Minority groups: Croats 54,000 (2.7%); Serbs 47,000 (2.4%); Muslims 26,700 (1.4%); Others (including Hungarians (8,500), Italians (3,000), 'unknown', and 'undeclared) 117,000 (6.0%).

Languages: Slovene, Serbo-Croat, Hungarian, Italian

II. International obligations

The 1991 Constitution of the Republic of Slovenia states in Article 8 that statutes and other legislative measures shall comply with generally accepted principles of international law and shall accord with international agreements which bind Slovenia. Proclaimed international agreements to which Slovenia adheres shall take immediate effect.

United Nations
- International Covenant on Civil and Political Rights (succession 6 July 1992)
- First Optional Protocol (accession 16 July 1993)
- International Covenant on Economic, Social and Cultural Rights (succession 6 July 1992)

Council of Europe
- Member (14 May 1993)
- ECHR (signature 14 May 1993, ratification 28 June 1994)
- Charter for Regional or Minority Languages (signature 3 July 1997, ratification 4 October 2000)
- Framework Convention for the Protection of National Minorities (signature 1 February 1995, ratification 25 March 1998, entry into force 1 July 1998)

Bilateral agreements
- 1975 – with Italy, Osimo Agreement concluded by the former Socialist Federal Republic of Yugoslavia to which Slovenia succeeded
- 1992 – with Hungary, Agreement on the rights of the Slovene national minority in Hungary and the rights of the Hungarian ethnic community in the Republic of Slovenia
- 1992 – with Hungary, friendship and cooperation
- 1992 – with Croatia and Italy, Memorandum on mutual understanding between Croatia, Italy and Slovenia on the protection of rights of the Italian minority in Croatia and Slovenia

III. National legislation

Constitution (23 December 1991 as amended on 14 July 1997)

Article 11
The official language of Slovenia shall be Slovenian. In those areas where Italian or Hungarian ethnic communities reside, the official language shall also be Italian or Hungarian.

Article 14 – Equality before the Law
In Slovenia each individual shall be guaranteed equal human rights and fundamental freedoms irrespective of national origin, race, sex, language, religion, political or other beliefs, financial status, birth, education, social status or whatever other personal circumstance. All persons shall be equal before the law.

Article 61 – Profession of National Allegiance
Each person shall be entitled to freely identify with his national grouping or ethnic community, to foster and give expression to his culture and to use his own language and script.

Article 62 – The Right to the Use of Language and Script
In order to give effect to his rights and obligations, and in all dealings with State bodies and other bodies having official functions, each person shall have the right to use his own language and script in such a manner as shall be determined by statute.

Article 64 – Special Rights of the Autochthonous Italian and Hungarian Ethnic Communities in Slovenia

1. The autochthonous Italian and Hungarian ethnic communities and their members shall be guaranteed the right to freely use their national symbols and, in order to preserve their national identity, the right to establish organizations, to foster economic, cultural, scientific and research activities, as well as activities associated with the mass media and publishing. Those two ethnic communities and their members shall have, consistent with statute, the right to education and schooling in their own languages, as well as the right to plan and develop their own curricular. The State shall determine by statute those geographical areas in which bilingual education shall be compulsory. The Italian and Hungarian ethnic communities and their members shall enjoy the right to foster contacts with the wider Italian and Hungarian communities living outside Slovenia, and with Italy and Hungary respectively. Slovenia shall give financial support and encouragement to the implementation of these rights.

2. In those areas where the Italian and Hungarian ethnic communities live, their members shall be entitled to establish autonomous organizations in order to give effect to their rights. At the request of the Italian and Hungarian ethnic communities, the State may authorize their respective autonomous organizations to carry out specific functions which are presently within the jurisdiction of the State, and the State shall ensure the provision of the Means for those functions to be effected.
3. The Italian and Hungarian ethnic communities shall be directly represented at the local level and shall also be represented in the National Assembly.
4. The status of the Italian and the Hungarian ethnic communities and the manner in which their rights may be exercised in those areas where the two ethnic communities live, shall be determined by statute. In addition, the obligations of the local self-governing communities which represent the two ethnic communities to promote the exercise of their rights, together with the rights of the members of the two ethnic communities living outside their autochthonous areas, shall be determined by statute. The rights of both ethnic communities and of their members shall be guaranteed without regard for the numerical strength of either community.
5. Statues, regulations and other legislative enactments which exclusively affect the exercise of specific rights enjoyed by the Italian or Hungarian ethnic communities under this Constitution, or affecting the status of these communities, may not be enacted without the consent of the representatives of the ethnic community or communities affected.

IV. Developments/events/comments

In mixed areas inhabited by Hungarian or Italian ethnic communities, the Hungarian or Italian languages are equal to Slovenian and can be equally used in the functioning of the administration and in judicial proceedings.

Media
The Republic co-finances radio and TV programmes.

Judicial procedures
The 1999 Code of Civil Procedure stipulates that the procedure shall be held in the officially used language, but the clients have the right to use their own language in accordance with Article 6 of the Code.

National bodies
The Commission for Ethnic Communities is a parliamentary body whose main task is to provide opinions, observations and proposals on legislative acts of importance for or concerning minorities.
   The Governmental Office of National Minorities undertakes the responsibilities of the State in the field of minorities. Its tasks are, *inter alia*, to

monitor developments and to harmonize the implementation of the legislation which is relevant for minorities; to cooperate with the organizations representing national minorities and to provide funds for their activities; as well as to prepare draft proposals for laws and other legal provisions on both national and local levels.

There is also the institution of the Ombudsman for the Protection of Human Rights established by a 1993 Law, who does not, however, deal particularly with the issue of minorities.

SPAIN

I. Demographic situation

Population (1994): Total 39,100,000. Minority groups: Catalans 6,250,000 (16.0%); Galicians 3,100,000 (7.9%); Basques 780,000 (2.0%); Roma/Gypsies 650,000-800,000 (1.7-2.0%); South and Central Americans 167,500 (0.4%); Moroccans 58,000 (0.1%); Asians 36,000 (less than 0.1%); Jews 20,000 (less than 0.1%).

Languages: Castilian (Spanish), Catalan, Valencian, Basque and Gallego (Galician).[28]

II. International obligations

Article 95, paragraphs 1 and 2, of the 1978 Constitution stipulates that the conclusion of an international treaty which contains stipulations contrary to the Constitution shall require a prior constitutional revision. The Government or either of the Chambers may request the Constitutional Court to declare whether or not such a contradiction exists. In accordance with Article 96, paragraph 1, the validly concluded international treaties once officially published in Spain shall constitute part of the internal legal order. Their provisions may only be abolished, modified, or suspended in the manner provided for in the treaties themselves or in accordance with general norms of international law.

---

[28] Under the 1978 Constitution Spain has a decentralized system of autonomous communities autonomy having been granted to 17 regions. In the regions in question the vernacular languages – Catalan, Galician and Basque – have official status.

United Nations
- International Covenant on Civil and Political Rights (signature 28 September 1976, ratification 27 April 1977)
- First Optional Protocol (accession 25 January 1985)
- International Covenant on Economic, Social and Cultural Rights (signature 28 September 1976, ratification 27 April 1977)

Council of Europe
- Member (24 November 1977)
- ECHR (24 November 1977 signature, 4 December 1979 ratification)
- Charter for Regional or Minority Languages (5 November 1992)
- Framework Convention for the Protection of National Minorities (1 February 1995 signature, 1 September 1995 ratification, 1 February 1998 entry into force)

III. National legislation

Constitution (29 December 1978)

Article 3
1. Castilian is the official Spanish language of the State. All Spaniards have the duty to know it and the right to use it.
2. The other languages of Spain will also be official in the respective autonomous communities, in accordance with their statutes.
3. The richness of the linguistic modalities of Spain is a cultural patrimony which will be the object of special respect and protection.

Article 20
3. The law shall regulate the organization and parliamentary control of the means of social communication owned by the State or any public entity and shall guarantee access to those means by significant social and political groups, respecting the pluralism of society and the various languages of Spain.

Article 148
1. The Autonomous Communities may assume jurisdiction in the following matters [...]
    17) assistance to culture, research and, as the case may be, for the teaching of the language of the Autonomous Community; [...]

IV. Developments/events/comments

The Statute of Autonomy of Catalonia, Valencia, the Balearic Islands and Aragon stipulates in Article 3 that the language in Catalonia is Catalan, which is the official language together with Spanish as the official language of the State.

The Resolution on the Situation of Languages in the Community and on the Catalan Language, adopted by the European Parliament on 11 December 1990, recognizes the identity, current validity and the use of Catalan within the context of the European Union.

Media
There are 7 official newspapers printed in Catalonia in the Catalan language. In addition, there are two TV channels and 192 local radio stations which broadcast programmes in the Catalan language.

SWEDEN

I. Demographic situation

Population (1994): Total 8,700,000. Minority groups: Finns 260,000 (3.0%); Citizens of other Nordic countries 90,000 (1.0%); Former Yugoslavs 75,500 (0.9%); Iranians 51,000 (0.6%); Turks and Kurds 35,900 (0.4%); Roma/Gypsies 15,000-20,000 (0.2%); Jews 16,000 (0.2%); Sami 15,000 (0.2%).

Languages: Swedish, Finnish.

II. International obligations

According to Chapter 10, Article 5(2), of the 1975 Swedish Constitution where it has been laid down in law that an international treaty shall have the force of Swedish law, Parliament may prescribe by a decision taken in the order laid down in paragraph 1 that any future amendment to the treaty, which is binding upon the Realm, also shall apply within the Realm.

United Nations
- International Covenant on Civil and Political Rights (signature 29 September 1967, ratification 6 December 1971)
- First Optional Protocol (signature 29 September 1967, ratification 6 December 1971)

- International Covenant on Economic, Social and Cultural Rights (signature 29 September 1967, ratification 6 December 1971)

Council of Europe
- Member (5 May 1949)
- ECHR (signature 28 November 1950, ratification 4 February 1952)
- Charter for Regional or Minority Languages (signature 9 February 2000, ratification 9 February 2000)
- Framework Convention for the Protection of National Minorities (signature 1 February 1995, ratification 9 February 2000, entry into force 1 June 2000)

III. National legislation

Constitution (1 January 1975, as amended)

Chapter 1

Article 2
4. Opportunities should be promoted for ethnic, linguistic and religious minorities to preserve and develop a cultural and social life of their own.

IV. Developments/events/comments

On the basis of the Report prepared by the Minority Language Committee, in June 1999 the Government recommended to the Swedish Parliament that the Sami, the Tornedal Finns, the Swedish Finns, the Roma and the Jews should be regarded as national minorities in accordance with the Council of Europe Framework Convention on the Protection of National Minorities. Accordingly, Sami (all varieties), Finnish, Meäkieli (Tornedal Finnish), Romany Chib (all varieties) and Yiddish should be recognized as historical, regional or minority languages in accordance with the European Charter for Regional or Minority Languages. In addition, it was proposed on the national level to include the study of the Sami language, culture and history as an optional subject. At the regional level, the Government has proposed new legislation providing for the right of individuals to use the Sami language in dealings with administrative authorities and in the courts. This will apply only to the four northern regions where the Sami language is used by a large number of individuals.

SWITZERLAND

I. Demographic situation

Population (1994): Total 7,000,000. Minority groups: French speakers 1,300,000 (18.0%) (of which Jurassiens number around 67,000); Italian-speakers 500,000 (7.0%); Former Yugoslavs 200,000 (2.8%); Portuguese 150,000 (2.1%); Spanish 120,000 (1.7%); Rhaetians/Romansh speakers 50,000 (0.7%); Roma/Gypsies 30,000-35,000 (0.4-0.5%); Jews 18,300 (0.3%).

Languages: Swiss-German, French, Italian and Romansh.

II. International obligations

Article 5, paragraph 4 of the 2000 Constitution, establishes that the Confederation and the Cantons do respect international law. Whereas in Article 166, paragraph 2, the Constitution stipulates that the Federal Parliament shall approve international treaties, with the exception of those which by statute or international treaty are within the powers of the Federal Government, it does not contain any provision providing for the primacy of international treaties over national laws.

United Nations
- International Covenant on Civil and Political Rights (18 June 1992 accession)
- Not a party to the First Optional Protocol
- International Covenant on Economic, Social and Cultural Rights (18 June 1992 accession)

Council of Europe
- Member (6 May 1963)
- ECHR (signature 21 December 1972, ratification 28 November 1974)
- Charter for Regional or Minority Languages (signature 8 October 1993, ratification 23 December 1997, entry into force 1 April 1998)
- Framework Convention for the Protection of National Minorities (signature 1 February 1995, ratification 21 October 1998, entry into force 1 February 1999)

III. National legislation

Constitution (of 14 April 1999, entered into force on 1 January 2000)

Article 4 – National Languages
The national languages are German, French, Italian, and Romansh.

Article 18 – Freedom of Language
The freedom of language is guaranteed.

Article 70 – Languages
1. The official languages of the Confederation are German, French, and Italian. Romansh shall be an official language for communicating with persons of Romansh language.
2. The Cantons shall designate their official languages. In order to preserve harmony between linguistic communities, they shall respect the traditional territorial distribution of languages, and take into account the indigenous linguistic minorities.
3. The Confederation and the Cantons shall encourage understanding and exchange between the linguistic communities.
4. The Confederation shall support the plurilingual Cantons in the fulfilment of their particular tasks.
5. The Confederation shall support the measures taken by the Cantons of Grisons and Ticino to maintain and to promote Romansh and Italian.

IV. Developments/events/comments

Languages in use
Switzerland has four official languages, which can all be used for administrative purposes. The official languages are German, French and Italian; Romansh is a national language in Switzerland, together with the other three languages. The three languages have equal protection at the federal level, which means that:

- all federal laws are published and translated into the three languages,
- all the three languages are considered equal concerning the interpretation of the contents of a statute and
- citizens can discuss and correspond with the federal authorities in all the three languages.

Romansh can, as a national language, be used as an official language for relations between the Confederation and its Romansh-speaking citizens. In the canton of Grisons Romansh is accepted as an administrative language. The Swiss Confederation provides financial support to maintain and promote the use of the Romansh and Italian languages in the cantons of Grisons and Ticino.

Judicial procedures
In Switzerland linguistic freedom is recognized by the Federal Court and two languages are used in the Swiss courts. These are German and French. Switzerland is divided into cantons. These are divided into *bezirken* or *kreisen*, and in these areas a 'court language' is appointed. Every lawsuit in this area should be done in the language of that area. In the mixed areas lawsuits are

conducted in the language of the defendant, unless the parties agree otherwise. In the cantonal courts the language to be used is the language which has been used at first instance.

The cantonal courts are allowed to change the borders of the *bezirken* and *kreisen* in such a way that homogeneity in the language of the areas in question will be maintained, even if this limits the rights of some individuals to use their own language in court. The changes should be proportional, however. They should not limit a person's freedom to use his own language further than is necessary.

Representation of linguistic minorities at the federal level
In Switzerland there is no system for the representation of minorities, in the sense that for each minority a number of seats in a national assembly are reserved. That is not necessary in Switzerland while all linguistic minorities are somehow organized as a majority within their cantons. Minority representation in federal councils is well protected by means of cantonal participation in these federal councils.

Problem of relations between the linguistic regions
According to a representative questionnaire distributed at the end of 1994, the Swiss population do not see the relations between the different language areas as a prominent problem. The Swiss do identify themselves with the Swiss Confederation.

There are some points which have to be made, however. Especially the linguistic minorities see the relations between the linguistic regions as problematic. The Romansh and Italian-speaking minorities do see a gap between the regions. The Romansh-speaking minority even see their language as a burden.

Grants for the maintenance and support of the Romansh and Italian languages and culture
On 6 October 1996 a Federal law was adopted regulating grants by the Confederation to the canton of Grison for the maintenance and the support of the Romansh and Italian languages and culture as well to the canton of Ticino for the maintenance of the Italian language and culture. The grants are aimed at supporting general measures for the maintenance and support of Romansh and Italian culture; of organizations and institutions which fulfil supraregional assignments for the maintenance and the support of the Romansh and Italian languages and culture; and, publishing activities in the Romansh and Italian-speaking part of Switzerland.

TAJIKISTAN

I. Demographic situation

Population (1994): Total 5,990,000. Minority groups: Uzbeks 1,500,000 (25.0%); Pamiri Tajiks 185,000 (3.0%); Russians fewer than 100,000 (1.7%); Tatars 84,000 (1.4%); Kyrgyz 63,800 (1.0%); Ukrainians 41,400 (0.7%); Germans 32,700 (0.5%); Turkmen 20,500 (0.3%); Koreans 13,400 (0.2%).

Languages: Tajik, Russian, Uzbek, Yagnobi, Pamiri.

II. International obligations

Article 10 of the 1994 Constitution of Tajikistan establishes, *inter alia*, that international legal documents recognized by Tajikistan are a constituent part of the legal system of the Republic. If Republican laws do not conform to the recognized international legal documents, the norms of the international documents shall be applied. International laws and documents recognized by Tajikistan apply following official publication.

United Nations
- International Covenant on Civil and Political Rights (accession 4 January 1999)
- First Optional Protocol (accession 4 January 1999)
- International Covenant on Economic, Social and Cultural Rights (accession 4 January 1999)

Council of Europe
- Not a member of the Council of Europe
- Not a party to the Charter for Regional or Minority Languages
- Not a party to the Framework Convention for the Protection of National Minorities

III. National legislation

Constitution (6 November 1994)

Article 2
The State language of Tajikistan is Tajik. Russian is a language of inter-ethnic communication. All nations and peoples residing on the territory of the republic have the right to use freely their native languages.

Article 17
All persons are equal before the law and the courts. The government guarantees the rights and freedoms of every person regardless of ethnicity, race, sex,

language, faith, political beliefs, education, or social or property status. Men and women have equal rights.

Article 65
The President is elected for a term of five years by the citizens of Tajikistan on the basis of general, equal, and direct voting rights by secret ballot. Any citizen who is age 35 to 65, is fluent in the State language, and has been resident on the territory of Tajikistan for at least the previous ten years may be nominated as a candidate for the office of President of the Republic. A candidate for the office of President of the Republic is any person who has so registered and has collected the signatures of nomination of no less than five percent of the voters. No one may be President for more than two consecutive terms.

Article 88
Judges review cases both on panels and individually. The judicial process is exercised on the basis of the principle of the adversarial nature and equality of parties. Hearings in all courts are open, except in cases anticipated by law. Judicial proceedings are carried out in either the State language or in the language of the majority of the people of a given locality. Persons who do not speak the language of the judicial proceedings are provided with the services of an interpreter.

IV. Developments/events/comments

The draft Constitution, published in 1992, reinforced the 1989 Language Law aimed at establishing Tajik as the sole State language by 1996, with Russian only used in inter-ethnic communications. This caused protests from non-Tajik ethnic national communities, among which the Uzbeks make up 25% of the total population. Whereas in education instruction is given in Tajik, Russian and Uzbek, in administration Tajik is the official language.

Media and education
Since 1992 the number of newspapers, TV broadcasts and schools in the Uzbek language has significantly decreased. TV and radio broadcasts are mostly in the Tajik and Russian languages. Russian is the language of inter-ethnic communication and is widely used in government. On the other hand, Uzbek, which is spoken by 25% of the total population, has no official status.

TURKEY

I. Demographic situation

Population (1993): Total 59,800,000; Kurds 13,000,000 (22%); Alevis 10,000,000 (17%); Zaza language group 3,000,000 (5%); Balkan origin 2,000,000 (3.3%); Circassian and other Caucasus groups 1,300,000 (2.2%); Arabs 1,200,000 (2%); Turkoman groups 500,000 (0.8%).

Languages: Turkish (the only official language), Kirmanji, Zaza Kurdish, Laz, Arabic.

II. International obligations

As established by Article 90 of 1982 Constitution the ratification of treaties concluded with foreign States and international organizations on behalf of the Republic of Turkey, shall be subject to adoption by the Turkish Grand National Assembly by law approving the ratification. International agreements duly put into effect carry the force of law. No appeal to the Constitutional Court can be made with regard to these agreements, on the ground that they are unconstitutional.

United Nations
- International Covenant on Civil and Political Rights (signature 15 August 2000)
- Not a party to the First Optional Protocol
- International Covenant on Economic, Social and Cultural Rights (signature 15 August 2000)

Council of Europe
- Member (13 April 1950)
- ECHR (signature 4 November 1950, ratification 18 May 1954)
- Not a party to the Charter for Regional or Minority Languages
- Not a party to the Framework Convention for the Protection of National Minorities

Other treaties
- 1923 – Treaty of Lausanne (Section III, Articles 37-45)

III. National legislation

Constitution (9 November 1982)

Article 3
The Turkish State, with its territory and nation, is an indivisible entity. Its language is Turkish.

Article 10
All individuals are equal without any discrimination before the law, irrespective of language, race, colour, sex, political opinion, philosophical belief, religion and sect, or any such considerations.

Article 14
None of the rights and freedoms embodied in the Constitution shall be exercised with the aim of violating the indivisible integrity of the State with its territory and nation, of endangering the existence of the Turkish State and Republic, of destroying fundamental rights and freedoms, of placing the government of the State under the control of an individual or a group of people, or establishing the hegemony of one social class over others, or creating discrimination on the basis of language, race, religion or sect, or of establishing by any other means a system of government based on these concepts and ideas.

Article 26
[...] No language prohibited by law shall be used in the expression and dissemination of thought. Any written or printed documents, phonograph records, magnetic or video tapes, and other means of expression used in contravention of this provision shall be seized by a duly issued decision of a judge or, in cases where delay is deemed prejudicial, by the competent authority designated by law. The authority issuing the seizure order shall notify the competent judge of its decision within twenty-four hours. The judge shall decide on the matter within three days.

Article 28
The press is free, and shall not be censored. The establishment of a printing house shall not be subject to prior permission or the deposit of a financial guarantee.
    Publication shall not be made in any language prohibited by law.

Article 42
No language other than Turkish shall be taught as a mother tongue to Turkish citizens at any institutions of training or education. Foreign languages to be taught in institutions of training and education and the rules to be followed by schools conducting training and education in a foreign language shall be determined by law. The provisions of international treaties are reserved.

IV. Developments/events/comments

Political parties, election laws, and associations
In Law No. 2820 on Political Parties, adopted on 26 April 1982, there are a number of provisions which are significant for minorities and minority languages. Firstly, Article 31(a) prohibits political parties from claiming that there are minorities within the country of the Turkish Republic, based on differences of race, religion, sect, culture and language. Of certain relevance are also Articles 5 and 12 of the Law which establish that political parties cannot be used with the aim of creating discrimination with respect to, *inter alia*, languages, and that party regulations cannot contain provisions pertaining to the language, race, sex, religion etc. of those who apply for membership. Similarly, Article 82 of the Law on Political Parties stipulates that political parties are not allowed to claim that minorities exist in the Turkish Republic based on national, religious, confessional, racial, or language differences, neither can they use a language other than Turkish in writing and printing the party's statute or programme, at congresses, at open-air meetings or indoor gatherings. At meetings and in propaganda one cannot use or distribute placards, pictures, phonograph records, voice and visual tapes, brochures and statements written in a language other than Turkish; one also cannot remain indifferent to these actions and acts committed by others. However, it is possible to translate party statutes and programmes into foreign languages other than those forbidden by law.

Similarly, the Law Concerning Fundamental Provisions on Elections and Voter Registries (No. 298 of 26 April 1961) in Article 58 forbids the use of any language or script other than Turkish in propaganda disseminated on radio or television as well as in other election propaganda.

Articles 5 and 76 of the Act on Associations (2908/1983) prohibits the formation of associations claiming that there are minorities based on differences of race, religion, sect, culture and language within the country of the Turkish Republic, or creating minorities by protecting, advancing or spreading languages and cultures other than the Turkish language and culture.

Demographic names
The Law on Provincial Administration (No. 5442, adopted on 10 June 1949 and amended in 1959 (No. 7267)), provides in Article 2/d/2 that village names that are not Turkish and give rise to confusion are to be changed within the shortest possible time by the Ministry of the Interior after receiving the opinion of the Provincial Permanent Committee.

Media
The Law Concerning the Founding and Broadcasts of Television and Radio (No. 3984 of 13 April 1994) stipulates in Article 4 paragraph (t), that radio and television broadcasts will be in Turkish; however, for the purpose of teaching or

of imparting news those foreign languages that have made a contribution to the development of universal cultural and scientific works can be used.

Education
According to Article 4 of the Fundamental Act on National Education (1739/1973) educational institutions are open to all, with no distinction as to language, race, gender and religion.

In addition, there is also a Law on Foreign Language Education and Teaching (No. 2923) which in Article 2 paragraphs (a) and (c) establishes that the mother tongue of Turkish citizens cannot be any language other than Turkish. However, by taking into consideration the view of the National Security Council, the Council of Ministers determines which foreign languages can be taught in Turkey. According to Decision No. 92/2788 of 1992 the Council of Ministers decided on 4 March 1992 that in official and private courses education and teaching may be in the following languages: English, French, German as well as Russian, Italian, Spanish, Arabic, Japanese, and Chinese.

TURKMENISTAN

I. Demographic situation

Population (1993): Total 4,254,000. Minority groups: Russians 404,100 (9.5%); Uzbeks 382,900 (9.0%); Kazakhs 106,350 (2.5%); Volga Tatars 39,000 (0.9%); Ukrainians 35,600 (0.8%); Azeris 35,000 (0.8%); Armenians 31,800 (0.7%); Baluchis 28,300 (0.7%).

Languages: Turkmen, Russian, Uzbek.

II. International obligations

According to Article 6 of the 1992 Constitution, Turkmenistan, *inter alia*, recognizes the primacy of generally recognized norms of international law.

United Nations
– International Covenant on Civil and Political Rights (accession 1 May 1997)
– First Optional Protocol (accession 1 May 1997)
– International Covenant on Economic, Social and Cultural Rights (accession 1 May 1997)

Council of Europe
- Not a member of the Council of Europe
- Not a party to the Charter for Regional or Minority Languages
- Not a party to the Framework Convention for the Protection of National Minorities

Bilateral agreements
- 1995 – with the Russian Federation, Treaty on the legal status of the citizens of the Russian Federation permanently residing in the territory of Turkmenistan, and the citizens of Turkmenistan permanently residing in the territory of the Russian Federation

III. National legislation

Constitution (18 May 1992)

Article 13
The State language of Turkmenistan shall be the Turkmen language.
All citizens of Turkmenistan shall be guaranteed the right to use their native language.

Article 17
Turkmenistan shall guarantee the equality of the rights and freedoms of citizens, as well as the equality of citizens before the law irrespective of nationality, origin, property status or official position, place of residence, language, attitude towards religion, political beliefs, or political party membership.

Article 106
Judicial procedure shall be conducted in the State language. Persons participating in the case who do not speak the language of the judicial procedure shall be ensured the right to acquaint themselves with the materials of the case and to participate in judicial action, and also the right to testify in court in their native language.

IV. Developments/events/comments

The 1990 Law on Language establishes the Turkmen language as the State language. The Russian language has the status of a language for inter-ethnic communication and can be used in public authorities, enterprises, institutions, education, science, culture and the administration of justice.

Article 18 (2) of the Citizenship Law of Turkmenistan of 30 September 1992 contains the requirement that a person applying for Turkmenistan citizenship must know the State language of Turkmenistan sufficiently well for the purpose of communication.

UKRAINE

I. Demographic situation

Population (1998): Total 50,500,000. Minority groups: Russians 11,400,000 (22.1%); Jews 486,300 (0.9%); Belarusians 440,000 (0.9%); Moldavians 342,500 (0.6%); Bulgarians 233,800 (0.5%); Poles 219,200 (0.4%); Hungarians 163,100 (0.3%); Romanians 134,800 (0.3%). According to some estimates in 1998 over 250,000 Crimean Tatars returned to the Autonomous Republic of Crimea. There are thirteen groups – Greeks, Armenians, Gypsies, Germans, Azerbaijanis, Gagauzes, Georgians, Chivashes, Uzbeks, Mordvinians, Lithuanians and Kazakhs – which count between 10,000-100,000 persons each.

Languages: Ukrainian, Russian.

II. International obligations

Article 9 of the 1996 Ukrainian Constitution stipulates that international treaties that are in force, and it has been agreed by the Verkhovna Rada of Ukraine that they will be binding, are part of the national legislation of Ukraine.

United Nations
- International Covenant on Civil and Political Rights (signature 20 March 1968, ratification 12 November 1973)
- First Optional Protocol (accession 25 July 1991)
- International Covenant on Civil and Political Rights (signature 20 March 1968, ratification 12 November 1973)

Council of Europe
- Member (9 November 1995)
- ECHR (signature 9 November 1995, ratification 11 September 1997)
- Charter for Regional or Minority Languages (signature 2 May 1996)
- Framework Convention for the Protection of National Minorities (signature 15 September 1995, ratification 26 January 1998, entry into force 1 May 1998)

Bilateral agreements
- 1991 – with Hungary, Treaty on neighbourliness and cooperation
- 1992 – with Hungary, Statement on the principles of cooperation in the field of minority rights

Ukraine has concluded bilateral agreements relevant to the protection of minorities with the Russian Federation and Romania. In addition, there are agreements concluded at government level on issues of international relations and protection of national minorities. These agreements have been entered into force with Moldova, Lithuania and the Russian Federation.

III. National legislation

Constitution (28 June 1996)

Article 10
The State language of Ukraine is the Ukrainian language.
The State ensures the comprehensive development and functioning of the Ukrainian language in all spheres of social life throughout the entire territory of Ukraine.
In Ukraine, the free development, use and protection of Russian, and other languages of national minorities of Ukraine, is guaranteed.
The State promotes the learning of languages of international communication.
The use of languages in Ukraine is guaranteed by the Constitution of Ukraine and is determined by law.

Article 53
[...] Citizens who belong to national minorities are guaranteed in accordance with the law the right to receive instruction in their native language, or to study their native language in State and communal educational establishments and through national cultural societies.

Article 92
The following are determined exclusively by the laws of Ukraine:
3. the rights of indigenous peoples and national minorities;
4. the procedure for the use of languages;

Article 103
[...] A citizen of Ukraine who has attained the age of thirty-five, has the right to vote, has resided in Ukraine for the past ten years prior to the day of elections, and has command of the State language, may be elected as the President of Ukraine.

Article 138
The competence of the Autonomous Republic of Crimea comprises:
8. ensuring the operation and development of the State language and national languages and cultures in the Autonomous Republic of Crimea; protection and use of historical monuments;

Article 148
A citizen of Ukraine who has attained the age of forty on the day of appointment, has a higher legal education and professional experience of no less

than ten years, has resided in Ukraine for the last twenty years, and has command of the State language, may be a judge of the Constitutional Court of Ukraine.

Foundations of the Legislation of Ukraine on Culture

Article 4
Equal rights and possibilities concerning using languages of all national minorities who reside in the territory of Ukraine, in the field of culture, are guaranteed by the State.

The Law on National Minorities in Ukraine

Article 2
Ukraine's citizens of all nationalities are obliged to observe the Constitution and laws of Ukraine, to defend its State sovereignty and territorial integrity, to respect languages, cultures, traditions, customs, religious originality of the Ukrainian peoples and all national minorities.

Article 6
The State guarantees all national minorities the rights for the national and cultural autonomy: using and studying a native language or learning a native language in State educational institutions or through national cultural societies, development of national cultural traditions, using national symbols, celebration of national holidays, professing own religion, satisfaction of needs in literature, arts, mass media, creation of national cultural and educational institutions. Monuments of history and culture of national minorities in the territory of Ukraine are protected by the law.

Article 8
[...] in the work of State authorities, public associations, as well as enterprises, institutions and organizations, situated in the places where the majority of population is formed by a national minority, its language may be used along with the State Ukrainian language.

Article 12
Each citizen of Ukraine has the right to use his (her) national surname, first name and patronymic. The citizens have the right of renewing, in the established order, their national surname, first name and patronymic.

IV. Developments/comments

Citizenship
The Citizenship Law of Ukraine adopted on 8 October 1991 in Article 17 (3) provides that sufficient knowledge of the Ukrainian language for communication is a condition for admission to Ukrainian citizenship.

Judicial proceedings
According to Article 18 of the Law on Languages in Ukraine national minorities the right to use their own language in legal proceedings, i.e. that legal proceedings may be conducted in the national language of the majority of the population residing in one locality or another. Documents in one's own language and an interpreter will be provided for persons taking part in criminal and/or civil legal proceedings

Education
Every child has the right to be educated in his/her native language (Article 25 of the Law on Languages in Ukraine). For this purpose a network of pre-school educational institutions and schools with teaching also in minority languages has been established.

The equality of all citizens in the enjoyment of the right to education and to free education in all State schools has been proclaimed. Additional measures have also been undertaken for providing education in and on minority languages. About 170 official publications have been issued in 19 minority languages. In addition, the State organs organize and finance the training of educational staff for teaching in minority languages. There are also some private institutions providing for the education of minority-schools professionals.

The 1998/99 statistics reveals that out of total of 21,246 educational institutions with 4,421,265 pupils there were: 2,561 (2,313,901 pupils) Russian educational institutions; 108 (27,776 pupils) Romanian; 65 (21,214 pupils) Hungarian; 18 (4,506 pupils) Moldavian; 6 (4,071 pupils) Crimean Tatar; and 3 (1,109 pupils) Polish. In addition, there were 2,469 mixed educational institutions of general education.

Toponyms
According to Articles 35 and 38 of the Law on Languages, national minorities have the right to inscribe toponyms, signboards, legends and other information in their own language. Since the beginning of the 1990s some places have had their historic national names returned to them.

National bodies
A special State Committee for Nationalities and Migration has been established with its task being, *inter alia*, to participate in the development and implementation of State policy; to prepare drafts of relevant laws and other legislative acts; to analyse the situation of minorities in Ukraine; and to assist in

providing for effective control of the implementation of national legislation relevant for minorities.

On 18 May 1999 the President of Ukraine, Leonid Kuchma, passed a Decree on the Establishment of the Council of the Representatives of the Crimean Tatar People, aimed at solving the politico-legal, socio-economic, cultural and other issues connected with the adaptation and integration of the Crimean Tatar People into the Ukrainian community.

Media

In the period 1996-1999 around 350 publications in 22 languages of national minorities were published.

Article 6 of the Law on National Minorities and Article 33, Part IV of the Law on Languages in Ukraine provide for the right to use national minority languages as well as the languages of other nationalities in the mass media (radio, TV, press). Every year 1,229 hours on TV and 1,988 hours on radio are broadcast in minority languages. The amount of hours in the various minority languages are proportionally determined according to the concentration of minorities in certain regions.

Statistics reveal that in January 1998 there were 1,300 newspapers and periodicals in Russian and around 95 in other minority languages.

Events

In January 1999 the school of Georgian language was opened in Sumy, the capital of the Sumskii region of Ukraine. Children will study their native language, the history of Georgia, they will learn national traditional dances, songs and at the same time will study Ukrainian at a deeper level than in other secondary schools of the city. Minorities from Armenia and Azerbaijan also decided to establish schools to study their native languages.

Ukrainian-Russian talks

During his visit to Ukraine, from 15-18 July 1999, the Russian Prime Minister, Sergei Stepashin, at a meeting held with the Ukrainian President, Leonid Kuchma, called for changes to Ukraine's legislation in order to make Ukrainian-Russian dual citizenship possible and to confer official status on the Russian language in Ukraine, along with Ukrainian. President Kuchma turned down both proposals. As he told a gathering of journalists from Ukraine's regions: 'there must be one State language in Ukraine – Ukrainian. An ever-larger number of (Russian) people in Ukraine accept of their own accord to learn Ukrainian. There are no fewer Ukrainians in Russia than there are Russians in Ukraine, yet there are no Ukrainian schools and newspapers in Russia (though there are Russian ones in Ukraine)'. President Kuchma added that Crimea only had four elementary schools and one secondary school with complete Ukrainian-language instruction. At the same time the Ukrainian President reaffirmed his 'categorical opposition to coercive methods of introducing the Ukrainian language into official use' in the Crimea and other Russified regions – a position held across

Ukraine's political spectrum. But he also underscored that he 'never promised to anyone that he would introduce a second official language in Ukraine'.

UNITED KINGDOM

I. Demographic situation

Population (1994): Total 57,900,000. Minority groups: Scots 5,100,000 (8.8%); Welsh 2,000,000 (3.5%); Northern Irish 1,500,000 (2.6%); Indians 840,800 (1.5%); Afro-Caribbeans 449,100 (0.9%); Pakistanis 475,800 (0.8%); Jews 300,000 (0.5%); Black Africans 207,500 (0.4%); Bangladeshis 160,300 (0.3%); Chinese 157,500 (0.3%); Roma 90,000-120,000 (0.16-0.2%)

Languages: English, Welsh, Gaelic, Bengali, Chinese, Gujarati, Urdu, Punjabi.

II. International obligations

United Nations
– International Covenant on Civil and Political Rights (signature 16 September 1968, ratification 20 May 1976)
– Not a party to the First Optional Protocol
– International Covenant on Economic, Social and Cultural Rights (signature 16 September 1968, ratification 20 May 1976)

Council of Europe
– Member (5 May 1949)
– ECHR (signature 4 November 1950, ratification 8 March 1951)
– Charter for Regional or Minority Languages (signature 2 March 2000)
– Framework Convention for the Protection of National Minorities (signature 1 February 1995, ratification 15 January 1998, entry into force 1 May 1998)

III. National legislation

Constitution

There is no written constitution or comprehensive Bill of Rights; Britain's Constitution is to be found partly in conventions and customs and partly in statute. The Act known as the Bill of Rights 1689 deals with the exercise of the royal prerogative and succession to the Crown.

IV. Developments/events/comments

In England, Northern Ireland and Scotland the language of State and administration is English. In Wales both the English and Welsh languages have equal status in public business and the administration of Justice (the 1993 Welsh Language Act).

Names and surnames
UK legislation allows individuals to maintain or change their surnames or to revert to a former surname. In Northern Ireland, Irish language personal names are recognized for all purposes.

Public notices, the names of places and road signs
There is nothing to prevent anyone from displaying road signs, public notices etc. in minority languages.

Under the Local Government (Miscellaneous Provisions (Northern Ireland) Order 1995, a District Council may, with the agreement of the occupiers of a street, erect a second nameplate in a language other than English.

In Wales, the use of place names, street names and similar information in both Welsh and English is well established. Relevant public authorities are required to make commitments in this respect in their statutory Welsh language schemes.

Media
Whereas the BBC provides a radio service in the Welsh language, the TV channel S4C broadcasts about 30 hours of programmes in Welsh each week.

Various steps are also being undertaken to provide for broadcasting in the Gaelic language. For example in 1990 an independent statutory body was established with responsibility for managing the Gaelic Broadcasting Fund which amounts to £8.5 million per year for financing the production of and the activities necessary for Gaelic programmes.

In addition, over twenty broadcasting licences have been issued by the Independent Television Commission aimed at the Asian, Chinese, Japanese, Turkish, Iranian and Afro-Caribbean communities.

Judicial and administrative procedures
In general, the English language is used in legal proceedings. However, in the areas of Scotland with a Gaelic-speaking population there is a bilingual policy, and in Wales the 1993 Welsh Language Act stipulates that public bodies provide their services in both the English and Welsh languages, in accordance with the so-called statutory Welsh language schemes. The Welsh language may also be used in all legal proceedings taking place in Wales, subject to the rules of court.

In public administration persons belonging to ethnic minorities may use their own language and will be provided with interpreting services.

Education

The National Curriculum does not provide for the teaching of mother tongues, one of the reasons being a great number of languages represented in British schools (about 200 different mother tongues, and in a particular school there might be as many as 60 languages represented). In this respect priority is given to English as a language of instruction in schools (except in Wales where the language of instruction is English or Welsh) which should equip children with the level of knowledge necessary to participate as adults fully in the working life.

At the secondary level pupils may have the opportunity to study their mother tongue, while many ethnic communities have set up supplementary schools aimed at maintaining their ethnic identity, language and culture.

In Scotland the Gaelic-medium education is financed by the Government which in 1999 provided £ 2.4 million to local authorities. Currently there are over 1,800 pupils in 56 primary schools providing instruction in the Gaelic language.

In Wales the Welsh language is used as a language of instruction in over 500 primary and secondary schools with in total 80,000 pupils. However, in all schools English is also taught although this is optional in Welsh-medium schools until the age of seven. Outside Wales there is one privately funded Welsh-language primary school in London.

UZBEKISTAN

I. Demographic situation

Population (1994): Total 21,600,000. Minority groups: Russians 1,792,000 (8.3%); Tajiks 1,015,000 (4.7%); Kazakhs 885,000 (4.1%); Volga Tatars 518.000 (2.4%); Karakalpas 453,000 (2.1%); Other smaller minorities.

Languages: Uzbek, Russian, Tajik, Kazak, Tatar.

II. International obligations

Whereas the Preamble of the 1992 Constitution of the Republic of Uzbekistan recognizes the priority of the generally accepted norms of international law, meaning that international provisions will be directly applicable in the territory of Uzbekistan, there is no specific provision dealing with the position of accepted international norms in the national legal system of Uzbekistan.

United Nations
- International Covenant on Civil and Political Rights (accession 28 September 1995)
- First Optional Protocol (accession 28 September 1995)
- International Covenant on Economic, Social and Cultural Rights (accession 28 September 1995)

Council of Europe
- Not a member of the Council of Europe
- Not a party to the Charter for Regional or Minority Languages
- Not a party to the Framework Convention for the Protection of National Minorities

III. National legislation

Constitution (8 December 1992)

Article 4
The State language of the Republic of Uzbekistan is Uzbek.
The Republic of Uzbekistan ensures a respectful attitude towards the languages, customs, and traditions of the nationalities and peoples living on its territory and ensures conditions for their development.

Article 18
All citizens of the Republic of Uzbekistan have equal rights and freedoms and are equal before the law regardless of differences in gender, race, nationality, language, religious, social heritage, convictions, and person or social position. Privileges may be established only by law and should be accord with the principles of social justice.

Article 115
Judicial proceedings in the Republic of Uzbekistan are conducted in Uzbek, Karakalpak, or the language of the majority of people of the area. Participants in a case who do not know the language of the judicial proceedings are ensured the right to acquaint themselves fully with the materials of the case and participate in the judicial proceedings through an interpreter, and also the right to address the court in their native language.

IV. Developments/events/comments

The Law on the State Language of Uzbekistan was adopted on 21 December 1995, and entered into force on 21 December 1995. A major change introduced by the Law concerns the Russian language which the Law no longer highlights. Uzbek and other languages are used if necessary in documentation relating to an individual's identity and rights; publishing; postal-telegraphic messages;

announcements; advertisements, etc. In localities with a compact residence of ethnic groups Uzbek and other languages are used in documents of local government institutions and pre-school institutions. Both Uzbek and other languages are used in radio and TV programmes; labels of goods; instructions; and in secondary, special secondary, technical and higher education. In everyday life, interpersonal relations, writing names, and religious practice any language may be used.

Criminal and Administrative liability
Article 42 of the Code on Administrative Liability contains a provision on liability for contravening the rights of citizens to the free choice of language in the upbringing of children, in the education of children and for placing obstacles and restrictions on the use of a language. In addition, Article 141 of the Criminal Code stipulates that a direct or indirect infringement or restriction of rights or the granting of direct or indirect privileges to citizens on the basis of race, nationality or language shall be punishable by a fine of up to 25 times the minimum wage or the deprivation of a specified right for a period of up to three years.

Judicial proceedings
Article 7 of the Act on the Courts stipulates that legal proceedings shall be conducted in the Uzbek or Karakalpak languages or in the language of the majority of the population of a given area. Article 9 of the Code of Civil Procedure contains a similar provision. In both cases, persons who are not proficient in the language of the proceedings will have the right to an interpreter.

Education
Secondary education is conducted in 7 languages: Uzbek, Karakalpak, Russian, Kazak, Turkmen, Tajik and Kyrgyz.

The admission test for undergraduate entry to the higher education institutions takes place in three languages: Uzbek, Russian and Karakalpak. At the same time in all institutions of higher education instruction is provided, alongside Uzbek, also in the Russian language. In a number of universities teaching is also provided in Kazak, Tajik, Turkmen and Korean. Textbooks and teaching materials in the minority languages are generally provided by the respective countries of the Commonwealth of Independent States.

Media
Newspapers and journals are published in 11 different languages, whereas three national TV channels devote considerable time to programmes in the Russian language. There is also a channel which broadcasts weekly programmes in the languages of other minorities.

YUGOSLAVIA, FEDERAL REPUBLIC OF

I. Demographic situation

Population (census 1991): Total 10,597,000. Minority groups: Albanians 1,727,500 (16.6%); Montenegrins 520,500 (5.0%); Hungarians 345,400 (3.3%); 'Yugoslavs' 344,000 (3.3%); Muslims 327,500 (3.1%); Roma 137,265 (1.3%); Croats 109,214 (1.0%); Others 270,497 (2.6%).

Other estimates: Albanians more than 2,000,000 (19%), Roma more than 500,000 (4.8%).

Languages: Serbian, Albanian, Hungarian.

II. International obligations

Article 10 of the 1992 Constitution states that the Federal Republic of Yugoslavia shall recognize and guarantee the rights and freedoms of man and the citizen recognized under international law. According to Article 16 the Federal Republic of Yugoslavia shall fulfil in good faith the obligations contained in international treaties to which it is a contracting party. International treaties which have been ratified and promulgated in conformity with the present Constitution and generally accepted rules of international law shall be a constituent part of the internal legal order.

United Nations
- International Covenant on Civil and Political Rights (signature 8 August 1967, ratification 2 June 1971)
- First Optional Protocol (signature 14 March 1990)
- International Covenant on Economic, Social and Cultural Rights (signature 8 August 1967, ratification 2 June 1971)

Council of Europe
- Not a member of the Council of Europe
- Not a party to the Charter for Regional or Minority Languages
- Not a party to the Framework Convention for the Protection of National Minorities

Bilateral agreements
- 1996 – with Croatia, Agreement on the normalization of relations

III. National legislation

Constitution (27 April 1992)

Article 11
The Federal Republic of Yugoslavia shall recognize and guarantee the rights of national minorities to preserve, foster and express their ethnic, cultural, linguistic and other peculiarities, as well as to use their national symbols, in accordance with international law.

Article 15
1. In the Federal Republic of Yugoslavia, the Serbian language in its ekavian and ijekavian dialects and the Cyrillic script shall be official, while the Latin script shall be in official use as provided for by the Constitution and law.
2. In regions of the Federal Republic of Yugoslavia inhabited by national minorities, the languages and scripts of these minorities shall also be in official use in the manner prescribed by law.

Article 20
1. Citizens shall be equal irrespective of their nationality, race, sex, language, faith, political or other beliefs, education, social origin, property, or other personal status.

Article 23
3. Every person taken into custody must be informed immediately in his mother tongue or in a language which he understands of the reasons for his arrest, and he shall be entitled to demand that the authorities inform his next of kin of his detention.

Article 46
1. Members of national minorities shall have the right to education in their own language, in conformity with the law.
2. Members of national minorities shall have the right to information media in their own language.

Article 49
Everyone shall be guaranteed the right to use his own language in proceedings before a tribunal or other authority or organization which in the performance of their public powers decide on his rights and duties and in the course of these proceedings to be informed of the facts in his own language.

Constitution of the Republic of Serbia (1990)

Article 8
In the Republic of Serbia the Serbo-Croatian language and the Cyrillic alphabet shall be officially used, while the Latinic alphabet shall be officially used in the manner established by law.

In the regions of the Republic of Serbia inhabited by national minorities, their own languages and alphabets shall be officially used as well, in the manner established by law.

Report on the State of Affairs and the exercise of national minority rights in the Federal Republic of Yugoslavia (adopted on 9 May 1996 and submitted to the Sub-Commission on Prevention of Discrimination and Protection of Minorities, UN Doc. E/CN.4/Sub.2/1996/35)

23. The constitutional right of persons belonging to national minorities to be taught in their language has been elaborated in a number of Republic laws and other regulations. The educational process is organized in minority languages from the pre-school level up to the university level.
24. Under the Law on Elementary Schools and the Law on Secondary Schools of the Republic of Serbia, persons belonging to national minorities may follow the curricula in their native language provided at least five pupils enrol in the first grade - even fewer subject to the educational minister's approval. The Law also provides for the possibility of bilingual schooling or additional classes in the minority language with elements of national culture as an elective subject. According to the data for the 1993/94 school year, elementary instruction in the Autonomous Province of Vojvodina is conducted in five teaching languages: Serbian, Hungarian, Slovak, Romanian and Ruthenian. In 38 out of Vojvodina's 45 townships, pupils are taught in one or several minority languages: in Hungarian in 29 townships, in Slovak in 12, in Romanian in 10, and in Ruthenian in 3 townships.
25. Education in the Bulgarian language or bilingual instruction is conducted in 38 primary schools in the townships with a higher percentage of ethnic Bulgarians (Bosilegrad and Dimitrovgrad). They are attended by 2,451 pupils.
26. Pupils belonging to the Hungarian national minority attend classes solely in their native language in 42, Slovak in 7, Romanian in 13, and Ruthenian in 1 elementary school in Vojvodina. Parallel instruction in Serbian and any of the minority languages is conducted in 100 elementary schools and in another 2 schools pupils are taught in three minority languages. Of the total school population in Vojvodina, 11.54 per cent attend elementary school in Hungarian, 2.19 per cent in Slovak, 0.82 per cent in Romanian and 0.35 per cent in Ruthenian, which is more or less proportionate to Vojvodina's overall ethnic structure. In areas where pupils are only taught in Serbian, the pupils

whose native language in other than Serbian have an elective 'Native language with elements of national culture' with two lessons a week from form 1 to form VIII.

27. In 37 secondary schools in Vojvodina, instruction is conducted in one of the four minority languages: in Hungarian in 27 schools, in Slovak in 2, in Romanian in 2 and in Ruthenian in 1 secondary school.

28. Teaching and education in national minority languages in secondary school facilities takes place under the Law on Secondary Schools, which, similarly to the Law on Elementary Schools, stipulates that at least 15 students in the first form of lycée, vocational and art schools are required for them to follow the curriculum in their national minority language. Instruction in a minority language in cases where the 15-student requirement has not been fulfilled is subject to approval by the Education Minister. The schools which provide instruction in national minority languages alone are likewise obliged to create the conditions for following Serbian language classes. Instruction in a national minority language - Hungarian, Slovak, Romanian and Ruthenian - is conducted in 18 of Vojvodina's townships, in 12 lycées, and in 20 vocational schools, involving 290 classes and 7,240 students. In elementary and secondary schools where pupils and students are taught in minority languages, the Law stipulates the requirement for teachers to keep records also in minority languages, and the public school report is issued in those languages as well. Under the provisions of the Law on Higher schools and the Law on the University of the Republic of Serbia, instruction is conducted in Serbian, hut may also be conducted in a minority language, subject to a decision by the founder of that school and approval from the University. Higher education in Hungarian is organized at seven faculties, in Slovak at two, in Romanian at two and in Ruthenian at two faculties.

29. The Law on Higher Schools and the Law on the university have provisions regulating the organization and conduct of instruction in minority languages, as well as record-keeping in registries of diplomas issued and public certificates issued attesting to completed studies. According to the data for the 1993/94 school year, 11 higher-schools in Vojvodina are attended by 717 students belonging to the Hungarian, Romanian, Slovak and Ruthenian national minorities, of whom 466 attend lectures in their native language. Of the total number of students belonging to national minorities, the following percentages study at higher schools in their respective native languages: 69.3 per cent of Hungarians; 32 per cent of Slovaks; 91.07 per cent of Romanians; and 4.76 per cent of Ruthenians. The 13 institutions of high learning in Vojvodina are attended by 1,592 students belonging to national minorities, of whom 357 study in their native language.

30. A similar education arrangement is applied in [Autonomous Province] AP Kosovo and Metohija, but ethnic Albanians are boycotting the legal educational system in elementary to high education facilities, which provide instruction in Albanian. Prior to the boycott, there were 904 Albanian schools

with 315,000 pupils, 69 secondary schools with 73,000 students, and the University in Pristina, which was attended by 37,000 students, 80 per cent of whom were Albanians studying in the Albanian language. Ninety-eight per cent of education-related costs were financed by the Republic of Serbia. By the number of students, the Autonomous Province of Kosovo and Metohija was in fourth place in the world (behind the United States, Canada and the Netherlands), while at the game time no more than 19,000 students were receiving their schooling at the University in Tirana.

31. The present state of affairs in education is characterized by the fact that persons belonging to the Albanian minority are taught in their native language in State-owned buildings and the Republic of Serbia has secured all that is necessary for the normal operation of schools, observing the principles enshrined in the relevant International documents. There are currently in Kosovo and Metohija 1,400 elementary schools in operation, 60 secondary schools and education centres and the University with 14 faculties. Teachers belonging to the Albanian minority use State-owned classrooms and teaching aids, teach in Albanian and only refuse to receive Information, publishing activities and culture.

Information, publishing activities and culture

40. It follows from the provision of the Constitution of FRY which lays down the right of national minorities to public information in their respective languages, and also from the relevant provisions of the Republic laws on public information, that the international standards have been met in this area as well.

41. The statistics for 1994 show that the following numbers of daily papers, magazines and different bulletins are published in FRY: 75 in Hungarian; 17 in Romanian and Ruthenian; 12 in Czech and Slovak; 25 in Albanian; 3 in Turkish; and 3 in Bulgarian. Nineteen papers and 36 magazines are published multilingually.

42. In keeping with the provisions of the Constitution of the Republic of Serbia and the Law on Public Information, a large number of public media in Serbia use national minority languages - Albanian, Hungarian, Slovak, Romanian, Ruthenian, Ukrainian, Turkish, Bulgarian and Romany. All the public media material in the minority languages is edited by persons belonging to the respective minorities. The Republic Law on Public Information in the Republic of Serbia makes it possible for everyone to publish papers even without any preliminary authorization, simply by entering the name of the paper into the competent court' s registry. AP Vojvodina is responsible for securing the required preconditions for public information in minority languages and scripts as well. For example, the 1994 provincial budget allocated funds for supporting the publication of 14 newspapers and 4 magazines in national minority languages.

43. Furthermore, Radio Television Pristina broadcasts television and radio programming in Albanian, and radio programmes are also broadcast in Albanian by six local radio stations. Twenty-five papers art published in Albanian with a total annual circulation of 21 million, and 40 magazines with a total annual circulation of 300,000 copies.
44. Radio Pristina broadcasts programming in the Albanian language every day after 15.30 hrs. The programming is basically of an informative nature and the speech to music ratio is 20:90. Apart from the news bulletin which is broadcast every hour on the hour, the following informative programmes are produced every day before 15.00 hrs: the 12 o'clock News (10 minutes); the Events of the Day at 15.00 hrs (30 minutes); the Evening News at 18.30 hrs (30 minutes); and the Daily Chronicle at 22.00 hrs (15 minutes). Radio Pristina also transmits every day Radio Yugoslavia's informative programme in Albanian, which is broadcast from 21 to 21.15 hrs.
45. Radio Pristina broadcasts programming in the Turkish language every day from 11 to 18.00 hrs. Apart from informative-political programmes, news bulletins and the evening news, the programming also features topics relating to culture, science, education, drama, entertainment, sports and music.
46. Radio Pristina also broadcasts two one-hour programmes (on Thursdays and Sundays) in Romany, covering the most important events related to the life, culture and customs of the Romanies.
47. Apart from Radio Pristina there are also local radio stations in the area of Kosovo and Metohija, for instance Radio Metohija (Pec) and Radio Kosovska Mitrovica, which broadcast programmes in minority languages - in Albanian, Turkish and Romany.
48. Television Pristina broadcasts in Albanian day-to-day news (duration 10 minutes) and evening news (25 minutes) and at present produces an average 47 minutes of programming in Albanian every day, that is 329 minutes a week or 17,019 minutes a year. In addition to the Albanian language, Television Pristina also broadcasts programmes in Turkish whose annual duration is 10,316 minutes, as well as an 'informative-magazine' programme in Romany with a total annual duration of 1,178 minutes.
49. The Radio Pristina and Television Pristina programmes in Albanian are organized as business units like the programmes in Serbian and in Turkish, and the units are led by responsible editors who look after the production of certain broadcasts and their contents.
50. There is a disproportion between the Serbian language programme and the Albanian language programme, largely due to the shortage of personnel needed for the production of programmes in Albanian. Vacancies remain unfilled because unqualified applicants are in short supply as persons belonging to the Albanian national minority are refusing to work at enterprises financed by the State.
51. Of a total of 285,827 hours of radio and television programming broadcast in FRY in 1994, 6,454 hours were in Albanian. In that year, 105 hours of radio

and television programming were broadcast in Bulgarian; 19,543 in Hungarian; 3,599 in Romanian; 1,803 in Ruthenian; 5,485 in Slovak; 3,149 in Turkish; 48 in Ukrainian; and 4,614 hours in other minority language.

52. The radio stations in Vojvodina broadcast programmes in eight languages: Serbian, Hungarian, Slovak, Romanian, Ruthenian, Ukrainian, Macedonian and Romany. Radio programmes in Hungarian are broadcast for 24 hours a day, in Slovak on average 7 hours a day, in Romanian 7 hours as well, and in Ruthenian for 4 hours a day. These data relate to Radio Novi Sad - the main station for Vojvodina's territory. However, there are also another 27 regional and local radio stations in this province of which 4 produce and broadcast programmes in 4 languages, 6 stations have programmes in 3 languages, 8 stations use 2 and 4 stations 1 language.

53. Television Novi Sad broadcasts regularly in five languages: in Hungarian every day; and in Slovak, Romanian and Ruthenian five to six times a week.

54. In 1993 the following numbers of books and brochures were published: 48 in Hungarian; 17 in Czech and Slovak; 16 in Romanian; 5 in Albanian; 1 in Bulgarian and 221 books in several languages.

55. In 1993, 41 books were published in Hungarian with an average circulation of 1,000 copies each, 7 books in Slovak with a circulation of 500 each and 6 to 7 books in Romanian and in Ruthenian with a circulation of 500 copies each. The library network across Vojvodina holds books In minority languages that correspond to the ethnic structure of the population: 76.67 per cent of these books are in Serbian; 15.65 per cent are in Hungarian; 1.12 per cent in Slovak; 1.04 per cent in Romanian and 0.22 per cent in Ruthenian.

56. In keeping with the provisions of the Law on Public Information of the Republic of Montenegro, several papers are published in the Albanian language in that Republic, as well as the monthly magazine 'Fati' which is published in Ulcinj and the weekly 'Polis' which is published in Podgorica. Television of Montenegro broadcasts daily 15 minutes of news in Albanian, and on Saturday a 60-minute informative cultural programme. Montenegrin radio stations broadcast 30 minutes of news in Albanian every day. The interests of minority populations in the area of creative work and culture are looked after by the respective mother nations, communities and societies which, in cooperation with relevant provincial cultural institutions, prepare programmes and carry out activities to maintain and cherish national identity, preserve and promote people's language, literature the arts and folklore.

57. Persons belonging to the Albanian national minority have not abandoned their work posts en masse and in an organized manner at the cultural institutions in Kosovo and Metohija. On the contrary, Albanians are employed in almost all cultural institutions and they make up a majority in many of them. Thus, for example, cultural centres or culture clubs in most towns in Kosovo and Metohija employ ethnic Albanians who outnumber Serb employees. Only three out o eight employees at the provincial Cultural Centre in Pristina are Serbs and all employees in the Municipal Cultural

Centre in Glogovac are Albanians; the same applies to the State archives and museums. For instance, of the 34 employees at the Kosovo and Metohija museum, 20 are ethnic Albanians, i.e. around 60 per cent.
[...]

The right to the official use of a native language and script

69. The FRY Constitution recognizes to the national minorities the right to develop, preserve and express their linguistic specificities, and in the parts of FRY inhabited by national minorities, their languages and scripts, too, are in official use, in accordance with the law. The minorities are likewise guaranteed, as set out above, the right to public information and schooling in their native language in accordance with the law.

70. There is no comprehensive law at the level of FRY regulating the official use of languages and scripts, but the Federal Government is currently working on one such project. The Republic of Serbia has passed the Law on the Official Use of Languages and Scripts, which stipulates that in the areas of the Republic of Serbia inhabited by minorities also their languages and scripts will be used together with the Serbian language in official communications.

71. According to the above-mentioned Law, the official use of languages and scripts entails the use of these languages and scripts by the State authorities, agencies of the autonomous provinces, towns and townships, institutions, enterprises and other organizations pursuing the activities set forth in this Law. The official use of languages and scripts also includes the use of languages and scripts for writing place names and other geographic names, the names of squares and streets, the names of agencies, organizations and firms, public announcements, information and warnings, am well as the writing of other public inscriptions. The Law further stipulates that the official use of languages and scripts entails in particular their use in verbal and written communications between government bodies and organizations, as well as clients, meaning individual citizens, the conduct of proceedings for the exercise and protection of civil rights, duties and responsibilities, prescribed record-keeping, issuance of identification documents and the exercise of their rights, duties and responsibilities by employed or formerly employed persons.

72. The Law stipulates that the townships inhabited by minorities shall decide when minority languages will be in official use in their territory, i.e. specify in the municipal statute which language or minority languages shall be in official use in their township.

73. We shall here illustrate how the constitutional and legal provisions on the official use of languages and scripts are enforced in practice by looking at AP Vojvodina, a province with a specific ethnic composition: Serbs account for 57.3 per cent of its population, Hungarians 16.9 per cent, Yugoslavs 8.4 per cent, Croats 3.7 per cent, Slovaks 3.2 per cent, Montenegrins 2.2 per cent,

Romanians 1.9 per cent, Romanies 1.2 per cent, Bunyevats 1.1 per cent, Ruthenians 0.9 per cent, Ukrainians 0.24 per cent and others 3.2 per cent.

74. The statute of AP Vojvodina, the basic legal act of the province, stipulates that in parallel with the Serbian language and the Cyrillic script (and in the Latin script as laid down by the law), the Government agencies of AP Vojvodina will officially use the Hungarian, Slovak, Romanian and Ruthenian languages and their respective scripts, as well as the languages and scripts of other national minorities as stipulated by law. Regular simultaneous interpretation into five languages is provided at the Vojvodina Assembly sessions. Communications between clients (citizens) and the provincial authorities take place in the languages of the national minorities. The courts of law in Vojvodina have the necessary capacities for the conduct of proceedings in the languages which are in official use in particular areas and in cases where such a possibility does not exist, a sworn-in court interpreter is provided.

75. Of the total 45 townships in AP Vojvodina, 37 have included in their statutes a provision governing the official use of the languages and scripts of the respective national minorities living in their territories so that one or several minority languages are in official use as well. in parallel with Serbian, the Hungarian language and script are in official use in 31 townships, Slovak in 12, Romanian in 10, Ruthenian in 6 and Czech in 1 township. (There are no more than 2,910 Czechs living in the whole of Yugoslavia, of whom 1,844 live in Vojvodina.) A considerable number of townships use several languages and scripts simultaneously and equally.

76. In the Republic of Montenegro, the relevant constitutional arrangements are carried out directly. In particular, Article 68 of the Constitution of the Republic of Montenegro guarantees persons belonging to national minority and ethnic groups the right freely to use their language and script and the right to be educated and informed in their language.

IV. Developments/events/comments

Education

Articles 4 and 5 of the 1992 Elementary Education Law of the Republic of Serbia determine that the language of instruction shall be Serbian. The instruction for members of nationalities shall be provided in the mother tongue or bilingually if not less than 15 pupils enrol in the first grade, subject to the consent of the Minister of Education. The Minister has competence to prescribe the mode of the bilingual instruction. In case the instruction is in the languages of nationalities, the pupils shall follow the syllabus of the Serbian language, whereas when the language of instruction is Serbian, the pupils who are members of nationalities shall have instruction in their mother tongue with elements of the national culture.

Similar provisions are embodied in the 1992 Secondary Education Law of the Republic of Serbia. The 1992 High School Law also determines that high school education shall be acquired in the Serbian language, however it can also be in the languages of nationalities or national minorities as well as in one of the world languages as decided by the founder.

According to Article 43 of the 1990 University Law of the Republic of Serbia, the language of instruction at universities shall be Serbo-Croatian. In the Socialist Autonomous Provinces the syllabi shall also be in the language of another nation and nationality when not less than 30 students of the same year of study opt therefor (paragraph 2). If the republican or provincial administrative agency responsible for educational affairs considers it necessary, a faculty may ensure instruction in the language of another nation or nationality for the whole course or for individual subjects for a lesser number of students (paragraph 3). However, Article 126 of the same law excluded the application of Article 43, paragraphs 2 and 3 in the territory of the Autonomous Province of Kosovo.